Horror Literature
through History

Horror Literature through History

An Encyclopedia of the Stories That Speak to Our Deepest Fears

VOLUME 2

MATT CARDIN, EDITOR

 GREENWOOD™

An Imprint of ABC-CLIO, LLC
Santa Barbara, California • Denver, Colorado

Library of Congress Cataloging-in-Publication Data

Names: Cardin, Matt, editor.
Title: Horror literature through history : an encyclopedia of the stories that speak
   to our deepest fears / Matt Cardin, editor.
Description: Santa Barbara, California : Greenwood, 2017. |
   Includes bibliographical references and index.
Identifiers: LCCN 2017000044 (print) | LCCN 2017000211 (ebook) |
   ISBN 9781440842016 (set : acid-free paper) | ISBN 9781440847561
   (volume 1 : acid-free paper) | ISBN 9781440847578 (volume 2 : acid-free
   paper) | ISBN 9781440842023 (ebook)
Subjects: LCSH: Horror tales—History and criticism—Encyclopedias.
Classification: LCC PN3435 .H665 2017 (print) | LCC PN3435 (ebook) |
   DDC 809.3/8738—dc23
LC record available at https://lccn.loc.gov/2017000044

ISBN: 978-1-4408-4201-6 (set)
      978-1-4408-4756-1 (vol. 1)
      978-1-4408-4757-8 (vol. 2)
      978-1-4408-4202-3 (ebook)

21 20 19 18 17   1 2 3 4 5

This book is also available as an eBook.

Greenwood
An Imprint of ABC-CLIO, LLC

ABC-CLIO, LLC
130 Cremona Drive, P.O. Box 1911
Santa Barbara, California 93116-1911
www.abc-clio.com

This book is printed on acid-free paper ♾

Manufactured in the United States of America

Contents

Guide to Related Topics

Interviews

Laird Barron
Ramsey Campbell
Ellen Datlow
Caitlín R. Kiernan
Joe R. Lansdale
Thomas Ligotti
Chelsea Quinn Yarbro

Horror Literature through History

Horror in the Ancient World
Horror in the Early Modern Era
Horror in the Middle Ages
Horror in the Eighteenth Century
Horror in the Nineteenth Century
Horror from 1900 to 1950
Horror from 1950 to 2000
Horror in the Twenty-First Century

Horror Types and Subgenres

Apocalyptic Horror
Dark Fantasy
Eco-horror
Ghost Stories
The Gothic Literary Tradition
Gothic Poetry
Horror Comics
Horror Literature and Science
    Fiction
Lovecraftian Horror
New Weird
Occult Fiction
Psychological Horror

Vampire Fiction from Dracula to Lestat
    and Beyond
Weird and Cosmic Horror Fiction
Young Adult Horror Fiction

Monsters, Creatures, Threats, and Villains

Devils and Demons
Doubles, Doppelgängers, and Split
    Selves
Gothic Hero/Villain
Incubi and Succubi
Mad Scientist
Monsters
Mummies
Vampires
Werewolves
Witches and Witchcraft
Zombies

Topical Studies

Body Horror
Cthulhu Mythos
Gender, Sexuality, and the Monsters of
    Literary Horror
Horror Anthologies
Horror Criticism
Horror Literature in the Internet Age
Horror Literature as Social Criticism
    and Commentary
Horror Publishing, 1975–1995: The
    Boom Years
Horror Video Games

Preface

Horror is not only one of the most popular types of literature but one of the oldest. People have always been mesmerized by stories that speak to their deepest fears. *Horror Literature through History*, in both the scope of its coverage and the currency of its contents, is uniquely suited to speak to this primal and perennial fascination.

It is also a pointedly timely work, as it arrives at a cultural moment when horror is experiencing a fierce resurgence after having gone through a relative cultural downswing during the previous decade. It was not that horror had ever actually died, for it is, as many have enjoyed noting, an undying—or perhaps undead—form of art and entertainment. But it had become somewhat sluggish in the mid- and late 1990s, aided by the flaming out of the great horror publishing boom of the previous decade-plus, whose high-water mark on the mass market end was represented by the soaring popularity of novels by the likes of Stephen King, Peter Straub, Anne Rice, Ramsey Campbell, and Dean Koontz. And so the revival of the early 2000s constitutes a distinct and discernable phenomenon.

Significantly, this revitalization of horror has not been just a literary matter; in this new era, horror's chief audience and consumer base, consisting largely of high school–aged and college-aged young people, has begun eagerly absorbing horror, especially of the supernatural variety, from a variety of sources. Along with novels and short fiction collections, there are television programs, movies, comic books, and video (and other types of) games. Weird horror fiction—a form to be defined and discussed in the pages to follow—has entered what some began to call a new golden age, not just in literary form but in film and television, as in HBO's *True Detective*, whose first season in 2014 displayed the distinct influence of such authors as Robert W. Chambers, Thomas Ligotti, and Laird Barron. Horror gaming—like other gaming—has rapidly attained new heights of technological and narrative sophistication. Horror movie subgenres both old (such as exorcism) and new (such as "torture porn" and the found-footage world of movies like *Paranormal Activity*) have become enormously popular and profitable. Armies of zombies have begun to infest the pages of comic books and the proliferating sea of screens both large and small.

And throughout it all, the various nonliterary forms continue to draw deeply on their literary cousins for their basic plots, themes, and ideas. This was always true of horror films, but it is critically important to recognize that it remains equally true during the present era of exploding new forms and media, when it might be possible for a partaker of these new forms—the horror video games, the creepypastas, and so on—to ignore or forget the literary foundations of the whole phenomenon.

Literary horror predates all of the other types. It has a vastly longer, and therefore richer and deeper, history. And this is where and why a reference work like the present one comes in: because it serves to illuminate the roots of modern horror, both literary and otherwise, by laying out the field's deep history and evolutionary development.

To this end, *Horror Literature through History* is presented in a three-part structure that is designed for maximum usefulness in assisting all kinds of readers, including those who seek a comprehensive overview of horror's rich literary heritage and those who want to conduct a focused study of specific authors, works, and/or topics. It is also well suited to piecemeal browsing.

Part One, titled "Horror through History," consists of eight essays presenting a comprehensive chronological overview of horror literature during different historical periods. These essays take the form of narrative and critical surveys that situate literary works within the social, cultural, historical, and intellectual currents of their respective eras, creating a seamless narrative of the genre's evolution from ancient times to the present

Part Two, "Themes, Topics, and Genres," contains twenty-three essays that show how otherwise unrelated works of horror have influenced each other, how horror subgenres have evolved, and how a broad range of topics within horror—such as ghosts, vampires, religion, and gender roles, as well as the academic study of these things—have been handled across time.

Part Three, "Reference Entries," presents nearly 400 alphabetically arranged reference entries on authors, works, and specialized topics. It serves as both a source of stand-alone reference reading in its own right and, importantly, a supplement to the encyclopedia's preceding sections. In effect, many of the reference entries serve as "close-ups" on information and concepts presented in the preceding two sections, allowing readers to understand specific authors, works, and topics within the wider context of horror literature's evolutionary history and thematic universe.

Supplementing the main entries are seven original interviews with important contemporary horror authors and editors plus nearly 150 sidebars featuring mini-analyses of literary works, excerpts from primary and secondary works, excerpts from reviews, timelines, trivia, information about media adaptations, and more.

With this unique structure, *Horror Literature through History* offers a variety of uses both to students and to general readers:

- The excerpts from horror novels and stories exemplify topics discussed in the entries, such as theme, language, and characterization. Students are thus able to read these excerpts critically in light of the entries. This supports Common Core State Standards for English language arts.
- The excerpts from background texts work in tandem with the entries by providing contextual material to help students read the literary works critically and understand how authors have engaged the major scientific, social, artistic, psychological, religious, and other issues of their respective eras.

- The historical overview essays in Part One and the topical essays in Part Two distinguish *Horror Literature through History* from works consisting of relatively short A–Z entries. These essays prompt readers to consider the nature of horror as a genre and the ways in which horror literature intersects with mainstream concerns such as religion, politics, education, and more.
- The information on such topics as film adaptations, television shows, video games, and other nonliterary matters helps readers connect horror literature to popular culture at large.
- The interviews provide insights from horror authors about what they have written and why, as well as their thoughts on other writers, works, themes, trends, and issues in the field. Students can apply these views and opinions to analyzing and evaluating the work of the interviewees, as well as many additional works, authors, and topics.

In sum, the encyclopedia enables readers to discover the roots of modern horror literature, trace the evolution of horror literature across time, recognize the influence of literary horror on popular culture, examine how works of horror have related to key issues at different periods in history, and conduct focused research on specific authors, literary works, genres, themes, and topics related to horror. Written by seventy scholars and authors from half a dozen countries, *Horror Literature through History: An Encyclopedia of the Stories That Speak to Our Deepest Fears* offers the reader an in-depth education, in two volumes, about the literary background of popular modern horror entertainments and the rich intrinsic value of this enduring art form in its own right.

Introduction: Spookhouses, Catharsis, and Dark Consolations

Why Horror?

From the outset, a reference work like this one begs an important question, and one that strikes right to the heart of the stated project: *Why horror?* Why do people seek stories, novels, movies, plays, and games that horrify? It is an old question, and one that has become virtually clichéd from overuse, as many horror novelists and movie directors can testify after years of having been asked some version of it by multiple interviewers, often with an affected attitude of mild amazement or disbelief: "Why horror? Why do you (or how can you) write, direct, imagine, envision, such unpleasant things? Why do you think your readers/viewers flock to them? Why are we insatiably addicted to tales of horror and dread?"

What Is Horror?

In answering this question, one could immediately jump into offering various theories and speculations, but to do this would be to beg yet another question, one that is usually missed or ignored by those attempting to deal with the "Why?" question, but that is properly prior to it: namely, the question of horror's *definition*. The very word and concept of "horror" is a noun, and also an adjective (as in "horror novel" and "horror movie"), that is too often left uninterrogated. Not by everyone, to be sure, but by a great many of the people who read the books, watch the movies, and play the games labeled as "horror" year in and year out. Many such people, if pressed, would likely say something to the effect that horror has something to do with being scared, and leave it at that. They would assert that "horror" is simply another word for "fear."

But a moment's reflection is enough to disabuse one of that notion. Certainly, horror does involve fear, but simple introspection shows that the word refers to something more than this, to fear *plus* something, fear with an admixture or addition of *something else*. A person may fear losing a job, or facing a tiger, or being mugged or beaten up; this does not mean someone in those positions is experiencing horror. Conversely, one may witness, say, the emotional abuse of a child, or the despoiling of an ecosystem, or the ravaging of a loved one by cancer—things that do not involve the supernatural trappings or operatic violence and gore associated with many books and movies bearing the "horror" label—and yet say in all honesty that one feels *horrified*. What exactly is it, then, about the emotional response to such situations that warrants the use of the "h" word to describe it?

These, along with a multitude of additional possible examples, may allow us to triangulate the inner element that makes horror horrifying, and to identify this element as some quality of *wrongness* or *repulsiveness*—physical, metaphysical, moral, or otherwise—that leads one to shrink from someone, something, some event, some idea, a monster, the sight of blood, a situation of gross immorality or injustice, or any number of other things. Horror, it seems, involves an irreducible element of revulsion or abhorrence, centered on a primal gut feeling, often implicit, that something *should not be*, that something is somehow fundamentally *wrong* about a given person, creature, act, event, phenomenon, environment, or situation. (Additionally, and significantly, there is a distinction to be made between horror and *terror*—another word that is of critical importance to the type of art generally labeled "horror" today—and this is addressed in the pages of this encyclopedia.)

In his 1990 study of the aesthetics of horror titled *The Philosophy of Horror, or Paradoxes of the Heart* (1990), the philosopher and film scholar Noël Carroll famously noted the interesting and revealing fact that horror as a genre is named for the chief emotional reaction with which it is concerned, the emotional reaction that we have here called into question. Horror *horrifies*: it sets out to inspire a sense of fear and dread mingled with revulsion. Or, if one follows the lead of Leo Tolstoy (1828–1910), R. G. Collingwood (1889–1943), and other significant representatives of the expressive theory of art, one might argue that the works of horror that actually achieve the true status of art as such (defined as imaginative works possessing and displaying an intrinsically higher level of quality than "mere" genre or formula fiction, whose purpose is to entertain) do not so much seek to inspire horror in the reader or viewer as to communicate a sense of horror that has been experienced by the author. The horror critic and scholar S. T. Joshi, in such books as *The Weird Tale* (1990) and *The Modern Weird Tale* (2001), has advanced the idea that what distinguishes the most important and enduring authors of weird and supernatural horror fiction is their tendency to imbue their work with a consistent vision or worldview. In keeping with this, and regardless of the overall merit of Joshi's specific assertion (which some have disputed), it may well be that one of the distinguishing qualities of the greatest authors in this area is an uncommonly and acutely deep personal sensitivity to the more fearsome, dark, and distressing aspects of life, so that these aspects become a true source of fear, suffering, and, yes, *horror*. Following Tolstoy and Collingwood, one would say that when this quality is present in an individual who possesses (or is possessed by) the inbuilt drive and skill that motivates some people to become writers and artists, it will naturally lead such an individual to tell the rest of us the truth about these dark insights and experiences. And it will empower such a person to use the vehicles of prose fiction, and/or poetry, stage drama, film, television, comic books, or video games, to communicate to others an actual experience of horror by recreating it, to some extent, in the reader, viewer, or player.

Interestingly, and as demonstrated repeatedly over the long history of horror literature, this does not necessarily mean that such writers and artists convey their horror in just a single, easily identifiable type of work that can automatically be given a category or genre label. Horror, as has been persuasively argued—perhaps most famously by Douglas E. Winter in his 1998 speech, and later essay, "The Pathos of Genre"—is not really a genre, defined as a type of narrative that has developed recognizable characteristics through repeated use, which can then be used as a kind of formula for producing other, similar works. Rather, it is "a progressive form of fiction, one that evolves to meet the fears and anxieties of its times. . . . [S]ometimes it wears other names, other faces, marking the fragmentation and meltdown of a sudden and ill-conceived thing that many publishers and writers foolishly believed could be called a genre" (Winter 2000, 182). In other words, horror in art is not a genre but a *mode* that can be employed in any form or genre. Horror has thus had a long and fruitful relationship with, for example, science fiction, from such Ur-texts as Mary Shelley's *Frankenstein* (1818) and H. P. Lovecraft's *At the Mountains of Madness* (1936), to the advent of the "New Weird" at the turn of the twenty-first century in such works as China Miéville's *Perdido Street Station* (2000), to the fifty-year reign of zombies over the realm of apocalyptic and postapocalyptic horror that began in 1968 with writer/director George Romero's *Night of the Living Dead*, which was itself partly inspired by Richard Matheson's classic 1954 horror/science fiction novel *I Am Legend*. And there are also horror Westerns, horror romance novels, religious horror stories, horror thrillers, horror mysteries, and so-called "literary" horror (with "literary" denoting nongenre writing).

Being so portable, as it were, horror can spread out into all types of storytelling, and indeed, this is what has been happening with increasing visibility and pervasiveness in the horror renaissance of the early twenty-first century, to the point where the creeping spread of horror throughout the literary and entertainment landscape is one of the defining characteristics of this new era. Horror has become unbound, and its fortunes have become those of literature at large. In this new state of things, horror's reputation has begun to transcend its former questionable status, as some darlings of the literary establishment have produced works that could be considered pure horror even though they do not bear the category label. In fact, if these had been published during the great horror boom of the 1980s, when not just Stephen King and Anne Rice but a host of lesser authors virtually owned drugstore bookshelves and bookstore window displays, they would have been every bit as horrifying as (if not more so than) any 1980s paperback novel with garish Gothic typography and a leering monster on the cover.

Again: Why Horror?

So these, then, are some of the issues involved in identifying and defining horror in life and art. But the question with which we opened still remains: *Why* horror? Even having answered—perhaps provisionally, arguably, necessarily incompletely—the question of why some writers write it (because they are themselves subject to a deeper-than-average experience of the horrors of life and consciousness), the question remains as to why readers read it. Fear and loathing are conventionally unpleasant emotions. Why do people seek to be subjected to them?

There are a number of customary answers to this question, many of which have been resorted to repeatedly by the interviewees mentioned above, and all of which carry some merit. For instance, what has sometimes been termed the roller coaster or funhouse theory of horror is surely true to an extent. There is something pleasant, even delightful—so this answer has it—about absorbing fictional stories of darkness, danger, and dread while remaining safely in one's easy chair. There is something purely entertaining and enjoyable about entering an imaginative world of horror, rather like a carnival funhouse ride, in order to enjoy the thrills to be found in such a place. From this point of view, seeking horror in fictional, cinematic, or any other form is no different in principle from seeking an adrenaline rush by reading a thriller or seeking a laugh by watching a comedy. And some people do approach all of these things on this very level. Some horror fiction, including most (but not all) of what appeared in *Weird Tales* and the other classic horror, fantasy, and science fiction pulps of the 1920s through the 1940s, as well as most of what was published during the late twentieth-century horror boom, seems precisely aimed at fulfilling this function.

There is also surely something to the more profound theory of horror as catharsis, a position first advanced by Aristotle in his *Poetics* and still invoked more than two thousand years later to explain all kinds of artistic engagements, but especially those of a powerfully stark and unpleasant nature. Aristotle was talking specifically about Greek tragic plays, which brim with grief, betrayal, dark secrets, and unhappy endings, not to mention supernatural horrors and gruesome violence (as in, for example, Euripides's *Medea* and Aeschylus's *Oresteia* trilogy, both from the fifth century BCE). Such productions, the great philosopher argued, serve to purge viewers of their pent-up emotions of fear and pity in a safely walled-off fictional world, thus preparing them better to deal with the anxieties of real life. One would be foolish and naïve to deny that today's horror fiction (and other forms) may serve this kind of function for some, and perhaps many, people.

But even granting the validity of these views, there is another and deeper answer to be given, and this is where the possible sensitivity of the reader meets the sensitivity of the writer who uses imaginative literature to convey his or her own sense of profound horror at the vicissitudes and strangenesses of life, the world, consciousness, and everything. Perhaps, for some people, the great works of horror provide a deep, visceral, darkly electrifying confirmation of their own most personal and profound experiences and intuitions. After the spookhouse ride has let out, and after the catharsis has come and gone, horror in art, as Thomas Ligotti put it in his essay "The Consolations of Horror," may actually, weirdly, provide some readers with a kind of *comfort* by showing that "someone shares some of your own feelings and has made of these a work of art which you have the insight, sensitivity, and—like it or not—peculiar set of experiences to appreciate" (Ligotti 1996, xxi). What is more, horror accomplishes this artistic-alchemical feat not by denying or diminishing the dark, dismal, dreadful, terrifying, and horrifying elements of life, but by *amplifying* them. Never mind the possible therapeutic or other conventionally beneficial results that might be imputed to such a thing; the point, for both writer and reader, is simply to confront, recognize, experience, name, and know horror as such, because it is in fact real. It is part of the human experience. We are, from time to time (and some of us more often than others), haunted by horror. The type of art named as such is an expression of this truth, a personal and cultural acknowledgment of and dialogue with it, a means by which we know it, and affirm it, and "stay with" it, instead of denying it and looking away, as is otherwise our wont.

Like all art, horror literature and its associated other forms play out in ways that link up with a host of additional issues: historical, cultural, sociological, ideological, scientific, artistic, philosophical, religious, spiritual, and existential. It is the story of how exactly this has played out over the long span of human history, especially, but not exclusively, since the birth of literary Gothicism in the eighteenth century with the publication of Horace Walpole's *The Castle of Otranto* (1764), that is the central focus of this encyclopedia. Whatever the reader's purpose in picking up this work, and whichever the level at which he or she tends to engage personally with horror—as funhouse ride, cathartic tool, or personal consolation—it is hoped that the contents herein will help to clarify and illuminate the history, present, and possible futures of horror in both literary and other forms, while also fostering an enhanced appreciation of the central mystery and core of darkness that lies at the heart of the whole thing. It is in fact this darkness that serves as horror's source of enduring power, and that makes it an undying and undead form of human literary and artistic endeavor.

Matt Cardin

Further Reading

Carroll, Noël. 1990. *The Philosophy of Horror, or Paradoxes of the Heart*. New York: Routledge.

Joshi, S. T. 1990. *The Weird Tale*. Austin: University of Texas Press.

Joshi, S. T. 2001. *The Modern Weird Tale*. Jefferson, NC: McFarland.

Ligotti, Thomas. 1996. *The Nightmare Factory*. New York: Carroll & Graf.

Winter, Douglas E. 2000. "The Pathos of Genre." In *The Year's Best Fantasy and Horror*, edited by Ellen Datlow and Terri Windling, 176–183. New York: St. Martin's Press. Also available at http://omnimagazine.com/eh/commentary/winter/pages/0799.html.

Timeline of Horror Literature Through History

ca. 2100 BCE	The *Epic of Gilgamesh*
ca. 750–700 BCE	Homer's *Iliad* and *Odyssey*, featuring tales of gods, monsters, magic, a trip to the underworld; Hesiod's *Theogony*, with additional descriptions of monstrous and supernatural entities
5th century BCE	Heyday of Greek tragedy in works of Aeschylus, Sophocles, and Euripides, featuring supernaturalism and grisly scenes of physical horror
3rd century BCE	Apollonius Rodius, *Argonautica*, showing Jason and the Argonauts encountering multiple monsters and supernatural threats
ca. 200 BCE	Plautus, *Mostellaria* ("The Haunted House")
1st century CE	Petronius, *Satyricon*, featuring the first extant account of a werewolf in ancient literature; Ovid, *Metamorphoses*, with tales of human beings transforming into plants and animals
2nd century CE	Apuleius, *Metamorphosis*, a.k.a. *The Golden Ass*, with transformation, witchcraft, and more
ca. 750–1000	*Beowulf*
12th century	Romance narratives rise to prominence in Europe, featuring many fantastical elements, including ghosts, fairies, werewolves, supernatural transformations, and mysterious castles
14th century	Middle English romances flourish, including tales of women seduced by demons (e.g., *Sir Gowther*), werewolves (*William of Palerne*, translated from Old French), and *Sir Gawain and the Green Knight*, which teems with supernaturalism and horror
1308–1320	Composition of Dante Alighieri's *Divine Comedy*, whose second section, *Inferno*, profoundly shapes Western Christian conceptions of demons, devils, Satan, and hell
1487	Heinrich Kramer and Jacob Sprenger, *Malleus Maleficarum* (*The Hammer of the Witches*)—the most famous (notorious) of the witch-hunting manuals

1572	English translation of Swiss theologian Ludwig Lavatar's *Of ghostes and spirites walking by nyght*
1584	Reginald Scot, *Discoverie of Witchcraft*
1587	Thomas Kyd, *The Spanish Tragedy*
1594	Christopher Marlowe, *Doctor Faustus*; Thomas Nashe, *The Terrors of the Night*; William Shakespeare, *Titus Andronicus*
1597	King James I, *Daemonologie*
1599	John Marsten, *Antonio's Revenge*
1600	William Shakespeare, *Hamlet*
1605	English translation of French scholar Pierre le Loyer's *A treatise of spectres or straunge sights, visions and apparitions appearing sensibly unto men*
1607	Thomas Middleton, *The Revenger's Tragedy*; William Shakespeare, *Macbeth*
1612	Thomas Middleton, *The Witch*
1621	Thomas Dekker, John Ford, and William Rowley, *The Witch of Edmonton*
1623	John Webster, *The Duchess of Malfi*
1634	Thomas Heywood and Richard Brome, *The Late Lancashire Witches*
1667	Publication of John Milton's *Paradise Lost*, with a profoundly influential depiction of Christian angels, demons, and Lucifer
1681	Joseph Glanvill, *Saducismus Triumphatus*, an apparition narrative arguing for the reality of both biblical/Christian supernaturalism and witches, revenants, and other horrific supernatural beings
1692	Beginning of the Salem witch trials
1693	Publication of Cotton Mather's *Wonders of the Invisible World*, focusing on the dangers of witchcraft, and published in the immediate wake of the Salem witch trials
1704	Publication of John Dennis, *Grounds of Criticism in Poetry*, an essay promoting the terror of the sublime as the most powerful driver of great poetry
ca. 1722–1751	Rise of the so-called Graveyard Poets, who wrote melancholy poetry set in graveyards and reflecting on death and mortality, e.g., Robert Blair's "The Grave," Edward Young's *The Complaint:*

	Or Night-Thoughts on Life, Death and Immortality, and Thomas Gray's "Elegy Written in a Country Churchyard"
1727	Daniel Defoe, *An Essay on the History and Reality of Apparitions*
1746	Publication of Antoine Augustin Calmet's "Dissertations on the Apparitions of Spirits and on the Vampires or Revenants of Hungary, Moravia, and Silesia"—an exhaustive study of angels, demons, witchcraft, lycanthropy, and related beings and occult phenomena (and a book of major importance in driving popular fascination with vampires for the next century)
1757	Publication of Edmund Burke's *A Philosophical Enquiry into the Origins of Our Ideas of the Sublime and Beautiful*, an essay articulating an aesthetics of death, pain, power, and cosmic immensity that proved hugely influential for subsequent Gothic and horror literature
1764	Horace Walpole, *The Castle of Otranto*
1774	August Bürger, *Lenore*
1778	Clara Reeve, *The Old English Baron*
1781	Henry Fuseli, *The Nightmare* (painting)
1786	William Beckford, *Vathek*
1787–1789	Friedrich von Schiller, *Der Geisterseher* (*The Ghost-Seer*)
1793	Christian Heinrich Spiess, *Petermännchen* (*The Dwarf of Westerbourg*)
1794	Ann Radcliffe, *The Mysteries of Udolpho*
1796	Matthew Lewis, *The Monk*
1797	Samuel Taylor Coleridge, *Christabel*; Matthew Lewis, *The Castle Spectre*; Ann Radcliffe, *The Italian*
1798	Charles Brockden Brown, *Wieland, or The Transformation*; Samuel Taylor Coleridge, *Rime of the Ancient Mariner*
1799	Charles Brockden Brown, *Edgar Huntly*
1801	Robert Southey, *Thalaba the Destroyer*
1816	Lord Byron, John Polidori, Percy Shelley, and Mary Shelley hold a ghost story contest while staying together for the summer at the Villa Diodati on the shores of Lake Geneva, giving rise to the literary vampire (via Polidori's "The Vampyre") and Mary's *Frankenstein*
1817	E. T. A. Hoffmann, "The Sand-man"; Lord Byron, *Manfred*

1818	Jane Austen, *Northanger Abbey*; Mary Shelley, *Frankenstein, or The Modern Prometheus*
1819	John Polidori, "The Vampyre"
1820	Washington Irving, "The Legend of Sleepy Hollow"; Charles Maturin, *Melmoth the Wanderer*
1824	James Hogg, *The Private Memoirs and Confessions of a Justified Sinner*
1826	Posthumous publication of Ann Radcliffe's essay "On the Supernatural in Poetry"
1831	Nikolai Gogol, *Evenings on a Farm Near Dikanka*; Victor Hugo, *Notre Dame de Paris* (*The Hunchback of Notre Dame*); Mary Shelley, *Frankenstein* (revised version)
1835	Nikolai Gogol, *Mirgorod* and *Arabesques*; Nathaniel Hawthorne, "Young Goodman Brown"
1837	Nathaniel Hawthorne, *Twice-Told Tales*
1838	Edgar Allan Poe, "Ligeia" and *The Narrative of Arthur Gordon Pym*
1839	J. Sheridan Le Fanu, "Schalken the Painter"; Edgar Allan Poe, "The Fall of the House of Usher"
1840	Edgar Allan Poe, *Tales of the Grotesque and Arabesque*
1842	Edward Bulwer-Lytton, *Zanoni*; Edgar Allan Poe, "The Mask of the Red Death" (revised in 1845 as "The Masque of the Red Death")
1843	Edgar Allan Poe, "The Black Cat," "The Pit and the Pendulum," "The Tell-Tale Heart," "The Conqueror Worm"
1844	Nathaniel Hawthorne, "Rappaccini's Daughter"; Karl Adolf von Wachsmann, "The Mysterious Stranger"
1845	Edgar Allan Poe, "The Raven"
1845–1847	James Malcolm Rymer and Thomas Peckett Prest, *Varney the Vampire* (published in installments)
1846	Edgar Allan Poe, "The Cask of Amontillado"
1847	Charlotte Brontë, *Jane Eyre*; Emily Brontë, *Wuthering Heights*; Thomas Peckett Prest, *Sweeney Todd, The Demon Barber* (first published as *The String of Pearls*); Count Jan Potocki, *The Manuscript Found in Saragossa*
1848	The young Fox sisters of Hydesville, New York, report hearing "spirit raps," leading to the explosive birth of Spiritualism,

	which will play a significant role in much supernatural horror fiction
1851	Nathaniel Hawthorne, *The House of the Seven Gables*
1855	Elizabeth Gaskell, "The Old Nurse's Story"
1857	Charles Baudelaire, *Les Fleurs du Mal* (*The Flowers of Evil*)
1859	Edward Bulwer-Lytton, "The Haunted and the Haunters"; Wilkie Collins, *The Woman in White*; Fitz-James O'Brien, "What Was It?"
1866	Charles Dickens, "The Signal-man" (first published as "No. 1 Branch Line: The Signal-man")
1869	Comte de Lautréamont, *The Songs of Maldoror*; J. Sheridan Le Fanu, "Green Tea"
1872	J. Sheridan Le Fanu, *In a Glass Darkly* (includes *Carmilla*)
1881	Robert Louis Stevenson, "Thrawn Janet"
1882	The Society for Psychical Research is founded in London.
1884	J. K. Huysmans, *A rebours* (*Against the Grain*); Robert Louis Stevenson, "The Body Snatcher"
1885	Rudyard Kipling, "The Phantom 'Rickshaw"; Robert Louis Stevenson, "Olalla"
1886	F. Marion Crawford, "The Upper Berth"; H. Rider Haggard, *She: A History of Adventure*; Robert Louis Stevenson, *The Strange Case of Dr. Jekyll and Mr. Hyde*
1887	Guy de Maupassant, "The Horla"
1888	Rudyard Kipling, *The Phantom 'Rickshaw, and Other Tales*
1889	W. C. Morrow, "His Unconquerable Enemy"
1890	Arthur Conan Doyle, "The Ring of Thoth"; Rudyard Kipling, "The Mark of the Beast"; Vernon Lee, *Hauntings*; Oscar Wilde, *The Picture of Dorian Gray*
1891	Ambrose Bierce, "An Occurrence at Owl Creek Bridge" and "The Death of Halpin Frayser"; Thomas Hardy, *Tess of the d'Urbervilles*; J. K. Huysmans, *Là-Bas* (published in English as *Down There* or *The Damned*); Henry James, "Sir Edmund Orme"; Rudyard Kipling, "The Recrudescence of Imray"
1892	Charlotte Perkins Gilman, "The Yellow Wall-Paper" Arthur Conan Doyle, "Lot No. 249"
1893	Ambrose Bierce, "The Damned Thing" and *Can Such Things Be?*

1894	George du Maurier, *Trilby*; Arthur Machen, *The Great God Pan and the Inmost Light*
1895	Robert W. Chambers, *The King in Yellow*; Arthur Machen, *The Three Impostors* (with "The Novel of the Black Seal")
1896	H. G. Wells, *The Island of Dr. Moreau*
1897	Arthur Machen, *The Hill of Dreams*; Richard Marsh, *The Beetle*; Bram Stoker, *Dracula*; H. G. Wells, *The Invisible Man*
1898	Henry James, *The Turn of the Screw*
1899	Vernon Lee, "The Doll"
1900	Lafcadio Hearn, "Nightmare-Touch"; Robert Hichens, "How Love Came to Professor Guildea"
1901	Arthur Conan Doyle, *The Hound of the Baskervilles*; M. P. Shiel, *The Purple Cloud*
1902	W. W. Jacobs, "The Monkey's Paw"
1903	Bram Stoker, *The Jewel of Seven Stars*
1904	Lafcadio Hearn, *Kwaidan: Stories and Studies of Strange Things*; M. R. James, *Ghost Stories of an Antiquary* (with "Oh, Whistle, and I'll Come to You, My Lad"); Arthur Machen, "The White People"
1905	F. Marion Crawford, "For the Blood Is the Life"
1906	Leonid Andreyev, "Lazarus"; Algernon Blackwood, *The Empty House*
1907	Algernon Blackwood, *The Listener and Other Stories* (with "The Willows")
1908	Algernon Blackwood, *John Silence: Physician Extraordinary*; F. Marion Crawford, "The Screaming Skull"; Hanns Heinz Ewers, "The Spider"; William Hope Hodgson, *The House on the Borderland*
1910	Algernon Blackwood, "The Wendigo"; Walter de la Mare, *The Return*; Gaston Leroux, *The Phantom of the Opera*; Edith Wharton, "Afterward"
1911	Hanns Heinz Ewers, *Alraune*; M. R. James, *More Ghost Stories of an Antiquary* (with "Casting the Runes"); Oliver Onions, *Widdershins* (with "The Beckoning Fair One"); Saki, "Sredni Vashtar"; Bram Stoker, *The Lair of the White Worm*
1912	E. F. Benson, *The Room in the Tower*; Walter de la Mare, "The Listeners"; William Hope Hodgson, *The Night Land*

1913	William Hope Hodgson, *Carnacki, the Ghost Finder*
1913–1914	Gustav Meyrink, *The Golem*
1914	Saki, "The Open Window"
1915	Franz Kafka, "The Metamorphosis"
1918	Sax Rohmer, *Brood of the Witch Queen*
1919	Sigmund Freud, "The Uncanny"; Stefan Grabiński, *The Motion Demon*; W. F. Harvey, "The Beast with Five Fingers"
1920	Maurice Renard, *The Hands of Orlac*
1921	A. E. Coppard, "Adam & Eve & Pinch Me"
1922	Walter de la Mare, "Seaton's Aunt"; H. P. Lovecraft, "The Music of Erich Zann"
1923	Walter de la Mare, *The Riddle and Other Stories* (with "Seaton's Aunt" and "Out of the Deep"); launch of *Weird Tales*
1924	H. P. Lovecraft, "The Rats in the Walls"
1925	Franz Kafka, *The Trial*; Edward Lucas White, "Lukundoo"; *Not at Night*, edited by Christine Campbell Thomson
1926	Cynthia Asquith, *The Ghost Book*; D. H. Lawrence, "The Rocking-Horse Winner"; H. P. Lovecraft, "The Outsider"
1927	F. Scott Fitzgerald, "A Short Trip Home"; H. P. Lovecraft, *The Case of Charles Dexter Ward*, "Pickman's Model," "The Colour out of Space," and *Supernatural Horror in Literature*
1928	Frank Belknap Long, "The Space Eaters"; H. P. Lovecraft, "The Call of Cthulhu"; Montague Summers, *The Vampire, His Kith and Kin*; H. R. Wakefield, *They Return at Evening* (with "He Cometh and He Passeth By"); *Great Short Stories of Detection, Mystery, and Horror*, edited by Dorothy Sayers
1929	Frank Belknap Long, "The Hounds of Tindalos"; H. P. Lovecraft, "The Dunwich Horror"; Montague Summers, *The Vampire in Europe*
1930	William Faulkner, "A Rose for Emily"; H. P. Lovecraft, "The Whisperer in Darkness"
1931	Conrad Aiken, "Mr. Arcularis"; Clark Ashton Smith, "The Return of the Sorcerer"
1932	Conrad Aiken, "Silent Snow, Secret Snow"; Jean Ray, "The Shadowy Street"; launch of Charles Birkin's *Creeps* anthology series

1933	Guy Endore, *The Werewolf of Paris*; H. P. Lovecraft, "The Dreams in the Witch House"; Clark Ashton Smith, "Ubbo-Sathla"
1934	Dennis Wheatley, *The Devil Rides Out*
1936	H. P. Lovecraft, *At the Mountains of Madness*, "The Shadow over Innsmouth" "The Shadow Out of Time," and "The Haunter of the Dark"
1937	H. P. Lovecraft, "The Thing on the Doorstep"; Edith Wharton, *Ghosts* (published posthumously)
1938	John W. Campbell, "Who Goes There?"; Robert E. Howard, "Pigeons from Hell"; Daphne du Maurier, *Rebecca*
1939	H. P. Lovecraft, *The Outsider and Others*—the first published collection of Lovecraft's fiction, from the newly founded Arkham House; founding of *Unknown* magazine
1940	John Collier, "Evening Primrose"; L. Ron Hubbard, *Fear*; Theodore Sturgeon, "It"; Jack Williamson, *Darker Than You Think*
1941	Fritz Leiber, "Smoke Ghost"; H. P. Lovecraft, *The Case of Charles Dexter Ward* (published posthumously)
1942	Clark Ashton Smith, *Out of Space and Time*
1943	Robert Bloch, "Yours Truly, Jack the Ripper"; Fritz Leiber, *Conjure Wife*; Jean Ray, *Malpertuis*
1944	Theodore Sturgeon, "Killdozer"; Jack Williamson, *Darker Than You Think: Great Tales of Terror and the Supernatural*, edited by Herbert Wise and Phyllis Fraser; *Sleep No More*, edited by August Derleth
1945	Robert Bloch, *The Opener of the Way*; Elizabeth Bowen, *The Demon Lover*; August Derleth (and H. P. Lovecraft), *The Lurker at the Threshold*
1946	Ray Bradbury, "The Homecoming"
1947	Ray Bradbury, *Dark Carnival*; rebranding of Educational Comics as Entertaining Comics by William Gaines, soon to publish *Tales from the Crypt*, *Haunt of Fear*, and *Vault of Horror*
1948	Shirley Jackson, "The Lottery"; Theodore Sturgeon, "The Perfect Host"
1949	Fritz Leiber, "The Girl with the Hungry Eyes"
1950	Richard Matheson, "Born of Man and Woman"
1951	Robert Aickman, *We Are for the Dark*; Ray Bradbury, *The Illustrated Man*; John Wyndham, *The Day of the Triffids*

1952	Daphne du Maurier, "The Birds"
1953	Sarban, *The Doll Maker and Other Tales of the Uncanny*
1954	Richard Matheson, *I Am Legend*
1955	Jack Finney, *The Body Snatchers*; Flannery O'Connor, "Good Country People"
1955	Ray Bradbury, *The October Country* (revised version of 1947's *Dark Carnival*)
1957	John Wyndham, *The Midwich Cuckoos*
1959	Robert Bloch, *Psycho*; Shirley Jackson, *The Haunting of Hill House*; the first *Pan Book of Horror Stories*, edited by Herbert van Thal; *The Macabre Reader*, edited by Donald A. Wollheim
1961	Richard Matheson, "Nightmare at 20,000 Feet"; Ray Russell, "Sardonicus"
1962	Ray Bradbury, *Something Wicked This Way Comes*; Shirley Jackson, *We Have Always Lived in the Castle*; Ray Russell, *The Case Against Satan*
1963	Manly Wade Wellman, *Who Fears the Devil?*
1964	Robert Aickman, *Dark Entries* (with "Ringing the Changes"); Ramsey Campbell, *The Inhabitant of the Lake and Less Welcome Tenants*; *Creepy* #1, from Warren Publishing
1966	*Eerie* #1, from Warren Publishing
1967	Ira Levin, *Rosemary's Baby*; Colin Wilson, *The Mind Parasites*; *Dangerous Visions*, edited by Harlan Ellison
1968	Robert Aickman, *Sub Rosa* (with "The Cicerones"); Fred Chappell, *Dagon;* launch of the magazine *Weirdbook;* creation of modern zombie archetype in George Romero's *Night of the Living Dead*
1971	William Peter Blatty, *The Exorcist*; T. E. D. Klein, "The Events at Poroth Farm"; Richard Matheson, *Hell House*; Thomas Tryon, *The Other*; *The Seventh Fontana Book of Great Ghost Stories*, edited by Robert Aickman
1973	J. G. Ballard, *Crash*; Ramsey Campbell, *Demons by Daylight*; Harlan Ellison, "The Whimper of Whipped Dogs"; Robert Marasco, *Burnt Offerings*; Thomas Tryon, *Harvest Home*
1974	James Herbert, *The Rats*; Stephen King, *Carrie*; Brian Lumley, *Beneath the Moors* and *The Burrowers Beneath*; Karl Edward Wagner, "Sticks"

1975   J. G. Ballard, *High-Rise*; Harlan Ellison, *Deathbird Stories*; James Herbert, *The Fog*; Stephen King, *'Salem's Lot*; establishment of the World Fantasy Award at the first World Fantasy Convention

1976   Ramsey Campbell, *The Doll Who Ate His Mother*; John Farris, *The Fury*; Russell Kirk, "There's a Long, Long Trail A-Winding"; Ray Russell, *Incubus*; *Frights*, edited by Kirby McCauley

1977   Gary Brandner, *The Howling*; Stephen King, *The Shining*; Fritz Leiber, *Our Lady of Darkness*; Joyce Carol Oates, *Night-Side*; *Whispers*, edited by Stuart David Schiff

1978   Stephen King, *The Stand* and *Night Shift*; Whitley Strieber, *The Wolfen*; Chelsea Quinn Yarbro, *Hotel Transylvania*; launch of the *Shadows* horror anthology series, edited by Charles L. Grant

1979   Ramsey Campbell, *The Face That Must Die* and "Mackintosh Willie"; Angela Carter, *The Bloody Chamber*; Charles L. Grant, *The Hour of the Oxrun Dead*; George R. R. Martin, *Sandkings*; David Morrell, *The Totem*; Peter Straub, *Ghost Story*; Thomas Tessier, *The Nightwalker*

1980   Jonathan Carroll, *The Land of Laughs*; Suzy McKee Charnas, *The Vampire Tapestry*; Jack Ketchum, *Off Season*; Russell Kirk, "The Watchers at the Strait Gate"; Michael Shea, "The Autopsy"; *Dark Forces*, edited by Kirby McCauley

1981   Dennis Etchison, *The Dark Country*; Thomas Harris, *Red Dragon* (the novel that introduced Hannibal Lecter); Stephen King, *Cujo* and *Danse Macabre*; Robert R. McCammon, *They Thirst*; Sandy Peterson, *The Call of Cthulhu* (role-playing game); Whitley Strieber, *The Hunger*; F. Paul Wilson, *The Keep*; launch of *Rod Serling's Twilight Zone Magazine*, edited by T. E. D. Klein, Michael Blaine, and Tappan King

1982   Thomas Tessier, *Shockwaves*

1983   William Peter Blatty, *Legion* (sequel to *The Exorcist*); Robert Bloch, *Psycho 2*; Susan Hill, *The Woman in Black*; *Black Water*, edited by Alberto Manguel; *Fantastic Tales*, edited by Italo Calvino; *The Guide to Supernatural Fiction*, edited by E. F. Bleiler

1984   Clive Barker, *The Books of Blood*; Octavia E. Butler, "Bloodchild"; Stephen King and Peter Straub, *The Talisman*; T. E. D. Klein, *The Ceremonies*; Alan Moore takes over DC's *Swamp Thing*; John Skipp and Craig Spector, *The Light at the End*; S. P. Somtow, *Vampire Junction*

1985	Clive Barker, *The Damnation Game*; Stephen King, *Skeleton Crew*; T. E. D. Klein, *Dark Gods*; Thomas Ligotti, *Songs of a Dead Dreamer*; Anne Rice, *The Vampire Lestat*; Ray Russell, *Haunted Castle: The Complete Gothic Tales of Ray Russell*; Dan Simmons, *Song of Kali*
1986	Clive Barker, *The Hellbound Heart*; Stephen King, *It*; Brian Lumley, *Necroscope*; Lisa Tuttle, *A Nest of Nightmares*; "splatterpunk" coined by David J. Schow
1987	Clive Barker, *Weaveworld*; Stephen King, *Misery*; Robert R. McCammon, *Swan Song*; Toni Morrison, *Beloved*; Michael Shea, *Polyphemus* and *Fat Face*; Whitley Strieber, *Communion*; founding of the Horror Writers Association (as Horror Writers of America) and establishment of the Bram Stoker Award Dean Koontz, *Watchers*
1988	Clive Barker, *Cabal*; Neil Gaiman, *Sandman* (launch of comic book series); Thomas Harris, *The Silence of the Lambs*; Anne Rice, *The Queen of the Damned*; John Skipp and Craig Spector, *The Scream*; *Prime Evil*, edited by Douglas A. Winter; revival of *Weird Tales* by George H. Scithers, John Gregory Betancourt, and Darrell Schweitzer
1989	Neil Gaiman, *Sandman* #1; Jack Ketchum, *The Girl Next Door*; Joe R. Lansdale, *On the Far Side of the Cadillac Desert with Dead Folks*; Patrick McGrath, *The Grotesque*; Anne Rice, *The Mummy, or Ramses the Damned*; Dan Simmons, *Carrion Comfort*
1990	Robert Bloch, *Psycho House*; Noël Carroll, *The Philosophy of Horror: Or, Paradoxes of the Heart*; Thomas Ligotti, "The Last Feast of Harlequin"; Robert R. McCammon, *Mine*; Anne Rice, *The Witching Hour*; *Lovecraft's Legacy*, edited by Robert Weinberg and Martin H. Greenberg; *Splatterpunks: Extreme Horror*, edited by Paul Sammon
1991	Clive Barker, *Imajica*; Bret Easton Ellis, *American Psycho*; Thomas Ligotti, *Grimscribe: His Lives and Works*; Alan Moore, *From Hell* (issue 1); launch of the Dell Abyss line of horror paperbacks; founding of the International Gothic Association
1992	Poppy Z. Brite, *Lost Souls*; Tanith Lee, *Dark Dance* and *Heart Beast*; Kim Newman, *Anno Dracula*
1993	Poppy Z. Brite, *Drawing Blood*; Ramsey Campbell, *Alone with the Horrors*; Stefan Grabiński, *The Dark Domain*; Laurell K. Hamilton, *Guilty Pleasures*
1994	Elizabeth Hand, *Waking the Moon*; Jack Ketchum, "The Box"; Joe R. Lansdale, *Bubba Ho-Tep*; Thomas Ligotti, *Noctuary* and

	The Agonizing Resurrection of Victor Frankenstein and Other Gothic Tales; Joyce Carol Oates, *Haunted: Tales of the Grotesque*
1995	Joyce Carol Oates, *Zombie*; establishment of the International Horror Guild Award (which will run to 2008)
1996	Poppy Z. Brite, *Exquisite Corpse*; Ramsey Campbell, *The House on Nazareth Hill*; Thomas Ligotti, *The Nightmare Factory*
1997	Thomas Tessier, *Fogheart*
1998	Tom Holland, *The Sleeper in the Sands*; Caitlín R. Kiernan, *Silk*
1999	Michael Cisco, *The Divinity Student*; Thomas Harris, *Hannibal*; H. P. Lovecraft, *The Call of Cthulhu and Other Weird Stories* (first of three Penguin Classics volumes that help to canonize Lovecraft as a major American author); Peter Straub, *Mr. X*; launch of the journal *Gothic Studies*
2000	Mark Z. Danielewski, *House of Leaves*; Stephen King, *The Bullet* (published online as a freely downloadable eBook for the first week); Sarah Langan, *The Keeper*; Patrick McGrath, *Martha Peake*; China Miéville, *Perdido Street Station*; Jeffrey Thomas, *Punktown*
2001	Tananarive Due, *The Living Blood*; Neil Gaiman, *American Gods*; Charlaine Harris, *Dead Until Dark* (first novel in *The Southern Vampire Mysteries*, later adapted for television as *True Blood*); Stephen King and Peter Straub, *Black House*; Kelly Link, *Stranger Things Happen*; Chuck Palahniuk, *Lullaby*; Jeff VanderMeer, *City of Saints and Madmen*
2002	Matt Cardin, *Divinations of the Deep*; Neil Gaiman, *Coraline*; Thomas Ligotti, *My Work Is Not Yet Done*; China Miéville, *The Scar*; David Morrell, *Long Lost*
2003	Brian Keene, *The Rising*; Reggie Oliver, *The Dreams of Cardinal Vittorini*; Mark Samuels, *The White Hands and Other Weird Tales*; Jeff VanderMeer, *Veniss Underground*; awarding of the National Book Foundation's Medal for Distinguished Contribution to American Letters to Stephen King; debut of Robert Kirkman's comic series *The Walking Dead*
2004	China Miéville, *Iron Council*; Adam Nevill, *The Banquet of the Damned*
2005	Elizabeth Kostova, *The Historian*; Octavia E. Butler, *Fledgling*; John Ajvide Lindqvist, *Handling the Undead*; Joe Hill, *20th Century Ghosts*; H. P. Lovecraft: *Tales*, edited by Peter Straub and published by Library of America; Stephenie Meyer, *Twilight*; Chuck Palahniuk, *Haunted*

2006   Max Brooks, *World War Z: An Oral History of the Zombie War*; Thomas Ligotti, *Teatro Grottesco*; launch of *The Irish Journal of Gothic and Horror Studies*

2007   Laird Barron, *The Imago Sequence and Other Stories*; Joe Hill, *Heart-Shaped Box*; Sarah Langan, *The Missing*; John Ajvide Lindqvist, *Let the Right One In*; Cormac McCarthy, *The Road*; Reggie Oliver, *Masques of Satan*; Dan Simmons, *The Terror*; establishment of the Shirley Jackson Awards

2008   John Langan, *Mr. Gaunt and Other Uneasy Encounters*; Mark Samuels, *Glyphotech and Other Macabre Processes*; *Poe's Children*, edited by Peter Straub; launch of Creepypasta.com

2009   Jane Austen and Seth Grahame-Smith, *Pride and Prejudice and Zombies*; Caitlín R. Kiernan, *The Red Tree*; John Langan, *House of Windows*; Joe McKinney, *Dead City*

2010   Laird Barron, *Occultation and Other Stories*; Matt Cardin, *Dark Awakenings*; Justin Cronin, *The Passage*; Joe Hill, *Horns*; Thomas Ligotti, *The Conspiracy against the Human Race*; Isaac Marion, *Warm Bodies*; Adam Nevill, *Apartment 16*; Helen Oyeyemi, *White Is for Witching*; debut of *The Walking Dead* television series on AMC; launch of the academic journal *Horror Studies*

2011   Laird Barron, *The Light Is the Darkness*; Livia Llewellyn, *Engines of Desire: Tales of Love and Other Horrors*; Adam Nevill, *The Ritual*; Mark Samuels, *The Man Who Collected Machen*; *The Weird*, edited by Ann and Jeff VanderMeer

2012   Laird Barron, *The Croning*; Richard Gavin, *At Fear's Altar*; Jack Ketchum, *I'm Not Sam*; Caitlín R. Kiernan, *The Drowning Girl: A Memoir*; Adam Nevill, *Last Days*

2013   Laird Barron, *The Beautiful Thing That Awaits Us All*; Joe Hill, *NOS4A2*; John Langan, *The Wide Carnivorous Sky and Other Monstrous Geographies*

2014   Kelly Link, *Magic for Beginners*; Adam Nevill, *No One Gets Out Alive*; Simon Strantzas, *Burnt Black Suns*; Jeff VanderMeer, the *Southern Reach Trilogy*

2015   Clive Barker, *The Scarlet Gospels*; Elizabeth Hand, *Wylding Hall*; Thomas Ligotti, *Songs of a Dead Dreamer and Grimscribe* (Penguin Classics edition with revised texts); Paul Tremblay, *A Head Full of Ghosts*; National Medal of the Arts awarded to Stephen King

2015–2016	Alan Moore, *Providence*
2016	Laird Barron, *Swift to Chase*; Joe Hill, *The Fireman*; John Langan, *The Fisherman*; Livia Llewellyn, *Furnace*; Jon Padgett, *The Secret of Ventriloquism*

JACKSON, SHIRLEY (1916–1965)

Best known for the 1948 short story "The Lottery" and the 1959 novel *The Haunting of Hill House*, Shirley Jackson was a prominent, albeit controversial writer during the 1950s and 1960s. Her legacy is largely as an author of horror and supernatural fiction, but Jackson's oeuvre crossed genres, from the campus novel to children's fiction to the domestic novel. She is considered to be the queen of Gothic literature in the twentieth century. With her husband, literary critic Stanley Edgar Hyman, Jackson raised four children, and the couple moved several times, most notably to

"The Lottery": Picture-Perfect Town with a Sinister Secret

"The Lottery," first published on June 26, 1948, in *The New Yorker*, is one of Jackson's best-known works, establishing her as a writer of horror and the macabre. It takes place on one day—June 27—in an unnamed small American town. The town is presented as completely normal and innocuous, as the reader is introduced to different townspeople, all of whom appear to be preparing for some sort of festival or town ritual, known only as the lottery. The tone becomes increasingly sinister until it is clear what is happening: the unlucky winner of the lottery will be stoned to ensure a healthy harvest.

The story's publication prompted a storm of readers to write letters to the editor, expressing their disapproval and outright disgust. Jackson said nearly three hundred letters arrived that summer, most of them negative, although some readers did express admiration for the story. "The Lottery" made such a lasting impression that Jackson received attention over it for the rest of her life from readers demanding answers to why she wrote it. She would eventually say that she had hoped the story would highlight the world's inhumanity and violence. A prevalent theme is not just brutality, as seen in the ancient ritual that is still alive and well in the small town, but also the random nature of that brutality. The townspeople have largely forgotten why they even participate in the lottery; it is simply a ritual that they follow because they have always done so.

"The Lottery" has been adapted for film and television, and it remains one of Jackson's most famous works. It is routinely anthologized and taught in high school and university literature courses, and fans celebrate "Lottery Day" every year on June 27.

Lisa Kröger

North Bennington, Vermont, a town that offered inspiration for her writing. Though she died in 1965 at the relatively young age of forty-eight, she was prolific.

After briefly attending the University of Rochester, Jackson withdrew to take a year to write, before enrolling in Syracuse University, where she published her first short story, "Janice" (1938), and met Hyman, a relationship that proved to be instrumental in her career. Together, Hyman and Jackson founded a university literary magazine, *Spectre*. By the time her first novel, *The Road Through the Wall*, was published in 1948, Jackson had long been immersed in the literary world and had published several stories; her first national story was the humorous "My Life with R. H. Macy" in a 1941 issue of the *New Republic*. *The Road Through the Wall* introduced readers to a theme that would become common in Jackson's work: an isolated community that is hostile toward or unwilling to interact with outsiders. The novel tells the story of the citizens of Pepper Street, who are all fine, upstanding citizens in their own minds, but who refuse to socialize with those who do not fit their narrow view of the world.

The same year her first novel was published, Jackson's most infamous story, "The Lottery," was printed in *The New Yorker*. Like *The Road Through the Wall*, the story introduces a seemingly moral community, but one that annually engages in murder to appease a long-standing tradition. The story immediately struck a chord with readers, many of whom hated the violence of the story's climax and wrote letters to the magazine, resulting in the largest amount of mail the publisher had ever received. Though "The Lottery" was widely criticized, the story also gave Jackson literary fame, and the story was first adapted to television in 1952. It would later inspire film adaptations. Though none of her other stories received as much attention as "The Lottery," a few did garner critical attention, including "The Summer People" (1951) and "One Ordinary Day with Peanuts" (1956), both of which appeared in *Best American Short Stories* in the years they were published. Her 1961 short story "Louisa, Please Come Home," a mystery involving the disappearance of a young woman the day before her sister's wedding, was awarded the Edgar Allan Poe Award, given by the Mystery Writers of America.

"The Lottery" established Jackson as a writer of "weird fiction," placing her in a long line of writers of the fantasy and horror genre. Jackson, though, defied categorization, as she was just as comfortable writing about her life at home as she was a grisly tale of murder. As a mother of four children and a homemaker, Jackson had a fountain of material, which she collected into essays for *Good Housekeeping* and a litany of other magazines, including *Woman's Day* and *Woman's Home Companion*, plus two domestic novels filled with sketches of her life as a wife and mother, often with a humorous tone: *Life Among the Savages* was published in 1952, and *Raising Demons* followed in 1957. Jackson's musings are unflinchingly honest at times, which sets them apart from the stylized and overly optimistic domestic writings of the time.

As is fitting for a Gothic writer, Jackson was greatly interested in studying witchcraft and the occult, a subject she wrote about in 1956's *The Witchcraft of Salem*

Village, an account of the events surrounding the Salem witch trials written for children. Jackson would go on to pen more children's stories, including a one-act play called *The Bad Children* (1959), which retold the fable of Hansel and Gretel, and two more books, *9 Magic Wishes* (1963) and *Famous Sally* (1966).

It was Jackson's novel *Hangsaman*, published in 1951, that established her career as a Gothic writer. On its surface it is a campus novel, telling the story of Natalie Waite as she attends her first year at a small liberal arts college that shares more than a passing resemblance to Bennington College, where Jackson's husband had taught. But as the novel progresses, the plot becomes darker as Natalie, a Gothic heroine, is sexually assaulted by a family friend and eventually unravels. The novels that followed all contain elements of Gothic horror. *The Bird's Nest* (1954) contains a heroine who, like Natalie in *Hangsaman*, has a tenuous grip on reality. The book tells the story of Elizabeth, who struggles with schizophrenia and multiple personalities after being molested by her mother's lover. The novel is a prime example of Jackson's interest in the field of psychology, which forms a recurring motif in her works. It was adapted into the 1957 film *Lizzie*, directed by Hugo Haas and starring Eleanor Parker. In *The Sundial* (1958), Jackson explored the idea of a Gothic mansion, this one run by the Halloran family, all of whom seem to be so removed from the outside world that they cannot be trusted to understand what is reality and what is fantasy.

The character of the outsider shunning the world in a Gothic castle is one that would become a favorite of Jackson's. In 1959, Jackson published her most famous novel, *The Haunting of Hill House*. In telling the story of Hill House, a mansion that Jackson describes as having been "born bad" (Jackson 1984, 70), Jackson enters into a long tradition of haunted house tales, following in the footsteps of Edgar Allan Poe and Henry James. The novel inspired two films, 1963's *The Haunting*, directed by Robert Wise and considered a masterpiece in its own right, and the lesser 1999 film of the same title, directed by Jan de Bont. Hill House, a haunted house with its writing on the wall (in blood) and mysterious noises, is most likely the prototype for many haunted houses to come, from the Overlook Hotel in Stephen King's 1977 novel *The Shining* to the Navidson family's new home in Mark Z. Danielewski's *House of Leaves* (2000).

Though not a haunted house novel, Jackson's *We Have Always Lived in the Castle* (1962), which was named one of the "Ten Best Novels" of the year by *Time* magazine, continued her development of the Gothic. Like many of Jackson's other novels, this one tells the story of a heroine who has become an outsider to society. Unlike a weaker or more innocent character such as *Hangsaman*'s Natalie or *The Haunting of Hill House*'s Eleanor, Merricat Blackwood maintains more control over her isolation in Blackwood Manor, and also, more significantly, over her older sister Constance. Merricat is protective of her sister, defending her against the antagonistic townspeople and a greedy relative, and making a home for the two of them, even as their family home is crumbling around them. The novel spawned several adaptations for the stage, the first in 1966 and another in 2010, as a musical for the

Yale Repertory Theatre. Film adaptations have been rumored, though as of 2016, none have come to fruition.

The Haunting of Hill House and *We Have Always Lived in the Castle* garnered more critical praise for Jackson than any of her other novels. Despite failing health, she continued to be a prolific writer, participating in conferences and lecturing at universities until her death on August 8, 1965, of heart failure.

Given Jackson's quite varied authorial career, many critics find it difficult to categorize her as merely a "horror" writer, out of concern that the title does not accurately represent the breadth of her canon. Jackson does manage to instill a sense of horror in her readers, particularly as she shows them the violence that can lie just beneath the surface of everyday life. Her characters are often on the verge of a mental collapse, and her stories have a profound psychological depth for readers to plumb. Her landscapes tend to be Gothic in nature (i.e., large mansions with murderous pasts), and her heroines are almost always escaping a hostile outside world. Perhaps due to her success in the Gothic and horror fiction, Jackson's legacy has been relegated to that genre, though late twentieth-century and early twenty-first-century critics began to show a renewed interest in her work.

In 1988, Judy Oppenheimer published the first biography of Jackson, *Private Demons: The Life of Shirley Jackson*. Many readers and critics questioned some of its claims that Jackson suffered from mental disease and possible childhood sexual abuse. Oppenheimer also makes the claim that Jackson's study into the supernatural and occult went beyond a scholar's interest, and that she believed in the existence of the supernatural. Many critics, however, take issue with this stance, asserting that Jackson probably held no such notion and citing the fact the characters in Jackson's works who experience the supernatural are often struggling with differentiating the real world from the inner world of imagination. Some have argued that the question of whether or not Jackson herself believed in the supernatural overshadows her authorial legacy, though this is beginning to change. Jackson's literary achievements continue into the twenty-first century, with her estate releasing previously unpublished works, including "Paranoia" (2013) and "The Man in the Woods" (2014), both of which appeared in *The New Yorker*. These stories, along with more of Jackson's previously unseen works, were collected and published in *Let Me Tell You: New Stories, Essays, and Other Writings* (2015), edited by two of Jackson's adult children, Laurence Jackson Hyman and Sarah Hyman DeWitt.

In some ways, the memory of Jackson herself has nearly eclipsed her writing, as readers are just as intrigued by Shirley Jackson the person as they are by Shirley Jackson the author. On June 27 (the same day the events of "The Lottery" take place), the town of North Bennington celebrates Shirley Jackson as one of their most illustrious citizens. Novelist Susan Scott Merrell wrote Jackson as a character in her 2015 psychological thriller *Shirley: A Novel*, which tells the tale of the disappearance of a young college student who attends the same university where Jackson's husband teaches. The novel takes true events from Jackson's life and the real disappearance of Paula Weldon (which also inspired Jackson's *Hangsaman* and

"The Missing Girl") and interweaves them with a fictional mystery. In 2016, a new biography of Shirley Jackson, *Shirley Jackson: A Rather Haunted Life*, written by Ruth Franklin, was published, demonstrating that Jackson still captivates audiences even half a century after her death. In a further example of her enduring influence, the Shirley Jackson Award was established in 2007 to be given annually in recognition of superior achievement in long and short fiction in the genres of thriller (particularly psychological thrillers, as Jackson herself would have preferred), horror, and dark fantasy. The first Shirley Jackson Awards were presented at the 2007 Readercon conference in Burlington, Massachusetts.

Lisa Kröger

See also: The Haunted House or Castle; *The Haunting of Hill House*; Shirley Jackson Awards; Witches and Witchcraft.

Further Reading

Anderson, Melanie R., and Lisa Kröger, eds. 2016. *Shirley Jackson, Influences and Confluences*. New York: Routledge.

Franklin, Ruth. 2016. *Shirley Jackson: A Rather Haunted Life*. New York: Liveright.

Friedman, Lenemaja. 1975. *Shirley Jackson: A Biography*. Boston: Twayne.

Hall, Joan Wylie. 1993. *Shirley Jackson: A Study of the Short Fiction*. New York: Twayne.

Hattenhauer, Darryl. 2003. *Shirley Jackson's American Gothic*. Albany: State University of New York Press.

Jackson, Shirley. [1959] 1984. *The Haunting of Hill House*. New York: Penguin Books.

Jackson, Shirley. 2015. *Let Me Tell You: New Stories, Essays, and Other Writings*. New York: Random House.

Miller, Laura. 2006. Introduction to *The Haunting of Hill House*, by Shirley Jackson, ix–xxii. New York: Penguin. http://lauramiller.typepad.com/lauramiller/shirley-jacksons-the -haunting-of-hill-house-an-introduction.html.

Murphy, Bernice M., ed. 2005. *Shirley Jackson: Essays on the Literary Legacy*. Jefferson, NC: McFarland.

Oppenheimer, Judy. 1988. *Private Demons: The Life of Shirley Jackson*. New York: Putnam.

JAMES, HENRY (1843–1916)

Henry James was an expatriate American writer who spent most of his adult life living in England and on the European continent. He was a prolific author of novels, short stories, essays, reviews, and travel writing, and was best known in his fiction writing for his sharp and incisive portraits of the psychological lives of his characters. James's vast output includes eighteen stories, most written before the turn of the twentieth century, which his biographer, Leon Edel, collected as *The Ghostly Tales of Henry James* (1948). Charles L. Elkins, writing in *Supernatural Fiction Writers*, speculates that James may have been drawn to the tale of the supernatural because ghost stories were a very popular type of fiction in the Victorian era and James wanted to be successful financially as well as critically. His most famous ghost story is an undisputed classic of the form, the short novel *The Turn of the Screw* (1898).

Although James's ghost stories are not traditional by most genre standards, some feature genuine ghostly presences. In "The Romance of Certain Old Clothes" (1868), a woman who is set on marrying the widower of her dead sister rummages through a trunk of clothes that her sister forbade anyone but her daughter to have, and is found dead beside it, her face and brow bearing "the marks of ten hideous wounds from two vengeful ghostly hands." "Sir Edmund Orme" (1891) literalizes the idea of the sins of the parents being visited upon the children when a mother is dismayed to see the ghost of a lover she once jilted pursuing her daughter, presumably to inflict misery upon her. In "The Real Right Thing" (1899), a journalist intent on writing the biography of a deceased writer with the cooperation of his widow changes his mind when the writer's ghost appears to them both to dissuade them.

In a number of James's stories, the ghosts and hauntings are more ambiguous. "The Ghostly Rental" (1876) concerns an elderly man, Captain Diamond, who is convinced that he sees the ghost of his dead daughter in the house where he disowned her for a past indiscretion. When his daughter later reveals to the narrator that she is alive and has been maintaining the charade of her death to punish her father, she is convinced that she sees *his* ghost in the house after he dies, although this may just be an expression of her own guilty feelings. In "Owen Wingrave" (1892), a young man who refuses to follow his family's tradition of entering military service agrees to sleep in a room supposedly haunted by the ghost of a colonel ancestor who killed his own son in it in a fit of rage. When the room is entered the next day the young man is found dead. The protagonist of "The Jolly Corner" (1908) returns to his boyhood home in New York as part of his quest to discover how his life might have turned out had he not left thirty years before, and encounters what appears to be the alternate identity that he might have had. *The Turn of the Screw* has long been regarded a masterpiece of ambiguous supernaturalism. Its heroine, a newly hired governess at a country estate, is convinced that the two children she is supervising have fallen under the malignant influence of the ghosts of her employer's ex-valet and her predecessor, although it is never clear whether the spectral figures she sees are real or projections of her own emotionally overwrought mind. The story was adapted memorably for the screen in 1961 as *The Innocents*.

Like the ghost stories of Edith Wharton, with whom James was friends, his ghost stories differ little from his more mainstream writing as regards the development of their characters and the insights provided for their motivations and behaviors. They are important examples of how the tale of the supernatural is just one of many possible approaches to fiction in a literary writer's repertoire.

Stefan R. Dziemianowicz

See also: Psychological Horror; Spiritualism; *The Turn of the Screw*; Unreliable Narrator; Wharton, Edith; *Part One, Horror through History*: Horror in the Nineteenth Century; *Part Two, Themes, Topics, and Genres*: Ghost Stories.

Further Reading

Edel, Leon. 1970. "Introduction." In *Henry James: Stories of the Supernatural*, v–xiv. New York: Taplinger.

Elkins, Charles. 1982. "Henry James." In *Supernatural Fiction Writers, Volume I: Fantasy and Horror*, edited by E. F. Bleiler, 337–344. New York: Scribners.

James, Henry. 1996. "The Romance of Certain Old Clothes." In *American Gothic Tales*, edited by Joyce Carol Oates, 103–120. New York: Penguin.

Lustig, T. J. 1994. *Henry James and the Ghostly*. Cambridge: Cambridge University Press.

Tuttle, Lisa. 1988. "Henry James." In *The St. James Guide to Horror, Ghost & Gothic Writers*, edited by Richard Bleiler, 298–301. Detroit, MI: St. James Press.

JAMES, M. R. (1862–1936)

Montague Rhodes "Monty" James was the youngest son of an evangelical Anglican divine (clergy). As indicated by his memoir's title, *Eton and King's* (1926), he attended Eton College, then King's College at Cambridge University, and worked at those two institutions for most of his life as a medievalist, biblical scholar, translator, museum director, and administrator. However, James's contemporary reputation rests not on a prolific academic output but on his occasional pastime as writer of about three dozen ghost stories, which some critics see as the apogee of the late nineteenth- and early twentieth-century English ghost story tradition. He published relatively few of these stories in periodicals, and some, such as "After Dark in the Playing Fields" (1924) and "Rats" (1929), appeared in small Eton magazines.

James's stories were often honed as oral tales to rapt fireside academic audiences on Christmas Eve nights or read at meetings of various literary societies. They often maintain informal, laconic, and understated tones appropriate to their original telling, glaze over plot details, and exhibit a flair for the minutiae of Edwardian academics' lives. For example, "The Mezzotint" (1904) includes a side gag about academics golfing.

Many of James's stories made their first print appearances in four thin collections of five to eight stories: *Ghost Stories of an Antiquary* (1904), *More Ghost Stories of an Antiquary* (1911), *A Thin Ghost and Others* (1919), and *A Warning to the Curious and Other Ghost Stories* (1925). A darkly humorous tale to scare Boy Scouts, *Wailing Well* (1928) first appeared as a chapbook. The nearly comprehensive *The Collected Ghost Stories of M. R. James* (1931) appeared in his lifetime. S. T. Joshi's two-volume *The Complete Ghost Stories of M. R. James* (2005–2006) rounds up remaining early and fugitive stories as well as James's limited but provocative theoretical writings on the form of the ghost story, mostly from prefaces to his own work or others' collections.

James is best remembered for his first two collections, especially *Ghost Stories of an Antiquary*. The enthusiasm of James's illustrator friend James McBryde spurred James to assemble the collection. However, McBryde's untimely death came after he produced only two illustrations each for "Canon Alberic's Scrap-Book" (1895) and "Oh, Whistle, and I'll Come to You, My Lad" (1904). James refused to let any

"Oh, Whistle, and I'll Come to You, My Lad"

This story, which takes its title from a song by Robert Burns, first appeared in 1903 in a reading by M. R. James before a Christmas gathering in King's College, Cambridge, before its inclusion in *Ghost Stories of an Antiquary* the following year. It has been widely anthologized and was adapted for television three times in Britain: as a reasonably faithful short film (1968), a dramatic reading (1986), and a loosely reworked metaphor for dementia (2010).

Professor Parkins, a resolute rationalist, notes someone following him at a distance the moment he uncovers a bronze whistle in the ruins of a Templar church, and he assumes this is merely another guest at his hotel. When he discovers inscriptions on both sides of the whistle, he ignores the Latin puzzle in the first, but feels sufficiently confident in his translation of the second—"Who is this who is coming?"—to set the whistle to his lips, bringing a gust of shrieking wind round the hotel, which bursts into the room and blows out the candles (James 2005, 88). Thereafter, dreams of pursuit along the beach join puzzling activity on the empty bed adjacent to his own, and sightings of a waving figure at his window, until he encounters a hideous "face of crumpled linen" (100).

James cleverly combines traditional motifs—the sheeted ghost, Gothic ruins, folk belief in whistling for the wind, and a skeptical observer—with an abbreviated form of the accumulated tension and inexorable weight of history that he had learned from J. Sheridan Le Fanu, then adds elements specific to his own interests, such as Latin tags, medieval artifacts, and an ironic detachment bordering on black humor. The result is as seamless as myth and as vivid as nightmare.

Jim Rockhill

Source: James, M. R. 2005. *Count Magnus and Other Ghost Stories.* New York: Penguin Classics.

other illustrator finish the work. McBryde's detailed rendering from a photograph of the interior of Saint Bertrand de Comminges Cathedral, the location of Canon Alberic's haunted scrapbook, became the frontispiece for the collection's first edition. McBryde models his drawing of the story's academic protagonist on James himself, and that character, Dennistoun, is mentioned again by the narrator of "The Mezzotint" and establishes the type for subsequent James protagonists. Another of McBryde's illustrations, the sheet-wrapped specter attacking in "Oh, Whistle," is iconic and graces many subsequent covers of James's work. As a tribute to his friend, James also oversaw the publication of *The Story of a Troll-Hunt* (1904), a fantasy story written and drawn by McBryde and based on his and James's trip with a third friend to Jutland. Another James editorial project was the recovery and publication of often anonymous ghost stories from his favorite writer of the genre, J. Sheridan Le Fanu, in *Madame Cowl's Ghost and Other Tales of Mystery* (1923).

James appeared to hold some contempt for the occult detective fiction of contemporaries William Hope Hodgson and Algernon Blackwood, but his work has overlays of detective fiction. He admired Charles Dickens and Arthur Conan Doyle's Sherlock Holmes, referenced *The Strand* in "A School Story" (1911), and wrote an introduction (1926) to Le Fanu's sensation novel *Uncle Silas* (1864). One might connect the Holmes cases' emphases on clues and physical objects and use of them for titles to James's practice. The vast majority of James's stories are titled after objects and places, the sources of the haunting. The haunted art of "The Mezzotint" is the most self-reflexive example, a motif James returns to in "The Haunted Dolls' House" (1923). Scholars dispute the interpretation of James's title "The Malice of Inanimate Objects" (1933), but it aptly summarizes his oeuvre. More direct influences from detective fiction are present. Despite his contempt for Edgar Allan Poe's "Ligeia" (1838), James's "The Treasure of Abbot Thomas" (1904) owes much to the cryptography of Poe's "The Gold-Bug" (1843). Other stories like "The Rose Garden" (1911) and "Two Doctors" (1919) are highly elliptical and rely on the reader to make inferences from their sparse details.

Mark Fisher's *The Weird and the Eerie* (2017) contrasts two categories of horror that many James stories straddle. James's playful, understated ghost stories might seem inimical to the cosmic bombast often associated with *Weird Tales* writing. As Joshi points out, James slyly criticizes weird writers in print, and in letters rails against H. P. Lovecraft, Arthur Machen, and others. But Lovecraft admires James, and not just for their shared disinterest in plots (Joshi 1990, 141–42). Lovecraft singles out the grotesque, bestial, and tactile qualities of James's ghosts, which can suggest weird writers' fascination with viscera, sinister evolutions, and the nonhuman. One might think of the burned giant spiders and the witch's black-haired skeleton revealed in the immolation of "The Ash-Tree" (1904) or the dried, cobwebbed baldness of the apparition in "The Tractate Middoth" (1911). As Joshi points out, many of James's tales operate on a strident binary between the academic, reserved, bourgeois qualities of his English male protagonists and the bestial violence of his sometimes feminine specters. In "Count Magnus" (1904), an overinquisitive English academic foolishly thrice wishes to gaze upon a dead Satanist Swedish nobleman and finds himself pursued back to England and to a grisly end by two mysterious cloaked figures, the revenant count and his nonhuman familiar. For Lovecraft and China Miéville, this story is the apotheosis of James's synthesis of the ghost story's typical religious and folkloric overtones, as well as indirect style, with the weird tale's characteristic madness and inexplicable otherness.

Robert Macfarlane intimately associates the mode of the eerie with James, both as a technique of slow-mounting dread and as a fascination with landscapes and what lies beneath: brutal histories of struggles for property and more overt supernatural intrusions. Macfarlane's central example is James's "A View from a Hill" (1925) as haunted binoculars reveal the ghosts of people and architecture of an English landscape. James's post–World War I stories largely surrendered his occasional prior interest in French and Scandinavian settings, and James's fiction turned to an English setting eerie with hidden landscapes and threatening yet never fully apprehensible history, such as "A Warning to the Curious" (1925). As Macfarlane traces it, this mode of James's inflects contemporary trends in music, poetry, and painting. Most notably, one can see its role in the filmic subgenre of folk horror, which had a heyday in the late 1960s and early 1970s, including *The Blood on Satan's Claw* (1970), *The Wicker Man* (1973), and *A Ghost Story for Christmas* (1971–1975), an annual television film series of James adaptations. This tradition has lately been revived in the films of Ben Wheatley, especially *A Field in England* (2013), and revivals of *A Ghost Story for Christmas*.

The most comprehensive collection of television film adaptations of James is the British Film Institute's *Ghost Stories for Christmas* (2013), which includes twenty-one different adaptations of James's stories along with adaptations of a few other ghost story writers, including Dickens and occasional James-imitator Ramsey Campbell. Many were broadcast on the BBC at Christmas. These adaptations range from eleven to fifty-two minutes in length and were made from 1968 to 2010. About half dramatize James's narratives; the other half are single actors performing partially dramatized readings, including three done by Christopher Lee playing M. R. James himself. Both visual and audio adaptations of James proliferate far beyond that single British Film Institute (BFI) collection. One volunteer-based, public domain source of audio adaptations of James is the website *LibriVox*, which hosts recordings of James's first three story collections as well as his only novel, the surreal children's fantasy *The Five Jars* (1922).

Bob Hodges

See also: Campbell, Ramsey; "Casting the Runes"; The Haunted House or Castle; Le Fanu, J. Sheridan; Occult Detectives; *Part One, Horror through History*: Horror from 1900 to 1950; *Part Two, Themes, Topics, and Genres*: Ghost Stories; Occult Fiction; Religion, Horror, and the Supernatural; Weird and Cosmic Horror Fiction.

Further Reading

Briggs, Julia. 1977. *Night Visitors: The Rise and Fall of the English Ghost Story*. London: Faber.

Ghost Stories for Christmas: Expanded 6 Disc Collection. 2013. DVD. London: BFI.

Joshi, S. T. 2005–2006. Introductions to *The Complete Ghost Stories of M. R. James*. 2 vols. New York: Penguin.

Joshi, S. T. [1990] 2003. *The Weird Tale*. Maryland: Wildside Press.

Lovecraft, H. P. [1927] 2012. *The Annotated Supernatural Horror in Literature*, edited by S. T. Joshi. New York: Hippocampus Press.

Macfarlane, Robert. 2015. "The Eeriness of the English Countryside." *The Guardian*, April 10. https://www.theguardian.com/books/2015/apr/10/eeriness-english-country side-robert-macfarlane.

Miéville, China. 2011. "M. R. James and the Quantum Vampire: Weird; Hauntological: Versus and/or and and/or or?" *Weird Fiction Review*, November 29. http://weirdfiction review.com/2011/11/m-r-james-and-the-quantum-vampire-by-china-mieville. Originally published in *Collapse* IV (May 2008): 105–126.

Sullivan, Jack. 1978. *Elegant Nightmares: The English Ghost Story from Le Fanu to Blackwood*. Athens: Ohio University Press.

THE JEWEL OF SEVEN STARS

The Jewel of Seven Stars is Bram Stoker's best-known novel after *Dracula*, and the only other of his works to have been adapted for the cinema. It was released in two very different versions in 1903 and 1912, the latter being significantly shorter, with a conventional romantic ending and a central, introspective chapter excised.

The novel opens in Edwardian London, where Abel Trelawny, a British Egyptologist, lies unconscious after having been mysteriously attacked during the night. The narrator, Malcolm Ross, is enamored of Margaret, Trelawny's daughter, and joins the beleaguered household in their nightly vigils. Ross learns through Corbeck, another Egyptologist, that Trelawny has plundered the grave goods of the female pharaoh Tera, transporting her mummy, its detached seven-fingered hand, a mysterious ruby—the jewel of the title—a sealed coffer, and some ritually significant lamps to London. The attacks appear to have been perpetrated supernaturally by Tera's mummified polydactyl cat, who acts as a sort of guardian both to the severed hand and the jewel. Having transported the whole assemblage to a cave in Cornwall, Trelawny attempts to revive the remarkably preserved mummy of Tera. In the first edition, a violent storm breaks into the chamber, disrupting what appears to be a successful revival of the body, and Ross, the sole survivor, is left to describe the horror that characterizes the fixed faces of his dead companions who have, clearly, witnessed something unspeakable. In the second edition, the mummy is destroyed without having been revived, nobody dies, and Ross and Margaret marry, the bride wearing Tera's robe and jewelry.

The Jewel of Seven Stars is, in many ways, a quite conventional Gothic work. It has an ambivalent supernatural content, and there is a suggestion of the promethean overreacher in the characterization of Trelawny. The novel is, further, saturated with doppelgängers—Margaret resembles Tera; her polydactyl cat may be confused with its mummified counterpart; the dead are at times mistaken for

---

Film Adaptations of *The Jewel of Seven Stars*

1970   "The Curse of the Mummy"—The final episode of the popular British television anthology series *Mystery and Imagination*.

1971   *Blood from the Mummy's Tomb*—The last entry in the popular series of mummy movies from Britain's Hammer Films that had started in 1959 with *The Mummy*.

1980   *The Awakening*—A big-budget production starring Charlton Heston, intended as a "serious" mummy film but emerging as a critical and commercial flop.

1998   *Bram Stoker's The Mummy*—A garish, low-budget production that was hastily made and released to cash in on the imminent reboot of Universal Studios' classic mummy series with 1999's big-budget *The Mummy*.

Matt Cardin

the living. As in *Dracula*, there is a central group of professional, educated gentlemen, accompanied by an appendant and resourceful woman, to balance the supernatural revenant—though here they appear to be easing, rather than opposing, the undead's access to British soil. The settings, both in urban London and rural Cornwall, are claustrophobic and sublime in their literally shadowed obscurity.

While *The Jewel of Seven Stars* superficially resembles Egyptological romances such as Conan Doyle's "Lot no. 249" (1892), or Marsh's *The Beetle* (1897), it is nonetheless an unusually thoughtful work. Tera's resurrection is rendered through the language of science rather than occultism, and science is implicitly tested by the uncanny. "Powers—Old and New," the cancelled chapter, likewise contemplates the existence of rival gods, thereby engendering a cosmological debate that the stridently Protestant author might well have deemed inappropriate for a second, popular edition. The Egyptological content of the novel is, incidentally, systematic and relatively accurate, being derived largely from the writings of the British Egyptologist E. A. Wallis Budge. Notable film adaptations include *Blood from the Mummy's Tomb* (1971), which was the last entry in the Hammer Films mummy series, and *The Awakening* (1980), a big-budget (and slow, and ponderous, and critically reviled) production starring Charlton Heston.

William Hughes

See also: Doubles, Doppelgängers, and Split Selves; Mummies; Stoker, Bram; *Part One, Horror through History*: Horror from 1900 to 1950.

Further Reading

Bridges, Meilee D. 2008. "Tales from the Crypt: Bram Stoker and the Curse of the Egyptian Mummy." *Victorians Institute Journal* 36, 137–165.

Hughes, William. 2000. *Beyond Dracula: Stoker's Fiction and Its Cultural Context*. New York: Palgrave.

Stoker, Bram. [1903] 1996. *The Jewel of Seven Stars*. Annotated and edited by Clive Leatherdale. Westcliff-on-Sea, Essex, UK: Desert Island Books.

JOHN SILENCE: PHYSICIAN EXTRAORDINARY

John Silence: Physician Extraordinary by Algernon Blackwood was one of the earliest and most influential books in the development of the occult detective genre. It was published in 1908 as a collection of five original stories. The character of Silence followed in the footsteps of Bram Stoker's Abraham Van Helsing, J. Sheridan Le Fanu's Dr. Martin Hesselius, and Heskith Pritchard's Flaxman Low.

The stories were originally intended by Blackwood to be independent examinations of different occult topics, but the publisher, Eveleigh Nash, requested him to tie them together with a single character. Because Silence was added secondarily, he sometimes has only a nominal role. The publisher excluded a sixth story, "A

The Psychic Doctor

In the opening paragraphs of the first John Silence story, "A Psychical Invasion," Blackwood paints a picture of the eponymous detective that is at once endearing and mysterious. After describing Silence as independently wealthy and inclined toward philanthropy—to the point of accepting only "unremunerative cases"—Blackwood begins to establish the doctor's mysterious credentials:

> But there was another side to his personality and practice, and one with which we are now more directly concerned; for the cases that especially appealed to him were of no ordinary kind, but rather of that intangible, elusive, and difficult nature best described as psychical afflictions; and, though he would have been the last person himself to approve of the title, it was beyond question that he was known more or less generally as the "Psychic Doctor."
>
> In order to grapple with cases of this peculiar kind, he had submitted himself to a long and severe training, at once physical, mental, and spiritual. What precisely this training had been, or where undergone, no one seemed to know,— for he never spoke of it, as, indeed, he betrayed no single other characteristic of the charlatan,—but the fact that it had involved a total disappearance from the world for five years, and that after he returned and began his singular practice no one ever dreamed of applying to him the so easily acquired epithet of quack, spoke much for the seriousness of his strange quest and also for the genuineness of his attainments. (Blackwood 1909, 3–4)

Matt Cardin

Source: Blackwood, Algernon. 1909. *John Silence, Physician Extraordinary.* Boston: John W. Luce & Company.

Victim of Higher Space," from the collection because he felt it was weaker than the others, but it was published in *The Occult Review* for December 1914 and has been added to recent reprints of the collection. It is far shorter than the others and lacks their mood and atmosphere.

Silence is an independently wealthy physician who only takes on cases that personally interest him, such as a haunting that causes a writer to lose his sense of humor in "A Psychical Invasion." As in "Green Tea" by Le Fanu, it involves a patient made vulnerable to a haunting by ingesting a drug. It was inspired by a haunted house Blackwood knew of in Putney. Other cases involve a fire elemental from ancient Egypt in "Nemesis of Fire," inspired by the home of an Egyptologist he knew, and a case of lycanthropy in "Camp of the Dog," set on a Swedish island where he had once camped with a group. Silence makes only nominal appearances in "Ancient Sorceries," in which he passively listens to a patient's tale of witchcraft and cats in a remote French village, and in "Secret Worship," in which he appears at the end to save someone from the spectral replay of a devil-worshipping cult in a southern German village.

The individual stories reflect Blackwood's interests both as an occultist and as an outdoorsman. A member of the Order of the Golden Dawn, an important occult and metaphysical organization at the turn of the twentieth century that numbered several prominent authors among its members, he believed in the supernatural and understood and treated his subject matter seriously. He also had a lifelong love of nature, which shows in his writings. The first five Silence stories were all set in locations Blackwood had visited, and they display his strength at creating atmosphere, a strength that also informed other, later works such as "The Wendigo" and "The Willows."

The book was heavily promoted on its release, and its popularity established Blackwood's name and reputation as a writer. It also paved the way for such later characters and series as William Hope Hodgson's Thomas Carnacki, Seabury Quinn's Jules de Grandin, and on television, *Kolchak the Night Stalker* and *The X-Files*.

Lee Weinstein

See also: Blackwood, Algernon; *Carmilla*; *The Devil Rides Out*; *Dracula*; "Green Tea"; Hodgson, William Hope; Occult Detectives; Quinn, Seabury; "The Willows."

Further Reading

Ashley, Mike. 2001. *Algernon Blackwood: An Extraordinary Life*. New York: Carroll & Graf.

Blackwood, Algernon. 1997. *The Complete John Silence Stories*. Edited by S. T. Joshi. Mineola, NY: Dover.

Fonseca, Tony. 2007. "The Psychic." In *Icons of Horror and the Supernatural: An Encyclopedia of Our Worst Nightmares*, edited by S. T. Joshi, 409–439. Westport, CT: Greenwood Press.

Joshi, S. T. 1990. "Algernon Blackwood: The Expansion of Consciousness." In *The Weird Tale*, 87–132. Austin: University of Texas Press.

JOSHI, S. T. (1958–)

Sunand Tryambak Joshi is a leading American scholar, critic, and editor of horror fiction, in particular of the work of H. P. Lovecraft. Joshi was born in India and immigrated to the United States in 1963. Considered to be the greatest living authority on the genre, Joshi has written multiple critical surveys, published many collections of horror fiction both classic and contemporary, and edited multiple academic journals.

The first phase of Joshi's career was devoted to researching and explicating Lovecraft's work: he made comprehensive and landmark contributions in textual editing, literary criticism, biography, and bibliography. The capstone of this work was the authoritative two-volume biography *I Am Providence: The Life and Times of*

H. P. Lovecraft (2010), for which he won the World Fantasy Award, and the publication of three volumes of Lovecraft's fiction under the prestigious Penguin imprint beginning in 1999.

Joshi's work is characterized not merely by critical acumen but also by diligence and thoroughness. He seems not merely to study but to envelop an author—researching and consulting all primary and secondary sources, reading the entire body of the author's work, and understanding the author's intellectual milieu. He often seeks to apprehend how an author's worldview is reflected in his or her fiction.

After writing several collections of comprehensive essay-reviews on the main writers in the genre, Joshi produced the only truly comprehensive survey of horror fiction yet published. In *Unutterable Horror: A History of Supernatural Fiction* (2012), Joshi evaluates both the famous and the obscure, from antiquity to the present, in 800 pages over two volumes. He concludes that the vast majority of horror fiction, like the vast majority of any genre fiction, is junk. Along the way Joshi does find a few gems amid the dross, and boosts such lesser lights as L. P. Hartley and Charles Beaumont. He also singles out a more thoughtful stream of contemporary authors—Robert Aickman, Ramsey Campbell, T. E. D. Klein, Caitlín R. Kiernan, and Thomas Ligotti—as contributors of effective work with significant depth and artistic finish. Some reviews of the book contended Joshi, who is an expert polemicist like his favorite, H. L. Mencken, was overly harsh in his criticisms, particularly of modern authors.

Joshi has edited numerous collections of horror fiction, many as editor of Dover Publications' supernatural fiction line. He has been the editor of many literary journals devoted to horror, most recently *The Lovecraft Annual: New Scholarship on H. P. Lovecraft* (2007–present) and *Studies in the Fantastic* (2008–present). He continues to resurrect neglected horror tales and elevate individual authors and the genre as a whole.

Steven J. Mariconda

See also: Aickman, Robert; Beaumont, Charles; Campbell, Ramsey; Hartley, L. P.; Kiernan, Caitlín R.; Klein, T. E. D.; Ligotti, Thomas; Lovecraft, H. P.; World Fantasy Award; *Part Two, Themes, Topics, and Genres*: Horror Anthologies; Horror Criticism; Small Press, Specialty, and Online Horror.

Further Reading

Joshi, S. T. 2014. *200 Books by S. T. Joshi: A Comprehensive Bibliography*. New York: Hippocampus Press.

Joshi, S. T. 2012. *Unutterable Horror: A History of Supernatural Fiction, Volume 1: From Gilgamesh to the End of the Nineteenth Century*. New York: Hippocampus Press.

Joshi, S. T. 2014. *Unutterable Horror: A History of Supernatural Fiction, Volume 2: The Twentieth and Twenty-first Centuries*. New York: Hippocampus Press.

Joshi, S. T. 2016. *S. T. Joshi's Web Site*. Accessed July 4, 2016. http://stjoshi.org.

JOYCE, GRAHAM (1954–2014)

Graham William Joyce was a British author of speculative fiction that combined elements of fantasy, horror, and science fiction. His novels and short stories relied upon an ambiguous perspective in which he allowed readers to decide for themselves whether something truly supernatural was taking place or the seemingly supernatural events were just manifestations of a character's mental breakdown, angst, delusion, hysteria, or alcohol- or drug-induced hallucination. Joyce was of the opinion that there was little difference between what his characters believed and what was real.

The son of a coal miner, Joyce grew up in Keresley, an English coal-mining town near Coventry that was destroyed during the Blitz in World War II. His grandmother— the seventh child of a seventh child, fictionalized in Joyce's *The Facts of Life* (2002), and the inspiration for Old Liz in his novel *Dark Sister* (1992)—had visions and uttered accurate prophecies laden with classic or modernized symbols. Joyce claimed that he also had uncanny experiences that inspired him when writing his novels.

After working at an odd assemblage of jobs during his twenties and early thirties, he turned from poetry (for which he won awards) to fiction. His first novel attracted some attention but was never published. In 1988, he married, quit his job with the National Association of Youth Clubs, and moved to the Greek islands of Lesbos and Crete, an experience that he fictionalized in *The House of Lost Dreams* (1993). During this year abroad, he completed *Dreamside*, which was published in England in 1991.

He believed stories require a strong sense of place because environment demands a certain response from readers. His novels alternated between being set in the English midlands, a region he felt was not represented in fiction very often, and exotic locales such as Jerusalem, Rome, Greece, and the south of France. *Smoking Poppy* (2001), about an electrician who travels to Thailand to rescue his daughter, is written with a thick regional accent.

His books were critically acclaimed in the United Kingdom, where he won four British Fantasy Awards and a World Fantasy Award for best novel between 1993 and 2003, but his work was initially deemed too British for American audiences. Eventually he found a publisher in the United States, where *Requiem*, his fourth novel, was chosen as his American debut in 1996. His novels explored such varied topics as lucid dreaming, spiritualism, mysticism, witchcraft, guilt's power to twist the psyche, coming of age, the corrupting power of secrets in families, the perception of reality, demons—both personal and literal—ghosts, and fairies.

He was awarded a PhD from Nottingham Trent University, where he taught creative writing from 1996 onward. He published fourteen novels, four books for young adults, a nonfiction football memoir, and more than two dozen short stories. His short fiction appears in three collections, the last of which, *25 Years in the Word Mines*, brought together the best of his previously published stories and appeared around the time of his death from cancer in 2014.

Bev Vincent

See also: Dark Fantasy; Devils and Demons; Dreams and Nightmares; Psychological Horror; Spiritualism; Witches and Witchcraft; World Fantasy Award; *Part One, Horror through History*, Horror in the Twenty-First Century; *Part Two, Themes, Topics, and Genres*: Religion, Horror, and the Supernatural.

Further Reading

"Ghost Writing" (interview with Graham Joyce). 2009. *Locus* 62, no. 4 (April): 6–7, 60–61.

"Graham Joyce." 2014. *Contemporary Authors Online*. Detroit: Gale.

Stableford, Brian. 2003. "Joyce, Graham 1954–." *Supernatural Fiction Writers: Contemporary Fantasy and Horror*. 2nd ed. vol. 1. Edited by Richard Bleiler, 503–508. New York: Charles Scribner's Sons, 2003.

K

KAFKA, FRANZ (1883–1924)

Franz Kafka was a Czech author of fantastic literature and one of the most important modernist writers of the early twentieth century. During his brief lifetime (Kafka died from complications of tuberculosis at the age of forty), he published only a few dozen stories, but these include classics such as "A Report to an Academy" (1917), about a captured ape who learns to imitate human behavior, and "In the Penal Colony" (1919), in which an elaborate torture device that inscribes the body with a record of its crimes is used for public executions. These tales established two of Kafka's abiding themes: the mutability of identity and the cruel power of fate—themes that come together powerfully in the greatest of his tales, "The Metamorphosis" (1915).

Gregor Samsa's Metamorphosis

The opening lines of Kafka's "The Metamorphosis" are among the most famous in all of world literature. Like the rest of the story, they are strange, unsettling, and utterly unforgettable. For sensitive readers, they act as a kind of chute, channel, or doorway that ushers them for a time into the unfortunate life space of Gregor Samsa, whose existence, like his bodily form, is unaccountably transformed one morning into an absurd and surreal nightmare:

> When Gregor Samsa woke one morning from troubled dreams, he found himself transformed right there in his bed into some sort of monstrous insect. He was lying on his back—which was hard, like a carapace—and when he raised his head a little he saw his curved brown belly, segmented by rigid arches atop which the blanket, already slipping, was just barely managing to cling. His many legs, pitifully thin compared to the rest of him, waved helplessly before his eyes.
>
> "What in the world has happened to me?" he thought. It was no dream. His room, a proper human room, if admittedly rather too small, lay peacefully between the four familiar walls.

Matt Cardin

Source: Kafka, Franz. [1915] 2016. *The Metamorphosis*. Translated by Susan Bernofsky. Edited by Mark M. Anderson. Norton Critical Editions. New York and London: Norton.

This novella chronicles the pathetic experience of Gregor Samsa, a traveling salesman who awakens one morning to find himself transformed into "some sort of monstrous insect" (Kafka 2016, 3). The transformation is narrated matter-of-factly, and no explanation is offered save for allegorical ones: Samsa, a meek man who has submerged his identity in routines of drudgery geared to support his lazy and ungrateful family, goes from being a metaphorical to a literal insect. At first horrified and repelled by his new appearance, his family gradually accommodate themselves to the change, and Gregor, locked in his room, alternates between bouts of morose self-pity and tentative explorations of his new insectile identity. Like Gogol's absurdist fictions of bizarre transformation, "The Metamorphosis" sustains a tone at once humorous and menacing, sharply satirizing the social mores of the lower middle class while capturing the claustrophobic environment of the Samsa household as it degenerates into a nest of lurking secrets and festering resentments.

When Kafka died, he left behind a cache of manuscripts, with instructions to his friend and executor, Max Brod, to destroy them. In one of the most consequential and humane decisions in literary history, Brod ignored the author's orders and released many of the unpublished works, beginning in 1925 with the novel *The Trial*. This novel focuses on a bank clerk named Josef K. who is subjected to a systematic, nightmarish prosecution for crimes that are never specified, by an authority whose jurisdiction and motives are never clearly articulated. This theme of paranoiac entrapment in inscrutable bureaucratic intrigues is even more powerfully conveyed by Kafka's novel *The Castle* (1926), wherein the protagonist, known simply as K., attempts to gain access to the faceless agents who inhabit the eponymous structure, which governs a small village in which he takes up residence. These two novels, when published and translated, secured for Kafka an international reputation as one of the most important satirists of modern experience, with its aimless anonymity, its subversion of the search for transcendent meaning, and its subordination of individual autonomy in abstract systems of management and control. The term "Kafkaesque" has been coined to describe the characteristic atmosphere of his fictions: bleak, darkly comic, full of a pervading sense of alienation and despair.

Kafka's influence on the genres of the fantastic during the twentieth and twenty-first centuries has been immense yet somewhat amorphous. An identifiable strain of Kafkaesque surreality runs through such mainstream authors as Dino Buzzati and José Saramago, yet locating a similar tradition within genre fantasy and horror is more difficult. Isolated works such as Christopher Fowler's *The Bureau of Lost Souls* (1989) and China Miéville's *The City and the City* (2009) have struck chords of macabre absurdism reminiscent of *The Castle* and *The Trial*, and arguably the creepy sense of alienation and sinister conspiracy that informs the best short fiction of Robert Aickman and Ramsey Campbell has roots in Kafka's chilly dreamscapes. Kafka has likewise influenced cinematic horror, as such strange and unsettling films as Roman Polanski's *The Tenant* (1976) and Patrick Bokanowski's

The Angel (1982) attest. Kafka's own *The Trial* was memorably filmed by Orson Welles in 1963.

Rob Latham

See also: Aickman, Robert; Body Horror; Buzzati, Dino; Campbell, Ramsey; The Grotesque; Miéville, China; Psychological Horror; Surrealism; Transformation and Metamorphosis; The Uncanny; *Part Two, Themes, Topics, and Genres*: Horror Literature as Social Criticism and Commentary.

Further Reading

Gross, Ruth V., ed. 1990. *Critical Essays on Franz Kafka*. Boston: G. K. Hall.

Kafka, Franz. [1915] 2016. *The Metamorphosis*. Translated by Susan Bernofsky. Edited by Mark M. Anderson. Norton Critical Editions. New York and London: Norton.

Pawel, Ernst. 1984. *The Nightmare of Reason: A Life of Franz Kafka*. New York: Farrar, Straus and Giroux.

Ternes, Hans. 1985. "The Fantastic in the Work of Franz Kafka." In *The Scope of the Fantastic: Theory, Technique, Major Authors*, edited by Robert A. Collins and Howard D. Pierce, 221–228. Westport, CT: Greenwood.

KEENE, BRIAN (1967–)

Brian Keene is a popular American author of horror in both novel and comic book mediums. He is noted as one of the most celebrated writers in the pulp tradition and is often credited with assisting in the rise of popular interest in zombies with his 2003 novel *The Rising*. He was born in 1967 in North Carolina and currently lives in Pennsylvania.

Keene won his first Bram Stoker Award for *Jobs in Hell*, an email newsletter in the late 1990s and early 2000s that published articles, commentary, and market news of the horror genre. After joining the horror world with his nonfiction work, Keene entered the horror fiction scene with the publication of his first novel, *The Rising*. Featuring a zombie apocalypse in which a particle accelerator experiment allows dead bodies to be possessed by demons, it won a Bram Stoker Award for Best First Novel. *The Rising* follows a diverse set of characters trying to survive in a nightmarish world that is a strange blend of classic zombie stories, cosmic horror, the occult, and science fiction. Keene expanded this fictional universe with subsequent sequels and short stories.

Keene's other work includes the Earthworm Gods series, set in a world ravaged by floods, strange creatures, and giant monstrous worms. The series is often compared to H. P. Lovecraft for its cosmic horror, though it maintains Keene's twenty-first-century writing style, which is distinct from Lovecraft's deliberately archaic style.

Keene also writes in other mediums, such as comic books. Representative titles include *Dead of Night: Devil Slayer*, *Doom Patrol*, and a twenty-five-issue run of his own original title, *The Last Zombie*.

Mark Athitakis describes Keene's work as being a product of the milieu established by Richard Matheson and Stephen King. His work is also often inspired by Lovecraft. Andrea Johnson approvingly notes that Keene writes "fiction that smacks you in the face" (Johnson 2015). An often-used setting for Keene is a postapocalyptic earth, where everyday people must find a way to survive harsh and brutal locales filled with monsters. Keene commonly explores the theme of faith in his writings, be it in the form of characters who worship strange and monstrous creatures or the author's requirement that his own readers have faith that his characters will survive and complete their goals.

Keene remains an active participant of the horror genre with his novels, stories, essays and blog posts, weekly podcasts, and Internet presence. He has won multiple Stokers and was given the World Horror Convention Grand Master Award in 2014.

Chun H. Lee

See also: Bram Stoker Award; King, Stephen; Lovecraft, H. P.; Matheson, Richard; Zombies; *Part One, Horror through History*: Horror in the Twenty-First Century; *Part Two, Themes, Topics, and Genres*: Apocalyptic Horror; Horror Comics.

Further Reading

Athitakis, Mark. 2004. "Horror Books: The Old Horror and the New Dark Fantasy." *New York Times*. October 31. http://www.nytimes.com/2004/10/31/books/review/horror -books-the-old-horror-and-the-new-dark-fantasy.html?_r=0.

"Brian Keene." 2009. *Contemporary Authors Online*. Detroit: Gale.

The Horror Show with Brian Keene. Accessed August 22, 2016. http://www.thehorrorshow withbriankeene.com.

Johnson, Andrea. 2015. "Interview with Brian Keene." *Apex Magazine*. February 3. http:// www.apex-magazine.com/interview-with-brian-keene.

KETCHUM, JACK (1946–)

Jack Ketchum is the pseudonym for Dallas Mayr, an American writer who has been given the title "the scariest guy in America" by Stephen King. Ketchum is a man who has held numerous titles, including actor, singer, and lumber salesman. He also worked at Scott Meredith Literary Agency, where he was responsible for acquiring Henry Miller's *Tropic of Cancer.* Ketchum himself is a prolific writer who has written more than twenty novels and novellas, five of which have been turned into movies.

In the 1980s, Ketchum's fiction contributed to the splatterpunk movement in the horror genre, characterized by extreme violence and visceral scenes of unflinching horror. *Off Season*, published in 1980 by Ballantine, established his reputation as one of the originators of extreme horror, as it tells the story of a group of tourists who encounter a family of cannibals in the woods. The novel also establishes a common theme in Ketchum's works: breaking down the ideas of civilization and savagery by examining the kind of circumstances in which normally peaceable people can turn to violence. Though the novel sold over 250,000 copies, it was also widely panned when readers were outraged at the gruesome detail in which Ketchum described the depravity of his characters. The publisher initially requested that Ketchum trim some of the excessive gore from his book; eventually, Ballantine retreated altogether, refusing any more printings after the first run, despite strong sales for the first-time novelist. His second novel, *Hide and Seek*, which was published in 1984, is a more restrained book, though his career had not yet recovered from *Off Season*. He continued to write, producing *Cover* (1987) and *She Wakes* (1989), a slight departure from true horror, focusing more on the supernatural. Ketchum returned to his original affinity for excessive gore and detailed, sometimes sexual violence with one of his more infamous novels, *The Girl Next Door* (1989), which portrays in brutal detail the torture and eventual murder of a teenage girl. *Joyride* (1994) and *Stranglehold* (1995) followed before Ketchum would begin to receive critical acclaim for his writing.

Ketchum's 1994 story "The Box" won him his first Bram Stoker Award for short fiction. The following years would be filled with award nominations. *Right to Life* (1999), a novella published by Cemetery Dance, was nominated for another Bram Stoker Award, this time for Best Long Fiction, as was *Gone* (2000, nominated for Best Short Fiction) and *The Lost* (2001, for Best Novel). He would win the Bram Stoker again—twice—in 2003 for *Peaceable Kingdom*, which won Best Collection, and *Closing Time*, which won Best Long Fiction. Ketchum's other novels include *Red* (1995), *Ladies' Night* (1997), *The Crossings* (2003), and *Old Flames* (2008); he also wrote *Masks* (1999), with Edward Lee, and *Triage* (2001), a collection of three novellas, written with Edward Lee and Richard Laymon. Ketchum's short fiction has been included in numerous collections and magazines.

Many of Ketchum's stories and novels have been adapted into films, including *The Lost* (2006), *The Girl Next Door* (2007), *Red* (2008), and *The Offspring* (2009). In 2008, Ketchum began a collaboration with horror film director Lucky McKee, director of movies such as *May* and *All Cheerleaders Die*. McKee was the original director of *Red*, and he was instrumental in bringing the novel to the screen; however, after production issues, McKee withdrew and was replaced by director Trygve Allister Diesen. McKee and Ketchum continued their collaboration, though, writing several books together: *The Woman* (2010), *I'm Not Sam* (2012), and *The Secret Lives of Souls: A Novel* (2016). *I'm Not Sam* was nominated for the Bram Stoker Award for Best Long Fiction and the Shirley Jackson Award for Best Novella. McKee directed the film version of *The Woman*, which caused a controversy when it premiered at the Sundance Film Festival in 2011. The story itself is a brutal one. *The Woman* tells the story of a seemingly average suburban family that finds a feral woman who has been living in the woods. When they try to civilize her, the line between savage and savior becomes unclear. Like many of Ketchum's works, its violence is unflinching, particularly in its scenes depicting rape and sexual torture; as such, the film drew attention when a theatergoer walked out during a screening, vocally protesting what he considered gratuitous cruelty and misogyny. The rant went viral when a video was posted on YouTube. Even with the negative press, *The Woman* still did well on the festival circuit, winning the Grand Prize and the Audience Award at the Festival Européen du Film Fantastique de Strasbourg. Ketchum's short story "The Box" was adapted for the horror anthology *XX* (2016), a collection of short horror films all directed by women, with female leads. "The Box" is directed by Jovanka Vuckovic. Ketchum can be seen in several of his films as an actor in small roles.

Ketchum was the 2011 Grand Master at the World Horror Convention. He was awarded the Lifetime Achievement Award and lifetime membership status from the Horror Writer's Association. He has collected some of his life stories and successes in his memoir, *Book of Souls*. Many of his books, including the original, fully detailed version of *Off Season*, have been republished, reintroducing readers to the man who has been called the "godfather of splatterpunk."

Lisa Kröger

See also: Bram Stoker Award; *The Girl Next Door*; Shirley Jackson Awards; Splatterpunk.

Further Reading

Boden, John. 2012. "Digging in the Dirt: A Conversation with Jack Ketchum." *Shock Totem* 5.

Castleberry, Gary. "The Scariest Man in America: An Interview with Jack Ketchum." *Living Dead* 4: 62–64.

Hall, Tina. 2013. "Jack Ketchum." *The Damned Book of Interviews*. Hertford, NC: Crossroad Press. Kindle edition.

Hatfull, Jonathan. 2013. "Jack Ketchum on Human Monsters and Writing Horror." *SciFiNow*, October 16. http://www.scifinow.co.uk/interviews/jack-ketchum-on-human-monsters-and-writing-horror.

Kelleghan, Fiona. 2003. "Ketchum, Jack 1946–." *Supernatural Fiction Writers: Contemporary Fantasy and Horror*, edited by Richard Bleiler. 2nd ed., vol. 2, 517–523. New York: Charles Scribner's Sons.

Ketchum, Jack. 2011. *Book of Souls*. Hertford, NC: Crossroad Press. Kindle edition.

KIERNAN, CAITLÍN R. (1964–)

Caitlín Rebekah Kiernan is an Irish American author who has produced a large, influential, and celebrated body of speculative fiction, most of it in a weird or dark fantastic vein. Kiernan has written in a wide variety of forms and genres, having published ten novels and more than two hundred works of short fiction in addition to scripting the comic book series *The Dreaming* (1996–2000, a series that spun off from Neil Gaiman's seminal *Sandman* books) and *Alabaster* (2013–2016, a series that follows Dancy Flammarion, a character who first appears in Kiernan's 2003 novel *Threshold*). Before turning to writing fiction full time, Kiernan trained as a vertebrate paleontologist, working both in a museum and as a university lecturer. Her scientific background is reflected in her research-intensive and precisely observational approach to fiction. Her career as a professional author began with the story "Persephone" in 1995, and her first novel, *Silk*, was published to critical acclaim in 1998. Her more recent, and thematically interlinked, novels *The Red Tree* (2008) and *The Drowning Girl* (2012) are Kiernan's most stylistically and structurally complex to date, and both have been optioned for development as feature films.

Kiernan's literary influences are numerous and include such varied figures as William Faulkner, Peter Straub, Angela Carter, William S. Burroughs, Harlan Ellison, Arthur Machen, and Lewis Carroll. However, probably the most important in shaping her work have been H. P. Lovecraft, whose concepts of cosmic indifferentism and deep time are central themes in Kiernan's fiction, and Shirley Jackson, whose understated modernization of the female Gothic informs Kiernan's sympathetic and immersive approach to character.

Despite its scope and diversity, over the course of her career Kiernan's writing has been unified by a number of shared characteristics. Inspired by the work of Swiss analytic psychologist C. G. Jung and American anomalous researcher Charles Fort, her approach fuses autobiography with fiction, coincidence with causality, randomness with pattern, and subject with object. She is known for testing the limits of genre writing and for experimenting with narrative convention. While Kiernan eschews foregrounding identity politics, viewing herself as chiefly "a writer" rather than a female writer or a queer writer, her experience as a transsexual and lesbian nevertheless deeply infuses her fiction. Kiernan often queers tropes and literary traditions associated with Gothic and horror fiction, an approach she describes as a "feminizing of the weird." Her fiction interrogates received wisdom not just about the relationship between gender and literary genre, but about that between sexuality and life, human as well as alien. In this respect, her work is more closely related to that of earlier speculative fiction writers James Tiptree Jr. and Octavia E. Butler than to that of contemporary horror writers such as Ramsey Campbell or Thomas Ligotti, despite the importance both these latter figures have had in shaping Kiernan's visions of the weird.

Unlike Campbell or Ligotti, who are largely content with the label "horror writer," Kiernan has consistently rejected it, viewing it as primarily an outdated marketing category that creates distorted expectations contrary to her authorial intentions. Rather than scaring, shocking, or disturbing the reader, Kiernan's writing is primarily concerned with empathetically portraying the alien, the outsider, and the other, and with expanding, in her words, readers' "mental and moral horizons" (Baker 2012). It was this emphasis on imaginative identification and empathy that, early in her career, led Neil Gaiman to characterize her as "the poet and bard of the wasted and lost" (Alexander 2013), and Jeff VanderMeer to declare more recently that "more than any other writer of the past thirty years, Kiernan places the reader somewhere alien and inhabits points of view that seem both luminous and edgy" (VanderMeer 2012).

Despite her rejection of the label "horror," Kiernan's emphasis on psychological alienation, dark eroticism, and the transgression of social, cultural, and generic boundaries, as well as her frequently harrowing use of supernatural elements, has led to her fiction's enthusiastic reception by self-identified readers and writers of horror. This is reflected in the number of genre awards that Kiernan's work has accumulated, including two Bram Stoker Awards, four International Horror Guild Awards, as well as two James Tiptree Jr. Awards, two World Fantasy Awards, and a Locus Award.

Sean Moreland

See also: Barker, Clive; Brite, Poppy Z.; Butler, Octavia E.; Campbell, Ramsey; *The Drowning Girl*; Jackson, Shirley; Ligotti, Thomas; Lovecraft, H. P.; Straub, Peter; VanderMeer, Jeff; *Part Two, Themes, Topics, and Genres*: Weird and Cosmic Horror Fiction.

Further Reading

Alexander, Niall. 2013. "Short Fiction Spotlight: *The Ape's Wife and Other Stories*." Tor.com, November 26. http://www.tor.com/2013/11/26/short-fiction-spotlight-the-apes-wife-and-other-stories.

Baker, Bill. 2012. "A Pale Rider Approaches: Interview with Caitlin R. Kiernan." *TMR*, April 5. http://www.themortonreport.com/books/news/comics-a-pale-rider-approaches.

"Caitlin R. Kiernan." 2015. *Contemporary Authors Online*. Detroit: Gale.

Jones, Jeremy. 2010. "Finding the Language I Need: An Interview with Caitlin R. Kiernan." *Clarkesworld* 45. http://clarkesworldmagazine.com/kiernan_interview.

Mann, James. 2002. "Caitlín R. Kiernan: Pain, Wonder, and Really Old Things." *Ink19*, March 28. http://ink19.com/2002/03/magazine/interviews/caitlin-r-kiernan.

VanderMeer, Jeff. 2012. "Caitlín R. Kiernan on Weird Fiction." *Weird Fiction Review*, March 12. http://weirdfictionreview.com/2012/03/interview-caitlin-r-kiernan-on-weird-fiction.

An Interview with Caitlín R. Kiernan

October 2016

In this interview Kiernan talks about her experiences as an author whose career was born at the dawn of the Internet age, and who has therefore had a front-row seat to, and a personal stake in, the dramatic changes that have rocked the publishing field since then. She also talks about some of her primary literary influences—specifically, H. P. Lovecraft, Shirley Jackson, Ray Bradbury, Angela Carter, and Harlan Ellison—and she discusses how her lifelong interests in religion, psychology, and the weird and paranormal have fueled her fiction. She also offers a rich list of recommended horror reading, even as she explains why she has consistently rejected the label of "horror author" for herself.

Matt Cardin: Your career as a published author was launched at a highly significant cultural inflection point, right at the beginning of the Internet era and the end of the twentieth century. Here in the second decade of the twenty-first century, what are some of the significant transformations in the literary environment that strike you as particularly momentous, whether on the publishing end or the purely literary end (as in, evolutionary changes in what's written or how it is written)? Especially when it comes to horror fiction, dark fantasy, and the like, how have things changed? Specifically, how have they changed for you?

Caitlín R. Kiernan: I'm really not the person to ask about how technology has changed publishing on a wide scale. I have too little contact with the wider world of publishing to be able to answer that question. Generally speaking, I choose not to have that sort of contact. But it's true that the emergence of the Internet at the beginning of my career had an enormous impact on the way things played out for me. I was online beginning in 1994, networking and promoting my writing, and in October 1995 I became one of the very first authors with a website, which I designed and built myself and shared with Billy Martin (aka "Poppy Z. Brite"). By 2001, I had a daily blog, which, fifteen years later, I'm still keeping, and it has been a very important promotional tool. In 2005, I started Sirenia Digest, which has been enormously important to my staying afloat financially, has given me a fantastic venue for my short fiction, and never would have worked as a print publication. In 2011, I used Kickstarter to raise $4,000 to fund a book trailer to support *The Drowning Girl*. And now I'm using Patreon to keep the bills paid while I write my next novel. So, yes, significant and momentous stuff.

I have a pretty classic love-hate relationship with the Internet, with computers in general, with the way they've changed the world and the way they've changed writing. I pine for fountain pens and manual typewriters, but since 1992—when I was twenty-eight years old—I've composed almost every word I've written on Apple computers. Indeed, the way I write, the evolution of my style, my voice, is largely facilitated by MS Word, and also the way I'm obsessed with sentence-level prose and getting a story or novel perfect in the first draft—I couldn't do that, not really, on a typewriter. This is the sort of thing I'm loathe to admit, but it's true.

MC: You have generally rejected the label of horror author even though you and your work have remained consistently associated with the field bearing that name. With the 1980s and 1990s horror publishing boom receding ever more fully and definitively in history's rear view mirror, and with genre boundaries growing ever more porous, has your position on this changed at all? Or does it have little to do with the current state of publishing categories and genre outlines at any given moment?

CRK: No, it hasn't changed, not at all. If anything, I believe more firmly than ever that the issue of genre horror has very little relevance to my writing. The primary goal of my work as a writer has never been about instilling horror or writing scary stories, and I think that's fairly obvious to anyone who's actually familiar with my work. From the beginning, I saw that getting pegged as a horror writer would not only be inaccurate, but it would be extremely limiting. I got pegged as a horror writer, regardless. I know that's how most people think of me. Never mind all the science fiction and fantasy and noir and what have you that I've published—my first two short fiction sales were SF—I still got pegged as a horror writer, and it happened largely because my publishers needed a way to market me and because readers are very open to the categories that publishers create to sell them things. But to try and accurately characterize the bulk of what I've written as "horror," as if I'm setting about to elicit above all else this one emotion, that's nonsense. If you have to have a shoebox, you can call my fiction dark, or weird, or you can use Robert Aickman's suitably vague "strange stories," but I'm not a horror writer. To me, that conjures up images of foil-embossed, blood-spattered paperbacks and slasher films and jump scares, and that's just not what I've ever been about. I'm working, and I have always worked—and I certainly hope this is true—with a much broader spectrum of human emotion and experience than fear and the evocation of horror.

MC: Your literary influences have included, among others, Shirley Jackson, Angela Carter, H. P. Lovecraft, Ray Bradbury, and Harlan Ellison—towering figures, all. What have you found especially powerful, memorable, and moving about these authors?

CRK: I don't know if I can put my finger on some commonality that unites the authors who have been the greatest influence on my own work. They're a very diverse bunch. Shirley Jackson, she helped me learn how to write about insanity and longing and loss and the treachery of social mores. Angela Carter opened up fairy tales for me, and she's one of the writers who taught me how to approach sex and informed the feminist aspects of my writing. Lovecraft nurtured my fascination with deep time and the insignificance of humanity on a cosmic scale—as did the existentialist philosophers, the modernist authors, and a great number of science writers. Very early on, when I was just a kid, Ray Bradbury ignited my fascination with language. I was immediately in awe of his magic with words, and I think it really was like seeing a magician and becoming obsessed with figuring out how the tricks are done and wanting to go them all one better. And Harlan Ellison, when I discovered him it was pretty much a wrecking ball to my small-town Southern sensibilities, someone who shows up with a book like *Deathbird Stories* or a tale like "I Have No Mouth and I Must Scream" and says, hey kid, forget everything you thought you knew about writing, because—look at what I can do. That happened to me again in college with James Joyce and with the magical realists. For me, it really has been a matter of standing on the shoulders of giants. Without these people I might still have become a writer, but whatever I'd have done in the absence of their influences would have looked nothing at all like what I'm doing now, what I've done over the past quarter century.

MC: Before becoming a writer, you had a career as a scientist. You have also been deeply interested in and influenced by the likes of Carl Jung and Charles Fort. Some might sense a tension here. How do you make sense of the connections among these things, centered in your own self and authorial sensibility? And is there perhaps something in this linkage of hard science, depth psychology, and the paranormal or supernatural that provides an especially fertile ground for growing, and appreciating, and understanding, works of fiction centered in horror, darkness, dreams, nightmares, and the fantastic?

CRK: I come from a background rife with superstition and religion. I was raised, by turns, a Catholic and a Methodist, in a Southern Appalachian environment where ghosts were real and demons were real and where hanging a dead snake in a tree would make it rain. Also, I grew up in the seventies, a decade obsessed with everything from reincarnation to Atlantis to Bigfoot to claims that ancient aliens had built the pyramids. And I was crazy about that stuff when I was young. I was raised in an environment that was, very often, hostile to science, especially to evolutionary biology and paleontology and historical geology, and I spent years learning that I had to figure out for myself what was true. Part of that was losing my faith in Christianity and learning, mostly on my own, critical thought and the scientific method. I had a junior high school earth science teacher who was a Pentecostal minister and wouldn't teach the parts of the textbook that he disagreed with, which was most of it. But, I think that no matter how much I have moved away from or outgrown those primitive, childish ways of seeing the world, those paradigms helped shape me. On some level, all that stuff is still there. I still get a thrill when I read claims of the paranormal, and I still feel awe at the sight of a church steeple. In fact, I think that much of what I've written has arisen from the frisson created by the conflict between the beliefs of my childhood and the way that I see the world as an adult. I don't think anyone can have been deeply religious and ever be free of those emotions and fears that religion has evolved to satisfy, ever be shed of what are, essentially, religious reactions to the world around them.

As for Jung—and also Joseph Campbell, James Frazer, and Bruno Bettelheim—they helped me understand the fundamental connections between myth and the way that the human mind works, which is, for me, like the Rosetta Stone or a source code for understanding all fantastic fiction, including science fiction and dark fiction. All writers should study human psychology and anthropology, just as surely as they should study the work of other authors—and especially if you want to understand primal emotions like fear, awe, terror, dread, and so forth. I found Jung's approach especially useful in grappling with the slippery mess that is the human psyche. Dreams figure very prominently in my fiction, and, in part, that's because Jung and Freud taught me that dreams cut the crap and get to the heart of the matter. They're the way we tell ourselves the truths our conscious minds are trying to avoid. Which is, of course, the object of dark and weird fiction, to entice us to look at things we'd rather not.

MC: In addition to the authors already named, what are some additional authors and works that you would recommend to those who are looking to explore the horror wing of the literary universe? Which ones strike you as especially important and profound both for this genre and for literature as a whole, and why?

CRK: I'd start with Mark Z. Danielewski's *House of Leaves*. Nothing more important or more amazing has been published since *House of Leaves* was published sixteen years ago. Also, if you can find the early novels of Kathe Koja—*The Cipher* (1991), *Skin* (1993), *Strange Angels* (1994)—beautiful and brilliant and sadly out of print. Same for T. E .D. Klein's *The Ceremonies* (1984) and *Dark Gods* (1985), brilliant and sadly out of print. Almost everything by Ramsey Campbell, but especially *The Doll Who Ate His Mother* (1976) and *Ancient Images* (1989). Thomas Ligotti, obviously. Peter Straub, obviously, particularly *Ghost Story* (1979). Ian Banks's *The Wasp Factory* (1984), Katherine Dunn's *Geek Love* (1989), and Clive Barker's short fiction. More recently, I'll point to Jeff VanderMeer, everything from *City of Saints and Madmen* (2004) to *The Southern Reach Trilogy* (2014). He's not a "horror writer," either, but he's doing a lot of the same things I'm doing, and often doing it better. Same for Michael Cisco, who's published a series of embarrassingly brilliant, surreal novels, beginning with *The Divinity Student* (1999). Gemma Files (*Experimental Film*, 2015) and Livia Llewellyn (*Furnace*, 2016), those are two names devotees of macabre fiction should be watching.

KING, STEPHEN (1947–)

Stephen Edwin King is an American author of horror fiction. The most popular and influential horror author of the twentieth century, he has sold upwards of 350 million books and ranks high on the list of best-selling authors of all time, regardless of genre. King is the winner of numerous prizes, including multiple Bram Stoker, British Fantasy, and World Fantasy awards. In 2003 he was awarded the Medal of Distinguished Contribution to American Letters by the National Book Foundation, a decision that was met with both applause and derision from the critical establishment. While he is predominantly considered a horror author, King's work frequently crosses generic boundaries, including traces of science fiction, fantasy, the thriller, and the Western, as well as several nonfiction reflections on genre and the writer's craft.

King was born in Portland, Maine, in 1947. He has spent most of his life in Maine and has set the great majority of his books there. He wrote avidly from a young age and sold his first story to *Startling Mystery Stories* in 1967. This story, "The Glass Elevator," is collected, along with much unpublished material, juvenilia, and errata, in the University of Maine Library.

King's career as a novelist began with the publication of *Carrie* in 1974. This short novel focuses on the suffering of the titular character at the hands of her high school peers and maniacally religious mother. A particularly traumatic episode at the beginning of the novel heralds the emergence of Carrie's latent telekinetic abilities. Another grand act of adolescent cruelty prompts Carrie to release the full extent of her powers, bringing an apocalyptic end to the school and town that have tormented her. *Carrie* is noteworthy for the prominence and range of its female voices. The bulk of the novel is seen through a female gaze, belonging to either Carrie, her mother, or Carrie's popular but benevolent high school classmate Susan Snell. King has been criticized throughout his career for his inability to write women, so it is interesting to note that he entered the published market with such a distinctly female-centric novel. In *Carrie*, men are largely peripheral and are shown to be almost entirely baffled by or actively hostile to the women in their lives. King's own inexperience in writing women nearly resulted in his discarding *Carrie* after only a few chapters. His wife, Tabitha, rescued the pages from the trash and encouraged him to continue. He did, and the paperback rights for the novel were bought for $400,000.

Carrie was followed by *'Salem's Lot* (1975) and *The Shining* (1977), both of which are now regarded as key texts in the birth of contemporary horror fiction. *'Salem's Lot* established the recurrent King conceit of great evil being visited upon a small New England town, while *The Shining* has attained "classic" status. It is King's fourth novel, however, that best expresses the scale of his early ambition.

The Stand (1978) is often considered King's magnum opus, and fans frequently credit it as their favorite among his novels. A sprawling, postapocalyptic fantasy, *The Stand* allows King the space to elaborate on the character building and textured back story that are hallmarks of his work. The genre-melding impulse is already evident, with the science fiction of a pandemic flu apocalypse giving way to supernatural fantasy in the novel's second half. *The Stand* is a big book in both length and theme, and it is key to the 1980s vogue for expansive horror-fantasy "epics," such as Robert McCammon's *Swan Song* (1987) and Clive Barker's *Weaveworld* (1987). Its influence is also evident in such recent epics as Justin Cronin's *The Passage* (2010) and Joe Hill's *The Fireman* (2016).

The Stand introduces the recurrent antagonist Randall Flagg, who is an embodiment of unspecified evil, and who appears in a number of King novels, including *The Eyes of the Dragon* (1984), *Hearts in Atlantis* (1999), and the eight-volume *Dark Tower* series (1982–2004). Often going by other names (but usually with the initials R. F.), Flagg is part of King's multiverse. This intertextual network centers on the eponymous "Dark Tower," a construct that links the various worlds presented in King's fiction. Some novels are more obviously included within this shared universe. *The Talisman* (1984), *It* (1986), *Insomnia* (1994), and *Hearts in Atlantis* are closely related to the world of *The Dark Tower* and its mythology. Flagg is not the only recurrent character; Father Donald Callahan reappears in the latter books of *The Dark Tower*, having been presumed dead at the end of *'Salem's Lot,* while other minor connections link much of King's oeuvre.

This connective mythology illustrates King's debt to the work of the iconic early twentieth-century American horror author H. P. Lovecraft. Like Lovecraft's Cthulhu Mythos, King's multiverse alludes to trans-dimensional entities, largely organized under the leadership of the pan-dimensional antagonist "The Crimson King." Randall Flagg is one such being, as is Pennywise the Clown, the antagonist of *It*, who, in a fashion typical of Lovecraft's extraterrestrial monstrosities, predates humankind's appearance on earth, and whose true physical form cannot be perceived by human cognition.

The general influence of Lovecraft is clearly evident in such things, but King has also dabbled more directly in the Lovecraftian world in short fiction such as "Jerusalem's Lot" (1978), "Crouch End" (1980), and "N" (2008). In *Danse Macabre*, King's nonfiction treatise on the history of horror, he describes his discovery of his father's collection of Lovecraftian pulps as "my first encounter with serious fantasy-horror" (King 1981, 102). Throughout the book he reiterates the tremendous impact that Lovecraft has had on twentieth-century horror, including his own.

However, King's style would seem to fit uneasily with Lovecraft's extravagant cosmic themes. King's fiction is concerned with the banal and the prosaic: the mundane conversations and petty angst of modern American small-town life. It is this realist backdrop that accentuates the inevitable supernatural disruption in his novels and stories. He cites the direct influence of nonhorror authors such as Frank Norris, but his most obvious antecedents are Richard Matheson and Shirley Jackson, both of whom worked in horror. King has repeatedly credited Matheson as the author who most influenced his own writing, while Shirley Jackson's *The Haunting of Hill House* (1959) has a substantial presence in King's early work. The rain of stones that falls upon Carrie White's house is lifted almost wholly from an episode in Jackson's novel, while Hill House itself is the bedrock for the recurrent King motif of "the bad place." The Marsten House in 'Salem's Lot and the Overlook Hotel in The Shining, as well as numerous other examples, are versions of "the bad place," where the residue of past evils exerts its potency upon the present. Other essential themes in King's fiction are memory, sexual abuse, and the strength (and evils) of community; each appears in some guise across the breadth of his work.

More persistent still is his focus on childhood and creativity. Children play an integral part in King's horror. In his short story "Children of the Corn"—published in his short fiction collection Night Shift (1978)—two adults stumble across an isolated town populated entirely by a cult of murderous children. The story has entered into modern popular culture as an early example of the now familiar trope of the "scary child." It is an anomaly in King's oeuvre, however, as his fiction more commonly emphasizes the romance, loyalty, and quiet heroism of childhood. This is foremost in It and the novella The Body (1982), better known through its adaptation into the film Stand by Me (1986). These stories render childhood in nostalgic hues. As the protagonist of The Body says: "I never had friends later on like the ones I had when I was twelve. Jesus, does anyone?" (King 1982, 505).

Most of all, King is interested in the imaginative capacity and resilience of children. Children are able to accept and confront the horrors of King's fiction because their imaginations have not yet atrophied. As Heidi Strengell points out: "Adults without imagination are the worst of his monsters" (Strengell 2005, 14). They are opposed by children and by adults who retain their childhood capacities for romance. Such adult characters are almost without exception represented as writers.

This focus on writers forms a distinct trope of its own in King's work, as a great number of his protagonists are authors. Through them he indulges in commentary on both the craft and the business of writing, often in defense of genre and accessibility. In 'Salem's Lot, King's first author protagonist, Ben Mears, describes literary analysis as an "intellectual game of capture-the-flag" (King 1975, 171). Mears dreams about selling a story to Playboy but laments that "they only do authors if their books are big on campus" (22). This antiacademic stance has waned in King's later work, but his early novels' staunch defense of the popular suggests an insecurity about his own literary status—something he has consistently denied. Nonetheless, the issue reaches a climax in the publication of Misery (1987) and The Dark Half (1989). These novels portray authors for whom writing accrues very real, very scary consequence. In The Dark Half, the protagonist, Thad Beaumont, is tormented by the corporeal manifestation of his pseudonym, George Stark, whom he has recently killed off.

The Dark Half seems to be a clear extension of King's revelation and termination of his own pseudonym. For years King had written under the name of Richard Bachman, producing tight, linear thrillers that avoid the grand canvases of King's typical work. These four short novels are collected in The Bachman Books (1985).

However, when one of the novels, *Rage*, was found in the locker of a Columbine High School shooter, King withdrew it from publication. All subsequent editions of *The Bachman Books* omit *Rage*.

King has continued to be a best seller, and a huge proportion of his fiction has been adapted to film. Though few filmmakers are able to convey the psychological interiority of King's fiction, a few exceptional films have been made from his work. Notable examples include *The Shining* (1980), *Stand by Me* (1986), *The Green Mile* (1999), and *The Mist* (2007). Of all King adaptations, perhaps the best known and most loved is *The Shawshank Redemption* (1994), directed by Frank Darabont, who also adapted the screenplay from King's novel (and who wrote and directed the adaptations of *The Green Mile* and *The Mist* as well). There is a bit of irony in the fact that *Shawshank* is credited as one of the greatest films ever made, since its source material is a minor novella from a relatively obscure King collection, *Different Seasons* (1982).

In 1999 King suffered a severe accident when he was hit by a car while walking in rural Maine. He suffered extensive and profound injuries, and his retirement was debated. But in the end he went only one year without releasing a novel, and then returned with *Dreamcatcher* in 2001. By his own admission, this novel is a failure, marred by his dependence on painkillers. In 2002 he released *Black House*, a sequel to *The Talisman* (1984), both of which he wrote in collaboration with fellow horror author Peter Straub.

Following *Black House*, King finally completed his prolonged *Dark Tower* series, and he has not slowed down in the years since. Though his more recent novels are less confined to the horror genre, they retain a fascination with the macabre and the dark potential of society. *Under the Dome* (2009) is a particular instance of this, depicting a town cut off from the outside world by a strange, transparent dome. It feels like a return to King's roots, filled with eccentric characters, a conflict between the everyman and the powerful, and a richly drawn community. When King also returned to the world of *The Shining* in its long-gestated sequel, *Doctor Sleep* (2013), it almost seemed as if he had exhausted his creative resources. However, he subsequently completed an entirely new trilogy of crime thrillers featuring detective Bill Hodges. The final installment, *End of Watch* (2016), marries the streamlined thrills of the Bachman books with King's own brand of supernatural horror. Tonally, it is something King has not attempted before, and it shows that although he is now in his fifth decade as an author, he is far from done. He has also found new life in collaboration with his sons, Joe Hill and Owen King, both of whom have emerged as professional authors. Hill, in particular, has catapulted into the foreground of contemporary horror, and his novel *NOS4A2* intersects with his father's work, both in theme and in direct reference to some of King's most iconic characters.

In light of King's many accomplishments, it is reasonable to speculate that there may never be another author who taps into the public consciousness in quite the same way that he has done. At the height of his popularity, he was a pop-culture icon. Though he may no longer reign quite so high in the best-seller hierarchy, his name still connotes excellence in the genre. The longevity of his career also gives his work added importance, as he was writing horror and mapping collective anxieties throughout some of the most tumultuous decades of American social life.

Neil McRobert

See also: Barker, Clive; Cthulhu Mythos; *The Dark Tower*; Hill, Joe; *It*; Jackson, Shirley; Lovecraftian Horror; Matheson, Richard; *Misery*; *Night Shift*; *The Shining*; Straub, Peter; Vampires.

Further Reading

Beahm, George, ed. 2015. *The Stephen King Companion: Four Decades of Fear from the Master of Horror*. New York: Thomas Dunn Books.

Gatta, John. 2000. "Stephen King." In *American Writers: A Collection of Literary Biographies, Supplement 5*, edited by Jay Parini. Scribner Writers Series. New York: Charles Scribner's Sons.

Hill, Joe. 2013. *NOS4A2*. New York: HarperCollins.

Indick, Ben P. 1982. "King and the Literary Tradition of Horror and the Supernatural." In *Fear Itself*, edited by Tim Underwood and Chuck Miller, 153–167. San Francisco: Underwood-Miller. Rpt. in *Children's Literature Review*, vol. 194, 2015, edited by Lawrence J. Trudeau. Farmington Hills, MI: Gale.

King, Stephen. 1975. *'Salem's Lot*. New York: Doubleday.

King, Stephen. 1982. *Different Seasons*. New York: Viking.

King, Stephen. 2000. *On Writing: A Memoir of the Craft*. New York: Scribner.

King, Stephen. [1981] 2010. *Danse Macabre*. New York: Gallery Books.

Magistrale, Tony. 1988. *Landscape of Fear: Stephen King's American Gothic*. Bowling Green, OH: Bowling Green State University.

Sears, John. 2011. *Stephen King's Gothic*. Cardiff: University of Wales Press.

Strengell, Heidi. 2005. *Dissecting Stephen King: From Gothic to Literary Naturalism*. Madison: University of Wisconsin Press.

Underwood, Tim, and Chuck Miller. 1988. *Bare Bones: Conversations on Terror with Stephen King*. New York: McGraw-Hill.

THE KING IN YELLOW

The King in Yellow (1895) is a story collection by Robert W. Chambers. It contains a time-slip romance, a group of poems, several mainstream stories, and, most importantly, four interconnected stories of supernatural horror set against a common mythological backdrop. It holds an important niche in the genre following Edgar Allan Poe and predating the modern era. The four interconnected stories revolve around a fictitious play titled *The King in Yellow*, which drives its readers to a state of illness and possibly insanity. It leaves its readers in a dazed state, speaking of such things as Hastur, Hali, Alar, the Pallid Mask, Carcosa, and the Mystery of the Hyades, terms that are never explained but serve to unify the stories. This common background anticipates Lovecraft's Cthulhu Mythos, but Lovecraft discovered the book

Chambers's oblique descriptions of the title play in *The King in Yellow* generate a powerful aura of sinister mystery. The narrator of "The Repairer of Reputations," for example, describes his experience of reading the play like this:

> I remember after finishing the first act that it occurred to me that I had better stop. I started up and flung the book into the fireplace; the volume struck the barred grate and fell open on the hearth in the firelight. If I had not caught a glimpse of the opening words in the second act I should never have finished it, but as I stooped to pick it up, my eyes became riveted to the open page, and with a cry of terror, or perhaps it was of joy so poignant that I suffered in every nerve, I snatched the thing out of the coals and crept shaking to my bedroom, where I read it and reread it, and wept and laughed and trembled with a horror which at times assails me yet. This is the thing that troubles me, for I cannot forget Carcosa where black stars hang in the heavens; where the shadows of men's thoughts lengthen in the afternoon, when the twin suns sink into the Lake of Hali; and my mind will bear forever the memory of the Pallid Mask. I pray God will curse the writer, as the writer has cursed the world with this beautiful, stupendous creation, terrible in its simplicity, irresistible in its truth—a world which now trembles before the King in Yellow. (Chambers 1902, 6–7)

Matt Cardin

Source: Chambers, Robert W. 1902. *The King in Yellow*. New York: Harper & Brothers.

late, after creating his mythos. The word "yellow" alludes to the "Yellow Nineties" and to contemporary French Decadent literature, as does the character name "Wilde."

"The Repairer of Reputations" is set in a future (1920) that may be a product of the narrator's imagination. The play provides him and his cohort, Wilde, with a plan to take over the United States. "The Mask" involves a chemical solution that turns living tissue to stone. The play impacts the relationship of the sculptor narrator with his model. His sculpture, "The Fates," also appears in the previous story. In "In the Court of the Dragon," the play opens the narrator's mind to a different and deadly plane of existence. In "The Yellow Sign," an artist and his model find the eponymous sign from the play, read the play, and suffer the consequences at the hands of a living corpse.

The unrelated fantasy "The Demoiselle D'Ys" is a haunting romance involving a modern man and a medieval woman. It has a human character named Hastur.

Chambers borrowed many mysterious terms from two stories by Ambrose Bierce to embellish his mythology. In Bierce's "Haita the Shepherd," Hastur is a benign god of shepherds. Bierce's "An Inhabitant of Carcosa" quotes the fictional author Hali and also contains references to Aldebaran, the Hyades, and Alar. Chambers repurposed Bierce's terms, making Hali a lake and Carcosa a city in the sky, and leaving the meaning of many terms, such as Hastur and Alar, unexplained.

Lovecraft alluded to these names in "The Whisperer in Darkness" (1930). They were later employed by August Derleth, who reimagined Hastur as an evil entity.

Thorns (1967) by Robert Silverberg alludes to *The King in Yellow*, and James Blish in "More Light" (1970) attempts to write out the actual play. The first season of the HBO television series *True Detective* (2014) alludes to the book and created a surge in its popularity.

Lee Weinstein

See also: Bierce, Ambrose; Chambers, Robert W.; Cthulhu Mythos; *Part One, Horror through History*: Horror in the Nineteenth Century; *Part Two, Themes, Topics, and Genres*: Weird and Cosmic Horror Fiction.

Further Reading

Chambers, Robert W. 2000. *The Yellow Sign and Other Stories: The Complete Weird Tales of Robert W. Chambers*, edited by S. T. Joshi. Hayward, CA: Chaosium.

Joshi, S. T. 2000. Introduction to *"The Yellow Sign" and Other Stories* by Robert W. Chambers, edited by S. T. Joshi, xi–xviii. Hayward, CA: Chaosium.

Punter, David. 1980. "Later American Gothic." In *The Literature of Terror: A History of Gothic Fictions from 1765 to the Present Day*, 268–290. London: Longman.

Weinstein, Lee. 1985. "Robert W. Chambers." In *Supernatural Fiction Writers*, edited by E. F. Bleiler, 739–745. New York: Charles Scribner's Sons.

KIPLING, RUDYARD (1865–1936)

Rudyard Joseph Kipling was a popular and important English writer (he won the 1907 Nobel Prize for Literature, becoming the first English-language writer to do so) who has often been condemned for his espousal of imperialist and colonialist attitudes, though in his presentation of these he was by no means uncritical. Horror figures often and almost ubiquitously in Kipling's work, and even the tales in such well-known juvenile works as *The Jungle Book* (1894) and the *Just So Stories* (1902) have their horrific elements: the mongoose Rikki-Tikki-Tavi battles two deadly cobras, the feral child Mowgli is abducted and must fight deadly animals, and were it not for his nose stretching, the inquisitive elephant child (in "How the Elephant Got His Trunk," a.k.a. "The Elephant's Child") would have ended as food for the crocodile. Kipling's best known work for adults is probably "The Man Who Would Be King" (1888), and in it Peachey Carnehan describes being crucified between two pine trees, "as Peachey's hand will show. They used wooden pegs for his hands and his feet; and he didn't die. He hung there and screamed, and they took him down the next day, and said it was a miracle he wasn't dead" (Kipling 1888, 102–103). (Carnehan has also been carrying about with him the "dried, withered head" [103] of his one-time friend Daniel Dravot.)

The horrors of untreatable and lethal sicknesses and diseases are likewise present in many of Kipling's stories, particularly those set in India, a country with whose people and beliefs Kipling was familiar: "now India is a place beyond all

---

"The Mark of the Beast": British Beasts in India

"The Mark of the Beast" (1890) is perhaps Kipling's best-known horror story. On New Year's Eve in Dharamsala, India, a group of English colonials get incredibly drunk, and Fleete, hitherto an amiable and inoffensive man, behaves abominably in the Temple of Hanuman, grinding his cigar into the image's forehead and calling it the "Mark of the Beast." A Silver Man—a disciple of Hanuman, a man so leprous that he is silver—lays his head against Fleete, leaving marks that blacken, and Fleete thereafter descends into bestial madness: he eats raw meat, grovels in the dirt, scares horses, and must be restrained from attacking others. The English doctor thinks it is hydrophobia (rabies), but Strickland, a police officer who knows much of India, captures the Silver Man with the narrator's assistance and tortures him until he releases Fleete, whose malady disappears. The doctor is astonished, and Fleete remembers nothing of his ordeal.

This is one of Kipling's more ambiguous stories. The title itself exemplifies this ambivalence, referring both to Fleete's desecration and the marks caused by the leper. But there is yet another level, for the "beasts" are the colonials, and the story depicts their religious comeuppance as well as a quasi-awakening to this by the narrator. Before Fleete's actions, he says he is fond of Hanuman, for all gods and priests have good points. Then he discovers that the Indian faiths and their magic and curses are real and devastating, and perhaps even more powerful than the British characters' Christianity: only by descending to a lower ethical level and actively torturing the Silver Man can the narrator and Strickland restore the uneasy status quo. In the end, the narrator and his fellow colonials are as beasts.

Richard Bleiler

---

others where one must not take things too seriously—the midday sun always excepted" (Kipling 1889, 20) states "Thrown Away" (1888), a tale of a callow suicide and the lies told following his passing. A lethal and terrible heat likewise figures in "The City of Dreadful Night" (1885), which concludes by recognizing that "the city was of Death as well as Night, after all" (Kipling 1891, 59). An energetic little boy is killed by fever in "The Story of Muhammad Din" (1886), and epidemics and the supernatural figure in "By Word of Mouth" (1887), in which the ghost of a deceased wife promises a meeting with her physician husband.

The living dead are encountered in the longer and more explicitly horrific "The Strange Ride of Morrowbie Jukes" (1885): the feverish hero, out riding, becomes trapped in a crater inhabited by people who were declared dead from cholera but recovered in time to escape being burned; they live in grave-like burrows and survive on crows and such meat as they can scavenge, and their leader is the murderous Brahmin Gunga Dass, who takes it upon himself "to torture me as a schoolboy would devote a rapturous half-hour to watching the agonies of an impaled beetle, or as a ferret in a blind burrow might glue himself comfortably to the neck of a rabbit" (1888, 52). The dead likewise walk and assist in battle in "The Lost Legion" (*The Strand,* May 1893), though the narrator worries that the English victory against the Afghanis is so neat that the dead regiment "is in danger of being forgotten" (Kipling [1888] 1893). One forgets the dead at one's peril in Kipling's work, however, for they remain active in human affairs, and their ways are not always sympathetic.

Richard Bleiler

See also: Haggard, H. Rider; "The Phantom 'Rickshaw"; "The Recrudescence of Imray"/"The Return of Imray"; "They."

Further Reading

Bauer, Helen Pike. 1994. *Rudyard Kipling: A Study of the Short Fiction.* New York: Twayne.

Kipling, Rudyard. 1888. *The Phantom 'Rickshaw and Other Eerie Tales.* Allahabad, India: A. H. Wheeler.

Kipling, Rudyard. 1889. *Plain Tales from the Hills.* New York: John W. Lovell Company.

Kipling, Rudyard. 1891. *Life's Handicap.* London: Macmillan.

Kipling, Rudyard. 1893. *Many Inventions.* London: Macmillan.

Kipling, Rudyard. 2008. *Rudyard Kipling's Tales of Horror and Fantasy.* New York: Pegasus Books.

Mallett, Phillip. 2003. *Rudyard Kipling: A Literary Life.* New York: Palgrave Macmillan.

Ricketts, Harry. 2000. *Rudyard Kipling: A Life.* New York: Carroll & Graf.

KIRK, RUSSELL (1918–1994)

Best known in his lifetime as one of the chief voices of American political conservatism, Russell Amos Kirk was also the author of superb ghost stories, many with strong religious elements, which Kirk himself described as exercises in "moral imagination." While he is often compared to M. R. James, he probably has more in common with the British fantasists and Christian writers C. S. Lewis or Charles Williams. Kirk's conservatism is part and parcel of his fondness for the supernatural. He was as resistant to change as H. P. Lovecraft; it is no surprise that one of his books is entitled *Enemies of Permanent Things.*

Kirk, who converted to Catholicism as an adult, took his religion seriously. Indeed, his most famous story, "There's a Long, Long Trail A-Winding" (1976; a winner of the World Fantasy Award) is explicable only in Catholic terms. The time slip, which enables the hobo protagonist to free himself of his earthly purgatory by performing a redemptive act in the past, is a miracle of divine grace.

In a sequel, "The Watchers at the Strait Gate" (1980), the hobo's ghost returns to help a priest into the hereafter. Typically, Kirk's ghost characters continue to play an active role after death. Something similar happens in "Saviourgate" (1976), in which the ghost of a man killed battling a spook in "Sorworth Place" turns up in a phantom street in the British city of York.

Kirk, born in Michigan, spent most of his life there, but he also had strong ties to northern Britain; he studied at the University of St. Andrews in Scotland after World War II, and he frequently used Scottish settings. Otherwise, his stories tend to be set in bleak, backwater districts in rural Michigan, which often contain nasty forces that are best left alone, as in "Behind the Stumps" (1950), where an obnoxious census-taker comes to a bad end through his persistence. Of course dangerous survivals are to be discovered in Scotland too, as the burglar protagonist of "Balgrummo's Hell" (1967) discovers when he tries to steal valuable paintings from a decaying manor in which a man has been suspended in a timeless hell for fifty years.

Kirk's first novel, *The Old House of Fear* (1961), partakes of Gothic conventions that date all the way back to Ann Radcliffe, but as in Radcliffe's novels, the seeming-supernatural is explained away, even if the sense of terror remains. *Lord of the Hollow Dark* (1979) combines threads from his other fiction and shares many of the characters. It features Manfred Arcane, world traveler and adventurer, plus two ghosts and others arrayed against an evil cult in a castle in Scotland. This time the magic, sorcery, and glimpses of the twilit hereafter are quite real.

Kirk wrote a total of twenty-two ghost stories over a long career. He excelled in eerie details and shadowy settings, but his main interest was to depict good and evil in conflict in a dark world of the spirit.

Darrell Schweitzer

See also: "There's a Long, Long Trail A-Winding"; *Part Two, Themes, Topics, and Genres*: Ghost Stories; Religion, Horror, and the Supernatural.

Further Reading

Birzer, Bradley J. 2015. *Russell Kirk: American Conservative*. Lexington: University Press of Kentucky.

Herron, Don. 1985. "Russell Kirk: Ghost Master of Mecosta." In *Discovering Modern Horror Fiction 1*, edited by Darrell Schweitzer. Mercer Island, WA: Starmont.

Person, James E., Jr. 1999. *Russell Kirk: A Critical Biography of a Conservative Mind*. Lanham, MD: Madison Books.

KLEIN, T. E. D. (1947–)

Theodore Eibon Donald "Ted" Klein is an American writer and editor who came to prominence during the horror fiction boom of the 1970s and 1980s. His work has been praised for its extension of the themes and approaches of classic horror fiction, in particular the work of H. P. Lovecraft and Arthur Machen, into the modern horror tale of the late twentieth century.

Klein had published several short stories in the early 1970s when, in 1972, his tale "The Events at Poroth Farm" appeared in an issue of the small press magazine

From Beyond the Dark Gateway. It is the story of Jeremy Freirs, a young academic who has removed himself to a remote farm in New Jersey to study the classic Gothic fiction that he will be teaching that fall, and who gradually becomes aware that he is under siege by horrors that his immersion in those works has invoked. The novella is richly atmospheric and memorable for its grounding of horrors with a cosmic scope in the mundane reality of its rural setting. In 1984 Klein used it as the foundation for his novel *The Ceremonies*, in which Jeremy's experiences are revealed to be part of a greater scheme being engineered by a cosmic entity named the Old One to bring about the destruction of the world. S. T. Joshi, in the *St. James Guide to Horror, Ghost & Gothic Writer*, called the novel "a conscious adaptation of Arthur Machen's 'The White People'" that provided "a kind of elaboration or clarification of the hints that Machen left perhaps too vague" (Joshi 1988, 330). *The Ceremonies* was awarded the British Fantasy Award for best novel in 1985.

Klein's first short-fiction collection, *Dark Gods* (1986), featured four novellas similar in their concerns and ambitions to "The Events at Poroth Farm." "Petey" (1979) is a semi-satirical tale in which guests indulging in banal small talk at a house party in Connecticut are unaware of the imminent threat posed to them by a monstrous creature raised as a pet by the house's former owner. "Black Man with a Horn," whose narrator is modeled on H. P. Lovecraft's friend and colleague Frank Belknap Long, is a Cthulhu Mythos tale about a writer who has lived in the shadow of a more famous writer friend only to discover that he is doomed to suffer a horrific fate typical of those experienced by victims in his friend's horror fiction. In "Children of the Kingdom," an ancient race of eldritch beings that supposedly died out eons ago emerges to menace the residents of New York City during the chaos of the city's blackout of 1977. The protagonist of "Nadelman's God" is a man who is horrified to discover that a nihilistic poem invoking a malignant god that he wrote in his disillusioned youth is being used as a blueprint by a zealous fan to create a monstrous servant for that god. The story won the World Fantasy Award in 1986.

In 1981 Klein was tapped to serve as editor of *Rod Serling's Twilight Zone Magazine*, a position he held until 1985. During his tenure with the magazine, Klein published the work of many writers whose careers are synonymous with the post–Stephen King horror boom. Klein himself wrote a series of pseudonymous columns for the magazine under the title "Dr. Van Helsing's Handy Guide to Ghost Stories," and his work as an editor informed his nonfiction guide for writing horror fiction, *Raising Goosebumps for Fun and Profit* (1988). Klein edited the true crime magazine *CrimeBeat* between 1991 and 1993. In 1993 he also wrote the screenplay for Dario Argento's film *Trauma*. Klein's second collection, *Reassuring Tales* (2006), brought together most of his previously uncollected short stories. His second novel, the urban horror story *Nighttown,* was announced shortly after the publication of *The Ceremonies* but has yet to be published.

Stefan R. Dziemianowicz

See also: The Ceremonies; Cthulhu Mythos; *Dark Gods*; Lovecraftian Horror; Machen, Arthur; *Part One, Horror through History*: Horror from 1950 to 2000; *Part Two, Themes, Topics, and Genres*: Horror Publishing, 1975–1995: The Boom Years; Weird and Cosmic Horror Fiction.

Further Reading

Joshi, S. T. 1988. "T(heodore) E(ibon) D(onald) Klein." In *The St. James Guide to Horror, Ghost & Gothic Writers*, edited by David Pringle, 329–330. Detroit, MI: St. James Press.

Joshi, S. T. 2001. "T. E. D. Klein: Urban Horror." In *The Modern Weird Tale: A Critique of Horror Fiction*, 95–114. Jefferson, NC: McFarland.

Mariconda, Stephen J. 1986. "The Hints and Portents of T. E. D. Klein." *Studies in Weird Fiction* 1 (Summer): 19–28.

Price, Robert M. "T. E. D. Klein." In *Discovering Modern Horror Fiction I*, edited by Darrell Schweitzer, 68–85. Mercer Island, WA: Starmont House.

Winter, Douglas E. 1985. "T. E. D. Klein." In *Faces of Fear*, 122–135. New York: Berkley.

KNEALE, NIGEL (1922–2006)

Nigel Kneale was the professional name used by Thomas Nigel Kneale, a British writer of fantasy and science fiction. He is best known for his work in television and movies, especially for the four films featuring his scientist Bernard Quatermass.

Kneale's first book and sole collection of short fiction, *Tomato Cain* (1949), collected twenty-nine stories, several of which veer into horror and the macabre. The book's most reprinted story, "The Pond," concerns an eccentric who stuffs and dresses frogs for fantasy dioramas, and the just deserts served him on his last visit to the nearby pond. Three stories feature ghosts: "Minuke," about a destructive poltergeist; "Peg," about a fourteen-year-old ghost killed during the London Blitz who pines for contact with the living; and "The Patter of Little Feet," in which a man is haunted by the ghost of the child his dead wife wanted but could never have. "Jeremy in the Wind" and "Oh Mirror, Mirror" both are dramatic monologues, the one spoken by a scarecrow-toting serial killer, and the other by a domineering aunt who persuades her niece to believe that she is repulsively ugly. "Enderby and the Sleeping Beauty" is a modern retelling of a classic fairy tale, while "The Tarroo-Ushtey" and "The Calculation of M'Bambwe" are contemporary folktales that hinge on the clash of science and superstition, a common theme in Kneale's work.

The streamlined prose and tightly focused scenarios of Kneale's short fiction anticipate his work as a screenwriter. His television play *The Quatermass Experiment* (1953) introduced the eponymous series scientist, a foe of bureaucrats and politicians who is sensitive to Earth's vulnerability to hostile invasion in the nascent space age. The three Quatermass television plays, written for the BBC—*The Quatermass Experiment* (a.k.a. *The Creeping Unknown*), *Quatermass II* (a.k.a. *Enemy from Space*), and *Quatermass and the Pit* (a.k.a. *Five Million Years to Earth*)—were later adapted as feature films, as was the novel *Quatermass* (a.k.a. *The Quatermass Conclusion*). All explored the horrific implications of their alien invasion theme, the most compelling being *Quatermass and the Pit*, in which it is revealed that an alien race influenced human evolution millions of years ago and encoded our species with divisive aggressions that continue to express themselves in contemporary times.

Kneale also adapted George Orwell's *1984* and Susan Hill's ghost novel *The Woman in Black* as television plays in 1954 and 1989, respectively. His television play *The Creature* (1955) was filmed by Hammer Studios as *The Abominable Snowman* (1957) from his screenplay. Hammer also filmed his adaptation of Norah Lofts's novel *The Devil's Own* (1960) as *The Witches* (1966). His other memorable adaptations include the television play *The Stone Tape* (1972) and the screenplays for *First Men in the Moon* (with Jan Read, 1964), *Look Back in Anger* (1958), and *The Entertainer*, the latter two both adapted from plays by John Osborne and filmed by Tony Richardson. Kneale was awarded the Bram Stoker Award of the Horror Writers Association (HWA) for Lifetime Achievement in 2001, and the Karl Edward Wagner Award of the British Fantasy Society in 2005.

Stefan R. Dziemianowicz

See also: Bram Stoker Award; *The Woman in Black*; *Part Two, Themes, Topics, and Genres*: Horror Literature and Science Fiction.

Further Reading

Murray, Andy. 2006. *Into the Unknown: The Fantastic Life of Nigel Kneale*. Manchester, UK: Headpress.

Rolinson, Dave, and Karen Devlin. 2008. "A New Wilderness: Memory and Language in the Television Science Fiction of Nigel Kneale." *Science Fiction Film and Television* 1, no. 1 (Spring): 45–65.

Westfahl, Gary. 1998. "Kneale, (Thomas) Nigel." In *St. James Guide to Horror, Ghost & Gothic Writers*, edited by David Pringle. Detroit, MI: St. James Press.

KOJA, KATHE (1960–)

Kathe Koja is an American writer, playwright, director, and producer known for her highly original, intense stream-of-consciousness prose and memorably grotesque horror fiction, often set in grimy urban postindustrial landscapes and imbued with a punk/Goth subcultural sensibility. She has been associated with the "splatterpunk" school of horror fiction, and also with the New Weird.

Koja was born in Detroit, Michigan, and lives there to this day with her husband Rick Lieder, an illustrator whose work has been featured on many of her print and e-book covers. *The Cipher* (1991), Koja's first novel, whose first edition featured a cover by Marshall Arisman, launched the Dell Abyss contemporary horror line in February 1991 and won that year's Bram Stoker Award for Superior Achievement in a First Novel. It also won a Locus Award for Best First Novel and was nominated for Philip K. Dick and Nebula awards, while Koja's third novel, *Skin* (1993), was nominated for a World Fantasy Award.

Koja's début novel narrates the story of Nicholas and Nakota, mired in an unhappy relationship, who discover a strange hole that grotesquely transforms everything that enters it, including human flesh. This was followed by *Bad Brains* (1992), *Skin*, *Strange Angels* (1994), and *Kink* (1996), all featuring tormented artistic outsiders who get pulled into bizarre and often harmful relationships with themselves and each other. Koja also compiled sixteen of her short stories in *Extremities* (1998), which had previously been published in magazines and collections such as *Fantasy and Science Fiction*, *Dark Voices*, *Omni*, and *A Whisper of Blood*. She has also collaborated with science fiction author Barry Malzberg on a number of short fictions. In the early 2000s she produced several fictions for young adults, including *Straydog* (2002), *Buddha Boy* (2003), *The Blue Mirror* (2004), *Talk* (2005), *Going Under* (2006), *Kissing the Bee* (2007), and *Headlong* (2008). She has also published a trilogy—*Under the Poppy* (2010), *The Mercury Waltz* (2014), *The Bastards' Paradise* (2015)—and a novel about Christopher Marlowe. In addition to her authorial work, she founded the immersive ensemble *nerve*, along with Loudermilk Productions, to create and perform works of her own devising as well as private commissions.

Koja's extraordinary, sensuous style has repeatedly been described as a distinctive "voice" and, as Paula Guran remarks, can only be presented accurately by providing a sample (Guran 1998). Here, for example, is a passage from *Skin*, in which welder Tess Bajac first encounters the avant-garde performance artist troupe for which she will eventually create kinetic sculptures, including dancer Bibi Bloss, who becomes Tess's lover:

> Sandrine changing the tape and now the music began, a spare rhythm, simple drum beat slow but somehow unsettling, a moment's close listening to discern why: deliberately uneven, it ran ¾ then skipped, a stuttering but no pattern even in that. Bibi in front, the others scattered triangular around her, all four heads down, arms hanging bonelessly loose. Tess saw a muscle moving in Bibi's thigh, was she consciously keeping time and how could she, there was no time to keep. And a keening, for a startled moment she thought it was coming from the tape but no, it was them, all three of the women in the same painful note, only Paul silent and then it was Bibi moving forward, still keening, still bent and now crouching, half her body frozen like a stroke patient, like a corpse, the other women swaying silent on their feet, arms like wind-cracked branches and Paul crablike, mouth open in Kabuki grimace as he crept sideways to Bibi, still in her terrible stasis, still keening like the warning of disaster unavoidable and then as Paul's outstretched arm reached the barest periphery of her skin, the flat landscape of her belly, she struck him, not in pantomime, not with an actor's false violence but truly hit him hard, Tess wincing instinctively at the dull meaty sound. (Koja 1993, 23)

Koja's work is notable for its exploration of love and obsession, as well as pain and loss in relationships, often with strongly feminist themes of women becoming especially powerful due to their suffering or monstrosity. In her story "The Neglected Garden" (1991), for example, Anne, who is being dumped by her former lover Richard, refuses to leave their house, impales herself with wire tethering her to the backyard fence, and begins an appalling transformation into a creature with flowers sprouting around her and in her mouth, and spiderwebs in her ear, even as she is somehow rotting, yet "lush with growth" (Koja 1998, 18). Richard's increasingly abusive attempts to get rid of her finally culminate in his spraying her with pesticide, which only transforms her further into a terrifying monster with blackened eyes, lips, and snake-like tongue, which chases after him with a smile. In another funhouse mirror of family and relationship, "Teratisms," first published in *A Whisper of Blood* (1991), Koja presents incestuous siblings Randle and Mitch, burdened with the care of monstrous younger brother Alex, who seems to be constantly covered in gore and who vomits out baby fingers in a fast-food restaurant.

Aalya Ahmad

See also: Body Horror; Bram Stoker Award; The Grotesque; New Weird; Transformation and Metamorphosis.

Further Reading

Arnzen, Michael A. 1995. "Behold the Funhole: Post-Structuralist Theory and Kathe Koja's *The Ciper.*" *Paradoxa* 1, no. 3: 342–351.

Guran, Paula. 1998. "Kathe Koja: Transcendence and Transformation." *Omni Online*, January. http://www.darkecho.com/darkecho/archives/koja.html.

Hantke, Steffen. 1995. "Deconstructing Horror: Commodities in the Fiction of Jonathan Carroll and Kathe Koja." *Journal of American Culture* 18, no. 3: 41–57.

Hantke, Steffen. 2003. "Kathe Koja." In *Supernatural Fiction Writers: Contemporary Fantasy and Horror*, edited by Richard Bleiler, 541–550. New York: Thomson/Gale.

Koja, Kathe. 1993. *Skin*. New York: Dell Abyss.

Koja, Kathe. 1998. *Extremities: Stories*. New York: Four Walls Eight Windows.

KOONTZ, DEAN (1945–)

Dean Koontz is arguably the most famous horror writer who does not want to be regarded as a horror writer. And indeed, despite the fact that he was widely identified as one of the driving forces behind the horror publishing boom of the 1980s, much of his fiction has defied typical horror genre expectations and stereotypes. Often, his stories are profoundly spiritual or uplifting. They frequently deal with tales of love and friendship defeating the evil forces of chaos and destruction. His protagonists are highly sympathetic heroes who are not two-dimensional, cardboard cutout supermen (or superwomen), but who are instead characters possessing great depth, for whom the reader has great empathy.

Born in Everett, Pennsylvania, and raised in Bedford, Pennsylvania, Koontz was a single child in a family with an abusive alcoholic father. Koontz said in an interview about this period of his life: "As a lonely child growing up in poverty, in the shadow of a violent and alcoholic father who repeatedly threatened to kill my mother and me . . . I found relief from fear and privation only in books" (Koontz 1997, 33). He attended Shippensburg University, part of the University of Pennsylvania State System of Higher Education, and later taught English at Mechanicsburg High School in Pennsylvania. After publishing his first novel, *Star Quest*, as part of a paperback "Ace Double" in 1968, Koontz went on to write prolifically in a variety of fiction styles ranging from fantasy, science fiction, and suspense to, of course, horror. Discussing his versatility as a popular writer, Koontz claims, "I've not only written SF and horror but psychological suspense like *Shattered* [1973] . . . and caper novels like *Blood Risk* [1973], *Surrounded* [1974], and *The Wall of Masks* [1975] as 'Brian Coffey.' And international intrigue as in *The Key to Midnight* [1979] as 'Leigh Nichols'" (Munster 1988, 5). Koontz, in fact, published under a variety of pseudonyms early in his literary career, including "David Axton," "Deanna Dwyer," "K. R. Dwyer," "John Hill," "Anthony North," "Richard Paige," "Owen West," and "Aaron Wolfe."

Today, Koontz may perhaps be more precisely defined as a writer of best-selling thrillers that contain elements or motifs of horror and terror within a larger narrative structure that also features a number of other popular genre tropes, such as romance, mystery, and action and adventure. Regarding his ability to work across genre boundaries, Koontz has said that "there's an infinite way to combine genres, and some are bound to please more than others. The fun for me is the challenge of it, finding new forms of fiction, new ways of telling stories, unexpected juxtapositions of mood and material" (Morrish 1999, 3). A perfect example of Koontz's use of "unexpected juxtapositions" can be found in his 1996 novel *Ticktock* (1996), which can be characterized as a wacky cross between screwball comedy and horror.

Addressing the limitations of the horror genre in an article entitled "Genre in Crisis," Koontz stated: "When a form of writing has become as inbred and self-consuming as the horror genre in the 1980s, frankness is not well received by its practitioners . . . in a spirit of boosterism that has . . . arisen from a sub-conscious awareness of the current lack of quality in the genre" (Greenberg, Gorman, and Munster 1994, 207). Koontz attempted to address that perceived lack of quality by reinventing stale genre fiction in novels such as 1988's *Lightning*. In her definitive *Dean Koontz: A Writer's Biography*, Katherine Ramsland quotes Koontz as saying, "*Lightning* was a bear of a novel to write because I was developing an idea that had never been used before—time travel from the past instead of from the future—plus a *very* unusual mix of genres" (Greenberg, Gorman, and Munster 1994, 334).

Transcendentalism of one sort or another also is an important concept in Koontz's fiction, whether it is seventeen-year-old Slim Mackenzie of *Twilight Eyes* (1987), who is able to see behind the façade of evil people the goblins that reside within, or Odd Thomas (appearing in a popular series beginning with the 2003 novel of the same title), a twenty-year-old small-town fry cook who is able to see the spirits of dead people and attempts to help them move on. Koontz's abused past as a child in a dysfunctional home also helped provide background material for such classic suspense novels as *Intensity* (1996), a story about twenty-six-year-old Chyna Shepherd, who is terrorized by a sociopathic madman named Edgler Vess.

Perhaps the best summation of Koontz's efforts as a horror writer can be found in Joan G. Kotker's study, *Dean Koontz: A Critical Companion* (1996), in which she argues that talking about Koontz's work as horror is inaccurate, unless the discussion "emphasizes that in most of Koontz's work, horror is based on the inhumanity of one human being to another rather than on stock supernatural devices" (Kotker 1996, 14). Kotker goes on to add that the reason Koontz's fiction affects his readers so profoundly is because "there is nothing comforting about Dean Koontz's descriptions of the horrors that we can and do inflict on each other" (Kotker 1996, 14).

Yet many of Koontz's heroes possess profound levels of compassion and understanding for those who suffer because of their own travails. Travis Cornell and his golden retriever Einstein (a genetically engineered dog that serves as an important protagonist) in the classic thriller *Watchers* (1987) are effective examples of these types of characters, as is the genetically challenged Christopher Snow from *Fear Nothing* (1998) and *Seize the Night* (1999). Often, Koontz's message to his readers is that courage and perseverance, along with love and the ability to overcome intense suffering, can triumph over the most despicable of human or inhuman behavior. Because of this foundational strain of indefatigable optimism, horror itself, for Koontz, becomes something that strengthens human will rather than destroying it.

Many film adaptations of Koontz's novels have been produced, including *Odd Thomas* (2013), *Phantoms* (novel 1983, movie 1998), and *Demon Seed* (novel 1973, movie 1977). In 1996 he received the World Horror Convention's Grandmaster Award.

Gary Hoppenstand

See also: Phantoms; Part One, Horror through History: Horror from 1950 to 2000; *Part Two, Themes, Topics, and Genres*: Horror Literature as Social Criticism and Commentary; Horror Publishing, 1975–1995: The Boom Years.

Further Reading

Greenberg, Martin H., Ed Gorman, and Bill Munster, eds. 1994. *The Dean Koontz Companion*. New York: Berkley Books, 1994.

Koontz, Dean. 1997. "Koontz on Koontz." In *Mystery Scene* 59, edited by Ed Gorman, 30–33. Cedar Rapids, IA.

Kotker, Joan G. 1996. *Dean Koontz: A Critical Companion*. Westport, CT: Greenwood Press.

Morrish, Bob. 1999. "Dean Koontz." In *Speaking of Murder, Volume II*, edited by Ed Gorman and Martin H. Greenberg. New York: Berkley Prime Crime.

Munster, Bill. 1988. "Interview with Dean Koontz." In *Sudden Fear: The Horror and Dark Suspense Fiction of Dean R. Koontz*, 5–31. Mercer Island, WA: Starmont House.

KUTTNER, HENRY (1915–1958)

Henry Kuttner was an American writer best known for his contributions to *Astounding Science-Fiction* and other Golden Age science fiction magazines, many of which he collaborated on with his wife, C. L. Moore, under his own name and a score of pseudonyms, notably Lewis Padgett. For the first decade of his career he wrote mostly weird fiction and contributed to the Cthulhu Mythos, the shared world of stories by diverse hands extrapolated from the myth patterns elaborated in H. P. Lovecraft's tales of cosmic horror.

Kuttner's first professional fiction sale, "The Graveyard Rats," appeared in the March 1936 issue of *Weird Tales*. The story of an unscrupulous New England gravedigger who gets his horrifying comeuppance when he plunders a grave for jewelry interred with a corpse, it showed the influence of Lovecraft, whom Kuttner had been introduced to as a correspondent by Robert Bloch. "The Secret of Kralitz," published in the October 1936 issue of *Weird Tales*, was Kuttner's first tale to explicitly reference elements from Lovecraft's fiction. "It Walks by Night" (1936) and "The Eater of Souls" (1937) were also imitative of Lovecraft, and indeed, much of Kuttner's early weird fiction was derivative of writers whose work he admired.

Over the next three years, under his own name and the pseudonym Paul Hammond, Kuttner wrote nearly a dozen stories for *Weird Tales* and *Strange Stories* that evoked the cosmic horrors of Lovecraft's fiction, his most accomplished being "The Salem Horror," a variation on the theme of Lovecraft's "The Dreams in the Witch House" that appeared in the May 1937 issue of *Weird Tales*. Kuttner's other contributions to *Weird Tales* included "I, the Vampire" (1937), one of the first sympathetic vampire stories, and four stories—beginning with "Thunder in the Dawn" (1938)—that featured Elak of Atlantis, a sword-and-sorcery hero derivative of Robert E. Howard's Conan the Conqueror, and companions to two similar tales, "Cursed Be the City" and "The Citadel of Darkness," featuring the supernatural adventures of swordsman Prince Raynor, that appeared in *Strange Stories* in 1939. Two of Kuttner's best-known *Weird Tales* stories were collaborations: "The Black Kiss" (1937), written with Robert Bloch, about a sea creature who seduces a man through his dreams in order to exchange bodies with him, and "Quest of the Starstone" (1937), written with C. L. Moore and bringing together Moore's science-fantasy hero Northwest Smith and her fantasy heroine Jirel of Joiry.

At the same time that he wrote for *Weird Tales* and *Strange Stories*, Kuttner placed more than a dozen stories in *Thrilling Mystery, Terror Tales,* and other so-called "shudder pulps," which featured modern Gothic stories with rationalized horrors. Formulaic by nature and often preposterous in their plots, Kuttner's contributions to these magazines showed some elements of originality, as in "A Skull Has No Ears," published in the July 1941 issue of *Thrilling Mystery,* which tangentially referenced the Lovecraft mythos, and "Hunger in the Dark," published in the March 1941 issue of *Terror Tales*, which left ambiguous whether its seeming supernatural horrors could be logically explained.

Some of Kuttner's best short weird fiction was published in *Unknown* (later *Unknown Worlds*), the magazine of "logical fantasy" fiction created as a companion to *Astounding Science-Fiction*, where Kuttner placed nine stories. "Threshold," published in the December 1940 issue, and "The Devil We Know," published in the August 1941 issue, were clever variations on the traditional deal-with-the-devil story in which deal-makers who think they have outwitted the devil are themselves outwitted. In "Compliments of the Author," published in the October 1942 issue, a vengeful sorcerer's familiar relentlessly stalks the killer of its master, systematically neutralizing the limited safeguards against death that a grimoire filched from the sorcerer has given him. The wit and sophistication of Kuttner's work for *Unknown* spread into his other writing at the time, including "Masquerade," a comic vampire tale published in the May 1942 issue of *Weird Tales* that was adapted memorably for the television program *Boris Karloff's Thriller* in 1961, and "Housing Problem" (1944), an amusing fantasy about a household's fairy infestation that was purchased for *Unknown Worlds* but published in the publisher's slick magazine *Charm* after the pulp suspended publication.

Several stories that Kuttner placed in science fiction magazines are ostensibly weird tales, including "The Touching Point," published in the April 1941 issue of *Stirring Science Stories*, a story of magical transformations dressed up as a tale of extradimensional adventure, and "The Tree of Life," published in the September 1941 issue of *Astonishing Stories,* which features a man-eating plant. In "Call Him Demon," published in the fall 1946 issue of *Thrilling Wonder Stories*, the children in a family discover that a beloved uncle is actually an extraterrestrial in disguise who feeds upon human beings. With C. L. Moore, Kuttner also wrote several short novels redolent of the lost world fantasies of A. Merritt, among them *Earth's Last Citadel* (1943), *The Dark World* (1946), and *The Valley of the Flame* (1946).

Stefan R. Dziemianowicz

See also: Bloch, Robert; Cthulhu Mythos; Howard, Robert E.; Lovecraftian Horror; Pulp Horror; *Weird Tales*.

Further Reading

D'Ammassa, Don. 1996. "Henry Kuttner: Man of Many Voices." In *Discovering Classic Fantasy Fiction: Essays on the Antecedents of Fantastic Literature*, edited by Darrell Schweitzer, 122–125. San Bernardino, CA: Borgo Press.

Dziemianowicz, Stefan, and Robert Morrish. 2001. "Introduction." In *Masters of the Weird Tale: Henry Kuttner*, edited by Stefan Dziemianowicz. Lakewood, CO: Centipede Press.

Moskowitz, Sam. 1967. "Henry Kuttner." In *Seekers of Tomorrow: Masters of Modern Science Fiction*, 319–333. New York: Ballantine.

Ramsey, Shawn. 1990. "Henry Kuttner's Cthulhu Mythos Fiction: An Overview." In *The Horror of It All*, edited by Robert M. Price, 120–124. Mercer Island, WA: Starmont. Originally published in *Crypt of Cthulhu* 51 (1987).

Roberts, Garyn G. 2013. "Henry Kuttner: Often-Overlooked Pillar of the Weird Tale and the Pulpwood Magazine." In *Critical Insights: Pulp Fiction of the 1920s and 1930s*, edited by Gary Hoppenstand, 109–127. Ipswich, MA: Salem Press.

KWAIDAN: STORIES AND STUDIES OF STRANGE THINGS

The title of this 1904 collection is an archaic Japanese word (sometimes rendered "kaidan") meaning "ghost story" or "weird tale." It is the most famous of Lafcadio Hearn's many books of Japanese supernatural stories. How much of it constitutes creative literature (i.e., original writing by Hearn) and how much is translation from Japanese sources is not clear. In some instances, Hearn refers to a word or line in an original Japanese text, but his beautifully rendered versions hover somewhere between translation and retelling. Certainly Hearn, in this book, did more than anyone else to introduce Japanese ghostly fiction to Western audiences, and he did so at the precise moment that Japan was rapidly modernizing. These are visions of Japan's past. Modern Japanese horror writers use other terms to describe their work. A story is only "kaidan" if it is intended to evoke an old-fashioned atmosphere.

In the world of Japanese fantasy, malevolent spirits abound. There are, for instance, the dangerous samurai ghosts of "The Story of Mimi-Nashi-Hoichi," vanquished warriors who summon a blind minstrel to perform for them the tragic story of their own defeat. It is clear they will tear him to pieces when he is done. To protect him, a priest and his assistant paint texts from sacred sutras all over Hoichi's body to render him invisible to the spirits. But they forget to protect his ears, which the spirits tear off. In "Mujina" the reader meets a faceless demon. In "Rokuro-Kubi" there is a whole group of ghastly beings whose heads detach from their bodies and fly around at night. In "Yuki-Onna" a beautiful snow demon has killed one man, but spares another because of his youth on the condition that he never tell what has happened. Later, he meets and marries a woman who looks much like the demon. They have children and live together for ten years. Then one night he confides the story to her, and she is revealed as the demon. She spares him again because of the children, but leaves, threatening to kill him if they ever have cause to complain about his parenting. This was apparently a folktale Hearn had heard from a farmer. "Jikiniki" tells of a corpse-eating monster, the ghost of a greedy priest being punished for his sins.

Overall, the stories represent a combination of romance and horror, and are occasionally closer to fairy tales. Instances of the latter variety include "The Dream of Akinosuke," in which a man goes to fairyland and marries a princess, spending many years there. When his wife dies, he snaps back into the normal world, only to find that just a few moments have passed and he was dwelling in an anthill. Some other stories are sentimental or moralistic. Also in the fairy tale vein is "The Story of Aoyagi," about a man who marries the spirit of a tree.

Kwaidan was memorably filmed by Masaki Kobayashi in 1964, although two of the four episodes are based on Hearn stories from other books.

Darrell Schweitzer

See also: Hearn, Lafcadio; *Part Two, Themes, Topics, and Genres*: Ghost Stories.

Further Reading

"The Ghost Story." 2003. In *Short Story Criticism*, vol. 58, edited by Janet Witalec. Detroit, MI: Gale.

Williams, Vera, 1946. *Lafcadio Hearn*. Boston: Houghton Mifflin.

L

LANE, JOEL (1963–2013)

Joel Lane was one of the most accomplished writers of short horror fiction to emerge in Britain during the 1990s. Like Iain Sinclair and Nicholas Royle, he chronicled the dark underside of London life, exploring the experiences of disturbed individuals subsisting on the tattered fringes of modern society. Following in the footsteps of such brilliant urban portraitists as Dennis Etchison and Ramsey Campbell (the latter an acknowledged influence), Lane crafted a series of elliptical, hallucinatory short stories, released in small-press outlets such as Ambit and Winter Chills, that surreally collapse psychic and physical topographies, evoking a crumbling, dream-like Britain peopled with alienated losers, drug-addled visionaries, and other noir-esque hard cases.

Lane's reputation rests exclusively on his stories, which have been gathered in *The Earth Wire* (1994), *The Lost District* (2006), and the World Fantasy Award–winning *Where Furnaces Burn* (2012). While compellingly written, his two novels, *From Blue to Black* (2000) and *The Blue Mask* (2003), generally shun fantastic elements. A committed socialist, Lane brought to his work a serious social consciousness that exposed the flaws in post–Margaret Thatcher, post-welfare-state Britain. When he died in 2013 with a number of major works unfinished or unpublished, horror fiction lost a crucial voice.

Rob Latham

See also: Body Horror; Campbell, Ramsey; Dreams and Nightmares; Etchison, Dennis; Novels Versus Short Fiction; Psychological Horror; Surrealism.

Further Reading

"Joel Lane." 2014. Contemporary Authors Online. Detroit, MI: Gale.

Valentine, Mark. 2013. "R.I.P. - Joel Lane, Author, Poet, Scholar." Wormwoodiana. Retrieved from http://wormwoodiana.blogspot.com/2013/11/rip-joel-lane-author-poet-critic.html.

LANSDALE, JOE R. (1951–)

Joe R. Lansdale is a prolific and multiple award–winning American author whose work spans several genres and numerous media. He has written Western, horror, mystery, and science fiction novels and short stories, and his work has been adapted for film and television. He has also written for comics, television, film, newspapers, and Internet sites, and has edited or co-edited several anthologies. Lansdale has produced more than forty-five novels and numerous stories, which have been collected in thirty volumes. Texas born and bred, he resides in the East Texas town of Nacogdoches with his wife, Karen.

Both Lansdale's affection for horror and his penchant for genre bending are evidenced by the fact that many of his works have been nominated for the Bram Stoker Award from the Horror Writers Association. He has received a total of nineteen nominations and has won ten times. Among his winning works are the visceral "Night They Missed the Horror Show" (1988), the zombie apocalypse novella *On the Far Side of the Cadillac Desert with Dead Folks* (1989), *The Events Concerning a Nude Fold-Out Found in a Harlequin Romance* (1992), *The Big Blow* (2000), the short fiction collection *Mad Dog Summer* (2004), and the graphic novel *Jonah Hex: Two Gun Mojo* (1993). In both his horror writings and his other work, Lansdale's unique, folksy, compelling voice unfailingly shines through. A typical Lansdale story will start out grounded in the mundane and everyday, and veer off into the unknown, as his characters suddenly find themselves under extreme duress with no hope in sight. Lansdale then proceeds to milk those extreme situations, squeezing every drop of humor, suspense, and tension out of them.

He is perhaps best known for his crime novels featuring the duo of Hap and Leonard (appearing in nine books and three novellas since 1990), and for Southern Gothics such as *Freezer Burn* (1999), *The Bottoms* (2000), *A Fine Dark Line* (2002), *Sunset and Sawdust* (2004), *Leather Maiden* (2008), and *The Thicket* (2013). These tales, which bring to mind the works of authors as diverse as Flannery O'Connor and James M. Cain, often take dark and bizarre turns, and include many elements that could be considered horrific.

Lansdale's novella *Bubba Ho-Tep* (1994) is one of his most widely known horror-related works, a fact aided by the story's adaptation to film by director Don Coscarelli (of the *Phantasm* horror movie franchise) in 2002. The novella features Elvis Presley (played in the movie by horror legend Bruce Campbell) and John F. Kennedy (played in the movie by Ossie Davis) as two senior citizens in a nursing home who battle a soul-sucking Egyptian mummy. The movie version is considered a cult classic.

Other extraliterary adaptations of Lansdale's work include his story "Incident On and Off a Mountain Road" (1991), which was adapted as the first episode of Showtime's *Masters of Horror* series in 2005; his zombie novella *Christmas with the Dead* (2010), which was adapted for the screen in 2012 by Lansdale's son Keith, and which features his daughter, Kasey, in a starring role; and the crime novel *Cold in July* (1989), adapted as a 2014 film starring Michael C. Hall, Sam Shepard, and Don Johnson. The latter movie was nominated for the Grand Jury Prize at the Sundance Film Festival. In 2016 Lansdale's novel *Savage Season* (1990) was adapted for television, serving as the basis for the first season of the Sundance original series *Hap and Leonard*.

Lansdale takes a practical, pragmatic view of his craft and profession. In the introduction to his miscellaneous fiction collection *For a Few Stories More*, titled

"Livestock, Roses, and Stories," he famously offered a "Guide to (Not Rules of) Writing," setting forth two tenets:

1. Put your ass in a chair and write. (Okay. I lied. This one is a rule.)
2. Turn off the TV and read. All kinds of things. Not just what you want to write. (This one is also a rule.) (Lansdale 2002, 17)

Seemingly fearless in his own writing, Lansdale explores both the best and worst aspects of humanity and infuses his work with an abiding sense of the absurdity of human existence.

Hank Wagner

See also: Bram Stoker Award; Mummies; Splatterpunk.

Further Reading

Benson, Eric. 2016. "Darkness on the Edge of Town." *Texas Monthly*, February 2016. http://www.texasmonthly.com/the-culture/darkness-on-the-edge-of-town.

Dziemianowicz, Stefan. 2003. "Lansdale, Joe R. 1951–." *Supernatural Fiction Writers: Contemporary Fantasy and Horror*, 2nd ed., vol. 2, edited by Richard Bleiler, 603–612. New York: Charles Scribner's Sons.

Hynes, James. 1997. "Joe R. Lansdale: Black Belt in Pulp Fiction." *Publishers Weekly*, Sept. 29: 59–60.

Lansdale, Joe. 2002. *For a Few Stories More*. Burton, MI: Subterranean Press.

Williamson, Chet. 2005. "Joe R. Lansdale: Dark Master of Texas Gothic." *Weird Tales* 62, no. 1: 30–35.

Interview with Joe R. Lansdale

October 2016

In this brief interview, Lansdale talks about his reasons for writing horror and for infusing horror frequently into the vast span of different genres and types of writing that he has produced. He goes on to talk about the reasons why readers are drawn to horror, and he ruminates on the long-term effects of the 1970s–1990s horror publishing boom. He also lists some of his major influences—ranging from the likes of Ray Bradbury, Richard Matheson, and Robert Bloch to the likes of Ernest Hemingway, Flannery O'Connor, and F. Scott Fitzgerald—and he recommends a few horror authors whose work is worth seeking out.

Matt Cardin: As an author, you have been not just prolific but strikingly broad in your focus, writing in multiple genres and forms for multiple media. Yet one of the notes you continue to hit over and over is that of horror—sometimes in outright works of horror as such, and other times as a mode that you bring to bear on works that are formally classified as something else. What keeps you coming back? Why does horror play such a critical role in your writing?

Joe R. Lansdale: I grew up a great fan of horror, so it only seems natural that it has become part of my writerly DNA. Now and again I specifically try and write a story that fits comfortably into one genre, but most of my work doesn't start out with as solid an intent. I just borrow from the things that interest me, and horror is one of them. I think of it and suspense as close cousins, and horror doesn't always have to be grisly or shocking, it can be creepy and unsettling as well. It depends on how you define it, but it is certainly a fine tool in any writer's tool box. As is understanding mystery and suspense. Loving and studying and writing all those genres led me eventually to whatever it is I do most of the time, which is, well, just me, but I'm very much aware of the tools available to me.

MC: Moving from the writer's to the reader's end of things, why do you think people are drawn to read horror? What draws you personally?

JRL: A delicious sense of the unknown. Controlled fear, something you can lay aside and go, "Wow, that's not real, but it sure is fun when I'm reading it, but now I can continue my life, which is far less stressful." I think it is a release system for a lot of us. I think that's true of all stories, but horror allows a kind of vibrant release.

MC: You made it onto the map as a writer in the very middle of the big horror boom of the late twentieth century. The story of how that particular publishing phenomenon flared and then flamed out is well known to everyone. What are some of the major differences between then and now when it comes to writing and/or publishing things that may be classified as "horror"? Do you see or feel any lasting impact on your own writing or that of others? Basically, what's different today because of what happened circa 1975 to 1995?

JRL: I don't think the story is nearly as well known as it should be. I think in its own way it was as important to horror, as well as crime, suspense, and other genres, as the New Wave in science fiction was to literature in general. In fact, I think the boom of that era, especially from mid-seventies to mid/late-eighties, was more instrumental in how it changed fiction in general. No one has really written about it or the authors of that time in an insightful manner. It collapsed under the weight of its own popularity and bad publishing choices. I would say that the writers of short fiction were what drove the undercurrent, and of the novels, there were several writers who pushed that forward, but in that arena Stephen King almost stands by himself. What he was doing really influenced short fiction as well, but I think it was more the eighties that represented this new trend in all its blooming glory. By the end of the eighties it was pretty much dead, though a few residual works floated on the dead waters for a few years to come. The influence of that time made its way into crime and suspense fiction specifically, but writers of literary fiction eventually embraced it as well. Its impact continues, if not directly under the label of horror.

MC: In the past you have named Richard Matheson, William F. Nolan, Ray Bradbury, and Robert Bloch as among your favorite writers and most important influences. What do you find particularly compelling about each? For someone just learning for the first time about one or all of these writers, what would you say is important to know?

JRL: They were my most important influences early on. But Flannery O'Connor, Raymond Chandler, James Cain, William Goldman, Chester Himes, Ernest Hemingway, John Steinbeck, F. Scott Fitzgerald, and so many other writers influenced me. They were engaging in a simple way that invited you in, but their styles are all very complex when you analyze them. They feel natural, but they have hidden items beneath the surface of their waters. All of those writers in one way or another are poetic, perhaps Cain less obviously so, but I would suggest his poetry is of a more subtle nature. They are all visual and for the most part character-driven. I never thought of Bradbury as particularly strong on character in the classic sense. But his stories themselves were the characters. Another thing about all of them, the obvious thing, is they are style-driven.

MC: Are there any additional authors and works that you would recommend to those who are looking to explore this wing of the literary universe? Which ones strike you as especially important both for this genre and for literature as a whole?

JRL: One that has elements of horror, but transcends genre, is Robert McCammon's *Boy's Life*, and to dive down into the blood and thunder of the old pulps, his *They Thirst*. Ramsey Campbell for creep-up-on-you nastiness. Stephen Graham Jones, who writes his own books, but many of which certainly have a lot of horror in them. I could be here all night, so on this subject, try the Jones and tip your waitress.

MC: If you had one insight or nugget or wisdom to offer readers interested in horror fiction, what would it be?

JRL: Horror never dies. It merely, as horror should, mutates.

"THE LAST FEAST OF HARLEQUIN"

Thomas Ligotti's story "The Last Feast of Harlequin" was first published in the April 1990 issue of *Fantasy and Science Fiction* magazine and was reprinted in his collections *Grimscribe: His Lives and Works* (1991) and *The Nightmare Factory* (1996). Arguably his most famous tale—and the earliest written of his published works— "Harlequin" is dedicated "To the memory of H. P. Lovecraft" (Ligotti 1994, 48).

Strongly echoing Lovecraft's "The Festival" (1923) and "The Shadow over Innsmouth" (1931), "Harlequin" follows the narrator, an anthropologist who specializes in clowns, as he investigates a midwinter festival held in Mirocaw, a strangely lifeless town in the American Midwest. Fashioning a costume that mimics the threatening aspect of some of the less gregarious clowns that roam the town's streets, he discovers that these unnerving figures transform into giant worms every year and feast on the flesh of young local women.

While the Lovecraftian elements are explicitly indicated in the dedication, "Harlequin" also draws on a wider tradition of American horror. Descriptions of the town as made up of unlikely angles and skewed perspective recall both Lovecraft's "The Dreams in the Witch House" (1932) and Shirley Jackson's *The Haunting of Hill House* (1959), while a poster for the state lottery calls to mind Jackson's infamous tale of small-town horror, "The Lottery" (1948). A scene in which the narrator follows one of the drab clowns harks back to Edgar Allan Poe's "The Man of the Crowd" (1840), while the depictions of mindlessly threatening townsfolk converging slowly around a horrified narrator allude both to zombie narratives and to Stephen King's *'Salem's Lot* (1975).

Ligotti often asserts in interviews that he feels human existence is little more than endless suffering and confusion. Many other stories in his *Grimscribe* collection, such as "The Spectacles in the Drawer" and "The Dreaming in Nortown," attempt to literalize this, set as they are in a nightmare realm with few historical or geographical markers, a postmodern version of E. T. A. Hoffmann's timeless fairy-tale settings. By contrast, "Harlequin" is situated within a relatively realistic, contemporary world, rendering its horrific revelations particularly effective.

Dara Downey

See also: The Haunting of Hill House; Ligotti, Thomas; Lovecraft, H. P.; Lovecraftian Horror.

Further Reading

Harris, Jason M. 2012. "Smiles of Oblivion: Demonic Clowns and Doomed Puppets as Fantastic Figures of Absurdity and Misanthropy in the Writings of Thomas Ligotti." *Journal of Popular Culture* 45, no. 6 (December): 1249–1265.

Langan, John. 2007. "Thomas Ligotti's Metafictional Mapping: The Allegory of 'The Last Feast of Harlequin.'" *Lovecraft Annual* 1: 126–144.

Ligotti, Thomas. 1994. *Grimscribe: His Lives and Works*. New York: Jove.

Schweitzer, Darrell, ed. 2003. *The Thomas Ligotti Reader: Essays and Explorations*. Holicong, PA: Wildside.

"LAZARUS"

This 1906 story by the Russian expressionist and symbolist writer Leonid Andreyev (1871–1919) was first published in English in 1918, translated for an anthology by the then head of the Slavic Division of the New York Public Library, Avrahm (Abraham) Yarmolinsky. Andreyev was a successful and critically acclaimed author in Russia, although he became increasingly isolated politically after the 1905 revolution, eventually dying in poverty as an exile in Finland at the relatively young age of forty-eight.

"Lazarus" concerns the biblical figure of the same name, but rather than focusing on the circumstances surrounding Jesus's restoration of Lazarus to life, Andreyev creates a vivid and starkly pessimistic account of the consequences of an event usually cast as miraculous. Lazarus, it transpires, has been irrevocably altered by the experience of death. After the "sinister oddities" (Andreyev 1918, 9) of Lazarus first become evident at a celebratory feast, he is cast out of his community, and rumors of the sanity-shattering effect of his gaze spread quickly to Rome. An Epicurean artist named Aurelius tries to glean Lazarus's secrets in order to apply them to his creations, but is instead rendered unable to do anything other than ruminate on the revelation that all beauty is "a lie" (22). Lazarus is eventually summoned before Emperor Augustus, and although Augustus is, like others, irrevocably altered by the encounter, he breaks Lazarus's gaze just in time to avoid permanent madness

The Horror of the Void in His Eyes

Andreyev conveys the galling, life-draining power of the resurrected Lazarus's gaze by describing it as a

> horror which lay motionless in the depth of his black pupils. Lazarus looked calmly and simply with no desire to conceal anything, but also with no intention to say anything; he looked coldly, as he who is infinitely indifferent to those alive. Many carefree people came close to him without noticing him, and only later did they learn with astonishment and fear who that calm stout man was, that walked slowly by, almost touching them with his gorgeous and dazzling garments. The sun did not cease shining, when he was looking, nor did the fountain hush its murmur, and the sky overhead remained cloudless and blue. But the man under the spell of his enigmatical look heard no more the fountain and saw not the sky overhead. Sometimes, he wept bitterly, sometimes he tore his hair and in frenzy called for help; but more often it came to pass that apathetically and quietly he began to die, and so he languished many years, before everybody's very eyes, wasted away, colorless, flabby, dull, like a tree, silently drying up in a stony soil. And of those who gazed at him, the ones who wept madly, sometimes felt again the stir of life; the others never.

Matt Cardin

Source: Andreyev, Leonid. 1918. "Lazarus." In *Lazarus by Leonid Andreyev and The Gentleman from San Francisco by Ivan Bunin*, translated by Abraham Yarmolinsky, 9–21. Boston: The Stratford Company.

and despair. Lazarus returns to the Holy Land having been blinded on Augustus's orders.

Allegorical in tone, "Lazarus" is startling in its subversive reiteration of the biblical message of hope into one of profound dread and anguish. There are distinct elements of cosmic horror conveyed in the testimony of those who have been "stricken" by the baleful gaze of Lazarus and now understand that "wrapped by void and darkness the man in despair trembled in the face of the Horror of the Infinite" (17). The celebrated social-realist writer Maxim Gorky described it as "the best . . . that has been written about death in all the world's literature" (Jackson 1993, 131). After its initial publication in English as an example of contemporary Slavic literature, it was included by Dorothy Scarborough in her 1912 collection *Famous Modern Ghost Stories*, which, by placing the story in the context of work by Algernon Blackwood, Arthur Machen, Edgar Allan Poe, and others, established it as a horror classic. The story was included in the 1927 issue of *Weird Tales*, where it proved popular with the readership, with one correspondent describing it several years later as "the greatest weird tale ever written" ("The Eyrie" 1932, 150). It has subsequently become a staple of horror anthologies and in 2009 was even co-opted into the zombie genre by its inclusion in the anthology *Zombies: Encounters with the Hungry Dead.*

James Machin

See also: Weird Tales; Zombies.

Further Reading

Andreyev, Leonid. 1918. "Lazarus." In *Lazarus by Leonid Andreyev and The Gentleman from San Francisco by Ivan Bunin*, translated by Abraham Yarmolinsky, 9–21. Boston: Stratford.

"The Eyrie." 1932. *Weird Tales* 20, no. 2 (August): 148–150, 271.

Jackson, Robert Louis. 1993. *Dialogues with Dostoevsky: The Overwhelming Questions*. Stanford, CA: Stanford University Press.

Newcombe, Josephine M. 1973. *Leonid Andreyev*. New York: Frederick Ungar.

Zhenevsky, Vlad. 2013. "An Introduction to Leonid Andreyev." *Weird Fiction Review*, October 30. http://weirdfictionreview.com/2013/10/an-introduction-to-leonid-andreyev.

LE FANU, J. SHERIDAN (1814–1873)

Few authors' lives reflect the dark and mysterious image of the horror writer as strikingly as does the life of Joseph Thomas Sheridan Le Fanu. Le Fanu is most remembered for a number of supernatural short stories, most notably "Schalken the Painter" (1839), "Squire Toby's Will" (1868), "Green Tea" (1869), and the influential vampire novella *Carmilla* (1872). He published fourteen novels that, while not in the horror genre, show the development of his talent for the subtle creation of dark and foreboding atmospheres. The most well received of these is *Uncle Silas* (1964). A prolific author working in multiple genres, Le Fanu had a successful career as newspaper publisher and editor that warrants some comparison to the careers of his two great contemporaries: Charles Dickens in England, and Edgar Allan Poe in America. Similarities to the latter in both life and fiction even led St. John Sweeney to dub Le Fanu "The Irish Poe" in *The Journal of Irish Literature* (Sweeney 1986). Like the work of both of these authors, Le Fanu's short tales of horror and the uncanny remain today among the very first rank in the genre.

A descendant of persecuted Huguenot emigrants, Le Fanu grew up as the son of a Protestant clergyman, Thomas Philip Le Fanu, who served as Dean of Emly in Abington, County Limerick, in southern Ireland throughout most of Joseph's childhood. Thomas Le Fanu's mother was the sister of the celebrated Irish dramatist Richard Brinsley Sheridan, and the Sheridan connection remains a source of pride throughout the Le Fanu family. Later in life, Joseph would acquire Brinsley Sheridan's writing desk, upon which he would compose some of his own work.

Unfortunately, Le Fanu came of age during a time of much religious and political strife between Catholics and Protestants. In his formative years, he witnessed protest violence and threats of violence brought about by religious and political power struggles, including perhaps the Limerick food riots of 1830. His brother William narrowly escaped stoning by a mob during the Tithe Wars of the early 1830s, an act of retribution against their father's position in the Church of Ireland. Others in his family also barely escaped violent confrontations by Irish nationalists against those of the Protestant ascendancy.

Le Fanu was nevertheless captivated throughout his childhood by the rich tradition of folk legends, superstitions, and supernatural tales spread throughout rural Ireland: tales of fairies, banshees, dearg-dues, and other restless spirits. Despite religious and political tensions, the Le Fanus were still well liked by many members of the parish whom they served well, and young Joseph found plenty of opportunities for listening to Irish legends and superstitions told firsthand by the local peasantry. From them he gained both a wealth of imaginative stories and an empathy for their plight. Both would later find expression in his writing and intrigue him throughout his life.

Le Fanu gained acceptance at Trinity College in Dublin in 1832. Always a bookish boy, he had taken early to writing stories and enjoying his father's large library and so was a proficient student despite some experience with an ineffectual childhood tutor who often took more interest in tying fishing lures than in teaching Joseph and his brother. Throughout their childhood, the Le Fanu children were educated at home and in a relaxed way that suited Joseph well, allowing him free time to be entertained by local legends and pore over his father's collection of classics and obscure religious texts. He flourished at Trinity, becoming an active officer in the College Historical Society and a talented debater. He graduated with honors in 1837 and continued to study law until called to the bar in 1939, a career path he ultimately decided to abandon, much to the disappointment of his peers, who saw in his debate skills a promising barrister.

Between 1838 and 1840, Le Fanu published a dozen short stories in the *Dublin University Magazine*, his first being "The Ghost and the Bonesetter" (1838), a tale set firmly in the Irish tradition in which Le Fanu treats an old superstition with both humor and the local color of legendary Irish yarns (complete with dialect). He demonstrated yet more promise in "Schalken the Painter" (1839), a tale of the fantastic in which supernatural portent is drawn thickly, leaving readers chilled and reeling with unanswered questions. That Le Fanu's stories were accepted so readily by a publisher encouraged him to indulge his budding talent and set him onto a new path.

By the time he was called to the bar, Le Fanu had instead flung himself into his passion for journalism, continuing to publish the short fictions that would later be collected and posthumously published as *The Purcell Papers* (1880). These initial stories are each presented as the manuscripts of a priest by the name of Father Francis Purcell. Le Fanu would later return to the presentation of the collected manuscript in his final collection, *In a Glass Darkly* (1872).

In 1841, Le Fanu purchased a newspaper of his own, *The Warder*, and settled into the busy life of newspaper owner and editor. In 1844, at the age of thirty and established in a career, he married Susanna Bennett. They remained happily married for fourteen years during which Le Fanu published his first two novels, *The Cock and Anchor* (1845) and *The Fortunes of Colonel Torlogh O'Brien* (1847). They had four children together, two sons and two daughters. Susanna's death in 1858 produced a profound sadness in Le Fanu, and he began to withdraw from public life shortly thereafter, entertaining fewer guests and engaging in a burst of prolific writing that produced twelve novels in ten years between 1863 and 1873, along with myriad short stories, articles, and lyrical ballads.

Le Fanu's copious literary output coincided with his purchase of the *Dublin University Magazine* in 1861, the same magazine that had published his first short stories. Over the next eight years, under Le Fanu's supervision, the publication returned to its former prominence. The majority of his novels were serialized in the magazine, and he continued to publish short ghostly tales and mysteries in its pages.

In 1864, midway through his tenure at the *Dublin University Magazine*, Le Fanu published what would become his most notable novel, *Uncle Silas*. While *Uncle Silas* does not venture into the supernatural, it does threaten unspeakable horrors and presents an unrelenting atmosphere of ominous foreboding and evil threat. Silas, the ill-reputed uncle of the orphaned Maud Ruthyn, cares for her at his estate, Bartram-Haugh. Upon his death, her father wills Maud the family fortune when she comes of age; however, a codicil stipulates that if she were to die before coming of age, the fortune would then go to Silas. As expected, Maud (and the reader) begins to understand that terrible menace awaits her at Bartram-Haugh. Le Fanu's adept building of dark suspense throughout the novel also permeates his horror tales, including the earlier "An Account of Some Strange Disturbances on Aungier Street" (1853), and with further sophistication in *Carmilla*.

Throughout this period, Le Fanu receded further into the shadows of Dublin. Le Fanu was known to "emerge like an apparition" at the local booksellers just at dusk to inquire "Any more ghost stories for me?" (Browne 1951, 27). Many anecdotes exist of Le Fanu's late-night requests for books on both ghosts and demons. Fellow Dubliners began to refer to the self-isolating Le Fanu as "the Invisible Prince," glimpsing him only at odd hours as he slipped quietly to and from his newspaper office. While remaining pleasant and welcoming to a tight circle of friends for some time, he became increasingly reclusive in later years, avoiding the public and at times even turning away his closest friends when they called at his home in Merrion Square.

Le Fanu sold the *Dublin University Magazine* in 1868, but did not cease writing. His late works are some of his most memorable and are marked with disturbing themes of death, guilt, and the supernatural. They also bear an eerie similarity to his personal afflictions. At least part of Le Fanu's reputation as the Invisible Prince stems from his acquired writing habits as, plagued by recurrent nightmares, he would often awake in the night and, propped up in bed, write by candlelight into the early hours of the morning. Five of his late tales, collected as *In a Glass Darkly*, introduce isolated and haunted characters whose torment stems as much from their own conscience or obsession as it does from supernatural presences. In stories like "Green Tea" (1869)—published in Charles Dickens's *All the Year Round*—one recognizes the aged Le Fanu in the character of Mr. Jennings, a scholar obsessed with the study of the Christian mystic Emanuel Swedenborg and his visions of the spiritual dimension: the realms beyond death.

Le Fanu's own interest in the writings of Swedenborg (1688–1772) first appear in *Uncle Silas* and feature more prominently in "Green Tea," in which the main character, the Reverend Mr. Jennings, experiences, to his horror, what happens when his "interior sight is opened" to a Swedenborgian spiritual realm. Jennings becomes tormented by a "spectral" monkey, a ghostly presence that will not leave him alone and seeks to drive him mad. For Jennings, the monkey may represent religious doubts, its form a symbol of the threat of Darwin's scientific theory to religious thought throughout the 1860s. For Le Fanu, the spectral presence may indeed represent a more personal torment: his continued anxiety over the soul of his beloved Susanna. Her religious doubts and anxiety before her death caused Le Fanu enormous grief, and he worried whether she might have doubted her soul into hell.

The last year before his death, Le Fanu completed what would become his most well-known and long-lasting work: the vampire tale *Carmilla*. In writing *Carmilla*, Le Fanu draws upon a few prior vampire tales, including John Polidori's "The Vampyre" (1819) as well as traditional Romanian folklore. Unflinching homoeroticism pervades the narrative of a female vampire visiting her desires upon Laura, the young female protagonist. Bram Stoker owes a debt to *Carmilla*, from which he borrowed not only the shockingly sexualized image of the vampire in *Dracula* (1897) but also the image of the vampire hunter. Stoker's Dr. Abraham von Helsing, with some alliteration, borrows heavily from Le Fanu's Dr. Martin Hesselius and Baron Vordenburg, Le Fanu's paternal characters who are also students of both science and the paranormal. Next to *Dracula*, *Carmilla* still ranks as one of the most influential narratives in all of vampire fiction.

Demonstrating his flair for the horror short story as early as 1838, Le Fanu developed his method and style of horror independently of Edgar Allan Poe, whose essay "The Philosophy of Composition" (1846) is often credited with setting forth the modern short story (and horror story) methodology. Le Fanu's inspirations sprang directly from his life: the violence and political turmoil of his childhood years, chilling Irish folklore and superstition, the pain and bereavement over the loss of his wife, his studies in Swedenborgian spiritualism, and his own recurring nightmare—as he once related to his doctor—of a huge and rotting mansion threatening to topple and crush him.

Le Fanu died at his home in Merrion Square, Dublin on February 7, 1873, having published some of his most enduring work only months before. Upon finding him in his bed, his doctor is reported to have said, "I feared this—that house fell at last" (Browne 1951, 31). Le Fanu's talent has been praised by authors as diverse as

Charles Dickens, Henry James, M. R. James, and Dorothy L. Sayers. His work has been a direct influence on some of the most prestigious Irish authors to follow him, including not only Bram Stoker, but also W. B. Yeats and James Joyce. His work, although highly esteemed and influential, has not been as prominently or widely recognized within the horror genre during the last century as may be warranted. More recently, though, it appears that this neglect is beginning to lift.

Mark Wegley

See also: Carmilla; Dracula; "Green Tea"; *In a Glass Darkly*; James, Henry; James, M. R.; Poe, Edgar Allan; "Schalken the Painter"; Spiritualism; Stoker, Bram; The Uncanny; Vampires.

Further Reading

Browne, N. 1951. *Sheridan Le Fanu*. New York: Roy.

Crawford, Gary William. 1995. *J. Sheridan Le Fanu: A Bio-bibliography*. Westport, CT: Greenwood Press.

Crawford, Gary William, Jim Rockhill, and Brian J. Showers, eds. 2011. *Reflections in a Glass Darkly: Essays on J. Sheridan Le Fanu*. New York: Hippocampus Press.

Harris, Sally. 2003. "Spiritual Warnings: The Ghost Stories of Joseph Sheridan Le Fanu." *Victorians Institute Journal* 31: 9–39.

McCormack, W. J. 1980. *Sheridan Le Fanu and Victorian Ireland*. Oxford: Clarendon.

Melada, I. 1987. *Sheridan Le Fanu*. Boston: Twayne.

Sweeney, J. 1986. "Sheridan Le Fanu: The Irish Poe." *Journal of Irish Literature* 15: 3–32.

Wegley, M. 2002. "Fear Unknowable: Le Fanu's Contribution to the Literary Fantastic." *Paradoxa* 17: 32–51.

LEE, TANITH (1947–2015)

Tanith Lee was a British author of fantasy, science fiction, dark fantasy, and horror. She published more than ninety novels and three hundred short stories, a great number of which contain horror elements, however they are classified.

The difficulty of categorizing Lee as an author is evident from the opening to her story "Death Dances," published in *Weird Tales* in 1988. The story begins: "Death came to Idradrud at suns' rise. She had appointments to keep." The city of Idradrud sounds a little like India, but it is clearly the sort of imaginary city familiar from the genre of fantasy fiction. However, there are two suns in the sky, and it is unclear whether this means the story is set on another planet and may therefore have affinities with science fiction. The personification of death, for its part, locates the story in horror territory. Lee's work always mixed genres and blurred boundaries.

Her fiction is vivid and sensual, with a style that is sometimes almost like prose poetry, as if it were written for the sheer delight of language and imagery. For example, her story "The Werewolf" (1976) does nothing particularly original with the werewolf legend, but makes it fresh by the immersive intensity of Lee's writing.

Her short fiction often shows a preoccupation with symmetry and form, very much like poetry. In the above-cited "Death Dances," Death enters the city and, in a series of short episodes, causes various people (including a harlot, a thief, and a priestess) to die and be reborn into one another's lives, with ironic results. In her World Fantasy Award–winning story "Elle Est Trois, (La Mort)" (1983), which draws its structure from a French rhyme that translates as "She is three, Death," three failures, a poet, an artist, and a composer, are visited by Death in three forms: seductress, thief, and slaughterer.

Lee also sometimes deflated the overt fantastic element in her stories, as in her other World Fantasy Award winner, "The Gorgon" (1982), in which a man ignores all warnings and swims to a haunted Greek isle. The "gorgon" there may just be a deformed woman, and he feels a definite loss at the destruction of his expectation of the mythic and marvelous. The "gorgon" has figuratively, if not literally, turned him to stone. "La Vampiresse" (2000) tells of a fabulously glamorous woman, now a recluse, and of the fading of her beauty. She may or may not be a vampire. The reader is given the impression that this is a delusion, but one that is accepted with regret.

Some of Lee's novels addressed horror themes directly. *Heart Beast* (1992) is about an unstoppable werewolf-like creature. Lee's Blood Opera sequence, consisting of three novels, was commissioned by the editor of the Dell Abyss horror line, so that it could be clearly placed, commercially, in the horror category. *Dark Dance* (1992), the first novel in the series, introduces Rachaela, a young woman with few prospects in life who turns in desperation to her long-lost relatives, the Scarabae, who are alleged vampires, although they are not actually blood-sucking wraiths. They are very long lived, surviving for centuries and maintaining the purity of their bloodline through multigenerational incest. Rachaela comes to share their hedonistic, mad, but claustrophobic existence, and achieves a sexual awakening in the bed of Adamus, her own father and the leader of the clan. Pregnant by Adamus, she briefly escapes, but gives birth to Ruth. The relationship between mother and daughter is grim. Adamus now lusts for Ruth. Rachaela is of no more use or interest. Her purpose was merely to continue the nearly immortal Scarabae genes. At the end, Ruth "stakes" several of the family through the heart with knitting needles, burns down the family manor, and vanishes. Arguably, a story like this, about the selective breeding of long-lived people, could be classified as science fiction with its speculative genetics reminiscent of Robert Heinlein's *Methuselah's Children* (1958). However, if horror is not a plot element but an emotion that can be evoked by many different kinds of fiction, as the critic Douglas Winter has suggested, then *Dark Dance* is undeniably a horror novel, with its horror found in Rachaela's slowly becoming everything she loathes and fears, that is, one of the Scarabae. In the sequel, *Personal Darkness* (1993), Rachaela sinks into despair, shut off from the world like most of the Scarabae, while Ruth becomes a serial killer and sexual avenger. Another of the terribly seductive Scarabae men attempts to tame Ruth, but she returns to killing and in the end must die. Meanwhile, Rachaela gives birth to a second daughter, Anna, who may be the reincarnation of Ruth. In the third volume, *Darkness, I* (1994), Anna meets the oldest of the Scarabae line, Cain, and becomes his lover. Anna by this point may have entirely reverted to the persona of the murderous Ruth.

Upon Lee's death from cancer in 2015, an obituary published in *The Guardian* provided just one of many recognitions of her significance to the field of speculative fiction: "Along with Jane Gaskell and Angela Carter, Tanith Lee was . . . one of the most influential revisionist and feminist voices in contemporary fantasy writing. Unlike them, she was principally published and known as a voice firmly rooted in the science-fiction, fantasy and horror world" ("Tanith Lee Obituary" 2015).

Darrell Schweitzer

See also: Dark Fantasy; Vampires; *Weird Tales*; Werewolves.

Further Reading

Cowperthwaite, David. 1993. *Tanith Lee, Mistress of Delirium*. Liverpool, UK: British Fantasy Society.

Haut, Mavis. 2001. *The Hidden Library of Tanith Lee*. Jefferson, NC: McFarland.

Moran, Maureen F. 2002. "Tanith Lee." *British Fantasy and Science-Fiction Writers since 1960*, edited by Darren Harris-Fain. *Dictionary of Literary Biography*, Vol. 261. Detroit, MI: Gale.

"Tanith Lee Obituary." 2015. *The Guardian*, June 1. https://www.theguardian.com/books /2015/jun/01/tanith-lee.

LEE, VERNON (1856–1935)

Vernon Lee was the pseudonym of Violet Paget. Born in France to expatriate parents, she was the half-sister of Eugene Lee-Hamilton, a career invalid whom she nursed for a long time until he decided to get up and get married. A pioneer of the British aesthetic movement (ca. 1850–1910), she is mostly remembered today for her supernatural stories. She never married and was widely reputed to be a lesbian, although she never confirmed or denied it; at any rate, she was able to insert into her literary accounts of sexual passion a kind of objectivity that construed erotic attraction as a dangerous fever, and evaluated its effects with a cutting sarcasm.

The novella *A Phantom Lover* (1886), reprinted in the landmark collection *Hauntings* (1890) as "Oke of Okehurst," describes the tragic unwinding of a family curse rooted in ancestral adultery. Two of the other items in the collection, the *femme fatale* stories "Amour Dure" and "Dionea," gradually release the repression exerted by their quasi-academic style to put on lurid displays of seductive power. "A Wicked Voice" is not quite a *femme fatale* story, because its alluring phantom is a castrato male rather than a female; calmer in consequence than its companions, it aspires—not without a telling ambiguity—to a higher degree of aesthetic purity.

The longest story in *Pope Jacynth and Other Fantastic Tales* (1907), "Prince Alberic and the Snake Lady," originally appeared in John Lane's *Yellow Book* and exhibits a studied ironic Decadence befitting that notorious periodical. As in other works based on the same anecdote from Philostratus's highly fanciful *Life of Apollonius of Tyana*, including John Keats's "Lamia" and Théophile Gautier's "Clarimonde," the reality principle intrudes upon the protagonist's fascination by a lamia (a demonic vampiric-type monster). The other supernatural tales in the volume are polished decorative fantasies contrasting sharply with the intense tales in *Hauntings*, but with their cynicism and license they can be seen as falling into the tradition of *contes cruels* (tales of brutality and cynicism).

For Maurice: Five Unlikely Tales (1927) assembled five more fanciful tales, including "Winthrop's Adventure" (first published 1874 as "A Culture-Ghost") and "The Virgin of the Seven Daggers" (1889), the most unrepentantly feverish of all Lee's sexual fantasies, featuring a quixotic Don Juan. "Marsyas in Flanders" (1900) features a pagan idol mistaken for a Christian image, whose true nature cannot be suppressed by adoption. Lee's other supernatural fiction includes one item with a significant element of horror, "The Legend of Madame Krasinska" (1890), a tale of ineptly repressed sexuality.

Lee did not see her supernatural stories as important elements of her literary endeavor, and never wrote anything of that kind as substantial as Eugene Lee-Hamilton's lurid historical novel *The Lord of the Dark Red Star* (1903). In spite of a marked tendency to neurasthenia (nervous exhaustion), she maintained her literary productivity far better than her half-brother, and her work always retains a methodical efficiency.

Brian Stableford

See also: Romanticism and Dark Romanticism.

Further Reading

Colby, Vinetta. 2003. *Vernon Lee: A Literary Biography*. Charlottesville: University Press of Virginia.

Gunn, Peter. 1964. *Vernon Lee: Violet Paget, 1856–1935*. London: Oxford University Press.

Pulham, Patricia. 2008. *Art and the Transitional Object in Vernon Lee's Supernatural Tales*. Aldershot, Hampshire, UK: Ashgate.

Stableford, Brian. 2001. "Haunted by the Pagan Past: An Introduction to Vernon Lee." *infinity plus*, December. http://www.infinityplus.co.uk/introduces/lee.htm.

"THE LEGEND OF SLEEPY HOLLOW"

Published originally in *The Sketch Book of Geoffrey Crayon, Gent.* (1819–1820), a pseudonymous collection of Washington Irving's first short prose pieces (including "Rip Van Winkle"), "The Legend of Sleepy Hollow" is one of Irving's best-known works of Gothic horror. Notable particularly for its reproduction of traditional

Dutch settler customs and local ghost fables, the narrative was inspired by the young Irving's familiarity with the real town of Sleepy Hollow in upstate New York.

While much of Irving's tale recounts in listless fashion the dreamlike qualities of life in Sleepy Hollow and the somewhat mundane rituals of the local schoolmaster, Ichabod Crane, Irving's strength as a writer of Gothic horror lies in his ability to intermittently lull the reader into comfort with his dreamy narrative style before quickly heightening suspense, marshaling local superstitions and stories of the now-famous headless horseman to tauten the atmosphere within the text.

Irving's story trades largely in the superstitions of old housewives' tales, and, in large part, "Sleepy Hollow" details the despairing effects a fearful imagination run wild has upon the individual. Indeed, this is a story about the irrationality of fear itself. The world of Sleepy Hollow is one in which old superstitions become in the minds of the locals fearful beliefs, and where people frequently report strange visions and ghostly encounters. It is with a fearful, ritualized pride, too, that the locals of Sleepy Hollow recount their shared fears and would-be myths of the headless horseman in particular. Fear and the collective cultural response to it is at the heart of "Sleepy Hollow."

Moreover, Irving's tale is quite explicit in linking this fear to America's historical past, and to the fervor for advancement and the migration of peoples away from the old colonies that characterized early modern America. Irving neatly suggests that America's ghost stories are tied to the old Dutch settlements precisely because the ghosts of the past (fears of the old world itself) are immobile, static reminders of early American frontier fears, against which the rationale of later modern America is defined.

Above all, "The Legend of Sleepy Hollow" presents a philosophical debate between illogical superstition and rational enlightenment thinking. Irving is mocking of Ichabod Crane, whom he describes as one of the "pioneers of the mind" (Irving 1994, 34), yet who is nevertheless a firm believer in the marvelous and the fantastic. In spite of his learnedness, Ichabod is of "small shrewdness and simple credulity" (Irving 1994, 39), and when his love rival, Brom Bones, dresses up as the fabled headless horseman, carrying a carved pumpkin for a head to scare off Ichabod, the credulous Ichabod is so overcome by his own illogical fears that he leaves town.

Irving's tale is a vindication of the values of rational thinking. That Ichabod actually believes his pursuer to be a Hessian solider who has literally lost his head in battle is an indictment of his own simple credulity. The real horror at the center of this story is the fear of losing one's head—not literally, but figuratively, like Ichabod—and the idea that irrational superstition should ever win over the values of logic and rationality—a distinctly American fear.

The story of "Sleepy Hollow" continues to appeal to popular culture and was brought to life in Tim Burton's 1999 film adaptation starring Johnny Depp (in which the ambiguity of Brom's deception of Ichabod in Irving's tale is made overt). More recently, the television network Fox adapted the story into a supernatural serial thriller that has generated a new wave of interest in Irving as a Gothic writer and continues to draw many more fans to his work.

Ian Kinane

See also: Irving, Washington.

Further Reading

Aderman, Ralph M., ed. 1990. *Critical Essays on Washington Irving*. Boston: G. K. Hall.

Anderson, Donald. 2003. "Irving's *The Legend of Sleepy Hollow*." *Explicator* 61, no. 4: 207–210.

Burstein, Andrew. 2007. *The Original Knickerbocker: The Life of Washington Irving*. New York: Basic Books.

Irving, Washington. [1820] 1994. *Rip Van Winkle and Other Stories*. London: Puffin.

Jones, Brian Jay. 2008. *Washington Irving: An American Original*. New York: Arcade.

Smith, Greg. 2001. "Supernatural Ambiguity and Possibility in Irving's 'The Legend of Sleepy Hollow.'" *Midwest Quarterly* 42, no. 2: 174–182.

LEIBER, FRITZ (1910–1992)

Fritz Leiber, born in 1910 in Chicago, was one of the most multifariously talented writers of popular fantastic literature who ever lived, widely celebrated—along with Robert Bloch and Ray Bradbury—as a pioneer of the modern horror genre in the United States. Over a sixty-year career, Leiber not only produced science fiction classics such as *The Big Time* (1958), but also pioneered the genre of sword-and-sorcery, with his "Fafhrd and the Gray Mouser" series. His best science fiction drew themes and tones from horror literature, with the 1943 novel *Gather, Darkness!* imagining a theocratic (religiously governed) dystopia where technoscience is disguised as sorcery, while the 1950 short story "Coming Attraction" depicts a desolate postapocalyptic future where sadomasochistic subcultures engage in startling acts of random violence, and the 1953 novel *You're All Alone* explores the theme of claustrophobic entrapment in a paranoid technological mindscape. As evidence of his enormous versatility, Leiber is one of only three authors (the others being Michael Moorcock and Harlan Ellison) to have won lifetime achievement awards from the Science Fiction Writers of America, the World Fantasy Association, and the Horror Writers of America (now the Horror Writers Association) combined.

Throughout his long career, Leiber proved remarkably adaptable to changing vogues within the field, being equally at home in John W. Campbell's pulp magazine *Astounding* during its 1940s Golden Age as in Michael Moorcock's avant-garde periodical *New Worlds* during the New Wave movement a quarter-century later. Yet the publication that gave him his most successful platform from which to launch a new breed of horror story was undoubtedly Campbell's *Unknown* (a.k.a. *Unknown Worlds*), which debuted in 1939. Through its mere four years of

"Smoke Ghost": The Specter of Urban Malaise

"Smoke Ghost," originally published in the pulp magazine *Unknown* (a.k.a. *Unknown Worlds*) and subsequently widely anthologized, pioneered the tale of modern urban horror and updates a classic horror theme—the ghostly revenant—for a contemporary setting.

As its title implies, "Smoke Ghost" recounts a ghastly haunting, but the eponymous specter is no conventional phantasm; rather, it is the veritable incarnation of big-city squalor and malaise. A grimy, shambling creature that spectrally incarnates the spirit of industrial civilization with its soot and pounding machinery, it stalks the protagonist relentlessly, first as a series of silhouettes glimpsed from his subway seat and high-rise office building, then as a demonic amalgam of all the psychological trials of urban life, and finally as a demonic idol demanding total subservience and devotion. Leiber's smoke ghost is, in short, the embodiment of all of urban modernity's compelling contradictions: its boundless creativity and entropic decay, its brutal dynamism and boring stasis, its exhilaration and despair. The protagonist, a representative urban everyman, is susceptible to its predatory wiles because it is, in essence, the embodiment of his own incipient dreads and smothered despairs.

The tone of the story—paranoid, borderline hysterical, nervously alert to subtle hints and lurking portents—would exert an enormous influence on future chroniclers of urban anxiety and dread. Indeed, Leiber's work during the 1940s, which located the uncanny not in the Gothic relics of the past but in modern sites and situations, made possible the explosion of urban horror that took place during the postwar period.

Rob Latham

existence, *Unknown* made an indelible mark on the genre, sweeping away a century of Gothic cobwebs and ushering in a skeptical, streamlined depiction of uncanny presences hovering on the margins of modern life. Arguably, Leiber was the most significant originator of this trend. He consistently managed to capture the potent blend of horror, science fiction, and urban noir for which *Unknown* came to be celebrated.

Leiber's best work for *Unknown* included the groundbreaking stories "Smoke Ghost" (1941) and *Conjure Wife* (1943), which updated, for a modern urban environment, classic ghost and witch stories, respectively. During the 1940s, Leiber published a series of similar efforts—in *Unknown*, *Weird Tales*, and elsewhere—that explored specifically contemporary forms of horror, usually in an urban milieu. In "The Hound" (1942), the werewolves of medieval folklore are replaced by a monster spawned by city-dwellers' fears and insecurities, with the title creature's animal sounds emerging from and merging with the noise of traffic and industry. Similarly,

"The Girl with the Hungry Eyes" (1949) updates the conventions of the vampiric femme fatale for a world of modern consumerism. Leiber continued producing such tales of urban dread throughout his career, interspersed with a wide range of other work; his best horror stories can be found in such seminal collections as *Night's Black Agents* (1947), *Shadows with Eyes* (1962), and *Night Monsters* (1969). In 1977, his novel *Our Lady of Darkness*, about occult presences in modern-day San Francisco, served as a fitting capstone for his rich and sophisticated contribution to the field.

In 1984, the retrospective collection *The Ghost Light* gathered much of Leiber's finest work, including the title story, an eerie novella of ambiguous spectral beings, and "Four Ghosts in Hamlet" (1965), a tale that drew on Leiber's experiences as a Shakespearean actor. The book is capped by an autobiographical essay in which the author muses on his long life and career.

Rob Latham

See also: Bloch, Robert; Bradbury, Ray; Bram Stoker Award; *Conjure Wife*; Dark Fantasy; "The Girl with the Hungry Eyes"; *Our Lady of Darkness*; Pulp Horror; The Uncanny; *Weird Tales*; Witches and Witchcraft; World Fantasy Award; *Part Two, Themes, Topics, and Genres*: Shakespearean Horrors.

Further Reading

Byfield, Bruce. 1991. *Witches of the Mind: A Critical Study of Fritz Leiber*. West Warwick, RI: Necronomicon Press.

Goho, James. 2014. "City of Darkness: The Beginnings of Modern Urban Horror." In *Journeys into Darkness: Critical Essays on Gothic Horror*, 181–204. New York: Rowman & Littlefield.

Schweitzer, Darrell. 1988. "Poetry of Darkness: The Horror Fiction of Fritz Leiber." In *Discovering Modern Horror Fiction II*, 18–29. Mercer Island, WA: Starmont House.

Szumskyj, Benjamin, ed. 2008. *Fritz Leiber: Critical Essays*. Jefferson, NC: McFarland.

LEWIS, MATTHEW GREGORY (1775–1818)

Matthew Gregory Lewis was commonly known by his contemporaries as Matthew "Monk" Lewis or simply "Monk" Lewis, a reference to his most infamous and influential novel, *The Monk* (1796). Lewis is best known for this scandalous first work, written when he was nineteen, during the short period he served as a member of Parliament (MP), and in part a response to Ann Radcliffe's novel *The Mysteries of Udolpho* (1794) and the "explained supernatural." Lewis's deviation from this approach would characterize his work for the rest of his life. *The Monk* showcases supernatural events as truly supernatural and favors graphic depictions of violence and gore over less descriptive insinuations. His work falls into the category of horror, as defined by Radcliffe, opposed to her preferred use of terror. In his work, one can see the influence of the German *schauerroman* literature (or shudder-novel), as well as French Revolution violence and an unstable family life, all of which would establish the foundations of the Gothic tradition.

Lewis's first work was not his last, though it is the work for which most students of the Gothic recognize him. He was careful to avoid another scandal in further work, but his oeuvre never strayed far from the realm of horror. A prolific writer of poetry and drama, such as his most important play, *The Castle Spectre* (1797), he was also a talented translator, and many of his works walked the fine line between translation, adaptation, and imitation. His poetry tended toward Gothic themes, but what contemporaries praised most was his skill at writing verse, particularly his experimental form in such poems as "Alonzo the Brave and Fair Imogine" (first published in *The Monk*), appropriately called "Alonzo meter." Lewis influenced many canonical Romantic poets, mentoring Sir Walter Scott, Percy Bysshe Shelley, and even Lord Byron, who sought his advice on his own work. Lewis's anthology of poetry, *Tales of Wonder* (1801), included works from several poets, Scott included, as well as his own translations, original poetry, and even a parody of one of his poems. The collection *Tales of Terror*, published shortly thereafter, was attributed to him by his nineteenth-century biographer, an error that has only recently been rectified. The author of this second collection remains unknown, but the text is widely understood to be a parody of (or tribute to) *Tales of Wonder*. Today's scholars take particular interest in approaches to sexuality, gender, and race in all of Lewis's works, as well as their unique and playful forms.

In 1812, Lewis's father Matthew—deputy secretary of war and a sugar plantation owner—died, leaving the writer his Jamaican property and its slaves, a charge that Lewis approached with seriousness and anxiety. While his own politics were fairly inconsistent, Lewis expressed concern for his slaves and an interest in their freedom. His last work was one of his most remarkable: *Journal of a West India Proprietor* (written 1815–1818 and published 1834). Lewis died at sea from yellow fever on a return trip from Jamaica. "Monk" Lewis not only penned one of the most defining texts within one of the most defining periods of the Gothic tradition, but he worked within that tradition's forms throughout his life, inspiring writers and audiences with his craft and the power of horror.

Laura R. Kremmel

See also: The Monk; Radcliffe, Ann; Romanticism and Dark Romanticism; Terror versus Horror.

Further Reading

Macdonald, D. L. 2000. *Monk Lewis: A Critical Biography*. Toronto: University of Toronto Press.

Robinson, Daniel. 2013. "Gothic Prosody: Monkish Perversity and the Poetics of Weird Form." In *Transnational Gothic: Literary and Social Exchanges in the Long Nineteenth Century*, edited by Monika Elbert and Bridget M. Marshall, 155–171. Surrey: Ashgate.

Thomson, Douglass H. 2008. "Mingled Measures: Gothic Parody in *Tales of Wonder* and *Tales of Terror*." In *Romanticism and Victorianism on the Net* 50. https://www.erudit.org /revue/ravon/2008/v/n50/018143ar.html.

"LIGEIA"

Edgar Allan Poe seems to have regarded the 1838 story "Ligeia" as one of his best, and to have revised it several times during its publication history. It is one of his stories about the death of a beautiful woman, a subject he claimed to be "the most poetical" in the world, and which he certainly made famous with his poem "Annabel Lee" (Poe 2003, 436).

"Ligeia" introduces a Poe narrator at his most obsessive and unreliable. The hero cannot even remember where he first met the Lady Ligeia (somewhere in Germany, perhaps), but he goes on for pages describing every aspect of her physical beauty (raven-black hair, marble complexion, high forehead, etc.), intellectual accomplishments, charms, and such. The prose is intense and fervid, not so much because Poe

---

In the story's opening lines, the first-person narrator of "Ligeia" is established as one of Poe's overwrought, high-strung, hyperintelligent, probably unreliable individuals whose perception of events is almost certainly skewed in dark and disturbing ways:

> I cannot, for my soul, remember how, when, or even precisely where, I first became acquainted with the lady Ligeia. Long years have since elapsed, and my memory is feeble through much suffering. Or, perhaps, I cannot *now* bring these points to mind, because, in truth, the character of my beloved, her rare learning, her singular yet placid cast of beauty, and the thrilling and enthralling eloquence of her low musical language, made their way into my heart by paces so steadily and stealthily progressive that they have been unnoticed and unknown. . . . And now, while I write, a recollection flashes upon me that I have *never known* the paternal name of her who was my friend and my betrothed, and who became the partner of my studies, and finally the wife of my bosom. Was it a playful charge on the part of my Ligeia? or was it a test of my strength of affection, that I should institute no inquiries upon this point? or was it rather a caprice of my own—a wildly romantic offering on the shrine of the most passionate devotion? I but indistinctly recall the fact itself—what wonder that I have utterly forgotten the circumstances which originated or attended it? And, indeed, if ever that spirit which is entitled *Romance*—if ever she, the wan and the misty-winged *Ashtophet* of idolatrous Egypt, presided, as they tell, over marriages ill-omened, then most surely she presided over mine.

Matt Cardin

Source: Poe, Edgar Allan. 1902. *Complete Works of Edgar Allan Poe.* Vol. 3. New York: Fred De Fau & Company. 192–193.

is overwriting but because the narrator's state of mind is already bordering on madness. Then Ligeia sickens and dies, but not before the narrator has read aloud to her the poem "The Conqueror Worm," which is actually by Poe, but which the story frames as Ligeia's own composition. This poem, with its triumph of the bloody grave worm, would seem to contradict the quote from Joseph Glanvill, a seventeenth-century English philosopher, that is both presented at the head of the story and repeated within the text, to the effect that the human will has the power to overcome death: "And the will therein lieth, which dieth not. Who knoweth the mysteries of the will, with its vigor? For God is but a great will pervading all things by nature of its intentness. Man doth not yield himself to the angels, nor unto death utterly, save only through the weakness of his feeble will" (Poe 1984, 262). (This passage has not been found among Glanville's works and may be Poe's invention.)

Having lost one wife, the hero moves to a remote part of England and, being fabulously rich, refurnishes an old abbey, decorating it fantastically, slipping into extreme decadence and aesthetic excess. In this state, now taking opium regularly, he marries the much more conventional (and blonde-haired) Lady Rowena, but soon hates her and longs for Ligeia. Rowena also sickens, and the narrator seems to sense the presence of the ghost of Ligeia in the bedchamber with the two of them. The narrator describes several suspicious red drops that appear in Rowena's wine, and it is unclear whether he did it himself, or whether the ghost of Ligeia did it, or whether the entire episode is nothing but a hallucination. The climax comes as Rowena, already presumed dead and wrapped for the grave, seems to revive and staggers into the middle of the room, but recoils from the narrator. She falls back on the bed. The grave-wrappings come loose, and her black hair is revealed. It is Ligeia, returned—but it is unclear whether she is alive or just another beautiful corpse.

Roger Corman filmed this story in 1964 as *The Tomb of Ligeia*, the last and least successful of his Poe films, but the influence of the story extends far beyond that. The hero's extreme aesthetic indulgence is more in the spirit of the "decadent" writers of the 1890s and later and it certainly influenced them. Traces of this story are visible in the works of J. K. Huysmans, M. P. Shiel, Oscar Wilde, and Clark Ashton Smith. It depicts the borderline where the pursuit of beauty and the indulgence of the senses overwhelm the senses and shade into horror.

Darrell Schweitzer

See also: "The Fall of the House of Usher"; Huysmans, J. K.; "The Masque of the Red Death"; Poe, Edgar Allan; Psychological Horror; Romanticism and Dark Romanticism; Shiel, M. P.; Smith, Clark Ashton; Unreliable Narrator.

Further Reading

Heller, Terry. 1980. "Poe's 'Ligeia' and the Pleasures of Terror." *Gothic* 2, no. 2: 39–48.
Holland-Toll, Linda J. 1997. "Ligeia: The Facts of the Case." *Studies in Weird Fiction* 21 (Summer): 10–16.

Jay, Gregory S. 1983. "Poe: Writing and the Unconscious." In *The American Renaissance: New Dimensions*, edited by Harry R. Garvin and Peter C. Carafiol, 144–169. London and Toronto: Associated University Presses.

Kennedy, J. Gerald. 1993. "Poe, 'Ligeia,' and the Problem of Dying Women." In *New Essays on Poe's Major Tales*, edited by Kenneth Silverman, 119–120. Cambridge: Cambridge University Press.

Poe, Edgar Allan. 1984. *Poetry and Tales*. New York: Library of America.

Poe, Edgar Allan. 2003. "The Philosophy of Composition." In *Edgar Allan Poe: The Fall of the House of Usher and Other Writings: Poems, Tales, Essays, and Reviews*, edited by David Galloway, 430–442. New York: Penguin.

Shi, Yaohua. 1991. "The Enigmatic Ligeia/'Ligeia.'" *Studies in Short Fiction* 28, no. 4: 485–496.

LIGOTTI, THOMAS (1953–)

Thomas Ligotti is an American pessimist and innovator in weird fiction. Noteworthy for avoiding traditional horror storytelling and for using language in an extremely precise and careful way, Ligotti's horror is pointedly philosophical; that is, the menace in a Ligotti story is an idea more often than it is a monster or a villain. Specifically, the menacing idea is the notion that existence is meaningless, that reality cannot really be distinguished from nothingness. Ideas such as these are often combined and labeled "nihilism," which means "belief in nothing." Nihilism has no institutions, no "rules," but is a name for a point of view that can be found anywhere, including in literature and philosophy, especially when the topic is a loss of faith in conventional values, or even in conventional ideas of what does or does not exist. This loss of faith is often called "disillusionment," and it may be said that it is disillusionment that Ligotti imparts to the reader through his fiction.

During the 1980s Ligotti published his first stories in small press magazines such as *Nyctalops*, *Eldritch Tales*, *Grimoire*, *Grue*, *Fantasy Macabre*, *Dark Horizons*, and *Crypt of Cthulhu*. His first collection, *Songs of a Dead Dreamer*, was published in a limited edition by Silver Scarab Press in 1985, expanded and reissued first in England by Robinson Publishing in 1989, and then in the United States in 1990 by Carroll and Graf, which would go on to publish three further collections, *Grimscribe* (1991), *Noctuary* (1994), and *The Nightmare Factory* (1996). *Songs of a Dead Dreamer* was highly praised for its originality and importance when it was published. *The Nightmare Factory* was the first mass market paperback of Ligotti's work, incorporating selections from his earlier collections alongside new material, and it won both the Bram Stoker and British Fantasy awards for Best Fiction Collection of 1996. During this period, Ligotti also published *The Agonizing Resurrection of Victor Frankenstein and Other Gothic Tales* (1994) (with an introduction by fellow horror master Michael Shea), a work that shows particularly well Ligotti's highly self-aware approach to horror as a literary genre.

Over a period of five years, Ligotti produced a series of four works in collaboration with the English experimental band Current 93, consisting of brief, limited-edition books released along with compact discs of original music inspired by the

"The Red Tower": The Universe as a Nightmare Factory

"The Red Tower" is among the most widely reprinted of Ligotti's stories, and it won a Bram Stoker Award for Long Fiction after it was first published in his collection *The Nightmare Factory* in 1996. The concluding story of the book, its subject is echoed by the title of, and serves as a coda to, that collection as a whole. More an unnerving prose poem than a plot-driven narrative, it consists of an unnamed first-person narrator's description of a three-story, ruined factory made of crumbling red brick, known as the Red Tower, that stands in an otherwise blank landscape. This factory, operating like an organism, without owners, employees, or even consumers for its products, industriously churns out a wide variety of grotesque "novelty items," until it begins to break down and fade from existence.

This building and its hostile, empty environment, apparently resentful of the factory's novelties, are the story's only major characters, for the reader learns nothing of the narrator beyond that he or she is part of a select group of alienated obsessives who share their "hallucinatory accounts" of the Tower's activities. These accounts inform the narrator's speculation that the factory's environs are attempting to return to a state of total vacancy. The narrator admires the factory's defiant production of absurd artifacts, while anxiously anticipating its inevitable dissolution.

With its eschewal of traditional plot and character; development of a highly stylized, abstract, and even opaque language; and highly wrought images of disintegration and entropy, the story showcases many of the techniques and themes for which Ligotti's name has become a sort of shorthand. Its atmosphere of decay is inextricable from its allegorical portrayal of a universe that is intrinsically hostile to creativity, consciousness, and even existence itself.

Sean Moreland

fiction, as well as readings of the fiction. These works were *In a Foreign Town, In a Foreign Land* (1997), *I Have a Special Plan for This World* (2000), *This Degenerate Little Town* (2001), and *The Unholy City* (2002).

In 2002, Ligotti's collection of stories all related to the idea of "corporate horror," entitled *My Work Is Not Yet Done*, won the Stoker and International Horror Guild awards for Best Long Fiction. The following year, he published a screenplay, *Crampton*, written in collaboration with Brandon Trenz, and originally intended as an episode of *The X-Files* television program. He remained highly active in publishing during this period, releasing *Sideshow and Other Stories* (2003), *Death Poems* (2004), *The Shadow at the Bottom of the World* (2005), and *Teatro Grottesco* (2006), all published by small presses instead of mainstream, mass market ones.

There followed a publishing hiatus of eight years. In 2007, however, a filmed adaptation of Ligotti's early story "The Frolic" was released, directed by Jacob Cooney, with a screenplay by Ligotti and Brandon Trenz.

Ligotti returned to publishing in 2014 with a collection of two stories, *The Spectral Link*, and the same year he was also the subject of a collection of interviews spanning twenty-five years of his career, titled *Born to Fear* and edited by Matt Cardin. His name and work gained additional prominence in 2014 when the first season of the HBO television series *True Detective* incorporated distinctively Ligottian elements into its dialogue and dark philosophical worldview, prompting an accusation of plagiarism (not leveled by Ligotti himself) that attained international media attention and brought Ligotti to the awareness of a massive mainstream audience for the first time. Ligotti's significance has also been acknowledged by the republication of his two earliest collections in one volume by Penguin Books, *Songs of a Dead Dreamer and Grimscribe*, in 2015.

Ligotti has acknowledged the influence of several philosophers on his work and his thought, most notably Romanian pessimist Emile Cioran and the early nineteenth-century German philosopher Arthur Schopenhauer. Since his stories tend to be more about ideas than about character or plot, except indirectly, the language and imagery Ligotti uses become accordingly more important, since it is the story itself that has to be frightening, rather than what the story is about.

Ligotti makes his point of view available to others by employing both new and familiar aspects of horror stories; the somewhat exaggerated nature of the dangers and fears in a conventional horror tale are used to make Ligotti's more subtle uncertainties large enough to see clearly. In stories such as "The Sect of the Idiot," "The Mystics of Muelenberg," and "The Voice in the Bones," rather than present the reader with a disillusioned character passively thinking in a single setting, simply reciting nihilistic ideas, Ligotti instead will introduce characters into situations that cause them to discover, or rediscover, the unreality and emptiness of the world and of themselves. By dramatizing this idea, turning it into a realization for characters, rather than the "message," Ligotti is able to infuse this idea with the emotions appropriate to it. In Ligotti's work, the discovery of unreality leads the reader to the possibility that nothing is real.

The student of horror fiction is familiar with stories revolving around sinister dolls and puppets. E. T. A. Hoffmann, whose story "The Sand-man" includes an "automaton" (robot) character, was one of the most important writers to deal extensively with dolls. The most famous section of the classic English anthology horror film "Dead of Night" (1945) involves a ventriloquist dummy come to life, as does an episode of the original *Twilight Zone*, "The Dummy" (1962). So does the Anthony Hopkins film *Magic* (1978). Dolls or dummies occur again and again in Ligotti's fiction, serving as important images of a kind of falseness in life. The idea that there is really no difference between a human being and a manikin is addressed in "Dream of a Manikin," for example; the narrator at one point is unable to determine whether or not the figures he sees are people impersonating dolls, or simply dolls. The dolls invite the narrator to become one of them, to "die into" them, but this death is more like the disappearance of the idea of life itself, a loss even greater than the loss of an individual life. As is typical in Ligotti's work, the question of reality is not treated separately from the question of life itself; if reality is unreal, then life is unreal, and death therefore is the truer reality.

Ligotti's stories seldom involve action or violence, although *My Work Is Not Yet Done* marries an element of supernatural violence to the meditations on emptiness. Heroes and villains are also typically absent from his work; the cosmos, or life itself, is the villain in Ligotti's fiction, with no hero to vanquish them. Instead, Ligotti's main characters are often dreamers. Actual dreams have an important place in Ligotti's work, but the figure of the dreamer is more than just a character who dreams a dream. A dreamer is, in a way, a reality-impaired person; someone who is less solidly connected to what is supposed to be real. The dreamer may or may not have a job, but usually that job will be a meaningless and solitary occupation. He will be isolated, either in real solitude, or so alienated from other people that he might as well be alone even in a crowd. Since the dreamer is only superficially participating in everyday life, which is all of reality for most people, the dreamer seems to be less real. The point of view of the dreamer, someone who does not see reality as real, is extensively explored in Ligotti's fiction. Sometimes the dreamer is someone who despises reality as a crude illusion, but more often Ligotti's dreamers are people who seem unable to manage to believe in reality, or in themselves.

Seen from this point of view, reality often seems absurd, which means that it seems pointless and silly. The point of view of the dreamer is ironic, that is, the dreamer does not fully believe in reality, but understands that the people around him do. This gives rise to sardonic humor, which means a kind of humor that is painful. Even though they find life to be empty and meaningless, Ligotti's characters do not want to die and will cling to their dream of life even though they cannot find any meaning in living. In the middle of his 2014 story "Metaphysica Morum," there is a long letter written in the style of American phantasmagoric author William S. Burroughs, which combines broad humor with the absurd contrast between the tone of the letter and the tone of the rest of the story. Ligotti's fiction often creates effects in this way, using aspects of style or tone alongside more familiar ways of creating effects using characters and situations. This passage resembles others in earlier stories that involve Hoffmann-like dream characters, unreal persons who are darkly sarcastic avatars of unreality, or agents of it.

Much of Ligotti's early work appeared in publications devoted in whole or in part to literary works inspired by H. P. Lovecraft, so that, for a time, Ligotti was regarded as a "Lovecraftian" writer. Stories such as "Nethescurial" and "The Prodigy of Dreams" are experiments in a more overtly Lovecraftian vein, both involving the creation of godlike otherworldly entities—Nethescurial itself, and Cynothoglys, respectively. Ligotti also invented his own dream city, "Vastarien," in the story of the same name. However, Ligotti's connection to Lovecraft actually redefined for many what "Lovecraftian" meant, as he did not simply ape the more obvious aspects of Lovecraft's work in his own, but instead adopted Lovecraft's own point of view. Lovecraft, a strict materialist, felt that existence was fundamentally meaningless, that tradition and stability were the greatest goods a society could possess, and that one should adopt a detached attitude toward reality. Ligotti extends this perspective and makes it less calm and more painful. He is a Lovecraftian in the sense that he writes horror fiction in order to express a philosophy of horror.

A part of Ligotti's appeal may be the consistency of his thinking and the reality of his commitment to the nihilism of his writing. In addition to his literary work, Ligotti has also written a philosophical book, *The Conspiracy against the Human Race* (2010), advocating that humanity bring itself to an end as a species by ceasing to reproduce. This idea is sometimes called "antinatalism," meaning "against birth."

Ligotti's story "The Red Tower" is a reflection on the sources of his own fiction. The story has no character other than a nameless narrator, really only a voice saying "I." There is no plot, but only a description of a mysterious red tower, which is continually producing horrific things. This tower does not seem to be inhabited, at least not in any normal sense. There is no reason why it should exist or create horrible things. In a way, the red tower is the imagination of the horror writer. One of the things that makes Ligotti's work is so distinctive, and one of his innovations in the writing of horror stories, is this kind of self-awareness. Many of Ligotti's stories "know" that they are stories; since he is usually writing about the unreality of what we think of as real, it is not inconsistent to write also about the reality of his stories. If reality is a fiction, then fiction and reality are not so different from each other. In other pieces like "Professor Nobody's Little Lectures on Supernatural Horror" and "Notes on the Writing of Horror: A Story," Ligotti transforms the discussion of horror fiction into horror stories, and so cancels the distance that would normally "protect" the reader from what he or she is reading. In this way, Ligotti is able to extend the work of the classic horror writers who influenced him—including Edgar Allan Poe, H. P. Lovecraft, Arthur Machen, M. R. James, and Algernon Blackwood—by introducing aspects of modern literary self-awareness, drawn from writers whose work is not normally considered horror fiction, such as Thomas Bernhard, William S. Burroughs, Vladimir Nabokov, or Bruno Schulz. Ligotti has himself gone on to influence a new generation of horror writers, makers of music, television, and film, who look to him for inspiration and guidance.

Michael Cisco

See also: Bram Stoker Award; Hoffmann, E. T. A.; International Horror Guild Award; "The Last Feast of Harlequin"; Lovecraft, H. P.; Shea, Michael; World Fantasy Award.

Further Reading

Calia, Michael. 2015. "A Master of Horror Blows Up." *Wall Street Journal—Eastern Edition*, September 25. D3.

Cardin, Matt, ed. 2014. *Born to Fear: Interviews with Thomas Ligotti*. Burton, MI: Subterranean Press.

Joshi, S. T. 2001. "Thomas Ligotti: The Escape from Life." In *The Modern Weird Tale*, 243–257. Jefferson, NC: McFarland.

Ligotti, Thomas. 2010. *The Conspiracy against the Human Race: A Contrivance of Horror*. New York: Hippocampus Press.

Schweitzer, Darrell, ed. 2003. *The Thomas Ligotti Reader*. Holicong, PA: Wildside Press.

Tompkins, Stephen. 2006. "The Nemesis of Mimesis: Thomas Ligotti, Worlds Elsewhere, and the Darkness Ten Times." *Studies in Modern Horror* 4: 1–28.

Interview with Thomas Ligotti

October 2016

Ligotti here talks about the use of dolls, dummies, puppets, and manikins in both his own writing and that of other horror writers. He does the same for the use of dreams and nightmares as well. He also talks about the differences between short-form horror fiction and novel-length horror fiction, the changing status and permanent importance of H. P. Lovecraft to the field, and the central purpose of horror literature.

Matt Cardin: One of the most characteristic elements of your stories is the frequent presence of dolls, dummies, scarecrows, manikins, puppets, and other artificial representations of the human form, used to uncanny, unnerving, and horrific effect. These are always tied into an extremely dark view of reality, and of the place of conscious life within it. Dolls and dummies also have a venerable history in horror literature at large, stretching back centuries. Why is this so? What is it about these effigies of human beings (and sometimes other life forms) that makes them such a powerful presence in horror fiction? And why do you personally find them so useful and expressive of your authorial calling?

Thomas Ligotti: It's probably not possible to offer a definitive explanation to the question, "Why is there a potential for alarm in all approximations of the human figure?" I use the word "potential" because such representations have seldom been intended to alarm in such a way that violates their nature as representations. Only our perception that a violation of this kind might occur, or has in fact occurred, instills in us a sense that something which should not be in fact *is*. This is the essence of the uncanny, and the uncanny is always alarming. One might argue that all horror fiction is based on some uncanny phenomenon. To some degree this is true, as in the case of people who are bitten by zombies and afterward themselves become zombies. There is a moment of the uncanny when one form of being turns into an entirely different form. Subsequently, though, the new form is normalized into a monster and bears no resemblance to what it once was. Monsters aren't uncanny. They're simply a threat to humans. Ghosts aren't uncanny. They're not even by nature alarming. And monster trucks driven by vengeful ghosts definitely aren't uncanny. The harm posed by these unusual things and many others featured in horror stories is a strictly physical harm to human bodies. The harm of the uncanny is psychological, that is, the wreckage of some metaphysical viewpoint deeply ingrained in us. It's a threat to how we believe the world should be and violates the categories, so often proven false, of our conception of existence in general and of our existence as persons in particular.

Cartesian dualism is a classic attempt to wrestle with our anxiety about what we are and how we work. Perhaps, as Descartes wrote, we really are because we *think,* but that doesn't mean we are the way we think we are. When dolls or puppets or manikins behave as we do, declaring their possession of a mind and a will like our own, there is a confusion of categories and an uncanny horror arises from this confusion. How can these lifeless things, these purely physical things of parts, also present themselves as being things that are whole, things that have a reality we thought belonged only to us? We feel there is something deranged about this, something fundamentally *wrong.* But is it deranged, is it wrong, because of the way these purely physical things of parts behave—and they always behave menacingly—or because they behave with the same appearance of mind and will as we seem to do? Two things can't be one. Things of parts can't amount to anything whole, anything real, and, above all, anything "human."

MC: Another typical trope in your work is the use of dreams and nightmares. These, too, are also staples of the Gothic and horrific literary traditions. Both for you individually and for the tradition in general, why?

TL: To play off my response to the previous questions, dreams and nightmares are the principal locus of uncanny experience, and looking back on what I've written it's the effect of the uncanny that is dominant in my stories. I didn't deliberately intend this to be the case. I don't think it's possible to do that. One simply has to be the kind of person who feels, as I indicated above, that there is something fundamentally wrong about being alive and aware in this world. When I contemplate how the whole melange of organic existence evolved, I can't help being overwhelmed by a sense of the weird and grotesque oddity of it all. Some people find the slide from bacteria to conscious beings to be something marvelous and enchanting. I don't. I'm not saying that those who don't share my perception of existence are wrongheaded. Quite obviously they possess a different sensibility from my own and find it easier to accept what I view as a maddening showcase of whimsical biology and pointless experience that trails off into nonexistence. I'm just saying that given the accidents of my personal evolution, I can't see the big picture of life as anything but a sequence of scenarios that add up to one great uncanny nightmare.

MC: With the exception of *My Work Is Not Yet Done* and *The Conspiracy against the Human Race*, you have published exclusively short-form work. Many people have noted that short stories and novellas seem an especially suitable vehicle for horror fiction, and that the mass birth of the horror novel in the late twentieth century represented a kind of combined literary and publishing experiment. Are there any long-form works of horror that you, as a reader, personally like and recommend, or do you find yourself drawn exclusively to the traditional short forms?

TL: It's not only horror novels that are perceived as freaks in the history of genre fiction. Excellent arguments have been made by better brains than mine that the novel itself was an artistic aberration in the march of literature. With the advent of modernism at the latest, writers have been attempting to do something different, something more expressive and faithful to human experience, than telling—or, even worse, "showing"—a lengthy story for the purpose of edification and entertainment. There's nothing inherently evil about a long work of fiction, but there's no argument that this form is for the most part rigidly conventionalized in subject matter as well as form, and everything else is relegated to minor, miniaturist, or cult status. Jorge Luis Borges once said that he could imagine a world without novels but not without tales. Admittedly, massive, mass-market page-turners make more people happy than any other literary form. How can anyone honestly say that this is a puke-making or terrible phenomenon? When it comes down to it, everyone reads for entertainment or they don't read at all. As for horror fiction as such, it's a fact that the classics of this genre and the works cherished by its most avid aficionados exist almost exclusively in short form.

MC: After decades of occupying a strange hybrid status as pulp author, respected literary author, cult author, and underground pop culture icon all at once, Lovecraft has now exploded onto the scene in an even stranger status. He is at once a canonized American writer and a controversial, polarizing, lightning rod–type figure who is both lauded and reviled. He is also, for you, as for so many other horror writers, a chief and cherished influence. What do you think readers need to know about him right now?

TL: Despite all attempts to derogate or trivialize them, Lovecraft's works will resonate down the ages for their brave and expansive view of the universe and a unique vision that hardly exists elsewhere in literature. The last thing on the mind of Lovecraft was the highly perishable effort to convey what it was like to live at a particular time and in a particular place in world history. His ambition went far beyond documenting the contemporaneous or an engagement in mere wordsmithing for art's sake. While superb work has been done in the field of illuminating Lovecraft's writing for a specialized audience, my hope has always been that the literary elites might better appreciate the mind behind the monsters, thereby enabling them to express a wider view of the human experiment.

MC: What is the point, purpose, or value of horror literature?

TL: To entertain and disillusion its readers at the same time.

MC: What do readers of horror literature need to know?

TL: If you read a lot of horror literature because you like to be scared, then you're probably a normal, healthy person. If you read horror literature to fulfill some deeply personal predisposition, be assured there is probably something odd and unwholesome about you. Don't ever let anyone tell you it's not all right to be that way.

LINK, KELLY (1969–)

Kelly Link is an author best known for her Fabulations, which are stories that draw from the treasury of science fiction, fantasy, and horror, but that are not readily identifiable as belonging to any of those sole genres specifically. Another way of thinking about her work, and of Fabulation in general, is to consider its disregard for genre divisions even as it demonstrates a reverence for genre traditions. In Link's hands Fabulation is neither parody nor pastiche (even if it sometimes incorporates these approaches), but a creatively and intellectually sincere engagement with the variety of motifs most broadly associated with speculative fiction. Additionally, it is important to note that her work is not defined by genre, but instead works in conversation with it. Her work differs significantly, then, from that of traditional genre writers in that it is more experimental at both a formal and a philosophical level.

Put another way, Link's work challenges genre readers precisely because it uses familiar tropes—ghosts, zombies, witches—in unfamiliar ways and with unfamiliar tones. Her stories engage, in some cases overtly, the storytelling tradition in all its diverse forms. Sometimes this means that plot and characters are secondary concerns. Often, her stories inhabit an indeterminate narrative state that eschews pat resolutions and closure. Her work is characterized by an ambiguity that resists interpretation. And yet, there is great, sometimes bleak, humor in her stories. Part of what makes Link so readable is that the heaviness often associated with experimental fiction is largely absent. There is always a sense of playfulness, of fun, running throughout her work that, sometimes ironically, intensifies its narrative.

Her work has been widely praised by critics outside the fields of science fiction, fantasy, and horror. For example, her 2016 fiction collection *Get in Trouble* was a finalist for the Pulitzer Prize, and her work has been included in such mainstream anthologies as *The Best American Short Stories* series (which usually adheres to traditionally realist fiction). At the same time, she has enjoyed much success within her home fields, having garnered Nebula, Hugo, and Locus awards, as well as the Theodore Sturgeon Award, the World Fantasy Award, the James Tiptree Jr. Award, and the Shirley Jackson Award.

To date Link has published four short story collections: *Stranger Things Happen* (2001), *Magic for Beginners* (2014), *Pretty Monsters* (2010; includes stories from the previous two collections along with new material), and *Get in Trouble*. Standout titles of individual stories that represent Link's nuanced complexity and breadth while incorporating elements of horror include "Water off a Black Dog's Back" and "The Specialist's Hat" in *Stranger Things Happen*; "Magic for Beginners," "Stone Animals," and "Catskin" in *Magic for Beginners*; and "The Summer People" and "Two Houses" in *Pretty Monsters*. Link has also been an active and prolific editor, overseeing, with husband Gavin Grant, Small Beer Press and the fiction zine *Lady Churchill's Rosebud Wristlet*. She has also edited the anthologies *Trampoline* (2003) and, with Grant, *Monstrous Affections* (2014).

Javier A. Martinez

See also: Monsters; New Weird; Shirley Jackson Awards; Vampires; World Fantasy Award; Zombies.

Further Reading

Baker, James Ireland. 2005. "Maverick Fabulist: Kelly Link, Rising Star, Goes Her Own Way." *Publishers Weekly*, July 22. http://www.publishersweekly.com/pw/print/20050725/20526-maverick-fabulist.html.

"Horror Stories Are Love Stories: Helen Oyemi interviews Kelly Link." 2015. *Los Angeles Review of Books*, May 26. https://lareviewofbooks.org/article/horror-stories-are-love-stories.

"Kelly Link." 2016. *Contemporary Authors Online*. Detroit, MI: Gale.

"THE LISTENERS"

Written in 1912 and published that year by Constable and Company in *The Listeners and Other Poems*, "The Listeners" is perhaps Walter de la Mare's most recognizable work for either adults or children in any form, noted particularly for its simple metric rhythm, its atmospheric setting, and its darkly romantic imagery.

"The Listeners" recounts in brief the arrival of an unnamed traveler to a moonlit house late one night, and his unsuccessful attempts to gain admittance. The poem's stark central image is that of the eponymous, silent listeners, a large group of (it is implied) phantoms who are thronging the halls of the house, and who remain steadfastly still and silent in response to the traveler's calls.

The horror underlining de la Mare's poem is that of the uncanny, otherworldly nature of the silent listeners, and the mysterious relationship between the traveler and those who dwell within the house. Indeed, "The Listeners" poses many questions that de la Mare deliberately leaves unresolved, thereby heightening the numerous mysteries at the heart of the poem. The subtle threat running throughout the poem, and that (along with its decidedly supernatural elements) accounts for the reader's increasing sense of discomfort, is the primal fear felt in the face of the unfathomable actions of the phantom listeners, who represent a collective predatory threat to the lone figure of the traveler.

Moreover, "The Listeners" compounds this sense of dread with the further existential fear of resolute silence, as de la Mare's pointed refusal to answer the many questions his narrative implicitly raises echoes in kind the silence that meets the traveler's repeated question: "Is there anybody there?" Like the traveler, the reader, too, encounters a void, an existential emptiness that de la Mare refuses to fill.

Finally, "The Listeners" captures the quiet menace of unexplained occurrences or incidences and suggests that the most threatening thing of all to the human mind is the unanswered (or unanswerable) question, to which we necessarily demand a meaningful response. The poem presents several questions, such as who the traveler is and where he has traveled to/from; what his relationship is to the people in the house; who the listeners are and why they won't answer him; what "word" he has kept, and to whom. De la Mare leaves the answers to these questions very much open, and the strength of "The Listeners" as a work of supernatural horror lies in the discomfort the reader feels at the poem's thorough lack of resolution.

Ian Kinane

"The Listeners" by Walter de la Mare

"Is there anybody there?" said the Traveller,
　　Knocking on the moonlit door;
And his horse in the silence champ'd the grasses
　　Of the forest's ferny floor:
And a bird flew up out of the turret,
　　Above the Traveller's head:
And he smote upon the door again a second time;
　　"Is there anybody there?" he said.
But no one descended to the Traveller;
　　No head from the leaf-fringed sill
Lean'd over and look'd into his grey eyes,
　　Where he stood perplex'd and still.
But only a host of phantom listeners
　　That dwelt in the lone house then
Stood listening in the quiet of the moonlight
　　To that voice from the world of men:
Stood thronging the faint moonbeams on the dark stair,
　　That goes down to the empty hall,
Hearkening in an air stirr'd and shaken
　　By the lonely Traveller's call.
And he felt in his heart their strangeness,
　　Their stillness answering his cry,
While his horse moved, cropping the dark turf,
　　'Neath the starred and leafy sky;
For he suddenly smote on the door, even
　　Louder, and lifted his head:—
"Tell them I came, and no one answer'd,
　　That I kept my word," he said.
Never the least stir made the listeners,
　　Though every word he spake
Fell echoing through the shadowiness of the still house
　　From the one man left awake:
Ay, they heard his foot upon the stirrup,
　　And the sound of iron on stone,
And how the silence surged softly backward,
　　When the plunging hoofs were gone. (De la Mare 1916, 13)

Source: De La Mare, Walter. 1916. "The Listeners." In *The Poetry Review of America*. William Stanley Braithwaite and Joseph Lebowich, editors. Vol. 1 (May). Cambridge, MA: Poetry Review Company.

See also: de la Mare, Walter; "Out of the Deep"; *The Return*.

Further Reading

Avery, Gillian, and Julia Briggs. 1989. *Children and Their Books: A Celebration of the Works of Iona and Peter Opie*. Oxford: Clarendon Press.

Bentinck, A. 1991. "De la Mare's 'The Listeners.'" *Explicator* 50, no. 1 (Fall): 33–35.

de la Mare, Walter. [1912] 2010. *The Listeners, and Other Poems*. Charleston: Nabu Press.

Duffin, Henry Charles. 1949. *Walter de la Mare: A Study of his Poetry*. London: Sidgwick & Jackson.

Pierson, Robert M. 1964. "The Meter of 'The Listeners.'" *English Studies* 45, no. 5 (October): 373–381.

Reid, Forrest. 1929. *Walter de la Mare: A Critical Study*. New York: Holt.

LONG, FRANK BELKNAP (1901–1994)

Frank Belknap Long was an American writer of fantasy, horror, and science fiction who was best known as a friend and disciple of groundbreaking weird fiction writer H. P. Lovecraft. He was the first writer to build on the mythology Lovecraft was elaborating in his stories and that would eventually serve as the foundation for the shared fictional universe referred to as the Cthulhu Mythos.

Lovecraft made Long's acquaintance in 1921 after reading his Edgar Allan Poe pastiche "The Eye Above the Mantel" in *United Amateur*, a magazine to which Lovecraft himself contributed. Several years later he recommended Long's fiction to *Weird Tales* editor Farnsworth Wright, who published Long's first professional sale, "The Desert Lich," in the magazine's November 1924 issue. The themes of Long's stories were typical of early *Weird Tales* fare: native curses in "Death Waters" (1924), giant sea monsters in "The Ocean Leech" (1925), and ancient sorceries in "The Black Druid (1930) and "A Visitor from Egypt" (1930). One of his most reprinted *Weird Tales* stories, "Second Night Out" (aka "The Dead Black Thing," 1933), nods to F. Marion Crawford's classic tale "The Upper Berth" in its account of a monster that regularly manifests aboard a ship at a particular nautical crossing. Another *Weird Tales* sale, "The Man with a Thousand Legs" (1927), incorporated significant science fiction elements, and, in fact, Long went on to write more science fiction than supernatural fiction over the course of his career.

Long first referenced elements from Lovecraft's fiction in his tale "The Dog-Eared God" (1926). His story "The Space Eaters" (1928), which features characters based on Lovecraft and himself attempting to survive an invasion by the titular otherworldly monsters, which are modeled on horrors in Lovecraft's own stories, is now regarded the first tale of the Cthulhu Mythos not written by Lovecraft himself. Although Lovecraft gave his blessing to the story and eventually referenced it in his own work, Long's failure to evoke a sense of horror commensurate with the cosmic horrors of Lovecraft's fiction showed, from the outset, the challenge that contributors to the Cthulhu Mythos other than Lovecraft faced when trying to work with the same thematic materials. "The Hounds of Tindalos" (1929), another

"The Hounds of Tindalos": A Cthulhu Mythos Classic

"The Hounds of Tindalos" was first published in the March 1929 issue of *Weird Tales*. It is Frank Belknap Long's best-known tale, and it became a part of the shared universe of Lovecraftian horror stories by diverse hands known today as the Cthulhu Mythos when H. P. Lovecraft, Long's friend and mentor, referenced the monsters named in its title two years later in his tale "The Whisperer in Darkness."

In Long's story, the main character, Halpin, is a writer of occult fiction who seeks to transcend the limits of known space and time under the influence of a mind-expanding drug. Describing his visions while under the drug's influence to an assistant named Frank, Chalmers travels back in time before the origins of organic life, where he finds another type of time that is *curved* and *angular*. When malignant beings of angular time that he refers to as the Hounds of Tindalos "scent" him, they begin their pursuit. Chalmers attempts to thwart the beings by plastering the architectural angles in his apartment into curves, since entities in angular time cannot enter curved time—but a freak earthquake shakes the plaster loose, with horrifying results.

The story features characters modeled on Lovecraft himself (Chalmers) and other members of the Lovecraft circle—a narrative quirk that, as much as the evocation of monstrous entities beyond space and time, was to become a trademark of Cthulhu Mythos fiction. It served as the title story for Long's first short-fiction collection, published by Arkham House in 1946, and August Derleth included it in the seminal 1969 anthology *Tales of the Cthulhu Mythos*. Over the years numerous horror writers including Brian Lumley, Thomas Monteleone, and John Ajvide Lindqvist have paid tribute to Long's story by referencing it in their own work.

Stefan R. Dziemianowicz

tale that evoked Long and Lovecraft's friendship in a plot involving ravening monsters from beyond space and time, would become the title tale of Long's first short-fiction collection, published in 1946. *The Horror from the Hills* (1931) was a collaboration of sorts between Long and Lovecraft, insofar as this tale of the monstrous entity Chaugnar Faugn's incursion into our world incorporated a chapter that was actually Lovecraft's transcription of one of his dreams.

Long was one of the few writers for *Weird Tales* who also wrote for *Unknown* (later *Unknown Worlds*), the magazine of logical fantasy fiction that was a sister publication to Golden Age science fiction magazine *Astounding Science-Fiction*. His contributions show greater sophistication than much of his work for *Weird Tales*, especially "Fisherman's Luck" (1940) and "Step into My Garden" (1942), which deploy elements of classical mythology, and "Johnny on the Spot" (1939), which presents a literal assignation with death in the style of a hardboiled crime story.

By the 1940s Long had shifted to writing science fiction almost entirely and eventually placed stories in nearly every major science fiction magazine, including *Astounding, Thrilling Wonder Stories,* and *Startling Stories.* He also wrote for a variety of comic books, most notably *Adventures into the Unknown.* In the 1950s and 1960s he served in an editorial capacity on a number of magazines, among them *Satellite Science Fiction, Fantastic Universe, Ellery Queen's Mystery Magazine,* and *Mike Shayne Mystery Magazine.* He also wrote nine modern Gothic romance novels, all but one under the pseudonym Lyda Belknap Long. Long was a published poet for nearly as long as he was a fiction writer, and his collections of verse include *A Man from Genoa and Other Poems* (1926), *The Goblin Tower* (1928), and *In Mayan Splendor* (1977). Collections of his weird tales and science fiction include *The Rim of Unknown* (1972), *Night Fear* (1979), and *The Early Long* (1975), which includes a lengthy autobiographical introduction.

Although Long wrote weird fiction sporadically through the 1980s, he is remembered today almost exclusively for his early stories for *Weird Tales* and his association with H. P. Lovecraft, whom he defended in *Howard Phillips Lovecraft: Dreamer on the Nightside* (1975) against what he thought was an inaccurate representation of his friend and mentor in L. Sprague de Camp's *Lovecraft: A Biography* (1975).

Stefan R. Dziemianowicz

See also: Arkham House; Cthulhu Mythos; Lovecraft, H. P.; Pulp Horror; *Weird Tales.*

Further Reading

Daniels, Les. 1985. "Frank Belknap Long." *Supernatural Fiction Writers*, edited by Everett F. Bleiler, 869–874. New York: Scribner's.

Dziemianowicz, Stefan. 1998. "Frank Belknap Long." *The St. James Guide to Horror, Ghost & Gothic Writers.* Detroit, MI: St. James Press.

Long, Frank Belknap. 1975. *Howard Phillips Lovecraft: Dreamer on the Night Side.* Sauk City, WI: Arkham House.

Long, Frank Belknap. 1975. "Introduction." *The Early Long.* New York: Doubleday.

"LOT NO. 249"

Arthur Conan Doyle's "Lot No. 249" first appeared in *Harper's Magazine* in 1892. The short story combines Doyle's enthusiasm for the supernatural with his interest in crime and detection. "Lot No. 249" is a tale of murder and mystery. Doyle sets his tale in Oxford, where Abercrombie Smith, a medical student, discovers that another student, Edward Bellingham, has become enamored with Egyptology, going so far as to have a mummy, Lot No. 249 at an auction, in his room. Several students are mysteriously attacked, and Smith eventually discovers that Bellingham has brought the mummy to life and is controlling him. Smith eventually confronts Bellingham and forces him to destroy the mummy and all objects connected with it.

Conan Doyle structures his story as a standard mystery. An intelligent man, in this case medical student Abercrombie Smith, comes across a series of unusual, unexplained events that suggest danger to the community. As the mysterious events grow more threatening, the protagonist must first uncover the true nature of the events, then who is behind them, and finally eliminate the threat by destroying or capturing the source of the evil. This is a typical plot structure of both mystery and horror narratives, and in "Lot No. 249" Conan Doyle, the creator of Sherlock Holmes, sets an amateur detective in the world of the fantastic.

"Lot No. 249," although one of Conan Doyle's lesser known works, is important for several reasons. First, it is an example of the interest in the fantastic that was a significant part of Victorian and Edwardian English culture. Conan Doyle was one of the founders of the British Society for Psychical Research in 1893 and published works on Spiritualism, telepathy, reincarnation, and the existence of fairies. He, like many others at the turn of the century, was fascinated by ancient Egypt, and the nineteenth century enthusiasm for Egyptian art, architecture, science, and spirituality led to what has been called Egyptomania, which was only heightened with Howard Carter's discovery of the tomb of Tutankhamun in 1923. "Lot No. 249" dramatizes the juxtaposition of modern realism (in Abercrombie Smith's medical science) with the actuality of the supernatural (a mummy brought back to life).

Conan Doyle's story is important for another reason: it was the first English story to depict a mummy being brought back to life by a modern man using ancient Egyptian texts. Previous tales of mummies being brought back to life had used galvanism, or electricity, as the rejuvenating force. But here, and in his other, more famous mummy tale, "The Ring of Thoth" (1890), Conan Doyle provided a groundwork narrative that served as a source for the film mummies that followed in the twentieth century.

"Lot No. 249" has been adapted more than once for other media, including a 1967 BBC television production and the opening segment of *Tales from the Darkside: The Movie* (1990).

Jim Holte

See also: Mummies; Occult Detectives.

Further Reading

Booth, Martin. 2000. *The Doctor and the Detective: A Biography of Sir Arthur Conan Doyle.* New York: St. Martin's Press.

Bulfin, Ailise. 2011. "The Fiction of Gothic Egypt and British Imperial Paranoia: The Curse of the Suez Canal." *English Literature in Transition 1880–1920* 54, no. 4: 411–443.

Curl, James Stevens. 1994. *Egyptomania: The Egyptian Revival, a Recurring Theme in the History of Taste.* Manchester, UK, and New York: Manchester University Press.

Pascal, Janet B. 2000. *Arthur Conan Doyle Beyond Baker Street.* Oxford and New York: Oxford University Press.

LOVECRAFT, H. P. (1890–1937)

Howard Phillips Lovecraft was an American author whose innovative approach to horror fiction ushered in a new era of the genre, and whose work is distinguished by exceptional artistry and philosophical depth. Writing in the early twentieth century, Lovecraft blended radical developments in science—physics, astronomy, biology, geology, anthropology, and psychology—into his tales, relocating the center of horror from outmoded superstition to human confrontation with an indifferent, unknowable, and chaotic cosmos.

The Long Shadow of H. P. Lovecraft

Lovecraft's influence on popular culture has been enormous, and actually preceded his canonization as a top-tier American literary author. The website www.hplovecraft.com features an extensive catalog of Lovecraft's influence on movies, television, games, music, art, comics, and more. So does the book *H. P. Lovecraft in Popular Culture* by Don G. Smith (McFarland, 2006).

The following is a highly selective sampling of Lovecraft's ubiquitous presence in pop culture.

Movies directly based on Lovecraft's stories:

- *The Haunted Palace* (1963) (From *The Case of Charles Dexter Ward*)
- *Die, Monster, Die!* (1965) (From "The Colour out of Space")
- *The Crimson Cult* (1968) (From "The Dreams in the Witch House")
- *The Dunwich Horror* (1970)
- *Re-Animator* (1985) (From *Herbert West—Reanimator*)
- *From Beyond* (1986)
- *The Curse* (1987) (From "The Colour out of Space")
- *The Unnamable* (1988)
- *The Resurrected* (1992) (From *The Case of Charles Dexter Ward*)
- *Dagon* (2001)

Movies featuring a distinct Lovecraftian influence or direct Lovecraftian references:

- *Alien* (1979)
- *The Evil Dead* (1982)
- *John Carpenter's The Thing* (1982)
- *Ghostbusters* (1984)
- *Army of Darkness* (1993)
- *In the Mouth of Madness* (1995)
- *Hellboy* (2004)
- *The Mist* (2007)
- *The Cabin in the Woods* (2012)

Lovecraftian television

- *Night Gallery*: "Cool Air" (1971), "Pickman's Model" (1972), "Professor Peabody's Last Lecture" (1971)
- *The Real Ghostbusters*: "Collect Call of Cthulhu" (1987), "Russian About" (1990)
- *Babylon 5*: Multiple elements inspired by Lovecraft

Lovecraftian music:

- Black Sabbath: "Behind the Wall of Sleep" (1970)
- Metallica: "The Call of Ktulu" (1984), "The Thing That Should Not Be" (1986)

Lovecraftian games:

- The Call of Cthulhu (role-playing game)
- Dungeons & Dragons (incorporates many Lovecraftian monsters and concepts)
- Digital games:
  - *Alone in the Dark* (1992)
  - *Call of Cthulhu: Dark Corners of the Earth* (2005)
  - *Eternal Darkness: Sanity's Requiem* (2002)
  - *The Lurking Horror* (1987)
  - *Silent Hill* (1999)

Matt Cardin

Lovecraft was born and spent much of his life in Providence, Rhode Island. His childhood was marked by tragedy: his father went mad, and his family lost their house and fortune. Lovecraft emerged from a period of seclusion in 1914 when he became a leading light in various amateur press associations. In this milieu he met his wife, and they lived in New York City for several years before splitting up. He returned to Providence and spent the last decade of his life creating his greatest stories, dying from cancer at forty-seven years old.

In Lovecraft's cosmology, the human race can no longer claim a privileged place in the universe; indeed, it can no longer claim a privileged place on the earth. Aliens came here millions of years ago, erected magnificent civilizations, and departed long before humanity arrived. These races, which occasionally still manifest themselves, are superior to humans—physically, intellectually, and aesthetically. Humanity is at best the inconsequential and accidental by-product of life-forms completely beyond its comprehension. Lovecraft is thus at the forefront of cosmic horror, where conventional notions are destabilized by transdimensional ruptures, by otherworldly intrusions, and by shadowy threats to the fundamental fabric of reality.

The notion of alien races was first used by Lovecraft in "The Nameless City" (1921) and most extensively treated in his last major tale, "The Shadow out of Time" (1934–1935). From the beginning, however, Lovecraft created a recurring set of unknown entities, geographical settings, and arcane books (e.g., the *Necronomicon*, a blend of grimore, demonology, and scripture regarding the extraterrestrial Old Ones, transcribed ca. 700 CE by Abdul Alhazred). This apparatus was collectively labeled the "Cthulhu Mythos" by Arkham House publisher August Derleth, but Lovecraft did not wish to segregate tales employing this pseudo-mythology from his other works.

Lovecraft's framework was not programmatic or rigid; it was, instead, a flexible aesthetic construct, adaptable to the author's developing vision and varying narrative requirements. He considered his strange entities (e.g., Cthulhu, Yog-Sothoth, etc.) to be *symbolic* rather than representative. Lovecraft created what we now call the Cthulhu Mythos because he needed a more powerful and aesthetically refined set of symbols than found in traditional superstition. Taken to task by a colleague about his use of a personal myth-cycle, Lovecraft defended himself this way:

> I really agree that Yog-Sothoth is basically . . . unfitted for really serious literature. The fact is, I have never approached really serious literature as yet. But I consider the use of actual folk myths as even more childish than the use of new artificial myths, since in employing the former one is forced to retain many blatant puerilities & contradictions of experience which could be subtilised or smoothed over if the supernaturalism were modelled to order for the given case. The only permanently artistic use of Yog-Sothoery, I think, is in symbolic or associative phantasy of the frankly poetic type; in which fixed dream-patterns of the natural organism are given embodiment & crystallization. (*Selected Letters* 3.293)

The impetus for Lovecraft's "symbolic phantasy" was his imaginative enchantment with the natural world. In a letter he explained how he tried to effect or embody his artistic impulses by using

> as many as possible of the elements which have, under earlier mental and emotional conditions, given man a symbolic feeling of the unreal, the ethereal, & the mystical—choosing those least attacked by realistic mental and emotional conditions of the present. Darkness—sunset—dreams—mists—fever—madness—the tomb—the hills—the sea—the sky—the wind—all these, & many other things have seemed to me to retain a certain imaginative potency despite our actual scientific analyses of them. Accordingly I have tried to weave them into a kind of shadowy phantasmagoria which may have the same sort of vague coherence as a cycle of traditional myth or legend. . . . [A]n artificial mythology can become subtler & more plausible than a natural one, because it can recognize & adapt itself to the information and moods of the present. (*Selected Letters* 4.70ff)

In his early years as an author, Lovecraft experimented with Dunsanian fantasy (e.g., "The White Ship," 1919), ethereal stories of fantastic, dreamlike worlds in the vein of those produced by one of his literary idols, the Irish writer Lord Dunsany (1878–1957). These works are sometimes termed the "Dreamlands" stories. (Like his other work, these stories never saw print during his lifetime beyond amateur journals, pulp magazines, and a few private press editions.) By 1926, however, he had established his unique and characteristic blend of literary realism and the weird. Literary realism uses detailed observation of everyday life with almost forensic levels of detail and precision to produce a sense of reality. But in Lovecraft, the generally accepted "sense of reality" is shown to mask something that is incoherent and inimical to sanity.

Above Dunsany, Lovecraft's primary fictional influence is Edgar Allan Poe. Poe's emphases on psychological terror using first person narration, on the cultivation of weird atmosphere, and on a high level of artistic finish all are amplified by Lovecraft. The literary stream than runs from Poe through Charles Baudelaire to the Symbolists, and ultimately to the Surrealists, is likewise manifest. Following the lead of the Decadents (notably J. K. Huysmans), Lovecraft carefully employed bursts of linguistic energy bordering on delirium. We find, too, an intense interest in dreams and what the Surrealists called *hasard*, roughly equivalent to "chance," but with connotations of disorder and the irrational.

Lovecraft saw horror fiction as his especial domain; his letters and essays reflect refinement of an aesthetic of the "weird" over his literary career (1918–1937). Its most notable exposition is the essay *Supernatural Horror in Literature* (written 1925–1926, published 1927), a survey from ancient times. Lovecraft declares: "Atmosphere is the all-important thing [in horror fiction], for the final criterion of authenticity is not the dovetailing of a plot but the creation of a given sensation" (Lovecraft 2012, 28). In all Lovecraft's stories, a characteristic atmosphere seems to flow from the very first sentence, as if a switch had been thrown. He typically employs the first-person voice of a refined, sensible, and slightly imperious narrator, modulating his tone to a hyperbolic and sometimes surreal rhetoric when describing his horrors. Lovecraft's skill as a poet is reflected in the metrical and rhetorical adroitness of his prose. (*Fungi from Yuggoth*, 1929–1930, a cycle of thirty-six sonnets, is a poetic achievement worthy of his best fiction.) He also developed a distinctive set of cosmic imagery—largely revolving around the concepts of chaos and asymmetry—to suggest the utterly nonhuman.

While Lovecraft emphasized the importance of atmosphere over plot in horror fiction, his tales show great skill in construction. The stories often nested narratives and documents, requiring the reader to participate in (as he writes in "The Call of Cthulhu," 1928) the "piecing together of dissociated knowledge" that reveals "terrifying vistas of reality" (Lovecraft 2002, 139). Lovecraft was also ingenious in foreshadowing, weaving explicative narrative content—including key phrases that become significant only in retrospect—into the prolegomena of his tales to clear the way for the creation of atmosphere. This technique, derived from detective fiction, makes his work endlessly re-readable. The remarkable merging of real and unreal gains force by Lovecraft's use of autobiographical materials—numerous aspects of the stories are transmuted from events, locales, and persons he knew.

"The Colour out of Space" (1927), Lovecraft's most accomplished tale, mesmerizingly recounts how intergalactic life-forms of an indeterminate nature came in a "meteorite" and spread gray death. In "The Whisperer in Darkness" (1930), local legends veneer extraterrestrials possessing "prodigious surgical, biological, chemical, and mechanical skill" (Lovecraft 2002, 267) that transport their victims' conscious brains to an interstellar outpost on Pluto. "The Dreams in the Witch House" (1932) identifies the spells of witchcraft with equations of non-Euclidean geometry that breach other dimensions. Always lurking at the edge of Lovecraft's indifferent universe is the threat that natural law may not hold, as hinted at by quantum mechanics: thus his concept of ultimate chaos, "wherein reigns the mindless daemon-sultan Azathoth" (Lovecraft 2004, 329).

Lovecraft joins Nathaniel Hawthorne and Mary E. Wilkins Freeman in using detailed New England local color—history, folkways, landscape, and architecture—as a foundation for supernatural incursions. Lovecraft had a specialist's knowledge of colonial history, and this is reflected throughout his fiction. In "The Shunned House" (1924), for example, descriptions of a sinister Providence residence are embellished with the convincing annals of its doomed inhabitants.

Many New Englanders in the early twentieth century viewed immigrants who came to work in industrialized cities as a threat to tradition, and Lovecraft was no exception. His upbringing created a fear of "foreigners" impervious to the rationality he showed in other areas of thought. The terrors of "Dagon" (1918), "The Lurking Fear" (1922), and other tales may be seen as veiled projections of fears regarding an overthrow of nineteenth-century culture through immigration. This theme, inflamed by the carnage of World War I and the paranoia of the Red Scare, grows in stories such as "He" (1925), "The Horror at Red Hook" (1925), and the brilliant prose poem "Nyarlathotep" (1920) to the scope of apocalyptic narrative.

But Lovecraft's racism is best understood in the context of his anthrophobia. In his most radically modern and innovative stories, the horror of "aliens" is supplanted by the horror of the self, the horror of being human. In "Facts Concerning the Late Arthur Jermyn and His Family" (1920) it is revealed that even a scion of an aristocratic English family is not immune from the savagery of human descent, as the protagonist discovers his great-great-great-grandmother was a Congo ape. Likewise, "The Rats in the Walls" (1924), "The Shadow over Innsmouth" (1936), and others cunningly cultivate sympathy with an ostensibly reasonable narrator who is revealed at the end to be monstrous.

Subsequent writers have been inspired by Lovecraft in varied ways. One way manifested prior to Lovecraft's death: contributors to *Weird Tales* began to festoon their horror stories with his alien beings, geographical settings, and arcane books, and also to invent their own. There soon developed a "fan fiction" subculture of pastiche, which generates hundreds of "Mythos" works each year. But Lovecraft's significant influence (in approach and in technique, rather than in embellishment) has been upon horror writers who offer their own unique talent: Ramsey Campbell, T. E. D. Klein, Thomas Ligotti, and others.

Thanks to a group of scholars led by S. T. Joshi, Lovecraft has ascended from the literary slums of the pulp magazines to the pantheon of American literature. He also has become something of a cult figure and pop culture phenomenon. Lovecraft the man has been featured as a character in fictional works, and his imaginary worlds have been employed in every aspect of modern-day media, from movies to comics to television to video games.

Steven J. Mariconda

See also: Arkham House; *At the Mountains of Madness*; "The Call of Cthulhu"; Campbell, Ramsey; *The Case of Charles Dexter Ward*; "The Colour out of Space"; Cthulhu Mythos; Dreams and Nightmares; "The Dunwich Horror"; Huysmans, J. K.; Joshi, S. T.; Klein, T. E. D.; "The Last Feast of Harlequin"; Ligotti, Thomas; Lovecraftian Horror; *The Mind Parasites*; "The Music of Erich Zann"; The Numinous; "Pickman's Model"; Poe, Edgar Allan; "The Rats in the Walls"; *Weird Tales*.

Further Reading

Dziemianowicz, Stefan. 2010. "Terror Eternal: The Enduring Popularity of H. P. Lovecraft." *Publishers Weekly*, July 12. http://www.publishersweekly.com/pw/by-topic/industry -news/publisher-news/article/43793-terror-eternal-the-enduring-popularity-of-h -p-lovecraft.html.

Eil, Philip. 2015. "The Unlikely Reanimation of H. P. Lovecraft." *The Atlantic*, August 20. http://www.theatlantic.com/entertainment/archive/2015/08/hp-lovecraft-125/401471.

H. P. Lovecraft: Fear of the Unknown. 2009. Directed by Frank Woodward. Los Angeles: Cinevolve Studios. DVD.

Joshi, S. T. 2010. *I Am Providence: The Life and Times of H. P. Lovecraft*. New York: Hippocampus Press.

Joshi, S. T. 2010. *A Subtler Magick: The Writings and Philosophy of H. P. Lovecraft*. Gillette, NJ: Wildside Press.

Joshi, S. T., and David E. Schultz, eds. 1991. *An Epicure in the Terrible: A Centennial Anthology of Essays in Honor of H. P. Lovecraft*. Rutherford, NJ: Fairleigh Dickinson University Press.

Joshi, S. T., and David E. Schultz. 2004. *An H. P. Lovecraft Encyclopedia*. New York: Hippocampus Press.

Loucks, Donovan K. 2016. *The H. P. Lovecraft Archive*, June 12. http://www.hplovecraft .com.

Lovecraft, H. P. 1965–1976. *Selected Letters* (five volumes). Sauk City, WI: Arkham House.

Lovecraft, H. P. 2002. *The Call of Cthulhu and Other Weird Stories*. Edited by S. T. Joshi. London: Penguin.

Lovecraft, H. P. 2004. *The Dreams in the Witch House and Other Weird Stories*. Edited by S. T. Joshi. London: Penguin.

Lovecraft, H. P. [1927] 2012. *The Annotated Supernatural Horror in Literature*. Edited by S. T. Joshi. New York: Hippocampus Press.

LOVECRAFTIAN HORROR

Lovecraftian horror is a subgenre categorized by a personal narrative chronicling a foreboding sense of what writer H. P. Lovecraft termed "outsideness"—detailing encounters with unknown external forces intruding upon the world of humans.

These forces may be alien, ultra-cosmic, or other-dimensional. And while they might operate in a manner suggesting that they are inimical to humanity, they are more correctly indifferent to human emotions and aspirations. More than merely unknown, they are unknowable, as the hapless narrator discovers by degree.

In 1927, Lovecraft expounded on his nascent vision, writing, "Now all my tales are based on the fundamental premise that common human laws and interests and emotions have no validity or significance in the cosmos-at-large. . . . when we cross the line to the boundless and hideous unknown—the shadow-haunted Outside— we must remember to leave our humanity and terrestrialism at the threshold" (Joshi 2008, 16).

Although there existed precursors to the worldview exemplified in Lovecraftian horror fiction—principally selected stories by Ambrose Bierce, Robert W. Chambers, William Hope Hodgson, and A. Merritt—it was Lovecraft who gathered together the thin threads of disparate ideas and sensibilities to weave together a tapestry that placed humans not at the apex of the known universe, but at the bottom of a cosmic food chain in which they were less than insects in the eyes of higher intelligences. Posthumously, a portion of Lovecraft's fiction has been categorized as belonging to the Cthulhu Mythos—a term not his own—despite scant evidence that the writer had any such fixed formal concept in mind.

One of the unique innovations of Lovecraftian horror posits that, while there may exist supernatural monsters such as vampires or ghosts, the true monsters are of cosmic origin—seemingly godlike and remote beings such as Cthulhu (one of Lovecraft's most famous fictional creations), with which humans are intellectually and emotionally unprepared to cope. Futility is a running theme, as well as the re-alization that ultimate reality lies beyond the senses of ordinary mortals and cannot possibly be comprehended by the human brain; otherwise, madness would result. Lovecraftian protagonists were therefore helpless in the face of cosmic forces be-yond their comprehension. In these works, happy endings are out of the question, although temporary and ultimately inconsequential victories might be achieved, as in Lovecraft's "The Dunwich Horror," which represents a mere holding back of the inevitable crushing defeat and unavoidable fall of humanity.

The type of stories H. P. Lovecraft and his adherents concocted were a direct response to the contrived formulaic horror fiction in which an intrepid investigator into the supernatural might overcome any manner of mundane monster, no matter how horrific, through ingenuity and the appropriate occult tools. Not so in Love-craftian horror fiction, which is antiheroic and nihilistic in the extreme, and which postulates a vision of the supernatural that is cosmic in scope and truly alien in nature.

Will Murray

See also: Bierce, Ambrose; Chambers, Robert W.; Cthulhu Mythos; "The Dunwich Horror"; Hodgson, William Hope; Lovecraft, H. P.

Further Reading

Joshi, S. T. 2008. *The Rise and Fall of the Cthulhu Mythos*. Poplar Bluff, MO: Mythos Books.

Joshi, S. T. 2010. *I Am Providence: The Life and Times of H. P. Lovecraft*. New York: Hippocampus Press.

Lovecraft, H. P. 2014. *The New Annotated H. P. Lovecraft*. New York: Liveright.

LUMLEY, BRIAN (1937–)

Brian Lumley is an author of horror fiction who began his career by adding to H. P. Lovecraft's Cthulhu Mythos, and proceeded to find his own voice and write a large body of work, often mixing horror with fantasy and science fiction. Other influences include classic tales by Robert W. Chambers, Robert E. Howard, and William Hope Hodgson. Lumley's stories have been characterized by some critics as Lovecraft stories turned into action-adventure. His protagonists do not swoon or faint, but fight back. His writing style has been described as "masculine," and his stories generally feature strong male protagonists who can think as well as fight. By all accounts, Lumley is a writer who enjoys storytelling for its own sake and tries to appeal to readers who like good stories with no hidden meanings. His efforts have won him many enthusiastic readers, as well as many prestigious awards.

Lumley was born in 1937 in Horden, County Durham, United Kingdom. The son of a coal miner, he was nonetheless raised in a home with books on the shelves, including two large anthologies of horror stories that he read as a child. He apprenticed as a woodcutting machinist, but was drafted and became a member of the Royal Military Police. He remained in the army for two decades while writing horror fiction as a hobby.

He discovered Lovecraft's stories as a teenager, and he corresponded with Lovecraft's protégé August Derleth, who encouraged him to write. Eventually Derleth became the first to publish Lumley's work; Lumley's earliest published stories appeared in the *Arkham Collector*, a horror and fantasy magazine edited by Derleth and published by Arkham House, the publishing house that Derleth and another Lovecraft protégé, Donald Wandrei, founded to preserve Lovecraft's work. These early Lumley stories were soon collected in Lumley's first book, *The Caller of the Black* (1971), which was likewise published by Arkham House. The stories were not pastiches of Lovecraft's style, but rather they employed the Cthulhu Mythos as a background. His first sale, "The Cyprus Shell" (1968), was inspired by Lovecraft's horror of the sea. His first two novels, *Beneath the Moors* and *The Burrowers Beneath*, both appeared in 1974.

Lumley went on to become an extremely prolific writer, creating several series of novels. The "Titus Crow" series (beginning with 1974's *The Burrowers Beneath*) is about the eponymous occult detective, who fights against wizards and occult magic by employing spells from such forbidden Cthulhu Mythos tomes such as the *Necronomicon*, *Cultes de Goules*, and *De Vermis Mysteriis* (all imaginary books of dark magical lore invented by Lovecraft and those who joined him in creating a horror mythos composed of interlinked stories). Crow was originally inspired by Dr. Van Helsing from Bram Stoker's *Dracula*, with other occult detectives such as Hodgson's Carnacki and Seabury Quinn's Jules de Grandin probably serving as additional inspirations. Lumley's Titus Crow stories are often narrated by a Watson-like figure named Henri-Laurent de Marigny, a descendant of Étienne-Laurent de Marigny, a character from Lovecraft's "Through the Gates of the Silver Key" (1934).

The "Dreamscape" series, beginning with *Hero of Dreams* (1986), follows protagonist David Hero, who is transported to the world of Lovecraft's "dreamland" stories. These novels are not horror but lighthearted sword and sorcery adventure. Hero and his sidekick Eldin have been compared to Fritz Leiber's Fafhrd and the Gray Mouser stories, but, according to Lumley, they were actually inspired by Bing Crosby and Bob Hope's series of "Road" film comedies from the 1940s through the 1960s.

Lumley's "Psychomech" series (from 1984) blends horror with science fiction. It involves an injured British soldier, a wealthy German industrialist, and a means of transferring minds. His most successful series, titled "Necroscope" (from 1986), features Harry Keogh, a "necroscope" (one who can speak with the dead) whose mission is to fight and destroy vampires from another planet. These stories combine horror, science fiction, and espionage. A spin-off series, "Vampire World," follows Keogh's twin sons, beginning with *Blood Brothers* (1993). A second spin-off, the "E-Branch trilogy," begins with *Invaders* (1999). A more recent entry is the collection *Necroscope: Harry and the Pirates and other Tales from the Lost Years* (2010). The original *Necroscope* novel has been optioned for a film.

Many volumes of Lumley's short stories have been published, including *A Coven of Vampires* (1998), *The Whisperer and Other Voices* (2000), *Beneath the Moors and Darker Places* (2002), *Brian Lumley's Freaks* (2004), *The Taint and Other Novellas* (2007), *No Sharks in the Med and Other Stories* (2012), and *Tales of the Primal Land* (2015).

Lumley won the British Fantasy Award in 1989 for "Fruiting Bodies," a tale inspired by William Hope Hodgson's "The Voice in the Night." He won the World Horror Convention's Grand Master award (1998), *Fear* magazine's Best Established Author (1990) award, the Bram Stoker Award for Lifetime Achievement (2010), and the World Fantasy Convention's Life Achievement Award (2010). His short story "Necros" was filmed as an episode of the Showtime series *The Hunger* (1997).

Robert Weinberg has described Lumley as "an author of astonishing skills" and "a gentleman of equally amazing talents" (Lumley and Wiater 2002, 21). Approaching his eighth decade, Lumley shows no signs of putting these talents to rest. He has developed a wide and devoted audience, and he continues to write.

Lee Weinstein

See also: Arkham House; Cthulhu Mythos; Derleth, August; Lovecraft, H. P.; Lovecraftian Horror; Occult Detectives.

Further Reading

"Brian Lumley." 2016. *Contemporary Authors Online*. Detroit, MI: Gale.

Joshi, S. T. 2004. *The Evolution of the Weird Tale*. New York: Hippocampus Press.

Lumley, Brian, and Stanley Wiater, eds. 2002. *The Brian Lumley Companion*, 747–751. New York: Tor.

Schweitzer, Darrell. 1994. "Brian Lumley." In *Speaking of Horror: Interviews with Writers of the Supernatural*, 75–80. San Bernardino, CA: Borgo Press.

THE LURKER AT THE THRESHOLD

The Lurker at the Threshold is a short novel of approximately 50,000 words published by Arkham House in 1945. It is attributed to H. P. Lovecraft and August Derleth, and is the first of more than a dozen "posthumous collaborations" published over the next thirty years in which Derleth took fragments or ideas found in Lovecraft's papers and wrote pastiches of Lovecraft's fiction based on them. The three fragments Derleth drew on for this novel amounted to approximately 1,200 words of text by Lovecraft.

The novel is divided into three parts. In the first part, Ambrose Dewart moves into a house on the outskirts of the Massachusetts town of Arkham abandoned by his ancestor Alijah Billington a century before. There he finds papers that mention accusations of sorcery aimed at several generations of Billingtons and references to strange noises, sights, and disappearances, all related to a circle of stones and a stone tower raised in the woods behind the house. Another document abjures whoever lives on the property not "to invite Him Who lurks at the threshold." From a decorative rose window in the house Ambrose sees glimpses of an alien world, and on the night of a new disappearance he discovers that he may have sleepwalked out to the tower. The second part of the novel is the narrative of Ambrose's cousin, Stephen Bates, whom Ambrose has summoned to the house. Stephen finds Ambrose acting peculiar, as though under the influence of another personality, and in time sees Ambrose performing a ritual on top of the tower invoking the name "Yog Sothoth." Bates's narrative ends with Ambrose informing him that he has hired a handyman by the name of Quamis, clearly a descendant or avatar of the Wampanaug Indian Misquamacus who taught sorcery to Dewart's ancestors. The novel's third part is the narrative of Winfield Phillips who, with his employer Seneca Lapham, a professor of anthropology at Miskatonic University, helps to piece together the mystery of Dewart's apparent possession by the spirit of his ancestor and to thwart Dewart's efforts to bring the monstrous entity Yog-Sothoth across the threshold into our world.

The Lurker at the Threshold was Derleth's most significant effort to present ideas in Lovecraft's fiction in terms of what he was defining as the Cthulhu Mythos, the name he gave to the myth pattern linking Lovecraft's stories and the stories of others writing in homage to Lovecraft and his fiction. Much mythos fiction written in its wake would follow its pattern of cataloguing otherworldly monsters and books of occult lore, giving characters names that resonate with those of Lovecraft's, and having "evil" monsters and their human servants defeated by the forces of good.

Stefan R. Dziemianowicz

See also: Arkham House; Cthulhu Mythos; Derleth, August; Lovecraft, H. P.; Love-craftian Horror.

Further Reading
Joshi, S. T. 2015. *The Rise, Fall, and Rise of the Cthulhu Mythos.* New York: Hippocampus Press.

Price, Robert M. 1982. "The Lovecraft-Derleth Connection." *Lovecraft Studies* 2, no. 2 (Fall): 18–24.

Price, Robert M. 1991. "The Shadow over Dunwich: A Neglected Subplot in Derleth's *The Lurker at the Threshold.*" *Crypt of Cthulhu* 10, no. 2: 5–7.

Tierney, Richard L. 1987. "The Derleth Mythos." In *Discovering H. P. Lovecraft*, edited by Darrell Schweitzer, 65–68. Mercer Island, WA: Starmont.

MACHEN, ARTHUR (1863–1947)

Arthur Machen was a Welsh author whose work has exerted a dramatic influence on the horror and fantasy genres. Often referred to as a "lost" writer, he nevertheless wrote works such as "The Great God Pan" and *The Three Impostors* that have resonated through ensuing horror fiction, and Machen's influence in that respect is evident throughout the twentieth and twenty-first centuries. He was regularly cited as an important benchmark by the coterie of writers associated with *Weird Tales*, particularly by H. P. Lovecraft. More recently, Ramsey Campbell, Stephen King, T. E. D. Klein, Mark Samuels, and numerous other horror writers have acknowledged Machen as having a profound impact on their writing and understanding of the genre. King, Klein, and Samuels have all written explicit homages to Machen. In the wider literary world, Machen has received plaudits from Sir Arthur Conan Doyle, John Buchan, Jorge Luis Borges, and Henry Miller, among many others. Film directors John Carpenter—who named a character Machen in *The Fog* (1980)—and Guillermo del Toro have also cited Machen as an important influence on their work, as especially evident in the latter's *Pan's Labyrinth* (2006). Del Toro also provided the foreword for a Penguin Classics edition of Machen's work, *The White People and Other Weird Stories* (2012).

Machen was born in Caerleon, a small town in south Wales on the river Usk. The isolated, wild countryside in which he grew up was to remain a persistent influence on his writing, and the fact that Caerleon was formerly a major Roman settlement shaped his childhood imagination. He was the son of a Church of England vicar, who at the time of Machen's birth was in the process of impoverishing his family through his construction of an extravagant new rectory, which became the home in which Machen was raised. Not having the finances necessary to attend university, Machen instead made an unenthusiastic attempt to enroll in medical school, before deciding to relocate permanently to London with the intention of becoming a "man of letters." He initially experienced only grinding poverty. After various engagements as a tutor, cataloguer, and translator, and the publication of a medieval pastiche, *The Chronicle of Clemendy* (1888), Machen's short stories began appearing in periodicals (then a burgeoning market), bringing him to the notice of Oscar Wilde, among others.

One of Machen's "society" stories, "A Double Return" (1890), angered the readership of the *St James's Gazette* to the extent that its editor declined to accept any more submissions from Machen. "The Lost Club" (1890), with its clear debt to Robert Louis Stevenson's *The Suicide Club* (1878), marked the beginning of an

1863	Arthur Machen is born in Caerleon, South Wales.
1894	*The Great God Pan and The Inmost Light* is published.
1895	*The Three Impostors* is published.
1895–1900	Machen writes "The White People," *The Hill of Dreams*, and *Ornaments in Jade*. None are published until after the turn of the century.
1900–1910	Following the death of his first wife, Amy, in 1899, a devastated Machen becomes involved in the Order of the Golden Dawn, an occult society. He will later become staunchly self-identified as a high church Anglican.
1903	Machen marries Dorothy Purefoy Hudleston.
1914	Machen's "The Bowmen" is published in the *Evening News* in September, giving rise to the legend—widely believed as fact—of the "Angels of Mons."
1916	*The Terror* is published.
1920s	Much of Machen's work is reprinted in *Weird Tales*, gaining him an enthusiastic American audience.
1926 and 1929	Machen has new supernatural fiction published in Lady Cynthia Asquith's *The Ghost Book* and *Shudders*.
1933	*The Green Round* is published.
1939	*The Children of the Pool* is published.
1947	Machen dies shortly after Dorothy.

Matt Cardin

influence that became one of the prevailing features of Machen's output for the first half of the 1890s. Machen gained wide and fleeting attention from the reading public with his two books published for John Lane, an imprint very much associated with the controversial new "Decadent" movement: *The Great God Pan and The Inmost Light* (1894) and *The Three Impostors* (1895). These exercises in weird horror were to be his most commercially successful achievements as an author, and they remain his most widely read works. Critical reaction to Machen's uniquely potent blend of Stevenson, Poe, scientific horror, and pagan mystery was mixed and often negative. While H. G. Wells complained that Machen had "determined to be weird [and] horrible" (Wells 1896, 48), the art critic Harry Quilter less soberly accused Machen of being an agent of dangerous moral corruption. Machen was disparaged for being at once too graphic in his descriptions of hideous bodily degeneration and horrific tortures, and remiss in keeping the central mysteries of his stories nebulous and unresolved. However, this latter aspect of his writing has become increasingly valorized over the years, to the point where it is now regarded as one of his definitive stylistic achievements.

The scandal surrounding the trial of Oscar Wilde in 1895 resulted in "unhealthy" literature such as Machen's becoming too controversial for publishers and readers alike. While the immediate effect of the trial on Machen's career can be gauged by the fact that Machen referred to it henceforth as "the disaster," a series of legacies from a Scottish branch of his family meant Machen felt no financial pressure to calibrate his writing to the new public mood. It was during this period (the second half of the 1890s) that he wrote what was to become one of his most celebrated contributions to the horror genre, "The White People," although it was not published until 1904. Intent on changing course from Stevensonian horror, a seam he considered by then exhausted, he also produced what are regarded as his most unambiguously Decadent texts: *The Hill of Dreams*, a novel, and *Ornaments in Jade*, an anthology of prose poems. At odds with the post-Wilde trial reticence of the closing years of the 1890s, both works did not see print until years after they were written, *The Hill of Dreams* in 1907 and *Ornaments in Jade* in 1924.

After the death of his first wife, Amy Hogg, a distraught Machen temporarily abandoned writing fiction altogether. He also had a brief dalliance with the occult society the Order of the Golden Dawn, which attracted a variety of notable fin-de-siècle personalities including W. B. Yeats and the notorious Aleister Crowley. Machen's temporary embroilment in the fractious internal politics of the group, characterized by claims of supernatural persecutions, resulted in or was contemporaneous with an episode that some have characterized as a nervous breakdown of sorts: the still-grieving Machen felt as though various extraordinary scenes from *The Three Impostors* were now being played out before him, with, for example, Yeats assuming the role of the novel's "Young Man with Spectacles," psychically threatened by Crowley's "Dr. Lipsius."

During a happier subsequent period as a "strolling player," or rather a repertory actor in the Benson Company, often playing various Shakespearean supporting characters, he met Dorothy Purefoy Hudleston, who became his second wife. Settled back in London with a young family, Machen found work as a journalist, an occupation that offered him financial stability, but that he bitterly resented. With his signature Inverness cape and pipe he became something of a Fleet Street character, regaling younger colleagues with an apparently endless repertoire of anecdotes in his sonorous Welsh accent. He was frequently assigned to more outré stories commensurate with his interests. It was during this period that he saw his second period of fleeting notoriety and success. Throughout the First World War, he produced morale-boosting pieces for the *Evening News*, including in September 1914 one with the simple title of "The Bowmen." It is presented as an account of a supernatural episode experienced by a retreating army unit, saved from extermination at the hands of the Germans by the appearance of ghostly Agincourt bowmen. The tale was taken by some readers at face value, and exaggerated and distorted versions of it spread across the country until it was popularly regarded as fact. Appalled, Machen made every effort to correct the misunderstanding, but the (by then) "Angels of Mons" legend clearly resonated intensely with the national mood, and gained such traction that it is still occasionally discussed as a genuine mystery to this day.

Most of Machen's output during the Great War could be fairly classed as propaganda, and his nonfiction *War and the Christian Faith* (1918) is explicitly so. A notable exception is perhaps the wartime serial *The Terror* (1916), the story of a revolt of the animal kingdom in response to the imbalance to the natural order of things created by the unprecedented scale of the human conflict. Rarely singled out for critical praise, it is nevertheless a well-executed and exciting shocker, and the horrific set-pieces suggest that Machen could have become a very capable thriller writer should he have been so inclined. *The Terror* is also noteworthy as an antecedent to, and possible inspiration for, Daphne du Maurier's story "The Birds," the source material for Hitchcock's celebrated film.

During the 1920s, and while he was still working as a journalist, Machen's work experienced something of a renaissance in America. A number of American writers and critics, most notably Vincent Starrett, were recovering Machen's earlier fiction from obscurity and positioning him as a great forgotten writer of the fin-de-siècle. Machen saw some immediate material benefit from their enthusiasm through revenue generated from U.S. reprints of his work. He was also at this time being enthusiastically discussed in the pages of *Weird Tales*—which reprinted "The Bowmen" in 1928—as a master of the form. Although it does not appear that Machen directly engaged with or was much aware of this pulp milieu, there is evidence that he read and thought highly of Lovecraft's discussion of his work in Lovecraft's influential survey *Supernatural Horror in Literature*. In 1916, Machen had, coincidentally, favorably reviewed Clark Ashton Smith's poetry anthology *The Star-Treader and Other Poems*.

Although Machen's output between the wars was prodigious in terms of his journalism, nonfiction, and memoirs, he only occasionally turned his hand to supernatural fiction. Much of his work in the genre at this time was the result of commissions from Lady Cynthia Asquith for the various highly regarded anthologies she edited and contributed to in that period. Collections such as *The Ghost Book* (1926) and *Shudders* (1929) saw Machen rubbing shoulders with the likes of D. H. Lawrence, Elizabeth Bowen, and L. P. Hartley, as well as fellow supernatural fiction specialists such as Algernon Blackwood. Some of this work was later anthologized in *The Cosy Room and Other Stories* (1936).

Two more substantial late efforts are *The Green Round* (1933) and *The Children of the Pool* (1936). The latter is a collection of original short stories that includes "The Bright Boy," noteworthy for its use of the trope of a malevolent, aged dwarf masquerading as a child. Once again, Machen anticipates du Maurier, this time her similar conceit in *Don't Look Now* (1971), and also the 2009 horror film *Orphan*. Associated with his interest in fairy lore (evident in his "The Novel of the Black Seal"), the association of child-like figures with malignant supernatural forces became increasingly oblique in his later writing. Examples include the cruel children in "Out of the Earth" (1915) who have wizened, repulsive faces, and the strange childlike entity persecuting the protagonist of *The Green Round*. M. John Harrison's short story "The Incalling" (1983) and also his novel *The Course of the Heart* (1992) offer clear debts to Machen in this respect, acknowledged by the author.

Machen's final—arguably underrated—novel *The Green Round* is usually dismissed as demonstrative of an aging writer's failing powers. It is composed in the same journalistic, anecdotal style that distinguishes much of his later fiction and is off-putting to some commentators. The story ostensibly relates the convalescence of Hillyer, a reclusive scholar who at the age of fifty-five has developed a nervous condition, in the picturesque Welsh seaside town of Porth. He is baffled when the other residents at the hotel at which he resides turn against him, and rumors spread of his complicity in a local murder, based on his alleged association with a small, evil-looking dwarf. Hillyer returns to London plagued by poltergeist-like disruptions, and the novel's potent atmosphere of disorienting paranoia intensifies. Although this is an accurate enough sketch in terms of plot fundamentals, it is perhaps misleading since in its execution Machen often interrupts the narrative with essayistic digressions on a range of matters including alchemy, religion, the nature of reality, and sanity and insanity.

Written, like *The Green Round*, when Machen was in his seventies, "N" was the only original contribution to *The Cosy Room and Other Stories*. This short story is a distillation of many ideas he had previously explored, but they are perhaps more perfectly expressed in this tale than in any other. Once again, the narrative is presented indirectly, anecdotally; it is an assembly of first-, second- and third-hand testimony regarding a recurring vision experienced by disparate visitors to a certain region of Stoke Newington in London. It is left up to the reader to piece together these strange fragments, tantalizing pieces of an unsolvable puzzle.

Apart from the works of specific horror interest mentioned above, Machen left a considerable wider legacy of both fiction and nonfiction, and three volumes of memoirs. Throughout the six- or seven-decade span of his writing career, Machen revisited certain tropes with something approaching monomania, although he steadily refined his treatment of the same material, moving generally away from horror toward something far more ambiguous and oblique. Ultimately, his central preoccupation was with what he considered to be the eternal mystery at the heart of all things. Despite his brief flirtation with the fin-de-siècle occult scene, and contrary to an erroneous assertion in his *Times* obituary of a deathbed conversion to Roman Catholicism, Machen remained a lifelong high church Anglican. Machen's profound religiosity informed much of his fiction, especially its visionary aspects and his insistence on the existence of a numinous "reality" inaccessible to human consciousness, but indistinctly refracted through symbol and ritual. He regretted that in his early horror fiction of the 1890s he only managed to render this mystery as something evil, rather than awe-inspiring.

Although much of his later life was marked by periods of impoverishment and financial uncertainty, his dotage was eased considerably by the securement of a civil list pension, petitioned for by a number of other writers including George

Bernard Shaw, T. S. Eliot, and Walter de la Mare. His eightieth birthday celebration was attended by, among other notables, W. W. Jacobs and Algernon Blackwood.

James Machin

See also: Blackwood, Algernon; *The Ceremonies*; du Maurier, Daphne; "The Great God Pan"; Lovecraft, H. P.; "The Novel of the Black Seal"; The Numinous; Samuels, Mark; "The White People."

Further Reading

Arizuno, Lee. 2012. "Leave the Capitol: The Weird Tales of Arthur Machen." *The Quietus*, October 31. http://thequietus.com/articles/08758-leave-the-capitol-the-weird-tales-of -arthur-machen.

Gawsworth, John. 2013. *The Life of Arthur Machen*. Leyburn: Tartarus.

Goldstone, Adrian, and Wesley Sweetser. 1965. *A Bibliography of Arthur Machen*. Austin: University of Texas.

Joshi, S. T. 1990. *The Weird Tale*. Holicong, PA: Wildside.

Lovecraft, H. P. [1927] 2012. *The Annotated Supernatural Horror in Literature*. Edited by S. T. Joshi. New York: Hippocampus Press.

Reynolds, Aidan, and William Charlton. 1988. *Arthur Machen*. Oxford: Caermaen.

Valentine, Mark. 1995. *Arthur Machen: A Short Account of His Life and Works*. Bridgend: Seren.

Wells, H. G. 1896. Review of "The Three Impostors" by Arthur Machen. *Saturday Review* 81, no. 2098 (January 11): 48–49. In *The Saturday Review of Politics, Literature, Science and Art*, vol. LXXXI. London.

"MACKINTOSH WILLY"

Written in 1977, British author Ramsey Campbell's short story "Mackintosh Willy" first appeared in Charles L. Grant's anthology *Shadows 2* in 1979, before publication in the collections *Dark Companions* (1982), *Dark Feasts: The World of Ramsey Campbell* (1987), and *Alone with the Horrors* (1993). It won a World Fantasy Award in 1980, has been translated into multiple languages, and is one of the author's most anthologized works.

The shambling, mumbling drunk dubbed Mackintosh Willy presents a vague threat to the neighborhood children, but most simply shun him when not teasing each other about the local bogeyman—most, if not all, because someone hated the tramp enough to destroy his eyes as he lay dead in a park shelter. As the years go by, something with a metallic glint to its eyes forms in the shadows of that shelter, increasing in strength and malevolence as it draws its prey to a reckoning.

If the trash-strewn park shelter beside a pool was far from welcoming, its walls not only defaced by graffiti but offering little protection from the rain, its occupancy by a belligerent drunkard made it a place shunned by children and subject to dares by adolescents, even after the derelict's death. Years afterward, the same fear that drove someone to screw bottle caps into the corpse's eyes continued to lend its aura to his former residence, imbuing it with sonic, visual, and tactile evidence of his vengeful, waiting presence.

Throughout the story, a fluid and constant tension blurs the lines between innocence and guilt, reality and imagination, which Campbell deftly channels through the eyes of a narrator suffering through the petty rituals that circumscribe how those growing through childhood into adolescence allow themselves to deal with fear, friendship, loyalty, responsibility, and the attractions of the opposite sex. He builds the narrow "loophole for a natural explanation" recommended by M. R. James (James 2001, 486) directly into the uncertainty and wariness of ridicule natural to children interacting with each other and adults. Thus, the words of strange import overheard in and around the shelter might be fragments of sounds from the radio, the fair, or other outside forces; that heavy sodden body might have been rubbish after all; and it could have been the wind that drove those glittering bottle caps forward like glaring eyes. Meanwhile, the doomed friend has no choice but to face his nemesis, driven not only by misdirection from the ghost, but the goading and embarrassment visited upon him by his friends.

Imagination and guilt play out simultaneously during a necking scene within the shelter, when the narrator takes delight in his girlfriend's sudden fear of the place by indulging his own dread, leading to a statement—"I was eager to let my imagination flourish, for it was better than reading a ghost story"—which casts light on a passage at the beginning: "One has to call one's fears something, if only to gain the illusion of control. Still, sometimes I wonder how much of his monstrousness we created. Wondering helps me not to ponder my responsibility for what happened" (Campbell 1982, 233, 224). The protagonist certainly did not create the ghost, as the graphically violent graffiti and the increasingly shallow, limping tracks in the drying concrete leading from the shelter had appeared prior to this scene; but it is possible he believes himself responsible for assisting in its further incarnation, given his girlfriend's escalating terror within and the widening of Willy's activity outside the shelter afterward.

Some of the elements in the story reveal Campbell to be cognizant of the tradition in which he was working, while reshaping it to fit his own concerns. The pair of gleaming bottle caps illuminating Willy's eyes are reminiscent of the "two small circular reflections, as it seemed to me of a reddish light" that signal the first appearance of the demonic monkey in Sheridan Le Fanu's "Green Tea" ([1869] 2002, 77). Similarly, the blurred voice that sounds as if it is emerging through interference on the radio is not dissimilar to "those soft husky mutterings one hears between items on the radio" in H. R. Wakefield's "Old Man's Beard" ([1929] 1996, 14), and the final image of the protagonist fearing to cover his eyes for fear of straying into the pool echoes the peril of the child running toward the river in terror of the ghosts in Wakefield's "The Red Lodge" (1928). In Campbell these occur in a recognizable location in his native Liverpool and are surrounded by a network of finely graded premonitions and disclosures, which strengthens the reality of the gritty urban setting and characters while infusing the whole with a creeping sense of unease. Campbell manages this through dialogue that is precise, yet natural and prose that, to quote from his story "The Trick" (1976), shows him "relishing each separate word" (1982, 153) while never calling attention away from the tale itself.

Jim Rockhill

See also: Campbell, Ramsey; James, M. R.; Le Fanu, J. Sheridan; Wakefield, H. R.; World Fantasy Award.

Further Reading

Campbell, Ramsey. 1982. *Dark Companions.* Glasgow: Fontana.

Campbell, Ramsey, Stefan Dziemianowicz, and S. T. Joshi. 1995. *The Core of Ramsey Campbell: A Bibliography and Reader's Guide.* West Warwick, RI: Necronomicon Press.

James, M. R. [1924] 2001. "Introduction to *Ghosts and Marvels.*" Oxford: Oxford University Press. In *A Pleasing Terror,* 486–490. Ashcroft: Ash-Tree Press.

Joshi, S. T. 2001. *Ramsey Campbell and Modern Horror Fiction.* Liverpool: Liverpool University Press.

Le Fanu, Joseph Sheridan. [1869] 2002. "Green Tea." In *The Haunted Baronet and Others: Ghost Stories 1861–70,* 65–88. Ashcroft: Ash-Tree Press.

Sullivan, Jack. 1982. "No Light Ahead." *Whispers* 4, no. 3/4: 34–41.

Wakefield, H. R. [1929] 1996. "Old Man's Beard." In *Old Man's Beard,* 3–20. Ashcroft: Ash-Tree Press.

MAD SCIENTIST

The figure of the "mad scientist" is one of the most recognizable archetypes in horror literature and film, highlighting a connection between specialized knowledge and sinister acts of godlike creation and Promethean arrogance. While the legendary Faust and other medieval alchemists are the likely historical sources of this icon, its modern incarnation owes everything to the figure of Victor Frankenstein in Mary Shelley's celebrated 1818 Gothic novel. *Frankenstein* established the basic lineaments of the mad scientist, which subsequent texts would deploy and develop: a Promethean artificer whose intellectual ambitions scorn traditional morality and challenge the prerogatives of God himself. In mad scientist narratives, science fiction shades into horror: Victor's bold commitment to unfettered experimentation makes him capable of both wondrous accomplishment—the creation of an artificial person endowed with superhuman strength and intelligence—and blinkered amorality.

During the nineteenth century, most major writers of fantastic literature essayed some version of this myth. In Nathaniel Hawthorne's "Rappaccini's Daughter" (1844), a secretive botanist turns his own child into a kind of poisonous plant; in Robert Louis Stevenson's *Dr. Jekyll and Mr. Hyde* (1886), a mild-mannered chemist invents a potion that unleashes his demonic id (the monstrous, rapacious underside of the psyche as characterized in Freudian psychology); in H. G. Wells's *The Island of Dr. Moreau* (1896), the eponymous vivisector (that is, someone who performs surgical experiments on living animals) creates a race of twisted human-animal hybrids. Like Shelley's *Frankenstein*, Wells's novel points up the ethical limitations of experimental science: Moreau's brilliance can mold a beast into a human semblance, but it cannot endow the result with virtue or a functioning conscience—thus suggesting a fundamental ambivalence regarding the processes and products of scientific inquiry.

During the twentieth century, the figure of the mad scientist flourished in the pulp magazines, in stories such as H. P. Lovecraft's "Herbert West—Reanimator" (1922), an overt echo of *Frankenstein* in which the title character revivifies a corpse, and Edmond Hamilton's "The Man Who Evolved" (1931), wherein a crazed inventor accelerates evolution with catastrophic results. The archetype found its most enduring representation, however, in the cinema, especially in the many adaptations of Shelley's *Frankenstein* that followed in the wake of James Whale's 1931 classic. These stories bequeathed to contemporary popular culture an enduring myth of science as an epochal threat to humanity and a source of moral corruption. In Stanley Kubrick's *Dr. Strangelove or: How I Learned to Stop Worrying and Love the Bomb* (1964), mad science even leads to the extermination of the human race in a global spasm of thermonuclear violence.

The mad scientist has now become something of a cliché in the genre, parodied and pastiched in scores of stories, films, comic books, and video games. The most culturally visible mad scientist of recent years is probably Sir John Hammond, creator of the out-of-control dinosaurs in the *Jurassic Park* film series (1993–2015), yet another avatar of Frankenstein.

Rob Latham

See also: Forbidden Knowledge or Power; Gothic Hero/Villain; *The Invisible Man*; *The Island of Doctor Moreau*; Shelley, Mary; *The Strange Case of Dr. Jekyll and Mr. Hyde*; Wells, H. G.

Further Reading

Colavito, Jason. 2008. *Knowing Fear: Science, Knowledge, and the Development of the Horror Genre*. Jefferson, NC: McFarland.

Haynes, Roslynn D. 1994. *From Faust to Strangelove: Representations of the Scientist in Western Literature*. Baltimore, MD: Johns Hopkins University Press.

Kirby, David A. 2011. *Lab Coats in Hollywood: Science, Scientists, and Cinema*. Cambridge, MA: MIT Press.

Skal, David J. 1998. *Screams of Reason: Mad Science and Modern Culture*. New York: Norton.

MALPERTUIS

Malpertuis is a novel by Belgian writer Jean Ray (1887–1964), first published in French in 1943. The first English translation appeared in 1998. *Malpertuis* is an example of a latter-day Gothic romance, employing frame narratives (i.e., stories within stories), set in and around a sinister old house filled with dark secrets, and centered on a doomed love affair. These story elements are employed without any regard for conventional realism, creating a dreamlike narrative that resembles the works of Hoffmann or Horace Walpole's short stories.

Jean-Jacques Grandsire is the young protagonist of the main story. According to the terms of a will left behind by a mysterious ancestor, Quentin Cassave, it is necessary for Grandsire to take up residence in Cassave's ancient mansion, named Malpertuis, in order to claim his inheritance. The mansion is home to a number of other beneficiaries and retainers as well, including a beautiful woman named Euryale. The house has an otherworldly atmosphere, and the others who live there are, for the most part, highly eccentric or even mad. One man, Lampernisse, is preoccupied with ensuring that the lights never go out. There are three sisters, a servant who can spit fire, and a beautiful young man with an enchanting singing voice, among others.

In time, Grandsire will determine the truth—that Quentin Cassave retrieved what remained of the gods and mythological figures of ancient Greece and brought them back to Belgium with him. They live cooped up in Malptertuis, disguised as more or less ordinary people. Lampernisse is Prometheus. The three sisters, including one with whom Grandsire has a brief affair, are the Furies. The old man named Eisengott is Zeus himself, and hence able to retain a greater degree of independence from Malpertuis. Grandsire's unknown mother may have been a supernatural being as well. Euryale is the only character to appear under her true name; a sister of Medusa, one of the Gorgons, she never looks directly at Grandsire.

The other dimensions of the story recount Cassave's discovery and capture of the gods on an island in the Mediterranean. In general, characters are able to tell only part of their stories before the novel switches to a new narrator or writer, so that the reader seems to piece together the overall story from fragmentary evidence.

The novel touches on many of Ray's favorite themes, including the reenchantment of urban settings and the subversion of bourgeois ideas of reality, the operation in human life of impersonal destiny, secret identities, and the parallels between hermetic magic and art. Like much of Ray's other work, *Malpertuis* favors the grotesque over the terrible. Ray's preference for the bizarre reflects an ambiguity in desire, which is at once frightened by and attracted to what is out of the ordinary. The figure of the Gorgon, altered here in that it is being seen by her, rather than seeing her, that turns one to stone, might be taken to reflect Ray's idea of the supernatural best.

Belgian director Harry Kuemel created a Flemish-language film adaptation of the novel, also called *Malpertuis*, in 1971. The film stars Orson Welles as Cassave, called "Cassavius" in the film. The novel was adapted for film by Jean Ferry, a French screenwriter who worked with internationally respected directors including Henri-Georges Clouzot and Louis Malle.

Michael Cisco

See also: Frame Story; Hoffmann, E. T. A.; Ray, Jean; Walpole; Horace.

Further Reading

Monteiro, António. 2011. "Ghosts, Fear, and Parallel Worlds: The Supernatural Fiction of Jean Ray." *Weird Fiction Review*, November 21. http://weirdfictionreview.com/2011/11/ghosts-fear-and-parallel-worlds-the-supernatural-fiction-of-jean-ray.
Thompson, David. 2002. "Auteur of Darkness." *Sight & Sound* 12, no. 8: 16–18.

THE MANUSCRIPT FOUND IN SARAGOSSA

Count Jan Potocki (1761–1815), a Polish nobleman, lived an itinerant life combining adventure and scholarship before he committed suicide by (according to some accounts) shooting himself in the head with a silver bullet. The publication history of his one surviving novel, *The Manuscript Found in Saragossa*, is a complex one. The original French manuscript is incomplete and some of the text has only survived in its translation into Potocki's native Polish. It is possible that Potocki began work on it in the 1790s and only completed it in the year of his death, although various extracts had already been published in Russia and France before then. After the first complete Polish translation was made in 1847, the novel eventually saw print in French in 1989, before Penguin published Ian Maclean's English translation in 1995.

Potocki claimed that *The Manuscript Found in Saragossa* was principally inspired by Ann Radcliffe's seminal works in the Gothic genre. However, Potocki's mind seems to have been too mercurial to follow Radcliffe's template in any ordinary or straightforward fashion. Instead, he presents the reader with a dizzyingly complicated arrangement of tales within tales, all themselves bookended with an overriding frame story. The resulting Russian-doll structure results in characters being introduced within a story, who then relate a further story, in which yet another character begins relating his or her own story, and so on. The reader quickly becomes hopelessly yet joyously lost in the maze-like palimpsest of narratives.

At the outset of the novel, the ostensible romantic hero, Alphonse Van Worden, a soldier lost in the wild Andalusian countryside, is apparently seduced by two Muslim sisters before waking to find himself lying beside the gyrating corpses of two executed bandits. Realizing he has been tricked by their malevolent spirits, he flees, but then finds himself similarly ensnared in another of their illusions. Potocki reboots the narrative several times in this manner, disorienting not only Van Worden, but also the reader, who struggles to keep up with the constant elision of reality and fantasy. This destabilizing effect is maintained throughout the novel, which is by turns ludic and terrifying, erotic and grotesque, but usually maintains a distinctly sardonic undercurrent. Populating the novel are demons, bandits, knights, kabbalists, princesses, scholars, soldiers, and inquisitors. The Wandering Jew stalks its pages, appearing in several stories as well as relating his own.

The tortured (and often torturous) hazing and repeated disorientation of Van Worden, and some of the other protagonists, in the face of horrors and wonders of consistently unresolved ontological status (including hallucinations, dreams, antagonistic human manipulation and misdirection, and the genuinely supernatural) goes somewhat beyond Radcliffe's rather more straightforward "explained supernatural." Thematically *The Manuscript Found in Saragossa* explicitly engages with the Occidental encounter with the Orient, where Spain, with its imbrication of Christian and Islamic cultures, represents a sort of liminal imaginative space between these two mutually fascinated and suspicious cultures. It has been suggested that the novel's complexity is the result of it being arranged according to an occult schema, possibly relating to the tarot deck. However, Potocki's frequent articulation of rationalist, enlightenment discourse within the novel and the often satirical tone of his treatment of, for example, the Spanish inquisition and kabbalism, at least complicates the notion of the author as a committed occultist.

Admirers of the novel include Neil Gaiman, Salman Rushdie, and Italo Calvino, the latter of whom regarded Potocki's work as an anticipation of Poe and used an excerpt to open his posthumously published 1998 anthology of nineteenth-century *Fantastic Tales*. The 1965 Polish film adaptation *The Saragossa Manuscript*, directed by Wojciech Has, is much admired by Martin Scorsese and Francis Ford Coppola. It successfully captures the quicksilver, expansive spirit of this unique novel, albeit in a necessarily truncated form.

James Machin

See also: Frame Story; Radcliffe, Ann; Unreliable Narrator.

Further Reading

Calvino, Italo. 2001. *Fantastic Tales*. London: Penguin.
Lachman, Gary. 2000. "The Mystical Count." *Fortean Times* 140 (November). http://web.archive.org/web/20020811153132/http://forteantimes.com/articles/140_potocki.shtml.
Maclean, Ian. 1995. "Introduction." In *The Manuscript Found in Saragossa*, by Jan Potocki. London: Penguin.

MARTIN, GEORGE R. R. (1948–)

George R. R. Martin is best known to contemporary audiences as the author of the ongoing fantasy series of novels *Song of Ice and Fire* and the massively popular television show *Game of Thrones* based on the same. He began his professional career in 1971 as a writer of science fiction short stories, but he quickly established himself as an author of great flexibility, moving seemingly without effort between science fiction, fantasy, and horror, and with great understanding of how these genres differ from, overlap with, and complement each other. Aside from the five novels in his *Song of Ice and Fire* series (with more projected at the time of this writing),

Martin has authored or co-authored six novels and edited or co-edited nearly three dozen science fiction, fantasy, and horror anthologies. His work has won him both critical acclaim and (mostly) commercial success, including four Hugo Awards, two Nebula Awards, a Bram Stoker Award, and a World Fantasy Award for Lifetime Achievement.

Fevre Dream (1982) is Martin's sole pure horror novel. An intensely readable and marvelously realized story of vampires and their human pawns and partners traversing the Mississippi River on ornate steamboats, the novel owes as much to its horror trappings as it does to the American historical novel. *The Armageddon Rag*, a thriller with supernatural underpinnings that seem forced at best, was published the following year. In his introduction to Martin's short story retrospective *Dreamsongs Volume I*, Gardner Dozois points to the commercial failure of *The Armageddon Rag* as the reason Martin abandoned the horror genre to focus on scripting and producing for television, including the relaunch of a new *Twilight Zone* (1985–1987) series and the more successful *Beauty and the Beast* (1987–1990). To that point Martin's published horror in short form included "Meathouse Man" (1976), *Sandkings* (1979), and "Nightflyers" (1980/1981). But Martin never completely left the horror field, and he continued to produce stories of high quality, such as "The Monkey Treatment" (1983), "The Pear-Shaped Man" (1987), and *Skin Trade* (1988).

Martin's horror fiction is distinguished by his ability to effectively blend genres together to achieve a maximum of narrative effect. "Meathouse Man," for example, relates through a mix of pre-cyberpunk imagery and body horror the story of a disaffected young male who is both sexually and socially frustrated, while "Nightflyers" reconceives the traditional haunted house story aboard a spaceship. *Sandkings*, too, belongs to this category of story. More traditional, yet no less powerful, stories like "The Pear-Shaped Man," wherein a female artist becomes obsessed with the odd loner who lives in the basement of her apartment complex, and "The Monkey Treatment," in which an obese man seeks a new treatment for his eating disorder and discovers that the cure is far worse than the ailment, demonstrate Martin's mastery of genre convention. The graphic novella *Skin Trade* shows the influence of splatterpunk, but remains distinctly Martin-ish in its telling of urban werewolves who are hunted by something far worse, and whose lead character, a middle-aged and out-of-shape reporter cum werewolf, undermines popular genre clichés.

As of this writing, George R. R. Martin's energies seem focused on completing *Song of Ice and Fire* and on further developing the *Game of Thrones* franchise, and one can hardly fault him given its enormous commercial success. While elements of horror can be found throughout the cycle—the Night King and his White Walkers, for example—it seems readers will have to wait for a more focused example of the horror fiction that Martin has proven so capable of producing.

Javier A. Martinez

See also: Body Horror; *Sandkings*; Vampires.

Further Reading

"Author George R. R. Martin 'Playing for Keeps.'" 2011. *Weekend All Things Considered.* NPR, July 17. http://info.nhpr.org/author-george-rr-martin-playing-keeps.

"George R. R. Martin." 2016. *Contemporary Authors Online.* Detroit, MI: Gale.

Levy, Michael. 1996. "George R. R. Martin: Dreamer of Fantastic Worlds." *Publishers Weekly,* 243: 70–71.

McMullen, E. C., Jr. 2003. "George R. R. Martin." In *Supernatural Fiction Writers: Contemporary Fantasy and Horror*, edited by Richard Bleiler, 667–672. New York: Thomson/Gale.

"THE MASQUE OF THE RED DEATH"

Edgar Allan Poe's short story "The Masque of the Red Death" was first published in the May 1842 issue of *Graham's Magazine* under the title "The Masque of the Red Death: A Fantasy." Allegorical in nature, the story is at once a deft rendering in Gothic horror fiction and a specimen of Poe's comic art in the short story. Fearing what they view as a contagion, Prince Prospero and his followers seclude themselves in his palace, imagining that they can thus escape blood and time, twin strongholds in life. The tale dramatizes their folly, concluding with death's overtaking the group in the form of a masked reveler who turns out not to be masked at all, but the actual personification of the plague they had feared. Poe's use of the term "masque" derives in part from an early form of English drama in which each performer represented a psychological or moral state, and although the characters in Poe's tale are revelers, they periodically register unease, betraying an awareness that they sense a futility in trying to control human realities of the body and of time, symbolized by the "Red Death," designating blood, and a striking clock, designating time's not standing still.

The chambers in Prospero's weird palace are decorated with colors that some readers think represent the stages in life from youth to old age. The red and black chamber, with its dual colors representing life and death, reveals that no delusion of the revelers will allow escape from reality. In Shakespeare's *The Tempest* (1611), from which in part Poe's tale derives, the Prospero character must return to real life from his paradise island, and even there an unsettling reality intrudes in the person of Caliban. In "Masque" no such reprieve is offered: all the would-be escapees from life's realities die, showing the futility of their endeavor.

Reading "Masque" is in part analogous to viewing the inside of a human head, with the characters in the tale representing the delusions of those who try to evade blood, time, and death—life's absolutes. Some also perceive comic undercurrents in the tale, particularly with "Masque" being viewed as a comic takeoff on Nathaniel Hawthorne's *Twice-Told Tales* (1837 and 1842), which Poe reviewed, there implying that Hawthorne had plagiarized from him.

The story was adapted, rather loosely, by screenwriters Charles Beaumont and R. Wright Campbell for an installment in director Roger Corman's popular series of

In Poe's story, the masked revelers are appalled, and Prospero is enraged, when someone appears among them who has had the audacity to dress as if afflicted by the Red Death, with his face and clothes sprinkled with blood. However, the story's apocalyptic climax reveals that this is not, in fact, a costume. The revelers are seized with awe as the figure makes its way through the colored rooms. Prospero makes pursuit. And then:

> He bore aloft a drawn dagger, and had approached, in rapid impetuosity, to within three or four feet of the retreating figure, when the latter, having attained the extremity of the velvet apartment, turned suddenly and confronted his pursuer. There was a sharp cry—and the dagger dropped gleaming upon the sable carpet, upon which, instantly afterwards, fell prostrate in death the Prince Prospero. Then, summoning the wild courage of despair, a throng of the revellers at once threw themselves into the black apartment, and, seizing the mummer, whose tall figure stood erect and motionless within the shadow of the ebony clock, gasped in unutterable horror at finding the grave-cerements and corpse-like mask which they handled with so violent a rudeness, untenanted by any tangible form.
>
> And now was acknowledged the presence of the Red Death. He had come like a thief in the night. And one by one dropped the revellers in the blood-bedewed halls of their revel, and died each in the despairing posture of his fall. And the life of the ebony clock went out with that of the last of the gay. And the flames of the tripods expired. And Darkness and Decay and the Red Death held illimitable dominion over all. (Poe 1984, 490)

Matt Cardin

Source: Poe, Edgar Allan. 1902. *The Works of Edgar Allan Poe.* Vol. 4. New York: Frank F. Lovell Book Co., Publishers. 14–15.

Edgar Allan Poe movies starring Vincent Price. Although the movie takes great liberties with Poe's story and also incorporates aspects of another Poe story, "Hop-Frog" (1849), it is an enjoyable production that remains somewhat true to the spirit of "The Masque of the Red Death." It was remade in 1989, with Corman producing and Larry Brand directing.

Benjamin F. Fisher

See also: Hawthorne, Nathaniel; Poe, Edgar Allan; *Part Two, Themes, Topics, and Genres*: Shakespearean Horrors.

Further Reading

Fisher, Benjamin F. 2002. "Poe and the Gothic Tradition." In *The Cambridge Companion to Edgar Allan Poe*, edited by Kevin J. Hayes, 72–91. Cambridge, UK: Cambridge University Press.

Regan, Robert. 1983. "Hawthorne's 'Plagiary'; Poe's Duplicity." In *The Naiad Voice: Essays on Poe's Satiric Hoaxing*, edited by Dennis W. Eddings, 73–87. Port Washington, NY: Associated Faculty Press. Originally published in *Nineteenth-Century Fiction*, 1970, 25: 281–298.

Roppolo, Joseph. 1963. "Meaning and 'The Masque of the Red Death.'" *Tulane Studies in English* 13: 59–69.

MATHESON, RICHARD (1926–2013)

Richard Burton Matheson was an American author of horror and science fiction whose work helped to shape the speculative fiction genres in the twentieth century. In the view of many critics and readers, Matheson captured the postmodern angst and existential predicaments that came to dominate the common person in the mid-to-late twentieth century better than his peers. Much of this was due to his anxieties and execution, where the hallmarks of his oeuvre included the intrusion of the extraordinary into daily life, a strong feeling (especially in his earlier output) of mistrust, and an all-inclusive desire to recognize the spiritual side of humankind (mostly in later works). Couple these characteristics with his footprint in mass media by way of an impressive career in film and television—in addition to his output in short fiction, novels, and song lyrics—and his import becomes clear upon even a cursory examination of his output.

He was born February 20, 1926, in Allendale, New Jersey, and was of Norwegian descent. Early on he found comfort in writing as a way to deal with the harsh realities of his alcoholic family life. After an honorable discharge from the Army during World War II, he obtained a degree in journalism from the University of Missouri. He wrote his first novels while submitting to short story and pulp markets; a breakthrough happened with the publication of his dystopian vampire work, *I Am Legend* (1954).

Matheson's follow-up book was another masterwork—*The Shrinking Man* (1956). In this novel, bleak notions about science, spiritualism, and humanity's place in the universe—themes that Matheson would revisit in later works—bubbled up, with astonishing results. Making his way to Los Angeles, he was given the chance (at his insistence as a gambit to establish himself in film) to adapt the book into script format (*The Incredible Shrinking Man*, 1957), thus demonstrating an additional ability: working in another medium. He was ahead of his peers in this respect, with the notable exception of his remarkable friend Charles Beaumont (*The Intruder*, 1959), and it was then that he and Beaumont were tapped by Rod Serling, by way of *The Martian Chronicles* (1950) author Ray Bradbury's intervention, to write for *The Twilight Zone*. During this time, he was part of a collective of creators and friends—known later as "The Southern California Writer's Group," but internally simply referred to as "The Group"—which included not only Matheson and Beaumont, but also William F. Nolan (*Logan's Run*, 1967), George Clayton Johnson (*Ocean's 11*, 1959), John Tomerlin (*Challenge the Wind*, 1967), and by extension Bradbury,

"Nightmare at 20,000 Feet": Monster on the Wing

Published in 1961, Matheson's short horror story "Nightmare at 20,000 feet" has become recognized as a classic. The basic plot is widely known in popular culture: On a nighttime passenger flight, a man named Arthur Jeffrey Wilson, who has a history of mental disturbance, believes he sees a man (or monster) outside the cabin inflicting damage to the wing of the airplane. When he alerts the other passengers, he is dismissed as either mistaken or having a mental breakdown. In the story's climax, Wilson attempts to kill the man by shooting out the window, nearly causing a catastrophe. The story ends with the damaged plane on the ground and Wilson being carted away on a stretcher by people who think he was trying to commit suicide.

Both the story and Matheson's eventual self-adapted episode of *The Twilight Zone* in 1963, starring William Shatner as Wilson, were groundbreaking. The unconventional themes—an everyman protagonist fragmented by paranoia, dovetailing with the use of the unreliable narrator technique; modern technology (air travel) as a menace; the focus on mental illness and its aftermath from a social lens—would eventually become hallmarks of Matheson's very personal approach to the modern horror story, and many of these treatments subsequently came into common usage. The story itself, especially in its *Twilight Zone* incarnation, has become iconic, to the point where parodies of it have appeared on everything from *The Simpsons* to *Saturday Night Live*.

"Nightmare at 20,000 Feet" was given another adaptation in 1983 as the fourth and final segment in the *Twilight Zone* anthology movie, with John Lithgow replacing Shatner as the protagonist. Once again, Matheson adapted the script from his own story, this time removing the mental illness angle and making the protagonist (now named John Valentine) suffer instead from a morbid fear of flying.

Jason V Brock

Robert Bloch (*Psycho*, 1959), and many others. By now, Matheson—in addition to being a successful novelist and writer for the screen—had also become a devoted husband and father.

Later, director Roger Corman would demonstrate similar vision as Serling by employing both Beaumont and Matheson to write his Poe series of films—*House of Usher* (1960), *The Pit and the Pendulum* (1961), and others. To this end, Matheson's personal demons—paranoia, fear of insanity, dread of unintended scientific repercussions, the dangers of modernity—began to be addressed directly in his output. As his career accelerated, he turned away from short fiction to write more for film and television. Though working frequently for the likes of directors such as Dan Curtis (*Dark Shadows*, 1966–1971) and a young Steven Spielberg (*Duel*, 1971), he continued to produce novels. Several of his standout books center on the ideas and thematic possibilities of the importance of the magical and the transcendent power of love. His output began to touch on themes and concepts that his friends' work did not.

Stylistically, a general lack of nostalgia (at least in his short work; a few of his novels have touched upon this emotion at length), yet cautious optimism and hope that there is more to the plight of humans, is another one of the things that separates Matheson's writing from his contemporaries in the genres he explored: Western, horror, science fiction, mainstream literary, and forays into nonfiction. In spite of Matheson's relatively modest literary output—he was never a consistent "best seller" or excessively prolific—he was nonetheless unusually important, even in his peer cohort. The reason for this most likely stems from Matheson's treatment of his personal concerns, which, at their core, strike at the root of human failing, technophobia, and anomie in ways that none of his colleagues ever managed, including his eminent, aforementioned equals, such as Charles Beaumont, William F. Nolan, and even the esteemed Ray Bradbury. Surrounded by family, Matheson passed away peacefully in his home on June 23, 2013.

Jason V Brock

See also: Beaumont, Charles; Bloch, Robert; Bradbury, Ray; Nolan, William F.; Vampires.

Further Reading

Brock, Jason V. 2014. *Disorders of Magnitude: A Survey of Dark Fantasy.* Lanham, MD: Rowman & Littlefield Publishing Group.

Dziemianowicz, Stefan. 2002. "The Matheson Zone." *Publishers Weekly* 249, no. 24 (June 17): 31–35. http://www.publishersweekly.com/pw/print/20020617/28779-the-matheson-zone.html.

Pulliam, June M., and Anthony J. Fonseca. 2016. *Richard Matheson's Monsters: Gender in the Stories, Scripts, Novels, and Twilight Zone Episodes.* Lanham, MD: Rowman & Littlefield Publishing Group.

Wiater, Stanley, Matthew R. Bradley, and Paul Stuve, eds. 2009. *The Twilight and Other Zones: The Dark Worlds of Richard Matheson.* New York: Citadel Press Books.

MATURIN, CHARLES ROBERT (1782–1824)

Charles Robert Maturin was a writer of Gothic novels and plays, most famously *Melmoth the Wanderer* (1820). A Protestant clergyman, he was born and lived most of his life in Dublin. He was an eccentric, a dandy, and a charismatic preacher.

Maturin was born in Dublin on September 25, 1782, into a line of Protestant clergymen, descendants of Huguenots who fled France to escape Catholic persecution. As a young man Maturin attended Trinity College. He then took religious orders and, following his ordination, became a curate in Dublin. He lived with his parents, and in 1803 married singer and society beauty Henrietta Kingsbury.

Maturin began to write out of his own interest and self-published his first books. Not wishing to harm his chances of advancement in the priesthood, Maturin wrote his first three novels under a pseudonym. They were not well received, but they attracted the notice of Sir Walter Scott, and Maturin and he struck up a correspondence. Scott was very supportive of Maturin's career and recommended his work to Lord Byron, who admired it.

A combination of factors—his Calvinism, the fact that he had offended a bishop, concern over the impiety of his fiction—meant Maturin was barred from clerical advancement. As he had to support his parents as well as his family, and his wages as a curate were small, he was forced to take on other jobs.

Then, in 1816, Maturin's tragic play, *Bertram*, was an unexpected success on the London stage. Maturin was suddenly famous, and the play earned him about £1,000, a sum that enabled him to give up the teaching he was doing on top of his priestly duties and devote more time to writing. Despite its popularity, *Bertram* was critically decried in Britain, with Samuel Taylor Coleridge blasting it in his *Biographia Literaria* (1817), describing the opening of its fourth act "as a melancholy proof of the depravation of the public mind" (Coleridge 2014, 398). However— and seemingly unsuspected by Maturin—internationally the play was not just popularly successful but critically acclaimed. It was performed in America, translated into French, used as the basis for operas in both France and Italy, and praised by the likes of Victor Hugo, Honoré de Balzac, Alexandre Dumas, and Johann Wolfgang von Goethe.

Further plays failed, however, so Maturin turned back to novel writing and, in 1820, published the work for which he is best known, *Melmoth the Wanderer*. Two other novels followed, but none of the three (*Melmoth* included) sold well or received many positive notices at the time.

Scott often, in his letters to Maturin, advised the Irishman to tone down his productions and introduce greater realism. Much about Maturin's aesthetic sense can be deduced from looking at the differences between his and Scott's approaches to writing as a career. Scott was developing a new tradition, a sober, plausible, and modern "historical romance," a mode designed to appeal to contemporary readers. Maturin's aim, by contrast, was to radicalize, to make more lurid and disturbing, the Gothic romance. Maturin was the archetype of the contrary horror writer who, out of step with public taste and frustrated by critical responses to his or her work, pushes more and more against the boundaries of decency. He aimed in his work at the intense, the sublime, the violent, the grotesque, and the comic, interweaving these moods to disconcerting effect.

Maturin died in penury and obscurity on October 20, 1824. In the 1890s, his literary reputation in Britain was revived, and *Melmoth*, which was translated into French in 1821, had a major influence on the Decadent and Surrealist movements.

Timothy J. Jarvis

See also: Byron, Lord; Frame Story; Romanticism and Dark Romanticism; The Sublime; Surrealism.

Further Reading

Coleridge, Samuel Taylor. [1817] 2014. *Biographia Literaria*. Edited by Adam Roberts. Edinburgh: Edinburgh University Press.

Sage, Victor. 2000. Introduction to *Melmoth the Wanderer* by Charles Robert Maturin, vii–xxix. London: Penguin.

MAUPASSANT, GUY DE (1850–1893)

Henri René Albert Guy de Maupassant was a French naturalist writer known for his virtuosic short stories, written between 1875 and 1891, including the remarkable "Le Horla" (1887), an early example of weird fiction that H. P. Lovecraft, in *Supernatural Horror in Literature* (1927), claims is "perhaps without a peer in its particular department" (Lovecraft 2012, 52). Indeed, Maupassant's horror tales, which often consist of hallucinatory encounters with the numinous that decenter the self as a privileged site for differentiating between the real and the unreal, have had an immeasurable impact on writers of weird fiction and cosmic horror similarly interested in subverting the rational.

A student of Gustave Flaubert, Maupassant is perhaps best known for the rollicking "Boule de suif" (Ball of Fat, 1880), published in Emile Zola's *Soirées de Médan* (Evenings at Médan), which brought him success as an author, and for the *conte cruel* (cynical tale of cruelty) "La Parure" (The Necklace, 1884), whose "twist" ending plays a cautionary role. Both stories explore French life in the nineteenth century with a spirit of playful mischievousness. Yet, as indicated by Arnold Kellett in the introduction to *The Dark Side: Tales of Terror and the Supernatural* (1989), there exists a "dark side" to the author's oeuvre, including some thirty tales that investigate the sometimes quiet, sometimes cosmic horrors of the weird and the unknown. Most of these stories are collected in Kellett's volume, which is the best introduction to Maupassant's horror fiction, where the reader can observe the ways in which Maupassant was inspired by the nineteenth-century German philosopher Arthur Schopenhauer's philosophical pessimism, the nineteenth-century French pioneer of neurology Jean-Martin Charcot's lectures on hypnotism, the German writer E. T. A. Hoffmann's Gothic stories, and the French writer Charles Baudelaire's translations of Edgar Allan Poe's macabre works.

Maupassant's horror tales, such as "Lui?" (tr. as The Terror; 1883), "La Nuit" (tr. as The Nightmare, 1887), and "Qui sait?" (Who Knows? 1890), straddle the line between the supernatural and realism, thereby allowing horror and terror to coexist in an atmosphere of uneasiness, often culminating in the narrator experiencing hallucinations, obsessions, and madness. Maupassant was fond of the frame story, frequently characterizing his narrators as persons of credible sanity whose encounters with the *outré* (the strange and unusual)—including doppelgängers, animate objects, and the undead—and whose subsequent devolutions into states of frenzy are rendered both believable and disturbing. Maupassant, who fought in the Franco-Prussian War, was equally interested in the notion of inhumanity, and he explored the horrors of war with a somber lucidity in stories such as "La Folle" (The Mad Woman, 1882), "Deux amis" (Two Friends, 1883), and "Le Père Milon" (Father Milon, 1883).

Maupassant lived a life of debauchery and, in his twenties, contracted syphilis, leading to the gradual dissolution of his physical and mental health. In 1892 he made a botched attempt at suicide and spent the remaining year of his life in an asylum, where he died at the young age of forty-two.

Sean Matharoo

See also: Doubles, Dopplegängers, and Split Selves; Dreams and Nightmares; Frame Story; The Haunted House or Castle; "The Horla"; The Numinous; Psychological Horror; Terror versus Horror.

Further Reading

Álvaro, L. C. 2005. "Hallucinations and Pathological Visual Perceptions in Maupassant's Fantastical Short Stories—a Neurological Approach." *Journal of the History of Neurosciences* 14 (2): 100–115.

Lerner, Michael G. 1975. *Maupassant*. New York: George Braziller.

Lovecraft, H. P. [1927] 2012. *The Annotated Supernatural Horror in Literature*. Edited by S. T. Joshi. New York: Hippocampus Press.

Marvin, Frederic R. 1915. "Maupassant and Poe." In *'A Hideous Bit of Morbidity': An Anthology of Horror Criticism from the Enlightenment to World War I*, edited by Jason Colavito, 148–152. Jefferson, NC: McFarland.

MCCAMMON, ROBERT R. (1952–)

Robert Rick McCammon is an American writer of horror and historical crime fiction who came to prominence in the 1980s and 1990s as a writer of best-selling paperback original novels. His work is distinguished by its optimistic portrayals of characters who draw on their greatest virtues as human beings to triumph over challenges, both supernatural and otherwise.

McCammon took a degree in journalism from the University of Alabama and was writing advertising copy for newspapers in Birmingham when his first novel, *Baal*, was published in 1978. The story of a child born of a rape committed by a demonic being who eventually grows into an antichrist-like figure with powers that threaten the world, it was the first of several novels in which McCammon tackled themes common in the then burgeoning horror market. *Bethany's Sin* (1980), which garnered comparisons to Thomas Tryon's *Harvest Home* (1973), is a small-town horror novel in which a family discovers that the Connecticut town they have recently moved to is home to a fertility cult possessed by the spirits of

Mine: Mind of a Human Monster

A suspense thriller published by Pocket Books in 1990, *Mine* marked a career turning point for McCammon, who up to then had been known primarily for writing supernatural horror. The two principal characters are Mary Terrell, a.k.a. Mary Terror, a former member of the Storm Front Brigade (a radical offshoot of the Weather Underground), and Laura Clayborne, an Atlanta suburbanite who is about to give birth to her first child. Since a shootout with the police in 1972 that resulted in the capture and disbanding of the Storm Front—and that caused her to lose her own unborn child— Mary has kept a low profile, living hand-to-mouth and frequently moving to hide her whereabouts. When she meets Laura, her long-simmering obsession with having a child boils over. Masquerading as a nurse, she steals Laura's infant son, David, and flees in the hope that, if she can track down Jack Gardiner (a.k.a. Lord Jack), the Storm Front's former leader, they will be able to reunite the brigade's surviving members.

Mine is a powerful character study in which McCammon compares and contrasts his two main characters. The psychotic Mary is frightening in the intensity of her desire to live in a past that the world has moved on from and in her pathological obsession to have a child. Although her actions represent a break with sanity, she is not completely unsympathetic, especially when she begins to show a sensitive, maternal side under David's influence. Although Laura seems to be living a life that is the complete opposite of Mary's—aloof, privileged, tradition-bound—the kidnapping of her child sets her on a more determined course of action as she pursues Mary across the country, becoming more ruthless and obsessive herself. *Mine* received the Bram Stoker Award for Best Novel of 1990.

Stefan R. Dziemianowicz

bloodthirsty Amazons unleashed during an archaeological excavation. *The Night Boat* (1980) was somewhat ahead of the horror genre's early twenty-first-century zombie craze with its account of a Nazi U-boat crew cursed by a voodoo priest to immortal existence as flesh-eating zombies. *They Thirst* (1981) proved to be McCammon's breakout novel: set in Los Angeles where an apocalyptic vampire invasion is gradually unfolding, its large cast of characters and epic scale showed him attempting more ambitious plots.

McCammon's next two novels were published as hardcovers. In *Mystery Walk* (1983), the struggle between human good and supernatural evil that serves as the foundation for many of his stories plays out in the relationship between two young men gifted with supernatural powers, one of whom uses his to heal the afflicted while the other uses his to further the campaign of his father, an evangelical Christian zealot. The premise of McCammon's Southern Gothic novel *Usher's Passing*

(1984) is that the doomed family in Edgar Allan Poe's "The Fall of the House of Usher" is a historically real American family that has made its fortune as arms merchants. Rix Usher, a contemporary descendant, repudiates his family's legacy, but finds that family obligations and his personal destiny as inheritor of a family business founded on a legacy of horrors are nearly impossible to escape.

Swan Song (1987) was another paperback original and the first of McCammon's novels to make the *New York Times* best-seller list. It is set in the aftermath of a nuclear war that has devastated the planet and left the survivors, some of whom are endowed with supernatural powers, to reestablish civilization and resist the ironically named "Friend," a shape-shifting monster trying to divide humanity against itself. McCammon's next novel, *Stinger* (1988), has been likened to a science fiction B-movie with its account of a small Texas town whose feuding residents pull together to assist a benign extraterrestrial who is fleeing the titular intergalactic bounty hunter. *Stinger* anticipates McCammon's *The Border* (2015), in which people from different, and often diametrically opposed, walks of life band together to assist a young man with an otherworldly pedigree who is the only possible salvation for an earth being decimated by opposing extraterrestrial armies that use it as their battleground. McCammon followed *Stinger* with *The Wolf's Hour* (1989), which gives a novel twist to the traditional werewolf theme: Michael Gallatin, the novel's werewolf, is a hero who fights for the Allied forces against the Nazis in World War II. Gallatin also serves as the protagonist in a handful of stories collected as *The Hunter from the Woods* (2015) and can be viewed as a prototype for Trevor Lawson, the benevolent vampire gunslinger in McCammon's period novels *I Travel By Night* (2013) and *Last Train from Perdition* (2016), both set in the American South in the aftermath of the Civil War.

McCammon shifted to writing nonsupernatural suspense fiction with *Mine* (1990), a novel about the dark side of America's counterculture in the 1960s, in which a former member of a radical underground front kidnaps the child of a privileged upper middle-class mother, setting off a cross-country chase that virtually radicalizes the mother in her determination to retrieve her child. *Boy's Life* (1991) is a Bradburyesque evocation of its main character's childhood in a small Southern town, one in which youthful imagination colors recollections of even the most dramatic events, infusing them with a fantastical quality. Like *Swan Song* and *Mine*, the novel won the Bram Stoker Award given by the Horror Writers Association for best novel. *Gone South* (1992) is yet another nonsupernatural novel concerning a fugitive on the run from bounty hunters whose pursuit through the Louisiana bayous bring him into contact with grotesques redolent of the fiction of Flannery O'Connor.

Ten years separate the publication of *Gone South* and *Speaks the Nightbird* (2002), during which McCammon, who was in disagreement with editors on the new direction he was taking in his work, unofficially retired from writing. *Speaks the Nightbird* is the first novel in a series that now includes *The Queen of Bedlam* (2007), *Mister Slaughter* (2010), *The Providence Rider* (2012), *The River of Souls* (2014), and *Freedom of the Mask* (2016), featuring Matthew Corbett, a "problem solver" (i.e., private detective) in prerevolutionary America whose adventures often verge on the macabre and occasionally suggest the supernatural through the superstitions and folk beliefs of their period characters. In this second act of his career, McCammon has alternated novels in his nonsupernatural series with supernatural fiction, including *The Five* (2011), in which a rock band's stalking by an assassin proves to be supernaturally motivated. McCammon is also the author of a collection of short fiction, *Blue World* (1989), several of whose stories have been adapted for television, including "Nightcrawlers," about a Vietnam veteran who brings the war home with him in the form of horrors that manifest from his dreams.

Stefan R. Dziemianowicz

See also: Bram Stoker Award; "The Fall of the House of Usher"; Splatterpunk; Vampires; Werewolves; Zombies.

Further Reading

Bleiler, Richard, and Hunter Goatley. 2003. "Robert R. McCammon." In *Supernatural Fiction Writers*, vol. 2, edited by Richard Bleiler, 705–712. New York: Scribner's.

Dziemianowicz, Stefan. 1998. "Robert R(ick) McCammon." In *The St. James Guide to Horror, Ghost, & Gothic Writers*, edited by David Pringle, 398–399. Detroit. MI: St. James Press.

Staggs, Sam. 1991. "PW Interviews: Robert R. McCammon." *Publishers Weekly* 238, no. 34 (August 2): 54–55.

Wiater, Stanley. 1990. "Robert R. McCammon." In *Dark Dreamers: Conversations with the Masters of Horror*, 145–153. New York: Avon.

MCDOWELL, MICHAEL (1950–1999)

Michael McEachern McDowell was an American screenwriter and novelist from Enterprise, Alabama. He is best known as the author of *Blackwater*, a six-part Southern Gothic serial novel, and for his work as a screenwriter, including two original scripts for Tim Burton and a Stephen King adaptation. King himself, in a much-quoted comment, once described McDowell as "the finest writer of paperback originals in America today" (Winter 1985, 177).

McDowell held degrees from Harvard (summa cum laude) and a PhD in English and American Literature from Brandeis, where his 1978 dissertation was titled *American Attitudes toward Death, 1825–1865*. While attempting six novels that failed to sell, he supported himself by working as a teacher, a theater critic, and a secretary at Massachusetts Institute of Technology.

After seeing a trailer for *The Omen* while attending a showing of *Barry Lyndon*, he was inspired to work on a horror script of his own. He novelized his script as an exercise, resulting in his debut, *The Amulet*, published in 1979. He continued in the Southern Gothic vein for several subsequent novels, including *Cold Moon over Babylon* (1980), *The Elementals* (1981), and *Blackwater* (1983), which was published in six monthly installments. Michael E. Stamm has noted that in his Southern Gothic novels, McDowell was "noticeably influenced" by Eudora Welty, the Pulitzer Prize–winning American Southern novelist (Stamm 1988, 51).

Roughly half of McDowell's approximately thirty novels, most published as paperback originals, appeared under his own name, while others were credited to various pseudonyms, including Mike McCray, Preston Macadam, and a pair of pen names used for his collaborations with Dennis Schuetz: Nathan Aldyne (four gay detective novels) and Axel Young. In addition to his horror novels, he wrote several historical novels, a trilogy of crime books, and a novelization for the movie *Clue*.

In the mid-1980s, McDowell received a phone call from the producers of the American anthology horror television series *Tales from the Darkside* inquiring after the rights to a story that was actually written by Michael P-Kube McDowell. He used the opportunity to send them a script and started writing for anthology television series, including *Amazing Stories*, *Monsters*, and *Alfred Hitchcock Presents*, as well as for two television specials. His feature film script of *Beetlejuice* (1988; based on a story co-written with Larry Wilson) followed, as well as scripts for *High Spirits* (1988), *Tales from the Darkside: The Movie* (1990), *The Nightmare before Christmas* (1993), and *Thinner* (1996), based on the Stephen King novel of the same name.

Following his discovery that he was HIV-positive in 1994, McDowell spent the last years of his life teaching classes on screenwriting at Boston and Tufts University. At the time of his death, he was working on treatments of a *Beetlejuice* sequel and a new version of *The Nutcracker*. After his death in 1999 from AIDS-related illness in Boston, Tabitha King, a personal friend, agreed to complete his final novel, *Candles Burning*, which was published in 2006.

McDowell's "Death Collection" of bizarre curios, some of which date to the sixteenth century, including pictures of women modeling burial gowns, spirit photographs, funeral cards, hair wreaths, morticians' supplies, crime scene photos, hanging and accident photos, and an infant-sized casket, is archived at Northwestern University.

Bev Vincent

See also: Dark Fantasy; King, Stephen; Welty, Eudora.

Further Reading

Cagle, Ryan. 2016. *Cold Moon over McDowell: The Life and Works of Michael McDowell*. Accessed August 11, 2016. http://coldmoonovermcdowell.blogspot.com.

Stamm, Michael E. 1988. "Michael McDowell and the Haunted South." In *Discovering Modern Horror Fiction II*, edited by Darrell Schweitzer, 51–62. San Bernardino, CA: Borgo Press.

Wiater, Stanley. 1988. "Horror in Print: Michael McDowell." *Fangoria* 40: 54–56.

Winter, Douglas E. 1982. "From Harvard to Horror" (interview with Michael McDowell). *Fantasy Newsletter* 5, no. 11 (December): 23–28.

Winter, Douglas E. 1985. *Faces of Fear: Encounters with the Creators of Modern Horror*. New York: Berkley Books.

MCGRATH, PATRICK (1950–)

Now predominantly residing in New York, the British novelist Patrick McGrath is a writer of some standing in the field of Anglo-American letters and Gothic literature. Since his debut novel *The Grotesque* (1989), he has penned several critically acclaimed fictions that stage and interrogate the complexities of madness, obsession, psychiatry, and familial relationships. A number of McGrath's novels have been read through critical lenses that are associated with Gothic studies, yet perhaps only a handful of his works—such as *Spider* (1990), his short story "The Smell" (1991), and his 2000 novel *Martha Peake*—are consistently Gothicized in their imagery, iconography, or narration. One of McGrath's most exquisite skills as a writer lies in the tendency of his crafted prose to transform sustained and slow-burning terror into moments of devastating horror or revelation. His greatest influences are from the Gothic tradition, Edgar Allan Poe in particular, but he is also an avid reader of the haunting tales of Joseph Conrad, the passionate love affairs of D. H. Lawrence, and the aesthetically intense prose of John Hawkes.

A landmark critical study, Sue Zlosnik's monograph *Patrick McGrath* (2011), makes the standout scholarly case for considering him as primarily a writer of modern Gothic fiction. For instance, Zlosnik suggests that even McGrath's *Asylum* (1996), the narrative style of which is influenced by Ford Madox Ford's 1915 modernist novel *The Good Soldier*, explores fundamentally Gothic concerns and themes; the book's "narrative voice resists a Gothic tone," but its "concerns are undeniably Gothic" as its thematics are "shaped around a powerful symbolic structure relating to boundaries" (Zlosnik 2011, 75). Indeed, *Asylum* is concerned thematically with the causes, limits, and contours of madness, betrayal, institutionalism, and sexual possession. Its setting in 1959 is particularly telling. The institutional practices critiqued in *Asylum* draw from Victorian principles of psychiatry that were soon to be revolutionized through the transformative legislation of the Mental Health Act in the United Kingdom. Of keen interest to those academics and scholars who work on the intersections between medical practices and literature, McGrath's father—Dr. Pat McGrath Sr.—was the last medical superintendent of Broadmoor Lunatic Asylum (as it was then known), and McGrath the writer spent a good portion of his youth growing-up in a house just outside of the asylum's grounds. The influence that these years have upon his writing is pronounced, and his fiction has been described as neuro-Gothic because of its fusion of Gothic atmosphere with medical matters.

McGrath's modern novels continue to impress critics, and posterity may judge his collection of three stories, *Ghost Town* (2005), as one of the most nuanced and moving meditations upon post-9/11 New York. The work of this millennial McGrath is more recognizably American, and in recent years he has continued to gain a global, transnational readership. For instance, his Gothic novel *Martha Peake* won Italy's Premio Flaiano Prize. Both *Trauma* (2008) and *Constance* (2013), his two most recent novels as of late 2016, produce devastating conclusions and revelations. McGrath's intensity as a writer is undiminished.

Reflecting a renewed interest in his writing, McGrath, in collaboration with the University of Stirling in Scotland, has created an archive of his professional materials, one that includes books of automatic writing, several drafts of his novels, early promotional materials, adapted screenplays—including for David Cronenberg's *Spider* (2002)—and a complete set of first editions of his works. The archive's opening in January 2016 was marked by an international symposium that both celebrated McGrath's work and was a testament to scholars' continuing fascination with his neuro-Gothic writings.

Matt Foley

See also: The Grotesque.

Further Reading

McGrath, Patrick. 1997. "John Hawkes' *An Irish Eye.*" *BOMB Magazine* 61 (Fall). http://bombmagazine.org/article/5188/john-hawkes-an-irish-eye.

McGrath, Patrick. 2012. "A Boy's Own Broadmoor." *The Economist*, September/October. https://www.1843magazine.com/content/ideas/a-boys-own-broadmoor.

McRobert, Neil. 2011. "Patrick McGrath Interviewed by Neil McRobert." *The Gothic Imagination* at University of Stirling, July 13. http://www.gothic.stir.ac.uk/blog/patrick-mcgrath-interviewed-by-neil-mcrobert.

Zlosnik, Sue. 2011. *Patrick McGrath*. Cardiff: University of Wales Press.

MELMOTH THE WANDERER

In works of literary history, *Melmoth the Wanderer: A Tale* (1820) is often said to mark the end of the high Gothic as a genre. Its author, Charles Robert Maturin, was a Protestant clergyman from Dublin and a writer of novels and plays. *Melmoth* is one of the most macabre and bizarre of all Gothic novels from the period, with frequent grotesque scenes and a very complex narrative structure.

Maturin struggled for money and, in his preface to *Melmoth*, claims to have resorted regretfully to the Gothic romance in an attempt to find popularity with the public at a time when the Gothic was seeing a late resurgence. But given the exuberance and relish with which *Melmoth* is written, it seems likely Maturin was being disingenuous. In truth, he had an affinity for the Gothic and had been writing in the vein for some years. Impoverished though he was, it is doubtful that he would ever have considered compromising his vision to meet the public taste; he wished to outdo in extremity the Gothic tales of earlier writers such as Ann Radcliffe and Matthew Lewis.

Melmoth has a complex structure consisting of nested narratives. Through manuscript and eyewitness accounts that are tortuous and labyrinthine, the novel unfolds the story of the eponymous Wanderer's Satanic bargain. Melmoth has pledged his soul to Satan in return for unnatural longevity, and he can only save himself if he is able to find someone willing to take his place. He attempts to corrupt those

Sebastian Melmoth the Wanderer

After being released in 1897 from two years of imprisonment for "gross indecency," Oscar Wilde, Victor Maturin's grand-nephew, exiled himself to France and took the name "Sebastian Melmoth," after the third-century Saint Sebastian and the title character in Maturin's *Melmoth the Wanderer*. He explained this choice of surname and commented on Maturin's novel in a letter to Louis Wilkinson:

"A fantastic name," he had called it in an earlier letter, "but I shall explain it to you some day."

"You asked me," he wrote later, "about 'Melmoth.' Of course I have not changed my name: in Paris I am as well known as in London: it wd. be childish.

"But to prevent postmen having fits—I sometimes have my letters inscribed with the name of a curious novel by my grand-uncle, Maturin: a novel that was part of the romantic revival of the early century—and though imperfect—a pioneer—: it is still read in France and Germany: Bentley republished it some years ago. I laugh at it, but it thrilled Europe—and is still played as a play in modern Spain." (Wilkinson 1914, 138)

Matt Cardin

Source: Wilkinson, Louis. 1914. "Oscar Wilde: Some Hitherto Unpublished Letters of the Last Phase." In *The Forum*, vol. 51, 130–139. New York and London: Mitchell Kennerley.

in great mortal suffering, but ultimately fails to do so. As allegory the novel is opaque and confused, but this only increases its imaginative power.

In *Melmoth*, Maturin brings together the poetics of Gothic extremity and the comic and skeptical tradition of Enlightenment satire. The effect of this is to make of the Gothic a critical mode. *Melmoth* is not a novel that, as most works of the high Gothic period do, confirms the status quo, but is instead one that mockingly and perversely questions it.

In light of this, it is ironic that most contemporary reviews of the novel were critical of Maturin's use of what they viewed as a worn-out Gothic mode. They also criticized the novel's perceived excesses, particularly as these were felt inappropriate given Maturin's role as a clergyman. One reviewer, John Wilson Crocker, in the *Quarterly Review* of January 1821, even went so far as to accuse Maturin of nonsense, lack of veracity, blasphemy, brutality, and "dark, cold-blooded, pedantic *obscenity*" (Crocker 1821, 311). At the same time, many critics were led to acknowledge, however grudgingly, Maturin's eloquence and skill. The reviewer in *Blackwood's Magazine* of November 1820, after rebuking Maturin for "copying the worst faults of his predecessors and contemporaries, in the commonest works of fictitious writing," claimed that "Maturin is gifted with a genius as fervently powerful as it is distinctly original" and called him "one of the most genuine masters of the dark romance" (Anonymous 1820, 161, 168).

In England *Melmoth* fell into obscurity after Maturin's death in poverty in 1824. There were some attempts to revive his reputation in Ireland during the nineteenth century, but it was not until the 1890s that the novel was reprinted, along with a memoir of Maturin for which Oscar Wilde and his mother, who was Maturin's niece by marriage, provided some biographical insights. Later, when Wilde left Reading Gaol to head to Paris to die, he took on the name "Sebastian Melmoth" in melancholy tribute to his great-uncle's creation.

But in France, where Maturin's play *Bertram* (1816) had been a popular success in translation, *Melmoth* had a much more sympathetic reception. The novel was translated into French in 1821 and was hailed as a classic of the Romantic sublime. Honoré de Balzac praised it as one of the most important works of the Romantic Gothic, and even wrote a satire based on its central conceit. The poet Charles Baudelaire saw Maturin not as a Romantic, but as a modern whose work demonstrated the demonic perversity of modernity. The strange poetic novel *The Songs of Maldoror*, by the self-styled Comte de Lautréamont, contains clear allusions to *Melmoth*. And André Breton, founder of Surrealism, thought it the greatest of all Gothic novels. The reputation of this odd and initially overlooked novel has only continued to rise since.

Timothy J. Jarvis

See also: Baudelaire, Charles; Gothic Hero/Villain; Lewis, Matthew Gregory; Radcliffe, Ann; Romanticism and Dark Romanticism; *The Songs of Maldoror* (*Les Chants de Maldoror*); Surrealism.

Further Reading

Anon. 1820. "Review of *Melmoth the Wanderer*." *Blackwood's Magazine* VIII: 160–168. https://babel.hathitrust.org/cgi/pt?id=mdp.39015030603925;view=1up;seq=9.

Crocker, John Wilson. 1821. "*Melmoth, the Wanderer*, by the Author of Bertram." *Quarterly Review* XXIV: 303–311.

Sage, Victor. 2000. Introduction to *Melmoth the Wanderer* by Charles Robert Maturin, vii–xxix. London: Penguin.

METCALFE, JOHN (1891–1965)

William John Metcalfe was an English writer who is best known for his macabre and supernatural horror stories. His best stories often present puzzles whose only solutions lead to additional puzzles accompanied by greater narrative unease.

His father, William Charles Metcalfe, was a successful writer of sea stories who imbued his son with a love of the sea. John Metcalfe matriculated at the University of London and received a degree in philosophy, taught in Paris, worked as a schoolmaster in London, and moved to the United States in 1928 to work as a barge captain in New York while writing. His early one-act play *T'Strike* (1921) uses English regional dialect to good effect to discuss the sociopolitical issues of his day, but although several stories in his first collection, *The Smoking Leg, and Other Stories* (1925) likewise use dialect, explicit discussions of politics are largely eschewed as Metcalfe concentrates on the horrors that can erupt from bizarre situations as well as exploring potentially horrific issues involving confusions of space and time. The titular story, first published in 1925, involves a cursed ruby implanted in a sailor's leg; it smokes and emits flames and causes ships to sink, but removing it is not an easy affair. "The Bad Lands" (1920) details two men's conviction that a remote house in the dunes and the surrounding countryside are the epitome of concentrated evil, though others see it as merely an old farmhouse; and "The Double Admiral," generally considered one of Metcalfe's best tales, takes another two men, one an admiral, on a journey to see a puzzling island in the distance, but they ultimately encounter themselves, and one of the admirals dies, to be replaced by the other, his doppelgänger.

Poorly chosen relationships and personality issues that resolve themselves horrifically are the subject of *Arm's-Length* (1930), which contains no overt supernaturalism, but *Judas, and Other Stories* (1931) again offers superior supernatural horrors: "Mortmain," set in the same areas as "The Double Admiral," concerns a haunting, with ghostly ships and horrible carrion moths. Religion plays a role in "Mr. Meldrum's Mania," in which Mr. Meldrum gradually and inexplicably becomes the Egyptian deity Thoth, and religious faith is depicted in "Time-Fuse," in which an elderly believer in spiritualism handles hot coals until her faith is destroyed, at which point she perishes horribly. "Funeral March of a Marionette" has grown dated and contains no supernatural horrors, but the central conceit—boys substitute a body for the effigy of Guy Fawkes—remains grotesquely effective. The titular boy in *Brenner's Boy* (1932) may not have been a guest in Winter's house, for his father insists that the boy is sick and never left home, but Winter's wife and friends saw something, even if he does not appear in photographs.

Following the Second World War, Metcalfe was unable to find an English publisher for his third collection of horrific stories, and he submitted them to August Derleth's Arkham House, but Derleth chose to publish only the longest, *The Feasting Dead* (1954). It is the story of a haunting, in which Colonel Hapgood's son Denis, for a while a guest in France, becomes oddly connected with Raoul Privache, perhaps a gardener or a servant, who follows him upon his return to England. The development, which involves psychic vampirism, possession, and utterly reprehensible human behavior, is horrible and disturbing. Additional horrific stories by Metcalfe exist in collections, but there is no comprehensive collection of Metcalfe's work readily available.

Richard Bleiler

See also: Arkham House; Derleth, August.

Further Reading

Dalby, Richard. 1985. "John Metcalfe." In *Supernatural Fiction Writers: Fantasy and Horror*, edited by E. F. Bleiler, 597–602. New York: Charles Scribner's Sons.

Dziemianowicz, Stefan. 2005. "Metcalfe, [William] John." In *Supernatural Literature of the World: An Encyclopedia*, edited by S. T. Joshi, 802–803. Westport, CT: Greenwood.

Metcalfe, John. 1998. *Nightmare Jack and Other Stories*, edited by Richard Dalby. Ashcroft, Canada: Ash-Tree Press.

Wilson, Neil. 2000. *Shadows in the Attic: A Guide to British Supernatural Fiction 1820–1950*. Boston Spa and London: British Library.

MEYRINK, GUSTAV (1868–1932)

Born Gustav Meyer, the Austrian writer Gustav Meyrink is best known for his supernatural fiction, most especially his novel *The Golem* (1914; first published in German as *Der Golem*). Other noteworthy works include *Das gruene Gesicht* (The Green Face) 1916), *Walpurgisnacht* (Walpurgis Night) (1917), and *Der Engel vom westlichen Fenster* (The Angel of the West Window) (1927).

Meyrink's supernatural fiction is permeated by philosophical uncertainty about religious faith. According to Meyrink, when he was twenty-four his suicide attempt was interrupted by the sudden appearance beneath his door of a pamphlet about the afterlife. He attributed to this incident the beginning of his intense interest in the occult; from that age on, he was an avid student of Western hermetic traditions and Eastern religions. He co-founded a financial company in 1889, and in 1902 he was arrested on charges that he was committing fraud by spiritualistic means. Thereafter, Meyrink was compelled to publish fiction and translations in order to make ends meet.

In general, Meyrink's fiction is characterized by a strong sense of place. Ordinary events are treated as only superficial indications of a more profound spiritual reality that is incomprehensible to unenlightened human beings. Very often, the narrator's experiences form not so much a coherent narrative with a clear plotline as a gathering of seemingly unrelated events that, when scanned for occult significance, reveal telling coincidences and similarities. So the reader of Meyrink's fiction undergoes a vicarious initiation into deeper mysteries, whose reality lies beyond the confines of the story or novel. In 2012 a high-profile collection of esoteric and spiritual literature, the Ritman Library in Amsterdam, also known as the Bibliotecha Philosophica Hermetica, held an exhibition devoted to Meyrink and his works.

Michael Cisco

See also: The Golem; *Part Two, Themes, Topics, and Genres*: Occult Fiction.

Further Reading

Irwin, Robert. 1995. "Gustav Meyrink and His Golem." In *The Golem* by Gustav Meyrink, translated by Mike Mitchell, 15–20. Monroe, OR: Dedalus.

Mitchell, Mike. 2008. *Vivo: The Life of Gustav Meyrink*. UK: Dedalus.

van den Berg, Erik. 2012. "Profile: Gustav Meyrink." Ritman Library/Bibliotheca Philosophica Hermetica, December 17. http://www.ritmanlibrary.com/2012/12/chotverdori-aschubliv.

MIÉVILLE, CHINA (1972–)

China Miéville is an award-winning British writer whose work combines elements of fantasy, science fiction, magic realism, and horror. Miéville studied social anthropology at Cambridge and earned a PhD in International Relations at the London School of Economics. A Marxist, Miéville brings a critique of contemporary capitalism into most of his work. A prolific as well as successful writer, Miéville has produced ten novels, two novellas, three short story collections, three comic books, one illustrated children's book, and three works of nonfiction.

Miéville sets his work in imaginary and often bleak or dystopic places. Three novels, *Perdido Street Station* (2000), *The Scar* (2002), and *Iron Council* (2004), form the Bas-Lag Series and explore the imagined city of New Crobuzon, where magic and technology mix in a futuristic steampunk universe (steampunk being the popular science fiction subgenre that imagines an alternate history and/or future and/or postapocalyptic world where technological evolution has been centered in nineteenth-century industrial steam-powered technology instead of electrical and digital technology). *Un Lun Dun* (2008) is a young adult novel. *Embassytown* (2011) is a science fiction novel set on a different planet, and describes the interactions of human colonists and intelligent aliens. Miéville continued to explore imagined places in *The City & The City* (2009), where two cities share the same physical space, but citizens of each city are not permitted to acknowledge the existence of the other. Miéville sets a crime narrative in this world of denial and rejection that serves as a metaphor of contemporary urban life. He continued to mix narrative styles and genres in his later novels: *Kraken* (2010) is a mystery novel in which a preserved body of a giant squid disappears from the London Museum of Natural History, and members of the Church of Kraken Almighty, who believe that the giant squid is God, are suspected. In *Railsea* (2012), a young adult novel based, very loosely, on *Moby Dick*, the captain and crew of an undersea train hunt a gigantic mole.

Miéville calls his writing "weird fiction," a genre of the fantastic that deliberately juxtaposes itself with the traditional high fantasy of such writers as J. R. R. Tolkien and C. S. Lewis by focusing on disruptions of reality and a sense of strangeness and surrealism. He is also associated with the "new weird" movement, in which the boundaries of fantasy, science fiction, and horror are blurred in stories characterized by urban settings, body horror, subversive social criticism, and a metaphysical and/or existential sense of strangeness and unease. His manipulation of genres and creation of dark futures make him one of the most significant writers working in genre fiction today.

Miéville has received numerous awards for his work. *Perdido Street Station* won the 2001 Arthur C. Clarke and British Fantasy awards. *The Scar* won the 2003

British Fantasy and Locus awards. *Iron Council* won the 2005 Arthur C. Clarke and Locus awards. *Un Lun Dun* won the 2008 Locus Award for Best Young Adult Book. *The City & The City* won the 2010 Arthur C. Clarke, Hugo, and World Fantasy awards. Miéville has been a guest of honor at numerous conventions and conferences, including Eastercon (the annual convention of the British Science Fiction Association) and the Society for the Fantastic in the Arts conference. In 2015 he became a Fellow of Britain's Royal Society of Literature.

Jim Holte

See also: New Weird; Surrealism.

Further Reading

Gordon, Joan. 2003. "Reveling in Genre: An Interview with China Miéville." *Science Fiction Studies* 30, no. 3: 355–373. http://www.depauw.edu/sfs/interviews/mievilleinterview .htm.

"Gothic Politics: A Discussion with China Miéville." 2008. *Gothic Studies* 10, no. 1: 61–70.

Williams, Mark. 2010. "Weird of Globalization: Esemplastic Power in the Short Fiction of China Miéville." *Irish Journal of Gothic Studies* 8 (June 14). https://irishgothichorror .files.wordpress.com/2016/04/ijghsissue8.pdf.

THE MIND PARASITES

Often discussed as a work of science fiction, Colin Wilson's *The Mind Parasites* (1967) strays from a stereotypical understanding of vampires as haematophagic (blood eating), but is very much a vampire story of stolen human autonomy, of psycho-emotive parasitism. Part of the vanguard of modern American vampire fiction, it sits alongside generic dominants such as the suburban mass infection in Richard Matheson's *I Am Legend* (1954) and the solipsistic self-reflection in Anne Rice's *Interview with the Vampire* (1976).

The central protagonist, archaeologist Professor Gilbert Austin, discovers that, in parallel with the growth of modern industrialism since the late eighteenth century,

Colin Wilson (1931–2013) was not just a novelist who sometimes wrote science fiction verging into horror, but a controversial intellectual and authorial dynamo whose ideas and books about a multitude of subjects, from the occult and paranormal to crime, philosophy, psychology, sexuality, history, and more, earned him an enthusiastic following even as it exiled him for most of his career from conventionally respectable intellectual and literary society. In both *The Mind Parasites* and another novel, *The Philosopher's Stone* (1969), he borrowed from and responded to the literary and philosophical world of H. P. Lovecraft to lay out some of his own ideas on the nature of consciousness and the enemies to humanity's full flourishing that may lie within people's very psyches.

Matt Cardin

humans have been cultivated as food for Mind Parasites, "alien intelligences, whose aim is either to destroy the human race or enslave it" (Wilson 2005, 113). These intelligences are variously referred to as "energy vampires" (52), "vampire bats of the soul" (71), "Great Old Ones" (36), and "Tsathogguans" (8) (these last two overtly influenced by H. P. Lovecraft's Cthulhu Mythos). *The Mind Parasites* has a horror pedigree born from a challenge to write a Lovecraftian tale issued by August Derleth, publisher and anthologist of Lovecraft's works.

Prior to *The Mind Parasites*, Wilson wrote about the effects of social dislocation through discussion of literary, artistic, and cultural figures ranging from Dostoyevsky to Van Gogh and Albert Camus in *The Outsider* (1956), first in a series of seven non-fiction texts that, over the subsequent decade, demonstrated a New Existentialist philosophical curiosity that fed into his fiction. This reflection upon disarticulation is, in *The Mind Parasites*, intensified by an exploitation of contemporary pre–moon landing unknowns surrounding space travel and alien antagonists, which caught popular imagination in the 1950s and 1960s.

The manipulation of humanity by unknown aliens positions horror in *The Mind Parasites* as holistic: what affects mind affects body, and what affects one affects all, within a narrative informed by the ideas of the eighteenth- and nineteenth-century German philosopher Edmund Husserl (who established the field of phenomenology, focused on investigating the first-person viewpoint of conscious experience), and also the idea of the collective unconscious as elaborated by the twentieth-century Swiss psychologist Carl Jung. Wilson thematically ranges across philosophy, psychology, academia, politics, and drug use, and yet his use of the human mind as a tangible space wherein terrible beasts dwell follows a straightforward overcoming-the-monster plot arc. These vampires channel humans toward a state of malleable pessimism: those who lack "the mental discipline to resist" (54) are a source of energy; those who challenge are destroyed. Unwilling to relinquish parasitic control, these aliens mount increasingly vicious attacks on the inner space of Austin and his fellow intellectual fighters, until their ultimate defeat. Wilson enhances this generic pastiche with Lovecraftian prose in which Austin apologizes for lacking erudition and resorting to conventional linguistic tropes employed in horror fiction, such as mental instability, slavery, grotesquerie, and glimpsed shadowy figures, in a bid to impress upon readers the concept that horror comes from a lack of foundation or meaning.

Jillian Wingfield

See also: Cthulhu Mythos; Derleth, August; *I Am Legend*; *Interview with the Vampire*; Vampires.

Further Reading

Lachman, Gary. 2016. *Beyond the Robot: The Life and Work of Colin Wilson*. New York: Tarcher.

Tredell, Nicolas. 1982. "Arrows to the Farther Shore: *The Mind Parasites* and *The Philosopher's Stone*." *The Novels of Colin Wilson*, 97–116. London and Totowa, NJ: Vision and Barnes & Noble.
Wilson, Colin. [1967] 2005. *The Mind Parasites*. Rhinebeck, NY: Monkfish.

MISERY

Misery is a horror/thriller novel by the American novelist Stephen King. Published in 1987, it was the first winner of the Bram Stoker Award for best novel. Often considered King's most autobiographical work, the novel centers on issues of authorship and the struggle for creative autonomy.

Misery is focused on two characters: the best-selling author Paul Sheldon and his obsessive fan Annie Wilkes. At the novel's opening, Paul has recently completed the final volume in a series of Gothic romances that has made his name, but that he regards as a barrier to creative fulfillment. Having killed off his heroine, Misery Chastaine, Paul sets off on a celebratory cross-country drive in inclement weather. He is carrying the only extant copy of his manuscript. Along the way he crashes his car and is rescued by Annie, who, upon his waking, professes herself his "number-one fan." Her ministrations, which initially seem benign, if odd, soon turn sinister once Annie reads Paul's manuscript. She is enraged at Misery's death and embarks on a regime of physical and psychological torture in order to coerce Paul into resurrecting her beloved character. The bulk of the novel concerns Paul's attempts to survive Annie's brutality while struggling with his own authorial anxieties.

Kathy Bates won an Oscar for her portrayal of Annie in Rob Reiner's 1990 adaptation of the novel. The film has become famous for the "hobbling" scene, in which Annie breaks Paul's ankles with a sledgehammer. Despite the scene's notoriety, it is actually toned down from the original, in which Annie amputates Paul's foot with an axe. In recent years *Misery* has been adapted for the theater by William Goldman (who also wrote the screenplay for the film). In 2012 the play moved to Broadway, where the role of Paul was played by Bruce Willis.

Paul and Annie's conflict is a microcosmic representation of the writing industry, where success breeds creative constraint and demanding fans reject deviation from type. Numerous critics have, therefore, associated the character of Paul with his creator. In the 1980s King was at the peak of his popularity as a horror writer. But in 1984 he had published *The Eyes of the Dragon*, a whimsical fantasy that stepped well outside of his usual fictional range. His fans' hostile response to this novel is seen by some as the genesis for *Misery*, in which the physical entrapment within Annie's cabin is a literal enactment of the confinement within genre boundaries that both Paul Sheldon and Stephen King experienced.

Together with *The Dark Half* (1989) and "Secret Window, Secret Garden" (1990), *Misery* forms a metafictional "trilogy" focusing on "writers and writing and that strange no-man's land between what's real and what's make believe" (King 1990, 237).

Despite his returning repeatedly to the figure of the writer in more recent years, *Misery* remains King's most potent and sophisticated reflection on the craft.

Neil McRobert

See also: Bram Stoker Award; Frame Story; King, Stephen.

Further Reading

Berkenkamp, Lauri. 1992. "Reading, Writing and Interpreting: Stephen King's *Misery*." In *The Dark Descent: Essays Defining Stephen King's Horrorscape*, edited by Tony Magistrale, 203–211. Westport, CT: Greenwood Press.

King, Stephen. 1990. *Four Past Midnight*. New York: Viking.

Magistrale, Anthony. 1989. "Art versus Madness in Stephen King's *Misery*." In *The Celebration of the Fantastic: Selected Papers from the Tenth Anniversary International Conference on the Fantastic in the Arts*, edited by Donald E. Morse, Marshall B. Tymn, and Csilla Bertha, 271–278. Westport, CT: Greenwood Press.

McRobert, Neil. 2013. "Figuring the Author in Modern Gothic Writing." In *The Gothic World*, edited by Glennis Byron and Dale Townshend, 297–308. New York: Routledge.

THE MONK

The Monk: A Romance largely shaped the course of the Gothic tradition in both the 1790s and subsequent decades, entering into conversation with its contemporaries and initiating new literary conversations. It is still considered to be one of the most shocking and graphic Gothic works. Written by the nineteen-year-old Matthew Gregory Lewis (known throughout his life as "Monk" Lewis), who claimed to have written it in ten weeks, it was published in five editions during his life, the first published anonymously in 1796. The second, published later in the same year, proudly bore his name and position as a member of Parliament (MP). Despite its popularity, it caused scandal for its graphic violence and sexual content, as well as its commentary on religion. Subsequent editions attempted to address these controversies, the fourth featuring the most evidence of self-censorship and, as a result, being the least interesting to scholars. All critical editions are based on the first edition.

The novel revolves around the young monk, Ambrosio, whose life of seclusion and asceticism fails to protect him from his own desires, incited when his faithful novice reveals him/herself to be a woman in disguise, Matilda. When she saves his life, he not only allows her to stay but to seduce him and guide him into a satanic pact to gain access to a more pure and innocent woman, Antonia. This constitutes the main plot but, like most Gothic novels of the period, it features several side plots. The second, and almost equally prominent, introduces Agnes, the sister of Antonia's suitor, Lorenzo, and a nun within Ambrosio's sister convent, who has been promised to religion by her family. When Ambrosio catches her with a note from her lover, Raymond (Lorenzo's best friend), he discovers that she is pregnant

Ambrosio's fate at the end of *The Monk* is fully as "extreme" as the rest of Lewis's novel, and serves as an appropriate capstone for a book brimming with garish extremes of wanton sin and horror. This involves a memorable appearance by Lucifer in Ambrosio's prison cell:

> A blaze of lightning flashed through the Cell; and in the next moment, borne upon sulphurous whirl-winds, Lucifer stood before him a second time. But He came not, as when at Matilda's summons He borrowed the Seraph's form to deceive Ambrosio. He appeared in all that ugliness, which since his fall from heaven had been his portion: His blasted limbs still bore marks of the Almighty's thunder: A swarthy darkness spread itself over his gigantic form: His hands and feet were armed with long Talons: Fury glared in his eyes, which might have struck the bravest heart with terror. (Lewis 1845, 124)

Then Ambrosio signs his soul over to Lucifer in exchange for being rescued from human punishment. His fate is far worse than the Inquisition could have managed:

> He [the Daemon] released the sufferer. headlong fell the Monk through the airy waste; The sharp point of a rock received him; and He rolled from precipice to precipice, till bruised and mangled He rested on the river's banks . . . The Sun now rose above the horizon; Its scorching beams darted full upon the head of the expiring Sinner. Myriads of insects were called forth by the warmth; They drank the blood which trickled from Ambrosio's wounds . . . The Eagles of the rock tore his flesh piecemeal, and dug out his eye-balls with their crooked beaks . . . six miserable days did the Villain languish. (127)

Matt Cardin

Source: Lewis, Matthew. [1796] 1845. *The Monk.* New York: Moore & Jackson.

and hands her over to the prioress, Mother St. Ursula, who punishes her by faking her death and entombing her alive within the catacombs.

It is easy to see how religion, sexuality, and gender stand out as prominent themes throughout the novel. Set in seventeenth-century Spain, Lewis's text is safely distanced from his own time and place, but it was clearly influenced by the violence of the French Revolution, discussions of the slave trade, and attitudes toward homosexuality at the time. Further, it demonstrates the evils of Catholicism characteristic of the Gothic and features a series of both tyrannical and pure women, culminating in the shape-shifting Matilda. Ambrosio, embracing his pact with the devil, murders Antonia's mother and fakes Antonia's death in order to fully possess and rape her, an act that culminates in her death and his arrest by the Inquisition. When word of what Mother St. Ursula has done reaches the people of Madrid, the crowd riots and tramples her in one of the most graphic scenes in Romantic literature: an act of the people against oppression. Agnes is found clutching the corpse of her baby, and Ambrosio, facing death, allows Matilda to entice him once more to sell his soul, an act that initiates his death and ends the novel. A short list of further side plots includes folkloric figures like the wandering Jew and the bleeding nun, encounters with bandits, family tyrannies, and incest.

The Monk was both inspired by and inspired other forms of literature. Lewis drew heavily on shorter texts, many of which he translated and stitched together with his own graphic twist. He admitted to being strongly influenced by Horace Walpole's *The Castle of Otranto* (1764), William Godwin's *Caleb Williams* (1794), and Ann Radcliffe's *The Mysteries of Udolpho* (1794), the last of which is often discussed in opposition to Lewis's novel as examples of female and male Gothic. Whereas Radcliffe's novels feature scenes of terror and the explained supernatural, Lewis's supernatural is real, and it leads to the graphic scenes of horror for which he is known. Radcliffe answered Lewis's novel with another of her own, *The Italian* (1797). *The Monk* incited a series of adaptations in the form of dramas, pantomimes, poems, and chapbooks. But growing interest in Gothic literature by women has drawn attention to the prominent rewriting of *The Monk*: *Zofloya* (1806), by Charlotte Dacre, referred to by some scholars as the "female monk" for her open idealization of the author. *Zofloya* features the same level of graphic gender and sexual engagement, with the added shock of its female authorship. Despite harsh criticism from reviewers such as Coleridge, Lewis's novel also inspired canonical writers, such as Lord Byron, Percy Bysshe Shelley, and Sir Walter Scott. It was, unsurprisingly, praised by the Marquis de Sade, who much preferred it over Radcliffe's work.

Twenty-first-century readers and scholars hail *The Monk* for its establishment of bold transgressions within institutions and identities, offering critiques of justice, religion, family, and tyranny as well as extensive explorations of morality and desire that would become trademarks of the Gothic tradition. Its use of underground and closed-off spaces creates a rich multilayered and recognizable comment on the dangers of repression and the power of the return of the repressed. It thus offers a keen illustration of claustrophobia in terms of both space and social structures. A novel preoccupied with excess, it presents a villain who is himself victimized by not only the devil and his temptations but the unrealistic expectations of the institutions that hold him in multiple layers of incarceration, making him an unsettlingly easy character with whom to sympathize. The extent to which the social structures within the text have its villains, victims, and monsters allows the Gothic to juxtapose them with the supernatural, exposing pervasive and, as such, invisible sociopolitical injustices. Unnatural repression of desire creates a master/slave relationship that causes rather than prevents damaging perversity. That Lewis offers readers the same enjoyment of excess through his prose creates a tense and uneasy bond between the reader and the novel's characters that would be replicated in subsequent Gothic works.

A renewed consideration of Gothic texts produced during the 1790s and their influences has brought *The Monk* into the twenty-first-century classroom, where its intertextuality has revealed its prominent place within the Romantic literary scene.

The 2013 edition of the novel through Valancourt Press includes an introduction by Stephen King, which outlines the extent to which current writers are also indebted to the vociferously transgressive moves of Lewis's first novel and its championship of horror.

Laura R. Kremmel

See also: The Castle of Otranto; Lewis, Matthew Gregory; *The Mysteries of Udolpho*; Radcliffe, Ann; Romanticism and Dark Romanticism; Terror versus Horror.

Further Reading

Brewer, William D. 2004. "Transgendering in Matthew Lewis's *The Monk*." *Gothic Studies* 6, no. 2: 192–207.

Lewis, Matthew Gregory. [1796] 2004. *The Monk: A Romance*. Edited by D. L. Macdonald and Kathleen Scherf. Ontario: Broadview Press.

Macdonald, D. L. 2000. *Monk Lewis: A Critical Biography*. Toronto: University of Toronto Press.

Miles, Robert. 2000. "Ann Radcliffe and Matthew Lewis." In *A Companion to the Gothic*, edited by David Punter, 41–57. Oxford: Blackwell.

"THE MONKEY'S PAW"

"The Monkey's Paw" is a short story by W. W. Jacobs (William Wymark Jacobs, 1863–1943), first published in the September 1902 issue of *Harper's* magazine and included in his collection *Our Lady of the Barge* that same year. Inspired by the tale of Aladdin and the magic lamp from *The Arabian Nights*, the story is about how people who interfere with fate do so to their sorrow. The theme is summed up in the epigram: Be careful what you wish for, you may receive it.

Sergeant-Major Morris, recently returned from India, visits the White family bearing the eponymous talisman, which he claims is cursed. It can grant three wishes, but greed clouds the holder's head. Its previous owner used his third wish to ask for death. Mr. White rescues the mummified paw from the fire after Morris attempts to destroy it. The wish for £200 to clear their debts is satisfied when their son Herbert is mangled by a machine the next day. Their second wish is for Herbert to be alive again. Herbert returns that night and, although his appearance is not described, his mother's actions in barricading the door against him indicate what a monster he must be. Mr. White's third wish is for Herbert to be dead again.

Although "The Monkey's Paw" is often cited as an example of great American literature, the author was born and lived in England all his life. The story is something of a departure for Jacobs, who wrote primarily humorous and satirical stories or seafaring tales. His early works were praised by the likes of Henry James, G. K. Chesterton, and Christopher Morley.

The story has had a pervasive influence on twentieth-century fiction and film, and it has been widely anthologized, including in literature textbooks widely used in American public schools. It was performed as a one-act play in 1907, has been filmed numerous times (as early as 1933), was adapted for an episode of *The Alfred Hitchcock Hour* in 1965, and provided the inspiration for works as diverse as operas, rock music lyrics, *Pet Sematary* by Stephen King, and episodes of the TV programs *The Monkees* and *The Simpsons*.

Bev Vincent

See also: Dark Fantasy; Forbidden Knowledge or Power.

Further Reading

Chesterton, G. K. 1953. "W. W. Jacobs." In *A Handful of Authors: Essays on Books and Writers*, edited by Dorothy Collins, 28–35. New York: Sheed and Ward.
Dziemianowicz, Stefan. 1997. "An Overview of 'The Monkey's Paw'" In *Short Stories for Students*, vol. 2, edited by Kathleen Wilson, 146–159. Detroit, MI: Gale.

MONSTERS

Horror literature and film have a long and productive history of engaging with and using monsters. Much of the early horror narratives drew from mythologies, folklore, and theological tradition, though they were limited by the moral standards of the day, so explicit detail is often vague rather than concrete. Early examples include the appearance of Satan as in Matthew Lewis's *The Monk* (1796), William Beckford's *Vathek* (1786), and Charlotte Dacre's *Zofloya* (1806). The monster narrative as it would be recognized today draws from these mythic, religious, and folkloric influences, and synthesizes these with more modern cultural concerns. Some of the most influential and notable texts in this tradition emerged from British romanticism and, particularly, the summer at the Villa Diodati in 1816 that served as the point of origin for two highly influential monster texts. One is John Polidori's "The Vampyre," which was published in 1819 and became one of the founding texts of modern vampire fiction, presenting the central monster as a romantic and aristocratic figure. The more famous text from 1818, and perhaps the most influential "monster" text in horror, is Mary Shelley's *Frankenstein, or The Modern Prometheus*. Shelley mixes theological and mythic narratives around the creation of humanity with new technological advances in science to create an extremely compelling new monster text. Both of these texts became extremely successful upon publication, spawning a host of theatrical adaptations throughout the 1800s.

The figure of the vampire with its mix of aristocratic hauteur, violence, and simmering eroticism became exceptionally popular throughout the nineteenth century. Key texts include James Malcolm Rymer and Thomas Peckett Prest's 1847 serial *Varney the Vampire* as well as Sheridan La Fanu's *Carmilla* of 1871–1872. These texts solidified the tropes and expectations of the vampire monster, which would reach its high point with the publication of Bram Stoker's *Dracula* in 1897.

Things That Should Not Be

The word "monster" comes from the Latin word *monstrum*, meaning a divine omen, portent, or warning, by way of the French *monstre*, meaning a creature afflicted with a birth defect or biological abnormality. Etymologically, therefore, a monster is a creature that exhibits some abnormality or deformation that serves as a warning or portent of something morally and/or metaphysically amiss. An understanding of this embedded meaning helps to illuminate the monstrosity of zombies (abnormally animated corpses), werewolves (abnormal hybrids of human and beast), vampires (undead bloodsuckers), Frankenstein's monster (a loathsome, animate mass of sewn-together corpse parts), serial killers (normal-looking people concealing murderously deranged psyches), the giant insects of atomic age horror movies (tiny natural creatures enlarged to abnormal proportions and thereby made lethal), and many other such things. In all of these cases, the monster is horrifying because it is, on some level, a "thing that should not be" (as Lovecraft might have put it), an entity that inspires fear and loathing not only, and not even primarily, because of what it does, but because of what it *is*.

Matt Cardin

As products of the cultural anxieties of their time, monsters have been subject to much critical attention as scholars trace their various contexts and analyze how this impacts the monsters of a particular era. The late nineteenth and early twentieth centuries, culturally shocked in the aftermath of Darwin's research on human nature and experiencing cultural change and instability at home and abroad, show a deep preoccupation with degeneration and devolution. This finds expression in a wide range of texts, including Arthur Machen's "The Great God Pan" (1890), Richard Marsh's *The Beetle* (1897), and Robert Louis Stevenson's famous *The Strange Case of Dr. Jekyll and Mr. Hyde* (1886). To become monstrous was to lose one's humanity. In a world where Darwinian evolution had replaced the religious as the source of human subjectivity, a person could become animal or abhuman with terrifying ease. The cultural and social upheaval of the early twentieth century further exacerbated this tendency as exemplified through the weird fiction of H. P. Lovecraft and his so-called Cthulhu Mythos, famously first presented in Lovecraft's short story "The Call of Cthulhu" in 1928.

As the twentieth century developed, historical changes forced change upon the presentation of the monster. The Universal Studios horror films of the 1930s made pop-culture icons out of both Frankenstein's monster and Dracula, with *Frankenstein* (dir. James Whale, 1931) and *Dracula* (dir. Tod Browning, 1931) becoming wildly popular. The performances of both Boris Karloff in *Frankenstein* and Bela Lugosi in *Dracula* created an enduring image of what these monsters were supposed to be, a conception that endures to the present day. The decades that followed featured new monsters as horror responded to new cultural stimuli. The age of the atomic bomb gave rise to new expressions of fear in science fiction–influenced horrors such as *Invasion of the Body Snatchers* (dir. Don Seigel, 1956; based on Jack Finney's 1955 novel *The Body Snatchers*), *Gojira* (dir. Ishirô Honda, 1954; known in the West as Godzilla), and *The Blob* (dir. Irvin Yeaworth, 1958).

As the Cold War ended and youth culture became increasingly important to cinema audiences, a new kind of monster was made: the slasher. Beginning with controversial films such as Michael Powell's *Peeping Tom* (1960), the new monsters were murderous figures that preyed upon the young and the reckless. Notable examples in this genre include *The Texas Chainsaw Massacre* (dir. Tobe Hooper, 1974), *The Last House on the Left* (dir. Wes Craven, 1972), and the *Nightmare on Elm Street* franchise. The slasher genre drew inspiration from director Alfred Hitchcock's 1960 film *Psycho*, often identified as the first slasher film, which was adapted from Robert Bloch's 1960 novel of the same title. Both the novel and the film are centered on the character of Norman Bates, whose twisted psyche makes him a true human monster. Meanwhile, even as this new trend developed, the more traditional monster narratives that drew on religious or spiritual themes became increasingly derivative after the successes of both *Rosemary's Baby* (dir. Roman Polanski, 1968) and *The Exorcist* (dir. William Friedkin, 1973), the former based on Ira Levin's 1967 novel and the latter adapted by William Peter Blatty from his best-selling 1971 novel.

In the late twentieth and early twenty-first centuries, the horror monster as killer was increasingly replaced with the horror of the zombie. Thanks to the success of films such as George A. Romero's *Living Dead* series (1968–2009) and novels such as Max Brooks's *World War Z* (2006), the figure of the zombie has increasingly been seen as a metaphor for the state of subjectivity under late capitalism, articulating a range of fears around race, the spread of disease, and the rise of consumerism. Zombies have become part of modern pop-culture, with Robert Kirkman's *The Walking Dead* comic books spawning a franchise that includes video games and a high-profile television show. Despite the notion that such monster texts may be considered "lowbrow," the zombie has become ubiquitous, suggesting that now, more than ever, there is a desire to experience new monster narratives.

Jon Greenaway

See also: Bloch, Robert; *Carmilla*; Cthulhu Mythos; *Dracula*; *The Exorcist*; "The Great God Pan"; *The Monk*; Mummies; Psychological Horror; *Rosemary's Baby*; *The Strange Case of Dr. Jekyll and Mr. Hyde*; Vampires; *Vathek*; Werewolves; Witches and Witchcraft; Zombies.

Further Reading

Asma, Stephen T. 2009. *On Monsters: An Unnatural History of Our Worst Fears*. Oxford: Oxford University Press.

Hogle, Jerrold E. 2014. *The Cambridge Companion to the Modern Gothic*. Cambridge: Cambridge University Press.

Skal, David J. 1994. *The Monster Show: A Cultural History of Horror*. London: Penguin Books.

MOORE, ALAN (1953–)

While he has produced short stories, novels, poetry and other, more difficult to classify literary and performance pieces, English writer, occultist, and magician Alan Moore is best known for his work in comic books and graphic novels. Moore is among the most important comics writers of the last half-century, having exerted an incalculable influence not only over that medium, but also over Anglo-American popular culture broadly since the 1980s. Moore often works in, around, and through the horror genre, and his work was crucial to the turn toward darker themes and Gothic aesthetics that spread through the world of British and American comics in the 1980s and 1990s. Many of Moore's fictions, both sequential art and literary, contain elements of supernatural horror.

Moore's darkly toned work with British independent comics magazines *Warrior* and *2000 AD* led to his assignment to work on DC's then fairly formulaic monster-focused series, *Saga of the Swamp Thing*. Moore scripted it from 1983 to 1987 to tremendous acclaim, contributing to a renewed popular interest in horror comics that would lead DC to create their new mature-readers imprint, Vertigo, which would publish some of the most important horror and fantasy titles of the late 1980s and 1990s, including Swamp Thing spin-off *Hellblazer* and Neil Gaiman's *Sandman*. Moore's work on *Swamp Thing* drew on his interest in American Gothic literature and folklore, flirting with a "monster of the month" approach while creating more complex narrative arcs. It fused classical horror tropes and monsters including werewolves and vampires with psychedelic science fictional concepts reminiscent of some of Philip K. Dick's darker moments and anticipatory of the approach taken by the 1990s TV series *The X-Files*. Moore would push his interest in complexly structured and maddeningly paranoid plots far further in the Victorian Gothic series *From Hell* (serialized 1989–1996, collected 1999), illustrated by Eddie Campbell. Combining horror and historical metafiction, this reimagining of the Jack the Ripper murders remains among the most ambitious graphic novels ever created, and was instrumental in the surge of popular interest in neo-Victorian Gothic fiction that continues to this day. It was adapted to film by the Hughes brothers in 2001.

Among Moore's many influences, none has been more important to his horror-focused work than H. P. Lovecraft, and Moore has contributed much to the resurgence of interest that Lovecraft's work experienced in the twenty-first century. Moore wrote many overtly Lovecraftian stories in the 1990s, some of which are now lost, but some of which are assembled in the collection *Yuggoth Cultures* (2003). He contributed a story titled "The Courtyard" to D. M. Mitchell's collection *The Starry Wisdom* (1994), subsequently using it as the basis for his horror comic limited series *Neonomicon* (2010–2011, illustrated by Jacen Burrows). Most recently, Moore has continued to draw extensively on Lovecraft's life and writings for the limited series *Providence* (2015–2016, also with Burrows).

Sean Moreland

See also: Dick, Philip K.; Gaiman, Neil; Lovecraft, H. P.

Further Reading

Di Liddo, Annalisa. 2009. *Alan Moore: Comics as Performance, Fiction as Scalpel*. Jackson: University Press of Mississippi.

Green, Matthew J. A. 2013. *Alan Moore and the Gothic Tradition*. Manchester: Manchester University Press.

Parkin, Lance. 2013. *Magic Words: The Extraordinary Life of Alan Moore*. London: Arum Press.

MORRELL, DAVID (1943–)

David Morrell is an American novelist who is perhaps best known for creating the character of John Rambo in his 1972 novel *First Blood*. He has also made contributions to the horror genre. Born in Kitchener, Ontario, Canada, Morrell immigrated to the United States in 1966 to attend Penn State University. While there, he was mentored by the science fiction writer Philip Klass, a.k.a. William Tenn. Under Klass's tutelage, Morrell followed the author's advice to exploit his own fears. Inspired by what he labeled "a waking nightmare," in which he was pursued through a forest by an unseen stalker, Morrell crafted his famous debut, *First Blood*, a seminal novel in the action/adventure/thriller genre.

Since 1972, Morrell has published numerous other novels and novelizations, among them *Last Reveille* (1977), *Testament* (1975), *Blood Oath* (1982), and the best-selling suspense novels *The Brotherhood of the Rose* (1984), *The Fraternity of the Stone* (1985), *The League of Night and Fog* (1987), *The Fifth Profession* (1990), and *The Covenant of the Flame* (1991). Other works include the fantasy *The Hundred Year Christmas* (1983) and thrillers *Assumed Identity* (1993), *Desperate Measures* (1994), *Extreme Denial* (1996), *Double Image* (1998), *Burnt Sienna* (2000), *The Protector* (2003), *Creepers* (2005), *Scavenger* (2009), *The Spy Who Came for Christmas* (2008), *The Shimmer* (2009), *The Naked Edge* (2010), *Murder as a Fine Art* (2013), and *Inspector of the Dead* (2015). *Fireflies*, a touching fictional memoir of the death from cancer of his fifteen-year-old son Matthew, was published in 1988. Since 2007, Morrell has also scripted several stories for Marvel Comics, featuring such classic heroes as Captain America, Spider-Man, and Wolverine.

Although he often explores the horrific in his novels (set pieces and themes in many of his books, especially *First Blood*, *Testament*, and *Creepers*, provide telling examples), only *The Totem* (1979) and *Long Lost* (2002) can be counted as pure works of horror. Inspired by Stephen King's *'Salem's Lot*, *The Totem* had two incarnations, both effective explorations of the zombie/werewolf/vampire and small town horror themes. Published in 1979, the first, slighter version earned a glowing entry in *Horror: 100 Best Books* (1988); a "complete and unaltered" version was published by Donald M. Grant in 1994. *Long Lost* is a horror novel/ghost story that was never really recognized as such. Although Morrell leads with classic revenge and chase motifs, his narrative also includes metaphorical monsters, tombs, and even a haunted house.

Morrell has written some of the most effective short horror of the last several decades. His shorter work has appeared in many major horror anthologies, including the *Whispers*, *Shadows*, *Night Visions*, and *Masters of Darkness* series. A number of these shorter works are showcased in *Black Evening* (1994) and *Nightscape* (2004). *Black Evening* contains stories written from 1972 through 1992, featuring the Bram Stoker Award–winning novellas "The Beautiful Uncut Hair of Graves" and "Orange Is for Anguish, Blue Is for Insanity." *Nightscape* includes many of Morrell's stories written since 1992. The major difference between the two collections is that the majority of the stories in *Black Evening* deal with the supernatural, whereas those appearing in *Nightscape* tend to be more realistic, treating themes of obsession, determination, and individual identity.

Hank Wagner

See also: King, Stephen; Vampires; Werewolves.

Further Reading

"David Morrell." 2016. *Contemporary Authors Online*. Detroit, MI: Gale.

Holt, Erika. 2014. "Author Spotlight: David Morrell." *Nightmare* 26 (November). http://www.nightmare-magazine.com/nonfiction/author-spotlight-david-morrell.

MORRISON, TONI (1931–)

Toni Morrison is one of the most recognized and influential American writers of the twentieth and twenty-first centuries, and in her work, her concern with presenting the African American experience coexists with elements of the supernatural. In interviews, she has emphasized the importance of the relationship between the language of haunting and her explorations of race, gender, memory, and the past.

She was born Chloe Wofford on February 18, 1931, in Lorain, Ohio. Her parents, George and Ramah, were migrants from Southern states. She studied the classics and humanities at Howard University (BA) and Cornell (MA). Her first novel, *The Bluest Eye*, was published in 1970. She has since published ten additional novels. A shortened list of her numerous awards and accolades includes the 1988 Pulitzer Prize, the 1993 Nobel Prize, the Presidential Medal of Freedom (2012), and the 2016 PEN/Saul Bellow Award for Achievement in American Fiction.

Morrison has influenced numerous writers, students, and readers. While she was writing her first novel, she worked at Random House, where she edited manuscripts by African American writers such as Angela Davis, Henry Dumas, and Toni Cade Bambara. She taught at Howard University, Texas Southern, Yale, and is Professor Emeritus at Princeton University.

Many critics note the influence of William Faulkner's Southern Gothic on Morrison's fiction and have suggested possible influences from magical realist writers.

While Morrison has acknowledged these precursors, she emphasizes that her work is grounded in African American culture, history, and literary tradition. In her turn, she has influenced writers such as, to name a few, Gloria Naylor, Amy Tan, and Louise Erdrich to use fiction (often with a supernatural component) to bring attention to elided histories of women and ethnic groups.

She is best known for her masterwork, *Beloved* (1987), an unflinching gaze at the horrors of slavery through a ghost story. In her collection of lectures *Playing in the Dark* (1992), she describes the marginalized and ghostly position of African American characters in American literature by white writers. In her fiction, characters, and sometimes narrators, speak from beyond the grave; living characters who are oppressed and marginalized become liminal presences; and specters appear in the return of the repressed to haunt individuals who have forgotten or are avoiding a traumatic past. Several of Morrison's novels include ghosts of the past, in particular *Song of Solomon* (1977), *Beloved* (1987), *Jazz* (1992), *Paradise* (1997), *Love* (2003), and *Home* (2012). Her play *Desdemona* (2011) gives Shakespeare's character a voice from the space between life and death as she tries to understand the trajectory of her life and her relationships by engaging issues of race and gender not present in *Othello*.

Morrison remains active in the literary and academic communities. Her papers are archived at Princeton University Library.

Melanie R. Anderson

See also: Beloved; Faulkner, William.

Further Reading

Denard, Carolyn C., ed. 2008. *Toni Morrison: Conversations*. Jackson: University Press of Mississippi.

Taylor-Guthrie, Danille K., ed. 1994. *Conversations with Toni Morrison*. Jackson: University Press of Mississippi.

MORROW, W. C. (1854–1932)

William Chambers Morrow was an American writer who wrote horror and science fiction that was popular in its day and has been compared at times to that of Edgar Allan Poe, Nathaniel Hawthorne, Ambrose Bierce, and other classic American horror writers. In 2009 the Library of America chose to include Morrow's 1889 story "His Unconquerable Enemy" in its two-volume retrospective anthology *American Fantastic Tales: Terror and the Uncanny*, effectively canonizing it.

Born in 1854 (although his birthdate was variously given), and raised and educated in Alabama, Morrow moved to California in 1879 and began writing for the San Francisco *Argonaut*, attracting favorable attention from Ambrose Bierce, among others, before joining the staff of William Randolph Hearst's *San Francisco Examiner*. His reputation as a horror writer exists largely because of *The Ape, the Idiot &*

"His Unconquerable Enemy": Revenge Horrific

"His Unconquerable Enemy" was first published in *The Argonaut* in 1889 as "The Rajah's Nemesis" and has been anthologized many times since, making it Morrow's best-known tale. The story is set in India and describes events in the earlier life of the narrator, an unnamed American doctor serving in the court of a local rajah. One of the rajah's servants is Neranya, whose temper leads him to stab a dwarf and who is sentenced to have his arm amputated. The narrator must clean up the messy amputation, but the insanely angry Neranya attempts vengeance on his master and thus has his other arm amputated. When the rajah's only son is found dead, Neranya is implicated and sentenced to be tortured, then killed, but after the doctor pleads for Neranya to have a quick death, the rajah changes his mind and has the doctor amputate Neranya's legs. Thereafter, the rajah keeps the limbless man in an aerial cage in his palace, in a room in which he often sleeps. One night the doctor watches Neranya wriggle his way out of the cage, whose rails are a foot taller than he, land on the sleeping rajah, and, as his dying act, bite the man to death.

Though contemporary readers encountering "His Unconquerable Enemy" for the first time are likely to be annoyed at its cultural clichés—the rajah, for example, possesses a "sense of cruelty purely Oriental" (Morrow 2015, 95)—as well as bothered by the extremely unethical behavior of its narrator, the situations described by Morrow remain vital and increasingly horrific. Furthermore and very ironically, while the rajah's progressive maimings of Neranya are horrible, they are also his undoing: had the rajah not been merciful but followed through with his original plan, his lineage would remain intact, as would his life.

Richard Bleiler

Source: Morrow, W. C. [1889] 2015. "His Unconquerable Enemy." In *In the Shadow of Edgar Allan Poe: Classic Tales of Terror 1816 to 1914*, edited by Leslie S. Klinger, 95–104. New York: Pegasus Books.

Other People (1897), a collection of fourteen stories including "His Unconquerable Enemy." Other notable stories include "The Monster Maker" (first published as "The Surgeon's Experiment" in 1887), "Over an Absinthe Bottle" (first published as "The Pale Dice-Thrower" in 1893), and "An Original Revenge." The first, a work of proto–science fiction, describes a young man, determined to conclude his life, who pays a surgeon $5,000 to kill him; the surgeon has other plans, and these culminate in the discovery of a brainless apelike monster: money can make monsters out of men. The latter two are fantastic: the first is heavily ironic, involving the chance meeting of a starving man and a bank robber, and a game of dice that seems to go well for the former but has a conclusion that owes much to Bierce's "An

Occurrence at Owl Creek Bridge," while the latter involves a haunting carried out as revenge.

In his later books, Morrow largely abandoned overtly horrific narratives, but *A Man: His Mark* (1900), though ostensibly a romance, contains scenes of accident and medical situations that will make a modern reader cringe and shudder. Morrow was a clever writer, unafraid to experiment and explore the ideas inherent in certain situations, and it is to be regretted that he ultimately found the writing of romances to be more lucrative than the writing of horrors.

Richard Bleiler

See also: Mad Scientist; Monsters.

Further Reading

Joshi, S. T. 2004. "W. C. Morrow: Horror in San Francisco." In *The Evolution of the Weird Tale*, 13–17. New York: Hippocampus Press.

Joshi, S. T. 2005. "Morrow, W[illiam] C[hambers]." In *Supernatural Literature of the World: An Encyclopedia*, edited by S. T. Joshi. Westport, CT: Greenwood Press.

Morrow, W. C. 2000. *The Monster Maker and Other Stories*, edited by S. T. Joshi and Stefan Dziemianowicz. Seattle, WA: Midnight House.

Moskowitz, Sam. 1992. "W. C. Morrow: Forgotten Master of Horror—First Phase." In *Discovering Classic Horror Fiction I*, edited by Darrell Schweitzer, 127–173. Mercer Island, WA: Starmont.

"MR. ARCULARIS"

"Mr. Arcularis" is a short story by the Pulitzer Prize–winning American poet, novelist, and short story writer Conrad Aiken. It was first published in *Harper's Magazine* in 1931 and later collected in *The Collected Short Stories of Conrad Aiken* in 1960. It was also chosen by the Library of America to appear in its two-volume retrospective anthology *American Fantastic Tales: Terror and the Uncanny* (2009), a semi-official mark of canonization that recognizes the story as a significant work of American literature in the vein of the fantastic.

Mr. Arcularis—his last name references an arc, and his first name is never given—is sent on a voyage to England following a serious operation, the ship leaving from Boston. It is June, but the weather is unseasonably cold, and he simply cannot get warm. One of his regular dinner companions is Miss Clarice Dean, a lovely young woman with whom he begins a gentle flirtation. He is disturbed to learn that the ship is also transporting a coffin containing a corpse, for such is a bad omen for a voyage, but more disturbing is his recently developed habit of sleepwalking. He shares this news with Miss Dean, along with the disturbing dream that accompanied it, and after another episode sees the ship's doctor for a bromide. The sleepwalking episodes begin to culminate with him awakening near the coffin with his memories slipping, and though he becomes more intimate with

Miss Dean, he is perpetually cold. The operation has failed, and Mr. Arcularis has died on the operating table.

In his introduction to *The Collected Short Stories of Conrad Aiken*, Mark Schorer states that Aiken "moves from the mundane into the mysterious, into hysteria, horror, hallucination, phobia, compulsion, dream, death, and, more often than not, back again into the mundane" (Aiken 1960, viii). Such is a reasonable assessment of the moods of "Mr. Arcularis," for the story is an unsettling combination of explicit detail and dreamlike development. At the same time, despite Aiken's literary skills, "Mr. Arcularis" cannot escape being pigeonholed: it is one of the works akin to Ambrose Bierce's "An Occurrence at Owl Creek Bridge," in which a dying mind attempts to create a narrative that provides an explanation for its passing. Once the conclusion is reached and the surprise revealed, everything falls into place. Its elements become clearer, but it does not transcend its literary inspiration.

Aiken later adapted "Mr. Arcularis" as a play that was first produced in 1949. It was published in 1957 by Harvard University Press as *Mr. Arcularis: A Play*. The play proved popular as material for mid-twentieth-century television: it was produced as an episode of the CBS television drama anthology series *Studio One in Hollywood* in 1956. Other American television productions followed in 1959 (for *ITV Play of the Week*) and 1961 (for *Great Ghost Tales*). A made-for-television movie adaptation of the story aired in West Germany in 1967.

Richard Bleiler

See also: Bierce, Ambrose; Dreams and Nightmares; "Silent Snow, Secret Snow."

Further Reading

Aiken, Conrad. 1960. *The Collected Short Stories of Conrad Aiken*. Cleveland and New York: World Publishing.

Pope, John A. 1957. "Conrad Aiken Revivifies 'Mr. Arcularis." *Harvard Crimson*. Accessed September 5, 2016. http://www.thecrimson.com/article/1957/3/1/conrad-aiken-reviv ifies-mr-arcularis-pin. Originally published in *The Harvard Crimson*, March 1, 1957.

Spivey, Ted R. 1997. "Fictional Descent into Hell." In *Time's Stop in Savannah: Conrad Aiken's Inner Journey*, 91–105. Macon, GA: Mercer University Press.

Tabachnick, Stephen E. 1974. "The Great Circle Voyage of Conrad Aiken's Mr. Arcularis." *American Literature* (January): 590–607.

MUMMIES

A mummy is a corpse of an animal or human preserved either intentionally or unintentionally by exposure to chemicals or extreme temperature and/or humidity. In its role as a character in horror literature, the mummy, like the vampire or zombie, is a revenant, a human being who returns from the dead. All revenants inspire fear as they represent a rupture of the natural and supernatural orders. Like the vampire and the zombie, the mummy also represents an assault on the normal rational world by an unexplained force that must be believed in, studied, and then destroyed before it destroys the modern rational world, usually represented by archaeologists, handsome young men, and beautiful women. The mummy is both ancient and foreign, and its appearance raises concerns about the power of the past, the power of the other, and the fear of incursion of the other.

Although mummification has occurred in China, Europe, and Central and South America, mummies in both fact and fiction are most often associated with Egypt, where mummification was practiced as early as 3400 BCE. Contrary to popular belief, mummification was not a process for royalty only; rather, it was used by most classes of society. Animals, especially pets, were also mummified in ancient Egypt.

Interest in mummies can be traced back to ancient Greece and Rome. In Europe during the Middle Ages (ca. 500–1500 CE), popular belief held that mummified bodies had healing properties, and a brisk trade in medicinal mummified ashes developed. Modern interest in mummies followed Napoleon Bonaparte's conquest of Egypt in 1798. He included a large number of scientists and scholars with his

Some Notable Mummy Fictions

Literary:

1890	"The Ring of Thoth" by Arthur Conan Doyle
1894	"Lot No. 249" by Arthur Conan Doyle
1903	*The Jewel of Seven Stars* by Bram Stoker
1918	*Brood of the Witch Queen* by Sax Rohmer
1938	"Beetles" by Robert Bloch
1947	"The Next in Line" by Ray Bradbury
1989	*The Mummy, or Ramses the Damned* by Anne Rice
1998	*The Sleeper in the Sands* by Tom Holland

Cinematic:

1932	*The Mummy* (the original mummy movies, from Universal Studios, launching a series)
1940	*The Mummy's Hand*
1942	*The Mummy's Tomb*
1944	*The Mummy's Ghost*
1959	*The Mummy* (first in Hammer Horror series)
1964	*The Curse of the Mummy's Tomb*
1966	*The Mummy's Shroud*
1971	*Blood from the Mummy's Tomb*
1999	*The Mummy* (Universal Studios reboot of classic series)

Matt Cardin

forces, and they in turn studied and made popular throughout Europe ancient Egyptian art and artifacts. The result has been termed "Egyptomania," an enthusiasm for all things Egyptian that swept Europe and the United States throughout the nineteenth century.

Two aspects of Egyptomania are important to the development of the mummy as a figure of horror. The first was the craze for mummy unwrapping, which led to the second, the development of mummy fiction. In Europe and the United States, a popular upper-class diversion was an "unwrapping party," in which a host who had purchased a mummy would invite friends for the "unwrapping." Writers soon turned this pastime into fiction.

One of the earliest mummy stories is Edgar Allan Poe's "Some Words with a Mummy" (1845), in which an unwrapped mummy is brought back to life through galvanism (electricity). Although Poe's story is comic, horror would follow. Arthur Conan Doyle, creator of Sherlock Holmes, wrote two mummy short stories, "The Ring of Thoth" (1890) and "Lot No. 249" (1894). In the former Conan Doyle introduces a magician/priest character into the narrative, thus establishing a figure that would become standard in later mummy horror stories. In the latter he creates the first monstrous mummy. Conan Doyle's friend Bram Stoker, best known as the creator of Dracula, published an influential mummy novel, *The Jewel of Seven Stars* (1903), in which Margaret, who is both the daughter of an Egyptologist and a reincarnated Egyptian princess, must reattach her lost mummified hand to the mummy of her former self in order to ensure immortality. In the original novel she fails, but in the 1912 edition she succeeds and marries the narrator, after which the mummy disappears.

Fact merged with fiction in 1922 when archaeologist John Carter opened the tomb of the Egyptian pharaoh Tutankhamun, popularly known as King Tut. The publicity surrounding this event, along with a now discredited story of a mummy's curse, reignited worldwide Egyptomania. Hollywood did not wait long before cashing in on the excitement. Universal Studios released *The Mummy* in 1932, and the success of that film established the mummy as one of horror's essential characters.

Universal Pictures producer Carl Laemmle, who also produced Universal's *Dracula*, commissioned screenwriter John Balderston, who in a former career as a journalist had reported on the opening of Tutankhamun's tomb, to create a screenplay for the film. The resulting narrative combines elements of "The Ring of Thoth," *The Jewel of Seven Stars*, and the discovery of Tutankhamun's tomb. It proved both a financial and critical success, and it also established the conventions adopted by most mummy films and novels that followed its release: the discovery of a mummy's tomb, the use of ancient scrolls to bring it to life, a curse on the tomb's discoverers, the mummy's revenge, the mummy's discovery of a lost reincarnated love, the invocation of ancient wisdom to combat the mummy, and the eventual destruction of the mummy and the reimposition of Western rationality and order.

Mummy movies rapidly became a thriving subgenre in the burgeoning world of horror and monster cinema. Between 1940 and 1955 Universal released a slew of additional mummy movies: *The Mummy's Hand* (1940), *The Mummy's Tomb* (1942), *The Mummy's Ghost* (1944), and *Abbot and Costello Meet the Mummy* (1955). In England, Hammer Films, which, like Universal, focused on the creation of horror films, released *The Mummy* (1959), *The Curse of the Mummy's Tomb* (1964), *The Mummy's Shroud* (1966), and *Blood from the Mummy's Tomb* (1971). In 1999, after a hiatus of nearly half a century, Universal retuned to making mummy movies with *The Mummy*, starring Brendan Fraser, which adapted the basic elements of the 1932 film for a modern audience, and which was followed by the sequels *The Mummy Returns* (2001) and *The Mummy: Tomb of the Dragon Emperor* (2008), as well as the spin-off *The Scorpion King* (2008), which is not a horror film but rather an adventure comedy employing the conventions of the earlier films.

The mummy has also reappeared in contemporary fiction, most notably in Anne Rice's *The Mummy, or Ramses the Damned* (1989). Rice employed many of the conventions established by the mummy film tradition, but she also made major changes. Her protagonist is not the priest Imhotep, but rather the pharaoh Ramses II, who discovered the secret elixir of eternal life from a Hittite priest and passed that secret on to Cleopatra, who chose death after the suicide of Mark Antony. Ramses falls in love with an Egyptologist's daughter, but when he discovers the mummy of Cleopatra, he attempts to bring her back to life. He succeeds, but Cleopatra is missing parts of her hands and face. The novel ends with her swearing eternal revenge on Ramses. In many ways the character of Ramses is closer to Rice's vampire Lestat from *The Vampire Chronicles* (1976–) than he is to earlier fictive or film vampires, as both creatures are larger than life and caught in immortality.

Jim Holte

See also: Ancestral Curse; *The Jewel of Seven Stars*; Lansdale, Joe R.; "Lot No. 249"; Monsters; Quinn, Seabury; Rice, Anne; Rohmer, Sax; *She*; Vampires; Werewolves.

Further Reading

Curl, James Stevens. 1994. *Egyptomania: The Egyptian Revival: A Recurring Theme in the History of Taste*. Manchester, UK, and New York: Manchester University Press.

Freeman, Richard. 2009. "*The Mummy* in Context." *European Journal of American Studies* 4, no. 1 (Spring). https://ejas.revues.org/7566.

Frost, Brian J. 2008. *The Essential Guide to Mummy Literature*. Lanham, MD: Scarecrow Press.

Luckhurst, Roger. 2012. *The Mummy's Curse: The True History of a Dark Fantasy*. Oxford: Oxford University Press.

"THE MUSIC OF ERICH ZANN"

In his letters, H. P. Lovecraft (1890–1937) wrote that of all his tales, his two favorites remained "The Colour out of Space" (1927) and "The Music of Erich Zann." Written in late 1921 and first published in *National Amateur* in March 1922,

"The Music of Erich Zann" was an early favorite for others as well. It quickly became one of Lovecraft's most popular works, republished twice in *Weird Tales* (May 1925; November 1934), anthologized in Dashiell Hammett's *Creeps by Night* (1931), and becoming the first Lovecraft tale printed in a literature textbook for use in schools: *The Short Story* (1956). More significant than its popularity is that "Zann" represents the seeds of Lovecraft's most enduring themes. It introduces the dream narrative, the forbidden knowledge narrative, and the narrative of cosmic horror—all major themes that would establish Lovecraft's unique contribution to horror literature in later works.

"Zann's" narrator, a once "impoverished student of metaphysics," provides a frame for the story by describing an experience that happened in his past, in an apartment and on a street that he can no longer find: the "Rue d'Auseil" (the name is a poor French construction loosely translatable as "street at the threshold"). The narrator emphasizes that, after an extensive search, he "cannot find the house, the street, or even the locality" (Lovecraft 2005, 15). Dislodging the setting from any verifiable external reality prefigures several of Lovecraft's dream narratives, including the early "Celephaïs" (1922), "The Silver Key" (1926), and "The Dream-Quest of the Unknown Kadath" (1926), in which settings become removed from physical reality and are difficult to reach or regain.

Elusive, forbidden knowledge plays an equally important role in the narrative. Curious about the "haunting" music of Erich Zann—an elderly viol player living in another apartment at the boardinghouse—the narrator slowly befriends Zann, finally convincing him to explain his unique music and his fear of allowing others to hear it. Unwilling to speak of it, Zann frantically scribbles his story in his native German, but as he is committing it to paper, the source of his horror returns. The narrator reports, "suddenly he rose, seized his viol, and commenced to rend the night with the wildest playing I had ever heard," and moments later, "A sudden gust, stronger than the others, caught up the manuscript and bore it toward the window" (Lovecraft 2005, 20). The papers are swallowed up by the horror outside the window, all explanation (and proof) lost forever. This theme of lost documents and forbidden and obscure knowledge would become a major theme of Lovecraft's work, most notably in the many stories referencing the dreaded *Necronomicon*.

The most powerful theme concerns the source of the horror itself, glimpsed by the narrator as he looks out the open window in Zann's apartment. He relates: "I saw no city spread below, and no friendly lights gleaming from remembered streets, but only the blackness of space illimitable; unimagined space alive with motion and music, and having no semblance to anything on earth" (Lovecraft 2005, 22). Confronting this dark and alien infinite, the narrator bolts from the apartment. While no physical embodiment of an alien other presents itself (as in later Lovecraft tales), the horror of the cosmic void—Lovecraft's most profound contribution to the genre—is presented starkly and memorably here.

Mark Wegley

See also: "The Colour out of Space"; Forbidden Knowledge or Power; Frame Story; Lovecraft, H. P.; Lovecraftian Horror; Pulp Horror; *Weird Tales.*

Further Reading

Airaksinen, Timo. 1999. "Fighting Nothingness: 'The Music of Erich Zann.'" In *The Philosophy of H. P. Lovecraft: The Route to Horror*, 7–15. New York: Peter Lang.

Burleson, Donald R. 1983. "Early Years: Beginnings and Foreshadowings (1920–1923)." In *H. P. Lovecraft: A Critical Study*: 39–96. Westport, CT: Greenwood Press.

Burleson, D. R. 1990. *Lovecraft: Disturbing the Universe.* Lexington: University Press of Kentucky.

Cannon, P. 1989. *H. P. Lovecraft.* Boston: Twayne.

Joshi, S. T., and David E. Schultz. 2001. *An H. P. Lovecraft Encyclopedia.* Westport, CT: Greenwood Press.

Ligotti, Thomas. 2003. "The Dark Beauty of Unheard of Horrors." In *The Thomas Ligotti Reader*, edited by Darrell Schweitzer, 78–84. Holicong, PA: Wildside Press.

Lovecraft, H. P. 2005. "The Music of Erich Zann." In *H. P. Lovecraft: Tales*, 15–23. New York: Library of America.

THE MYSTERIES OF UDOLPHO

Published in 1794 by Ann Radcliffe in four volumes, *The Mysteries of Udolpho: A Romance* is considered by many scholars to be the greatest Gothic novel of the eighteenth century. Already an established writer at the time of *The Mysteries of Udolpho*'s publication, Radcliffe was paid £500 to write *The Mysteries of Udolpho*, making her the most well-paid novelist at the time. *The Mysteries of Udolpho* proved an immediate success—it had a direct influence on the Gothic novels of the 1790s and subsequent decades, and is directly referenced in the works of writers such as Jane Austen, Edgar Allan Poe, and Herman Melville. A lengthy text that is filled with intellectual themes and a melodramatic plot, *The Mysteries of Udolpho* is the progenitor of female Gothic fiction (sometimes called Radcliffean Gothic) and has been an influential text on horror writers for more than two hundred years.

Set in France, *The Mysteries of Udolpho* focuses on the long plight of Emily St. Aubert. Emily is an only child and resides with her parents at their country estate. While the family is trying to cope with difficult economic times, Emily's mother suddenly passes away. This event results in father and daughter deciding to travel the countryside to reflect on the natural beauty of Europe, studying the sublime landscape of the mountains and forests in order to expand their appreciation of the natural world. The two meet a young man named Valancourt, who falls in love with Emily, before returning to their estate in France. Emily's father becomes sick and eventually dies. His sister, the superficial Madame Cheron, takes control of his estates and Emily, forcing the young girl to relocate to Italy, where Cheron marries a sinister Italian named Montoni. An authoritarian tyrant who only weds Cheron because he desires to take control of her estates, Montoni moves himself, his wife, and Emily to the castle Udolpho. There he abuses and threatens his wife and Emily

In describing Emily's first sight of Castle Udolpho, Radcliffe wrings every last bit of the sublime from the scene, in a descriptive passage that is arguably the most famous paragraph in the whole novel:

"There," said Montoni, speaking for the first time in several hours, "is Udolpho."

Emily gazed with melancholy awe upon the castle, which she understood to be Montoni's; for, though it was now lighted up by the setting sun, the gothic greatness of its features, and its mouldering walls of dark grey stone, rendered it a gloomy and sublime object. As she gazed, the light died away on its walls, leaving a melancholy purple tint, which spread deeper and deeper, as the thin vapour crept up the mountain, while the battlements above were still tipped with splendour. From those, too, the rays soon faded, and the whole edifice was invested with the solemn duskiness of evening. Silent, lonely, and sublime, it seemed to stand the sovereign of the scene, and to frown defiance on all who dared to invade its solitary reign. (Radcliffe 1794, 438)

Matt Cardin

Source: Radcliffe, Ann. June 1794. "The Mysteries of Udolpho." *The London Review*. London: J. Sewell.

until he gets what he wants: Cheron eventually passes away, yet Emily is subjected to various horrors at Udolpho until she eventually escapes Montoni with the help of friends. Emily later finds herself in the company of a French count and his family. She and her friends have an adventure at a nearby chateau that is believed to be haunted. She is soon after reunited with Valancourt, who had fallen on hard times, but marries Emily at the conclusion of the narrative.

At the center of Radcliffe's text is a conservative concern of balance between human emotions and eighteenth-century rational thought. Very much a young woman who has been taught to engage and explore her emotions, Emily is nonetheless prone to too much sentimentality, something her father openly discusses with his daughter on his deathbed. Emily's singular flaw, which is persistent throughout the majority of the text, is that she never develops the rational self-control embodied by her father. She thus lacks a balance between her emotional side and her rational mind, which manifests in an unrestrained imagination that terrifies her more than it should. To be certain, Emily's experiences throughout the text are terrifying, but her unrestrained imagination exacerbates it all, making her prone to superstitious sightings of ghosts that are not there and believing the worst even when the situation might not be as grave as she perceives. It is not until the text nears its conclusion, in the last hundred or so pages, that Emily finally develops controllable rationality when she subdues the powerful feelings that she has for Valancourt, whom she has come to believe has engaged in questionable moral behavior. By the text's conclusion, Emily is a woman mentally balanced by the emotional aspects of sentimentality and eighteenth-century rational thought.

One unintended consequence of *The Mysteries of Udolpho* was the publication of Matthew Lewis's *The Monk* in 1796. Although the only novel ever published by Lewis, *The Monk* was a direct challenge to the form of Gothic fiction envisioned by Radcliffe. Where Radcliffe made constant use of the explained supernatural throughout her novel, in accordance with her eighteenth-century beliefs against superstition, Lewis made his supernatural occurrences unquestionably real, with the use of sorcery, ghosts, and demons all present throughout. He likewise put more emphasis on his Gothic villain, the monk Ambrosio, over his pursued protagonist, a reversal of Radcliffe's focus on Emily over Montoni. More horrifying than terrifying, *The Monk* likewise utilizes different effects than *The Mysteries of Udolpho* in order to produce fear in its reader. Within two years of the publication of *The Mysteries of Udolpho*, Gothic fiction was divided into two subtypes, one represented by Radcliffe, the other by Lewis, showing the genre was open to experimentation and innovation that previously had not really been present.

The Mysteries of Udolpho stands as one of the greatest Gothic novels ever written. While it is not free from flaws within its narrative (many find the explained supernatural incredibly forced, and others have noted problems with the fourth volume involving the haunted chateau), Radcliffe's novel has nonetheless had a lasting impact upon the horror genre. Its publication marks a high point in the history of Gothic fiction, and it continues to hold strong cultural relevancy as evident in the many works that have come to reference it in some way. While the explained supernatural has not exactly fared well in the horror genre, Radcliffe's ability to create atmosphere, suspense, and terror set a standard that very few have been able to surpass.

Joel T. Terranova

See also: *The Castle of Otranto*; Lewis, Matthew Gregory; *The Monk*; Radcliffe, Ann; The Sublime; Terror versus Horror; Walpole, Horace.

Further Reading

Albright, Richard S. 2005. "No Time Like the Present: *The Mysteries of Udolpho*." *Journal for Early Modern Cultural Studies* 5, no. 1: 49–75.

Russett, Margaret. 1998. "Narrative Enchantment in *The Mysteries of Udolpho*." *ELH* 65, no. 1: 159–186.

Schillace, Brandy Lain. "'Temporary Failure of Mind': Déjà vu and Epilepsy in Radcliffe's *The Mysteries of Udolpho*." *Eighteenth-Century Studies* 42, no. 2: 273–287.

Whiting, Patrica. 1996. "Literal and Literary Representations of the Family in *The Mysteries of Udolpho*." *Eighteenth-Century Fiction* 8, no. 4: 485–501.

NEW WEIRD

In 2003, speculative-fiction author M. John Harrison posted a question on his "Third Alternative" message board: "The New Weird. Who does it? What is it? Is it even anything? Is it even New?" (quoted in VanderMeer and VanderMeer 2008, 317). This prompted a formative discussion about the genre that some have come to refer to as the "New Weird." Editors Ann and Jeff VanderMeer's anthology *The New Weird* (2008) provides the best entry point into this contested field, and includes such stories as K. J. Bishop's "The Art of Dying" (1997), Brian Evenson's "Watson's Boy" (2000), China Miéville's "Jack" (2005), Steph Swainston's "The Ride of the Gabbleratchet" (2007), and Alistair Rennie's "The Gutter Sees the Light That Never Shines" (2008).

In the introduction to *The New Weird*, Jeff VanderMeer points to the mainstream success of Miéville's genre-bending masterpiece *Perdido Street Station* (2000) as the event that most clearly defined the emergence of the movement. Using the novel as a springboard, VanderMeer offers one definition of the New Weird, emphasizing gritty urban settings that distort genre conventions, an intellectual sensibility influenced by New Wave science fiction writers such as J. G. Ballard and Michael Moorcock, a visceral corporeality (a focus on bodily reality) stemming from Clive Barker's horror fiction from the 1980s, and an embrace of the weird that often refers to the existential politics of modern life in a subversive or transgressive mode.

The New Weird, then, may be positioned in a genealogy of weird fiction that reaches back to Franz Kafka's bureaucratic horror, the French Surrealists' attacks on consensus reality, the cosmic dread of the Lovecraft school, and Mervyn Peake's *Gormenghast* saga (1946–1959), and then moves through Jack Vance's *Dying Earth* series (1950–1984), Harrison's Viriconium books (1971–1985), the splatterpunk of Barker and Poppy Z. Brite, and the metaphysical horror of Thomas Ligotti and Kathe Koja. In the 1990s, magazines such as Andy Cox's *The Third Alternative* and Ann VanderMeer's *The Silver Web* played a significant role in publishing New Weird fiction. Other examples of the New Weird include Kelly Link's *Stranger Things Happen* (1995), Jeff VanderMeer's *City of Saints and Madmen* (2001), Bishop's *The Etched City* (2003), and Reza Negarestani's *Cyclonopedia: Complicity with Anonymous Materials* (2008). More recently and in the context of visual media, the first season of Nic Pizzolatto's *True Detective* (2014) television series, David Robert Mitchell's pastiche film *It Follows* (2014), and Robert Eggers's supernatural film *The Witch* (2015) have brought New Weird sensibilities into the cultural mainstream.

However, like slipstream fiction and interstitial writing (writing that falls on or between the boundaries of genres and forms), works associated with the New Weird embrace multiplicity in both form and content, and therefore challenge taxonomic categorization, leading many authors and critics, aware of the pressures of marketability, to question the validity of the term. Art-horror writer Laird Barron, for instance, instead affirms the persistence of the weird itself as a speculative mode that cuts across genres by disrupting natural laws, thereby giving rise to an atmospherics of unease.

Sean Matharoo

See also: Barker, Clive; Barron, Laird; Brite, Poppy Z.; Kafka, Franz; Koja, Kathe; Ligotti, Thomas; Link, Kelly; Lovecraftian Horror; Miéville, China; Surrealism; VanderMeer, Jeff.

Further Reading

Miéville, China. 2003. "Long Live the New Weird." *The Third Alternative* 35: 3.

Sederholm, Carl H., and Jeffrey Andrew Weinstock, eds. 2016. *The Age of Lovecraft*. Minneapolis: University of Minnesota Press.

VanderMeer, Ann, and Jeff VanderMeer. 2008. *The New Weird*. San Francisco: Tachyon Publications.

Walter, Damien G. 2008. "The New World of New Weird." *The Guardian*, January 22. https://www.theguardian.com/books/booksblog/2008/jan/22/thenewworldofnewweird.

NEWMAN, KIM (1959–)

Kim James Newman is one of the most ingenious and media-literate authors of horror fiction to emerge during the 1980s. His earliest works were film novelizations and "sharecropper" novels set in the secondary worlds of gaming franchises, published under the pseudonym "Jack Yeovil," along with critical studies such as the excellent survey of horror cinema, *Nightmare Movies* (1988; rev. ed. 2011). Newman's knowledge of genre film, both classic and obscure, is nothing short of magisterial, and he continues to review movies for numerous venues, such as *Video Watchdog*.

Newman's wide-ranging erudition in twentieth-century popular culture deeply informed his first serious works of fiction. His debut novel under his own name, *The Night Mayor* (1989), is a potent fusion of noir, science fiction, and horror, in which characters are trapped in virtual-reality scenarios borrowed from Hollywood movies. Newman's second novel, *Bad Dreams* (1990), is a delirious dark fantasy in which a demonic vampire attempts to ensnare a young woman in his self-made dreamscape, only to be foiled by her willful, ingenious resistance. *Anno Dracula* (1992), Newman's first real breakthrough, is an alternate history in which the attempted undead invasion of England chronicled in Bram Stoker's 1897 novel was actually a success, with the count marrying Queen Victoria and their vampiric progeny coming to dominate the twentieth century. The novel spawned a number of sequels, all prolific with allusions to vampire literature and film: *The Bloody Red Baron* (1995), *Dracula Cha Cha Cha* (1998), and *Johnny Alucard* (2013). Newman's short fiction—gathered in such collections as *The Original Dr. Shade, and Other Stories* (1994) and *Famous Monsters* (1995)—has also engaged cleverly with the literary and cinematic history of horror.

Newman's favored form is the pastiche, involving the ironic recycling of familiar motifs and materials: his tales offer both the pleasure of recognition, as the densely textured layers of allusion register on the reader, and a sense of estrangement from the familiar genre patterns these allusions summon up. Newman's basic impulse is not merely to borrow but to subvert: his allusions always bear a critical edge. Yet at the same time, they suggest a bond of complicity linking author and reader in an ironic nostalgia for the icons and plot structures he has so ruthlessly plundered and satirically redeployed. The joy of reading *Anno Dracula*, for example, lies not only in its shrewd exposure of the patriarchal and imperialist power dynamics of classic nineteenth-century vampire stories, but also in the sheer profusion of loving detail with which Newman evokes them, the sense he conveys that this popular material, while ideologically suspect, is irrepressibly imprinted on our memories and appetites. Perhaps due to his restless genre-switching and his uncanny talent for mimicry, Newman's remarkable originality as an author has not been as widely recognized as it should be.

Rob Latham

See also: Dark Fantasy; New Weird; Vampires.

Further Reading

Hills, Matt. 2003. "Counterfictions in the Work of Kim Newman: Rewriting Gothic SF as 'Alternate-Story Stories.'" *Science Fiction Studies* 30 (30): 436–455.

Latham, Rob. 2001. "VR Noir: Kim Newman's *The Night Mayor*." *Paradoxa: Studies in World Literary Genres* 16: 95–122.

Wilkinson, Gary. 2000. "Stepping through the Silver Screen: The Fiction of Kim Newman." *Vector* 210 (March/April): 15–18.

THE NIGHT LAND

The Night Land is a visionary fantasy by William Hope Hodgson, first published in 1912. It constitutes a kind of allegorical summation of Hodgson's metaphysical and moral ideas. Critical opinion of the work has always been sharply divided; its admirers regard it as an unparalleled masterpiece by virtue of its imaginative reach and the phantasmagorical elaboration of its imagery, while its detractors consider it to be almost unreadable because of its mock-archaic style.

In the novel's frame narrative—set in a past sufficiently remote to justify the use of an ornate narrative style—the death of the narrator's beloved Mirdath stimulates visions of the remote future in his grief-stricken mind. In the world of those visions, the sun's radiation is fading away, leaving the Earth unfit for human habitation. The people who believe themselves to be the last representatives of humankind live in a huge metal pyramid, the Last Redoubt, which is supplied with power by an Electric Circle that draws energy from the dwindling Earth-Current. As well as life support, the power in question supplies the necessary defense against various monsters and enigmatic observers, seemingly waiting to inherit the Earth.

When a message is unexpectedly received from another precarious abode, whose sole surviving inhabitant, Naani, is a reincarnation of Mirdath, the narrator's dream-self embarks upon an arduous odyssey across the phantasmagorical landscape of the dying Earth, hoping to rescue her. He reaches her, but their return journey is even more dangerous. Eventually, Naani is killed by emanations from the mysterious House of Silence, the dwelling of the giant Silent Ones, but she is miraculously resurrected by the Earth-Current in order to secure the narrator a more fortunate end in his dream than he can possibly attain in life.

Hodgson's vision of the world's end is derived from Lord William Thomson Kelvin's theory that the sun's radiation was produced by gravitational collapse and could not last for more than a few million years. Other fictional extrapolations of the theory had been produced, most notably H. G. Wells's *The Time Machine*, but none had complicated the tragedy of the Earth's demise with such a dramatic metamorphosis of life on its surface, explained in terms of the breakdown of dimensional barriers. No previous work had contrived to communicate such an acute sense of the utter insignificance of one species inhabiting one world in a vast, bleak, intrinsically malign and essentially incomprehensible cosmos—the sensibility that H. P. Lovecraft called "cosmic horror." The artificiality of the novel's prose attempts to support the cultivation of that aesthetic reaction by provoking a sense of alienation in the reader; the many descriptive terms rendered with an initial capital letter do not refer in a simple sense to aspects of the imaginary landscape, but emphasize its status as a metaphorical model of the human mind under the stress of grief and angst. The allegory is only partly decipherable, by necessity, deliberately leaving a dark margin of mystery.

Brian Stableford

See also: Frame Story; Hodgson, William Hope; *The House on the Borderland.*

Further Reading

Bell, Ian. 1986. "A Dream of Darkness: William Hope Hodgson's *The Night Land.*" *Studies in Weird Fiction* 1 (Summer): 13–17.

Bloom, Harold. 1995. "William Hope Hodgson." In *Modern Horror Writers*, 93–107. New York: Chelsea House.

Bruce, Samuel W. 1997. "William Hope Hodgson." In *British Fantasy and Science-Fiction Writers Before World War I*, edited by Darren Harris-Fain, 121–131. *Dictionary of Literary Biography*, vol. 178. Detroit, MI: Gale.

Gafford, Sam. 1992. "Writing Backward: The Novels of William Hope Hodgson." *Studies in Weird Fiction* 11 (Spring): 12–15.

Hodgens, Richard. 1981. "The Deep World of Hodgson's *Nightland*." *Trumpet* 12 (Summer): 14–18, 44.

The Night Land: The Weird Fiction of William Hope Hodgson. Accessed August 15, 2016. http://nightland.website.

Warren, Alan. 1992. "Full Fathom Five: The Supernatural Fiction of William Hope Hodgson." In *Discovering Classic Horror Fiction I*, edited by Darrell Schweitzer, 41–52. Mercer Island, WA: Starmont.

NIGHT SHIFT

Night Shift is a collection of twenty stories by Stephen King, with an introduction by John D. Macdonald (who was one of King's writer idols) published in 1978. It was King's first short-fiction collection, and most of its contents had first been published in *Cavalier* and other men's magazines. The book showcases the many different types of fiction King attempted up to that point: Lovecraftian horror in "Jerusalem's Lot," an epistolary narrative about an ancient evil that overruns a small Maine town in the nineteenth century; science fiction in "I Am the Doorway," in which an astronaut returned from space discovers that his body is turning into a conduit to an alien dimension; suspense in "The Ledge," about a man blackmailed into undertaking a death-defying act by the husband whose wife is the man's lover; and even mainstream fiction in "The Woman in the Room," in which a man secretly facilitates the death of his mother, a cancer victim.

The majority of the book's stories are examples of King's trademark approach to horror, turning the ordinary and commonplace into objects of menace: laundry machinery is endowed with malevolent life in "The Mangler"; toy soldiers are magically animated as aggressive combatants in "Battleground"; rats infesting a decrepit mill grow to monstrous size in "Graveyard Shift"; a can of spoiled beer causes a grotesque transformation in the man who drinks it in "Gray Matter"; and childish fear of the boogeyman proves to be horrifyingly warranted in "The Boogeyman." The stories are set for the most part in recognizable American towns, cast with everyday people who are products of their environments and peppered with recognizable references to contemporary popular culture and consumer culture that help to situate their horrors in the familiar. The vampire story "One for the Road" is a sidebar to King's novel *'Salem's Lot* (1975). Most of the book's stories were later adapted as movies, notably "Trucks" as *Maximum Overdrive* (1986), which King himself directed; "Graveyard Shift" (film version 1990), and "Children of the Corn" (1984), the latter concerned with a cult of children in rural Nebraska who waylay unsuspecting travelers to sacrifice them to a monstrous entity that lives in the cornfields. The film version of *Children of the Corn* spawned a horror franchise that continues to this day.

In his lengthy foreword to the book, King relates his "marketable obsession" (King 2011, xix) to write horror to the reader's taste for horror fiction, noting that "great horror is almost always allegorical" in its depictions of death, and that "the horror tales live most naturally at that connection point between the conscious and the subconscious" (King 2011, xxxviii). In his opinion, the tale of horror fiction speaks to that commingling of interest and revulsion that compels us to contemplate what King refers to "the body under the sheet," that is, the reality of death, especially one's own. His observations anticipate those that would shape his book-length study of horror in popular culture, *Danse Macabre* (1981).

Stefan R. Dziemianowicz

See also: King, Stephen; Lovecraftian Horror; Vampires.

Further Reading

Collings, Michael, and David Engbretson. 1985. *The Shorter Works of Stephen King.* Mercer Island, WA: Starmont House.

Herron, Don. 1982. "Horror Springs in the Fiction of Stephen King." In *Fear Itself*, edited by Tim Underwood and Chuck Miller, 57–82. San Francisco: Underwood-Miller.

King, Stephen. 2011. *Night Shift.* New York: Anchor Books.

Reino, Joseph. 1988. "Night Shift: Harbinger of Bad News." In *Stephen King: The First Decade, Carrie to Pet Sematary*, 100–116. Boston: Twayne.

NOLAN, WILLIAM F. (1928–)

William Francis Nolan is an American science fiction, horror, and fantasy author. He is the creator, by his own estimation, of more than 2,000 pieces of fiction and nonfiction, and he has edited or co-edited roughly 26 anthologies in his nearly 60-year career. He was born in Kansas City, Missouri, and originally worked as an artist for Hallmark Cards and in the comic book industry before becoming a writer. Though married since 1970, he has been estranged from his wife for more than ten years. He is continually working on new projects and is a frequent guest of honor at industry conventions and festivals, including the World Horror Convention, the World Fantasy Convention, and smaller regional events.

In the 1950s, Nolan was an integral part of the writing ensemble known as "The Group," which included many well-known genre writers such as Ray Bradbury, Charles Beaumont, John Tomerlin, Richard Matheson, George Clayton Johnson (with whom he co-wrote *Logan's Run* in 1967), and others. Tomerlin, Beaumont, and Nolan were also avid auto racing fans and participated in local races themselves throughout the 1950s and 1960s. Nolan is considered a leading expert on Dashiell Hammett and pulps such as *Black Mask* and *Western Story*, and he is the world authority on the works of prolific scribe Max Brand, the creator of Dr. Kildare. In addition to writing biographies of both men, he has also written books on director John Huston, actor Steve McQueen, and racing legend Barney Oldfield. Also adept at poetry and screenwriting—with more than twenty produced scripts to his credit—he was co-writer, with Dan Curtis (of *Dark Shadows* fame), of the screenplay for the classic 1976 horror film *Burnt Offerings* (based on the 1973 novel of the same name by Robert Marasco), as well as co-writer, with his friend Richard Matheson, of the classic American television movie *Trilogy of Terror* (1975), directed by Curtis. Curtis and Nolan teamed up on several other productions as well, including *The Kansas City Massacre* (1975), *Turn of the Screw* (1974), and *The Norliss Tapes* (1973).

Though he has written in a variety of genres, Nolan's main output is in horror and science fiction. His style has changed over the years, and what began as a tendency toward the lush flourishes of his mentor Ray Bradbury has evolved into a leaner approach more influenced by noir, hardboiled fiction, and Ernest Hemingway. Many of his works are populated by loners, or, conversely, young female (and even alien/nonhuman) protagonists and are frequently narrated in the first person. With respect to themes, Nolan often utilizes plot-driven narratives with sparse characterizations and descriptions; many of his works focus on the juxtaposition of the uncanny and the commonplace, life given to inanimate objects, or the violent reaction of everyday people to unexpected circumstances.

Jason V Brock

See also: Beaumont, Charles; Bradbury, Ray; Matheson, Richard.

Further Reading

Brock, Jason V. 2014. *Disorders of Magnitude: A Survey of Dark Fantasy.* Lanham, MD: Rowman & Littlefield Publishing Group.

Morton, Lisa. 2015. "Interview: William F. Nolan." *Nightmare* 32 (May). http://www.night mare-magazine.com/nonfiction/interview-william-f-nolan.

Nolan, William F. 2013. *Nolan on Bradbury: Sixty Years of Writing about the Master of Science Fiction.* New York: Hippocampus Press.

Zicree, Marc Scott. 1992. *The Twilight Zone Companion*, 2nd ed. Los Angeles, CA: Silman-James Press.

NORTHANGER ABBEY

Although it was the first of her novels completed for publication, Jane Austen's *Northanger Abbey* was not published until 1818, a year after her death. *Northanger Abbey* is a parody of both a novel of manners and the Gothic novel, an eighteenth-century literary form made popular by such works as Horace Walpole's *The Castle of Otranto* (1764), Ann Radcliffe's *The Mysteries of Udolpho* (1794), and Matthew Lewis's *The Monk* (1796). These and similar novels combined ruined medieval castles or abbeys as settings, supernatural or paranormal occurrences, dark and threatening men who were often aristocrats or religious figures, a threatened young woman, and overwrought emotions often accompanied by overwrought prose. Although formulaic, Gothic novels were wildly successful and established many of the conventions of later horror fiction and film.

In *Northanger Abbey* Austen employs the conventions of the Gothic novel to subvert the genre. It begins with young Catherine Morland, an English teenager who is inordinately fond of reading Gothic novels, traveling to the city of Bath for a season of balls, tea in the Pump Room, and meeting eligible young gentlemen. There she is befriended by Isabella Thorpe, who shares her enthusiasm for Gothic fiction; Isabella's brother John; Henry Tilney, the son of a general; and his sister Eleanor. At Bath she is attracted to Henry Tilney but isolated by the Thorpes, who think she is wealthier than she is and who plan for her to marry John, for whom she has little affection. Invited by the Tilneys to visit their estate at Northanger Abbey, Catherine is delighted by the anticipation of staying at a Gothic abbey, where she imagines all kinds of excitingly dreadful experiences await her. While at the Abbey she imagines it to be haunted, believes it contains secret rooms with ominous histories, and convinces herself that the general has murdered his wife. Mysteriously, General Tilney cuts short her visit and orders her to leave. All turns out well, however. Catherine learns of the Thorpes' intentions, Henry Tilney proposes to her, and the general eventually consents to the marriage. Catherine, now older and wiser at age eighteen, realizes that life is not like a work of Gothic fiction as she prepares for her upcoming marriage.

Northanger Abbey is both a parody of the Gothic novel and a commentary on its readers. Catherine Morland is naïve and gullible. She believes everyone she meets has her best interests at heart, and more significantly, because she has immersed herself in reading Gothic novels, she believes that real life is a delightfully dreadful adventure full of danger and the supernatural. She interprets every event at the Abbey in light of her reading, and of course she is always wrong. In *Northanger Abbey* Austen is also satirizing the novel of manners, a form focused on matters of social class and convention, for while Catherine is in Bath in the first half of the novel, she has no clue whatsoever what is going on around her and simply follows the advice of others. Successful marriage in *Northanger Abbey* is the consequence of pure chance.

The novel has been adapted for stage and screen multiple times, including for PBS, the BBC, and the A&E Network. In 2014 a new version of the novel, written by best-selling crime writer Val McDermid and transforming it into a modern-day teen thriller (with the protagonist now called Cat Morland), was published as part of HarperCollins's Austen Project, in which popular and critically respected modern-day writers were hired to rework Jane Austen's six complete novels for modern audiences.

Jim Holte

See also: The Castle of Otranto; Lewis, Matthew Gregory; *The Monk*; *The Mysteries of Udolpho*; Radcliffe, Ann; Walpole, Horace.

Further Reading

Ford, Susan Allen. 2012. "A Sweet Creature's Horrid Novels: Gothic Reading in *Northanger Abbey*." *Persuasions: The Jane Austin Journal On-Line* 3, no. 1 (Winter). http://www.jasna.org/persuasions/on-line/vol33no1/ford.html.

Gill, Linda. 2013. "Jane Austen's Northanger Abbey." *Pennsylvania Literary Journal* 5, no. 3: 36–57.

Levine, George. 1975. "Translating the Monstrous: Northanger Abbey." *Nineteenth-Century Fiction* 30, no. 3: 335–350.

Skinner, Karalyn. 2013. "'Horrid' Gothicism: Austen's *Northanger Abbey*." *Explicator* 71, no. 3: 229–232.

"THE NOVEL OF THE BLACK SEAL"

Arthur Machen's "The Novel of the Black Seal" was originally published as one of the constituent tales of *The Three Impostors* (1895), a portmanteau work (that is, a work composed of multiple parts) consisting of several short stories connected by a frame story. In its title Machen invokes the (even then) antiquated French meaning of "novel," implying "novelty" rather than a book-length text.

The tale is presented as the alleged testimony of Miss Lally, an educated young woman fallen into poverty, who is rescued from starvation by employment as a governess to the children of Professor Gregg, an ethnologist. Relocating from

---

In "The Novel of the Black Seal," Machen advanced an idea that would exert a significant influence on H. P. Lovecraft (and, largely through him, on many other writers of horror and dark fantasy). He lays out the heart of the idea in what he frames as a document left by a professor who has recently disappeared after a series of strange events:

> I became convinced that much of the folk-lore of the world is but an exaggerated account of events that really happened, and I was especially drawn to consider the stories of the fairies, the good folk of the Celtic races. Here, I thought I could detect the fringe of embroidery and exaggeration, the fantastic guise, the little people dressed in green and gold sporting in the flowers, and I thought I saw a distinct analogy between the name given to this race (supposed to be imaginary) and the description of their appearance and manners. Just as our remote ancestors called the dreaded beings "fair" and "good" precisely because they dreaded them, so they had dressed them up in charming forms, knowing the truth to be the very reverse. Literature, too, had gone early to work, and had lent a powerful hand in the transformation, so that the playful elves of Shakespere are already far removed from the true original, and the real horror is disguised in a form of prankish mischief. But in the older tales, the stories that used to make men cross themselves as they sat around the burning logs, we tread a different stage. (Machen 1895, 105–106)

Matt Cardin

Source: Machen, Arthur. 1895. *The Three Impostors*. Boston: Roberts Brothers.

London to Professor Gregg's home on the edges of the remote Grey Hills in Wales, Lally is puzzled and terrified by a series of anomalous incidents. Discovering Gregg's journal, she reads of his work investigating the "reality" behind Celtic fairy lore: the persistence of prehuman hominids lurking in the isolated countryside.

The story is partly informed by the Euhemerist theories of David MacRitchie (1851–1925), who argued that, through analysis of folk traditions, one could gain information about premodern peoples, including (he speculated) a race of "Turanian" pygmies. Machen used this central idea in two other magazine stories also published in 1895, "The Shining Pyramid" and "The Red Hand." It was a theme he would return to repeatedly throughout his ensuing career, albeit in increasingly oblique ways, for example "Out of the Earth" (1915) and *The Green Round* (1933).

"The Novel of the Black Seal" should also be seen in the wider context of the late-Victorian preoccupation with biological and cultural atavism (a focus on the supposed barbarity and awfulness of earlier and "lower" stages of evolution), an anxiety in part precipitated by the wider acceptance of Darwin's evolutionary theory and concerns about biological and cultural degeneration. Comparable stories from the era include Grant Allen's "Pallinghurst Barrow" (1892) and John Buchan's "No-Man's Land" (1899), in which Buchan resituates Machen's malevolent little people within his native Scotland. However, the peculiar potency of Machen's use of this theme lies in his decision to keep his malignant prehuman entities "off screen," their ensuing ambiguity provoking in the reader a sense of queasy uncertainty and dread.

"The Novel of the Black Seal" is notable for the influence it had on Robert E. Howard and, particularly, H. P. Lovecraft. It is unlikely that many of Lovecraft's most celebrated stories would exist in any recognizable form divested of the influence of "The Novel of the Black Seal," specifically the notions of modern survival of ancient cults and prehuman intelligences, the dizzying contemplation of deep history, and the transient contingency of modernity (the idea that human civilization is not an inevitable or invulnerable phenomenon). Several stories by Howard, including "Worms of the Earth" and "The Little People," are essentially reworkings of Machen's central conceit, the latter story explicitly so.

James Machin

See also: "The Great God Pan"; Howard, Robert E.; Lovecraft, H. P.; Machen, Arthur; "The White People."

Further Reading

Joshi, S. T. 1990. *The Weird Tale*. Holicong, PA: Wildside.

Lovecraft, H. P. [1927] 2012. *The Annotated Supernatural Horror in Literature*. Edited by S. T. Joshi. New York: Hippocampus Press.

Trotter, David. 1995. "Introduction." In *The Three Imposters*, by Arthur Machen, xvii–xxxi. London: Everyman.

NOVELS VERSUS SHORT FICTION

Novels and short fiction are the two major literary forms in which Gothic literature and horror fiction can be found (although horror comics and Gothic and horror poetry form two important subgenres in their own right). Both allow fear, horror, and unease to be conveyed to the reader through the use of dramatic plot twists, supernatural elements, eerie landscapes, and uncanny atmospheres. The novel, in being a longer narrative form, makes for the development of complex narrative structures and in-depth explorations of psychological mechanisms, whereas the short story, in being a condensed form, plays on dramatic plot twists, drastic ellipsis, and elisions in order to shock or surprise the reader.

Gothic literature consists mainly of novels and short stories, even though some instances of Gothic theater and poetry can be found in the works of Lord Byron (*Manfred, Childe Harold's Pilgrimage*) or the graveyard poets ("Elegy Written in a Country Churchyard," "Night-Piece on Death"). In spite of the Gothic movement being born from the poetic tradition of dark romanticism, narrative prose was what made the genre highly popular in the late eighteenth century, as it allowed reaching out to a broader, more mainstream, and mostly feminine audience. Hundreds of Gothic novels were published over the period 1764–1820, fashioning what was known at the time as the "great Gothic craze" (Hansen 2010, 238).

Early Gothic fictions were short novels or romances, a mass-market literary form that focuses on relationships and love interests. Authors such as Horace Walpole (*The Castle of Otranto,* 1764), Ann Radcliffe (*The Mysteries of Udolpho,* 1794), and Matthew Lewis (*The Monk,* 1796) adopted this narrative format, as it was popular at the end of the eighteenth century. The publication of sentimental novels such as Samuel Richardson's *Pamela* (1740) and Jean-Jacques Rousseau's *Julie; or the New Héloïse* (1761) had seen a rise in the popularity of romances and had given credibility to a literature that had otherwise been held in contempt.

Gothic novels combined elements of sentimental novels with that of medieval folklore and dark romanticism: a complex love intrigue, mysterious threatening events, dilapidated castles, dark forests, supernatural creatures, and so on. The length of the novel allowed for many plot twists, and also movements and travels within the narrative, thus heightening its tension. As the genre picked up, short romances became full-fledged novels that focused on the development of characters and psychological drama. Examples of lengthy Gothic novels include Mary Shelley's *Frankenstein* (1818), Emily Brontë's *Wuthering Heights* (1847), and Bram Stoker's *Dracula* (1897). Victorian novelists such as Charles Dickens (*Great Expectations,* 1860–1861; *Bleak House,* 1852–1853) Thomas Hardy (*Tess of the D'Urbervilles,* 1891; *Jude the Obscure,* 1894–1895) or George Eliot (*Middlemarch* (1871–1872) also incorporated Gothic elements in their novels in spite of their more naturalist style.

While Gothic novels thrived in Britain at the turn of the eighteenth century, the short form started gaining popularity, mostly in America, where the genre would see a revival in the mid-nineteenth century. Being strongly influenced by folklore and popular tales, Gothic fiction already had the quality of short fiction, and authors such as Edgar Allan Poe and Nathaniel Hawthorne would immediately exploit this feature of the genre. Influenced by German folk tales (such as those passed along by E. T. A. Hoffmann and Jakob and Wilhelm Grimm) as well as early American Gothic short novels (such as *Wieland* and *Edgar Huntly* by Charles Brockden Brown), both would bring the art of Gothic tales to its pinnacle with short stories such as Hawthorne's "Young Goodman Brown" (1835), "Rappaccini's Daughter" (1844), and "The Minister's Black Veil" (1832), and Poe's "The Black Cat" (1843), "The Tell-Tale Heart" (1843), and "Berenice" (1835). In the literary essay "Philosophy of Composition" (1846), Poe praises the value of short fiction over lengthy writing, claiming that short fiction is better than novels in conveying shock, surprise, and fear to the reader since it can be enjoyed in "the limit of one single sitting" (Poe 2006, 525).

Short fiction would then become a widely popular form for Gothic and horror fiction in America, especially in the subgenre of Southern Gothic fiction. Major figures of Southern Gothic literature, including William Faulkner, Flannery O'Connor, Alice Walker, and Joyce Carol Oates, not only wrote many short stories but also defended their literary choice in claiming, much like Poe, that the writing of short stories is highly demanding creative art, particularly effective in creating uncanny, eerie narratives. As of today, collections of horror stories are published regularly in America and still manage to find the broad audience they were designed for in the first place.

At the same time, horror fiction in novel-length form continues to be popular, with one of the legacies of the horror publishing "boom" of the 1970s and 1980s being the creation of a unique subtype of horror novel that, in the words of horror and science fiction anthologist David Hartwell, "constitutes an avant-garde and experimental literary form which attempts to translate the horrific effects previously thought to be the nearly exclusive domain of the short forms into newly conceived long forms that maintain the proper atmosphere and effects" (Hartwell 1987, 3). The interesting relationship and significant distinctions between short works and novel-length works of horror continue to play a significant role in the evolution of horror literature as a whole.

Elsa Charléty

See also: The Brontë Sisters; Faulkner, William; Hawthorne, Nathaniel; Hoffmann, E. T. A; Oates, Joyce Carol; O'Connor, Flannery; Poe, Edgar Allan; Radcliffe, Ann; Romanticism and Dark Romanticism; Shelley, Mary.

Further Reading

Hansen, Christopher, ed. 2010. *Ruminations, Peregrinations, and Regenerations.* Newcastle-upon-Tyne, UK: Cambridge Scholars Publishing, 2010.

Hartwell, David. 1987. *The Dark Descent.* New York: Tor.

O'Connor, Flannery. 1969. *Mystery and Manners: Occasional Prose*, edited by Robert Fitzgerald and Sally Fitzgerald. New York: Macmillan.

Poe, Edgar Allan. 2006. *The Portable Edgar Allan Poe*. New York: Penguin.

Potter, Franz. 2005. *The History of Gothic Publishing, 1800–1835: Exhuming the Trade*. New York: Palgrave Macmillan.

THE NUMINOUS

The numinous is not a genre, but an aspect of some horror fiction. The term "numinous," which was coined by the nineteenth- and twentieth-century German theologian and philosopher Rudolf Otto, generally refers to the more spiritual or existential side of the supernatural encounter. While a supernatural entity may frighten a character by threatening him or her, the reason for this terror is clear. However, even when a supernatural entity is not threatening a character personally, the very existence of a supernatural being threatens a character's idea of what reality is. This may be owing to an intolerantly rationalistic attitude, but, in horror fiction, the numinous does not depend exclusively on a clash with any materialistic prejudice to make itself felt. The numinous experience is disturbing simply because it shows the characters there is another form of existence, and that reality as it is commonly known is only a smaller part of a much larger, invisible whole.

The numinous can be mystical. Noteworthy examples of the mystical numinous can be found in the writings of Arthur Machen and Algernon Blackwood. The numinous can also be more in keeping with scientific speculation, as was more often the case in H. P. Lovecraft's stories of "cosmic horror." Where Machen and Blackwood give the reader the impression that ancient spiritual mysteries continue to manifest themselves in modern reality, Lovecraft draws more on the boundlessness of relativistic space and time and on the limitations of human knowledge to create his numinous effects.

In formulating the concept of the numinous, Otto was greatly influenced by the German philosopher Immanuel Kant (1724–1804), in whose philosophy the linguistically distinct but thematically related idea of the *noumenal* plays an important role. Kant identified as noumenal those things that seem to lie just beyond the limits of possible human experience, things as they are "in themselves," as distinct from human perception and knowledge of them. The noumenal, Kant argued, cannot be experienced, but it is possible to experience the *limits* of human experience. With this as a deep background to Otto's concept, the numinous experience would then be the sense of almost experiencing what is just beyond the human, and so it is very close to the aesthetic idea of the sublime.

Horror fiction that dwells more on physical threats and direct emotional consequences would not be considered numinous. Numinous horror fiction may involve physical or direct threats and pay considerable attention to character, but in general the numinous horror tale is philosophical and will often downplay physical or personal aspects of a supernatural menace in order to emphasize the danger posed to an idea of the world itself. Such stories depend less on sympathy with characters in jeopardy and more on encouragement of the reader to question his or her reality.

For this reason, a numinous story will often be unsensational, set in familiar places, and involve ordinary people; the supernatural intrusion will be subtle and uncertain, and the points of view of the various characters will become correspondingly more important. However, a story like Henry James's *The Turn of the Screw* would not likely be considered numinous, for the considerable doubt thrown on the sanity of the governess in that story undermines the supernatural reality of the ghosts in that tale.

One significant example of a numinous story is "Cecilia de Noel," published by English writer Mary Elizabeth Hawker in 1891. This story is composed of a number of different narratives from different narrators, who all relate tales touching on a haunting. Numinous uncertainty, more than terror, is the overall effect of the story. Another, later example is the 1959 *Twilight Zone* episode "And When the Sky Was Opened," in which the main characters, a group of test pilots who have by chance stumbled across some mysterious threshold during an experimental flight in a new kind of aircraft, are edited out of existence; apparently, the cosmos wishes to preserve its secrets. This episode was based on a 1953 short story by Richard Matheson titled "Disappearing Act."

Michael Cisco

See also: Blackwood, Algernon; Lovecraft, H. P.; Machen, Arthur; Samuels, Mark; The Sublime; "The Willows."

Further Reading

Geary, Robert F. 1992. *The Supernatural in Gothic Fiction: Horror, Belief, and Literary Change.* Lewiston, Queenston, and Lampeter: Edward Mellon Press.

Varnado, S. L. 1987. *Haunted Presence: The Numinous in Gothic Fiction.* Tuscaloosa: University of Alabama Press.

OATES, JOYCE CAROL (1938–)

The American author Joyce Carol Oates is one of the most celebrated mainstream writers to be associated with the field of horror literature. A significant portion of her vast literary output has been cast in the Gothic mold, has deployed themes of the grotesque and uncanny, or has been self-consciously modeled on previous work in the genre.

Oates has openly acknowledged her debts to the fiction of Edgar Allan Poe and H. P. Lovecraft; indeed, she has written movingly about how their fiction, with its focus on "the interior of the soul," links personal fears and anxieties with nightmares of cosmic dread (Oates 1996). More broadly, Oates has articulated, in a 1998 essay on "The Aesthetics of Fear," a vision of horror literature as a cathartic mode, which, by evoking "an artful simulation" of an emotion that is "crude, inchoate, nerve-driven and ungovernable," prepares readers to confront real-world terrors when they arise (Oates 1998, 176). Oates sees the experience of terror as central to American literature in particular, as her superb anthology *American Gothic Tales* (1996), which traces a lineage from Charles Brockden Brown and Nathaniel Hawthorne to Stephen King and Thomas Ligotti, makes clear.

Oates's engagement with horror was evidenced in her early collection *Night-Side* (1977), which gathers eighteen stories—including the title tale, an evocative exploration of occult research—that treat themes of haunting, dark obsession, and morbid diablerie (sorcery aided by the devil). Many subsequent story collections—such as *Haunted: Tales of the Grotesque* (1994), *The Corn Maiden and Other Nightmares* (2011), and *The Doll Master and Other Tales of Terror* (2016)—have been organized around similar topics. A number of works explicitly harken back to classics in the field: "The Accursed Inhabitants of the House of Bly" (in *Haunted*), for example, is a retelling of Henry James's *The Turn of the Screw* (1898) from the perspective of the ghosts, while "Death-Cup" (in *Corn Maiden*) cleverly invokes Poe's ambiguous doppelgänger story, "William Wilson" (1839). These allusions function not as mere pastiches but rather as energetic reimaginings, in which Oates unpacks the subtexts of the originals with subtlety and a shrewd eye for psychological nuance. Oates's short fiction has been celebrated within the field: "Fossil-Figures," a tale of macabre vengeance, won a World Fantasy Award in 2011, while the collection in which it appeared, *Corn Maiden*, won a Bram Stoker Award.

Oates's novels have flirted with Gothic elements from the very start of her career. Perhaps her most abiding theme—of thwarted, enslaving, or embittered love—has always cast a Gothic shadow: novels such as *With Shuddering Fall* (1964), *Wonderland*

(1971), and *Do with Me What You Will* (1973) feature characters driven literally mad with unrequited passion. Her 1996 short novel *First Love: A Gothic Tale* turns an unsparingly brutal story of sexual abuse into a rich meditation on themes of vampirism and demonic possession (these themes are metaphorical, not literal, however). Similarly, *Beasts* (2003) analyzes the masochistic impulse that drives obsessive love, twisting desire into grotesque fantasies of abasement and devourment. Oates's fascination for tales of love gone wrong has led her to write several narratives of serial killers whose transgressive desires emerge out of sexual loneliness and a perverse yearning for human connection. For example, her Stoker Award–winning novel *Zombie* (1995), inspired by the grisly career of Jeffrey Dahmer, features a murderer who attempts to create a slavish companion whose love cannot be retracted or revoked. Oates first essayed this controversial topic in her widely anthologized 1966 story of sorcerous seduction, "Where Are You Going, Where Have You Been?"

Oates's most overt engagements with the horror genre can be found in her so-called "Gothic Saga," which includes *Bellefleur* (1980), *A Bloodsmoor Romance* (1982), *Mysteries of Winterthurn* (1984), *My Heart Laid Bare* (1998), and *The Accursed* (2013). Historical tales that self-consciously echo past masters of the field, as well as evoking and updating archaic forms, such as the sensation novel (which flourished in Great Britain in the 1860s and 1870s), these are rich and deeply rewarding works that weave occult elements—hauntings, psychic powers, ancestral curses—into a densely observed fabric of everyday life in the late nineteenth and early twentieth centuries. While the earliest installments in the series, though coinciding with the boom in horror publishing during the 1980s, did not enjoy a wide crossover audience, the more recent books have been warmly embraced within the field, with Stephen King calling *The Accursed* "hypnotic" in a *New York Times* review (King 2013).

Since the 1990s, Oates herself has cultivated intimate connections with the horror genre and has endeavored to build bridges between it and the larger literary marketplace. Indeed, she is probably the most distinguished ambassador for horror in the hallowed halls of mainstream publishing, issuing polemical manifestos for the centrality of terror to the modern imagination, and defending Lovecraft against his detractors as an author with an authentically spiritual and tragic sensibility. Though now in her sixth decade of writing, Oates shows no signs of slowing down; if anything, her Gothic preoccupations continue to provide a vital compulsion to her work.

Rob Latham

See also: Ancestral Curse; Bram Stoker Award; Dreams and Nightmares; The Grotesque; The Haunted House or Castle; Psychological Horror; World Fantasy Award; Zombies.

Further Reading

Colognes-Brooks, Gavin. 2014. "The Strange Case of Joyce Carol Oates." In *A Companion to American Gothic*, edited by Charles L. Crow, 303–314. Hoboken, NJ: John Wiley.

Egan, James. 1990. "Romance of a Darksome Type: Versions of the Fantastic in the Novels of Joyce Carol Oates." *Studies in Weird Fiction* 7 (Spring): 12–21.

King, Stephen. 2013. "Bride of Hades: 'The Accursed' by Joyce Carol Oates." *New York Times*, March 14. http://www.nytimes.com/2013/03/17/books/review/the-accursed-by -joyce-carol-oates.html?_r=0.

Milazzo, Lee. 1989. *Conversations with Joyce Carol Oates.* Jackson: University of Mississippi Press.

Oates, Joyce Carol. 1996. "The King of Weird." *New York Review of Books*, October 31. http://www.nybooks.com/articles/1996/10/31/the-king-of-weird.

Oates, Joyce Carol. 1998. "The Aesthetics of Fear." *Salmagundi* 120 (Fall): 176–185.

O'BRIEN, FITZ-JAMES (1828–1862)

Born Michael O'Brien in County Cork, Ireland, he changed his name to Fitz-James upon emigration from London to New York in 1852. In New York, as a regular contributor of fiction, poetry, and humor to U.S. periodicals, he helped form a literary circle at Pfaff's beer cellar with fellow Edgar Allan Poe admirers like his probable lover T. B. Aldrich and Fitz Hugh "Hashish Eater" Ludlow. He provides an early landmark for Irish American, supernatural, queer, and science fictions. Literary critics often bemoan his untimely death as a Union officer in the U.S. Civil War and unrealized potential for more tales or longer Hawthorne-esque romances.

O'Brien's first collection of poetry and tales, along with friends' reminiscences, was published in 1881. Despite the New York literati's fond post–Civil War recollections of O'Brien's machismo, dandyism, extravagance, and geniality, a second volume never found a publisher. Editor and anthologist Jessica Salmonson suggests this was the result of homophobia and O'Brien's probable bisexuality. Salmonson's 1988 two-volume edition divides O'Brien's supernatural tales between light fantasies and the macabre. The early 1850s fantasies were largely uncollected. Several have dream or Orientalist topics, such as O'Brien's first published tale, "An Arabian Night-Mare" (1851), in the magazine of Charles Dickens, another O'Brien idol, and "The Dragon-Fang Possessed by the Conjuror Piou-Lu" (1856). O'Brien's poetry and fantasies are forgotten. His macabre tales of the late 1850s like "The Golden Ingot" (1858), "What Was It?" (1859), and "The Wondersmith" (1859) endure. *Weird Tales* chose to reprint many of these in the 1920s and 1930s.

The frantic narrator of "The Diamond Lens" (1858) communes with the spirit of Anton von Leeuwenhoek on microscope construction, steals a rose-diamond for a lens from a caricatured French Jew (who stole it from an enslaved Brazilian), and obsesses over a woman his new microscope reveals in a water drop. The tale remained well regarded. Science fiction pulp magazine *Amazing Stories* reprinted it twice. Another disturbed narrator presents "The Lost Room" (1858). He reflects on mnemonic associations of his boardinghouse room's treasured objects (remembering a piano performance evoking H. P. Lovecraft's "The Music of Erich Zann"). The narrator is dispossessed of his room by the house's caricatured Congolese waiter and a ghoulish dinner party recalling Poe's "King Pest" (1835). The grotesque racial

"What Was It?": An Invisible Assault

O'Brien wrote "What Was It? A Mystery" (1859) while homeless and living with his probable lover, writer T. B. Aldrich. It was initially published alongside a translation of Théophile Gautier.

In a New York boardinghouse, opium-tranced Dr. Hammond and Harry Escott rhapsodize over Orientalist phantasmagorias and supernatural art. An invisible humanoid ghoul assaults Escott in bed, and the opium smokers study the possible cannibal for weeks before it starves. The tale is anthologized across several genres, but many reprints omit the concluding byline and editor's note about the display of a plaster cast of the ghoul.

Escott also narrates O'Brien's ghost tale "The Pot of Tulips" (1855). The scientific, systematic nature of Escott's paranormal investigations may make him fiction's first occult detective (before J. Sheridan Le Fanu's Hesselius) and fiction's second recurring detective (after Edgar Allan Poe's Dupin and before Harriet Prescott Spofford's *Harper's* detective Furbush). "What Was It?," in one of many metatextual instances, suggests "Tulips" was written in-story by Escott, which may account for Escott's happy, rich marriage in "Tulips" versus his being a doomed addict-renter in the later tale. "What Was It?" alludes to occult or grotesque art from Shakespeare, Jacques Callot, C. B. Brown, E. T. A. Hoffmann, Edward Bulwer-Lytton, Tony Johannot, Catherine Crowe, and Gustave Doré. O'Brien's works often feature grotesque racial caricatures, here a drunken black butler.

"What Was It?" is O'Brien's best remembered tale for its erudite steeping in prior supernatural art and wide influence. It informs invisibility in the fiction of Guy de Maupassant ("The Horla"), Ambrose Bierce ("The Damned Thing"), and H. P. Lovecraft ("The Dunwich Horror" and "The Colour out of Space"). The enigmatic descriptions of the captured ghoul raise questions about Victorian notions of science and public display, monstrosity, enslavement, queer desire, and invisible economic relations.

Bob Hodges

caricatures accompanying the tales' sense of the weird proves a barrier for contemporary interest.

Despite years of sparse recognition for "the Celtic Poe," critics increasingly see him and fellow *Harper's* contributor and Poe disciple H. P. Spofford as key late U.S. Romantics and a bridge in U.S. short fiction between antebellum Nathaniel Hawthorne and Poe and postbellum Bret Harte and Ambrose Bierce.

Bob Hodges

See also: Weird Tales.

Further Reading

Burdine, W. H. 2015. "'What Was It?': The Immaterial Self & Nineteenth-Century American Panic." *ESQ: A Journal of the American Renaissance* 61, no. 3: 441–473.

Franklin, H. Bruce, ed. 1995. *Future Perfect: American Science Fiction of the Nineteenth Century: An Anthology*. Rev. ed. New Brunswick, NJ: Rutgers University Press.

"The Golden Ingot." 1952. *Tales of Tomorrow* television series. May 9, 1952. *Horror Habit*. Edited by Jolie Bergman. 2016. http://horrorhabit.blogspot.com/p/watch-it-now-tales -of-tomorrow-1959-1960.html.

Salmonson, Jessica. 1988. Introductions to *The Supernatural Tales of Fitz-James O'Brien*. 2 vols. New York: Doubleday.

Taylor, Matthew. 2013. "Ghost-Humanism; or, Specters of Materialism." *J19: The Journal of Nineteenth-Century Americanists* 1, no. 2: 416–422.

Whitley, Edward, and Rob Weidman, eds. 2016. *The Vault at Pfaff's: An Archive of Art & Literature by the Bohemians of Antebellum NY*. Lehigh University. http://lehigh.edu /pfaffs.

OCCULT DETECTIVES

The occult or psychic detective is a character who specializes in identifying and dealing with paranormal phenomena and their causes. Such characters as Arthur Machen's Mr. Dyson, J. Sheridan Le Fanu's Dr. Hesselius in "Green Tea" (1869), and Bram Stoker's Dr. Abraham van Helsing in *Dracula* (1897), often cited as the earliest examples, are prototypes but are neither professional investigators nor series characters. Le Fanu's collection *In a Glass Darkly* has the conceit of being taken from Hesselius's files, but he appears in just one story.

The earliest series character to combine the supernatural and detective genres is Flaxman Low (1898–1899), created by Hesketh and Kate Pritchard. He is a professional ghost-hunter called in to investigate hauntings as Sherlock Holmes is to investigate crimes.

The first such character to become well known was John Silence, created by Algernon Blackwood. The collection *John Silence: Physician Extraordinary* (1908) was a best-seller. Silence, like Low, investigated occult phenomena employing logic and his broad knowledge of the paranormal.

Thomas Carnacki (1910–1912), created by William Hope Hodgson, a professional ghost-hunter like Low, used instead a scientific, or pseudoscientific, approach to deal with hauntings that were of Hodgson's own imaginative devising, such as "Saiitii" and "Aeiirii" phenomena. Carnacki stories are still being written today by various authors.

Many other similar characters have followed through the decades. Moris Klaw (1913–1920), created by Sax Rohmer (known for his Fu Manchu stories), was different in that he solved mundane crimes using psychic means. He slept on a special pillow and used his dreams to provide the clues.

The more typical Jules de Grandin was featured in a long series of stories by Seabury Quinn that ran in *Weird Tales* magazine from 1925 to 1951. It was the most popular series ever to run in the magazine. De Grandin solved a variety of crimes, sometimes purely supernatural, and sometimes, as in the Carnacki stories, of a more science fictional nature.

The Secrets of Dr. Taverner (1926) by occultist author Dion Fortune concerned the exploits of another doctor specializing in the paranormal. Taverner was supposed to have been modeled on a real doctor, and the stories are supposed to be composites of actual case histories.

Brian Lumley's Titus Crow series (1970–1989) combined the form with the Chthulhu Mythos.

Occult investigators have also appeared on television. Two Carnacki stories were televised respectively in 1953 and 1971. The original character Carl Kolchak, a reporter who investigates outré phenomena, appeared in two television movies and the series *Kolchak: The Night Stalker* (1974), which inspired *The X Files* (1993–2000).

The occult detective is still present in fiction, but has shifted from the Sherlock Holmes model toward a more hard-boiled detective model. Examples are Jim Butcher's novels about detective-wizard Harry Dresden (2000–) and Mike Carey's novels about freelance exorcist Felix Castor (2007–).

Lee Weinstein

See also: Blackwood, Algernon; *Dracula*; "Green Tea"; Hodgson, William Hope; *In a Glass Darkly*; *John Silence: Physician Extraordinary*; Le Fanu, J. Sheridan; Quinn, Seabury; Rohmer, Sax.

Further Reading

Fonseca, Tony. 2007. "The Psychic." In *Icons of Horror and the Supernatural: An Encyclopedia of Our Worst Nightmares*, edited by S. T. Joshi, 409–439. Westport, CT: Greenwood Press.

Hendrix, Grady. 2013. "The Terrible Occult Detectives." *Tor.com*, December 18. http://www.tor.com/2013/12/18/haunted-holidays-the-terrible-occult-detectives.

Jones, Stephen, ed. 1998. *Dark Detectives: Adventures of the Supernatural Sleuths*. Minneapolis, MN: Fedogan & Bremer.

Valentine, Mark, ed. 2009. *The Black Veil & Other Tales of Supernatural Sleuths*. Ware: Wordsworth Editions.

O'CONNOR, FLANNERY (1925–1964)

A noted practitioner of Southern Gothic and Southern grotesque, Mary Flannery O'Connor merged Christian demonic horror, violence, absurdity, and revelation in her harsh narrative landscapes. Her works are rife with elements of horror fiction; as Jon Lance Bacon notes, "she made extensive, strategic use of motifs from the horror genre" (Bacon 2010, 89). Indeed, some reviewers have classified O'Connor's tales as "the very best of horror literature," even if her fiction does not fit neatly into a standard definition (Pelfrey 1995, 5). Magistrale and Morrison's edition on contemporary American horror fiction even places O'Connor as a formative figure of the genre.

O'Connor was born in Savannah, Georgia, on March 25, 1925. She died prematurely of complications related to lupus on August 3, 1964. For a decade before her death, O'Connor lived as a veritable cripple on her mother's farm, Andalusia. Her illness gave her a unique worldview, which deeply affected her fiction: a literary vision of horrors distinctly Southern and grotesque. O'Connor had diverse influences from the surrealist satire and grotesquerie of the Russian author Nikolai Gogol (e.g., "Diary of a Madman"), to the dark comedy of *The Humorous Tales of Edgar Allan Poe*. Her style was shaped by the theological philosophy of scholars like Pierre Teilhard de Chardin (1881–1955). O'Connor is heavily anthologized, from Norton Editions of American Literature to editor David Hartwell's classic horror anthology *The Dark Descent*, and she has impacted the writing of everyone from Bruce Springsteen to Anne Rice.

During her lifetime, O'Connor produced two novels and two story collections, receiving numerous awards and accolades. While earning an MFA in creative writing at Iowa State University, O'Connor published her first short story, "The Geranium" (1946). It made her an instant literary success. But O'Connor produced the bulk of her work at Andalusia, where she moved in 1951 after being diagnosed with systemic lupus erythematosus.

O'Connor's first novel, *Wise Blood* (1952), attracted national attention, mixed reviews, and a spectrum of critical reactions. Some reviewers derisively compared *Wise Blood*—with its violence and sadism—to William Faulkner's *Sanctuary* and Erskine Caldwell's *Tobacco Road*. O'Connor's novel captures the absurd, grotesque, and antireligious exploits of a destructive and murderous World War II veteran named Hazel Motes. Motes is a prodigal prophet figure who lines his shoes with glass shards and wraps his chest with barbed wire as a form of self-mortification.

After *Wise Blood*, O'Connor published her first short story collection, *A Good Man Is Hard to Find and Other Stories* (1955). Early critics unleashed a barrage of tongue-in-cheek associations between her writing and popular fiction with a horrific edge. A reviewer for *Time* magazine, for example, allied her work with the "sardonic brutality" of "the early Graham Greene" ("Such Nice People" 1955, 114). Within this collection, several stories stand out as signature examples of her craft. "A Good Man Is Hard to Find" is her best-known work. It is punctuated by O'Connor's strategic use of moral horror. The character "the Grandmother" faces her "moral and emotional limits," as is typical of horror literature (Botting 1998, 130). Another heavily anthologized short story from this collection is "Good Country People." The piece is full of distorted dichotomies that lapse into grotesquerie through hyperbole, caricature, and absurdism. Hartwell suggests this story relies on "a non-supernatural strain of American psychological horror" (Hartwell 1987, 576). Likewise, "The Artificial Nigger" capitalizes on what Louis D. Rubin Jr. calls the "profound terror" of being lost and "confronted with the unknown"

(Rubin 1958, 36). Less often anthologized due to the offensive nature of its title, this short story uses imagery of Dante's inferno to project modernity as hell, a horrible labyrinthine purgatory of concrete and demonic corruption. The labyrinth, as Botting points out, is a common motif of horror. It generates the fear of entrapment and the dread of impending doom lurking around any corner. For O'Connor, the monsters hiding in the maze are people.

O'Connor's second novel, *The Violent Bear It Away*, came out in 1960 to a flurry of controversy catalyzed by its portrayal of murder, arson, kidnapping, and homosexual rape. The title originates in Matthew 11:12: "the kingdom of heaven suffereth violence, and the violent bear it away." Again O'Connor uses verbal, physical, and symbolic violence in tandem with human deformities to produce horror filled with immorality in which characters are shocked and bedeviled. The protagonist is a fated prophet named Francis Tarwater who resists his destiny with revolting and often inhuman actions. The devil assaults him. He then sets a conflagration and submits to his vocation. Tarwater resembles the character "Reverend" Powell, who is the homicidal and fraudulent religious man in Davis Gruber's classic 1953 horror-thriller *Night of the Hunter*. The Misfit of "A Good Man Is Hard to Find" is a similar permutation of this figure. Hank Wagner analyzes the Misfit as an icon of the genre, the serial killer (Wagner 2007, 483). O'Connor's prophets exemplify this archetype, recast within her own spiritual and moral vision.

Submitted to her editor in the final months of her life, O'Connor's last anthology of short stories, *Everything That Rises Must Converge* (1965), depicts moments of rage and redemption, violent derangements, alienation, and the wildly grotesque. This collection is darker in tenor and more spiritual.

During her career, O'Connor was the recipient of three O. Henry Awards and myriad other distinctions. Her form of grotesque comes out of a tradition of Southern humor that has evolved and twisted its aesthetic mode into nightmarish visions of reality, associated with comedic horror. She is linked to foundational Southern Gothic writers such as Faulkner and Carson McCullers through her use of violence and realism. Many horror writers consider O'Connor an influence on their fiction. Contemporary horror, thriller, and Southern Gothic writer Joe R. Lansdale credits O'Connor among his literary influences. The nightmares of O'Connor impact Joyce Carol Oates, as in her anthology *Haunted: Tales of the Grotesque*, and Stephen King, reflected in his musings on horror in *Danse Macabre*. Even Cormac McCarthy alludes to her influence in his infrequent interviews.

O'Connor succumbed to kidney failure at Baldwin County Hospital in Milledgeville, Georgia, on August 3, 1964. Among her posthumous publications, *Manners and Mysteries* (1969) contains O'Connor's selected essays and lectures. They are now an important part of scholarship on the grotesque in American literature. Recent biographies such as Brad Gooch's *Flannery* (2009) and Jean Cash's *Flannery O'Connor* (2002) link her personal context to her artistic output. Posthumous honors include a National Book Award, an O. Henry Award for her story "Revelation," induction into the American Poet's Corner in 2014, a National Endowment, and several international conferences that focus on O'Connor's dark, nuanced writing and its literary impact.

Naomi Simone Borwein

See also: Gogol, Nikolai; "Good Country People"; The Grotesque; Lansdale, Joe R.; Psychological Horror; Oates, Joyce Carol.

Further Reading

Bacon, Jon Lance. 2010. "Gory Stories: O'Connor and American Horror." In *Flannery O'Connor in the Age of Terrorism: Essays on Violence and Grace*, edited by Avis Hewitt and Robert Donahoo, 89–112. Knoxville: University of Tennessee Press.

Botting, Fred. 1998. "Horror." In *The Handbook of Gothic Literature*, edited by Marie Mulvey-Roberts, 123–131. London: Macmillan.

Hartwell, David G, ed. 1987. "Flannery O'Connor." In *The Dark Descent*, 576–590. New York: Tom Doherty Associates.

Magistrale, Tony, and Michael A. Morrison, eds. 1996. "Introduction." In *A Dark Night's Dreaming: Contemporary American Horror Fiction*, 1–7. Columbia: University of South Carolina.

Pelfrey, David. 1995. "Spooky Stories." *Santa Fe Reporter*, October 25–31: 5.

Rubin, Louis D., Jr. 1958. "Flannery O'Connor: A Note on Literary Fashions." *Critique* II: 11–18.

"Such Nice People." 1955. *Time*, June 6: 114.

Wagner, Hank. 2007. "The Serial Killer." In *Icons of Horror and Supernatural*, edited by S. T. Joshi, 473–506. Westport, CT: Greenwood.

THE OCTOBER COUNTRY

The American speculative fiction writer Ray Bradbury wrote a significant amount of horror fiction throughout his career, particularly early on. *The October Country* (1955) is a revised version of his first book, *Dark Carnival* (1947), and has become one of the classics of the field. Stephen King, in *Danse Macabre,* characterized *Dark Carnival* as "the *Dubliners* of American fantasy fiction" (King 2010, 346), alluding to the classic James Joyce collection.

While not all of the entries collected in *The October Country* are supernatural or horror, the book as a whole offers a treasure trove of eerie stories. The main themes, as in much of Bradbury's fiction, are childhood and death. "Jack-in-the-Box," for example, is about a boy raised by his fearful, psychotic mother in total isolation from the outside world. He thinks their house is the entire world, bounded only by endless forest. When she dies, he ventures out, and he thinks this is death. Death is also denied in the almost-comic "There Was an Old Woman." Aunt Tildy refuses to believe she is dead, even when the undertakers come for her body, and as a ghost she goes to the morgue and gets it back. An overtly horrific story is "The Small Assassin," in which a mother becomes convinced that her infant is out to kill her. It succeeds.

Other stories mix horror with macabre humor. "Skeleton" is about a man obsessed with the idea that there is a ghastly skeleton inside his body. He manages to remove it and go on as a blob-creature. In "The Man Upstairs" a boy discovers that the lodger his mother has taken in is a vampire. He kills and dissects the vampire, bringing strange organs, one by one, into the kitchen for Mom to identify. In "The Wind" an explorer discovers that the world's winds are alive and are determined to keep their secret. In "The Scythe" a Dustbowl refugee of the 1930s finds a deserted farm and a field of wheat, and begins to harvest. He soon discovers that he has become Death and is reaping lives, including those of his own family. Perhaps the strongest of the new stories in *The October Country* (not appearing in *Dark Carnival*) is "The Next in Line," a powerful meditation on the inevitability of death, inspired by the mummies in catacombs that Bradbury saw on a trip to Mexico.

The two stories that have probably most intrigued many younger readers are about the "weird" Elliot family. "Homecoming" concerns the one "normal" boy in a family of ghouls, vampires, and other monsters. He longs to be like them, but he does not have fangs or magical powers. In "Uncle Einar," the apparent problem posed by a bat-winged relative is solved when a boy is able to tie a string around him and fly him like a kite.

Bradbury's stories were revolutionary when they first began to appear in *Weird Tales* in the early 1940s, as they were entirely modern in their technique and told in spare prose that bordered on poetry. Bradbury had spent time reading not just pulp fiction but Ernest Hemingway, John Steinbeck, Thomas Wolfe, and other representatives of the high modern tradition, and the fusion of these influences with fantastic subject matter made for a unique effect, as vividly illustrated in the stories that were collected in *Dark Carnival* and then its altered incarnation as *The October Country*.

Darrell Schweitzer

See also: Arkham House; Bradbury, Ray; Dark Fantasy; *Weird Tales*.

Further Reading

King, Stephen. [1981] 2010. *Danse Macabre.* New York: Simon & Schuster.

Mogen, David. 1986. "Weird Tales: The Landscape of October Country." In *Ray Bradbury*. Twayne's United Authors Series 504. Boston: Twayne.

Pierce, Hazel. 1980. "Ray Bradbury and the Gothic Tradition." In *Ray Bradbury*, edited by Martin H. Greenberg and Joseph D. Olander, 186–194. New York: Taplinger.

Schweitzer, Darrell, 1988. "Tales of Childhood and the Grave: Ray Bradbury's Horror Fiction." In *Discovering Modern Horror Fiction II*, edited by Darrell Schweitzer, 29–42. Mercer Island, WA: Starmont House.

OLIVER, REGGIE (1952–)

Reggie Oliver is an English writer, dramatist, actor, theater director, illustrator, and the biographer of his aunt, Stella Gibbons (author of *Cold Comfort Farm*). He is the author of stage plays, essays, a regular review column for Mark Valentine's journal *Wormwoodiana*, more than 100 stories, novellas, and vignettes, *The Dracula Papers: The Scholar's Tale* (2011, the first volume in a projected tetralogy), the spiritual thriller and comedy of manners *Virtue in Danger* (2013), and what he describes as "a sort of children's book," *The Hauntings at Tankerton Park* (2016), for which he provided all sixty illustrations. His work has been much anthologized, and it has been gathered into seven collections: *The Dreams of Cardinal Vittorini & Other Strange Stories* (2003), *The Complete Symphonies of Adolf Hitler & Other Strange Stories* (2005), *Masques of Satan* (2007), *Madder Mysteries* (2009), *Mrs. Midnight and Other Stories* (2011, winner of Children of the Night Award), *Flowers of the Sea* (2013), and *Holidays from Hell* (2017)]. It has also appeared in three volumes of representative selections alongside previously uncollected work: *Dramas from the Depths* (2010), *Shadow Plays* (2012), and *The Sea of Blood* (2015).

Like Ramsey Campbell, Oliver is unashamed of being perceived as a horror writer, though he takes issue with the common misconception that narrows the field "to mean a lot of blood and sordid sex, and physical torment" (Slatter 2015); therefore, he prefers the term J. R. R. Tolkien's colleague Charles Williams used to describe his novels: spiritual shockers. In the "Introductory" to *Masques of Satan*, he states that his stories are "not *divertissements* . . . I have become convinced that to write ghost stories of lasting merit it is necessary to believe in the possibility of eternal damnation. . . . The protagonists of the supernatural tale at its best need to be playing for the highest stakes conceivable. . . . I write what I write, because it is the best way of saying what I want to say about what matters to me most" (Oliver 2007, x).

In other hands, this prescription might lead to a spate of predictable tracts masquerading as fiction in which a dichotomous morality invariably leads to the villain receiving his just deserts and the innocent emerging wiser but relatively unscathed. The worldview in Oliver's fiction, reflecting the slippery slopes that lead people to act against their own best interests and the clashes life poses between individuality and egoism, belief and obsession, aspiration and achievement, love and need, professionalism and callousness, comes closest to that of Euripides, in whom the human response to a dilemma dictates whether the outcome is tragic, grotesque, or merely humbling. Oliver evinces a remarkable degree of compassion toward all but the most predatory of his characters, contrasting their delusions against the reality that threatens to overwhelm them, and revealing that all actions, and many thoughts, have consequences.

On occasion, the vindictive ("Blood Bill," 2005) and the zealot ("Mr. Poo-Poo," 2007) become capable of making their delusion the prevailing, destructive vision in one of Oliver's tales; in other cases, such as "The Dreams of Cardinal Vittorini" (2003), a vision invoked willingly opens vistas of abysmal and utterly hopeless terror that no amount of time or effort can erase. One of his stories about dementia ("Flowers of the Sea," 2011) carries this phenomenon to an unforgettably poignant level that is simultaneously terrifying and heartbreaking.

Throughout his work, a person's character is often the only decisive factor leading to the safe(r) course when a decision is necessary. Sometimes life offers the opportunity to make the correct choice between alternatives ("The Road from Damascus," 2007), but it is filled just as often with damned if you do/damned if you don't situations whose implications might not be perceived until long afterward ("Love at First Sight," 2016).

In all of this, Oliver's command of atmosphere, characterization, and incisive dialogue are critical. He has acclaimed atmosphere as "the supreme ingredient" in crafting fiction, "evoking a mood that will bring about in the reader a sense of wonder, unease and deep reflection about the underlying nature of the universe" (Schettin 2013). Through this he often evokes a dread that strikes deeper than the threat of mere physical harm. Allied to this is the actor's knack for capturing a person's character through his or her use of language, and the ability to make each word of dialogue count, ironically or ominously, toward the denouement. His use of language also instills many of the stories with a vein of sly humor—"Mr. Poo-Poo," "Mmm-Delicious" (2007), "Mrs. Midnight" (2009)—which serves to sharpen the edge of unease.

Also on the subject of language, none excel and few equal the ventriloquial ease with which he captures the tone, cadence, and vocabulary of periods ranging from the present decade through the past, in stories set in the decadent underbelly of the Weimar Republic ("Singing Blood," 2011), a late Victorian courtroom ("Miss Marchant's Cause," 2003), the home and psyche of the mad nineteenth-century artist Richard Dadd ("A Child's Problem," 2011), the Restoration stage ("The Constant Rake," 2005), the ecclesiastical courts of sixteenth-century Italy ("The Dreams of Cardinal Vittorini"), and many more, including many stories revolving around stage productions, several stories reexamining the antiquarian underpinnings of M. R. James's ghost stories, and that grim *tour de force* "The Lord of the Fleas" (2012), which writer D. F. Lewis has aptly described as an "eighteenth century quilt of documents" (Lewis 2013).

Jim Rockhill

See also: Campbell, Ramsey; James, M. R.

Further Reading

Gevers, Nick. 2013. "An Interview with Reggie Oliver." *SF Site*. https://www.sfsite.com/12a/ro405.htm.

Griffin, Jude. 2015. "Author Spotlight: Reggie Oliver." *Nightmare* 36 (September). http://www.nightmare-magazine.com/nonfiction/author-spotlight-reggie-oliver.

Lewis, D. R. 2013. "Flowers of the Sea—Reggie Oliver." *Dreamcatcher—Gestalt Real-Time Reviews*, November 15. https://dflewisreviews.wordpress.com/2013/11/15/flowers-of-the-sea-reggie-oliver.

Oliver, Reggie. 2007. *Masques of Satan: Twelve Tales and a Novella*. Ashcroft, British Columbia: Ash-Tree Press.

Schettin, Silvia. 2013. "Reggie Oliver: The Art of the Short Story." *Fata Libelli*, September 16. http://fatalibelli.com/blog/2013/09/16/reggie-oliver-the-art-of-the-short-story.

Slatter, Angela. 2015. "Horrorology Interviews: Reggie Oliver." *Horrorology*, September 22. http://www.angelaslatter.com/horrorology-interviews-reggie-oliver.

ONIONS, OLIVER (1873–1961)

Oliver Onions was a prolific English author, best known for his ghost stories. Onions made his living as a writer of novels in almost every popular genre, including romance, historical fiction, science fiction, fantasy, and detective fiction. His horror fiction, however, consists of short stories, tending to focus on the theme of insanity.

"The Beckoning Fair One": Haunting of the Artist

Paul Oleron, the protagonist of Oliver Onions's classic story, rents a house with an eye toward completing his new novel there. But shortly after moving in, Paul finds it impossible to get any writing done, and his attitude begins to change toward his characters. Whereas Paul had previously believed that this novel would be his masterpiece, he now thinks everything about it is wrong, especially the title character, whom he has based on his girlfriend, Elsie. She grows increasingly concerned at his changing personality and erratic behavior. When Paul inquires about the house's previous history, he is informed that it has been vacant for twelve years and that the previous tenant, an artist, died there of apparent intentional starvation. During her visits to the house, Elsie is repeatedly injured by loose boards and exposed nails—almost as though the house is trying to hurt her. Elsie and Paul become estranged, and when Paul finds it more and more difficult to leave the premises, he realizes that a presence the house is imbued with is clinging to him like a terribly jealous lover. In the end Elsie dies under mysterious circumstances—maybe murdered by Paul—and Paul is removed from the house in a terrible state, suffering from starvation.

As a ghost story, "The Beckoning Fair One" is notable for its complete absence of any ghostly manifestations. The impact of the haunting is seen entirely in Paul's psychological and physical decline under the influence of the presence that has taken hold of him. The story's denouement resonates strongly with the fate suffered by the house's previous tenant, and it suggests that Oleron's is just one in a succession of similar fates suffered by others under the house's influence. The identity of who—or what—is haunting the house is never definitively established. "The Beckoning Fair One" has been praised by Robert Aickman, Everett F. Bleiler, and other authorities on supernatural fiction as one of the best ghost stories in the English language.

Stefan R. Dziemianowicz

During his lifetime, Onions published five collections of ghost stories: *Back o' the Moon* (1906), *Widdershins* (1911), *Ghosts in Daylight* (1924), *The Painted Face* (1929), and *Bells Rung Backward* (1953). His *Collected Ghost Stories* appeared in 1935. Of these, it was his second collection, *Widdershins*, which contains his most highly regarded work, particularly an influential tale called "The Beckoning Fair One," which was first published in *Widdershins*. This story is considered the single best treatment of Onions's preferred theme in horror: an artist who becomes so engrossed in his own imagination that he loses touch with reality. In this case, that loss of contact is facilitated by an invisible, feminine presence that is apparently the heroine of the novel he is writing; he imagines her so vividly that she appears to take on an independent existence and begins to dominate his life entirely.

Whether or not this "Beckoning Fair One" is anything more than his hallucination is never demonstrated clearly one way or the other. The story is distinguished not only by its thoughtful approach to the theme, but by the sophistication and beauty of its prose, which establishes Onions among the most skilled stylists in the genre.

Many of Onions's other stories likewise involve a mysterious figure who may or may not be real, and who acts as a focal point for the fantasies of an imaginative main character. In this, Onions may be said to extend a line in weird fiction that runs back through Henry James and E. T. A. Hoffmann. In his novella entitled "The Real People," a writer's characters take on an independent existence. In stories such as "The Rosewood Door" and "The Rope in the Rafters," characters assume past identities, or are taken over by archaic consciousnesses; the subject is treated largely psychologically, not unlike Walter de la Mare's novel *The Return*. However, Onions tended to specialize in main characters who are more aware of the suicidal or self-destructive aspects of their fantasies, but who are unable to resist them anyway. His characters often reach a point when they embrace demise rather than abandon a dream, which imparts a special mood of despair or fatalism to their tales. He adopts the figure of the doppelgänger, the fear of death by possession or replacement, in stories like "Rooum" and "The Painted Face," although in the latter story the main character commits suicide in order to save the one she loves from an evil spirit.

Onions is best remembered for his extreme attention to plausibility in his stories. His ghosts have no conventional trappings and are represented only in highly subtle, unsensational ways, which not only make it more difficult to discern what is and what is not psychological in the story, but which also ensures that the ghostliness is not ruined by clichés. In this way, he also carries forward the legacy of writers like Joseph Sheridan Le Fanu, who began the process of separating horror fiction from Gothic backgrounds and introducing it into contemporary settings that would have been more familiar, and more close to home, for the reading audience.

Michael Cisco

See also: Psychological Horror.

Further Reading

Ashley, Mike. 1992. "Oliver Onions: The Man at the Edge." In *Discovering Classic Horror Fiction I*, edited by Darrell Schweitzer, 120–126. Mercer Island, WA: Starmont.

Donaldson, Norman. 1985. "Oliver Onions." In *Supernatural Fiction Writers*, edited by E. F. Bleiler, 505–512. New York: Scribner's.

THE OTHER

The Other (1971) was the first novel by American novelist and former Hollywood actor Thomas Tryon, and it offers much in terms of horror. The narrator, thirteen-year-old Niles, is twin to his brother Holland, who seems to be one of the most destructive individuals in fiction. The novel is set in 1935 on an ancestral family farm in Connecticut, and it details the increasingly sinister and sociopathic acts of Holland, as told from Niles's viewpoint, during a summer when their family has gathered to mourn the passing of the boys' father, who died in a horrible accident. It is eventually revealed that the portrayal of Holland is false, and is a fantasy of Niles's, who is the novel's real villain.

Tryon's authorial skill is evident throughout, from the lushness of his descriptive writing in portraying the bucolic setting to his effective creation of a believable narrator in Niles, who truly seems to be reliable through much of the story as he draws readers from one episode of horror to another. This renders the final reveal all the more shocking and unsettling.

Like Mark Twain's *Adventures of Huckleberry Finn* or Tryon's *Harvest Home*, *The Other* offers a picture of what initially appears to be an inviting rural life, where all is idealistic and pleasant, only to expose, gradually, the horrors that may lurk—and lurk not very deeply—beneath seemingly pleasant surfaces. Reviewer I. P. Heldman has characterized the novel as "a Jamesian nightmare of psychological tension in a brooding atmosphere of insidious terror and madness" (quoted in "Thomas Tryon" 2003). Horror scholar S. T. Joshi has asserted that both *The Other* and Tryon's next novel, *Harvest Home*, had a significant impact on the horror genre itself: ""What *The Exorcist* did for the tale of supernatural horror, *The Other* and *Harvest Home* did for the non-supernatural tale of psychological horror: they legitimized it and showed that in the hands of a master it formed a genuine sub-genre of the weird tale" (Joshi 2001, 190). *The Other* was adapted for film in 1972 by director Robert Mulligan.

Benjamin F. Fisher

See also: *Harvest Home*; Psychological Horror; Unreliable Narrator.

Further Reading

Chaon, Dan. 2012. "Afterword." In *The Other* by Thomas Tryon, 253–258. New York: New York Review of Books.

Joshi, S. T. 2001. *The Modern Weird Tale*. Jefferson, NC and London: McFarland.

"Thomas Tryon." 2003. *Contemporary Authors Online*. Detroit, MI: Gale.

OUR LADY OF DARKNESS

Fritz Leiber's 1977 novel *Our Lady of Darkness*, expanded from a novella published in 1971 as "The Pale Brown Thing," is a compelling work of contemporary urban Gothic. Winner of the 1978 World Fantasy Award for best novel, it capped Leiber's long career as a pioneer of tales of urban dread and modern occult horror.

Set in San Francisco, the novel features as protagonist an aging horror writer and bibliophile named Franz Westren, who is clearly an autobiographical projection; indeed, Westren occupies the Geary Street apartment house where Leiber himself lived during the 1970s. Like Alfred Hitchcock's *Vertigo* (1958), *Our Lady of Darkness* offers a subtle evocation of the City by the Bay's buried history of supernatural legend, deeply connected to a local tradition of the fantastic that goes back to Ambrose Bierce and Clark Ashton Smith. The story centers on a (fictitious) secret book, Thibaut de Castries's *Megapolisomancy: A New Science of Cities*, which elaborates a theory of "paramental entities" (Leiber 2010, 39), hostile emanations of "all that stuff accumulating in big cities, its sheer liquid and solid mass" (22). In an eerie echo of the narrative of Leiber's classic short story "Smoke Ghost" (1941), our hero hurries anxiously through a city growing more estranged, "searching the dark sea of roofs" for "a swift pale brown thing stalking him," confident in its mastery of the landscape and "taking advantage of every bit of cover" (105) to stalk him relentlessly. Each feature of the skyline is a latent menace, each familiar scene transformed into an incipient wasteland of "electro-mephitic city-stuff" (81), the entropic sediment of human conglomeration rife with ghostly predators.

The culmination of a lifetime of reading in the field, *Our Lady of Darkness* not only draws upon influences as diverse as M. R. James and H. P. Lovecraft, it weaves them into a tapestry that takes on an almost metafictional dimension in its direct and self-conscious allusions to classic works of horror fiction and the biographies of major horror writers. At the same time, Leiber develops a unique and compelling form of modern occultism, the aforementioned "megapolisomancy," a form of secret knowledge that permits adepts to scry the city as one would a crystal ball, searching for portents and prophecies unleashed by the local concentration of paramental energies. *Our Lady of Darkness* is similar to Whitley Streiber's *The Wolfen* (1978) and Ken Eulo's *The Brownstone* (1980) in depicting the contemporary city as a breeding ground for malign supernatural presences, but it is considerably more ambitious in conception and more skillful in execution.

Rob Latham

See also: Bierce, Ambrose; Dark Fantasy; Forbidden Knowledge or Power; Leiber, Fritz; Lovecraftian Horror; Smith, Clark Ashton; World Fantasy Award.

Further Reading

Leiber, Fritz. [1977] 2010. *Our Lady of Darkness*. New York: Tom Doherty Associates.

Pardoe, Rosemary. 2004. "*Our Lady of Darkness*: A Jamesian Classic?" *Fantasy Commentator* 11 (Summer): 151–168.

Waugh, Robert. 2004. "Fritz Leiber's *Our Lady of Darkness*: Lovecraft, the Compound Ghost." *Studies in Modern Horror* 3: 7–17.

"OUT OF THE DEEP"

Published originally in 1923 as part of the collection *The Riddle and Other Stories*, Walter de la Mare's short psychological horror story "Out of the Deep" is one of the author's most well-known inconclusive ghost stories. In keeping with de la Mare's usual themes of the supernatural, "Out of the Deep" is also one of the author's foremost examples of the haunted house story.

The narrative follows Jimmie, who has returned to the house in which he was raised, following the death of his uncle. De la Mare's flair for suspenseful atmospheric writing can be seen throughout, as Jimmie is besieged by fearful memories of his childhood that take the form of ghostly apparitions of the household's serving staff. Unable to discern between the present reality and his ghostly memories, Jimmie dies mysteriously at the story's climax.

Much like the protagonist, the reader undergoes several psychological turns throughout the story, and the characteristic ambiguity of de la Mare's storytelling leaves the reader haunted by the narrative's lack of resolve. The descriptively Gothic elements of the household setting—particularly the shadowy and adorned recesses of the room in which Jimmie sleeps—are visually representative of de la Mare's unwillingness to cast a light upon the latent supernatural horrors that underlie the more explicit psychological horror.

Freudian psychology is, once again, not far from the heart of the narrative, and de la Mare makes it clear that it is from the recesses of the human psyche—from memory, from our childhood past—that long-buried and unrealized fears arise out of the deep and most successfully inhabit and augment our fearful imaginations.

Jimmie's childhood fears seem to be overtly linked to the bell cord that his aunt and uncle pulled to summon the servants. Moreover, the overwhelming terror that afflicts Jimmie at the thought of summoning the household's serving staff—compounded by the appearance of several phantoms in answer to his summons—suggests, perhaps, that a deeply ingrained classism is to be found at the center of the story.

Much like the silent crowd of phantoms that throng the seemingly empty house in de la Mare's most famous poem, "The Listeners" (1912), Jimmie is haunted by the collective presence of others. In particular, the phantasmic presence of the servants is not only supernatural, a reversal of the natural order; it is also an inversion of the social order, in which those who should remain invisible within the household (the serving staff) become visible to its occupants. In this way, "Out of the Deep" very much details the upper class's fears of their subordinates.

Ian Kinane

See also: de la Mare, Walter; "The Listeners"; *The Return.*

Further Reading

Clute, John. 1985. "Walter de la Mare." In *Supernatural Fiction Writers: Fantasy and Horror Vol. 1*, edited by E. F. Bleiler, 497–504. New York: Scribner Sons.

Crawford, Gary William. 1992. "On the Edge: The Ghost Stories of Walter de la Mare." *Discovering Classic Horror Fiction I*, edited by Darrell Schweitzer, 53–56. Rockville, MD: Wildside Press.

de la Mare, Walter. 1923. *The Riddle, and Other Stories.* London: Selwyn & Blount.

Stableford, Brian. 2005. "Walter de la Mare." In *The A to Z of Fantasy Literature.* Lanham, MD: Scarecrow Press.

PALAHNIUK, CHUCK (1962-)

Charles Michael "Chuck" Palahniuk is an American novelist and journalist. As of 2016, he has published fourteen novels, a short story collection, and several pieces of non-fiction. Though only a small portion of his work can categorically be considered "horror," his transgressive style and bleak worldview have made him a central figure in the contemporary macabre.

Palahniuk is best known for his first novel, *Fight Club* (1996). The novel met with lukewarm attention upon release, but after being adapted for film by director David Fincher it has gathered a cult following. *Fight Club*'s cynical and at times nihilistic indictment of contemporary corporate life has cemented its status as a key text of the Generation-X literary zeitgeist. All of Palahniuk's fiction is marked by an inclination toward the grotesque, the transgressive, and the nihilistic. Yet his contribution to the horror genre is largely concentrated within a sequence of three novels that Palahniuk has himself termed his "horror trilogy."

Lullaby (2001) concerns the search for a poem that, when read aloud, has the power to kill. At the beginning of the novel this "culling song" has resulted in the accidental death of the protagonist's family. The plot concerns his attempt to track down and eradicate the threat. In addition to this basic plot, which is clearly influenced by the success of urban-legend horror in films such as *Ringu* (1998), *Lullaby* also features a necrophiliac paramedic and an estate agent who specializes in haunted houses.

Diary (2002) is a more conventional piece of American Gothic. Its depiction of the sinister recesses of small-town America is clearly influenced by the work of Shirley Jackson and Stephen King. *Diary* is the story of Misty Wilmot, an aspiring artist who relocates to her husband's isolated island community. Once there she discovers that she is part of a sinister conspiracy in which her art, and her life, are to be sacrificed for the good of the town. Though there is little of the body horror that typifies Palahniuk's other work, *Diary* achieves a quiet eeriness that stands alone in his writing so far.

Of all Palahniuk's novels, *Haunted* (2005) is most clearly situated in the horror genre. It has an unusual structure, comprising nearly two dozen short narratives, framed within a wider story of confinement and abuse. The protagonists have each volunteered to be part of a writing retreat under the control of the elderly Mr. Whittier. They are taken to an abandoned theater and locked inside, under the proviso that they will be released once their writing is complete. Soon, however, the group descends to barbarity, eschewing literary creation in favor of a horror story that they can make (and sell) out of their own experience. They each tell their own tales, while brutalizing themselves and each other. Cannibalism and bodily dismemberment ensues. Nothing in the violence of the framing narrative can compete with the opening tale, "Guts." This story is infamous for making audience members faint during live readings.

A possible inspiration for this turn to outright horror is the real-life murder of Palahniuk's father in 1999. Palahniuk was asked to contribute to the legal discussion regarding whether the murderer should receive the death sentence. Critics have seen his horror trilogy as an attempt to deal with his responsibility in deciding the fate of another human being.

Though Palahniuk has gone on to write prolifically, releasing a novel per year since 2007, he has yet to match the potency of his horror trilogy. The first two installments of another trilogy, *Damned* (2011) and *Doomed* (2013), are horror-inflected, but they prioritize satire over any darker intent. However, a return to the world of *Fight Club* in a graphic novel sequel (2015–2016), does suggest that Palahniuk's violent, nihilistic sensibility may make a startling reappearance in future work.

Neil McRobert

See also: Body Horror; Frame Story; King, Stephen; Jackson, Shirley.

Further Reading

Kuhn, Cynthia, and Lance Rubin, eds. 2009. *Reading Chuck Palahniuk: American Monsters and Literary Mayhem*. New York: Routledge.
Palahniuk, Chuck. 2004. *Non Fiction*. London: Vintage.
Sartain, Jeffrey, ed. 2009. *Sacred and Immoral: On the Writings of Chuck Palahniuk*. Newcastle, UK: Cambridge Scholars Press.

PENNY DREADFUL

Penny dreadful is a name that was bestowed on penny newspapers filled with tales of adventure and horror that were published in England in the 1830s and 1840s. They were also referred to as "penny bloods" in reference to their blood-and-thunder style of storytelling. In the decades since, the term penny dreadful has become a catch-all phrase denoting publications with sensational or exploitative content.

Penny dreadfuls were made possible through the new machine manufacture of paper in the early nineteenth century and the invention of the rotary steam printing press, both of which allowed publishers to mass-produce printed publications relatively inexpensively. They were printed as pamphlets with dense, multicolumn text, usually adorned with a lurid cover engraving, and sold primarily to working-class readers as cheap entertainment. Penny dreadfuls were the successors to the Gothic bluebooks, or "shilling shockers," themselves the successors to the Gothic novels of the late eighteenth and early nineteenth centuries, and their contents were often redolent of both. Some featured self-contained stories, but most offered serial installments of longer works meant to entice readers to buy succeeding weekly or bi-weekly installments. By their nature the serial stories were written to run as long as they were popular with readers, meaning that their plots were often very loosely constructed, and they were often padded with chapters of history not essential to the story, unresolved subplots, and repetitive short lines of dialogue.

The best-known penny dreadfuls include James Malcolm Rymer and Thomas Peckett Prest's *Varney the Vampire* (serialized in 220 chapters between 1845 and 1847), G. W. M. Reynolds's *Wagner the Wehr-Wolf* (1846–1847), and Rymer's *The String of Pearls* (possibly written in collaboration with Thomas Peckett Prest), which is the best-known version of the story of Sweeney Todd, "The Demon Barber of Fleet Street," who murdered his patrons and gave their remains to his partner in crime, Mrs. Lovett, to be baked into meat pies for public consumption. A number of penny dreadfuls were the work of serial writers, hence their slapdash execution: *The Mysteries of London* was a four-series story about the seedy underbelly of street life in London begun in 1844 by G. W. M. Reynolds and finished several years later by Thomas Miller and Edward L. Blanchard.

Not all penny dreadfuls featured horror themes. The *Newgate Calendar*—a monthly account of imprisonments and executions in England's Newgate Prison, first published in book form in 1774—provided fodder for the penny papers, as did *The Terrific Register* (1825), an anthology of exotic atrocities and gruesome crimes from around the world. Dick Turpin, the infamous highwayman executed in 1739, was the hero of a number of penny dreadfuls, among them *Black Bess; or, The Knight of the Road*, which ran for 254 installments between 1867 and 1868. Spring-Heeled Jack, a leaping bandit reputed to have preyed upon women in London in the 1830s (and whose exploits were later conflated with those of Jack the Ripper), was the main character in several penny dreadfuls. Pirates, outlaws, freebooters, revolutionaries, robbers, and cowboys all put in appearances in the penny dreadfuls, as did folk heroes such as Robin Hood and celebrities from real life, including Buffalo Bill. Some of the more popular penny dreadfuls were plagiarized from the work of Charles Dickens and other celebrity writers of the era.

W. M. Clarke, Edward Lloyd, and others founded their publishing empires on the strength of their penny dreadful sales. By the 1850s, public disapproval of the content of penny dreadfuls and its impact on the sensibilities of young readers contributed to the conversion of penny papers to more genteel publications for young boys, among them *The Boy's Own Paper, Boys of England,* and *The Young Gentleman's Journal*. These papers were forerunners of the nickel weeklies and dime novels published at the end of the nineteenth century, which in turn paved the way for the pulp fiction magazines of the first half of the twentieth century.

In May 2014 the Showtime cable television channel premiered *Penny Dreadful*, a horror series set in Victorian England with a mash-up plot featuring characters from classic nineteenth-century horror fiction, including Bram Stoker's *Dracula*,

Mary Shelley's *Frankenstein*, Oscar Wilde's *The Picture of Dorian Gray*, and Robert Louis Stevenson's *Strange Case of Dr. Jekyll and Mr. Hyde*.

Stefan R. Dziemianowicz

See also: Dracula; The Picture of Dorian Gray; Pulp Horror; The Strange Case of Dr. Jekyll and Mr. Hyde; Vampires; Varney the Vampire; or, The Feast of Blood; Werewolves.

Further Reading

Angelo, Michael. 1977. *Penny Dreadfuls and Other Victorian Horrors*. London: Jupiter Books.
Haining, Peter, ed. 1976. *The Penny Dreadful*. London: Gollancz.

THE PHANTOM OF THE OPERA

The Phantom of the Opera began as a French Gothic novel published in 1910 by the prolific journalist and mystery-adventure novelist Gaston Leroux (1868–1927). Building on Leroux's knowledge of the real Paris Opera, begun in the 1860s under architect Charles Garnier, and fictionalizing several of that era's headlines to provide a news-like authenticity (including the actual fall of a chandelier into the Opera audience in 1896), the novel focuses on a musician-composer-architect-builder calling himself "Erik," supposedly one of the Opera's original designers.

Erik sequesters himself deep in the lower cellars underneath the Opera—indeed, on the shores of the underground lake (which actually exists because swampland had to be drained before the Opera could be built)—and hides himself there, while often trying to affect what happens in the world above. He is ashamed of the skull-face he bears from birth, over which has grown only thin and parchment-yellow skin, a visage suggested to Leroux by *danse macabre* paintings descended from medieval times and rarely used as the phantom's real visage in most adaptations.

The action of the novel commences after Erik witnesses a girl from the country, Christine Daae, join the opera chorus. After hearing her sing, he becomes her unseen voice teacher (and Freudian father-figure) from behind her dressing-room's walls and falls in love with her (regarding her at times as a replacement for his mother, since Freud's concepts were taking hold by 1910). Soon, though, Christine's improvement starts making her a rival for major roles with the Opera's diva, Carlotta—whom the phantom chases off the stage by cutting down the chandelier—and she welcomes visits from her childhood sweetheart, the Vicomte Raoul de Chigny, a patron of the Opera delighted to find his former love after many years.

To get closer to Christine, Erik disguises himself—except that he uses his actual skull-face—as the figure of "Red Death" (from an 1845 story by Poe) at the Opera's gala masked ball, a real annual event from the 1870s to the present. Alarmed by his pupil drifting from him, he captures her and takes her to his underground lair, where he woos her by rehearsing Verdi's *Otello* with her while wearing a black mask—adding racial, even miscegenistic overtones not present in any later

Leroux's novel became a popular subject for stage and screen adaptations soon after its publication. Some of the more significant English-language movie adaptations are as follows.

1925   *The Phantom of the Opera* (Universal Studios), starring Lon Chaney Sr. Chaney was the most significant horror movie actor of the silent period, and Leroux himself was involved in negotiating with Universal to get this adaptation made. The scene in which the heroine unmasks Chaney's truly horrifying-looking Phantom is among the most memorable in early cinema.

1943   *The Phantom of the Opera* (Universal Studios), starring Claude Raines. A remake of the 1925 version, this version made strong use of Technicolor and sumptuous set design and costuming to generate a general air of operatic spectacle.

1962   *The Phantom of the Opera* (Hammer Films), starring Herbert Lom. Hammer made this one in partnership with Universal, right on the heels of Hammer's massive success in rebooting and reimagining the classic Universal Frankenstein, Dracula, and Mummy horror series. Their Phantom film fell short of these others but still produced a few memorable moments.

1974   *Phantom of the Paradise* (20th Century Fox), starring Paul Williams. Directed by Brian De Palma, this cult movie mixes Leroux's original Phantom plot with elements of Faust and Oscar Wilde's *Picture of Dorian Gray* to produce a fairly delirious result. It received Academy Award and Golden Globe nominations for its music.

1989   *The Phantom of the Opera* (21st Century Film Corporation), starring Robert Englund. This gory adaptation is mainly notable for featuring Englund, best known for playing the character of Freddy in the *Nightmare on Elm Street* movies, in the title role.

2004   *The Phantom of the Opera* (Warner Bros. Pictures), starring Gerard Butler. Joel Schumacher directed this big-budget cinematic adaptation of the popular stage musical adaptation by Andrew Lloyd Webber.

Matt Cardin

adaptation—until she abruptly unmasks him and recoils at beholding Death incarnate.

Meanwhile, Raoul joins forces with a Persian detective (who has chased Erik to Paris from the Middle East, where he used to do magic and construct torture chambers for a shah) and climbs down a labyrinth of dark passages toward the cellars to rescue Christine. There they face exotic Oriental obstacles that Erik now puts in their way, a symptom of the racist Orientalism that was quite common at the Paris Opera—and in Europe generally—at the time of the novel.

This story conflates many mythical, literary, and contemporary sources, starting with several Greek myths about Death and the Maiden, the best known of which is

Pluto and Persephone (in which the god of the underworld kidnaps the daughter of Demeter, goddess of the harvest). It also carries forward several features from Victor Hugo's *Hunchback of Notre Dame* (1831), Honoré de Balzac's *Sarrasine* (1830), Bram Stoker's *Dracula* (1897), and the notorious French scandal of the 1890s known as the Dreyfus Affair, on which Leroux reported and in which a Jewish officer in Paris was falsely charged with espionage and returned from imprisonment for a retrial as emaciated as a skeleton.

Leroux's novel lost popularity after 1912 until the author himself negotiated the adaptation of it as a silent film released by Universal in 1925 and starring Lon Chaney, the premier star of silent horror pictures. That version, though it changed the novel significantly, set a standard for many that have come after it on the stage, film, and television. The most successful of these has been the stage-musical version by Andrew Lloyd Webber, Charles Hart, and Richard Stilgoe, which debuted in London in 1986 and then on Broadway during the 1987–1988 season. Since then, it has become the longest-running play in Broadway history, augmented by many touring companies and a film version that have carried it around the world.

Jerrold E. Hogle

See also: Body Horror; *Dracula*; Gothic Hero/Villain; Hugo, Victor; "The Masque of the Red Death"; Poe, Edgar Allan; Stoker, Bram.

Further Reading

Hogle, Jerrold E. 2002. *The Undergrounds of the Phantom of the Opera: Sublimation and the Gothic in Leroux's Novel and Its Progeny.* New York: Palgrave.

Perry, George, and Jane Rice 1987. *The Complete Phantom of the Opera.* New York: Henry Holt.

Wolf, Leonard, ed. and trans. 1996. *The Essential Phantom of the Opera, Including the Complete Novel by Gaston Leroux.* New York: Plume/Penguin.

"THE PHANTOM 'RICKSHAW"

Rudyard Kipling's "The Phantom 'Rickshaw" was originally published in *Quartette,* the Christmas Annual of the *Civil and Military Gazette* for 1885, and later collected in *The Phantom Rickshaw and Other Eerie Tales* (1888). It was Kipling's first supernatural story, and on one level, it is a traditional ghost story, the tale of a wrongdoer haunted and done in by those he wronged. In the judgment of Kipling scholar Louis Cornell, "The Phantom 'Rickshaw" is reminiscent of Edgar Allan Poe's "The Tell-Tale Heart" and "The Black Cat," but more than that, the story is actual superior to those two because of its deployment of traditional Gothic elements in a recognizable contemporary setting.

The story is presented as the deathbed narrative of Theobald Jack Pansay, an Englishman resident in Simla, India. While en route from Gravesend to Bombay, Pansay had an affair with Agnes Keith-Wessington, the wife of an officer, destroying her marriage. Although Pansay attempted to break off his relations, she followed him to Simla, over the course of the next year repeatedly letting him know from her 'rickshaw that she was there for him. A thoroughgoing cad, Pansay disregarded her and pursued others, becoming engaged to Kitty Mannering. Mrs. Keith-Wessington dies, but to his horror, Pansay finds himself haunted by her as well as her four liveried servants and the 'rickshaw from which she used to speak to him, although there is incontrovertible evidence that all (including the servants) are dead and that the 'rickshaw has been destroyed. Nobody else can see the ghosts, but Pansay's behavior attracts attention among the English colonials. The local doctor, Heathlegh, attempts to treat Pansay for hallucinations, but the 'rickshaw is present when the treatment concludes, and when the history of his treatment of Mrs. Keith-Wessington emerges, Pansay finds his engagement concluded. Pansay realizes that his days in India are numbered, and though he cannot understand why he must face punishment in this world rather than the next, he has conversations with Mrs. Wessington and accepts his fate before dying.

Certainly Pansay deserves what happens to him, for he is as unpleasant a character as Kipling ever created. Adding depth to the story is the depiction of the world of the English colonials residing in India: theirs is a closed society in which a transgression leads inevitably to ostracism. At the same time, Heathlegh's solution offers readers a different perspective, one that is rational and rejects the supernatural: that Pansay merely suffered from a mental problem, in which the haunting is a manifestation of his conscience. Finally, there is the pathos of Mrs. Keith-Wessington: hers is not a vengeful ghost, merely one who wants the love that has been denied to her when she was alive, and in attempting to get her due, she emerges as a surprisingly sympathetic specter.

In his autobiography *Something of Myself* (1937), Kipling said "The Phantom 'Rickshaw" was one of the first things that he wrote under the clear influence of his "Personal Daemon," a creative force that he experienced as being external to him, and that he described as guiding him in his authorial career.

Richard Bleiler

See also: Kipling, Rudyard; "The Recrudescence of Imray"/"The Return of Imray"; "They."

Further Reading

Cornell, Louis L. 1966. *Kipling in India*. New York: Macmillan.
Dillingham, William B. 2005. *Kipling: Hell and Heroism*. New York: Palgrave Macmillan.

PHANTOMS

The prolific American writer Dean Koontz has published numerous types of novels and has disputed being identified as a horror fiction writer. Though elements of horror do frequently appear in his stories, he is more correctly identified as a novelist of thrillers. He states in an afterword to a 2001 paperback reprint of his 1983 novel *Phantoms*, "Writing *Phantoms* was one of the ten biggest mistakes of my life," because this novel (which has sold more than 60 million copies worldwide) "earned for me the label of 'horror writer,' which I never wanted, never embraced, and have ever since sought to shed" (Koontz 2001, 432).

Nevertheless, *Phantoms* is generally regarded as a first-rate horror story, perhaps one of the finest in the genre. It narrates the story of two sisters—Lisa and Jenny Paige—who travel to Jenny's hometown of Snowfield, California, there to find the ski resort town to be entirely deserted. Jenny is a physician and Lisa is her fourteen-year-old sister. When they arrive at Jenny's home, they discover the corpse of Jenny's housekeeper lying on the floor, looking as if "she died in the middle of a scream" (15). Investigating the town, they discover more hideous corpses, some of them mutilated in sadistic fashion. They are able to contact the county authorities in Santa Mira, Sheriff Bryce Hammond and Lt. Talbert Whitman, who arrive in Snowfield to lead the investigation there. The most important clue they discover is the name "Timothy Flyte" written by one of the victims. Flyte, it appears, is a destitute British academic who once published a book entitled *The Ancient Enemy*, which recounts the mysterious mass disappearances of communities and populations through history.

Assisted by the Biological Investigations Unit of the American military, the group discovers that the "Ancient Enemy" is a massive creature able to shape parts of itself into any form or "phantom" that it desires. Growing in mass and size with each killing, this intelligent amoeba-like creature kills many of the investigators, including Flyte himself, who is brought to Snowfield at the creature's insistence in order to write its biography. A scientific solution is eventually discovered that defeats the monster via a bacteria solution that consumes its amorphous petroleum-like cell structure. A thought-provoking subplot also appears in the story about Fletcher Kale, a sociopath, who becomes a type of apostle of the Ancient Enemy, which presents itself to him as the Devil. The novel concludes with the possibility of Kale being infected by the Ancient Enemy before its destruction, thus leaving a dark, open-ended resolution to the story.

In an essay comparing and contrasting the central evil in *Phantoms* with that in two of Koontz's other novels, *Whispers* and *Darkfall*, Michael A. Morrison characterizes *Phantoms* as "the monster tale as police procedural" and notes that it focuses crucially on the mindset of the human protagonists as they confront something beyond their ken: "They are men and women of reason: systematic, scientific, rational. And much of *Phantoms* examines the responses of such people to the presence of an unknown" (Morrison 1998, 128–129). D. W. Taylor points out that the novel also engages not just its protagonists but its readers in a confrontation with this presence, and even turns this back upon the reader themselves: "[B]y the end of *Phantoms*, the hoary concept of a predestined evil from Hell has been turned upon the reader like a mirror, who suddenly finds himself staring rather uncomfortably into his own inexplicable, evil image" (Taylor 1998, 108).

Phantoms was released as a film in 1998, directed by Joe Chappelle and starring Peter O'Toole. Koontz wrote the screenplay based on his novel.

Gary Hoppenstand

See also: Koontz, Dean.

Further Reading

Koontz, Dean. [1983] 2001. *Phantoms*. New York: Berkley.

Lehti, Steven J. 1997. "Dean R. Koontz's *Phantoms*." *Cinefantasique* 29, no. 4/5 (October): 16–21.

Morrison, Michael A. 1998. "The Three Faces of Evil: The Monsters of *Whispers*, *Phantoms*, and *Darkfall*." In *Discovering Dean Koontz: Essays on America's Bestselling Writer of Suspense and Horror Fiction*, edited by Bill Munster, 120–143. San Bernardino, CA: Borgo Press.

Taylor, D. W. 1998. "Mainstream Horror in *Whispers* and *Phantoms*." In *Discovering Dean Koontz: Essays on America's Bestselling Writer of Suspense and Horror Fiction*, edited by Bill Munster, 97–111. San Bernardino, CA: Borgo Press.

"PICKMAN'S MODEL"

"Pickman's Model" is a short story by H. P. Lovecraft that was first published in the October 1927 issue of *Weird Tales*. It is among Lovecraft's most reprinted stories and it has been adapted numerous times for extraliterary media, notably by screenwriter Alvin Sapinsley for the December 1, 1971, episode of Rod Serling's *Night Gallery*.

Set in Boston, the story is a narrated as a monologue in the first person by a man named Thurber to his friend Eliot. Thurber refuses to travel with his friend via the city's subway system and by way of explanation he recounts his relationship with Richard Upton Pickman, a recently disappeared artist of the macabre who is shunned by the artistic establishment. It's less the horrific subject matter of Pickman's work—which frequently features dog-faced ghouls feeding—than its graphic realism that so distresses the art world.

Thurber relates how his admiration of Pickman's work compelled him to accept the artist's invitation one evening to visit his studio in Boston's North End, where Pickman points out that many of the houses are connected by a network of subterranean tunnels that date to the earliest years of New England's settling. Thurber is disturbed by several of Pickman's recent canvases hanging in the studio, including the painting "Subway Accident," which depicts the ghoul creatures emerging from train tunnels to attack a crowd on a platform, and "The Lesson," which appears to feature elder ghouls teaching a young human changeling how to feed on a corpse. When sounds are heard in the nearby room where the house's boarded-up tunnel entrance is located, Pickman investigates, fires several shots, and then returns to hastily conclude his meeting with Thurber. In his excitement, Thurber accidentally snatches a photo affixed to a corner of one of Pickman's works in progress. When

Lovecraft's description of Pickman's paintings demonstrates the power of written fiction to generate effects that would be difficult to capture with literal visual representations, for Pickman's paintings of ghouls, which Lovecraft describes as "beyond the power of words to classify," are obviously meant to exude a kind of primal horror that would be difficult, if not impossible, for an actual painting to achieve.

> There's no use in my trying to tell you what they were like, because the awful, the blasphemous horror, and the unbelievable loathsomeness and moral foetor came from simple touches quite beyond the power of words to classify.
>
> . . . The madness and monstrosity lay in the figures in the foreground—for Pickman's morbid art was preëminently one of daemoniac portraiture. These figures were seldom completely human, but often approached humanity in varying degree. Most of the bodies, while roughly bipedal, had a forward slumping, and a vaguely canine cast. The texture of the majority was a kind of unpleasant rubberiness. Ugh! I can see them now! Their occupations—well, don't ask me to be too precise. They were usually feeding—I won't say on what. They were sometimes shewn in groups in cemeteries or underground passages, and often appeared to be in battle over their prey—or rather, their treasure-trove. And what damnable expressiveness Pickman sometimes gave the sightless faces of this charnel booty! Occasionally the things were shewn leaping through open windows at night, or squatting on the chests of sleepers, worrying at their throats. One canvas shewed a ring of them baying about a hanged witch on Gallows Hill, whose dead face held a close kinship to theirs. (Lovecraft 2013, 93)

Matt Cardin

Source: Lovecraft, H. P. 2013. *The Thing on the Doorstep and Other Weird Stories*. New York: Penguin.

he looks at it later, expecting to see an image that Pickman is using for background detail, he discovers the truth about why Pickman's painted monsters appear so realistic.

Although not regarded as one of Lovecraft's tales of the Cthulhu Mythos, "Pickman's Model" can be appreciated in the same context as one of his efforts to depict an otherworldly race of beings that exists parallel to the human race, and largely unseen. References in the story suggest that the race of ghouls dates back at least to the Salem witch trials and the earliest years of New England history. Lovecraft lards the story with historic and geographic details that depict the ghoul culture as inextricable from the culture of those on whom they feed: the blue-blood stock of New England. The story has inspired a number of homages by other writers, including Robert Barbour Johnson's "Far Below" (1939) and Caitlín R. Kiernan's *Daughter of Hounds* (2006) and "Pickman's Other Model (1929)."

Stefan R. Dziemianowicz

See also: Arkham House; Lovecraft, H. P.; Lovecraftian Horror; Monsters; Pulp Horror; *Weird Tales*.

Further Reading

Anderson, James. 2002. "Pickman's Model: H. P. Lovecraft's Model of Terror." In *A Century Less a Dream: Selected Criticism on H. P. Lovecraft*, edited by Scott Connors, 195–205. Holicong, PA: Wildside.

Lovecraft, Howard P. [1927] 1999. "Pickman's Model." In *More Annotated Lovecraft*, edited by S. T. Joshi and Peter Cannon. New York: Dell.

Sederholm, Carl. 2006. "What Screams Are Made of: Representing Cosmic Fear in H. P. Lovecraft's 'Pickman's Model.'" *Journal of the Fantastic in the Arts* 16, no. 4 (Winter): 335–349.

THE PICTURE OF DORIAN GRAY

The Picture of Dorian Gray is Oscar Wilde's only novel, a supernatural tale of moral degeneration and hidden guilt. It began as a story told to his friends, but Philadelphia publisher J. M. Stoddart, on a visit to London, requested him to write it out for his magazine. It was published in *Lippincott's Monthly Magazine* for July 1890, where its thinly veiled homoeroticism stirred up controversy. Wilde extensively revised it before its book publication in 1891, toning down the homoeroticism and adding six chapters and a preface with the French Aestheticist argument that books are neither moral nor immoral but exist for their own sake.

Youthful Dorian Gray meets the hedonistic Lord Henry Wotton as he sits for a portrait. During the sitting Dorian wishes aloud to remain young while the portrait ages. He soon discovers his wish has been magically granted, but that it also reflects his evil deeds. Wotton gives him a yellow book, which helps to entice him into a corrupt, hedonistic lifestyle. The portrait, his symbolic conscience, gradually changes, reflecting his moral descent. Ashamed, he locks it in an unused upstairs room. Finally, he destroys the hated portrait with a knife, destroying himself in the process.

The book bears many similarities to Robert Louis Stevenson's *The Strange Case of Dr. Jekyll and Mr. Hyde*. Both involve moral decay, the separation of the good and evil aspects of human nature, and the self-destruction of the protagonist. Hyde's activities and Dorian's are largely left to the imagination.

Other major influences on it were Wilde's mother's translation of *Sidonia the Sorceress* by J. W. Meinhold with its double portrait of the good and evil versions of Sidonia; and *Melmoth the Wanderer* by Wilde's great-uncle, Charles Maturin, which has a hidden painting of a character who bargained with the devil to live 150 years. Other possible influences are Poe's "The Oval Portrait" and "William Wilson." The name Dorian alludes to the ancient Greek Dorian tribe, noted for homosexuality in their military. Dorian's character is partially based on Wilde himself and on his lover, Lord Alfred Douglas. The enticing yellow book is presumably the French Decadent novel *A Rebours* by J. K. Huysmans.

Critics attacked the magazine version, calling it immoral, unclean, and poisonous. It was used as evidence by the prosecution when Wilde was later tried for indecency. The book version received slightly less vehement criticism. An uncensored, annotated edition was published by Belknap Press in 2011.

The story has been adapted to ballet and opera and has been filmed many times between 1918 and 2009. Albert Lewin's version (1945), the most notable, won Academy and Golden Globe awards, as well as a retro Hugo. To this day, it is often said of youthful-appearing people that they "must have a portrait hidden in the attic."

Lee Weinstein

See also: Huysmans, J. K.; *Melmoth the Wanderer*; Poe, Edgar Allan; *The Strange Case of Dr. Jekyll and Mr. Hyde.*

Further Reading

Beckson, Karl E. 1998. *The Oscar Wilde Encyclopedia*. New York: AMS Press.

Belford, Barbara. 2000. *Oscar Wilde: A Certain Genius*. New York: Random House.

Gomel, Elana. 2004. "Oscar Wilde, *The Picture of Dorian Gray*, and the (Un)Death of the Author." *Narrative* 12, no. 1: 74–92.

Wilde, Oscar. [1890] 2011. *The Picture of Dorian Gray: An Annotated, Uncensored Edition*, edited by Nicholas Frankel. Cambridge, MA: Belknap Press.

POE, EDGAR ALLAN (1809–1849)

Edgar Allan Poe did not invent Gothic fiction, or supernatural fiction, or horror fiction, but he was certainly a significant heir of Gothic tradition, which he fashioned to his own purposes, thus refreshing literary Gothicism. Horror is indeed a signal feature in much of his work, but it is not horror for mere horror's sake. Critics taxed him for creating too much "German" (for which, read "Gothic" or "horror") substance, notably in his fiction. In the "Preface" to *Tales of the Grotesque and Arabesque* (1840), his first collection of his tales, most of which had been originally published in magazines or newspapers, he stated: "I maintain that terror is not of Germany but of the soul," adding that he composed those tales with that principle uppermost in mind (Poe 1984, 129). That this principle is evident in many of his poems, tales, and, certainly, in *The Narrative of Arthur Gordon Pym* (1838), Poe's only completed novel, is unmistakable.

Poe's biography is often thought to be sensational. Actually, his life was not extraordinary. He was no legendary drunkard as malicious gossip portrayed him; no drug addict, contrary to another misconception; and no debaucher—of young women, black cats, or ravens. If author Poe was pursued by any demon, that demon was poverty. His literary income for twenty-plus years' authorship was roughly ten thousand dollars, poverty level even in his day. Far too often, Poe's personal life has been presented as the basis for his creative writings, but that interpretation is also inaccurate.

"The Black Cat": A Sophisticated Rendering of Madness

First published in 1843, this popular story draws on the legend that cats, black cats in particular, understand human circumstances. The cat in Poe's tale, accidentally walled up alive, howls when its master, who has murdered his wife and wants to conceal her body behind a wall in the cellar, unwittingly disturbs the wall, thus prompting the cat's reaction, which leads to the opening of the wall, thus revealing the wife's decomposing corpse.

The cat's owner is a typical Poe first-person narrator who relates horrifying circumstances in what seems like a wholly rational manner. He has perpetrated a violent crime and is tortured by guilt, to the point where he reveals what he has done. The tale is rife with gory details of the narrator's physical abuse and murder of cats, but the reader may well wonder whether the image of a hanged cat that appears to the overwrought man's senses is a genuine image or a delusion of the murderer's imagination.

"The Black Cat" is one of Poe's excellent Gothic tales, which may be read with equal validity as a straight horror story or a sophisticated rendering of human emotion driven to madness, as readers from Poe's day to the present have recognized. Moreover, the role of the wife offers tantalizing ambiguities, notably, whether she is an innocent or, given the bond between her and the black cat, a witch, with the cat her familiar. Particulars connected with the narrator's supposed murders of the first cat and his wife furnish horror via violence, as well as providing the narrator's hallucinations about pain and death. These scenarios foreshadow his execution by hanging, which is associated with the horrors of strangling or the violence of the neck being broken.

Benjamin F. Fisher

Born January 19, 1809, as Edgar Poe, to actors David Poe Jr. and Elizabeth Arnold Hopkins Poe, he was the second of their three children. His siblings were William Henry Leonard Poe (1807–1831), usually known as Henry, and Rosalie Poe (1810–1874), adopted by the Mackenzies of Richmond, Virginia, so typically known as Rosalie Mackenzie Poe. David Poe Jr. deserted his family in 1811, and no documentary evidence has been discovered that details the rest of his life. Elizabeth died from tuberculosis later that year. Edgar became the foster child of John and Frances Allan, a childless couple of Richmond, so he came to sign his name as Edgar A. Poe, as if Allan were genuinely part of his name. John Allan, an immigrant from Scotland and a successful businessman, was a no-nonsense guardian. Frances Valentine Allan was far more sympathetic to their ward.

Edgar's early life with the Allans was fairly pleasant. He received a good education in English and American schools. He then attended the University of Virginia (February–December 1826), but Allan's scant financial support led to Poe's accumulating high gambling debts and his withdrawal, despite his academic credibility.

Poe quarreled with Allan, went to Boston, where he enlisted in the Army as "Edgar A. Perry," and published his first book, *Tamerlane and other Poems* "by a Bostonian" (1827). Poe's ambitions for authorship displeased the more practical-minded Allan.

Poe desired to be a poet akin to Lord Byron, Mary Shelley, and other British Romantic poets. He published two more slim books of verse, *Al Aaraaf, Tamerlane, and Minor Poems* (1829) and *Poems* (1831). He had also enrolled at West Point Military Academy, but tired of the regimen, got himself court martialed, and went to Baltimore, where he lived with his widowed, invalid grandmother, Elizabeth C. Poe, her daughter, Maria Poe Clemm, and Mrs. Clemm's daughter, Virginia, and Henry Poe (who died in August 1831). Henry, too, had literary ambitions, but his endeavors in authorship have sometimes been confused with Edgar's, given the practices of authorial anonymity then prevalent.

Poe's poems reveal undeniable links to Gothicism, for example, in the fearful or emotionally unsettled speakers in *Tamerlane*, "The Lake. To—," or "Spirits of the Dead," among early pieces, where weird, claustrophobic settings increase psychological unease. More intense psychological fears enhance later poems, for example, "The Raven" (1845), "The Conqueror Worm" (1843), and "Ulalume" (1847). The speakers are prey to anxieties, which seem mysterious, but which in "The Raven" prove to be grief for Lenore, who, in delightful ambiguity, may be literally dead or representative of a feminism "dead," that is, absent from the speaker's life. Likewise, Ulalume is no longer part of the speaker's normal life, but memories of her haunt him, much as a more literal ghost might torment its victim.

Poe's poems reveal his abilities to achieve exquisite mingling of sound with sense. Implications of scene and emotion closing in to overwhelm the speaker with claustrophobic, destructive feelings in "The Lake. To—," for example, are plausibly combined. The lyrical effects in "The Raven," "The Conqueror Worm," or "Ulalume" create a "music" that coalesces deftly with the decreasing rationality of the speaker, who ultimately succumbs to hypnotic effects of rhythms couching negative influences or what he imagines are negative influences.

Poe's early years in Baltimore, 1831–1833, still remain shadowy. Realizing, perhaps, that he was unlikely to achieve financial security from publishing verse, he began to write short stories or, as he preferred, "tales," emulating popular Gothic tales in *Blackwood's Edinburgh Magazine* and like periodicals. Poe entered five tales in a contest sponsored in late 1831 by the Philadelphia *Saturday Courier*; none won the prize, but all were published, unsigned, during 1832. In another prize competition for the best poem and the best tale, sponsored in 1833 by the Baltimore *Saturday Visiter*, Poe's tale "MS. Found in a Bottle" and his poem "The Coliseum" were chosen first in each category. The judges, though, didn't want to award both prizes to a single author, so the poetry prize went to John Hill Hewitt. He was connected with the *Visiter*, so Poe took umbrage.

Thanks to the kindness of John Pendleton Kennedy, an established Baltimore author who was a judge in the *Visiter* contest, Poe was hired by Thomas W. White, who established a new monthly magazine in Richmond, Virginia, the *Southern Literary Messenger*. Poe was managing editor for the magazine, though White had the final word on content. Although Poe published revised versions of some of his poems and tales, along with new pieces, in the *Messenger* during 1835–1836, he actually gained national fame for his reviews, which were accurate, if often stringent.

Poe rapidly perceived how much Gothic horror literature had become trite, featuring too many protagonists haunted by vague angst, in grim, often crumbling ancient castles as backdrops, and seemingly supernatural, too incredible horrors, multiplying to cause unease—all expressed in high-flown language. Alternatively, diabolic physical tortures and pain were inflicted on helpless victims of temperamental tyrants. Poe's literary artistry repeatedly transformed such clichéd settings, characters, and language into artistic symbolic representations of troubled human psychology.

In the early 1830s Poe's awareness of potential weaknesses in horror fiction also led him onto another path. Like many young people, he reacted against what he perceived as extremes and weaknesses—here, those in popular horror fiction—by confronting them with humor. He toyed with the idea of creating a book, "Tales of the Folio Club," featuring a group of pretentious authors, all caricatures of well-known writers of the times, who would meet monthly, enjoy ample drink and food, then proceed to read to each other an original tale, which the group would then criticize. The tales debated and the critical methods, too, would be discussed within a comic framework. The person whose tale was designated the worst had to host the next gathering. After several successive such penalties occurred to the same club member, he would decide to expose the pretentiousness and weaknesses in the club members and their productions, fleeing to a publisher to make public such folderol.

Thus Poe composed tales that parodied and satirized the themes and techniques of some much admired contemporary authors. Unfortunately, since no publisher would accept Poe's book because of financial uncertainties about its success with the reading public, Poe published the tales individually, thereby causing a confusion about his own aims and intentions that persists to the present.

Such tales as "Ligeia" (1838), "The Fall of the House of Usher" (1839), "The Masque of the Red Death" (1842), or "The Black Cat" (1843), to cite but a few, exemplify Poe's artistic, convincing portrayals of disintegrating minds. Although the surfaces in such tales may be horrific, they are the more terrifying because they are plausible. The narrators in the first two named tales and Prospero and his followers in the third represent destructive emotional forces that wreak horrors on the minds and perhaps the bodies of such characters.

Although he learned much about what would constitute best-selling horror fiction from models in *Blackwood's* and others of a similar nature, which were popular reading in his day and, in the case of *Blackwood's* in particular, which published horror fiction as a staple, Poe collected his stories, revised, into two volumes dated

1840 (actually published in late 1839). The book's title, *Tales of the Grotesque and Arabesque*, has continued to create confusion among critics, and clear distinctions between "grotesque" and "arabesque" have never been established.

Poe twice ventured beyond the tale as his venue. First, heeding the advice of James Kirke Paulding, an older, established author, Poe turned to writing a novel, *The Narrative of Arthur Gordon Pym*, which appeared in book form in 1838, though early chapters appeared in the *Messenger* in early 1837, during which time Poe left the magazine. Poe's second experiment in novel writing, *The Journal of Julius Rodman*, was serialized and left uncompleted in *Burton's Gentleman's Magazine* (January–June 1840). Poe had become editor of that magazine, though he also aspired to launch a literary magazine of his own, but those attempts failed. Poe and Burton ultimately clashed, so Poe accepted the offer of George R. Graham to edit *Graham's Magazine*, there publishing some of his most notable work, which included "The Murders in the Rue Morgue" (1841).

After unsuccessfully enlisting Graham to join his magazine project, Poe in 1843 went to New York City, where he would eventually publish the extended version of *Pym* and where he engaged in journalistic work, ultimately to become editor, then editor and proprietor of the *Broadway Journal*, a weekly literary periodical, during 1845–1846. Again Poe published revised versions of his stories and poems, along with perceptive reviews.

After he abandoned the *Broadway Journal*, Poe no longer had means of responding to antagonists (such antipathies caused chiefly by his often caustic reviews of some publisher's darling's book), and he became targeted by those who disliked him. Virginia Poe, who had long been suffering from tuberculosis, died in January 1847. In the wake of his devastation, Poe apparently sought understanding and compassion from other women, which has also led to many prurient speculations about his nature. Homeward bound from a successful visit to his onetime home, Richmond, where he had gone to lecture on poetry and politics, Poe was discovered in very poor physical condition in Baltimore in early October 1849. He was hospitalized, remained incoherent, died on October 7, 1849, and was buried in Westminster Presbyterian graveyard. In 1876, a memorial service was held, during which Poe's remains were moved to a new grave, replete with an imposing monument, in the front of the graveyard.

Because of a scurrilous, inaccurate biographical sketch of Poe by Rufus W. Griswold, then considered a prominent author and editor, Poe's reputation has repeatedly been called into question. There are persisting notions that Poe was diabolic and that he modeled all his literary protagonists on his own emotionally disordered self. The real reason for Poe's continuing fascination for readers is, however, that the weird, frightening characters and situations in his fiction and poems evince a "terror of the soul," which, in the "Preface" to *Tales of the Grotesque and Arabesque*, he himself called the mainstay of his creative endeavors.

Benjamin F. Fisher

See also: "The Fall of the House of Usher"; "Ligeia"; "The Masque of the Red Death"; Psychological Horror; Romanticism and Dark Romanticism; Unreliable Narrator.

Further Reading

Fisher, Benjamin F. 2008. *The Cambridge Introduction to Edgar Allan Poe.* Cambridge, UK: Cambridge University Press.

Poe, Edgar Allan. 1984. *Edgar Allan Poe: Poetry and Tales.* New York: Library of America.

Poe, Edgar Allan. 2008. *The Collected Letters of Edgar Allan Poe.* 2 vols. Edited by John Ward Ostrom. Revised, corrected, and expanded by Burton R. Pollin and Jeffrey A. Savoye. New York: Gordian Press.

Thomas, Dwight, and David K. Jackson. 1987. *The Poe Log: A Documentary Life of Edgar Allan Poe 1809–1849.* Boston: G. K. Hall.

Wagenknecht, Edward. 1963. *Edgar Allan Poe: The Man behind the Legend.* New York: Oxford University Press.

POSSESSION AND EXORCISM

Exorcism is the religious or spiritual practice of casting out demons from those who are under a state of possession from demonic or satanic spiritual forces. While possession and exorcism appear in many cultures and religious traditions, in the popular imagination they are most commonly part of Christian religious traditions. They are also extremely popular subjects for horror fiction and film, where they are commonly represented as being generally Catholic phenomena.

Within the Catholic Church, a distinction is drawn between "prayers of deliverance," which can be offered by anyone, and formal exorcism, which can only be performed by a priest during baptism or with the permission of a bishop. The Catholic rite for a "Major Exorcism" is given in Section Eleven of the *Rituale Romanum*. The exorcism is performed through the recitation of prayers listed in the rite, invoking the name of Jesus, God the Father, and the Holy Spirit; and it may, though not necessarily, involve the use of religious symbols and sacraments such as communion wafers, relics, crucifixes, and holy water. The authority and power of the exorcism comes from the invocation of the Trinity, and the efficacy of the exorcism is dependent upon the faith of the practitioner and the legitimacy of the authorizing body that allows it to take place.

The manifestation of demonic possession has been variable throughout history, but signs listed in the Roman Ritual include, but are not limited to, speaking foreign or ancient languages of which the possessed has no prior knowledge; supernatural strength; knowledge of hidden things that the possessed has no way of obtaining; an aversion to anything holy; and profuse blasphemous language. With clergy often criticized for mistaking undiagnosed mental illness for possession, recorded cases of episcopal approval for exorcism rites have become increasingly rare, although modern media attention (particularly in the aftermath of key horror texts such as *Rosemary's Baby* and *The Exorcist*) has often led to spikes in requests for exorcisms among established churches. Those under possession are often not held accountable for their actions, and thus the exorcism rite is understood not as a punishment but as an act designed to restore their individual subjectivity.

Representations of possession and exorcism in Gothic and horror literature and film tend to focus upon the process by which an individual can fall under demonic influence, the manifestation of the various demonic powers, and, although not always, the final restoration of normality and the "saving" of the possessed individual. Beginning with the satanic encounters in early horror texts such as Matthew Lewis's *The Monk* (1796), as well as Charlotte Dacre's *Zofloya the Moor: A Romance of the Fifteenth Century* (1806), possession has been a regular occurring theme throughout horror history. By the late nineteenth century, concerns around evolution and degeneration led to possession being represented as a loss of humanity, frequently shown in animalistic terms. Notable examples include Richard Marsh's *The Beetle* (1897) and Arthur Machen's "The Great God Pan" (1890). The ambiguity of possession in the era of increasing secularity is another repeated concern, reaching its high point with Henry James's novella *The Turn of the Screw* (1898). The early twentieth century saw a decline in the possession narrative, although the weird fiction of H. P. Lovecraft was often concerned with the annihilation of the subject after an encounter with a powerful spiritual reality. The possession narrative reemerged in the 1960s with Ray Russell's *The Case Against Satan* (1962) and William Peter Blatty's *The Exorcist* (1971), the latter of which became a critical and commercial success.

Film has also been an extremely fruitful area for possession and exorcism narratives, several of which have become well-regarded horror classics. Key texts from horror cinema in this area include *Rosemary's Baby* (dir. Roman Polanski, 1968) and the highly influential *The Exorcist* (dir. William Friedkin 1973), as well as Sam Rami's *Evil Dead* franchise (1981–2013). Postmillennial horror has featured a resurgence in possession and exorcism narratives—*The Exorcism of Emily Rose* (dir. Scott Derrickson, 2005) as well as *The Last Exorcism* (dir. Daniel Stamm, 2010) being high-profile examples. These films, which are relatively inexpensive to produce, generally generate high returns, despite an increasingly lukewarm critical response. This suggests that even in an era of ostensible secularity, the possession narrative and the fears that it taps into still continue to resonate with horror fans.

Jon Greenaway

See also: Devils and Demons; *The Exorcist*; "The Great God Pan"; *The Monk*; *Rosemary's Baby*; Russell, Ray; "Thrawn Janet"; *The Turn of the Screw*; Witches and Witchcraft.

Further Reading

Cardin, Matt. 2007. "The Angel and the Demon." In *Icons of Horror and the Supernatural*, edited by S. T. Joshi, 31–64. Westport, CT and London: Greenwood Press.

Mäyrä, Frans Ilkka. 1999. *Demonic Texts and Textual Demons: The Demonic Tradition, the Self, and Popular Fiction.* Tampere, Finland: Tampere University Press. http://people.uta.fi/~frans.mayra/Demon_2005/Demon.pdf.

Schober, Adrian. 2004. *Possessed Child Narratives in Literature and Film.* New York: Macmillan.

THE PRIVATE MEMOIRS AND CONFESSIONS OF A JUSTIFIED SINNER

James Hogg's 1824 novel *The Private Memoirs and Confessions of a Justified Sinner* can validly be considered a work ahead of its time. It is arguably the first psychological horror novel in literature, and certainly its ambiguities, which allow for either psychological or supernatural readings or both, is more to the taste of the twentieth and twenty-first centuries than the nineteenth.

In the late seventeenth century, George Colwan, a Scottish laird, marries an appalling religious bigot. This new wife is so offended by the merrymaking at the wedding that she refuses to come to his bed, and, very likely, he rapes her. A son born of this union, also called George, grows up to be personable and fun-loving, like his father. A year later Mrs. Colwan gives birth to another son, Robert Wringhim, apparently fathered by her hypocritical religious mentor. Young Robert becomes a fanatical believer in extreme Calvinism, convinced that he is predestined to go to heaven, regardless of what acts he may perform on Earth. The logical extension of this is that anything he does is God's work, including murder, starting with his half-brother, George. He attempts to push George to his death off Arthur's Seat, a height above Edinburgh, but is deterred by an apparition, which can be explained as a mirage.

Later, George is murdered, but witnesses clearly see someone else leaving the scene of the crime. However, the novel is told as a frame narrative with different points of view, and the "Editor's Narrative" now switches to Robert's "Confession," which presents the reader with a very different version of events. Robert has encountered a doppelgänger of himself called Gil-Martin, who urges him on to further crimes. While Robert believes that Gil-Martin is really the Russian czar Peter the Great traveling incognito, a better interpretation is that Gil-Martin is the Devil who leads him to destruction by telling him exactly what he wants to hear. It is clear that Robert's mind is disintegrating, but the question remains as to whether he is truly in the company of the Devil. Gil-Martin can assume any identity, and it is possible, but not certain, that he killed George.

More crimes ensue. Robert has large gaps in his memory. Gil-Martin may be a projection of Robert's, but this is never made clear, even after Robert comes to fear Gil-Martin, tries to flee, and ultimately commits suicide, at which point the "Editor's Narrative" resumes. The text analyzes itself and fails to come to a conclusion. The editor even inquires of the novel's author, Mr. Hogg, who, in an amusing in-joke, is too busy with a deal in sheep to show much interest.

The sheep joke fits because James Hogg was known as "The Ettrick Shepherd." He really had been a shepherd before he became a poet, and as a rustic bard he was acceptable to the Scottish literary establishment. But when he moved on to books like *Justified Sinner,* he was rejected, and the work fell into obscurity before being rediscovered and appreciated in the twentieth century. Today it is recognized as a precursor of such classic double and doppelgänger tales as Edgar Allan Poe's "William Wilson" and Robert Louis Stevenson's *The Strange Case of Dr. Jekyll and Mr. Hyde.* Like these and other such tales, Hogg's novel explores the question of human identity and possible duality, and it offers acute insight into the fears and anxieties surrounding Calvinism and predestination.

Darrell Schweitzer

See also: Doubles, Doppelgängers, and Split Selves; Frame Story; Poe, Edgar Allan; *The Strange Case of Dr. Jekyll and Mr. Hyde.*

Further Reading

Carey, John. 1959. Introduction to *The Private Memoirs and Confessions of a Justified Sinner*, ix–xvi. New York: Grove Press.

Jackson, Richard D. 2001. "The Devil, the Doppelgänger, and the *Confessions* of James Hogg and Thomas De Quincey." *Studies in Hogg and His World* 12: 90–103.

Smith, Nelson C. 1985. "James Hogg." In *Supernatural Fiction Writers: Fantasy and Horror*, vol. 1, edited by E. F. Bleiler, 177–183. New York: Charles Scribner's Sons.

PSYCHOLOGICAL HORROR

Psychological horror is a subgenre of horror that focuses on the inner psychological states and experiences of characters to generate horror, fear, and dread. Horror in general, as an artistic genre or mode, consists of prose fiction (or poetry, drama, or film) that elicits emotions of intense fear, revulsion, and dread. Horror is a subgenre of the fantastic, and it may be almost infinitely subdivided, with the major subdivisions including what might be called killer horror (centering on violent and murderous people as villains), monster horror, paranormal/supernatural horror, extreme horror (emphasizing gore and bodily destruction), and psychological horror. Unlike killer and monster horror, psychological horror does not rely on a physical, external threat to produce fear. Unlike paranormal/supernatural horror, it does not posit, or at least does not focus solely upon, the existence of a paranormal or supernatural universe as the chief source of dread. Unlike extreme horror, psychological horror emphasizes inner rather than external conflicts and brutality to produce the central emotions of fear and dread. Significantly, the boundaries between such subgenres are fluid, and many horror narratives move between genres.

Although first recognized as a subgenre of horror in film studies in the mid-twentieth century, psychological horror has a long literary history. Nathaniel Hawthorne's "Young Goodman Brown" (1835), with its depiction of a nightmarish walk

Edgar Allan Poe's "The Tell-Tale Heart": The Blurring of Sanity and Insanity

Poe's "The Tell-Tale Heart" (1843) reads on the one hand as a gruesome horror-supernatural story but on the other as a realistic, if terrifying, psychological fiction in which sanity and insanity blur. It is one of his most popular tales, and it has been anthologized countless times.

Attempting justification for murdering an old man for whom he has served as caretaker, the story's first-person narrator states that the latter's eye appalled him, so he murdered the old man to negate the repellent eye, carefully dismembered the corpse, and buried the parts under the floor. The narrative proceeds detail by detail, as if such careful, seemingly rational explanation of the circumstances will demonstrate the narrator's sanity. Such obsession as he reveals concerning his opinion about the old man's eye initially indicates that this account is rational, only to lead to a conclusion in which the narrator's guilty conscience causes him to imagine that his crime is perfect, so that he feels emboldened to invite the police to search his home. But he has begun to hear a strange noise, which to him seems to be the beating of the old man's heart, and ultimately this sound drives him into frenzy; he tells his visitors to tear up the floor boards, exposing the truth he tried to conceal. What the narrator hears may be the sound made by an insect, colloquially called "the Lesser Death-Watch," though no precise origin has been established. But more important than any specific source is the fact that the imagined sound drives the narrator to his undoing, thereby ironically undercutting all of his careful planning.

"The Tell-Tale Heart" remains as popular today as it was with its original readers. It has been adapted many times for radio, television, and film.

Benjamin F. Fisher

through the forest outside colonial Salem Village, Massachusetts, can be read as an early example, since it winds up to an ambiguous conclusion in which the title character may have witnessed an actual satanic gathering in the woods or may have simply had a dream or vision that left him forever suspicious of and alienated from his family and fellow villagers. Likewise, many of Edgar Allan Poe's stories, such as "Ligeia" (1838), "The Fall of the House of Usher" (1839), and "The Tell-Tale Heart" (1843), generate and rely on psychological horror. Charlotte Perkins Gilman's "The Yellow Wall-Paper" (1892) and Henry James's *The Turn of the Screw* (1898) are excellent examples of the genre with their depictions of progressive psychological deterioration narrated in the first person. More recent examples of psychological horror fiction include L. Ron Hubbard's *Fear* (1940), Shirley Jackson's *The Haunting of Hill House* (1959), Robert Bloch's *Psycho* (1959), and Stephen King's *Misery* (1987) and *The Shining* (1977), all of which dramatize the terror of growing psychosis and attendant violence.

Film has provided a welcoming medium for horror, and psychological horror has played an essential part in film history. Sometimes this has been linked to literary sources; adaptations of *Psycho* (directed by Alfred Hitchcock, 1960), *The Haunting of Hill House* (filmed as *The Haunting,* directed by Robert Wise, 1963), and *The Shining* (directed by Stanley Kubrick, 1980) are considered film classics. Cinema began to explore psychological horror very early, especially in the case of German Expressionism (1919–1933), which created a striking visual style by exteriorizing characters' often dark inner states by means of exaggerated and surreal lighting and set design. Robert Wiene's *The Cabinet of Dr. Caligari* (1920), which is set in an asylum, and Fritz Lang's *M* (1931), which follows a murdering pedophile through Berlin, use composition and lighting to reflect inner disorientation and fear. Also often cited as early examples of cinematic psychological horror are *The Black Cat* (1934), *Cat People* (1942), and *White Zombie* (1932), the latter of which, despite its title, is more a psychological film than monster movie.

Given the fluid boundaries between horror subgenres, a number of horror narratives can be read or viewed from a variety of critical perspectives that unite psychological horror with something else. For example, both Jack Finney's classic horror/science fiction novel *The Body Snatchers* (1955) and its several film adaptations as *Invasion of the Body Snatchers*—as in Dan Siegel's 1956 version, Philip Kaufman's 1978 version, and Abel Ferrara's 1993 version—are as much psychological studies of disorientation in the face of an almost inconceivable and unbearable event—the sinister replacement of one's friends, acquaintances, and loved ones by alien duplicates ("pod people," as they are commonly referred to in popular culture)—as they are science fiction invasion narratives. Both Thomas Harris's 1988 novel *The Silence of the Lambs* and its superlative 1991 film adaptation by director Jonathan Demme stand more as studies in madness, inhering in the almost transcendent and magisterial insanity of the genius, psychologist, and serial killer Hannibal Lecter, than they do as killer thrillers.

Jim Holte

See also: Bloch, Robert; "The Fall of the House of Usher"; *Fear*; Harris, Thomas; *The Haunting of Hill House*; "Ligeia"; *Misery*; *The Shining*; *The Turn of the Screw*; "The Yellow Wall-Paper"; "Young Goodman Brown."

Further Reading

Colavito, Jason. 2008. *Knowing Fear: Science, Knowledge, and the Development of the Horror Genre*. Jefferson, NC: McFarland.

Hoppenstand, Gary. 2001. "Horror Fiction." In *The Guide to United States Popular Culture*, edited by Ray B. Browne and Pat Browne, 406–408. Madison: University of Wisconsin Press.

Massé, Michelle A. 2015. "Psychoanalysis and the Gothic." In *A New Companion to the Gothic*, edited by David Punter, 307–320. Malden, MA: Wiley-Blackwell.

Spratford, Becky Siegel, and Tammy Hennigh Clausen. 2004. "Psychological Horror." In *Horror Readers' Advisory: The Librarian's Guide to Vampires, Killer Tomatoes, and Haunted Houses,* 90–97. Chicago: American Library Association.

Wisker, Gina. 2005. *Horror Fiction: An Introduction.* New York: Continuum.

PULP HORROR

The term "pulp horror" refers to a brand of horror fiction chiefly but not exclusively limited to twentieth-century popular magazines printed on cheap paper and catering to lower- and middle-class readers. Pulp horror is marked by an adherence to formula writing and stereotypical characters and themes at the expense of originality.

Horror fiction had been comparatively rare in the general-interest pulp magazines of the twentieth century until the advent of *Weird Tales* in 1923. Titles such as *Argosy* were formulated to appeal to a broad audience, and individual issues typically contained general fiction and the commonly accepted popular genres, such as mystery, Western, and romance. Horror was considered "off-trail," an editorial term denoting a story out of the mainstream of acceptability, and only the most compelling horror stories by reputable authors found their way into print.

For its first decade, *Weird Tales* had the field virtually to itself, and its readers were largely content with the traditional subgenres of supernatural fiction—vampires, werewolves, ghosts, and like monsters. It set the standard for magazine horror fiction in its day, and although it claimed to have no editorial taboos, in reality its contents hewed to common and comfortable horror conventions, with the contributions by H. P. Lovecraft, Clark Ashton Smith, and very few others representing notable exceptions.

The first wave of Hollywood horror talkies in 1931–1932 directly inspired a parallel trend in pulp detection fiction. *Dracula, Frankenstein, The Old Dark House,* and other now-classic films demonstrated that the general public was open to horror stories. This led to a wave of "menace" tales appearing in pulp magazines such as *Detective-Dragnet* and *Dime Mystery Magazine,* in which detective protagonists battled ghoulish fiends, the classic Prohibition-era gangster antagonist having become passé.

In 1933, menace detective fiction evolved into the mystery-terror story, becoming a distinct subgenre unto itself. In the fall of that year, Popular Publications reformulated *Dime Mystery Magazine* as a vehicle for horror-themed suspense stories with a specific mystery—but not deductive—slant.

Publisher Harry Steeger cited the horrific Grand Guignol Theater in Paris as the inspiration for this unique new brand of pulp story, but Edgar Allan Poe and the Marquis de Sade were equally influential. Editor Rogers Terrill described the rigid formula writers were required to follow slavishly: "Our stories usually concern a young man and a young woman in love, either married or sweethearts, and terror menaces both of them. The emotional effect of terror felt for someone else is far stronger than fear for oneself. Where a terrible menace threatens a man and woman in love, they will fight like hell for each other. . . . We want an eerie, uncanny type of menace, which may seem supernatural as the story progresses, but which can be logically explained at the end—or it may be definitely supernatural" (Lenninger 1935, 16).

Dime Mystery's rising circulation proved Steeger correct. The title was followed by *Terror Tales* (1934) and *Horror Stories* (1935), in which the new mystery-terror formula was relentlessly codified by writers such as Norvell W. Page, Frederick C. Davis, Wyatt Blassingame, Hugh B. Cave, Arthur J. Burks, Paul Ernst, and John H. Knox. "Weird Menace" became the operative term for these super-specialized stories wherein lay protagonists—as distinct from official or semiofficial crime solvers—confront and defeat seemingly supernatural situations and survive, if not triumph. One conceit of the formula avoided admitting that any actual supernatural agency was at work. The ghouls, fiends, vampires, and other depraved monsters were usually revealed as diabolical frauds, giving the stories a climactic twist in the direction of normalcy triumphant. A sprinkling of supernatural denouements were offered to create an element of uncertainty. The editorial need to push the boundaries of taboo situations inevitably led to excesses in the areas of sex and sadism, as typical Weird Menace titles such as "Death's Loving Arms," "Girls for the Devil's Abattoir," and "Daughter of Dark Desire" suggest, resulting in censorship pressures that culminated with the banning of such magazines in 1940 and their extinction in 1941.

With variations, the Weird Menace formula has been periodically revived. The so-called "Men's Sweat" magazines of the 1950s and 1960s flirted with it without success. Readers preferred Nazi torturers and naturalistic wildlife encounters instead of the faux-supernatural horror element. However, Weird Menace continues to thrive in Hollywood, as exemplified by the cycles of *Scream*, *Saw*, and *Nightmare on Elm Street* film franchises, in which hapless teenage protagonists endlessly reenact the grisly Ten Little Indians formula of classic mystery fiction, but with horrific trappings.

Will Murray

See also: Lovecraft, H. P.; Occult Detectives; Penny Dreadful; Smith, Clark Ashton; Splatterpunk; *Weird Tales*.

Further Reading

Jones, Robert Kenneth. 1978. *The Shudder Pulps: A History of the Weird Menace Magazines of the 1930s*. New York: New American Library.
Lenninger, August. 1935. "Six of a Chain." *Writer's Digest*, January. Cincinnati, Ohio.

Q

QUINN, SEABURY (1889–1969)

Born in the nation's capital during America's Gilded Age, and infamous today as the creator of the supernatural sleuth Jules de Grandin, Seabury Grandin Quinn was more than a prolific pulpsmith. He also led a varied career as a soldier during World War I, processed secret documents for military intelligence during World War II, acted as legal consultant to various chemical and mortuary concerns, and contributed extensively to the funeral trade through his skills in teaching, writing, and editing.

Quinn's first professional fiction sale, "The Stone Image," appeared in the May 1, 1919, issue of *The Thrill Book* followed by a prodigious amount of fiction throughout the 1920s, 1930s, and early 1940s, with 146 tales in *Weird Tales* alone. Although his output slowed with the impact of the paper shortage on magazine publication during World War II, he continued to write for a variety of markets, contributing to Robert A. W. Lowndes's *Magazine of Horror* in 1965.

Conventional wisdom denigrates Quinn for earning more money as a writer for *Weird Tales* than H. P. Lovecraft, Robert E. Howard, and Clark Ashton Smith combined by cranking out one formulaic tale after another, mindful only of word-count and the obligatory nude scene; but even the fastidious Lovecraft acknowledged in a 1936 letter to fellow fantasist Catherine L. Moore that Quinn was one of several "brilliant figures" while lamenting his "literary ruin" through the "effect of commerce on the writer" (Lovecraft 1976, 327).

It is true that works like the ambitious de Grandin novel *The Devil's Bride* (1932) fail to gel and have more than their share of faults despite episodes of great imagination and the high quality of some of their intercalated narratives. Nonetheless, two collections with overlapping contents, *Is the Devil a Gentleman?* (1970) and *Night Creatures* (2003), demonstrate just how brilliant Quinn could be in top form. The former contains four stories that are not shared with its 2003 counterpart, and these are quite interesting in idea. However, they are not developed with particular finesse. For instance, in spite of the enthusiasm Quinn and Virgil Finlay expressed for "The Globe of Memories" (1937) while Finlay was creating its *Weird Tales* cover art, the stilted antique dialogue compromises the shifts between medieval Italy and contemporary New York it is meant to reinforce. *Night Creatures* more consistently represents Quinn at his best. That he treated lycanthropy with rare sympathy and an unusual variety of approaches is evinced by the first of its six unshared stories, the simultaneously moving and unnerving "The Phantom Farmhouse" (1923)—filmed as part of Rod Serling's *Night Gallery* in 1971—and the contrast it presents with the malevolent lycanthrope engaged in a battle of wits with the doughty Jules de Grandin in "The Thing in the Fog" (1933) a decade later. "Mortmain" (1940) revolves around issues the author would have encountered under less perilous circumstances while offering advice about mortuary law. Sympathy for the victims of social injustice appears repeatedly in his work and manifests here in two quite different stories from 1941, "There Are Such Things" and "Two Shall Be Born." Particularly impressive among the less familiar stories is "The Golden Spider" (1940), a supernatural *tour de force* in a medieval French setting reminiscent of Clark Ashton Smith's Averoigne, with mythic undertones and a measure of sweetness that brings it closer to the fairy tale. If, when compared to the rest of these, "The Gentle Werewolf" (1940) is enjoyable but unremarkable in its convoluted plot and its transplantation of common fairytale motifs to a thirteenth-century Asian setting, the other four among the shared stories show Quinn adept at weaving plot and character into a setting that seems natural to both. "Glamour" (1939) is a superior specimen of the type of rural supernaturalism best known today from Stephen Vincent Benet's "The Devil and Daniel Webster" (1936) and the work of Quinn's friend Manly Wade Wellman. "Uncanonized" (1939) tells the love story of a suicide turned werewolf, with an odd ecclesiastical twist again worthy of Averoigne. "Is the Devil a Gentleman?" (1942) revolves around the moral dilemma of accepting supernatural aid from dubious forces or submitting to persecution and death from the superstitions of colonial New England. Another paradox faces attendees at the "Masked Ball" (1947), who discover that the dead fear the living at least as intensely as the living fear them.

It is this yoking of the conventional with surprising ethical or mythical twists that makes Quinn's best work a continued pleasure to read, so that even a novella as sentimental as the 1938 Christmas trilogy *Roads* entertains precisely because the legend he creates to account for the figure of Santa Claus through the unusual mixture of Norse mythology with court intrigue and the life of Christ from infancy to crucifixion is handled with such conviction.

The ninety-three case studies of Jules de Grandin present an interesting, if not always entirely successful, succession of crime stories and supernatural adventures, while also offering a fascinating view of American society during the years in which they were written. The predominant setting, Harrisonville and its environs, encompasses aspects of the idyllic small town and the bright, cold city of the hard-boiled school; the dark, superstitious forests of the Old World and a wide assortment of immigrant peoples and supernatural forces from every portion of Europe and Asia. As a result the tone of the tales is not as uniform as Quinn's detractors claim. Tales such as "The Devil People" (1929) have a gritty, hard-boiled quality. Others, such as "The House of Three Corpses" (1939), mix elements of traditional and hard-boiled detection with a strong dose of humor. "Ancient Fires" (1926) has a dreamlike quality, as does "Pledged to the Dead" (1937).

Many of the tales are also interesting ethically. In "The Isle of Missing Ships" (1926) and "Stealthy Death" (1930) hypocritical missionaries preying on the wealth and women of the foreign peoples they have been sent to assist precipitate horrendous events off the coast of Malaysia and present-day Harrisonville. The history behind the murders in the latter tale is even more horrible than the murders themselves. In "The Devil's Rosary" (1929), not only is the protagonist to blame for the assassinations launched against his family, but de Grandin sympathizes with the "villains" sufficiently to return their lost treasure to them and set the latest would-be assassin free. Sometimes Quinn repeats situations to explore a theme from more than one perspective, as when he deals sympathetically with the supplantation of personality in "Ancient Fires" and "A Gamble in Souls" (1933), but handles it with horror in "Trespassing Souls" (1929) and "The Brain-Thief" (1930), often revealing what is happening not only from the victims' viewpoint, but from the miscreant's viewpoint as well. The creation of de Grandin allowed Quinn to rail against the puritans, hypocrites, bigots, bullies, and snobs in a world in which he was outwardly comfortable, defending the rights of the individual regardless of their social status, race, or sins. Flying against convention, de Grandin has no more concern about burying a black woman in a white cemetery or an unshriven strumpet whose body had been the altar for the Black Mass in consecrated ground than he has in slitting the throat of a man who treated him treacherously or spilling down the stairs to his death an old man he knows will otherwise get away with murder.

Another remarkable feature of de Grandin's adventures is Quinn's talent for creating tableaux described with such care that they live in the memory long afterward. They are too numerous to list here, but the girl enwrapped and enraptured by the deadly embrace of a titanic snake in "The Tenants of Broussac" (1926), the butchering of the shipwrecked survivors in "The Isle of Missing Ships" (1926), the mummy standing silently in the room of death with its lips and staff smeared with blood in "The Grinning Mummy" (1926), the flight from death by supernatural winds along the Himalayas in "The Devil's Rosary" (1929), the ghost jeering through the nursery skylight in "The Jest of Warburg Tantavul" (1943), Amelie awaiting her lover beside her lonely tomb in "Pledged to the Dead" (1937), the statue's final appearance in the courtyard in "Stoneman's Memorial" (1942), and the mummy tracking its prey by sound alone in "The Man in Crescent Terrace" (1946) are all worthy examples that give the lie to any notion that the de Grandin corpus, let alone Quinn's work as a whole, is uniformly bland or carelessly written.

Jim Rockhill

See also: Mummies; Occult Detectives; Pulp Horror; *Weird Tales*.

Further Reading

Hoppenstand, Gary. 2013. "Seabury Quinn's Jules de Grandin: The Supernatural Sleuth in Weird Tales." In *Critical Insights: Pulp Fiction of the 1920s and 1930s*, edited by Gary Hoppenstand, 166–178. Ipswich, MA: Salem Press.
Lovecraft, H. P. 1976. *Selected Letters, Vol. V: 1934–1937*. Sauk City, WI: Arkham House.

Quinn, Seabury. 1966. "By Way of Explanation." In *The Phantom Fighter.* Sauk City, WI: Mycroft & Moran. Reprinted in *The Compleat Adventures of Jules de Grandin*, Volume 1 by Seabury Quinn, xxi. Shelburne, Ontario: Battered Silicon Dispatch Box.

Quinn, Seabury, Jr. 2001. "My Father and I." In *The Compleat Adventures of Jules de Grandin,* Volume 2 by Seabury Quinn, v. Shelburne, Ontario: Battered Silicon Dispatch Box.

Ruber, Peter, and Joseph Wrzos. 2003. "Introduction." In *Night Creatures* by Seabury Quinn, ix–xiii. Ashcroft, British Columbia: Ash-Tree Press.

Weinberg, Robert W. 2001. "My Life with Jules de Grandin." In *The Compleat Adventures of Jules de Grandin,* Volume 1 by Seabury Quinn, ix–xi. Shelburne, Ontario: Battered Silicon Dispatch Box.

QUIROGA, HORACIO (1878–1937)

Horacio Quiroga was a Uruguayan author who pioneered a breed of magical realism that would flower in Latin American fiction in the late twentieth century. An avid reader of Edgar Allan Poe and Guy de Maupassant, Quiroga was drawn to literature that explored humanity's dark unconscious, a landscape that took form for him in the tropical rainforests of Argentina, where he briefly operated a failing plantation. His *Jungle Tales* (1918), crafted in imitation of Rudyard Kipling's *The Jungle Book* (1894), featured a magical world of human-animal communication, a realm of dreamy fantasy whose obverse, darker side were the stories gathered in *Tales of Love, Madness, and Death* (1917). Deeply indebted to Poe, these were strikingly brutal and hallucinatory explorations of psychic extremity and graphic physical horror. "The Feather Pillow," for example, relates the tale of a vampiric parasite inhabiting the eponymous object, which slowly drains the life from a beautiful young woman, while "The Decapitated Chicken" is a *conte cruel* (a tale of cynicism and cruelty) in which a degenerate family is riven by an act of grisly violence.

This latter story was included, along with numerous others from the author's brief but prolific career, in a retrospective volume of English translations, *The Decapitated Chicken and Other Stories* (1976). Not included in this collection is the 1927 tale "The Vampire," a pioneering work about the predatory nature of cinema and its seeming ability to revivify the dead, which has spawned a minor tradition of what might be called "celluloid horror" stories (as in, for example, the works gathered in David J. Schow's 1988 anthology *Silver Scream*). The best compilation of Quiroga's horror-inflected tales is the Spanish-language collection *Cunetos de Horror*, published in 2012 by Ediciones Traspiés in Grenada, Spain.

Quiroga's two novels, *History of a Troubled Love* (1908) and *Past Love* (1929), while less overtly fantastic, explore themes of obsessive desire in a way that continued his fascination with morbid psychology, but it is his short fiction that has contributed most to the genre. Grim and pitiless, yet with a streak of macabre irony, his horror stories illuminate a world devoid of beauty and hope, yet whose denizens, driven by perverse obsessions, refuse to recognize that they are damned. Along with fellow modernist Kafka, he contributed to the development of an absurdist strain of modern horror fiction, counterpoised, in its matter-of-fact grotesquery, with the more extravagant cosmic horrors of the Lovecraft school. A haunted and sickly man, Quiroga committed suicide in 1937.

Rob Latham

See also: Body Horror; The Grotesque; de Maupassant, Guy; Kafka, Franz; Lovecraftian Horror; Poe, Edgar Allan; Surrealism.

Further Reading

Flores, Angel. 1955. "Magical Realism in Spanish American Fiction." *Hispania* 38 (2): 187–192.

Rueda, Jose A. B. 2004. "Horacio Quiroga (1878–1937)." In *Latin American Science Fiction Writers: An A-to-Z Guide*, edited by Darrell B. Lockhart, 158–163. Westport, CT: Greenwood.

Wong-Rusell, Michael E. 1996. "Science and the Uncanny in the Fiction of Horacio Quiroga." PhD Dissertation, Boston University.

RADCLIFFE, ANN (1764–1823)

The best paid novelist of the eighteenth century, Ann Radcliffe was a literary celebrity during her lifetime whose Gothic novels were incredibly popular with the British reading public. Born in 1764, the year the first Gothic novel, *The Castle of Otranto*, was published, Radcliffe was a reclusive middle-class writer who published a series of Gothic novels at the end of the eighteenth century during the height of the genre's popularity. Within an eight-year period, Radcliffe produced five Gothic novels, the last three of which proved incredibly successful in terms of commercial and aesthetic value; her works are *The Castles of Athlin and Dunbayne* (1789), *A Sicilian Romance* (1790), *The Romance of the Forest* (1791), *The Mysteries of Udolpho* (1794), and *The Italian* (1797). A historical romance, *Gaston de Blondeville* (1826), was published posthumously. Since her death in 1823, Radcliffe has continued to influence writers in the horror genre with many of them referencing her works within their own.

Radcliffe's biography has long been a challenge for literary historians. Much of her early life is unknown and she lived a private life during her years as a respected

---

An Ann Radcliffe Chronology

1764   Ann Radcliffe is born—the same year the first Gothic novel, Horace Walpole's *The Castle of Otranto*, is published.

1789   Radcliffe publishes her first novel, *The Castles of Athlin and Dunbayne.*

1790   Radcliffe publishes *A Sicilian Romance.*

1791   Radcliffe publishes *The Romance of the Forest.*

1794   Radcliffe publishes *The Mysteries of Udolpho.* It will become one of the most influential and highly regarded examples of the Gothic novel.

1797   Radcliffe publishes *The Italian.*

1823   Radcliffe dies at the age of fifty-eight.

1826   Radcliffe's historical romance *Gaston de Blondeville* is published. So is her essay "On the Supernatural in Poetry," containing her ideas on terror and horror in Gothic fiction, which will become enduringly relevant.

2014   Radcliffe's sole surviving letter of correspondence, to her mother-in-law, is discovered.

Matt Cardin

writer. Unlike other popular authors of the period, like Horace Walpole, only a single letter of correspondence, discovered in 2014, to her mother-in-law survives. The Victorian poet Christina Rossetti even attempted to write a book-length biography of Radcliffe but was forced to abandon her plans when it became evident that the historical sources simply do not exist. Radcliffe's place in the history of horror fiction, however, is an accepted fact despite the lack of biographical details. After Walpole published *The Castle of Otranto*, the Gothic novel slowly but surely took hold on the British reading public's imagination. By 1777, the second Gothic novel, *The Old English Baron* by Clara Reeve, was published, each following year seeing the publication of more Gothic novels until the trend finally began to slow down in the early years of the nineteenth century. Radcliffe was among the many literate middle- and working-class individuals who saw fit to write in the form presented by Gothic fiction with her first novel, *The Castles of Athlin and Dunbayne* appearing in 1789 and *A Sicilian Romance* a year later. Neither novel is an outstanding work on its own, both owing much to the earlier works by Walpole and Reeve as they are more imitative than anything else. It was the publication of her third novel in 1791, *The Romance of the Forest,* that not only demonstrated her complex growth as a writer but her mastery of Gothic fiction and subsequently earned her the adoration of the reading public.

Following the success of *The Romance of the Forest*, Radcliffe was advanced £500, an unheard-of sum for a novelist at the time, for her next novel, which would subsequently become her magnum opus, *The Mysteries of Udolpho*. The immediate success of *The Mysteries of Udolpho* established Radcliffe as a household name among middle- and upper-class families, making her perhaps the most influential figure in Gothic fiction for decades. Two years after the publication of *The Mysteries of Udolpho*, a young member of Parliament named Matthew Lewis published his own Gothic novel, *The Monk* (1796), a work that seemingly countered many of the themes and motifs presented by Radcliffe's brand of Gothic fiction. Radcliffe's response to Lewis was her final novel published during her lifetime, *The Italian*, a work she was paid £800 for, that took issue with the more masculine style of Gothic fiction found in *The Monk*. After *The Italian*, Radcliffe quietly disappeared from public life and died in 1823 at the age of 58. In 1826, an essay by Radcliffe, entitled "On the Supernatural in Poetry," was posthumously published, in which she states her ideas on the function of terror and horror in Gothic fiction, a distinction that has continued to be relevant ever since.

Radcliffe's contributions to Gothic fiction are immense. Many of her works, especially *The Mysteries of Udolpho*, utilize major eighteenth-century philosophical ideas such as the sublime and sensibility that illustrate a strong intellectual complexity that is lacking in other Gothic texts of the period. Her focus on the picturesque and description add depth to a genre already dependent on aesthetics and the imagination. Her own brand of Gothic fiction, sometimes called female Gothic (in direct opposition to the male Gothic best represented by Lewis) or Radcliffean Gothic, tends to focus on a young female protagonist who is normally pursued by a man of power, the use of terror over horror, the explained supernatural (true supernatural occurrences do not exist in Radcliffean Gothic—what is perceived to be supernatural is always logically explained by the conclusion of the text), and an integration of the aforementioned eighteenth-century concepts like sensibility and the sublime.

Radcliffe had an immediate influence on Gothic fiction during her literary career, influencing many of her contemporaries, like Eliza Parsons, Francis Lathom, and Regina Maria Roche, to fashion Radcliffean Gothic novels of their own. Later writers of the horror genre have been greatly influenced by her as well. For example, Edgar Allan Poe references Radcliffe and her work in several works of his own, most notably his "The Oval Portrait" (1842). Charlotte and Emily Brontë are among other nineteenth-century writers who are clearly inspired by Radcliffe, and the aforementioned Christina Rossetti found Radcliffe's biography a topic worthy of study. Strong parallels with Radcliffe and modern writers like Shirley Jackson, Anne Rice, and Susan Hill can also be found, once again demonstrating Radcliffe's lasting legacy on the horror genre.

Joel T. Terranova

See also: The Brontë Sisters; *The Castle of Otranto*; Hill, Susan; Jackson, Shirley; Lewis, Matthew Gregory; *The Monk*; *The Mysteries of Udolpho*; Poe, Edgar Allan; Rice, Anne; The Sublime; Terror versus Horror; Walpole, Horace.

Further Reading

Durant, David. 1982. "Ann Radcliffe and the Conservative Gothic." *Studies in English Literature, 1500–1900* 22, no. 3: 519–530.

Michasiw, Kim Ian. 1994. "Ann Radcliffe and the Terrors of Power." *Eighteenth-Century Fiction* 6, no. 4: 327–346.

Norton, Rictor. 1999. *Mistress of Udolpho: The Life of Ann Radcliffe*. London: Bloomsbury T&T Clark.

Rogers, Deborah D. 1996. *Ann Radcliffe: A Bio-Bibliography*. Westport, CT: Greenwood.

Townshend, Dale. 2014. *Ann Radcliffe, Romanticism, and the Gothic*. Cambridge: Cambridge University Press.

THE RATS

The Rats was the first novel by British horror writer James Herbert. It was published in the United Kingdom in 1974 by New English Library a few months before they also published Stephen King's first book, *Carrie*. The novel tells the story of a horde of large, savage, mutant rats invading London's docklands and killing people, an incursion investigated by a secondary school teacher named Harris. Herbert was inspired by a passage in Bram Stoker's *Dracula* (1897) in which Dracula's servant Renfield dreams of thousands of rats with red eyes. He was also inspired by his own impoverished upbringing in rat-infested slums in East London.

The Rats established the signature style and themes that would form the hall-mark of Herbert's future works: sparse and direct prose, explicit depictions of sex and violence, the vision of an empty metropolis, and a heavily political subtext. The book opens with the rats eating a former salesman who was drummed out of his job due to his homosexuality and is now drinking himself to death in abandoned buildings. As London is overrun, the disenfranchised—the homeless, the addicted, the poor, and the young—suffer at the rats' hands (or paws) while the government does nothing. Herbert has both main political parties, Labour and Conservative, blaming each other for the living conditions of the poor that allowed the mutant rats to breed, and it is not Foskins, the pompous and ineffective under-secretary of state, who saves the day, but the ordinary, working-class Harris.

Through this working-class focus, Herbert's novel democratized British horror by depicting characters who were not aristocrats or intellectuals as they were in other British horror staples such as the novels of Dennis Wheatley and the films produced by Hammer Studios. His protagonists were ordinary working people with the courage to act. Moreover, his emphasis on the explicit depiction of violence, while it alienated many people—famously, high-street book chain WH Smith initially refused to sell the book—effectively opened horror up to a new proletarian readership and ushered in a new era of British horror literature.

The Rats was loosely adapted as the 1982 Canadian horror movie *Deadly Eyes*, which was poorly received, and which Herbert himself repudiated.

Simon Brown

See also: Herbert, James.

Further Reading

Cabell, James. 2013. *James Herbert—The Authorised True Story 1943–2013*. London: John Blake.

Jones, Stephen. 1992. *James Herbert: By Horror Haunted*. London: Hodder and Stoughton.

Spark, Alasdair. 1993. "Horrible Writing: The Early Fiction of James Herbert." In *Creepers: British Horror & Fantasy in the Twentieth Century*, edited by Clive Bloom, 147–160. London and Boulder, CO: Pluto Press.

"THE RATS IN THE WALLS"

Written in August or September of 1923 and published in *Weird Tales* for March 1924, "The Rats in the Walls" by H. P. Lovecraft must have seemed, given the rather poor content of the early *Weird Tales*, an absolute miracle, probably the strongest American horror story since Poe. It was one of Lovecraft's early triumphs, and it remains one of his most widely read and anthologized works.

The story in fact bears a visible relationship to Poe: like "The Fall of the House of Usher," "The Rats in the Walls" concerns the dissolution of the "house"—in both an architectural and a genealogical sense—of an ancient and now extinct family, whose final representative comes to a bad end. In this case, the last of the de la Poers, whose only son has died from injuries suffered during World War I, restores and moves into Exham Priory in England, the family seat from which an ancestor fled centuries before under very mysterious circumstances. He finds himself haunted by spectral rats, which seem to be streaming by the thousands inside the walls, *downward*, into depths below the lowest cellars.

This is not merely a job for the exterminator, because apparently only he and his pet cats can hear the rats; but it is not a case of delusion, either, because further investigations, in the company of scientific men and Captain Norrys, his late son's war comrade, reveal hidden grottos and caves filled with thousands of human and animal bones, plus blasphemous altars and ultimately, it is implied, a pathway to the Earth's center where Nyarlathotep, "the mad, faceless god, howls blindly to the piping of two amorphous idiot flute players." Generations of de la Poers had indulged in unspeakable cultic practices, including human (and subhuman) sacrifice and cannibalism. As the last de la Poer penetrates the abyss, he reverts to atavistic type, his mind sliding back through the centuries, gibbering first in Elizabethan English, then older languages all the way back to a bestial gurgle. Even then he does not make it all the way to the throne of Nyarlathotep, because he is overtaken in the dark by his colleagues, having apparently killed and partially devoured Captain Norrys, although he insists that he is innocent and the rats did it.

This is a story of a man overwhelmed by accursed hereditary "influences." His attempt to live as a modern, moral person fails precisely because of who he actually is and what his ancestors have done. His reversion to the monstrous is brought on by uncovering what was best left hidden. A parallel to "The Fall of the House of Usher" recurs. In the Poe story the fissure in the wall that the narrator observes clearly symbolizes the unsoundness of Roderick Usher's mind, so that when the house literally falls to pieces, so does he, psychologically. Lovecraft's character, too, as he descends lower and lower through caves and tunnels, is delving into his own mind, the contents of which predate not only his own individual existence, but humanity itself. Barton Levi St. Armand's *The Roots of Horror in the Fiction of H.P. Lovecraft* contains a cogent analysis of this story in terms of dream imagery and Jungian archetypes.

Darrell Schweitzer

See also: Ancestral Curse; "The Fall of the House of Usher"; Lovecraft, H. P.; Poe, Edgar Allan.

Further Reading

Lévy, Maurice. 1988. "The Depths of Horror." In *Lovecraft: A Study in the Fantastic*, translated by S. T. Joshi, 63–72. Detroit, MI: Wayne State University Press.

Lovecraft, H. P. 1999. "The Rats in the Walls." In *The Call of Cthulhu and Other Weird Stories*, 89–108. Annotations by S. T. Joshi. New York: Penguin Books.

Monteleone, Paul. 1995. "'The Rats in the Walls': A Study in Pessimism." *Lovecraft Studies* 32 (Spring): 18–26.

St. Armand, Barton Levi. 1977. *The Roots of Horror in the Fiction of H. P. Lovecraft.* Elizabeth-town, NY: Dragon Press.

RAY, JEAN (1887–1964)

Jean Ray is the best-known pseudonym of Belgian writer Raymundus Joannes de Kremer. His fiction combines elements of the Gothic and modernist fiction; his stories involve both sensational and philosophical elements, laid out with a self-awareness in the story itself that bridges the gap between the more straightforward textual qualities of Gothic fiction—the reliance on frame narratives, the use of letters and other documentation alongside or instead of direct narration—and the formal experimentation of surrealist and modernist writers. His stories are characterized by a rapid switching between wonder and horror; they are often whimsical even as they are terrible. Destiny, Faustian bargains, and demonic presences, who

---

"The Shadowy Street": A Netherworld of Living Darkness

Also translated as "The Tenebrous Alley" (original title: "*La Ruelle Tenebreuse*"), Jean Ray's short story "The Shadowy Street" first appeared in his second collection, *Le Croisiere des Ombres* (1932), and was first published in English in his 1956 collection *Ghouls in My Grave*. It is generally regarded as one of Ray's best stories, and it shows him using the narrative strategy of multiplying accounts. The narrator finds two letters, in two different languages, written by two different persons, both of which independently describe certain related curious events in Hamburg. The first letter, written in German by a woman named Frida, relates how the city seems to have become haunted by a terrifying darkness, deeper than night. Dozens of people vanish without a trace, even from within the supposed safety of their homes. On one occasion, she describes how her sister fought off an invisible assailant, not unlike Guy de Maupassant's "Horla," wounding it with a sword. Her story breaks off abruptly. The second letter, in French, was penned by a schoolteacher living in Hamburg. He has found a street that no one else can see, Saint Beregonne's Lane, which seems to lead out of this world. Like certain localities in the stories of the Irish fantasist Lord Dunsany, the lane seems to select who will be able to find it. The far end of the lane is a netherworld of malevolent, living darkness, shadowing the city, occupied by shades who venture forth into the real Hamburg by night to wreak havoc. The schoolteacher finally burns down that part of the city, trying to close off the aperture. The narrator investigates further, but succeeds, as is not unusual in Ray's stories, only in deepening the mystery.

Michael Cisco

are associated with madness as much as they are with malice or temptation, are his preferred themes.

Ray was born in the Belgian town of Ghent, also known as Gand; his father was an official in maritime affairs and his mother ran a girls' school. Ray did not complete college, worked in low-level city clerical jobs, got involved in writing, and worked for a time as an editor on local periodicals. He married in 1912.

Ray's first book was a collection of grotesque and fantastic short stories called *Les Contes du Whisky*, or "Whisky Stories," published in 1925. These tales reflected Ray's lasting interest in England and America, his penchant for wildly unusual ideas, and his love of Hoffmann-esque experts, mad scientists, and other ominous officials.

Charged with participation in a scheme of embezzlement in 1926, Ray was found guilty, and in 1927 he was sent to prison. It was as a prisoner that he wrote two of his best known works, "The Shadowy Street" and "The Mainz Psalter." Although he had been sentenced to a six-year term, Ray was released in 1929. From this point forward, the exact details of his life are hard to pin down. Since Ray deliberately obscured or even falsified many of the facts of his life, it is not certain whether he really did engage in smuggling, rum running, or piracy, as he sometimes claimed. It is clear that he earned his living as a sailor for a time.

Financial troubles and a lack of opportunities made him a very prolific writer. Jean Ray was only one of many pen names, John Flanders being the one he preferred when writing in Flemish, which is one of the two languages commonly spoken in Belgium. Ray had been asked to translate a series of German-language stories about a fictional detective named Harry Dickson, the "American Sherlock Holmes." Ray didn't think the stories were that good, and he began writing his own, expanding the adventures of Harry Dickson by hundreds of new tales.

It is not clear what Ray did during World War II, but after the war's end he published six books in rapid succession: *Le Grand Nocturne* (1942), *La Cité de l'Inidicible Peur* (1943), *Malpertuis* (1943), *Les Cercles de l'Epouvante* (1943), *Les Derniers Contes de Canterbury* (1944), and *Le Livre des Fantomes* (1947). The first English edition of his work was *Ghouls in My Grave*, published in 1965.

In 1955, French author Raymond Queneau helped to bring *Malpertuis* back into print in France; this helped Ray avoid disappearing from public view. In 1959, he met with Alain Resnais, the French filmmaker known for *Hiroshima Mon Amour* and *L'Année Derniere á Marienbad*. Resnais was interested in building a film around Harry Dickson. While the film never happened, it is likely that this encounter was responsible for the involvement of Resnais's screenwriter, Jean Ferry, in creating the screenplay for Harry Kuemel's 1971 film adaptation of *Malpertuis*. There was also a film adaptation of *La Cité de l'Inidicible Peur* by Jean-Pierre Mocky in 1964.

Michael Cisco

See also: Dreams and Nightmares; *Malpertuis*; Surrealism.

Further Reading

Monteiro, António. 2011. "Ghosts, Fear, and Parallel Worlds: The Supernatural Fiction of Jean Ray." *Weird Fiction Review*, November 21. http://weirdfictionreview.com/2011/11/ghosts-fear-and-parallel-worlds-the-supernatural-fiction-of-jean-ray.

Van Calenbergh, Hubert. 1999. "Jean Ray and the Belgian School of the Weird." *Studies in Weird Fiction* 24 (Winter): 14–17.

"THE REACH"

"The Reach" is a story by Stephen King that was published under the title "Do the Dead Sing?" in the November 1981 issue of *Yankee* magazine and later collected in *Skeleton Crew* (1985). It is one of King's most evocative depictions of life in small-town Maine, and thus can be considered a sidebar to his tales of horror set in the fictional Maine town of Castle Rock.

Although its narrative point of view is omniscient, the story is essentially a glimpse into the mind of Stella Flanders, a woman who lives on Goat Island off the coast of Maine. In her ninety-five years, Stella has never once crossed the reach, the name given to the stretch of water that separates the island from the mainland. Suffering from cancer, Stella has begun to see ghosts, notably that of her dead husband Bill, who invites her to cross the reach to join him. Stella's thoughts about Bill and the life and family she had with him leads her to reflect on her many years on the island and the people she has known. Her random memories conjure the image of a self-sufficient, close-knit community who have looked out for one another and lived their lives largely independent of the world beyond their island. At the height of a severe snowstorm, Stella bundles up and sets out to cross the frozen-over reach to the mainland. En route, she finds herself helped out by Bill and friends who passed away over the years. The next day she is found frozen to death on the mainland—and the discovery that she's wearing a hat that Bill handed to her during her crossing dispels any doubt that the friends who accompanied her were only in her imagination. Her fate also confirms that crossing the reach was not just a physical journey, it was metaphoric for passing from life into the afterlife.

Auspiciously, "The Reach" was published one year before *Different Season*, a collection of four short novels in which King applied the techniques and approaches he had honed in his macabre fiction to stories with mainstream literary appeal. The tale is one of his most successful demonstrations of the potential for fantastic and supernatural fiction to address concerns universal to fiction irrespective of genre pigeonholing—an appraisal that has gained considerable traction in the twenty-first century with King's embrace by the literary mainstream. The title "Do the Dead Sing?" alludes to a passage in the story—"Do the dead sing? Do they love?" (King 1986, 566)—made in reference to the souls of the dead singing over the dying into the warm embrace of their community in the afterlife. It casts in a reassuring light the proximity of the dead to the living that is more often depicted as menacing in tales of the supernatural.

Stefan R. Dziemianowicz

See also: King, Stephen.

Further Reading

Collings, Michael, and Engbretson, David. 1985. *The Shorter Works of Stephen King.* Mercer Island, WA: Starmont House.

King, Stephen. 1986. *Skeleton Crew.* New York: Signet.

Reino, Joseph. 1988. *Stephen King: The First Decade, Carrie to Pet Sematary.* Boston: Twayne.

Winter, Douglas. 1986. *Stephen King: The Art of Darkness.* New York: Signet.

"THE RECRUDESCENE OF IMRAY"/ "THE RETURN OF IMRAY"

"The Recrudescence of Imray" by Rudyard Kipling was published in America, in 1891, in Kipling's fiction collection *Mine Own People*, the same year that it was published in England in *Life's Handicap, Being Stories of Mine Own People* under the title "The Return of Imray." The story is a loose sequel to Kipling's "The Mark of the Beast," and like that story it features the character of Strickland, a British police investigator living in India who has a deep knowledge of the Indian people and their ways. Also like "The Mark of the Beast," "The Recrudescence of Imray" touches on the "imperial Gothic," the late nineteenth- and early twentieth-century literary subgenre in which traditional Gothic motifs were drawn upon and transformed to show the dominant Western values of the British Empire being threatened by contamination from the "other" represented by colonial subjects, particularly in India and other Eastern locales.

"The Recrudescence of Imray" is in fact set in India, and it begins with the disappearance of Imray, apparently a very genial man-about-town. After Imray has been missing some months, Strickland of the police and his dog Tietjens move into Imray's bungalow, though Tietjens refuses to enter and sleeps on the veranda. When the narrator visits, he feels and shares Tietjens's unease, and when he and Strickland investigate some snakes that are living between the ceiling cloth and the bungalow roof, they discover the corpse of Imray. Strickland realizes the murderer could only be Imray's servant, Bahadur Khan, and he confronts Khan, who confesses: he believed that Imray's patting the head of his child was the casting of an evil eye, for the child died soon thereafter. But though Strickland wants to hang Bahadur Khan, the man escapes European justice.

Although the two titles of the story hint at humor, "The Recrudescence of Imray" is grim. A benevolent gesture is misinterpreted, for the different cultures have failed to communicate, and the conclusion offers no real hope for better relations: the narrator realizes only that his servant has been with him just as long as Bahadur Khan was with Imray. It can be debated whether the story is a primitive detective story, for Strickland does very little detecting, but in its borderline supernaturalism and in its denouement—the revelation of the rotting corpse of a murdered man hidden in the ceiling of his bungalow—it is remarkably horrific. The only one to escape unscathed is Tietjens, whose entrance into the bungalow at the conclusion reveals that everything has been satisfactorily resolved.

Richard Bleiler

See also: Kipling, Rudyard; "The Phantom 'Rickshaw"; "They."

Further Reading

Morey, Peter. 2000. "Gothic and Supernatural: Allegories at Work and Play in Kipling's Indian Fiction." In *Victorian Gothic: Literary and Cultural Manifestations in the Nineteenth Century*, edited by Ruth Robbins and Julian Wolfreys, 201–217. New York: Palgrave.

Punter, David, and Glennis Byron. "Imperial Gothic." In *The Gothic*, 44–49. Malden, MA: Blackwell.

THE RETURN

The Return is the second of three novels written by prolific British writer Walter de la Mare (1873–1956), and the second of his two longer works (the first being *Henry Brocken,* 1904) to deal with themes of supernaturalism, for which his short stories and poems such as "The Listeners" are more famous.

Published in 1910 and revised in both 1922 and 1945, *The Return* tells the story of Arthur Lawford, who, having fallen asleep on a grave on unconsecrated ground, is possessed by the spirit of the grave's occupant, and who begins to take on the physical (though not entirely the psychological) characteristics of the dead man. Unrecognized by his family and loved ones, Lawford's condition is the premise for de la Mare's mournful meditation on death, self-enforced isolation, and the fragility of personal identity and social bonds.

With echoes of Washington Irving's short story "Rip Van Winkle" (1819), Edgar Allan Poe's "William Wilson" (1839), and Robert Louis Stevenson's *Dr. Jekyll and Mr. Hyde* (1886), de la Mare's story engages early modernist, twentieth-century anxieties concerning Freudian psychology and the (at the time) growing awareness of the tenuous nature of individual personality.

Lawford's physical transmogrification is really a foil for de la Mare's subtler psychological probing into the fundamentals of self and the spiritual and emotional horrors that people would experience were family and loved ones suddenly unable to recognize them. In this way, Lawford's experience is very much an inversion of the traditional Capgras syndrome frequently found in alien invasion narratives (such as Jack Finney's 1955 science fiction novel *The Body Snatchers*), in which the protagonist's loved ones physically resemble themselves but have otherwise been psychologically taken over by invaders. In this particular instance, it is Lawford's wife, Sheila, who struggles with the belief that he is, in fact, still her husband.

De la Mare raises questions as to the validity of personal (and religious) faith in the face of logic and reason, and part of the narrative's horror for the reader derives from the supernatural impossibilities of Lawford's metamorphosis, as something very much against nature. Moreover, *The Return* illustrates the notion that body and mind are nondualistic, that they are in fact separate, and that the individual is at all times inherently a stranger to him/herself.

Beyond supernatural horror, *The Return* is also a painfully human tale about the disintegration of love between a husband and wife, and the psychologically destructive effects of domestic trauma. While Lawford, at first, fears the loss of his family's love due to his physical change (his wife believes that he is an impostor), his self-imposed retreat from her, and the acceptance he finds from another woman, makes it clear that the emotional horror underpinning this story is the unfathomable power of love and the tragedy that ensues when love between two people fades. Indeed, Lawford's internalized self-loathing, manifested in the story as a literal transformation into another person, is echoed somewhat in de la Mare's own personal history; for after his wife became an invalid from Parkinson's disease, de la Mare himself was cared for by a sick-nurse, whom he in turn loved deeply.

Ian Kinane

See also: de la Mare, Walter; Irving, Washington; "The Listeners"; "Out of the Deep"; Poe, Edgar Allan; Psychological Horror; *The Strange Case of Dr. Jekyll and Mr. Hyde.*

Further Reading

Clute, John. 1985. "Walter de la Mare." In *Supernatural Fiction Writers: Fantasy and Horror Vol. 1*, edited by E. F. Bleiler, 497–504. New York: Scribner Sons.
de la Mare, Walter. [1910] 2012. *The Return.* London: John Murray.
Lovecraft, H. P. [1927] 2012. *The Annotated Supernatural Horror in Literature.* Edited by S. T. Joshi. New York: Hippocampus Press.
McCrosson, Doris Ross. 1966. *Walter de la Mare.* New York: Twayne.

RICE, ANNE (1941–)

Anne Rice is a leading American horror and Gothic writer who made her mark with her debut novel *Interview with the Vampire* (1976). She was born to a New Orleans Catholic family, and her work as a writer has been indelibly influenced by these surroundings and religious upbringing, as well as her years living with her poet-husband Stan Rice in Haight-Ashbury and the Castro district in San Francisco, before settling once again in New Orleans. San Francisco and New Orleans are the home of many of her most iconic characters, offering an ideal backdrop for many of her literary explorations of religious belief, Catholic doctrine, sensuality, sexuality, morality, mortality, and the nature of good and evil. These themes and atmospheres underpin her writing. Since the success of her first novel, her writing career has been diverse, following *Interview with the Vampire* with historical period dramas such as *Feast of All Saints* (1978) and *Cry to Heaven* (1982), alongside two series of erotic novels written under the pseudonyms Anne Rampling (*Exit to Eden,* 1985;

Belinda, 1986) and A. N. Roquelaure (The Sleeping Beauty Series, 1983–1985/2015). In the 2000s, in a period in which she reembraced her religious upbringing, she turned to Christian fiction, telling stories about Jesus Christ (The Life of Christ series, 2005/2008) and angels (Songs of the Seraphim series, 2009/2010). While these genres of literature appear on the surface to be contrasting, they share a preoccupation with negotiating identity—of the author as well as her characters.

Despite her taste for generic experimentation, Rice's most substantial literary contribution has been within horror, returning repeatedly to familiar monsters such as the vampire, the mummy, witches, spirits, and werewolves, and reimagining them in distinct and provocative ways. Her storytelling is both personal and epic, with storylines that often privilege the first-person perspective, inviting introspection, but also positioning her characters within broader cultural and social histories that extend beyond individual books and into long-running series. The most significant of these is her Vampire Chronicles (1976–2015), totaling eleven

Novels by Anne Rice

Anne Rice has written nearly forty novels, not all of which have to do with horror. Here is a list of those that do.

1976	*Interview with the Vampire*
1985	*The Vampire Lestat*
1988	*The Queen of the Damned*
1989	*The Mummy, or Ramses the Damned*
1990	*The Witching Hour*
1992	*The Tale of the Body Thief*
1993	*Lasher*
1994	*Taltos*
1995	*Memnoch the Devil*
1996	*Servant of the Bones*
1997	*Violin*
1998	*Pandora* and *The Vampire Armand*
1999	*Vittorio the Vampire*
2000	*Merrick*
2001	*Blood and Gold*
2002	*Blackwood Farm*
2003	*Blood Canticle*
2012	*Claudia's Story* and *The Wolf Gift*
2013	*The Wolves of Midwinter*
2014	*Prince Lestat*
2016	*Prince Lestat and the Realms of Atlantis*

Matt Cardin

novels so far as well as a spin-off series, New Tales of the Vampires (1998–1999), which includes a further two books. This is followed by three books within The Lives of the Mayfair Witches series (1990–1994) and The Wolf Gift Chronicles (2012–2013), which to date is comprised of two books. While these books are largely self-contained narratives, with the exception of the Mayfair Witches, which is structured in a more serialized form, they are interconnected pieces within a broad supernatural matrix, creating a fully realized and complex universe in which to position her characters and immerse her reader. The worlds of the Vampire Chronicles and the Mayfair Witches are also interlinked and go so far as to directly intersect when one of the witches is turned into a vampire in Merrick (2000). The historical background of her stories often spans centuries, and even millennia in the case of The Mummy (1989), harking back to the time of Cleopatra, and The Queen of the Damned (1988), which reveals the origins of vampirism as emerging from ancient Egypt. These extensive timespans can reflect the personal immortal existence of her vampires or the many generations of the Mayfair Witches, inter-weaving real historical moments within her fictional universe. In her work, these supernatural characters clearly exist within or on the periphery of the real world, haunting the shadows, and that is part of their allure and horror.

As a horror writer, Rice undermines expectations about monsters, inviting the reader to love them while acknowledging the horrific things that they do and thus implicating the reader in complex moral dilemmas. Interview with the Vampire set the tone for her approach to the genre through its first-person narrative, told by the vampire Louis to a journalist, while its sequel, The Vampire Lestat (1985), is written as an autobiography of the vampire who "turned" Louis. Many of the later novels in the series continue to focus on Lestat, Rice's brat prince of the vampire world—a character who flaunts his evilness and revels in vampirism—but others open up the storytelling world to recurring characters within Lestat and Louis's universe, such as Marius, Armand, and Pandora. Together these novels encourage the reader to see the world from the vampires' perspective, emphasizing the sensuality and romanticism of the vampires alongside their brutality. In this manner, Rice's work stands as a pivotal moment within the evolution of the sympathetic vampire, a trajectory that runs from the Byronic heroes of Lord Byron and Dr. John Polidori to the twenty-first-century vampire works of Charlaine Harris and Stephenie Meyer, as well as the proliferation of sympathetic vampires in television series such as Angel (1999–2004), Buffy the Vampire Slayer (1997–2003), and Being Human (2008–2013) and films such as Byzantium (2012) and Only Lovers Left Alive (2013).

Notably, her first vampire novel emerged in the 1970s when horror was under-going a transition in which audiences no longer feared the monstrous outsider but rather identified with it, highlighting the destabilizing nature of horror in which the status quo is overturned. In Rice's Vampire Chronicles, the reader comes to understand vampires' experience of the world by seeing it through their eyes and hearing about it via their voices as they take control of the storytelling, dramati-cally explaining their appreciation of beauty, art, music, literature, the wonders of nature, and their near-orgasmic pleasure in the kill. While wallowing in the allure of vampirism, Rice's novels embrace the inherent moral ambiguity of their characters and confront readers with tough questions that challenge their understanding of evil. These include the questions of whether the characters are evil because they kill to survive; how readers rationalize their sympathy for characters with such passion for killing; and whether such characters, while they celebrate death, may not also offer a model of living to the fullest, as they revel in life and love as well as death.

While Rice does not always take a direct first-person point of view in each of her stories, her work is always informed by the perspective of the "other," extending this approach to the other monsters in her creative universes, such as Ramses in *The Mummy* and the werewolf Reuben in the *Wolf Gift* Chronicles, two monsters that have generally been rendered the least knowable within horror fiction. The mummy is the regenerated dead driven by a curse and a desire for revenge and therefore often lacking in consciousness, while the werewolf is typically presented as too primal to understand, devoid of human identity when in animal form and therefore impenetrable to the reader. Ramses and Reuben, however, remain highly articulate and thought-provoking creations, offering an alternative to mainstream conceptions of life and living and raising questions about morality. For instance, rather than feeling cursed by his lycanthropy, Reuben is empowered physically and morally, savoring his newfound strength and choosing to hurt those who hurt others; his first killing saves a woman from a rapist and murderer.

Rice's work explores existential questions about the meaning of good and evil and invites the reader to question the existence and nature of God within a world that allows such monsters to exist. This is particularly prevalent in *Interview with the Vampire*, but as a theme it recurs across much of her work. The very existence of her characters, whether they are vampires, immortals, regenerated dead, or spirits, challenges traditional conceptions of an afterlife that promises heaven. Her characters provide no such spiritual comfort but rather question the existence of heaven. Vampires, mummies, and spirits, after all, represent a pragmatic perception of an afterlife that is earthbound. More significantly, these monsters are also bound within their bodies, defined by their physicality rather than spiritual transcendence. For instance, the Mayfair Witches achieve their power through the support of a spirit known as Lasher that covets physical form, seeking rebirth through the pregnancy of one of the witches by entering her womb and joining with the fetus. Once born, it develops into a full-grown man and once again seduces and impregnates her and other witches within the family in order to spread its new species, all of which leads to miscarriage and death for the mothers. Through such tales, Rice explores the sensuality and horror of monstrosity, inviting readers to indulge their fascination with monsters while forcing them to question the implications of their sympathies.

Stacey Abbott

See also: Devils and Demons; Mummies; Vampires; Werewolves; Witches and Witchcraft.

Further Reading

Auerbach, Nina. 1997. *Our Vampires, Ourselves.* Chicago: University of Chicago Press.

Carter, Margaret L. 1997. "The Vampire as Alien in Contemporary Fiction." In *Blood Read: The Vampire as Metaphor in Contemporary Culture*, edited by Joan Gordon and Veronica Hollinger, 27–44. Philadelphia: University of Pennsylvania Press.

Hoppenstand, Gary, and Ray B. Browne, eds. 1996. *The Gothic World of Anne Rice.* Bowling Green, OH: Bowling Green State University Press.

Mulvey-Roberts, Marie. 1999. "Interviewing the Author of *Interview with the Vampire*." *Gothic Studies* 1, no. 2: 169–181.

Smith, Jennifer. 1996. *Anne Rice: A Critical Companion.* Westport, CT and London: Greenwood Press.

"RINGING THE CHANGES"

"Ringing the Changes" is the best known of all of Robert Aickman's "strange stories." It was first published in his fiction collection in *Dark Entries* (1964), then reprinted in *Painted Devils* (1979), which contains revised versions of earlier stories. It also appeared in *The Magazine of Fantasy and Science Fiction* in 1971. It was a very significant story for Aickman's career; Herbert Van Thal, a well-known literary agent, read it and was impressed, and this led to the publication of *Dark Entries* as well as Aickman's first novel, *The Late Breakfasters* (1964).

"Ringing the Changes" is one of only a small number of Aickman's tales to feature a customary horror trope, here the dead raised to a kind of life. But it is far from a conventional zombie story. Gerald and Phrynne have married after a very short courtship and go away on a belated honeymoon to Holihaven, a faded resort. There is a significant age gap between them; Gerald is twenty-four years Phrynne's senior. As they arrive, all the churches in town begin ringing their bells to—as another character, Commander Shotcroft later explains—"wake the dead." And the dead do wake, and dance with the living—an ecstatic revel in which Phrynne is caught up.

The story, as many of Aickman's works do, explores the Freudian linking of sex and death, of *eros* (the sexual force) and *thanatos* (the death drive). When the dead awake, Gerald and Phrynne are making love. The morning after their terrifying experience, as they are walking back to the train station and pass a graveyard where many men are digging, Phrynne flushes with excitement.

Aickman had a sensitivity to the atavistic, to the way ancient and dark rites lie just beneath the surface of civilized modern life. "Ringing the Changes," along with other Aickman stories such as "Bind Your Hair," bear similarities to the films of the folk horror movement in British cinema of the era, which expressed similar thematic concerns. The plot of "Ringing the Changes" also illustrates a common Aickman technique: the literalization of a figure of speech or metaphor—in this case, "ringing to wake the dead"—to strange and uncanny effect.

In 1968 a television adaptation of the story under the title "The Bells of Hell" appeared as part of the BBC 2 series *Late Night Horror*. There have also been two radio play versions, one in 1980 on the CBC series *Nightfall*, and another in 2000 as a BBC Radio Four production that was adapted by Jeremy Dyson and Mark Gatiss from the League of Gentlemen. "Ringing the Changes" is one of Aickman's most accessible stories, but it is still characteristically ambiguous and profoundly unsettling.

Timothy J. Jarvis

See also: Aickman, Robert; The Uncanny; Zombies.

Further Reading

Challinor, Philip. 2012. "Till Death Do Us Part: Some Notes on 'Ringing the Changes.'" In *Insufficient Answers: Essays on Robert Aickman*, edited by Gary William Crawford, 8–21. Baton Rouge, LA: Gothic Press.

Crawford, Gary William. 2011. *Robert Aickman: An Introduction*. Ashcroft, British Columbia: Ash Tree Press. Kindle edition.

"THE ROCKING-HORSE WINNER"

D. H. Lawrence's weird tale "The Rocking-Horse Winner" renders an early twentieth-century version of the haunted child trope that would later become prevalent in modern and contemporary horror fictions. Written in February 1926, the story was published in several places: the July 1926 edition of *Harper's Bazaar Magazine*; Cynthia Asquith's edited collection *The Ghost Book* of the same year; and the 1928 Secker edition of Lawrence's *The Woman Who Rode Away and Other Stories*. The story might never have come to fruition if Asquith had not rejected Lawrence's initial contribution to her *Ghost Book*, "Glad Ghosts" (1925), a tale in which a Lawrentian artist is visited in his guest chamber by a ghostly, sexualized figure that Asquith took to be a distasteful version of herself.

In "The Rocking-Horse Winner," an aristocratic mother, Hester, is a proxy for the Asquith whom Lawrence saw as rejecting him. Hester is cold-hearted, stoic, and recognizes her coldness toward her children, something that they too experience as unspoken but distinct. Rosemary Reeve Davies has argued that the genesis of the tale was suggested "by the tragic illness of Lady Cynthia's oldest son John and by the Asquith marriage itself" (Davies 1983, 121). At times, Lawrence acted as a pseudo-analyst for the Asquith family, particularly for John, who may have been autistic.

It is revealed that Hester's son Paul, who can thus be read as an extraordinary incarnation of John Asquith, has an uncanny and portentous ability to predict winning racehorses. As his powers heighten, so, too, does a disturbing refrain that echoes throughout his playroom, one that demands that he make more and more money. At the climax of this cautionary but speculative allegory—which warns against the monomaniacal pursuit of wealth—Paul dies after correctly predicting the success of the horse Malabar. While these winnings may clear debts, the family's betrayal of Lawrentian ideals leads, ultimately, to spiritual and emotional ruin.

"The Rocking-Horse Winner" has been widely anthologized. In 1949 it was adapted as a British feature film.

Matt Foley

See also: Part One, Horror through History: Horror from 1900 to 1950; *Part Two, Themes, Topics, and Genres*: The Gothic Literary Tradition; Horror Literature as Social Criticism and Commentary.

Further Reading

Davies, Rosemary. 1983. "Lawrence, Lady Cynthia Asquith, and 'The Rocking Horse Winner.'" *Studies in Short Fiction* 20, 2/3: 121–126.

Hollington, Michael. 2011. "Lawrentian Gothic and 'The Uncanny.'" *Anglophonia* 15 (2004): 172–184. Reprinted in *Short Story Criticism*, edited by Jelena O. Krstovic, Vol. 149. Detroit, MI: Gale.

ROHMER, SAX (1883–1959)

Sax Rohmer is the pseudonym of Arthur Sarsfield Ward, creator of Dr. Fu Manchu, a sinister supercriminal genius and dispenser of innumerable scientific and biological horrors. A former Fleet Street journalist, Rohmer debuted with a short story, "The Mysterious Mummy" (1903). Despite the author's frequent forays into horror, he belonged to the British thriller school of mystery fiction. Consequently, Fu Manchu was in the tradition of Guy Boothby's Dr. Nikola and Arthur Conan Doyle's Professor Moriarty, but was a distinct distillation of the Yellow Peril theme that traced back to the eighteenth century.

His creator memorably described Fu Manchu as a seemingly supernatural figure of horror: "Imagine a person, tall, lean and feline, high-shouldered, with a brow like Shakespeare and a face like Satan. . . . one giant intellect, with all the resources of science past and present. . . . Imagine that awful being, and you have a mental picture of Dr. Fu-Manchu, the yellow peril incarnate in one man" (Rohmer 1970, 17). Introduced in *The Mystery of Dr. Fu-Manchu* (later retitled *The Insidious Fu Manchu*) in 1913, the devil doctor most often battled British police official Nayland Smith and his cohorts. Contrary to accepted fictional portrayals of Asian malefactors, the character was portrayed with a strange mixture of subtle horror and sympathy. A Chinese physician and scientist, Dr. Fu Manchu was brilliant, bound by a strict code of honor, yet utterly diabolical in pursuit of his lofty goals, which typically centered around world domination by China through the Si-Fan, a secret society he controlled.

Although depicted as a coldly intellectual embodiment of evil, Fu Manchu was neither supernatural nor employed occult means to pursue his objectives, even though, as a consequence of imbibing the elixir of life, he was preternaturally ancient and inexplicably possessed the transparent inner eyelid of a feline. The horrors inflicted on his adversaries were most often venomous reptiles and insects, exotic poisons and fungi, and sinister agents of death such as Dacoits or Thuggees. The author was skilled in weaving an atmosphere of horror about the proceedings, and so indelible was Rohmer's portrayal of Fu Manchu that numerous imitations of Fu Manchu followed. Thirteen novels and a handful of short stories featuring the devil doctor were produced over a thirty-five-year period. By the time the series had run its course in 1959, cultural sensitivities made the iconic but stereotypical figure undesirable, if not entirely passé.

A student of the occult, Rohmer wrote a handful of short stories and novels exploring overtly supernatural themes, chief of which was his acknowledged masterpiece—praised by H. P. Lovecraft, among others—the mummy-themed *Brood of the Witch-Queen* (1918), followed by *The Green Eyes of Bast* (1920), a short story collection revolving around an occult detective, *The Dream Detective* (1920), and others. The author was also instrumental in introducing a strain of Egyptian-themed horror into the popular consciousness of his era, and in 1914 he produced a well-researched nonfiction survey of the occult, *The Romance of Sorcery*. Two lesser novels, *The Orchard of Tears* (1918) and *Wulfheim* (1950), were inspired by the author's Theosophical leanings. Sax Rohmer died in London on June 1, 1959, ironically succumbing to the Asian flu.

Will Murray

See also: Mummies; Occult Detectives; Pulp Horror.

Further Reading

Briney, R. E. 1998. "Rohmer, Sax (1883–1959)." *Mystery and Suspense Writers: The Literature of Crime, Detection, and Espionage*, vol. 2, edited by Robin W. Winks and Maureen Corrigan, 791–804. New York: Charles Scribner's Sons.

Rohmer, Sax. [1913] 1970. *The Insidious Dr. Fu Manchu*. New York: Pyramid Books.

Van Ash, Cay, and Elizabeth Sax Rohmer. 1972. *Master of Villainy: A Biography of Sax Rohmer*. Bowling Green, OH: Bowling Green University Popular Press.

ROMANTICISM AND DARK ROMANTICISM

During the eighteenth century in Europe, a major cultural movement took place, now known as "the Enlightenment," and those who participated in this movement celebrated reason above tradition. In politics, religion, and art, they tried to break with tradition and with historical trends, with the idea that a new, much better society could be formed along strictly rationalistic lines. The Enlightenment period gave rise to some of the most sophisticated literature, philosophy, and political thought in European history. In France in 1789, a revolution put people in power who were determined to rebuild the government, and indeed all of France, along

As a literary, aesthetic, and general cultural movement, romanticism was something of a reaction against what was perceived by some to be the soulless rationalism of the Enlightenment. Romantics championed heightened emotion and depth of feeling, and focused on human subjectivity and extreme psychological states.

What has been termed *dark* romanticism focused on the most pointedly Gothic aspects of the basic Romantic position, with the focus on the human psyche assuming a decidedly darker slant and emerging as a deep dread of the monstrous and sinister forces that might lurk within—and emerge from—the unconscious mind. It is dark romanticism, allied with the Gothic, that serves as the progenitor of modern Western horror fiction.

Matt Cardin

lines spelled out by important theoretical works of Enlightenment thinkers, many of whom were also important for the leaders of the American Revolution. Despite many accomplishments, the French Revolution finally produced what became known as "the Terror." More than 16,000 people were executed for being antirevolutionary in a period of not much more than a single year. For many, both in France and throughout the Western world, this was taken as a sign that the Enlightenment was a failure.

The cultural movement known as romanticism was, if anything, even more widely influential than the Enlightenment thinkers were. For some, romanticism was the rejection of Enlightenment ideals. While they did not dismiss reason as unimportant, they saw it as being soulless; the full human being is more than just a rational mind, being also an often tumultuous or chaotic emotional soul. What reason was to the Enlightenment, the will was to romanticism. However, there were many who participated in the Romantic movement who saw in it an extension of the best aspects of the Enlightenment, building on the best ideas of the previous generation while avoiding their errors.

It is important to distinguish between romanticism and dark romanticism, because a conflict existed between these two artistic directions within romanticism overall. While those who tended to write darker, more Gothic material simply went their own way, other writers who publicly identified themselves as leaders of a Romantic movement, including William Wordsworth and Lord Byron, took issue with the more fantastic and grotesque writing being published as "Romantic literature." These leaders came to represent the more utopian or uplifting side of romanticism, although even they went on to write a few "dark" pieces themselves.

Important Romantic authors include, in Germany, Johann Gottlieb Fichte, Johann Wolfgang von Goethe, E. T. A. Hoffmann, Friedrich Hölderlin, Heinrich von Kleist, Friedrich Schelling, and Ludwig Tieck; in England, William Blake, Lord Byron, Samuel Taylor Coleridge, William Hazlitt, John Keats, Charles Lamb, Sir Walter Scott,

Mary Shelley, Percy Bysshe Shelley, and William Wordsworth. In the United States, many canonical authors, including Nathaniel Hawthorne, Herman Melville, and Edgar Allan Poe, are considered either Romantics or to have been strongly influenced by romanticism.

Romantic literature often presents the reader with isolated characters whose psychological states are described in great detail. The concept of the unconscious mind becomes extremely important in Romantic writing and usually appears in some combination with nature; that is, nature is understood as the image or mirror of the unconscious mind. Very often the emotional or mental state of a character will be reflected in the weather or in landscape features; *Wuthering Heights* is a late example of this, providing in its stormy, remote setting a psychologically appropriate background for a novel about passionate, isolated characters.

This close association of the unconscious mind with nature is often described in terms of the supernatural. Coleridge, for example, believed that the imagination could produce knowledge, just as reason can. The inspired artistic genius was, for him, a seer. From the Romantic point of view, the artist of the Enlightenment was trying to create art by using a sort of recipe; true art, however, was supposed to have a mysterious origin. The artist did not create ideas consciously, but was receptive to the appearance of ideas that originated somewhere beyond the mind.

Modern Western horror fiction has its roots in dark romanticism, which is the more Gothic aspect of the Romantic movement. For some, the unconscious mind was seen as a gateway to higher, loftier thinking, but for others, the unconscious mind was a terrifying presence, an evil twin. Vampires, doubles, specters, all manner of beings meant to represent the guilt or the evil impulses of the main character abound in Dark Romantic writing. Frankenstein's monster is at times described as an evil double of Frankenstein himself, relentlessly pursuing him, refusing to allow him to forget or abandon his responsibilities. James Hogg's influential 1824 novel *The Private Memoirs and Confessions of a Justified Sinner* has a similar plot; in Edgar Allan Poe's story "William Wilson," the roles are reversed, and the pursuing twin is the main character's better side, rather than his evil side.

As the nineteenth century continued, aspects of dark romanticism cropped up in the fiction of later generations. Robert Louis Stevenson's novel *The Strange Case of Dr. Jekyll and Mr. Hyde* embodies both halves of one character in two distinct persons, while Arthur Machen's novella "The Great God Pan" revolves around a malevolent woman who represents something like the collective unconscious of all humanity, rather than of a single individual. Many ghost stories of this later era involve considerable uncertainty about the existence of the ghost. It is impossible to say with any certainty that the ghostly woman or double of the main character in Charlotte Perkins Gilman's story "The Yellow Wall-Paper" is an objectively other entity, or only some other part of her own mind.

Dark romanticism also became mingled with the literary movement known as decadence, which developed around the year 1890. The "Decadents" were writers and artists who also turned away from official rationalism and embraced the unconscious, treating it as a form of cultural exhaustion. Oscar Wilde was often included among the Decadents, as was French author J. K. Huysmans, whose novel about black magic, entitled *La-Bas* (literally translated as "Down There," although it has also been published in English under the title *The Damned*), was influential on H. P. Lovecraft, Clark Ashton Smith, and other horror writers. The Decadents were as concerned with society as the Romantics were, but had none of the optimistic utopianism of the Romantics; for the Decadents, society was like one huge work of art, and the decay of both society and individuals was regarded as beautiful.

Dark romanticism has since become associated with the aesthetics of a renewed Gothic cultural movement, while many of the aesthetic discoveries and ideas of the Romantics, especially with regard to the unconscious, remain in circulation today. The term is also sometimes used to describe a hybridization of the modern "romance novel," or love story, and horror fiction.

Michael Cisco

See also: The Brontë Sisters; Byron, Lord; Coleridge, Samuel Taylor; "The Great God Pan"; Hawthorne, Nathaniel; Poe, Edgar Allan; *The Private Memoirs and Confessions of a Justified Sinner*; Shelley, Mary; *The Strange Case of Dr. Jekyll and Mr. Hyde*; "The Yellow Wall-Paper."

Further Reading

Fiedler, Leslie. 1966. *Love and Death in the American Novel*. New York: Stein and Day.

Thompson, G. R., ed. 1974. "Romanticism and the Gothic Tradition." Introduction to *The Gothic Imagination: Essays in Dark Romanticism*. Pullman, WA: Washington State University Press.

ROSEMARY'S BABY

Rosemary's Baby is an American horror novel written by Ira Levin, first published in 1967. Levin's novel, a story of a woman who becomes the center of a plot by a coven of witches to bring about the Antichrist in New York City, was the beginning of a trend of devil and demon-possession horror novels in the late 1960s and 1970s. It was a bestseller for Levin, and the subsequent film adaptation cemented its status as a horror classic.

Ira Levin was already an established writer when he wrote *Rosemary's Baby*, his second novel. His first novel, *A Kiss Before Dying* (1953), won Levin an Edgar Award for Best First Novel. *Rosemary's Baby* tells the story of Rosemary Woodhouse, a naïve young woman who has just moved to a New York City apartment with her actor husband. Experiencing a difficult pregnancy, she grows suspicious of her neighbors, who she believes are witches, and eventually comes to the conclusion that she is impregnated with the spawn of Satan. The plot is firmly rooted in the Gothic tradition, as a helpless young heroine is isolated in a Gothic-style building with people who want to do her harm. Levin, however, adds depth to his novel by highlighting the powerlessness of Rosemary, who is repeatedly ignored when she seeks help. Her doctor, recommended by her neighbors, dismisses her early concerns when she expresses the painful symptoms of her pregnancy. Later, when her friends, frightened by the mother-to-be's gaunt and sickly appearance, push Rosemary to get help, Rosemary's husband, Guy, convinces her that her friends are meddling, hysterical women. When Rosemary finally escapes to a hospital and a doctor who is not under the coven's control, that doctor promptly calls her husband to pick her up, dismissing Rosemary's claims as the cries of a paranoid and anxious mother. The true horror, perhaps, lies in Rosemary's lack of agency as she tries to navigate a patriarchal society that dismisses her as a weak woman rather than one controlled by the satanic threat.

Levin would later return to this premise of women meeting horror at the hands of the men in their life in his next novel, *The Stepford Wives* (1972). *Rosemary's Baby* was met with enormous critical acclaim and commercial success. Levin wrote a sequel titled *Son of Rosemary* in 1997, but it did not earn the same praise as its predecessor.

Horror film director William Castle bought the rights to *Rosemary's Baby* before the novel was even published, eager to bring Levin's tale to the silver screen. The adaptation was a passion project for Castle, who was known more for his promotion gimmicks than his craft. He hoped that *Rosemary's Baby* would make him a respected director; however, the studio refused to make the film if Castle was directing. Instead, Castle took the role of producer, and Roman Polanski wrote and directed. *Rosemary's Baby*, the film, debuted in 1968 to enormous critical and popular praise. The movie, starring Mia Farrow as Rosemary, was nominated for several awards, including the Academy Award for Best Adapted Screenplay and several Golden Globes, earning nominations for Best Screenplay and Best Original Score. Ruth Gordon, who played Minnie Castavet, won an Academy Award and a Golden Globe for Best Supporting Actress. Mia Farrow also earned a nomination at the Golden Globes for Best Actress. Polanski's film is considered to be a classic horror film, often earning spots on best film lists. It was selected for preservation in the United States' National Film Registry.

Like the novel, the film adaptation of *Rosemary's Baby* spawned sequels and remakes. In 1976, a television film was made titled *Look What's Happened to Rosemary's Baby*, which was intended to be a sequel. Ruth Gordon reprised her role as Minnie Castavet, but Rosemary was played this time by Patty Duke. The film was universally disliked. In January 2014, NBC released a four-hour television miniseries of the original novel. Zoe Saldana was cast as Rosemary, and the setting was changed to Paris. This television adaptation received lukewarm reviews.

Lisa Kröger

See also: Devils and Demons; Incubi and Succubi; Witches and Witchcraft.

Further Reading

Adler, Renata. 1968. "Movie Review: *Rosemary's Baby*." *New York Times*, June 13. http://www.nytimes.com/movie/review?res=EE05E7DF1738E271BC4B52DFB0668383679 EDE.

Fisher, Lucy. 1992. "Birth Traumas: Parturition and Horror in 'Rosemary's Baby.'" *Cinema Journal* 31, no. 3: 3–18.

Langan, John. 2008. "A Devil for the Day: William Peter Blatty, Ira Levin, and the Revision of the Satanic." In *American Exorcist: Critical Essays on William Peter Blatty*, edited by Benjamin Szumskyj, 45–70. Jefferson, NC: McFarland.

Levin, Ira. 2012. "'Stuck with Satan': Ira Levin on the Origins of *Rosemary's Baby*." *Criterion.com*, November 5. https://www.criterion.com/current/posts/2541-stuck-with-satan-ira-levin-on-the-origins-of-rosemary-s-baby.

Lima, Robert. 1974. "The Satanic Rape of Catholicism in Rosemary's Baby." *Studies in American Fiction* (Autumn): 211–220.

Valerius, Karyn. 2005. "*Rosemary's Baby*, Gothic Pregnancy, and Fetal Subjects." *College Literature* 32, no. 2: 116–135.

RUSSELL, RAY (1924–1999)

Ray Russell was an American writer and editor. He was known for his work as fiction editor for *Playboy* magazine in the 1950s and 1960s, during which time he was responsible for making the magazine a prime market for short fiction, especially horror and science fiction. He was also an accomplished horror writer in his own right, publishing several novels and short stories until his death in 1999.

As fiction editor for *Playboy*, Russell was responsible for publishing science fiction and horror writers such as Kurt Vonnegut, Richard Matheson, and Ray Bradbury, to name only a few. It was during his time at *Playboy* that he discovered Charles Beaumont, a writer with whom he would later work. More than fifty of Russell's own works appeared in Hugh Hefner's magazine, including the short story "Sardonicus" (1961), which was later published as part of a trio of stories and adapted into film as *Mr. Sardonicus* (1961), for which Russell wrote the screenplay. He also penned the script for Roger Corman's *X: The Man with the X-Ray Eyes* (1963), as well as several other film projects, including *The Horror of It All* (1964) and *Chamber of Horrors* (1966). *X: The Man with the X-Ray Eyes* won Russell, along with his fellow screenwriter Robert Dillon, an award at the Trieste International Film Festival in 1963. He continued his work with Charles Beaumont when the two worked together on a screen adaptation of Edgar Allan Poe's story "The Premature Burial" (1962). The film was directed by Roger Corman.

Russell's other works include the 1962 novel *The Case Against Satan*, which tells the story of two priests who come to the aid of a young demon-possessed girl. The novel is remarkable in that it came before William Peter Blatty's 1971 novel *The Exorcist*. Russell's 1976 novel *Incubus* combined the shock of sex and the gore of horror as a demon tries to impregnate human women, mostly with horrific results. A movie based on *Incubus* was made in 1982, starring John Cassavetes. In the 1970s,

The Case Against Satan: Demonic Possession or Disturbed Psyche?

Russell's *The Case Against Satan* (1962) is a classic tale of demon possession and exorcism, notable for the fact that it appeared nine years before William Peter Blatty's *The Exorcist* (1971).

The plot is a familiar one: teenager Susan Garth begins to act unusually, her behavior marked by explosions of violence and profanity. The Catholic Church sends two priests to perform an exorcism, though the younger of the two priests is skeptical, believing more in modern-day psychology than in biblical demons. The battle between the two priests is perhaps more important to Russell's novel than is their battle with the demon. Unlike Blatty, who later used a similar plot to espouse his own Christian—specifically Catholic—ideology, Russell sows the seeds of doubt. The clergymen, the Garth family, and the readers are left wondering if the events were supernatural or due to the derangement of an unstable mind.

Given this, *The Case Against Satan* is less of a supernatural horror novel and more of an intellectual adventure. Most readers will close the book unsure of what exactly transpired, and Russell maintains a sparse tone throughout, offering some sort of distance to the subject matter. Still, though the supernatural is not proven per se, the novel seems to acknowledge a spiritual realm, though maybe not one related to any particular religion.

Russell's novel was successful in launching a renewed interest in supernatural books that featured demon possession, including Blatty's novel and Ira Levin's *Rosemary's Baby* (1967). Though Blatty's and Levin's books take a hard stance on the supernatural, Russell's lays the groundwork for the skeptic's possession novels of the twenty-first century, particularly novels such as Paul Tremblay's *A Head Full of Ghosts* (2015), in which a reality television crew tapes a teenage girl's exorcism, which may or may not be supernatural in nature.

Lisa Kröger

Russell continued to work with *Playboy*, editing several story anthologies (sometimes anonymously) including *The Playboy Book of Horror and the Supernatural* (1967). In 1985, a collection of his short stories was released, titled *Haunted Castles: The Complete Gothic Tales of Ray Russell*. Penguin released a new edition in 2013.

Russell's work earned him two Bram Stoker awards (in 1991 and 1992), as well as the World Fantasy Award for Lifetime Achievement in 1991. Penguin released a new edition of *The Case Against Satan* in 2015.

Lisa Kröger

See also: Beaumont, Charles; Bradbury, Ray; Bram Stoker Award; *The Exorcist*; Incubi and Succubi; Matheson, Richard; "Sardonicus"; World Fantasy Award.

Further Reading

Adrian, Jack. 1999. "Obituary: Ray Russell." *The Independent*, March 26. http://www.inde
pendent.co.uk/arts-entertainment/obituary-ray-russell-1083246.html.

Errickson, Will. 2014. "The Summer of Sleaze: Ray Russell's Incubus." Tor.com. September
19. http://www.tor.com/2014/09/19/summer-of-sleaze-ray-russell-incubus.

Morgan, Chris. 1998. "Ray Russell." In *St. James Guide to Horror, Ghost, and Gothic Writers*,
edited by David Pringle, 494–496. Detroit, MI: St. James Press/Gale.

Staggs, Matt. 2016. "Sardonicus Rising: Horror Master Ray Russsell's Unexpected Revival."
Unbound Worlds, September 30. http://www.unboundworlds.com/2016/09/sardonicus
-rising-horror-master-ray-russells-unexpected-revival.

SAKI (1870–1916)

Saki was the pen name of Hector Hugh Munro, whose macabre stories frequently appear in horror anthologies, especially "The Open Window" (1914) and "Sredni Vashtar" (1911). Celebrated for his sly and witty portrayals of the English upper middle classes, Saki's horror stories introduce bizarre incidents to an Edwardian England full of flappers, languid aristocrats, country homes, garden parties, and cynical young dandies or "feral ephebes" (Byrne 2007, 15).

Munro was born the youngest of three children to an imperial military family serving the British Raj in Akyab, northwest Burma (now Myanmar), on December 18, 1870. His mother died following a miscarriage, and at the tender age of two, young Hector was sent, with his siblings Charlie and Ethel, to his grandmother's house in England, where the children were in constant fear of two strict aunts who appear as the monstrous female relatives in Saki stories such as "The Lumber-Room" (1914) or "Sredni Vashtar."

Munro at first chose to follow his father into the Burmese military police, but illness drove him back to England, where he worked as a journalist for various newspapers and magazines. His first short story was published in 1899 and his first book, a historical study of the Russian Empire, in 1900. From 1902 to 1908, Munro worked abroad as a foreign correspondent for the *Morning Post*, but then returned to London, where he wrote satires on the politics of the day as well as collections of short stories revolving around his ephebe characters Bassington, Reginald, and Clovis Sangrail.

Elements of the horrific fantastic crept into the latter fiction. Saki's second collection of short stories, *Reginald in Russia* (1910), included "Gabriel-Ernest," a chilling tale of a beautiful boyish werewolf with a taste for child-flesh. "Sredni Vashtar," "Esmé," "The Music on the Hill," and "The Easter Egg" all appear in his subsequent collection, *The Chronicles of Clovis* (1911), and "The Open Window" in *Beasts and Super-beasts* (1914), while *The Toys of Peace* (1919) featured "The Interlopers," "The Penance," and "The Wolves of Cernograst."

Munro enlisted for World War I in 1914, when he was in his forties, refusing an officer's commission. He was shot and killed by a German sniper on November 14, 1916 near the village of Beaumont-Hamel on the river Somme. His last words were reported to have been, "Put that bloody cigarette out!" (Byrne 2007, 3).

Saki's tales are extremely funny, mingling what A. A. Milne called his "careless cruelty" with graceful satires on upper-class society (Milne 2016, 6). For example, in "Louis" (1919), an irritated husband conspires with his sister to gas his wife

"The Open Window": Ghosts of the Imagination

The most anthologized of all Saki's stories is "The Open Window" (1914), with a devastating twist and charmingly cruel practical joker. Suffering from nerves, Framton Nuttel comes to the countryside for a rest but is obliged by his sister to visit her acquaintances. At the Sappleton residence, he is greeted by fifteen-year-old Vera, who weaves a tall tale for Mr. Nuttel. She tells him that their hostess, Mrs. Sappleton, constantly leaves her French window open in the hopes that her husband and two brothers, dead in a hunting tragedy, will someday return. When Mrs. Sappleton joins them, she soon cheerily points out her husband and brothers coming across the lawn with their spaniel trotting at their side, just as Vera has described them. Nuttel believes he is seeing their ghosts and hastily departs, terrified. Mrs. Sappleton's bewilderment at Nuttel's abrupt exit is Vera's cue to produce another tall tale about Nuttel.

Practical jokes are a fixture of Saki's fiction, and this is a characteristically Saki tale, full of mischievous jabs at conventional society that by no means detract from the "chill shock of nameless fear" (Saki 1976, 261) the reader shares with Nuttel at the sight of the figures approaching the open window. His social awkwardness is contrasted with Vera's self-possession and the authority with which she defines their moment of shared surreality.

The conventional Nuttel is also portrayed as an unappealing bore. In contrast, the shock that Vera delights in producing, even going so far as to feign "dazed horror" upon spotting the hunters (261), is a welcome interruption to the yawns that Nuttel induces in his hostess as he drones on about his nerves. As with many other horror fictions, the dullness of everyday life is compared unfavorably to the thrill of imagination, however terrifying those thrills might be.

Aalya Ahmad

Lena's Pomeranian lapdog, only to discover that Lena has been cuddling a lifelike facsimile as an excuse to avoid accompanying him to social engagements. In "Esmé," an escaped hyena devours a Roma (Gypsy) child in front of two horrified lady hunters, one of whom recounts this episode in a highly amused fashion years later, revealing that she pretended the hyena was her dog in order to obtain a valuable brooch as compensation from a gentleman who accidentally ran it over.

Saki pits the elegant, highly artificial manners of the Edwardian drawing room against the raw violence of the natural world, most often in the form of animals and children. In his homoerotic werewolf story, "Gabriel-Ernest" (1909), which combines the animal with the child, the hapless gentleman Van Cheele is powerless before both the predations of the werewolf and the overtures of another overbearing aunt, who tries to make the lycanthropic boy her protégè, allowing him to carry off one of the infants from her Sunday-school class. The alluring queerness of the feral boy, reflecting Munro's own suppressed homosexuality, is mirrored by the god Pan, who appears as a beautiful, laughing boy in "The Music on the Hill" (1911), in which a domineering bride is gored to death by a stag as a punishment for taking an offering of grapes from his shrine.

While many of Saki's women are similarly punished, leaving the impression that they won't be missed, and his social comedies abound with disparaging references to the militant suffragettes of his time, he also has a soft spot for the younger, cheekier "flappers" of the early twentieth century. Another of his recurring characters is the precocious flapper Vera, who figures as the niece in "The Open Window."

Saki's adults occasionally live to regret their confrontations with the innocent ruthlessness of Nature. In "The Penance" (1919), three children (whose circumstances closely resemble those of Munro's own childhood) remorselessly pursue their neighbor, who has killed their pet cat, mistakenly under the impression that it was raiding his chickens. Taking advantage of his efforts to placate them, they kidnap his two-year-old daughter and drop her into the muck of the pigsty, refusing to help retrieve her until the frantic father vows to do penance by standing by the cat's grave holding a candle and declaring himself a "miserable Beast" (Saki 1976, 427). The "inexorable" cruelty of the children—"We shall be very sorry when we've killed Olivia," said the girl, "but we can't be sorry till we've done it" (426)—accentuates the coldness in what might otherwise be simply a cute story of childish revenge. But there is nothing cute about Saki's youngsters; their hatred of adult injustices is seething, bitter, and heartfelt.

Saki was clearly influenced by Oscar Wilde and Rudyard Kipling, both of whom have contributed major works of horror to world literature. His later contemporaries P. G. Wodehouse and M. R. James can be compared to him both in point of social satire and, in the case of the latter, the ability to introduce horrifying and shocking elements into scenes of utter normalcy. He has also been compared to the American writer of twist endings, O. Henry. Apart from his best known stories, Saki's work remains rather obscure, and scholarship on him has occurred but rarely. However, his fiction has been highly praised as inspirational by other authors, including G. K. Chesterton, A. A. Milne, Noël Coward, Christopher Morley, H. P. Lovecraft, V. S. Pritchett, and Graham Greene.

Aalya Ahmad

See also: James, M. R.; Lovecraft, H. P.; "Sredni Vashtar."

Further Reading

Birden, Lorene. 2004. "'People Dined against Each Other': Social Practices in Sakian Satire." *Literary London: Interdisciplinary Studies in the Representation of London* 2.2.

Birden, Lorene M. 2012. "Saki as Dauphin of the Wildean Witticism." *Anachronist* 17: 117.

Byrne, Sandi. 2007. *The Unbearable Saki: The Work of H. H. Munro.* Oxford: Oxford University Press.

Frost, Adam. 1999. "A Hundred Years of Saki." *Contemporary Review* 275, no. 1607, 302–304.

Gibson, Brian. 2014. *Reading Saki: The Fiction of H. H. Munro.* Jefferson, NC: McFarland.

Milne, A. A. [1911] 2016. Introduction to *The Chronicles of Clovis.* Createspace Independent Publishing Platform. 5–6.

Saki (H. H. Munro). 1976. *The Complete Works of Saki.* Introduction by Noël Coward. New York: Doubleday.

Salemi, Joseph S. 1989. "An Asp Lurking in an Apple-charlotte: Animal Violence in Saki's *The Chronicles of Clovis.*" *Studies in Short Fiction* 26, no. 4: 423.

Spears, George James. 1963. *The Satire of Saki: A Study of the Satiric Art of Hector Hugh Munro.* New York: Exposition Press.

SAMUELS, MARK (1967–)

Mark Samuels is a British writer of weird horror, primarily known for his short fiction. He is also a former general secretary of the Friends of Arthur Machen, a society devoted to the works of the visionary late nineteenth- and early twentieth-century writer.

Samuels was born in Clapham, South London. He began publishing short fiction in 1988. His debut collection, *The White Hands and Other Weird Tales*, was published in 2003, and both it and its title story were nominated for British Fantasy Awards in 2004. He has, as of this writing, published four subsequent collections of fiction and one novel, *The Face of Twilight* (2005), which was also nominated for a British Fantasy Award. In addition, he has had numerous short stories included in horror and weird fiction anthologies.

Much of Samuels's fiction is set in London. He is influenced in his approach to the city by that of Machen, who saw London as a place where atavistic and/or esoteric forces might at any time erupt. In Samuels's *The Face of Twilight*, a recurring character of his, Alfred Muswell (whose initials are a nod to Machen), is quoted as having written, "there are London streets that lead to another world impinging on this one" (Samuels 2006, 20). In Samuels's work there are two Londons, with a visionary city laid on top of the ordinary one.

Also like Machen, Samuels is intensely interested in the mystical side of Christianity. This can be seen in the tendency for his protagonists' encounters with the weird to end not in madness and death, as such encounters generally do in much weird fiction, including Lovecraftian fiction (and Lovecraft is another of Samuels's chief influences), but in ecstasy and transmutation, with the self animated by some primal animism or blinding numinous force.

In addition to Machen and Lovecraft, Samuels's work also bears the particular mark of Edgar Allan Poe, Thomas Ligotti, Bruno Schulz, Stefan Grabiński, and Ramsey Campbell. But his erudite and densely allusive fiction incorporates much more of the supernatural fiction tradition than just these writers. As in the stories of Jorge Luis Borges, who is another key influence, evocations of weird tales; scholarly, occult, and spiritual works; and historical events, both real and fabricated, are braided together in Samuels's stories into a bizarre yet convincing tissue of quotations.

His story "The Man Who Collected Machen," the eponymous entry in his 2011 collection *The Man Who Collected Machen*, is a representative example of Samuels's approach. A man who refuses to give up a rare edition of a work by Machen is therefore made a member of the Lost Club (a reference to a Machen story of that name) by a jealous collector and banished to a London transmuted by Machen's vision. But for him it is not a dreadful exile but an ecstatic one, for he sees the wonder in that awful place.

Samuels's writing has had an important influence on the modern weird fiction tradition. A tribute to his work, *Marked to Die*, featuring stories by a number of contemporary writers of weird horror, was published in June 2016.

Timothy J. Jarvis

See also: Borges, Jorge Luis; Campbell, Ramsey; Grabiński, Stefan; Ligotti, Thomas; Lovecraft, H. P.; Machen, Arthur; The Numinous; Poe, Edgar Allan; Schulz, Bruno.

Further Reading

Cardin, Matt. 2006. "Interview with Mark Samuels: A Sense of Charnel Glamour." *The Teeming Brain*, August. http://www.teemingbrain.com/interview-with-mark-samuels.

Samuels, Mark. 2006. *The Face of Twilight*. With an introduction by Mark Morris. Hornsea, England: PS Publishing.

SANDKINGS

Sandkings is a novella written by George R. R. Martin that was first published in the August 1979 issue of *Omni* magazine; it has since been reprinted numerous times in various anthologies. *Sandkings* was awarded the Hugo Award by the World Science Fiction Society in 1979 and the Nebula Award by the Science Fiction and Fantasy Writers of America in 1980. It was adapted into a graphic novel by DC Comics in 1987 and was filmed as the first episode of the relaunched *The Outer Limits* television series that premiered in 1995.

Sandkings opens with Simon Kress, a wealthy collector of exotic animals who lives on the planet Baldur, discovering a shop, Shade & Wo, he has never seen before in an otherwise familiar city. Inside he meets the shop's proprietress, Jala Wo, who, in response to Kress's request for an unusual animal, presents him with the insect-like Sandkings. There are four colonies of Sandkings, differentiated by their color scheme—red, orange, black, and white—that live in the four corners of a large terrarium buried in the sand; the queen, or Maw, remains unseen, buried deep below, but directs the Sandkings via telepathic signals. Wo promises Kress that so long as he keeps the Sandkings fed they will provide him countless hours of amusement with their warfare and strategic, purposeful maneuvering. She also informs him that the creatures will grow according to their environment, which heartens Kress, who had expressed reservations about their diminutive size.

Kress purchases the Sandkings and has them delivered to his home, where he keeps them in a terrarium much larger than the one used in the shop. A showman and braggart, Kress organizes viewing parties with fellow elites, calling attention especially to the reproduction of his likeness that the Sandkings sketch on the sides of their homes. While the partygoers are generally satisfied with the warring of the Sandkings, Kress eventually grows bored and begins withholding food from them, making them increasingly vicious. Kress's abusive treatment escalates and soon he is engaging them in fights with other exotic alien species. Wo warns him against this behavior. When Kress notices that one of his visages has taken on a twisted appearance, he lashes out at the Sandkings queen, gouging a stick deep into her lair and most likely injuring her. The next day Kress is visited by his former lover Cath, who resents his treatment of the Sandkings. She smashes their tank but is injured in the resulting tumult. Kress flees, leaving Cath behind. When he returns much later he finds that the red, black, and white factions of Sandkings have taken over the grounds and consumed Cath. Kress takes steps to exterminate them, but is forced to enlist Wo's aid. The Sandkings, she explains, have evolved to a point of sentience, but because of Kress's mistreatment they are pathological and fixated on revenge. Wo and her partner Shade, who is revealed to be an evolved Sandking, assume responsibility for the escaped Sandkings, much to Kress's relief. Fleeing the scene, Kress eventually stumbles upon a solitary home. Thinking he has found refuge, he discovers that the home is actually a large sandcastle built by the escaped orange Sandkings, which have adopted Kress's size and likeness. Their captive now, Kress is dragged away screaming, presumably to be devoured by the Maw.

While *Sandkings* initially reads as pure science fiction, complete with extraterrestrial creatures and an alien world that serves as the story's backdrop, it also functions as an example of psychological horror. As the story develops Kress experiences a gradual yet ever-increasing sense of dislocation from his environment. His sense of control over the Sandkings gradually erodes, leading to a break with his circle of acquaintances (one hesitates to call them his friends), expulsion from his home, and ultimately a complete separation from his role in Baldur's culture of wealth and leisure. The closing scene—in which Kress is mobbed by Sandkings who have adopted his visage—effectively blends existential crisis and physical violence as Kress's identity is symbolically and literally consumed.

Javier A. Martinez

See also: Martin, George R. R.; Psychological Horror.

Further Reading

Bischoff, David. 1995. "The New Outer Limits." *Omni* 17, no. 7: 34.

Cotman, Elwin. 2013. "The Colonial Nightmares in 'Sandkings.'" *Weird Fiction Review*, March 19. http://weirdfictionreview.com/2013/03/wfrs-101-weird-writers-22-george-r-r-martin.

"THE SAND-MAN"

"The Sand-man" (a.k.a. "Der Sand-mann") is a short story by the nineteenth-century German Romantic writer E. T. A. Hoffmann. Originally published in German in 1817, it first appeared in English in *Tales from the German, Comprising Specimens from the Most Celebrated Authors* in 1844. One of Hoffmann's most complex stories, "The Sand-man" exists in several translations and has different versions of its characters' names, but the story is at its core one of perceptions, with madness and identity and obsession being several of its themes.

The never-seen titular character is folkloric, a "wicked man, who comes to children, when they will not go to bed and throws handfuls of sand into their eyes, so that they start out bleeding from their heads" (Oxenford and Feiling 1844, 141);

The richness of "The Sand-man," especially in terms of philosophical and psychological content, comes through in passages like the following, which is one of many that articulate ideas, dreads, and suspicions that often lurk unexpressed in human minds and hearts until someone with Hoffmann's authorial acumen gives them voice.

> If there is a dark and hostile power, laying its treacherous toils within us, by which it holds us fast and draws us along the path of peril and destruction, which we should not otherwise have trod; if, I say there is such a power, it must form itself inside us and out of ourselves, indeed; it must become identical with ourselves. For it is only in this condition that we can believe in it, and grant it the room which it requires to accomplish its secret work. Now, if we have a mind which is sufficiently firm, sufficiently strengthened by the joy of life, always to recognize this strange enemy as such, and calmly to follow the path of our own inclination and calling, then the dark power will fail in its attempt to gain a form that shall be a reflection of ourselves. Lothaire adds that if we have willingly yielded ourselves up to the dark powers, they are known often to impress upon our minds any strange, unfamiliar shape which the external world has thrown in our way; so that we ourselves kindle the spirit, which we in our strange delusion believe to be speaking to us. It is the phantom of our own selves, the close relationship with which, and its deep operation on our mind, casts us into hell or transports us into heaven.

Matt Cardin

Source: Hoffmann, E. T. A. [1817] 1999. "The Sand-man." Translated by John Oxenford. *19th-Century German Stories*. http://germanstories.vcu.edu/hoffmann/sand_e.html.

he then takes the naughty children to his loved ones, where the children's eyes are plucked out. The Sand-man is one of young Nathanael's obsessions, and the story begins with his writing a letter to Lothair, brother of his fiancée Clara, in which he describes his childhood memories of the Sand-man and concludes with recounting a disastrous meeting with the domineering lawyer Coppelius. Coppelius is also an alchemist, and his fiery magical experiments almost lead to Nathanael's death; they do later lead to the death of Nathanael's father and the disappearance of Coppelius. But Nathanael believes Coppelius has reappeared as Coppola, a seller of barometers. Nathanael's letter is sent to Clara, however, who offers Nathanael sympathy, then concludes by telling him that his fears are from his own mind and that he should stop obsessing about Coppelius/Coppola. Nathanael's next letter reveals that he was wrong in his identification of Coppelius with Coppola, for the two are different people. He additionally reveals that his professor, Spalanzani, has vouched for Coppola and has a beautiful daughter, Olimpia. This letter is sent to Lothair and is correctly delivered.

The above motifs and situations being semi-established, there are more narrative complexities. There are issues of obsession, identity, and reality, for a person can be machine-like in behavior, and machines may have the appearance of people. Nathanael's actions reveal that he has become thoroughly unhinged, ultimately dangerously so, though he fails to kill Clara, Coppola, and Coppelius, and concludes by committing suicide, throwing himself from a balcony and leaving Clara to find happiness with another, which she does.

According to the introduction by the story's original English translators, "the story of the *Sand-man* had its origin in a discussion which actually took place between La Motte Fouqué and some friends, at which Hoffmann was present. Some of the people found fault with the cold, mechanical deportment of a young lady of their acquaintance, while La Motte Fouqué defended her. Here Hoffmann caught the notion of the automaton Olympia [sic], and the arguments used by Nathaniel [sic] are those that were really employed by La Motte Fouqué" (Oxenford and Feiling 1844, xii–xiii). At the same time, the story is much more than a simple assessment of behavior, and it remains one of Hoffmann's most complex and idea-driven tales. Significantly, it was used by Sigmund Freud as a chief focus in his 1919 essay "The Uncanny," where he dwells on the living doll Olimpia, the significance of the Sand-man's violence to eyes, and the theme of the double or doppelgänger, and avers that "E. T. A. Hoffmann is the unrivalled master of the uncanny in literature" (Freud 2003, 141).

Richard Bleiler

See also: Doubles, Doppelgängers, and Split Selves; Hoffmann, E. T. A.; Psychological Horror; The Uncanny.

Further Reading

Freud, Sigmund. [1919] 2003. "The Uncanny." In *The Uncanny*, translated by David McLintock, 121–162. New York: Penguin.

Mahlendorf, Ursula. 1975. "E. T. A. Hoffmann's *The Sand-man*: The Fictional Psycho-Biography of a Romantic Poet." *American Imago* 32, no. 3: 217–239.

Oxenford, John, and C. A. Feiling, trans. 1844. *Tales from the German, Comprising Specimens from the Most Celebrated Authors*. London: Chapman and Hall.

Willis, Martin T. 1994. "Scientific Portraits in Magical Frames: The Construction of Preternatural Narrative in the Work of E. T. A. Hoffmann and Arthur Machen." *Extrapolation* 35, no. 3: 186–200.

SARBAN (1910–1989)

"Sarban" was the pseudonym under which John William Wall, a British career diplomat, published three books of weird fiction between 1951 and 1953. Sarban's work is considered a bridge between the work of writers in the classic supernatural tradition, such as Algernon Blackwood and Arthur Machen, and contemporary weird fiction. His stories are especially memorable for their evocative descriptions of foreign lands and exotic cultures for whom mythic survivals are not uncommon.

Sarban's first book, *Ringstones and Other Curious Tales* (1951), collects five previously unpublished short stories. The title tale tells of a young woman, Daphne, who cares for three children in a manor house in the Northumbrian moorlands built near an ancient stone circle. The eldest, Nuaman, expresses a vibrant sexuality seemingly beyond his years. The evidence mounts by the story's end that Nuaman is the avatar of an ancient god in league with the fairy race who built the ringstones, and that Daphne has submitted to his primitive sexual dominance in dreams, if not in waking life. As Peter Nicholls has noted, dramatic tension in the story derives from the juxtaposition of the forbidden primitive sexuality that Nuaman represents to the repressions of modern life that govern Daphne. Survivals from the past infused with primitive sexuality are also elements in "The Khan" (1951), in which an Englishwoman traveling with her stodgy husband in the Persian desert strays into a mystical forest glade where she is groomed to become the sexual partner of a woodland spirit who assumes the form of a massive bear, and "Capra" (1951), in which a satyr from antiquity becomes the victim of a party of sexually uninhibited modern couples in contemporary Greece.

Sarban's best-known work, the short novel *The Sound of His Horn* (1952), is an alternate history tale (with none of the traditional science fiction underpinnings) whose protagonist, a prisoner escaped from a POW camp during World War II, slips into a future in which Germany has won the war. That future is not a futuristic extrapolation of the Third Reich, but rather a throwback to the legendary past in which a master forester, Count von Hackleberg, plays the role of the legendary Wild Huntsman, organizing hunts of members of subjugated races for the benefit of senior members of the Reich. The count's "harriers"—biologically altered females outfitted as naked catlike huntresses—gives the book's treatment of the themes of dominance and submission a patina of perverse sexuality.

Dominance and submission recur again in *The Doll Maker and Other Tales of the Uncanny* (1953), which collects three stories, including the title tale, in which a teenage girl discovers that the handsome young man who lives on the estate next door to her boarding school, and who encourages her romantic inclinations toward him, intends to capture her soul magically in a doll to serve as his plaything. In one of the book's other stories, "The Trespassers," a reclusive girl in a country estate uses her sexual allure to persuade two schoolboys who have strayed onto its premises to help her capture a unicorn.

The posthumous collection *The Sacrifice and Other Stories* (2002) collects four stories, of which two capture the same sense of sexual menace that imbues Sarban's other fiction: "The King of the Lake," an Arabian Nights–style fable in which two women lost in a sandstorm are taken to an underground lake by a mysterious stranger whose mythic destiny is bound up with his unsavory designs on them; and "Number Fourteen," about a religious cult's obsession with a dancer in (then) contemporary London. *Discovery of Heretics: Unseen Writings* (2010) collects a number of fragmentary and previously unpublished works, including the novella "The Gynarchs," about a postapocalyptic matriarchal utopia.

Stefan R. Dziemianowicz

See also: Blackwood, Algernon; Machen, Arthur.

Further Reading

Nicholls, Peter. 1986. "Sarban." In *Supernatural Fiction Writers, Volume II*, edited by Everett F. Bleiler, 667–673. New York: Scribners.
Valentine, Mark. 2010. *Time, A Falconer: A Study of Sarban*. North Yorkshire: Tartarus Press.

"SARDONICUS"

"Sardonicus" is a short story written by Ray Russell, originally published in the January 1961 issue of *Playboy* magazine. It is an example of a Gothic story in both its Bohemian castle setting and damsel-in-distress plot, prompting Stephen King to call it "perhaps the finest example of the modern Gothic ever written" (del Toro 2013, xii). The story was later collected in *Unholy Trilogy* (1967) with two other tales, "Sagittarius," which takes place in part in Paris at the infamous Grand Guignol (a theater specializing in horror plays, presented with copious gore), and "Sanguinarius," a fictional account of the murderous Countess Elizabeth Bathory.

"Sardonicus" tells the story of Robert Cargrave, a doctor, who is called to an ancient estate to help a former love interest, Maude, who is now married to Sardonicus, the owner of the impressive manor. Sardonicus is suffering from a rare medical condition that makes it impossible for him to move his face, which has been frozen in a horrific grin ever since he looked upon the corpse of his father in its grave. He is a prime example of a man who has turned into a monster, specifically, a ghoul. Sardonicus proves to be both an unkind host and an abusive husband, and after he psychologically tortures Robert, the doctor finally retaliates, determined to save

William Castle: Master of Gimmickry

The American filmmaker William Castle, who produced and directed the movie adaptation of Russell's *Sardonicus*, achieved lasting fame, albeit of a gaudy sort, for his low-budget thriller and horror films in the 1950s and 1960s (as well as for his one "high-class" producing effort, 1968's *Rosemary's Baby*). The "punishment poll" that he created for *Mr. Sardonicus* was only one of many gimmicks that he conceived to market his movies. For *Macabre* (1958), he provided audience members with (fake) life insurance policies in case they died of fright. For *The House on Haunted Hill* (1959), he had a skeleton fly out over audiences on a wire during the climactic scene (a gimmick given a fond homage thirty-eight years later in director Wes Craven's *Scream 2* [1997]). For *The Tingler* (1959) he had some of the seats in certain theaters rigged with a vibrating motor to provide a "shock" during the finale, when a monster called "the tingler" gets loose in a movie theater. Today these and Castle's many other promotional stunts are the stuff of Hollywood and horror movie legend.

Matt Cardin

Maude. Robert uses his own knowledge of psychology to convince Sardonicus that his mouth will no longer open or close, leaving him to die from starvation.

The same year of its publication, Russell's story was adapted to film by director William Castle under the title *Mr. Sardonicus*. The film was released by Columbia in October 1961, with Guy Rolfe playing the titular character. Castle, a master at creating gimmicks to fill theater seats, advertised two endings and let the audience participate in a "punishment poll" to vote on whether Mr. Sardonicus should live or die. The reviews were mixed at best, but even so, *Mr. Sardonicus* is considered by many to be the best of Castle's career, due in large part to the makeup effects used to create the horrific smile on Rolfe's face.

In 2013 Penguin included Russell's story in *Haunted Castles: The Complete Gothic Stories*, an anthology for Penguin Classics edited by filmmaker Guillermo del Toro. In his foreword, del Toro effectively highlighted the significance of "Sardonicus" as both a backward-looking and forward-looking tale when he described it as "a tale of enormous originality that remains, at the same time, a grand homage and a reinvention of the Gothic" (del Toro 2013, xiii).

Lisa Kröger

See also: Monsters; Psychological Horror; Russell, Ray.

Further Reading

Brottman, Mikita. 2004. "Afterword: Risus Sardonicus." In *Funny Peculiar: Gershon Legman and the Psychopathology of Humor*, 141–153. Hillsdale, NJ: Analytic Press.

Conners, Scott. 2007. "The Ghoul." In *Icons of Horror and the Supernatural: An Encyclopedia of Our Worst Nightmares*, edited by S. T. Joshi, 243–266. Westport, CT: Greenwood Press.

Del Toro, Guillermo. 2013. "Foreword." In *Haunted Castles: The Complete Gothic Stories* by Ray Russell, xi–xix. New York: Penguin.

Staggs, Matt. 2016. "Sardonicus Rising: Horror Master Ray Russsell's Unexpected Revival." *Unbound Worlds*, September 30. http://www.unboundworlds.com/2016/09/sardonicus -rising-horror-master-ray-russells-unexpected-revival.

"SCHALKEN THE PAINTER"

Although Irish author Joseph Sheridan Le Fanu's (1814–1873) most celebrated work remains the vampire novella *Carmilla* (1871–1872), and to a lesser extent the supernatural short story "Green Tea" (1869), "Schalken the Painter," one of his earliest supernatural tales, is considered by connoisseurs of the uncanny to be one of his finest offerings. The story has long been a favorite among anthologists, including Montague Summers, Peter Haining, and E. F. Bleiler. M. R. James, who generally held Le Fanu's writing in high regard, singled out this story in his introduction to *Ghosts & Marvels* (1924) as being "one of the best of Le Fanu's good things" (James 2001, 488).

"Strange Event in the Life of Schalken the Painter," to give the tale its full title, was first published in the *Dublin University Magazine* in the May 1839 issue. The story originally bore the subtitle "Being a Seventh Extract from the Legacy of the Late Francis Purcell, P.P. of Drumcoolagh," and was part of a loosely linked series of tales and poems, collected posthumously under the title *The Purcell Papers* (1880). "Schalken," which is set in Holland, is further notable as being Le Fanu's first story to be set outside of Dublin.

The titular protagonist Godfrey Schalken is based on the Dutch painter Godfried Schalcken (1643–1706), whose chiaroscuro style (an art style that highlights the contrast between light and shadow) informs Le Fanu's narrative technique, especially the way in which descriptive details are carefully revealed to great uncanny effect. The tale concerns the inspiration for a painting by Schalken depicting a white-robed female figure whose arch smile is illuminated solely by the lamp she bears; in the background is a man with his hand on the hilt of his sword, in the act of drawing it. Whether or not this painting is based on one that Le Fanu had actually seen is a frequent topic of debate among scholars.

Schalken, apprenticed to Gerard Douw (Gerrit Dou, 1613–1675), falls in love with his master's ward, Rose Velderkaust, who is "possessed of all the dimpling charms of the fair, light-hearted Flemish maidens" (Le Fanu 2014, 78). One evening a sinister stranger appears in the studio—Mynher Vanderhausen, from Rotterdam—whose bluish leaden face is described as "malignant, even satanic" (89). Vanderhausen offers Douw a box of golden ingots in exchange for Rose's hand in marriage. Despite Schalken's affection, Douw accepts, and Vanderhausen leaves for Rotterdam with his bride. Some time later, Rose returns to Douw's house "wild and haggard, and pale with exhaustion and terror" (92). With the aid of an old clergyman, Schalken and Douw attempt to shelter her, but she is taken one night by some unseen hand. Schalken encounters Rose once more in a church in Rotterdam. With an arch smile she leads him to the crypt, where he witnesses a charnel bed and the livid and demoniac form of Vanderhausen.

"Schalken" shares with *Carmilla* horrific sexual undertones, especially in its climax, in which sexual congress between the living and the dead is strongly implied. This theme of innocence ruined by the otherworldly can also be found in two of Le Fanu's later stories, "The Child That Went with the Faeries" (1870) and "Laura Silver Bell" (1872). However, "Schalken" remains Le Fanu's cruelest and most chilling variation on the demon lover theme.

Le Fanu often reworked his stories throughout his career. For his first collection, *Ghost Stories and Tales of Mystery* (1851), he included a rewritten version of "Strange Event in the Life of Schalken the Painter," with the truncated title "Schalken the Painter," and accompanied it with an illustration by frequent Dickens collaborator "Phiz" (Hablot K. Browne, 1815–1882). While neither version of the story is considered better than the other—each has its own merits and flourishes of supernatural subtlety—they do have their differences, notably in the rewritten opening paragraphs and the addition of a Bible quote (Job 9:32–34).

In 1979 the BBC adapted Le Fanu's story for television. *Schalken the Painter* was written and directed by Leslie Meaghy and first aired on December 23. Though a drama, *Schalcken* was filmed for the arts documentary program *Omnibus*. It is now considered part of the *Ghost Stories for Christmas* series along with adaptations of M. R. James and Dickens. Meaghy's faithful adaptation, with its slow build toward the final horrific scene, is also notable for its lush cinematography, reproducing as it does the styles, tones, and compositions of the Dutch masters.

Brian J. Showers

See also: Bleiler, E. F.; *Carmilla*; "Green Tea"; Haining, Peter; *In a Glass Darkly*; James, M. R.; Le Fanu, J. Sheridan; Summers, Montague.

Further Reading

Hervey, Ben. 2014. *Schalcken the Painter*. BFI Flipside: 1–9.

James, M. R. 2001. Introduction to *Ghosts and Marvels*. In *A Pleasing Terror: The Complete Supernatural Writings* by M. R. James, edited by Christopher Roden and Barbara Roden, 486–490. Ashcroft, British Columbia: Ash-Tree Press. Originally published in *Ghosts and Marvels: A Selection of Uncanny Tales from Daniel Defoe to Algernon Blackwood*, edited by Vere H. Collins (Oxford: Oxford University Press, 1924).

Le Fanu, Sheridan. [1839] 2014. "Strange Event in the Life of Schalken the Painter." In *Horror Stories: Classic Tales from Hoffmann to Hodgson*, edited by Darryl Jones, 76–98. Oxford: Oxford University Press.

Pardoe, Rosemary. 1988. "Schalken the Painting." *Ghosts and Scholars* 10: 28, 34.

Rockhill, Jim. 2002. Introduction to *Schalken the Painter and Others* by J. S. Le Fanu, ix–xxxiii. Ashcroft, British Columbia: Ash-Tree Press.

Sullivan, Jack. 1978. *Elegant Nightmares: The English Ghost Story from Le Fanu to Blackwood*. Athens, OH: Ohio University Press.

SCHULZ, BRUNO (1892–1942)

Bruno Schulz was a Polish author and artist of Jewish heritage, best known for his collections of fantastic short stories. He wrote atmospheric, phantasmagorical fiction that dwelt on humdrum images and scenes in a way that saturated them with a curious beauty. In some ways, Schulz's work seems to anticipate what would later be called magical realism, in association primarily with Latin American literature. He was more interested in mystery, wonder, and the play of the grotesque and the beautiful than he was in terror, although much of his fiction does involve a kind of intense emotion of expectancy, if not dread. In modern horror fiction his presence and significance can be felt through his impact on a number of authors, including the American writer Thomas Ligotti and the British writer Mark Samuels.

Schulz was born in Drohobycz, Poland (but now part of Ukraine), where he lived almost his entire life, and which was the backdrop and subject of his fiction. He left home to study art and architecture, then returned, and supported himself by teaching.

Schulz had already been writing for some time, starting no later than 1925, when a friend showed some of his letters to Zofia Nalkowska, a Polish novelist and an important member of the Polish Academy of Literature. She saw Schulz's extraordinary talent, and encouraged him to publish his work. Schulz's first collection was published in 1934. Entitled *Sklepy Cynamonowe*, or *Cinnamon Shops*, it consisted of a series of linked, dreamlike stories drawn from Schulz's own childhood and adolescent experiences. The collection was published in English under the title *The Street of Crocodiles* in 1963. A masterpiece of Polish prose, of delicate fantasy and subtle characterization, the work attracted enough praise to prompt a second book in 1937, *Sanatorium Pod Klepsydra*, published in English as *The Sanatorium Under the Sign of the Hourglass* in 1988.

In 1938, Schulz won the Golden Laurel, a prestigious award presented by the Polish Academy of Literature, identifying him as one of the most important living Polish authors. His reputation outside Poland took longer to develop, but he is now internationally recognized as one of the greatest fantasists of all time.

Schulz managed to avoid being forced to enter a concentration camp like many other Polish Jews during the Nazi occupation, mainly because he had the protection of Felix Landau, a Gestapo officer who appreciated Schulz's art. However, in 1942, Schulz was murdered in the streets of Drohobycz by Karl Guenter, another officer of the Gestapo.

There are three primary recurring characters in Schulz's stories, apart from the narrator, who is usually more or less a stand-in for Schulz himself. The first is his father, a quixotic, imaginative man who is not referred to by name; while benign, he has attributes of a sorcerer, alchemist, or mad scientist. Many of the most fantastic elements of the stories center on him. The second character is a female servant named Adela; while she works for the family, Adela is no menial, and seems to fill the void in authority, and real solidity, left behind by the remoteness of the father. The third character is Drohobycz; one dimension of Schulz's work is the animation and expressiveness he attributes to landscape, weather, and above all the town—its buildings, streets, various objects. The moods and desires of the characters are always reflected in local variations in the spirit of the setting, which always plays a dynamic role in these stories.

In 1973, Polish filmmaker Wojciech Jerzy created a feature film version of *The Sanatorium Under the Sign of the Hourglass*, called "The Hourglass Sanatorium." A story from *Cinnamon Shops*, entitled "The Street of Crocodiles," was adapted into a stop-motion animated film by the Quay Brothers in 1986.

Michael Cisco

See also: Dreams and Nightmares; The Numinous.

Further Reading

Banks, Brian R. 2006. *Muse & Messiah: The Life, Imagination, & Legacy of Bruno Schulz*. Ashby-de-la-Zouch: InkerMen Press.

Ficowksi, Jerzy. 2004. *Regions of the Great Heresy: Bruno Schulz, a Biographical Portrait*. New York: W. W. Norton.

Grossman, David. 2009. "The Age of Genius: The Legend of Bruno Schulz." *The New Yorker*, June 8. http://www.newyorker.com/magazine/2009/06/08/the-age-of-genius.

Nolen, Larry. 2013. "The Fragile Reality of 'Sanatorium Under the Sign of the Hourglass." *Weird Fiction Review*, June 4. http://weirdfictionreview.com/2013/06/101-weird-writers-25-bruno-schulz.

SCHWEITZER, DARRELL (1952–)

Darrell Schweitzer is known to the horror community as principal or co-editor of *Weird Tales* magazine from 1987 to 2007, a man behind numerous horror anthologies, a ubiquitous critic and reviewer, and the most active interviewer of authors in the horror field. Alongside these efforts, Schweitzer has generated several novels and more than 300 short stories in the horror, fantasy, science fiction, and historical fiction genres.

Schweitzer's critical reputation is of long standing. Tackling the most famous of modern horror writers, his early *The Dream Quest of H. P. Lovecraft* (1978) is a standout piece of scholarship: a critique of Lovecraft's work from a writer/editor's perspective that yields refreshingly frank assessments. His "Readers" series of essay collections, focusing on Thomas Ligotti, Robert E. Howard, and Neil Gaiman, gathers the views of the best of today's genre critics, and is well known to devotees of horror.

This same community is somewhat less aware of Schweitzer's own fiction. His outright horror stories can be found in *Transients* (1993), and his Cthulhu Mythos tales in *Awaiting Strange Gods* (2015); all hinge on intrusions of the strange and supernatural into contemporary life and are written in a disarmingly understated prose style, often in the first person. The imagery is nightmarish, and the events typically fateful. His characters—innocents, frequently children—explore Schweitzer's themes of suffering, sacrifice, the meaning of courage, and bewilderment in the face of the unknown. The bright themes that Schweitzer links with the dark—humility, grace, transformation, holiness—share an equal place.

Allowing for invented settings and mythic/religious overtones, Schweitzer's fantastic fiction can easily be gathered under the horror umbrella as well. The terror of these fantasies is profound and direct: Schweitzer scorns any "Dunsanian restraint" (i.e., the practice of shying delicately away from direct depictions of horror in the manner of the Irish fantasist Lord Dunsany) and presents chilling images of horror and scenes of bloody death that are shocking and effective. And while he keeps well to the "mythic" tradition in fantasy, the gods that weave the destinies of his characters work to a pattern that these characters will never understand.

In his harrowing best novel, *The Mask of the Sorcerer* (1995), the child Sekenre, son of a sorcerer, is driven to an act of parricide, by which he himself becomes a sorcerer. This is like contracting Soul Cancer, and it fills him with the souls of all the sorcerers his father had killed. Schweitzer meets the challenge of portraying the psychology of a child whose head is stuffed with the evil, dehumanized spirits of the dead. His "Goddess" series (*The Shattered Goddess* [1982] and a dozen stories) explores a far-future earth reeling from the death of this titular deity, a time of random horrors and miracles. The linked stories of *Living with the Dead* (2008) find Schweitzer working in a new palette, spare, pale, absurdist: a town must eternally suffer the cargo-ship loads of undecaying corpses left stacked on its docks.

Schweitzer has been awarded a World Fantasy Award for his editing of *Weird Tales*. He lives and works in Philadelphia.

Steve Behrends

See also: Cthulhu Mythos; Dark Fantasy; Lovecraft, H. P.; *Weird Tales*; World Fantasy Award.

Further Reading

Behrends, Steve. 1989. "Holy Fire: Darrell Schweitzer's Imaginative Fiction." *Studies in Weird Fiction* 5 (Spring): 3–11.

Loban, Leila. 1996. "The Sorcerer behind the Mask: Darrell Schweitzer Interviewed." *Interzone* 111 (September): 35–39.

Rand, Ken. 2004. "Darrell Schweitzer" (interview). *The Internet Review of Science Fiction*, January. http://www.irosf.com/q/zine/article/10014.

Schweitzer, Darrell. 1997. *Windows of the Imagination: Essays on Fantasy Literature*. San Bernardino, CA: Borgo Press.

"THE SCREAMING SKULL"

F. Marion Crawford, a popular and successful American novelist, wrote a small number of ghost stories in the course of a long career. His ghost stories were sufficiently atypical of his work—he mostly wrote mainstream novels set in Italy—that they were only collected posthumously in *Wandering Ghosts* (1911). Most of them have become anthology standards. And while one of these, "The Screaming Skull" (first published in 1908), is a powerful story, it is the tale's technique that most singles it out for study.

It was common for writers of Crawford's era (the late nineteenth and early twentieth centuries) to frame a story by carefully describing the circumstances under which it is told. Here Crawford builds a spooky atmosphere by taking this technique to an extreme. Two retired sea captains are talking on a dark night. The story is told as a monologue, almost stream of consciousness, by one of them, who also acts out part of the continuing drama as he relates the tale—for example, by fetching the box in which the skull of the title is kept, only to discover it missing. According to the narrative, the skull, which has the disconcerting habit of screaming if moved from where it wants to be, was found in the possession of the late Dr. Pratt. The sea captain narrator has a guilty conscience because he told Pratt how a murder was committed by drugging the victim, then pouring hot lead in through an ear. The doctor's wife, Mrs. Pratt, mysteriously died soon thereafter, and it is uncertain whether the screaming skull, which belonged to Dr. Pratt, is actually hers or just a medical specimen (although something does rattle inside it). Later, the doctor himself was found dead, as if something bit his throat and crushed his windpipe. The narrator says he has inherited the doctor's house, skull and all. He is convinced that it hates him.

While the reader can easily conclude that the skull is indeed screaming, as opposed to the sound merely coming from the wind, and that Pratt indeed killed his wife and that this is her skull with a lump of lead rattling inside it, the narrator uses his own diffuse narration to avoid coming to terms with these facts until it is too late, and he is likewise found dead "by the hands or teeth of some person unknown."

The story was adapted to film—although the screenplay's source in Crawford's story was unacknowledged and uncredited—in the 1950 low-grade American horror film *The Screaming Skull*, about a woman who thinks her new husband's first wife is haunting her.

Darrell Schweitzer

See also: Crawford, F. Marion; *Part One, Horror through History*: Horror from 1900 to 1950; *Part Two, Themes, Topics, and Genres*: Ghost Stories.

Further Reading

Joshi, S. T. 2004. "F. Marion Crawford: Blood-and-Thunder Horror." In *The Evolution of the Weird Tale*, 26–38. New York: Hippocampus Press.

Moran, John C. 1981. *An F. Marion Crawford Companion*. Westport, CT: Greenwood Press.

Morgan, Chris, 1985. "F. Marion Crawford." In *Supernatural Fiction Writers*, edited by E. F. Bleiler, 747–752. New York: Charles Scribner's Sons.

SHE

She: A History of Adventure is a novel by H. Rider Haggard. It was serialized in *The Graphic* between October 1886 and January 1887 and then published in book form in America in 1886 and England in 1887. Haggard was an extremely popular writer, and *She* was his most popular book, rivaled only by his *King Solomon's Mines* (1885). It remains one of the best-selling novels in publishing history, and its influence on subsequent writers of fantasy and horror has been extensive and profound, with its concepts of ancient immortals and lost civilizations influencing writers as diverse as Michael Crichton, Anne Rice, and J. R. R. Tolkien.

She at first appears to be a traditional ethnographic adventure story, which is to say, an adventure story in which the narrative core depicts Anglo-European travels to another land, often for personal gain but occasionally to resolve ancestral issues, and the travelers' interactions with the indigenous peoples. *She* is thus told from the viewpoint of Horace Holly, a middle-aged Cambridge professor, guardian of the young and handsome Leo Vincey. Leo's father told Holly of his family's heritage, left Holly with an iron box not to be opened until his son was twenty-five, and died that evening. Holly raised Leo, and on Leo's twenty-fifth birthday, the two open the box and find in it the Sherd of Amenartas, which gives them traveling instructions.

In East Africa they are captured by the Amahaggers, who are ruled by a mysterious white queen, "She-who-must-be-obeyed." Leo has married Ustane, one of the Amahaggers, when there is a fight in which he is wounded. He is near death when they are taken to the lost city of Kôr, which predates the Egyptians, and meet She, also known as Ayesha, whose scientific knowledge is incredible and whose lifespan is in excess of 2,000 years. She has lived in Kôr following the death of her Greek lover Kallikrates, whom she slew in a jealous rage. She has not seen the ailing Leo, but when she does, she believes him to be the reincarnation of Kallikrates and heals him. She is jealous of Ustane and kills her, and though Holly and Leo object, She is overwhelming. She wants Leo to join her as an immortal ruler, a process that involves an immersion in the Pillar of Fire. To show Leo that it is safe, She immerses herself again, but this second time undoes the benefits and She withers away. Her last words are a promise to return.

The character and story of *She* proved immensely popular with Haggard's late Victorian readership, and the book was immediately dramatized, parodied, and pastiched. (Haggard himself assisted in some of these.) She was a strong and independent woman, something relatively rare in Victorian ethnographic adventure stories, which focus on the men; indeed, so strong was She that the Swiss psychologist Carl Jung later used her as the embodiment of an archetype, the woman as sustainer and devourer. In addition, Haggard's presentation of the "Other," while leaving no doubt of the superiority of the English, is neither patronizing nor demeaning: his characters are sympathetic, even when their ends are, to European eyes, objectionable. She's "scientific" knowledge and abilities are likewise intriguing, but most intriguing of all, *She* is riddled with erotic imagery and behavior, presented almost explicitly. These include Holly's sexuality, Leo's marriage with Ustane, and the character Bilali's obsessions, but even She/Ayesha is depicted as having slept next to the corpse of Kallikrates for 2,000 years. Even if they could not put a word to it, Haggard's audience undoubtedly responded to this.

Haggard wrote continuations and sequels to *She*: *Ayesha: The Return of She* (1905), *She and Allan* (1920), and *Wisdom's Daughter: The Life and Love Story of She-Who-Must-Be-Obeyed* (1923). His attitudes toward the characters gradually shifted and evolved until, at the end, the love triangle resolved itself with She being Kallikrates/Leo Vincey's destined bride and Amenartas/Ustane being the interloper. All of these works remain readable, and *She* remains consistently fascinating. Its cultural reach has been extended by multiple extraliterary adaptations. It was adapted for the stage and first filmed in 1899 by cinema pioneer Georges Méliès; there have been many additional productions for film, radio, and other media, including a rock opera.

Richard Bleiler

See also: Haggard, H. Rider; Mummies.

Further Reading

Brantlinger, Patrick. 2001. Introduction to *She: A History of Adventure*, edited by Patrick Brantlinger, vii–xxviii. London and New York: Penguin.

Deane, Bradley. 2008. "Mummy Fiction and the Occupation of Egypt: Imperial Striptease." *English Literature in Transition 1880–1920* 51, no. 4: 381–410.

Luckhurst, Roger. 2012. "Rider Haggard among the Mummies." In *The Mummy's Curse: The True History of a Dark Fantasy*, 185–208. Oxford: Oxford University Press.

Nelson, Dale J. 2006. "Haggard's *She*: Burke's Sublime in a Popular Romance." *Mythlore* 24, nos. 3–4: 111–117.

SHEA, MICHAEL (1946–2014)

Michael Shea was one of the most versatile, brilliant, and sadly neglected talents in modern horror and dark fantasy literature. He began publishing short fiction in 1979 and had soon authored one of the most brilliantly horrific tales in the contemporary canon, "The Autopsy" (1980). His early tales were gathered in a 1987 Arkham House collection, *Polyphemus*; the eponymous novella, like "The Autopsy," fuses science fictional and horror elements, depicting the grotesque biology of extraterrestrial beings in imagery and language straight out of H. P. Lovecraft. Shea's debts to that author were profound, most evident in his 1984 novel *The Color out of Time*, a Cthulhu Mythos tale of malign alien presences infesting a secluded New England valley. Shea produced several more stories in a Lovecraftian vein, which were eventually gathered into *Copping Squid and Other Mythos Tales* (2010). Some of these stories evoke the antiquarian milieu of the originals, while others deploy more modern settings, such as his 1987 novella *Fat Face*, in which a prostitute down on her luck runs afoul of an eldritch monstrosity.

"The Autopsy": An Alien Parasite That Feeds on Terror

Shea's "The Autopsy" (1980) is a World Fantasy Award–nominated story about an alien parasite that invades and controls human bodies. As with much of Shea's other work, it is atmospheric and bleak, as well as vivid and cinematic. "The Autopsy" straddles the line between classic weird fiction and contemporary horror. A continuation of Lovecraftian cosmic dread, it shows humanity coming face-to-face with a cruel and malefic universe; at the same time, it is a forerunner of splatterpunk fiction in its matter-of-fact depiction of bodily violation and bloodletting.

The story centers on Dr. Carl Winters, a pathologist called in to perform autopsies on a number of bodies killed during a mining disaster. One of these cadavers turns out to be infested by the parasite, a highly intelligent and fiendishly manipulative entity with which Dr. Winters engages in a high-stakes battle of wits. The malign creature feeds on human terror, and the tale sustains a tone of barely suppressed hysteria as the full dimensions of the monster's evil purpose become apparent. Dr. Winters's ultimate gambit, a self-sacrificial act that turns the tables on the monster, is both ingenious and horrifying.

Written in a style that moves from the grimly clinical to the visionary, "The Autopsy" is one of the most compelling examples of a horror–science fiction crossover in contemporary genre literature. The scene in which the alien reveals itself to Dr. Winters is strikingly unnerving, and the dialogue that ensues between them resonates with the finest works of "first contact" in the science fiction canon, especially stories that depict a form of extraterrestrial life whose biomorphic difference from humanity leads to a fundamental gulf of understanding.

Rob Latham

Shea's uncanny ability to capture the sensibility of a major forerunner of modern dark fantasy was clear from his first publication, the 1974 novel *A Quest for Symbilis*, which is set in the decadent far future of Jack Vance's "Dying Earth" series. Shea crafted his own lush science-fantasy venue, reminiscent of Vance and Clark Ashton Smith, in his 1982 novel *Nifft the Lean* (1982), a picaresque tale with horror elements that was continued in two sequels, *The Mines of Behemoth* (1987) and *The A'rak* (2000). The series was well received by critics, with the first book winning a World Fantasy Award, though it did not connect with readers, perhaps because of its unsettled genre status—part sword-and-sorcery, part weird fiction, part quest fantasy—and its tendency to revel in scenes of baroque Gothic excess. His best work simply defies categories: the World Fantasy Award–winning story "Growlimb" (2004), for example, is science fiction in conception but horror in execution, while his 1985 novel *In Yana, The Touch of Undying* is sui generis (of its own unique kind):

an other-world fantasy teeming with bizarre invention. By contrast, Shea's final novel, *Assault on Sunrise* (2013), is a more conventional tale of dystopian apocalypse, intended as part of an unfinished trilogy.

Shea's sudden death in 2014 deprived the genre of one of its most unusual and compelling voices. An excellent "tribute" anthology—*And Death Shall Have No Dominion*, edited by S. T. Joshi—was released by Hippocampus Press in 2016 and may perhaps begin to revive Shea's dormant reputation. It is, at present, the only book of his work in print.

Rob Latham

See also: Cthulhu Mythos; Dark Fantasy; Lovecraft, H. P.; Lovecraftian Horror; Splatterpunk.

Further Reading

Cox, Arthur J. 1988. "The Grim Imperative of Michael Shea." In *Discovering Modern Horror Fiction II*, edited by Darrel Schweitzer, 115–120. Mercer Island, WA: Starmont House.

"Michael Shea." 1996. In *St. James Guide to Fantasy Writers*, edited by David Pringle. New York: St. James Press.

Stableford, Brian. 2003. "Michael Shea." In *Supernatural Fiction Writers: Contemporary Fantasy and Horror*, 2nd ed., vol. 2, edited by Richard Bleiler, 839–843. New York: Charles Scribner's Sons.

SHELLEY, MARY (1797–1851)

Despite her accomplished literary life, Mary Wollstonecraft Shelley is known for two things: writing the novel *Frankenstein* (1818, 1831) and keeping company with a crowd of highly significant literary figures. This included her mother, the feminist writer Mary Wollstonecraft (who died giving birth to her), and her father, the political philosopher and novelist William Godwin, from whom she inherited a political and literary mindset. It also included her husband, the poet Percy Bysshe Shelley, who complicated the authorship of her work, and Lord Byron and John Polidori, with whom she participated in a famous ghost story contest while staying in the Villa Diodati on the shores of Lake Geneva, Switzerland, in 1816. Her novel, *Frankenstein*, arose from this contest and would not only alter the course of the Gothic tradition with its relatable, tortured monster and its universal questions of life, death, and scientific pursuit, but its creation would also become a scholarly and popular obsession for the next 200 years. It has been a source of inspiration for countless works within Gothic literature, film, and visual art, and recent scholarship has increasingly considered Mary for her own genius rather than for her relationship to the writers around her.

Part of the reason why Mary Shelley continues to fascinate is because early political and social manipulations of her biography caused its veracity to be in a constant state of fluctuation. What is certain is that Shelley's life was fraught with traumatic births and deaths, the first of both being her entrance into the world, when Mary Wollstonecraft suffered puerperal fever following childbirth. It is rumored that young Mary made frequent visits to her mother's grave, learning to read by tracing the name in the stone, and eventually holding a courtship with her future husband over the burial plot. Her family life was unconventional for the time, including illegitimate siblings from both her mother's previous relationship and her father's remarriage after Wollstonecraft's death, establishing an early progressive view of human relationships beyond the limitations of law and social structure. She also experienced a high intellectual expectation in such a family, which received frequent visits from the great political and literary minds of the day. It was an expectation she had no difficulty meeting.

At the age of sixteen, she eloped with Percy Bysshe Shelley, then twenty-one and already married, accompanied by her step-sister Claire Clairmont. It was a tempestuous relationship that would occasion two suicides (Mary's half-sister Fanny and Shelley's wife, Harriet). The group expanded to include Byron, who fathered a child with Claire and who would add to the scandal already brewing, as the group was dubbed the "league of incest." The Shelleys married shortly after the famous summer of 1816 in an attempt to gain custody of Percy's children via Harriet. They failed in this, with courts questioning Percy's morality and lifestyle. He and Mary would relocate between England and the continent many times throughout their life together, creating their own circle of friends who shared their political, intellectual, and moral beliefs.

The death of Mary's first child soon after its birth left a lasting mark on the author, and she notes in her journal that she dreamed it had returned to life after she rubbed it by the fire to warm it. It would be the first glimmering of the central concept (of gaining the power to animate the dead) in *Frankenstein*, her first novel, which she would write more than a year later. The first edition was published anonymously in 1818, with a revised edition that bore Mary's name following in 1831. The extent of Percy's involvement in the writing of these editions and earlier drafts has been a matter of intense scholarly debate, a matter complicated by the Shelleys' frequent literary collaboration throughout their relationship. The novel became and remained popular in England through its many dramatizations.

Mary was a voracious reader, growing up in her father's library, finding a haven in her husband's library, and participating in the latest literary discussions among her intellectual circles. Surrounded by scientific and literary thinkers, she was impressively knowledgeable about the latest in scientific and medical research and political thought, a background that has kept scholars busy in their analysis of the historical and medical context of *Frankenstein* and her other novels. In the character of Victor Frankenstein, the scientific creator, critics also read motherhood and artistic creation, following the lead of Mary's biography in their analyses, as intensified by the recovery work of Ellen Moers and the idea of the "Female Gothic" that Moers established in the 1970s. As *Frankenstein* demonstrates, much of Mary's work articulates her parents' politics, particularly the politicization of the domestic sphere—family and education—and individual power and responsibility for egalitarian reform and positive change.

Frankenstein was far from Shelley's only literary progeny; she wrote six novels, many short stories, several poems, and extensive travel narratives, journals, and letters. In 1818 her one-year-old daughter, Clara, died of dysentery, and less than a year later her son, William, died of malaria at the age of three. These two deaths, in combination with tensions caused by Mary and Percy's notoriously open relationship, devastated her, driving her into a deep depression. She channeled this grief into the writing of *Matilda*, originally titled *The Fields of Fancy* after her mother's unfinished *The Cave of Fancy*. Though it was written in 1819, *Matilda* was not published until 1959 due to its preoccupation with incest and suicide: a father, obsessed and in love with his daughter when they are reunited after a long absence commits suicide when she fails to return this love. While the psycho-biographical approach taken by current scholars confirms the novel to be the product of a deeply depressed mind, the tendency of earlier critics to assign biographical status to much of Shelley's work becomes problematic here. Godwin, Mary's father, was disgusted by the text and urged her to hold its publication to prevent adding further scandal to her already unconventional domesticity, a relationship that Godwin did not support until she and Percy married, despite its similarity to his own romantic relationships. She agreed that it would not be published in her lifetime.

In her next three novels, Mary shifted to more historical themes. Written in Italy and influenced by her time there, *Valperga* (1823) involved extensive research into fourteenth-century Italian politics. Mixing a fictionalized version of this history with the politics of her own day, the novel follows conflicts between two political parties, the Guelphs and the Ghibelines, and attempts by the central characters, Castruccio and Euthanasia, to create a bond between the parties with their love, one that would eventually fail with the fall of Valperga, with Euthanasia's fictional castle representing republicanism and peace. The novel takes on themes of violence and power, with shades of Machiavellianism and Napoleon. As was the case for many of Mary's works, however, critics would take the cue of female authorship to prioritize the love story over its political commentary and experimentation.

In 1822, shortly before *Valperga*'s publication and less than a month after Shelley had suffered a miscarriage, Percy went sailing in the Bay of Spezia and drowned. When Byron died in Greece in 1824, Shelley would write in her journal of feeling like "the last man," left behind by her children, husband, and friend (Bennett 1998, 83). In her next novel, *The Last Man* (1826), she embraced biographical connection to its fictional characters as a way of grieving, reserving a place for the central figures in her life within the central characters of her novel. The plot, a kind of fictionalized future history, is one part romance, one part sociopolitical intrigue, and one part Gothic apocalyptic disease narrative. It follows efforts by a first-person narrator and his circle as they successfully replace the monarchy with a republic, but even its leaders are no match for the plague, which systematically dismantles institutions and their laws, leaving men and women as equals and devoid of the restrictions imposed on them by society, before wiping out all of humanity. The narrator soon becomes the last man alive, leaving his narrative behind as a testament to the works and fate of humanity, just as Shelley would strive to memorialize and document her husband's lifeworks.

Percy's father, Sir Timothy, approved of his relationship with Mary even less than Godwin did, and he made several attempts to prove that her marriage to his son was invalid and to assume custody of his remaining grandchild, Percy Florence, all of which failed. He agreed to support the dwindling family financially, but only if Shelley agreed to move back to England, which she had no choice but to do. He also forbade her from publishing his son's biography, and, while Mary waited for the end of his life to lift that ban, she did go ahead and publish a collection of Percy's poetry, with extensive biographical annotations and additions.

She returned to history in her authorship of *The Adventures of Perkin Warbeck* (1830), a text that is rarely read and little studied today. It was largely a response to the conservative, transitional sociopolitical environment she found in England when she returned with her son. Historical and cultural research for this novel found her reaching out to friends in Ireland and Scotland, including Walter Scott, to collect folklore and regional histories. The title character Warbeck historically claimed to be Richard, Duke of York, one of the princes imprisoned in the Tower of London by Richard III. He was forced to confess the falsity of this claim and was executed, but Shelley's novel presents his case as truthful and explores questions of citizenship and national and personal identity.

In a drastic turn from the historical novel, Shelley situated her last two novels in her own present day. *Lodore* (1835) and *Falkner* (1837) are often discussed together and widely believed to be the least dynamic of her novels, written to support her family. *Lodore* demonstrated a return to her parents' radical views on education and gender that surfaced in *Frankenstein*, though the story itself is a conventional tale of a mother/daughter relationship and a father's education of his daughter. Its inclusion of multiple forms of education amid this common plot has caused critics to disagree drastically as to its radical or conservative leanings. *Falkner*, written after Godwin's death, continues the father/daughter theme and is described by some as a rewriting of *Lodore*. In it, the orphaned Elizabeth has been cut off from a Catholic family that disapproved of her parents' marriage. When she interrupts Falkner's suicide (inspired by the guilt of ruining and abandoning a woman), he takes her under his wing, involving her in his past life and its consequences, showing a repetition of some of the themes found in *Matilda*. Despite its lukewarm reception, Shelley claimed that it was her favorite.

The end of Shelley's writing career saw a turn from fiction to biographical and travel works, as well as short periodical pieces. While writing *Falkner*, she took on five volumes of *Lives of the Most Eminent Literary and Scientific Men* (1835–1839), in which she chronicled the lives of great thinkers who asserted the ideals of social reform and liberty that she shared. Her last work, *Rambles in Germany and Italy in 1840, 1842, 1843* (published 1844) detailed her travels alongside her trademark political commentary. Throughout her work, she championed equal education, individual responsibility, egalitarian reform, travel and mobility, rationality, independence, imagination, and science, all sociopolitical topics glossed over by the critics of her day in favor of more "womanly" literary products. This has only recently begun to change, with scholars making concentrated efforts to recover a biography and system of thought that has been sanitized since the nineteenth century.

In the last years of her life, Mary Shelley traveled with her son, Sir Percy Florence, and his wife, Jane, while continuing to prepare her husband's writings and biography. In 1851, she fell into a week-long coma and died of a brain tumor that had plagued her for many years. She wished to be buried with her parents. They were disinterred from St. Pancras Churchyard, the historic site of her mother's grave where Mary had spent so much of her youth, and moved to Bournemouth to join the daughter who inherited and built upon their sociopolitical ideologies and intellectual gifts to claim a gradually recognized position of her own within Gothic studies, women's writing, progressive politics, and the English novel.

Laura R. Kremmel

See also: Byron, Lord; *Frankenstein*; Mad Scientist; Monster; Romanticism and Dark Romanticism.

Further Reading

Allen, Graham. 2008. *Critical Issues: Mary Shelley*. London: Palgrave Macmillan.

Bennett, Betty T. 1998. *Mary Wollstonecraft Shelley: An Introduction*. Baltimore: Johns Hopkins University Press.

Fisch, Audrey A., Anne K. Mellor, and Esther H. Schor. 1993. *The Other Mary Shelley: Beyond Frankenstein*. New York and Oxford: Oxford University Press.

Mellor, Anne K. 1989. *Mary Shelley: Her Life, Her Fiction, Her Monsters*. New York: Routledge.

Montillo, Roseanne. 2013. *The Lady and Her Monsters: A Tale of Dissections, Real-life Dr. Frankensteins, and the Creation of Mary Shelley's Masterpiece*. New York: William Morrow.

Schor, Esther, ed. 2003. *The Cambridge Companion to Mary Shelley*. Cambridge: Cambridge University Press.

SHIEL, M. P. (1865–1947)

Matthew Phipps Shiell, who dropped the final letter of his name for all purposes after coming to England in 1885, was a British writer of supernatural horror and science fiction. He was born in Monserrat in the West Indies, the son of a lay preacher, Matthew Dowdy Shiell. Much research has been carried out into the elder Shiell's ancestry, in association with the supposition that he was the son of a female slave, thus rendering the younger Shiel's insistence that he had "no black blood" suspect, although the small quantity in question hardly seems relevant now.

"Xélucha": A Dark and Decadent Parable

Shiel's "Xélucha" (1896), published first in *Shapes in the Fire: Being a Mid-Winter-Night's Entertainment in Two Parts and an Interlude*, uses abstruse vocabulary and a mythic depiction of London to build a dark and decadent parable about the powers of female sexuality.

The story's events are from the diary of Mérimée, an aged roué once known as a "Destroyer of Women," who is now dead. As Mérimée roams the streets of London, he recollects his dead friend Cosmo's pursuit of the feminine ideal, Xélucha. He encounters a woman—apparently a prostitute—and accompanies her to her house, which is lavishly furnished, though with a few discordant details. There, after an intense discussion of life and philosophy, of creation, intellect, and will, Mérimée recognizes the woman and declares that she is Xélucha, though she insists that Xélucha died of cholera at Antioch ten years previously. Mérimée rushes to embrace her but is rendered unconscious, and when he awakens, it is by himself, in a room of the utmost poverty.

Shiel's language is deliberately abstruse, allusive, dense, wild, and even playful. This matches the setting, for it is a London as conceived by Robert Louis Stevenson and presented in the *New Arabian Nights* (1882), a city cosmopolitan and urbane yet ancient and decadent, where the world's mysterious travelers cross paths and share adventures. The narrative likewise owes much to Edgar Allan Poe, and indeed may be seen as a retelling of "Ligeia" (1838), a statement of feminine will and its survival and eventual triumph, even after death. In addition, as Shiel's subtitle indicates, "Xélucha" is but a part of an entertainment; it is in fact the first of the three shapes, all involving aspects of femininity and the female.

Richard Bleiler

Shiel liked to tell the story of how his father once took him to the uninhabited islet of Redonda and crowned him king, thus entitling him to create the mythical literary kingdom of Redonda in England, bestowing theoretical titles on many of his friends. That institution still exists, although it is possible that Shiel borrowed and adapted the anecdote, along with the plot of his novel *The Lord of the Sea* (1900), from Camille Debans's *Les Malheurs de John Bull* (1884; translated as *The Misfortunes of John Bull*), whose hero assumes the kingship of the uninhabited island of Pola and similarly distributes titles to his associates.

Shiel's early literary endeavors were heavily influenced by Edgar Allan Poe and the French writers who had adapted Poe's work as key exemplars for the late nineteenth-century Decadent movement. *Prince Zaleski* (1895) features a detective whose lifestyle and posturing are based on Poe's detective Auguste Dupin, but extrapolated to extremes of bizarrerie in the spirit of Decadent style and lifestyle.

Shapes in the Fire (1897), similarly issued by *Yellow Book* publisher John Lane, performs the same function for several of Poe's other subjects, with an unparalleled flamboyance; alongside five stories and a narrative poem it provides a literary manifesto, "Premier and Maker," in the form of a dialogue between an alter ego of Shiel and a prime minister identifiable as Lord Rosebery. The cream of Shiel's short fiction is contained in the collection, including "Xélucha," in which the eponymous "splendid harlot" returns from the grave in the guise of a Piccadilly whore, and "Vaila," a vivid transfiguration of Poe's "The Fall of the House of Usher." The stories in *The Pale Ape and Other Pulses* (1911) are watered down by concessions to convention, but *Here Comes the Lady* (1928) contains transfigurations of Poe's "The Cask of Amontillado" and "A Descent into the Maëlstrom" in "The Primate of the Rose" and "Dark Lot of One Saul."

Shiel's only full-length Decadent fantasy, *The Purple Cloud* (1901), is a transfiguration of the biblical book of Job, in which the population of the Earth is destroyed, except for Adam Jeffson, who spends seventeen years as emperor of the empty Earth, assailed more sharply than any potentate of old by the classic Decadent afflictions of *impuissance, ennui,* and *spleen* (weakness, listlessness, and bad temper), before he is obliged to move on by the discovery of a female born as the world died and raised in ignorance of its plight. Stephen King has cited *The Purple Cloud* as one of the inspirations for his apocalyptic novel *The Stand*, and Eugene Thacker has identified it as arguably "the text that establishes the blueprint" for the type of modern story in which fogs or mists are portrayed "as gothic, malevolent forces, often that serve as cover for ghosts, monsters, or unknown miasmas," with examples of texts that follow this blueprint including James Herbert's *The Fog* (1975), Stephen King's *The Mist* (1980), and director John Carpenter's movie *The Fog* (1980) (Thacker 2011, 83, 84).

Few of Shiel's other novels contain substantial elements of horror, although *The Last Miracle* (1906) and *Dr Krasinski's Secret* (1929) feature the imprisonment and torture of innocents by seeming villains possessed of allegedly respectable ideals. In 1975 Arkham House published a collection of the thirteen stories that Shiel considered his best, *Xélucha and Others*, some three decades after the book had first been announced. This was followed by a second Arkham House collection, *Prince Zaleski and Cummings King Monk*, in 1977.

Brian Stableford

See also: Arkham House; Dark Fantasy.

Further Reading

Bleiler, E. F. 1999. "Shiel, M. P. (1865–1947)." In *Science Fiction Writers: Critical Studies of the Major Authors from the Early Nineteenth Century to the Present Day*, 2nd ed., edited by Richard Bleiler, 697–704. New York: Charles Scribner's Sons.

Morse, A. Reynolds, ed. 1983. *Shiel in Diverse Hands: A Collection of Essays on M. P. Shiel.* Morse Foundation.

Stableford, Brian. 1995. "The Politics of Evolution: Philosophical Themes in the Speculative Fiction of M. P. Shiel." In *Algebraic Fantasies and Realistic Romances: More Masters
of Science Fiction*, 73–98. The Milford Series: Popular Writers of Today 54. San Bernardino, CA: Borgo Press.

Thacker, Eugene. 2011. *In the Dust of This Planet: Horror of Philosophy Vol. 1*. Winchester,
UK: Zero Books.

THE SHINING

The Shining (1977) is a horror novel by American author Stephen King. It is King's
third published novel, following *Carrie* (1974) and *'Salem's Lot* (1975). Its success
established King's prominence in the horror genre and introduced motifs that recur
throughout his body of work, such as childhood trauma, uncanny psychic abilities, and anxiety regarding creative freedom.

The novel depicts the plight of the Torrance family during their overwinter stay
as caretakers in Colorado's isolated Overlook Hotel. The Torrances—Jack, Wendy,
and five-year-old Danny—experience horrors both human and supernatural as
they unearth the hotel's monstrous history. Danny's latent psychic power (the
eponymous "Shining") provides fuel for the hotel's evil, while his father begins to
unravel mentally under the pressure of isolation, alcoholism, and writer's block.
Eventually the secure family dynamic degenerates as Jack is driven into a murderous rage directed at his family, whom he sees as a barrier to his own happiness and
literary success.

As with so many of King's novels, it is possible to trace autobiographical links
between author and protagonist. In the case of *The Shining*, King concedes the association, admitting that the novel addresses his own ambivalent feelings toward
his young family at the start of his writing career. In an interview with *Playboy*,
King spoke of feeling "pressure" and "experiencing a range of nasty emotions from
resentment to anger to occasional outright hate, even surges of mental violence
that, thank God, I was able to suppress" (Norden 1988, 32). Pressure and suppres-
sion are key themes in *The Shining*, where the ever-building pressure within the
hotel boiler serves as an external metaphor for the violence rising within Jack.

The novel's psychological subtext is overt. *The Shining* offers a Freudian triangle
in microcosm, where the struggle between son and father is cast against the blank
canvas of the hotel and its snowy surroundings. So central is Sigmund Freud to the
plot of *The Shining* that, when Steven Bruhm makes the point that the contemporary Gothic is distinguished by its self-conscious application of psychoanalytic
theory, he uses this novel as the definitive example (see Bruhm 2002, 263–268).

Though *The Shining* is a foundational text of modern horror fiction, it is perhaps
more widely known in its cinematic adaptation. Directed by Stanley Kubrick, the
1980 film is regarded as a classic of horror cinema, though King himself famously
dislikes Kubrick's interpretation. The most famous scene, in which a deranged Jack
Nicholson demolishes a bathroom door with an axe, regularly tops lists of "scariest

scenes of all time." The film itself has occasioned much scholarly debate. The 2012 documentary film *Room 237* presents several elaborate analyses of the film, ranging from a reading of it as a commentary on the Native American genocide to "proof" that Kubrick was involved in the moon-landing hoax.

Such obsessive devotion to Kubrick's film often overshadows the impact that King's novel had on horror fiction. As the most influential haunted house story since Shirley Jackson's *The Haunting of Hill House* (1959), *The Shining* helped launch a new era of horror. Such is the power of *The Shining* that when King returned to Danny Torrance nearly four decades later in the sequel, *Doctor Sleep* (2013), he did so with trepidation, admitting that "nothing can live up to the memory of a good scare" (King 2013, 484).

Neil McRobert

See also: The Haunted House or Castle; *The Haunting of Hill House*; Psychological Horror; Unreliable Narrator.

Further Reading

Bruhm, Steven. 2002. "The Contemporary Gothic: Why We Need It." In *The Cambridge Companion to the Gothic*, edited by Jerrold Hogle, 259–276. Cambridge: University of Cambridge Press.

Indick, Ben P. 1982. "King and the Literary Tradition of Horror and the Supernatural." In *Fear Itself*, edited by Tim Underwood and Chuck Miller, 153–167. San Francisco: Underwood-Miller. Rpt. in *Children's Literature Review*, vol. 194, 2015, edited by Lawrence J. Trudeau. Farmington Hills, MI: Gale.

King, Stephen. 2013. *Doctor Sleep*. London: Hodder and Stoughton.

Luckhurst, Roger. 2013. *The Shining*. London: British Film Institute.

Norden, Eric. 1988. "Interview with Stephen King." In *Bare Bones: Conversations on Terror with Stephen King*, edited by Tim Underwood and Chuck Miller, 24–56. New York: McGraw-Hill.

SHIRLEY JACKSON AWARDS

The Shirley Jackson Awards were created to acknowledge excellence in the literary genres of the dark fantastic, horror, and psychological suspense. Named after the late Shirley Jackson, the Shirley Jackson Awards also acknowledge the lasting impact that Jackson has had on modern writers of numerous genres. The Shirley Jackson Awards thus honor the contributions of Jackson while simultaneously recognizing those works that best carry on her legacy in fiction.

First presented in 2007 with approval from the Jackson family and delivered every year at Readercon (a science fiction convention established in the 1980s by Bob Colby and Eric Van) in Burlington, Massachusetts, the Shirley Jackson Awards are given for six categories: novel, novella, novelette, short fiction, single-author collection, and edited anthology. The awards are voted on by a five-person jury that consists of academics, critics, editors, and writers. An advisory board offers input and recommendations to the jurors, but does not have voting power. There is also a board of directors made up of the jurors from the 2007 awards and the administrator. The awards maintain a website and social media presence for publicity purposes. Previous recipients of the awards include Alison Littlewood, Greer Gilman, Jeffrey Ford, Elizabeth Hand, Neil Gaiman, Stephen King, Yoko Ogawa, Lucius Shepard, Gemma Files, Steve Duffy, Lynda E. Rucker, Kelly Link, Simon Strantzas, and Laird Barron.

Despite their relatively young age, the Shirley Jackson Awards have nonetheless served an important role in the field of horror literature by honoring talented authors of genre-specific fiction who might otherwise be overlooked. The awards have received praise from publishers, commentators, and academics alike, with many noting the significance the awards have had on the genres they acknowledge. Likewise, the awards have helped raise awareness of Jackson's own literary accomplishments, most notably "The Lottery" (1948), *The Haunting of Hill House* (1959), and *We Have Always Lived in the Castle* (1962), which did not receive much attention outside of horror circles for many years after her death, until the transition to the twenty-first century. Although the awards are not the sole indicator of an increased awareness of Jackson's literature in recent years, they are certainly an important one that has helped secure her position as a major figure in American literature. With an impressive list of recipients and nominees every year, along with a rise of appreciation for Jackson's work, the Shirley Jackson Awards have provided an important outlet for the horror fiction community and are likely to continue to do so for the foreseeable future.

Joel T. Terranova

See also: Barron, Laird; Bram Stoker Award; Dark Fantasy; Gaiman, Neil; Hand, Elizabeth; *The Haunting of Hill House*; Jackson, Shirley; King, Stephen; Link, Kelly; Psychological Horror; World Fantasy Award.

Further Reading

Miller, Laura. 2010. "Is Shirley Jackson a Great American Writer?" *Salon*, July 14. http://www.salon.com/2010/07/14/shirley_jackson.

The Shirley Jackson Awards. Accessed December 1, 2016. http://www.shirleyjacksonawards.org.

"A SHORT TRIP HOME"

"A Short Trip Home" is a ghost story by the American author F. Scott Fitzgerald, written in October 1927 and first published in *The Saturday Evening Post* on December 17 of that year. Its plot concerns the rescue of Ellen Baker, a young female student at home for Christmas vacation who has been seduced by an incubus— dead man Joe Varland, who in life had been a petty swindler of women traveling alone by train. At the story's climax, narrator Eddie Stinson defeats Varland's ghost by professing his love for Ellen, freeing her from Varland's malign supernatural influence.

Recalling Henry James's *The Turn of the Screw*, whose ambiguous ending it both evokes and simplifies, the story reads as a Gothic allegory dramatizing sexual corruption and the redemption of innocence through love. Whereas James treated these themes with characteristic obscurity, Fitzgerald's story presents them in terms of a fairy tale–like triumph of good over evil. Varland's phantom incubus, like the would-be sex-ghosts of *Turn of the Screw*, "possesses" his innocent victim, making Ellen complicit in her own moral destruction. By this means, Fitzgerald's story develops a symbolic equation between supernatural threat, corrupt adult (implicitly male) sexuality, working-class criminality, and death.

The way the rhetoric of romance ("bewitchment," falling "under the spell" of the beloved [Fitzgerald 2003, 372, 376]), which characterizes Stinson's feelings for Ellen, lapses perversely into signs of sexual/supernatural predation/seduction in the story's symbolic register is one of the story's more disturbing elements, since it suggests that redemptive love and corrupting sexuality are part of the same ill-defined continuum. The story's ambiguous evocation of "home," which is not a place of safety, but a place of danger, associated both with Ellen's seduction and with the ghost's criminality, is similarly unsettling. Stinson's heroic rescue of his demonically "possessed" beloved from Varland's incubus has the quality of a successful exorcism, but it also suggests that the story may have been a wish-fulfillment for Fitzgerald, who was coping with his wife Zelda Fitzgerald's increasingly worsening schizophrenia throughout the period of the story's composition.

Fitzgerald regarded this critically neglected tale highly enough to include it in his fourth collection of short fiction, *Taps at Reveille* (1935), a companion volume to his novel *Tender Is the Night* (1934), which, published at the height of the Great Depression, was a commercial and critical failure. "A Short Trip Home" is noteworthy for being Fitzgerald's first foray into the ghost story genre, and also because Fitzgerald repurposed the story's description of Varland's ghost to describe another street hustler in *Tender Is the Night*. Although Fitzgerald typically sets his fiction in a realistic social world, his writing is also widely marked by forays into surrealism, romance, and fantasy, notable not only in this story but also in works such as "The Curious Case of Benjamin Button" (1922; loosely adapted to film in 2008) and "The Diamond as Big as the Ritz" (1922).

Brian Johnson

See also: Incubi and Succubi; Possession and Exorcism; *The Turn of the Screw*.

Further Reading

Buell, L. 1982. "The Significance of Fantasy in Fitzgerald's Fiction." In *The Short Stories of F. Scott Fitzgerald: New Approaches in Criticism*, edited by Jackson R. Bryer, 23–38. Madison: University of Wisconsin Press.

Fitzgerald, F. Scott. 2003. *The Short Stories of F. Scott Fitzgerald: A New Collection.* Edited by Matthew J. Bruccoli. New York: Scribner.

Petry, A. H. 1989. *Fitzgerald's Craft of Short Fiction: The Collected Stories 1920–1935.* Ann Arbor: UMI Research Press.

"SILENT SNOW, SECRET SNOW"

Written by the Pulitzer Prize–winning poet, novelist, and short story writer Conrad Aiken, "Silent Snow, Secret Snow" was first published in *Virginia Quarterly Review* in 1932 and later collected in *The Collected Short Stories of Conrad Aiken* in 1960. Perhaps Aiken's best-known story, it is a recognized classic that stands as one of the most widely read works of American short fiction from the twentieth century.

"Silent Snow, Secret Snow" focuses on twelve-year-old Paul Hasleman, an intelligent boy who is gradually and semi-deliberately becoming estranged from everybody and cut off from his world. He envisions snows that cover everything and muffle all noises, obscuring footfalls of postmen; ultimately, the snows communicate with him, sending him messages only he can perceive. Paul's distracted behavior causes concerns for his parents, and they summon a doctor, who can find nothing physically wrong with him, but the snows are telling him what to do, and he retreats to his room. When his mother knocks on his door, he yells for her to go away, that he hates her. This said, his world fills completely with the snow that only he can perceive.

Opinions differ on how Aiken's story is to be received. Some have seen it in an essentially Freudian light, interpreting the story as a retreat from the dirty maturity of adulthood into a dream world of pure white snow, and Aiken did indeed claim to be inspired by Sigmund Freud. Others have assessed the story in more abstract terms, with Paul's behavior seen as an act of creation, making Paul into what is essentially an artistic figure attempting to bring form and meaning into a structureless world. Still others have seen Paul's withdrawing from humanity as marking the onset of a mental illness, perhaps schizophrenia, and in this they reference Aiken's life, in which his respected father killed Aiken's mother and committed suicide, leaving young Conrad (age eleven) to discover their bodies. Because it is so open, presenting details without providing facile explanations, the story remains idiosyncratically powerful, horrible by implication.

"Silent Snow, Secret Snow" was recognized early for being appreciable as part of the canon of terror and horror literature. Herbert A. Wise and Phyllis Fraser chose to include it in their classic 1944 Modern Library anthology *Great Tales of Terror and the Supernatural.* The story was also adapted as a segment for a 1971 episode of Rod Serling's horror-themed television series *Night Gallery*, with narration provided by Orson Welles.

Richard Bleiler

See also: Dreams and Nightmares; "Mr. Arcularis"; Psychological Horror.

Further Reading

Gossman, Ann. 1964. "'Silent Snow, Secret Snow': The Child as Artist." *Studies in Short Fiction* 1, vol. 2 (Winter): 123–128.

Spivey, Ted R. 1997. "Fictional Descent into Hell." In *Time's Stop in Savannah: Conrad Aiken's Inner Journey*, 91–105. Macon, GA.: Mercer University Press.

Stevenson, Simon. 2004. "The Anorthoscopic Short Story." *Oxford Literary Review* 26: 63–78.

SIMMONS, DAN (1948–)

Dan Simmons is an American writer who has published award-winning novels in genres as diverse as mainstream literary fiction, science fiction, dark fantasy, historical fiction (featuring such characters as Ernest Hemingway, Charles Dickens, Henry James, Wilkie Collins, George Custer, Vlad Tepes, Mark Twain, Sherlock Holmes, and the crew of the HMS *Terror* and HMS *Erebus*), hard-boiled crime fiction, and psychological suspense and horror. His work is often informed or influenced by classical poets such as Dante, T. S. Eliot, John Keats, Gerard Manley Hopkins, Proust, Chaucer, and Homer.

Simmons was born in Peoria, Illinois, in 1948. His family moved around the Midwest when he was a child. One of their stops, Brimfield, Illinois, became the fictional Elm Haven of his novels *Summer of Night* (1991) and *A Winter Haunting* (2002). He received a BA in English from Wabash College, along with a Phi Beta Kappa award for creativity in writing and art. During his time at Wabash, he and his roommate published an underground paper called *The Satyr*. He earned a master's in Education from Washington University in St. Louis, where his thesis was on television's effects on cognition and IQ.

In 1969, while working as a teacher's aide at a school for the blind, he lived in an attic apartment in the Germantown section of Philadelphia, where he witnessed the gang battles and race riots that later appeared in his apocalyptic vampire novel *Carrion Comfort* (1989). For the next eighteen years, he taught in Missouri, New York, and Colorado, and ended his career in education teaching gifted and talented children. During his years teaching sixth grade, he told an epic story half an hour per day for six months to his students. It featured the first incarnation of the character that would later become the Shrike in his Hyperion Cantos series of science fiction novels, but he lost the manuscript during a move.

His first short story sales were to *Galaxy* and *Galileo*, but both magazines folded before his contributions appeared. The American science fiction author Harlan Ellison critiqued Simmons's story "The River Styx Runs Upstream" at the Writer's Conference in the Rockies in the summer of 1981. Ellison encouraged Simmons, who was on the verge of quitting writing, to submit his story to *Twilight Zone* magazine's short fiction contest for beginning writers, where it tied for first place, won the Rod Serling Memorial Award, and was published in February 1982, on the day Simmons's daughter was born.

During the summer of 1982, he wrote the horror novel *Song of Kali*, about an American writer who travels to Calcutta and gets caught up in a horrific cult that worships the eponymous Hindu goddess. It took three years to find a publisher because of the darkness of the story and its failure to follow genre formula. Tor published the book in 1985, and it became the first-ever first novel to win the World Fantasy Award for best novel, although Simmons himself has said that he does not consider it a fantasy. After the success of *Kali*, he retired from teaching to write full time.

In interviews and essays, Simmons has explained that he vowed to himself that if he had any success in writing, he would not be bound to one form—that he would write whatever moved him, and never allow an editor or publisher to dictate what he worked on. He acted on the assumption that if one publisher was uninterested in a given work, he would be able to find another publisher for it. This proved to be the case, but it has also meant that he is often forced to find different publishers for projects that deviate from prior expectations, as with his Joe Kurtz noir crime novels. This has had the effect of dividing his audience, and he has acknowledged that, for example, only a very small percentage of the people who read his horror novels also read his science fiction works.

In 1989, Simmons released three books, *Phases of Gravity*, *Carrion Comfort*, and *Hyperion*. He tackled the two long science fiction novels—*Fall of Hyperion* came out in 1990—because the advance allowed him to make a down payment on a house.

Simmons is known for his extensive research and attention to detail and has traveled as far as Romania and Thailand for research. He brought to life the Darwin Awards (the Internet meme that mocks supposedly true stories of people being killed in foolish accidents) in *Darwin's Blade* (2000), about an insurance investigator who looks into wrecks caused by vehicular stupidity; and he fictionalized the creation (and near-destruction) of Mount Rushmore in *Black Hills* (2010). One of his stated rules when using historical figures—even those who are fictional—is to have them refrain from doing anything that contradicts the known facts of their lives; however, the unknown interstices and gaps in their biographies are fair game.

Simmons's contributions to horror literature include vampires—of the blood-sucking and psychic varieties—ghosts, a godlike killing machine called the Shrike, malicious deities, ancient evils, and soul-devouring monsters. His version of space travel involves being crushed to death and painfully resurrected at the destination.

The author of nearly thirty books and roughly the same number of short stories and novellas, Simmons is the recipient of several Bram Stoker Awards, nearly a dozen Locus Awards, an International Horror Guild Award, a Hugo, a British Fantasy Award, a British Science Fiction Award, and two World Fantasy Awards, and he has been nominated for many others, including the Nebula and the Arthur C. Clarke Award.

While many of his books have been optioned for film and television over the years, none have been produced yet, although Simmons did write two teleplays for the *Monsters* television series in 1990. His script of his 1992 novel *Children of the Night* was almost the first to be filmed, but the project collapsed. Plans to film his original film treatment "The End of Gravity" aboard the International Space Station did not come to fruition. *Darwin's Blade* was green-lit for an ABC series that never launched. Screenwriters have been stymied by the multiple viewpoints and scope of the Hyperion Cantos. Director Guillermo del Toro acquired the rights to Simmons's novel *Drood* (2009), about dark goings-on during the final years of Charles Dickens's life as told by Dickens's friend Wilkie Collins, but del Toro put the project on the back-burner when he was hired to direct *The Hobbit* (which ended up being directed by Peter Jackson instead). In 2016 AMC announced plans to turn Simmons's historical novel *The Terror* (2007), which fictionalizes the disastrous arctic journey of Captain Sir John Franklin in the 1840s, into a horror series to air in 2017.

In 1995 Wabash College awarded Simmons an honorary doctorate for his contributions in education and writing. In 2013 he received the World Horror Convention Grand Master Award.

Bev Vincent

See also: Bram Stoker Award; *Carrion Comfort*; International Horror Guild Award; *Song of Kali*; World Fantasy Award.

Further Reading

Clasen, Mathias. 2011. "Primal Fear: A Darwinian Perspective on Dan Simmons' *Song of Kali.*" *Horror Studies* 2, no. 1 (May): 89–104.

"Dan Simmons: A Man for All Genres." 2002. *Locus* 49, no. 4 (October): 6–7, 59, 61.

Shindler, Dorman T. 2000. "Dan Simmons: Between Two Worlds." *Publishers Weekly* (November 6): 65–66. http://www.publishersweekly.com/pw/by-topic/authors/interviews/article/33845-dan-simmons-between-two-worlds.html.

Shindler, Dorman T. 2001. "Dan Simmons." *The Writer* 114, no. 2: 30–33.

SMITH, CLARK ASHTON (1893–1961)

Clark Ashton Smith was an American writer of fantasy, horror, and science fiction who is often grouped with H. P. Lovecraft and Robert E. Howard in discussions of the most significant writers who contributed regularly to *Weird Tales* in the 1930s. He was also an accomplished poet and sculptor whose dark and powerful imagination gave birth to an extraordinary body of creative work.

Smith was born in Long Valley, California, and spent most of his life living in a cabin built by his parent near the town of Auburn. He did not attend high school, and he completed his education himself, with his parents' assistance. An inveterate reader blessed with an exceptional memory, he read and digested *Webster's Dictionary* and the *Encyclopedia Britannica*. He began writing exotic adventure fiction at an early age and published a number of stories in his teens.

"Ubbo-Sathla": Decadent Prose-Poetry Meets the Cthulhu Mythos

Clark Ashton Smith's short story "Ubbo-Sathla" was first published in the July 1933 issue of *Weird Tales* and reprinted in the collection *Out of Space and Time* (1942). Like Smith's "The Return of the Sorcerer," it is a Lovecraftian story with an affiliation to the so-called Cthulhu Mythos, and deliberately links the substance of that Mythos to Smith's own developing mythical history of the lost continent of Hyperborea, adding a text by the Hyperborean sorcerer Eibon to the register of the Lovecraftian "forbidden books" and helping to broaden the mythical background, to the advantage of later writers recruited to the subgeneric cause.

The story begins with a quote from the *Book of Eibon* indentifying Ubbo-Sathla as a protoplasmic mass ancestral to all terrestrial life, which is fated also to be the end-product of that life's decay. The protagonist Paul Tregardis, a modern occultist, finds a magic lens in a curio shop, which unites him with the personality of the Hyperborean sorcerer who once used and employed it, and allows him to share the sorcerer's visionary quest to retreat through his past incarnations all the way to Ubbo-Sathla—which turns out, unsurprisingly, to be vast, horrific, and loathsome.

"Ubbo-Sathla" is terse and economical by the somewhat prolix standards of the subgenre, albeit loaded with exotic terminology. Once the initial purchase is made and Tregardis is alone with his crystal, the concluding visionary sequence of "Ubbo-Sathla" becomes close in style and spirit to Smith's Decadent prose-poetry: an effective injection from which the subgenre has always benefited.

Brian Stableford

Smith's literary vocation reached its first important landmark when he made the acquaintance of the "Bohemian" poet George Sterling, who was heavily influenced by Charles Baudelaire and other French Decadent writers; Smith became an enthusiastic translator of such material. His first poetry collection, *The Star Treader and Other Poems* (1912), won some critical acclaim, but he had difficulty following it up; his health was frequently poor and his production slow. A second landmark was reached when he became part of a circle of literary correspondents that included H. P. Lovecraft, who waxed enthusiastic about Smith's exceedingly exotic narrative poem "The Hashish Eater; or, The Apocalypse of Evil," in his third collection, *Ebony and Crystal* (1922).

When Smith was forced to attempt to make money from his pen in order to care for his aged parents, it was Lovecraft's lead that he followed, although he did so with a stylistic and thematic extravagance that was unique to him. The stories he produced during his one brief phase of hectic productivity, between 1929 and 1934, constitute one of the most remarkable oeuvres in imaginative literature. His highly ornamented prose was directed to the purpose of building phantasmagoric dream-worlds stranger than any that had ever been described before. It was not enough for his fantastic narratives to escape the mundane world; Smith wanted to outdo in imaginative reach all the established mythologies of past and present. These tales were first collected in the Arkham House collections *Out of Space and Time* (1942), *Lost Worlds* (1944), *Genius Loci and Other Tales* (1948), *The Abominations of Yondo* (1960) and *Tales of Science and Sorcery* (1964), but they have since been sampled in many other collections and anthologies.

Smith had some difficulty finding an appropriate milieu for his fiction. The imaginary French province of Averoigne allowed scope for pastiches of French fantasy, but not for the products of his wilder imaginings. The lost continent of Hyperborea suited him better, employed in heavily ironic "grotesques" that combined elements of horror and sharp wit evident in the savagely sarcastic "The Testament of Athammaus" (1932) and "The Seven Geases" (1934), in which a prideful magistrate is condemned to descend through a series of hell-like realms to "the ultimate source of all miscreation and abomination." "Ubbo-Sathla" (1933) accommodated Hyperborea to the Lovecraftian schema that became known as the Cthulhu Mythos, as did the magnificently bizarre "The Coming of the White Worm" (1941).

The most dramatically appropriate of Smith's imaginary worlds was far-future Zothique, "the world's last continent," in which science and civilization are extinct, and everything that happens is a mere prelude to final annihilation. Some stories set there are as ironic as the Hyperborean grotesques, but the best are possessed of an unparalleled dramatic momentum that carries them through a mass of bizarre detail to devastating conclusions, juxtaposing the necrophiliac eroticism of "The Witchcraft of Ulua" (1934) and "The Death of Ilalotha" (1937) with the savage cruelty of "Xeethra" (1934), "The Dark Eidolon" (1935), and "Necromancy in Naat" (1936).

These features are not evidence of depravity on the author's part, but represent a determined effort to confront the most nightmarish products of the imagination and render them intellectually manageable. Even so, they resulted in numerous tales being censored by their original editors; where original texts could still be found they were restored in a series of booklets published by the Necronomicon Press.

Smith's mother died in 1935 and his father in 1937. Having already slowed down considerably, Smith then gave up writing fiction almost completely, although he continued to write poetry. At the age of 61 he married a widow with children, Carolyn Jones Dman, and lived with them in Pacific Grove, but his health was poor and he eventually died of a stroke at the age of 68.

Brian Stableford

See also: Arkham House; Baudelaire, Charles; Cthulhu Mythos; Howard, Robert E.; Lovecraft, H. P.; Pulp Horror; *Weird Tales.*

Further Reading

The Eldritch Dark: The Sanctum of Clark Ashton Smith. Accessed August 15, 2016. http://www.eldritchdark.com.

Joshi, S. T. 2013. "A Triumvirate of Fantastic Poets: Ambrose Bierce, George Sterling, and Clark Ashton Smith." *Extrapolation* 54, no. 2: 147–161.

Lovecraft, H. P. [1927] 2012. *The Annotated Supernatural Horror in Literature*. Edited by S. T. Joshi. New York: Hippocampus Press.

Sidney-Fryer, Donald. [1963] 1997. *The Sorcerer Departs*. West Hills, CA: Tsathoggua Press.

Stableford, Brian. [1995] 2006. "Outside the Human Aquarium: The Fantastic Imagination of Clark Ashton Smith." In *The Freedom of Fantastic Things: Selected Criticism on Clark Ashton Smith*, edited by Scott Connors, 148–167. New York: Hippocampus Press.

Wolfe, Charles K. 1973. "Introduction." In *Planets and Dimensions: Collected Essays of Clark Ashton Smith*, edited by Charles K. Wolfe, ix–xii. Baltimore: Mirage Press.

SOMETHING WICKED THIS WAY COMES

Something Wicked This Way Comes is a modern Gothic novel by Ray Bradbury that was published in 1962. It represents the culmination of the dark carnival theme that Bradbury had explored in a number of earlier works, notably his short story "Black Ferris" (1948) and the frame story that wraps the contents of his collection *The Illustrated Man* (1951), which themselves had been influenced by *The Circus of Dr. Lao* (1935), a short novel by Charles G. Finney that Bradbury had reprinted in the anthology *Circus of Dr. Lao and Other Improbable Stories* (1956). The novel is also set in the same Midwestern milieu as the mostly nonfantastic stories that Bradbury assembled for his novel *Dandelion Wine* (1957)

The novel's two main characters, Will Halloway and Jim Nightshade, are best friends living in Green Town, Illinois. Will was born one minute before midnight on October 30, and Jim one minute after on October 31, Halloween, a distinction that seems relevant to Will's more cautious behavior and Jim's attraction to life's dark side. On October 24 in their thirteenth year a traveling carnival, Cooger & Dark's Pandemonium Shadow Show, sets up magically overnight in their town, much later than such seasonal entertainments usually operate. When the boys patronize the fair they discover things seriously amiss: the carnival has a house of mirrors that appears to trap people with images of what their lives might have been, and a carousel that can accelerate or reduce aging depending on the direction in which it spins. Will's father Charles, the only adult who believes in what the boys claim to have seen, is of the opinion that the carnival's crew are "autumn people" (Bradbury 1998, 193), steeped in death and the grave, who "live off the poison of the sins we do each other, and the ferment of our most terrible regrets" (204). Both Charles and Jim are tempted by the "empty promises" the carnival offers—Charles with the promise of youth that he is now beyond, and Jim with the promise of maturity that he has yet to grow into—before the three find a way to resist its allure and neutralize its threat.

Something Wicked This Way Comes crystallizes themes and approaches that had characterized Bradbury's writing for the two decades preceding its publication. It extends the investiture of ordinary life with aspects of the Gothic and grotesque that characterizes the stories he collected in *Dark Carnival* (1947) and *The October Country* (1955). It also shows Bradbury deploying familiar tropes of weird fiction to address concerns about the everyday lives of people that transcend most genre treatments—notably, the temptation to enjoy experiences that have not been earned and regret for life's missed opportunities. The novel marks a turning point in Bradbury's fiction, which, at the time of its publication, was increasingly inclined toward the literary mainstream.

Something Wicked This Way Comes exerted an enormous influence on subsequent fantasy and horror fiction, and has been adapted for radio, stage, and screen, including a 1983 movie produced by Disney and written for the screen by Bradbury himself.

Stefan R. Dziemianowicz

See also: Bradbury, Ray; Dark Fantasy; The Grotesque.

Further Reading

Bradbury, Ray. [1962] 1998. *Something Wicked This Way Comes*. New York: Avon.

Eller, Jonathan R. 2004. *Ray Bradbury Unbound*. Champaign: University of Illinois Press.

Eller, Jonathan R., and William F. Touponce. 2004. "Fathering the Carnival: Something Wicked This Way Comes." In *Ray Bradbury: The Life of Fiction*, 256–309. Kent, OH: Kent State University Press.

King, Stephen. [1981] 2010. *Danse Macabre*. New York: Gallery Books.

Wolfe, Gary K. 1983. "Something Wicked This Way Comes." In *Survey of Modern Fantasy Literature*, Vol. 4, 1769–1773. Englewood Cliffs, NJ: Salem Press.

SONG OF KALI

Song of Kali is a novel by Dan Simmons, published by Tor in 1985. It was the first debut novel to win the World Fantasy Award for Best Novel. The plot concerns a supposedly mythical cult devoted to Kali, which attempts to introduce the goddess of violence to the larger world through an epic poem.

In the novel, a protégé of Nobel laureate Rabindranath Tagore, Bengali poet M. Das, has been presumed dead for eight years. Recent reports from Calcutta claim he is alive and has produced a new manuscript. *Harper's* magazine sends poet Bobby Luczak on assignment to India for an interview article and to acquire Das's poetry for publication. Luczak takes his Indian-born wife Amrita along as a translator, together with their infant daughter, Victoria.

Das's new poetry is a rambling tribute to the goddess Kali, Calcutta's namesake. One man Luczak meets claims Das was reanimated during a Kapalika cult initiation. Luczak is constantly assailed by various factions with murky motives, and ultimately his daughter is kidnapped and murdered, her body used in a failed attempt to smuggle gemstones out of India. Seduced by the violent message of the Song of Kali, Luczak returns to Calcutta after burying his daughter, intending to kill everyone he blames for her death, but he overcomes the temptation.

In 1977, Simmons spent ten weeks in India as part of a group Fulbright Fellowship of visiting educators. He came home from that trip with notebooks filled with details and sketches, planning to write an article for *The Atlantic* magazine. However, after receiving encouragement from author Harlan Ellison at a writing workshop, Simmons decided to use the material as the basis for his first novel, which he wrote in the summer of 1982.

Though he spent only a couple of days in Calcutta, the city made an impression on him, and not a particularly favorable one based on the way he portrays it. The notion that a city could be "too evil to be allowed to exist" or "too wicked to be suffered" (Simmons 1985, 1) permeates the novel, as does the overcrowded city's miasma, arising from its oppressive climate and environment.

Simmons wrote without a specific genre in mind. The potentially supernatural elements in *Song of Kali* have alternate rational explanations. Many of the details he incorporated into the novel came from things he either witnessed personally or heard about second-hand. For example, a day spent attending the Calcutta Writers' Workshop, run by famous poet P. Lal in an ancient hotel with unreliable electric power in stifling heat, inspired the character of M. Das. The novel's success allowed Simmons to retire from teaching and become a full-time writer.

Bev Vincent

See also: Simmons, Dan; World Fantasy Award.

Further Reading

Bryant, Edward. 1988. "On *Song of Kali*." In *Horror: The 100 Best Books*, 2nd ed., edited by Stephen Jones and Kim Newman, 277–280. New York: Carroll & Graf.

Schweitzer, Darrell. 2002. "Dan Simmons." In *Speaking of the Fantastic: Interviews with Writers of Science Fiction and Fantasy*, 158–171. Holicong, PA: Wildside Press.

Simmons, Dan. 1985. *Song of Kali*. New York: Tor.

"Song of Kali." 1987. In *Contemporary Literary Criticism*, vol. 44, edited by Sharon K. Hall, 253–255a. Detroit, MI: Gale.

THE SONGS OF MALDOROR (*LES CHANTS DE MALDOROR*)

The Songs of Maldoror was first printed in its complete form in late 1869. It had been composed in the two years prior by Isidore-Lucien Ducasse, a Uruguay-born Frenchman living in Paris. It is a bizarre, fragmented work of heightened prose, which tells of the cruel deeds of its eponymous antihero.

The first *Chant*, or "Song," of *Maldoror* was published at Ducasse's expense in late 1868. It received a review in a literary journal, which praised the work's originality and strange savageness, but otherwise it went unnoticed. It was published anonymously, but subsequent printings gave the author as the Comte de Lautréamont, a pseudonym Ducasse took from Latréaumont, the eponymous character of an 1838 Gothic novel by Eugène Sue.

In writing *Maldoror*, Ducasse was influenced by Edgar Allan Poe, whom he read and admired at a young age, and by Adam Mickiewicz, John Milton, Charles Baudelaire, Théophile Gautier, William Shakespeare, Percy Bysshe Shelley, Lord Byron, and Charles Robert Maturin—all writers who had dealt with the theme of evil. Ducasse wished to explore evil in a new and shocking way; the name Maldoror is likely a pun on *mal d'aurore* or "evil dawn."

Ducasse's use of the word *chants* in his title is interesting. *Chants* implies "canto," "lay," or "epic," as well as "song." This leads the reader to expect verse and musicality, but *Maldoror* is, in fact, a prose work, and a jarring patchwork of many different genres. There are textual appropriations from diverse literary sources: Homer, Shakespeare, the Bible, Dante, Baudelaire, and Maturin's *Melmoth the Wanderer*. At some points, long descriptions of fauna and flora, many transcribed from textbooks, are interpolated. At others the book breaks into gothic horror, serial-novel melodrama and sentimentality, and passages of sexual transgression reminiscent of the Marquis de Sade. *Maldoror* is predatory in its borrowings. It divests itself of an authorial voice, as well as any claim to authority or even significance. It also has an amorphous, hybrid quality. Its metamorphoses can be seen as protean attempts to escape from morality and law.

Ducasse died of uncertain causes on November 24, 1870, at his lodgings in a modest Parisian hotel, during the siege of the city by the Prussian army. At the time, his work was unknown. The original printer of the full texts of *The Songs of Maldoror*, perhaps fearing a prosecution for blasphemy, did not distribute copies to booksellers. But they were eventually circulated in small numbers, and the book slowly gained a minor following among Symbolist writers. However, it was not until 1890, when the publisher Léon Genonceaux reprinted the work in France, that the book's reputation was sealed.

The text subsequently has had a major impact, in particular on the Surrealists, who saw in it an almost mystical dimension. It has also had an influence on cinema; Kenneth Anger admired the book and attempted to film it, but could not get together the funds, and a film adaptation in parts by London's Exploding Cinema Collective and Germany's Filmgruppe Chaos was completed in 2000.

Timothy J. Jarvis

See also: Baudelaire, Charles; Byron, Lord; Gautier, Théophile; Gothic Hero/Villain; The Grotesque; Maturin, Charles; *Melmoth the Wanderer*; Surrealism; Transformation and Metamorphosis.

Further Reading

Lautréamont, Comte de. 1994. *Maldoror and the Complete Works of the Comte de Lautréamont*. Trans. and with an introduction, notes, bibliography, and afterword by Alexis Lykiard. Cambridge, MA: Exact Change.

Thacker, Eugene. 2015. *Tentacles Longer Than Night: Horror of Philosophy*, vol. 3. Winchester, UK: Zero Books.

SPIRITUALISM

The term "Spiritualism" refers to a religion that began in the 1840s in North America and that emerged out of modest and controversial origins to make an indelible mark on the literature of horror and the supernatural. The most significant belief of Spiritualism is that it is possible for the living and the dead to communicate. In 1848, two young sisters from Hydesville, New York, reported making contact with a disembodied entity called Mr. Splitfoot. This was later revealed as a ruse by the girls, but not before their elaborate codes of communication using handclaps and reciprocal "spirit rapping" inspired a generation of mesmerists (hypnotists), psychical researchers, and Spiritualists eager to communicate with the dead. It was Spiritualism that gave rise to the famous Victorian subculture of séances led by spirit mediums who manifested supernatural marvels and conveyed messages from the spirits.

The arcane and obscure nature of Spiritualism also saturated Victorian literary culture, which incorporated the movement's expanding range of strategies, including "spirit raps," clairvoyance (psychic seeing), clairaudience (psychic hearing), telekinesis (the movement of objects through sheer mental power), trance talking, and the manifestation of phantom odors, "spirit lights," and ectoplasm, a gooey substance emitted by mediums and attributed to a spirit's physical materialization). The influence of Spiritualism on the literature of horror and the supernatural was likewise diverse. When Spiritualism first appeared, it appealed to people who had grown frustrated with conventional religion and were turning away from mainstream belief systems to more liberal and scientific explanations of reality and human life (and death). Committed advocates of Spiritualism such as Edgar Allan Poe, Florence Maryatt, and Elizabeth Phelps included variations of Spiritualism, mesmerism, and Transcendentalism (the influential mid-nineteenth-century American philosophical and social reform movement) in stories that centered on themes of loss and contributed to a growing idealization of the dead—those same stories were often macabre in nature.

Spiritualism was also a powerful social movement, especially in terms of women's rights, since most mediums were women, and the movement thus enabled women to hold positions of authority. The purported female sensitivity to the spiritual world helped to establish a strong community of female writers of the transgressive supernatural tale, including Vernon Lee, Margaret Oliphant, and Edith Wharton.

However, by the turn of the century Spiritualism was beginning to lose its viability as a social and religious movement of reform, and its associated literature began to represent an increasing culture of ambivalence and unease surrounding both the authenticity and the nature of the movement. Bram Stoker's *Dracula* (1897) and Henry James's *The Turn of the Screw* (1898), for example, represented the prevalent fear that Spiritualism was a vehicle for social and sexual violation. Arthur Machen's stories of Spiritualist villains also echoed this concern. By the mid-twentieth century, many of the beliefs surrounding communion with the dead had dissipated altogether, but Spiritualism continued to be a vital, if distorted, underpinning of supernatural horror. In some rare cases such as Richard Matheson's *Hell House* (1971), psychic phenomena remained a horrifying reality. However, increasingly in twentieth- and twenty-first-century horror, Spiritualism became a source of psychological ambiguity. Shirley Jackson's *The Haunting of Hill House* (1959), for instance, used mediums and Spiritualists to subvert reader expectations about the meaning of haunting, locating spirits and ghosts not in the beyond but within the psyche of the novel's characters.

Eleanor Beal

See also: Dracula; Ewers, Hanns Heinz; *The Haunting of Hill House*; *Hell House*; Lee, Vernon; Machen, Arthur; Poe, Edgar Allan; *The Turn of the Screw*; Wharton, Edith.

Further Reading

Bloom, Clive. 2010. "Do You See It?: The Gothic and the Ghostly." In *Gothic Histories: The Taste for Terror, 1764 to the Present*, 141–162. London and New York: Continuum.

Braude, Ann. 1989. *Radical Spirits: Spiritualism and Women's Rights in Nineteenth Century America*. Bloomington: Indiana University Press.

Geary, Robert F. 1992. "The Gothic Transformed: The Victorian Supernatural Tale." In *The Supernatural in Gothic Fiction: Horror, Belief, and Literary Change*, 101–120. Lewiston, Queenston, and Lampeter: Edwin Mellen Press.

Grimes, Hilary. 2013. *The Late Victorian Gothic: Mental Science, the Uncanny and Scenes of Writing*. Surrey and Burlington: Ashgate.

Leonard, Todd Jay. 2005. *Talking to the Other Side: A History of Modern Spiritualism and Mediumship*. Lincoln: iUniverse.

SPLATTERPUNK

Splatterpunk refers to a specific subcategory of the horror genre marked by extreme violence and graphic descriptions of gore, often blended with explicit sexual content. Splatterpunk originated in the 1980s, predominantly among a small group of American horror writers, reaching its height in the late 1980s and early 1990s.

The term was coined by writer David J. Schow in 1986 at the twelfth World Fantasy Convention in Providence, Rhode Island. The term "splatterpunk" was meant as a kind of off-handed joke, a play on the term "cyberpunk" that had been recently coined to describe the movement of science fiction writers who focus on how high technology affects the lower classes in a futuristic society. The genesis of

American Psycho: Splatterpunk as Literary Fiction?

American Psycho (1991) is a controversial novel about a serial killer written by mainstream author Bret Easton Ellis. When published, it sparked furious debates about the fictional representation of violence, with the critical treatment mirroring discussions regarding the extreme methods of splatterpunk authors.

It is narrated by Patrick Bateman, a New York investment banker who casually and brutally rapes and murders a series of colleagues, prostitutes, and homeless persons, in sequences of unsparing brutality. Some of the more grotesque scenes of gendered violence—which include acts of cannibalism and necrophilia—sparked outrage both before and after publication: the originally planned publisher, Simon & Schuster, declined the manuscript (despite Ellis's substantial literary reputation), and it was eventually published by Vintage Books, prompting the National Organization for Women to seek a boycott, which led to widespread debates about censorship and sexual objectification.

This public furor obscured the fact that the novel was not celebrating Bateman's misogyny but offering a ruthless satire of an ambitious and egotistical social climber. Indeed, it is a savage critique of the superficial materialism and amoral lifestyle of wealthy yuppies, whose contempt for their social inferiors takes, in Bateman's case, a literally violent turn. Bateman's narration is calm and emotionless, whether detailing his murderous rampages, describing scenes of debauched revelry, or offering his views on 1980s pop stars. There are strong suggestions that some of the events he narrates may be imaginary, as he begins to suffer hallucinations and lapses in memory. Reading the novel can be a challenge not only because of its graphic violence but also due to Bateman's highly confusing and sometimes tedious reveries.

The novel was memorably filmed in 2000, with Christian Bale capturing Bateman's slick and sleazy persona. A musical adaptation premiered in London in 2013.

Rob Latham

the movement is usually traced to Michael Shea's 1980 story "The Autopsy." Though the movement did not have any sort of true organization, several writers in the early to mid-1980s began writing similar fiction, all in reaction to what had previously been published in the horror world, specifically, the rather restrained style popular in the 1960s and 1970s. Robert Bloch, one of the older writers whose style was being exploded by the so-called "splatterpunks," famously criticized the subgenre, saying that "there is a distinction between that which inspires terror and that which inspires nausea" (Ross 1989, 64).

In many ways, splatterpunk is a type of pulp fiction, especially in its big and graphic descriptions of violence used for entertainment purposes. While critics complained that the movement cheapened horror literature by simply aiming to "gross out" readers, supporters of splatterpunk praise its ability to push the boundaries and become a subversive medium, much like the role of punk music; in this way, the subgenre could be considered an amalgamation of the popular (and joyfully gory) "splatter" films and the irreverent punk rock bands of the 1980s. Taboo topics are explored widely in splatterpunk because nothing is truly off limits. This inclusivity has made many argue that splatterpunk is a progressive subgenre, and in a way, that is true. Men and women are equal victims, as are gay or transgendered characters and characters of all ethnicities. No one is exempt from the pain and suffering.

Because of the indefinite boundaries that surround splatterpunk and its somewhat nebulous beginnings, defining splatterpunk writers is a difficult task, and one that is debated and contested. Writers who could be considered as writing in the splatterpunk tradition include David J. Schow, John Skipp, Robert McCammon, Joe R. Lansdale, Clive Barker, Poppy Z. Brite, Jack Ketchum, Richard Laymon, Richard Christian Matheson (not to be confused with his father, horror writer Richard Matheson), and Edward Lee. One of the earliest examples of splatterpunk is Clive Barker's *Books of Blood* (1984–1985), a collection that included such stories as "Rawhead Rex" and "The Midnight Meat Train," which pushed the boundaries of horror with its visceral descriptions of bodily horror. Barker's books marked a shift to the new style of horror, influencing novels such as Joe R. Lansdale's *The Nightrunners* (1987), which tells the story of a young married couple trying to deal with the aftermath of the wife's rape. Lansdale uses the brutal attack as a contrast to the supernatural God of the Razor who emerges as the novel progresses. Both the real crime and the supernatural serve to shock the readers with vivid imagery of dismemberment, skinning, and sexual violence. Another exemplary novel of the splatterpunk subgenre is *The Scream* (1988), written by John Skipp and Craig Spector. Skipp and Spector's novel, about a rock-and-roll group that turns its fans into zombified maniacs, is over the top in its blood and gore, but the tale is also tongue-in-cheek, riffing off the long history of religious leaders criticizing rock music for introducing Satan to the country's youth. More than any other writers, Skipp and Spector seem to truly embrace the title of "splatterpunk" as they relish the outlandish nature of exploding body parts and spewing bodily fluids. They continued to work together, establishing themselves as the leaders of the splatterpunk movement, writing such novels as *The Cleanup* and *The Light at the End*. Other notable texts are David J. Schow's novel *The Kill Riff* (1988) and *Silver Scream* (1988), a splatterpunk anthology edited by Schow; Richard Christian Matheson's short story collection *Scars* (1987); Joe R. Lansdale's *The Drive-In* (1988); and Edward Lee's *The Bighead* (1997). Though the splatterpunk movement was primarily active in the late 1980s, writers such as Edward Lee kept it alive throughout the 1990s and into the new millennium.

Paul M. Sammon, who edited the 1990 anthology *Splatterpunk: Extreme Horror,* called this group of writers the "outlaws" of the horror genre. Not all writers who have been classified as splatterpunk, however, accept the label. Joe R. Lansdale has said in interviews that he does not like it, mainly due to the fact that it restricts his writing to just one idea, and he wants to be more than just a label. Other authors have also spoken out against the categorization, such as Richard Laymon, who said in a *New York Times* article, "I don't want to be identified with that group, especially that one" (Tucker 1991).

Lisa Kröger

See also: Barker, Clive; Body Horror; Brite, Poppy Z.; Ketchum, Jack; Lansdale, Joe R.; McCammon, Robert; Pulp Horror; Shea, Michael.

Further Reading

Bail, Paul. 1996. *John Saul: A Critical Companion.* Westport and London: Greenwood Press.

Errickson, Will. 2015. "Evil Eighties: The Hollywood Horrors of David J. Schow." *Tor.com*, March 13. http://www.tor.com/2015/03/13/evil-eighties-david-j-schow.

Joshi, S. T. 2004. "David J. Schow and Splatterpunk." In *The Evolution of the Weird Tale.* New York: Hippocampus Press.

Kern, Louis J. 1996. "American 'Grand Guignol': Splatterpunk Gore, Sadean Morality and Socially Redemptive Violence." *Journal of American Culture* 19, no. 2: 47–59.

Latham, Rob. 2007. "Urban Horror." In *Icons of Horror and the Supernatural: An Encyclopedia of Our Worst Nightmares*, edited by S. T. Joshi, 591–618. Westport, CT: Greenwood Press.

Ross, Jean W. 1989. "Bloch, Robert (Albert)." In *Contemporary Authors*, New Revision Series, vol. 5. Detroit, MI: Gale Research.

Sammon, Paul. 1990. *Splatterpunks: Extreme Horror.* New York: St. Martin's Press.

Tucker, Ken. 1991. "The Splatterpunk Trend, and Welcome to It." *New York Times*, March 24. http://www.nytimes.com/1991/03/24/books/the-splatterpunk-trend-and-welcome -to-it.html?pagewanted=all.

"SREDNI VASHTAR"

"Sredni Vashtar," the tenth story in Saki's second collection *The Chronicles of Clovis* (1911), is widely considered to be a masterpiece of short fiction and one of Saki's most horrifying tales. Ten-year-old Conradin is a delicate boy, treated harshly by his domineering female guardian, Mrs. de Ropp, whom he eventually contrives to do away with via a large polecat ferret he keeps hidden away in a hutch as his only solace. The story concludes with the child calmly eating a previously forbidden treat of buttered toast as his guardian's mauled body is discovered.

Similarities exist between the life of Saki (Hector Hugh Munro) and Conradin, the protagonist of "Sredni Vashtar." Like Conradin, young Hector was thought to be a sickly boy, subjected to "illnesses and coddling restrictions and drawn-out dullnesses" (Saki 1976, 136). Hector spent his childhood in his grandmother's house under the reign of two aunts, who are supposed to be the originals for Conradin's guardian. Like Mrs. de Ropp, the aunts did their duty by the Munro children, but showed little love, imposing "a regime of seclusion, restraint and arbitrary rules" marked by beatings and "coldness, removal of privileges and guilt" (Byrne 2007, 17). In "Sredni Vashtar," Mrs. de Ropp's treatment of Conradin leads to the development of a fierce hatred in the boy, "which he was perfectly able to mask" (Saki 1976, 137). In fact, "Sredni Vashtar" may be interpreted as one of the first sightings of that twentieth-century human monster, the amoral psychopath, and Conradin an ancestor of Robert Bloch's *Psycho*, with its outwardly meek, mother-obsessed serial killer who cleverly masks his violent impulses. As much as the reader may sympathize with the bullied boy and enjoy his revenge, the conclusion that a cold-blooded murderer might have been unleashed upon the world still lingers.

As in other Saki stories, the animals that Conradin keeps hidden away in his haven, a disused toolshed, represent the feral impulses of Nature versus the oppressive artifice of adult institutions. Thus, the "lithe sharp-fanged beast" (137), the polecat-ferret itself, mirrors Conradin in its eventual escape from the toolshed, passing bloodstained but free into the world after killing Mrs. de Ropp. Like his fictional counterpart, Hector kept a Houdan fowl as a pet. It had to be euthanized, and his sister Ethel described the "hateful smile" on their aunt's face when this occurs (Byrne 2007, 21). In "Sredni Vashtar," the first animal to succumb to Mrs. de Ropp's incursions on Conradin's retreat is his Houdan hen. In taking this pet from him, she crosses the line, unleashing Conradin's hatred and inspiring him to pray to his idol, the ferret, for her to be punished.

The transformation of the mundane by the supernatural is a perennial horror trope. In "Sredni Vashtar," Saki leaves open the possibility that more may be at work than the natural world reasserting itself. Conradin comforts himself by inventing a "god and a religion" around Sredni Vashtar, which is the exotic name he gives the polecat-ferret. Conradin's worship, in contrast to Christ's injunction to make peace, values "the fierce impatient side of things" and calls for the death of Sredni Vashtar's enemies. Mrs. de Ropp's churchgoing is contrasted with these bloodthirsty rites. Saki leaves it to the reader's imagination as to what exactly happened to Mrs. de Ropp in the toolshed; Conradin's "simple brown ferret" may indeed have been a god after all.

Aalya Ahmad

See also: Saki.

Further Reading

Byrne, Sandi. 2007. *The Unbearable Saki: The Work of H. H. Munro.* Oxford: Oxford University Press.

Drake, Robert. 1963. "Saki's Ironic Stories." *Texas Studies in Literature and Language: A Journal of the Humanities* 5.3 (Autumn): 374–388.

Harding, James. 1994. "Sredni Vashtar: Overview." In *Reference Guide to Short Fiction*, edited by Noelle Watson, 1038. Detroit, MI: St. James Press.

Saki (H. H. Munro). 1976. *The Complete Works of Saki*. Introduction by Noël Coward. New York: Doubleday.

Salemi, Joseph S. 1989. "An Asp Lurking in an Apple-charlotte: Animal Violence in Saki's *The Chronicles of Clovis*." *Studies in Short Fiction* 26, no. 4: 423.

STEVENSON, ROBERT LOUIS (1850–1894)

Robert Louis Stevenson was a Scottish novelist, essayist, travel writer, and short story writer. An extremely productive figure, he is best known for his longer narratives *The Strange Case of Dr. Jekyll and Mr. Hyde*, *Kidnapped*, and *Treasure Island*. Although he was a literary celebrity within his own time, Stevenson was, after his death, critically regarded as being a second-rate writer, known for children's stories and horror narratives. In recent years, however, there has been a resurgence of critical interest in Stevenson, with greater attention being given to his imaginative

"Olalla": Ancestral Sin and Biological Degeneration

Robert Louis Stevenson's short story "Olalla" was first published in 1885 in *The Court and Society Review* Christmas issue. Like his longer and more famous work *The Strange Case of Dr. Jekyll and Mr. Hyde* (1886), this story draws on issues such as degeneration and tendency toward violence in human nature.

The story follows an English soldier's residence in a once-noble Spanish household. The unnamed protagonist falls for the daughter of the house, Olalla, who lives with her brother and her mother. The protagonist admits his love for Olalla, who tells him he must leave. Later he cuts his hand and seeks assistance from the mother, who, on seeing the blood, attacks him. Olalla tells him that her family is cursed. He leaves, seeing Olalla only once more, while she prays.

The Spanish setting draws on traditional Gothic narratives from the late eighteenth century as well as anti-Catholic sentiments. The protagonist finds himself disgusted and horrified by the behavior of Olalla's brother and mother, who are described as like animals. He is also perturbed by the resemblance between Olalla and ancestral portraits. The curse on the family has been read variously as lycanthropy or vampirism.

Stevenson fuses the traditional Gothic elements of ancestral sin with the horror of degeneration. Though Olalla suggests that she is cursed, the narrative also suggests that the family is returning to an animal-like state. Moving away from superstition and toward scientific explanations for human violence, "Olalla" is indicative of the addition of science to Gothic horror that can be seen in the literature of the late nineteenth century.

Kaja Franck

Source: Wasson, Sara. 2010. "Olalla's Legacy: Twentieth-Century Vampire Fiction and Genetic Previvorship." *Journal of Stevenson Studies* 7: 55–81.

writing, religious and folkloric interests, and deeply nuanced explorations of guilt, duality, and morality. His works have been adapted numerous times, and he is the twenty-sixth most translated author in the world.

Born in Edinburgh to a leading lighthouse engineer of the day, Stevenson was a rather ill child, and poor health would dog him his entire life. Often confined to bed, he was impacted from an early age by his nanny, Alison Cunningham, a devoutly Calvinist woman who was herself deeply influenced by Scottish folk stories. Religious ideas and the folklore of Scotland were to be enduring influences on Stevenson throughout his work. After a sporadic but thorough education, including studying both engineering and law, Stevenson left Scotland for London and by late 1873 was active on the London literary scene, publishing his first essay in *The Portfolio*. Much of his time was spent occupied in travel (often to warmer climes) for the benefit of his deeply fragile health. His first full-length publication was *An Island Voyage* (1878), inspired by a canoe trip taken around France and Belgium. The following year he traveled to America to be with his then lover and future wife Fanny Van de Grift Osbourne. The trip would result in the publication of *The Amateur Emigrant* but would also result in his health failing completely—it almost cost Stevenson his life. Between 1880 and 1887, Stevenson traveled extensively, seeking a climate beneficial to his health, summering in various places across the United Kingdom. In this period he was at his most productive, writing *Treasure Island* (1883)—his first successful book—*Kidnapped* (1886), and, most famously, *The Strange Case of Dr. Jekyll and Mr. Hyde* (1886), as well as several notable short stories. Over the course of the next two years, Stevenson resumed traveling, spending time in New York, Tahiti, and the Samoan Islands. In 1890, he purchased a tract of land of around 400 acres on one of the Samoan Islands, and it was there he wrote *The Beach of Falesa*, *Catriona* (titled *David Balfour* in the United States), *The Ebb-Tide*, and the *Vailima Letters*, as well as enjoying excellent relations with the local people.

While Stevenson was well regarded during his lifetime, the rise of modernism left him behind. His work was seen as being inferior, less realistic, and thus less skilled. This is principally attributable to Stevenson's own views on the creative act. Unlike his close friend Henry James, who believed that art should be a reflection of reality, Stevenson argued that the novel exists and thrives through emphasizing its difference from the actualities of life. As a result, much of Stevenson's fiction does not aim for the unity and psychological insight that the modernist writers so praised, preferring instead to show the divided nature of existence. This duality between the appearance of things and their actuality is a consistent theme throughout his writing and a strong contribution to the tradition of horror literature, as Stevenson explored the divisions between public respectability and private vices on multiple occasions. This was best exemplified in *The Strange Case of Dr. Jekyll and Mr. Hyde*, which has gone on to enter the cultural vernacular in reference to a divided self and become one of the most adapted horror texts of all time. This division between the public and private, between the benign and the immoral, also appears in several of his short stories, drawing upon the Calvinism of his youth and the folklore of Scotland that he was raised with. As a result, Stevenson's narratives frequently tend toward psychological simplicity and the fantastic, which explains his enduring popularity. However, this also contributed to his critical neglect during the advent and rise of literary modernism soon after his death.

The burgeoning interest in Stevenson has sought to connect him to other more plot-based writers of the day, seeing him as a contemporary of figures such as Joseph Conrad (*Heart of Darkness*, 1899) and H. Rider Haggard (*She*, 1886–1887), as well as J. M. Barrie (*Peter Pan*, 1904) and Arthur Conan Doyle (*The Hound of the Baskervilles*, 1901–1902). Rather than praising psychological sophistication and narrative realism, Stevenson's focus on imaginative and fantastic plot with the aim of provoking readers into emotional investment lends itself well to Gothic and horror writing and has been highly influential and much imitated. With the increasing popularity of horror fiction and the commensurate rise of horror scholarship, proper and much overdue critical work is more common on Stevenson as one of the most successful and popular writers of the Gothic canon. His wide range of literary works, including children's stories, poetry, novels, short stories, literary theory, and essays, shows a great breadth of talent, and his enduring popularity is testament to the power his works still hold in engaging the imagination of readers.

Stevenson died very suddenly at the age of forty-four on December 3, 1894, possibly from a cerebral hemorrhage. He was buried at Mount Vaea on the island of Upolu in Samoa, overlooking the sea.

Jon Greenaway

See also: Doubles, Doppelgängers, and Split Selves; Psychological Horror; *The Strange Case of Dr. Jekyll and Mr. Hyde*; "Thrawn Janet."

Further Reading

Ambrosini, Richard, and Richard Dury, eds. 2006. *Robert Louis Stevenson: Writer of Boundaries*. Madison: University of Wisconsin Press.

Fielding, Penny. 2010. *The Edinburgh Companion to Robert Louis Stevenson*. Edinburgh: Edinburgh University Press.

Gray, William. 2004. *Robert Louis Stevenson: A Literary Life*. New York: Palgrave Macmillan.

Harman, Claire. 2010. *Robert Louis Stevenson: A Biography*. London: HarperCollins.

Livesey, Margot. 1994. "The Double Life of Robert Louis Stevenson." *The Atlantic* (November): 140–146.

STOKER, BRAM (1847–1912)

Abraham ("Bram") Stoker is best remembered today as the author of the most famous vampire novel ever written, *Dracula* (1897), but in his day he was most notable for his association with his friend and employer, the celebrated English actor-manager Sir Henry Irving of the Lyceum Theatre in London. Stoker served as business manager for Irving's Lyceum for nearly thirty years and published in the interim a number of fictional works (many of which appropriated Gothic themes), including more than seventeen short stories and works of poetry, three short story collections (one posthumously), and twelve novels. One of these, *The Jewel of Seven Stars* (1903), although it was long considered a relatively minor work, has gradually (with the help of multiple movie adaptations) come to be regarded as a semiclassic mummy novel. Stoker continued to write until his death in London in 1912.

Stoker was born and raised in Dublin, Ireland. Born a sickly child, he suffered from a mysterious illness that kept him bedridden through much of his youth. During his bedridden years he was kept entertained by his mother's stories and legends from her native town of Sligo. Her stories bore themes of the supernatural, as well as death and disease, themes that would resurface in Stoker's fiction, especially *Dracula*. Stoker entered Trinity College, Dublin, in 1864, but by then he was

---

Meeting Dracula for the First Time

Stoker imagined Dracula quite differently from the way most later representations have painted him. Here is the initial description of the eponymous count in Stoker's novel:

His face was a strong—a very strong—aquiline, with high bridge of the thin nose and peculiarly arched nostrils, with lofty domed forehead, and hair growing scantily round the temples but profusely elsewhere. His eyebrows were very massive, almost meeting over the nose, and with bushy hair that seemed to curl in its own profusion. The mouth, so far as I could see it under the heavy moustache, was fixed and rather cruel-looking, with peculiarly sharp white teeth. These protruded over the lips, whose remarkable ruddiness showed astonishing vitality in a man of his years. For the rest, his ears were pale, and at the tops extremely pointed. The chin was broad and strong, and the cheeks firm though thin. The general effect was one of extraordinary pallor.

Hitherto I had noticed the backs of his hands as they lay on his knees in the firelight, and they had seemed rather white and fine. But seeing them now close to me, I could not but notice that they were rather coarse, broad, with squat fingers. Strange to say, there were hairs in the centre of the palm. The nails were long and fine, and cut to a sharp point. As the Count leaned over me and his hands touched me, I could not repress a shudder. It may have been that his breath was rank, but a horrible feeling of nausea came over me, which, do what I would, I could not conceal. (Stoker 1897, 18)

Matt Cardin

Source: Stoker, Bram. 1897. *Dracula: A Mystery Story.* New York: W. R. Caldwell & Co.

a strong young man who competed in athletics and received awards for debate and oratory.

Even before graduating in 1870, Stoker had already started following in his father's footsteps in the Irish civil service in Dublin, accepting a position there in 1866. In 1875, he was still working for the civil service when he purchased his master's degree (a common practice at the time that continues to this day), but in the meantime he indulged his creative passions by writing theater reviews and short fiction. Indeed, it was his review of *Hamlet* that led to a face-to-face meeting with actor Henry Irving. The encounter changed the course of Stoker's life, so that in 1878, two years after his father's death, Stoker accepted Irving's offer to become the manager of the new Lyceum Theatre, and then immediately moved to London with his new bride (and former Oscar Wilde sweetheart), Florence Balcombe.

Stoker's demanding responsibilities at the Lyceum and the lengths he went to organize Irving's English provincial and American tours, including several trips to America by himself, provided experiences that greatly informed his writing of *Dracula*, which he started in 1890 and continued intermittently until the novel's publication in 1897. *Dracula* was immediately popular throughout the English-speaking world, and literary critics showered it with praise through at least the 1910s. However, although *Dracula* serves suitably well as an autobiographical lens into Stoker's life, perhaps its greatest value is in laying bare the many tensions of fin de siècle (i.e., late nineteenth-century) England, including the evolving role of women, advancements in science and technology, criminality, and religion.

Stoker suffered two strokes and his health gradually declined after the death of his longtime friend and employer, Irving, in 1905. Still, Stoker wrote several works, including two more Gothic novels, *The Lady of the Shroud* (1909) and *The Lair of the White Worm* (1911), before dying at home on April 20, 1912. His body was cremated and his remains were interred at Golders Green in London. Stoker's title character Count Dracula remains one of the most recognizable fictional characters in the world, and his novel *Dracula* remains one of the most reprinted works in history.

John Edgar Browning

See also: *Dracula*; *The Jewel of Seven Stars*; Mummies; Vampires.

Further Reading

Belford, Barbara. 1996. *Bram Stoker: A Biography of the Author of Dracula*. New York: Alfred A. Knopf.

Browning, John Edgar, ed. 2012. *Bram Stoker's Dracula: The Critical Feast, An Annotated Reference of Early Reviews and Reactions, 1897–1913*. Berkeley, CA: Apocryphile Press.

Farson, Daniel. 1975. *The Man Who Wrote Dracula: A Biography of Bram Stoker*. London: Michael Joseph.

Hopkins, Lisa. 2007. *Bram Stoker: A Literary Life*. London: Palgrave Macmillan.

Hughes, William. 2000. *Beyond Dracula: Bram Stoker's Fiction and Its Cultural Context.* London: Palgrave Macmillan.

Murray, Paul. 2004. *From the Shadow of Dracula: A Life of Bram Stoker.* London: Jonathan Cape.

Murray, Paul. 2014. "Bram Stoker: The Facts and the Fictions." In *Bram Stoker: Centenary Essays*, edited by Jarlath Killeen, 56–72. Dublin: Four Courts Press.

THE STRANGE CASE OF DR. JEKYLL AND MR. HYDE

Robert Louis Stevenson's novella *The Strange Case of Dr. Jekyll and Mr. Hyde* was first published in 1886. Like Mary Shelley's *Frankenstein*, the inspiration for the story came, at least partly, from a dream the author had. In October 1885, Stevenson's wife Fanny was awakened one night because Stevenson was crying out in his sleep. Thinking he was suffering from a nightmare, Fanny woke him, only to find Stevenson was quite angry at being disturbed in the midst of his nocturnal imaginings, with the author exclaiming that he had been dreaming a wonderful frightening

---

In film and stage treatments of Stevenson's famous story, the scene of transformation from Jekyll to Hyde or vice versa is always a spectacular centerpiece. In this analogous scene from the original text, in which Hyde transforms back into Jekyll, Stevenson's sure hand as an author leavens the event's spectacular quality with an authentic sense of grim gravitas.

He put the glass to his lips and drank at one gulp. A cry followed; he reeled, staggered, clutched at the table and held on, staring with injected eyes, gasping with open mouth; and as I looked there came, I thought, a change—he seemed to swell—his face became suddenly black and the features seemed to melt and alter—and the next moment, I had sprung to my feet and leaped back against the wall, my arm raised to shield me from that prodigy, my mind submerged in terror.

"O God!" I screamed, and "O God!" again and again; for there before my eyes—pale and shaken, and half-fainting, and groping before him with his hands, like a man restored from death—there stood Henry Jekyll!

What he told me in the next hour, I cannot bring my mind to set on paper. I saw what I saw, I heard what I heard, and my soul sickened at it; and yet now when that sight has faded from my eyes, I ask myself if I believe it, and I cannot answer. My life is shaken to its roots; sleep has left me; the deadliest terror sits by me at all hours of the day and night; I feel that my days are numbered, and that I must die; and yet I shall die incredulous. (Stevenson 1886, 101)

Matt Cardin

Source: Stevenson, Robert Louis. 1886. *The Strange Case of Dr. Jekyll and Mr. Hyde.* New York: Charles Scribner's Sons.

tale. Stevenson often found inspiration from his dreams: his short story "Olalla," published in 1885, was also prompted by his nighttime visions. Stevenson referred to these dreams as "brownies," benign spirits that would take his unconscious imaginings and shape them into material for his stories as he slept.

Despite the interruption, Stevenson worked on his story feverishly. His stepson Lloyd Osbourne later recalled that writing the first draft took Stevenson no more than three days, and the processes of writing and editing were completed in six weeks.

The story opens not with Dr. Jekyll, nor even with Mr. Hyde, but with the respectable lawyer Mr. Gabriel Utterson. The entire story is told from his perspective, despite the fact that he is eliminated from nearly all film and television adaptations of the work. Utterson is out for a weekly walk around London with his cousin Mr. Enfield when the conversation turns to a repulsive, violent man named Edward Hyde whom Enfield has encountered. Mr. Hyde is somehow connected to a mutual acquaintance, the upstanding and respectable Dr. Henry Jekyll, who pays for the damage Hyde causes. Jekyll refuses to answer questions about Hyde, but as time passes he becomes withdrawn and reclusive. Eventually, Hyde commits murder and Jekyll vanishes from society. His friends break down his door and find Hyde dead from suicide, dressed in Jekyll's clothes. The solution is found in a letter left by Jekyll: he discovered a "draught" to turn himself into Mr. Hyde and enact his repressed, socially unacceptable desires while maintaining his respectable reputation as Dr. Jekyll. He lost control of his alter ego and Hyde took over. Wanted for murder, Hyde killed himself, and so the sorry tale of the doctor's split personality ends.

The hastily written novella was an immediate success, which is ironic, given that Stevenson had previously labored for eight years on a novel called *Prince Otto* (1885) that has languished in obscurity ever since it was published. The novella has been interpreted as a detective story, a Gothic tale, and a sensation novel (akin to the Victorian penny dreadful) by literary critics. Like many Gothic and horror tales, *Jekyll and Hyde* expresses fears and uncertainties prevalent at the time of its writing. Unlike many Gothic tales, however, these fears are not supernatural, but are rooted in apprehensions about science and progress. It expresses these anxieties through tropes and ideas common to both Victorian and Gothic fiction, notably the concept of the double.

The double appears in other late Victorian and early Edwardian fictions such as Wilde's *The Picture of Dorian Gray* (1890) and Joseph Conrad's "The Secret Sharer" (1910). It also appeared in the scientific theory of the era through Sigmund Freud's theory of the unconscious versus the conscious mind, which raised the frightening prospect of the repressed, unconscious self taking control of the conscious personality. The double, or the doppelgänger, appears in numerous Gothic texts ranging from *Jane Eyre* (1847) to episodes of *Buffy the Vampire Slayer*, but *Jekyll and Hyde* remains the most famous example of the double in literature.

Furthermore, the fear of degeneration permeates the story. Degeneration was a notion that developed after Charles Darwin published his *Origin of Species*, detailing his theory of biological evolution. Degeneration was the fear that Darwin's theory could be inverted, and that humanity could *regress* into a beastlier, more vicious version of itself, like the repulsive Hyde. Degeneration was a widespread concern in Victorian society and found expression in other literary works such as H. G. Wells's *The Island of Dr. Moreau* (1896), various stories by H. P. Lovecraft, and Stevenson's own short story "Olalla." It was not confined to literature: several major scientific works were written about the theory, notably Max Nordau's *Degeneration* (1892).

Jekyll and Hyde also expresses fears about the city and the rise of urban living. Not for nothing is London chosen for its setting; the city in Stevenson's novel is represented as a dark, threatening space where crime can flourish. Only a few years later, in 1888, Jack the Ripper would bring terror to the streets of Whitechapel. Although the nature of Jekyll's nastier, unrestrained self is never explained, all sorts of criminality (particularly sexual deviance) is implied. Literary critic Elaine Showalter even suggests that Hyde is an outlet for Jekyll's repressed (illegal) homosexuality.

The story about the doctor's ill-fated experiments concerning his split personality is so well known that it is strange to remember that the story was originally written as a mystery. It has been adapted on numerous occasions for stage and screen, with the earliest stage versions appearing only a year after the book's first American publication in Boston. There are also plenty of works "inspired" by the tale that depict Jekyll's unfortunate descendants or else put a new twist on the transformation, such as the film *Dr. Jekyll and Sister Hyde* (1971), in which Jekyll turns himself into a wicked woman. Perhaps the most impressive indicator of the book's profound and pervasive cultural impact is that the phrase "Jekyll and Hyde" has passed into the English language as a figure of speech to describe someone with a split personality or severe mood swings.

Carys Crossen

See also: Body Snatching Doubles, Doppelgängers, and Split Selves; *The Picture of Dorian Gray*; Psychological Horror; Romanticism and Dark Romanticism; Stevenson, Robert Louis.

Further Reading

Dryden, Linda. 2003. *The Modern Gothic and Literary Doubles: Stevenson, Wilde and Wells.* Basingstoke: Palgrave Macmillan.

Frayling, Christopher. 1996. "Dr. Jekyll and Mr. Hyde." In *Nightmare: The Birth of Horror*, 114–161. London: BBC Books.

Harman, Claire. 2006. *Robert Louis Stevenson: A Biography*. London: Harper Perennial.

Luckhurst, Roger. 2006. "Introduction." In *Strange Case of Dr. Jekyll and Mr. Hyde and Other Tales*, edited by Roger Luckhurst, vii–xxxii. Oxford: Oxford University Press.

Maixner, Paul. 1995. *Robert Louis Stevenson: The Critical Heritage*. London: Routledge.

Showalter, Elaine. 1992. *Sexual Anarchy: Gender and Culture at the Fin de Siècle*. London: Virago.

Stepan, Nancy. 1985. "Biology: Races and Proper Places." In *Degeneration: The Dark Side of Progress*, edited by J. Edward Chamberlain and Sander L. Gilman, 97–120. New York: Columbia University Press.

STRAUB, PETER (1943–)

Peter Straub is a best-selling American novelist, poet, and editor who is most famous for his horror novels, some of which were among the central texts that drove the horror publishing boom of the late twentieth century. He is a two-time recipient of the World Fantasy Award, ten-time winner of the Bram Stoker Award, two-time winner of the International Horror Guild Award, Grandmaster of the World Horror Convention, and recipient of the International Horror Guild's Living Legend Award. His work has helped to shape the face of American popular literary culture, especially, but not solely, in the field of horror publishing, where his status is iconic.

Peter Francis Straub was born in 1943 in Milwaukee, Wisconsin. In 1965, he received a BA from the University of Wisconsin; a year later, he earned a master's degree in Contemporary Literature from Columbia. He currently resides in Brooklyn, New York, with his wife Susan. He is father to a son, Ben, and a daughter, Emma. Emma has also pursued a writing career, to date having published three well-received novels and a short story collection.

Straub began his writing life as a poet; among his first published works were a series of six pamphlets that he and longtime friend, horror writer Thomas Tessier (*The Nightwalker*), put out under the name Seafront Press. Other volumes include *My Life in Pictures* (1971), *Ishmael* (1972), and *Open Air* (1972). Probably the most readily available volume of his poetry is *Leeson Park and Belsize Square: Poems 1970–1975*, published in 1983 by Underwood Miller, the closest thing the author has to a "collected works" volume of his poetry.

Straub soon gravitated to writing novels, publishing the mainstream works *Marriages* in 1973 and *Under Venus* in 1974. He followed these two efforts with his first forays into the macabre, publishing *Julia* in 1975 and *If You Could See Me Now* in 1977.

In 1979, he became something of a brand-name horror author with the publication of his breakout novel *Ghost Story*. His friend (and later collaborator) Stephen King lauded its virtues in a lengthy chapter in *Danse Macabre*, his nonfiction survey of horror fiction, where he described it as "the best of the supernatural novels to be published in the wake of the three books that kicked off a new horror 'wave' in the seventies—those three, of course, being *Rosemary's Baby*, *The Exorcist*, and *The Other*" (King 2010, 266). It also was included as a title in Stephen Jones and Kim Newman's *Horror: 100 Best Books*, where it was deftly analyzed by speculative fiction scholar Peter Nicholls.

Interestingly, the only books in Straub's canon to be adapted to film were two of the early works noted above. *Julia* appeared in 1976 as *Full Circle* and was later re-released as *The Haunting of Julia*. In Straub's mind, much of the casting was suspect, and the film's script did not hold up very well. *Ghost Story* appeared in movie theaters in 1981. Although the film received praise for its effective casting of John Houseman and Fred Astaire as the central characters of Sears James and Ricky Hawthorne, and for the debut of Alice Krige as the preternaturally threatening Alma Mobley, it was not a critical success, as Straub's plot was severely downsized. It did do respectable business at the box office, though.

Shadowland was published in 1980, a novel heavily influenced by John Fowles's *The Magus*. Straub followed that effort with *Floating Dragon* (1983), an expansive, bombastic story of terror set in suburban Connecticut.

His next project was a collaboration with Stephen King titled *The Talisman* (1984), a fantasy that chronicled the adventures of a boy named Jack Sawyer in a parallel universe. King and Straub published a sequel, *Black House*, in 2001. Besides updating fans on Jack's doings, it also established specific links to the worlds that King created as part of his epic *Dark Tower* saga. The two have discussed a third book in the series, but have not written it as of 2016.

In 1988, Straub published *Koko*, the first book in what was to become known as his Blue Rose Trilogy. A *New York Times* best seller, *Koko* appeared on that list simultaneously with another memorable novel, Thomas Harris's *The Silence of the Lambs*. Their appearance there signaled the beginning of a new era in thriller fiction, that of the serial killer as enigmatic antihero.

Like Harris, Straub had not yet finished wringing the last ounce of story value from his situations and characters; unlike Harris, Straub's subsequent forays into this strange landscape proved just as intriguing as their predecessor, as the author found numerous and creative ways to riff on the situations he set up in *Koko*, penning two additional novels—*Mystery* (1990) and *The Throat* (1993)—and writing several striking short stories that gave insight into the characters featured therein (including "Blue Rose," "The Juniper Tree," "The Ghost Village," and "Bunny Makes Good Bread"). In 2010, Straub collaborated with actor Michael Easton to write the graphic novel *The Green Woman*. Illustrated by John Bolton, the book looks in on serial killer Fee Bandolier, who featured heavily in *The Throat*.

The Blue Rose Trilogy introduced the character of Tim Underhill, a writer (he purportedly wrote the story "Blue Rose") who became both Straub's alter ego and, according to subsequent works, his collaborator. Underhill also played key roles in the novels *lost boy, lost girl* (2003) and *In the Night Room* (2004).

Straub introduced one of his most memorable and beloved villains, the despicable Dick Dart, in 1985's *Hellfire Club*. He delved into Lovecraftian themes in 1999's *Mr. X*. His most recent novel, *A Dark Matter*, a reflection on the counterculture of the late 1960s and early 1970s, appeared in 2010. An alternate version of this story, the novel *The Skylark,* was published by Subterranean Press that same year.

Although rightfully famous for his novels, Straub has also penned short stories, which have been showcased in his collections *Houses Without Doors, Magic Terror,* and *5 Stories*. In 2016, he published *Interior Darkness: Selected Stories*. That book, originally conceived as a two-volume edition of his collected stories, features sixteen shorter works, written over the course of some three decades. Writing about the collection in the *Washington Post*, reviewer Bill Sheehan stated, "There may be no better introduction to Straub's accomplishments than this new, aptly titled career retrospective" (Sheehan 2016).

Besides his work as a novelist and short story writer, Straub has paid his dues as an editor, helming the Horror Writers Association anthology *Peter Straub's Ghosts* in 1995, guest editing an edition of *Conjunctions* in 2002 (Issue 39, titled *The New Wave Fabulists*), selecting stories for the Library of America's *H. P. Lovecraft: Tales* (2005) and editing a volume titled *Poe's Children*, subtitled "The New Horror" (2008). Most recently, he served as editor for a two-volume set, again from the Library of America, titled *American Fantastic Tales: Terror and the Uncanny from Poe to Now* (2009). As an editor, Straub has sought to point out the richness and diversity of the genre, including stories from horror stalwarts such as Ramsey Campbell and Stephen King, but also promoting the talents of relative newcomers to the genre such as Kelly Link, Glenn Hirschberg, and Nalo Hopkinson, or such unlikely suspects as Dan Chaon and Jonathan Lethem.

Jazz informs much of Straub's work. His novella "Pork Pie Hat" is a good example, featuring a character based on jazz legend Lester Young. This influence extends to the titles he has used and the names he has chosen for his characters over the years. Jazz-influenced titles include *Koko*, "The Blue Rose," and *The Skylark*. Names such as Teagarden, Mobley, and Parker, and characters such as Henry Leyden of *Black House* in his guise as Symphonic Stan, the Big Band Man, proliferate. The final few pages of *Koko* are especially illuminating. There, a minor character named Spanky Burrage explores the differences between two tunes with the novel's name, one by Duke Ellington and another by Charlie Parker, who borrowed his song's chord progression from the song "Cherokee," written by Ray Noble. Parker's improvisation "bends" those chords, producing an entirely new tune. In a way, this is what Straub does with his stories, using variations on a theme to explore ideas and search for meaning; he often turns his stories inside out, looking at the same events from other angles, all in an effort to get at core truths.

Childhood trauma has always played an important part in Straub's fiction, from the sexual molestation endured by the narrator of the extremely disturbing short story "The Juniper Tree" (1988) to the terrible car accident that Tom Pasmore, the protagonist of *Mystery*, suffered in that novel. Not surprisingly, pieces of Straub's fiction are deeply informed by the events in his own life. In the May 1993 edition of the *Village Voice Literary Supplement*, Straub described one such event: "As a child, I was hit by a car. I was killed in effect, momentarily, and slowly and to some degree unwillingly returned to an unhappy, pain-ridden, angry frustrated life. I was crazy both with the physical pain and the horrible dread that kind of pain brings—and also, I now know, with anger at having been slapped down so severely" (Stokes 1993, 25). Fortunately for readers of horror fiction, the author has found ways to channel that anger and frustration into some of the most exquisite horror and thriller writing of the modern era.

Hank Wagner

See also: Bram Stoker Award; *Ghost Story*; International Horror Guild Award; King, Stephen.

Further Reading

Bosky, Bernadette L. 1996. "Mirror and Labyrinth: The Fiction of Peter Straub." In *A Dark Night's Dreaming: Contemporary American Horror Fiction*, edited by Tony Magistrale and Michael A. Morrison, 68–84. Columbia: University of South Carolina Press.

Collings, Michael. 2000. *Hauntings: The Official Peter Straub Bibliography*. Woodstock, GA: Overlook Connection Press.

King, Stephen. [1981] 2010. *Danse Macabre*. New York: Gallery Books.

Sheehan, Bill. 2000. *At the Foot of the Story Tree: An Inquiry into the Fiction of Peter Straub*. Burton, MI: Subterranean Press.

Sheehan, Bill. 2016. "'Interior Darkness' for Those Who Love Horror—and Even Those Who Don't." *Washington Post*, February 8. https://www.washingtonpost.com/enter tainment/books/interior-darkness-for-those-who-love-horror--and-even-those-who -dont/2016/02/08/53b1210a-ce6f-11e5-b2bc-988409ee911b_story.html.

Stokes, Geoffrey. 1993. "Ghosts: The Many Lives of Peter Straub." *Village Voice Literary Supplement* 115 (May): 25–26.

Tibbets, John C. 2016. *The Gothic Worlds of Peter Straub*. Jefferson, NC: McFarland.

Wolfe, Gary K., and Amelia Beamer. 2010. "Peter Straub and Transcendental Horror." In *Evaporating Genres: Essays on Fantastic Literature*, edited by Gary K. Wolfe, 151–163. Middletown, CT: Wesleyan University Press.

STURGEON, THEODORE (1918–1985)

Over the course of a publishing career that spanned nearly five decades, Theodore Sturgeon established himself as one of the most important short story writers in the field of science fiction, fantasy, and horror. His nearly 200 published stories, the best of which were published in the late 1940s and throughout the 1950s, are characterized by emotional depth and stylistic maturity unmatched by other writers in the field at the time. Even his lighter stories demonstrate a quality and craftsmanship achieved by few of his contemporaries. His attention to matters of narrative style and character was profoundly important for a field that was at the time moving away from its roots in the pulp magazines, and his influence has helped shape the science fiction, fantasy, and horror field that we have today. While he is best known as a science fiction writer who addressed issues of difference and sexuality—as in his best-known work, *More Than Human* (1953), and in works such as *Venus Plus X* (1960) and "The World Well Lost" (1953)—Sturgeon's work often makes use of supernatural elements or pathological behavior to create a sense of terror.

As early as 1940, with the publication of the story "It," Sturgeon was crafting polished and intense tales of horror. The titular It in this case is a swamp creature, prefiguring DC Comics' Swamp Thing by more than thirty years. Motivated by neither anger nor revenge, the creature nevertheless cuts a violent swath across the countryside in its futile attempts to come to terms with its environment and its emerging consciousness. The destruction It wreaks on one family, and on one teen-aged girl in particular, is especially heart-wrenching, all the more so for the creature's total lack of awareness of the consequences of its actions. "Killdozer" (1944) presents a very different kind of monster, a bulldozer possessed by an ancient alien entity that has been unintentionally unearthed by a construction corps. A story of possession masquerading as a hard science fiction story, "Killdozer" presents the entity's exorcism as an engineering problem to be solved, which of course it is by the highly competent engineer who is the story's lead. It remains a readable and at times intense working out of what would be an absurd notion in the hands of a lesser writer. In this sense Sturgeon laid the foundation for what followed decades later in Richard Matheson's *Duel* and Stephen King's "Trucks" (1978) and *Christine* (1983). Another story of possession, and one of Sturgeon's finest, "The Perfect Host" (1948) explores the emotional devastation a body-hopping entity leaves in its wake—and does so through a narrative ploy that contemporary audiences would consider postmodern.

These stories and most others in Sturgeon's oeuvre can be characterized as horror, fantasy, or science fiction, but "Bianca's Hands" (1947) eschews these trappings for a study in psychological pathology that is all too believable and all the more disturbing for it. The story follows a man who becomes obsessed with the hands of a possibly mentally deficient teenaged girl, the titular Bianca. After a brief courtship, Bianca's mother agrees to let them marry, and the man moves in. His obsession grows and worsens, and the ensuing downward spiral that all their lives take is vividly rendered in Sturgeon's polished prose. An even more powerful portrayal of deviance is played out in "Bright Segment" (1955), in which a solitary man rescues a woman after an auto accident and nurses her back to health in his apartment. As she becomes the focal point of his life, his ministrations turn to imprisonment and torture.

Sturgeon's work often features protagonists, often children or young adults, confronted by threatening or overwhelming forces. "The Professor's Teddy Bear" (1948) incorporates time travel into a story of a possessed teddy bear that affects its owner from childhood into adulthood, with a terrifying resolution that effectively undermines its innocuous imagery.

In "Shadow, Shadow on the Wall" (1951) an entity, either alien or supernatural, inhabits the shadow of a child's room and wreaks destruction on his family. "Prodigy" (1949), one of Sturgeon's shortest but best stories, relates the fate of a special child and raises disturbing questions about how society manages and reacts to difference. The monstrous child motif, in this case an all-powerful adolescent who can do anything he thinks, appears in "Talent" (1953)—the same year that Jerome

Bixby's classic short story "It's a Good Life," about an omnipotent child terrorizing a small town (adapted as the iconic *Twilight Zone* of the same title), was published. "Twink" (1955) demonstrates Sturgeon at his most humane in a story that explores the burgeoning telepathic relationship between a child in utero and her father. The terror here is one of birth, but it is a trauma elided by familial and human connection—another dominant theme in Sturgeon's work.

Surgeon was adept at producing stories in various modes. Examples of his lighter, if still darkly tinged work include "Shottle Bop" (1941), "Blabbermouth" (1947), and "Fluffy" (1947), all of which can be read as prefiguring the popular urban fantasy that emerged in the late 1980s and the paranormal romance that has existed as a marketing category since the middle of the first decade of the twenty-first century. "So Near the Darkness" (1955) is a noir mystery that hints at a lurking supernatural presence. "The Graveyard Reader" (1958), with its protagonist who learns how to read the life stories of the dead by examining their gravestones, anticipates in tone and mood the early work of Neil Gaiman. And "Vengeance Is" (1980) anticipates the HIV/AIDS crisis through a disturbing exploration of rape and revenge via the transmission of a sexually transmitted virus.

Of Sturgeon's handful of novels, *Some of Your Blood* (1961) is most relevant here. Told through a series of letters and personnel files, the novel gradually unpacks the life of a soldier committed to a psychiatric ward. What gradually emerges is a childhood history of abuse and neglect and an adult life marked by loss, instances of extreme violence, and blood drinking. It is a remarkable study of aberrant psychology that implies a supernatural underpinning that is left tantalizingly unconfirmed.

The Complete Stories of Theodore Sturgeon (1994–2010) collects in thirteen volumes all the short fiction along with insightful story notes from the editors. Taken as a whole, the retrospective illuminates a career of importance, influence, and sustained brilliance.

Javier A. Martinez

See also: Novel versus Short Fiction; Possession and Exorcism; Psychological Horror.

Further Reading

Hartwell, David G. 1989. "An Interview with Theodore Sturgeon, Part 1." *New York Review of Science Fiction* 7 (March): 1, 8–11.

Hartwell, David G. 1989. "An Interview with Theodore Sturgon, Part 2." *New York Review of Science Fiction* 8 (April): 12–15.

Schweitzer, Darrell, ed. "Theodore Sturgeon." In *Science Fiction Voices #1*, 4–18. San Bernardino, CA: Borgo Press.

Stableford, Brian M. 1985. "Theodore (Hamilton) Sturgeon." In *Supernatural Fiction Writers: Fantasy and Horror*, Volume 2, edited by Everett Franklin Bleiler, 941–946. New York: Charles Scribner's Sons.

Williams, Paul. [1976] 2010. "Theodore Sturgeon: Storyteller." In *Case and the Dreamer, Volume XIII: The Complete Stories of Theodore Sturgeon*, 327–354. Berkeley, CA: North Atlantic Books. Also at http://www.theodoresturgeontrust.com/williams.html.

THE SUBLIME

"Sublime" is a term belonging to aesthetics, which is a branch of philosophy devoted to the study of artistic values. It designates an affect (subjective emotional state) or experience that exceeds the ordinary limits of an individual's capacities. Since horror fiction often deals with overwhelming emotions—whether fear, disgust, or denial—as well as the existence of some other realm beyond the everyday world, the concept of the sublime can be an important tool in understanding horror.

The sublime in ancient literature signified some event or person, or perhaps a thing, that rose above its own level and took on something of a divine aspect. The sublime was the object of considerable attention among eighteenth-century thinkers

---

The Strongest Emotion

In a section of his *Philosophical Enquiry* titled "On the Sublime," Edmund Burke not only begins to define the sublime and identify its sources, but he characterizes it as the single strongest emotion a person can feel:

> Whatever is fitted in any sort to excite the ideas of pain and danger, that is to say, whatever is in any sort terrible, or is conversant about terrible objects, or operates in a manner analogous to terror, is a source of the *sublime;* that is, it is productive of the strongest emotion which the mind is capable of feeling. (Burke 1757, 131)

In a later section titled "Of the Passion Caused by the Sublime," Burke, in addition to refining and clarifying the nature of the sublime, describes it as so powerful and primal that it precedes reason and compels its course:

> The passion caused by the great and sublime in nature, when those causes operate most powerfully, is astonishment; and astonishment is that state of the soul, in which all its motions are suspended, with some degree of horror. In this case the mind is so entirely filled with its object, that it cannot entertain any other, nor by consequence reason on that object which employs it. Hence arises the great power of the sublime, that, far from being produced by them, it anticipates our reasonings, and hurries us on by an irresistible force. (95)

Matt Cardin

Source: Burke, Edmund. 1757. *A Philosophical Entry into the Sublime and Beautiful*. London: Printed for J. Dodsley in Pall-mall.

who endeavored to define laws governing the human response to beauty in art and nature. One of these thinkers, Edmund Burke (1729–1797), published a treatise titled *A Philosophical Enquiry into the Origin of Our Ideas of the Sublime and Beautiful* in 1756, which would become an important early critical text for scholars of horror literature. Rather than seeing the sublime as a form of superior beauty, Burke separated it from beauty and identified the sublime instead with horror. Much of the current discussion of horror literature still draws on Burke's idea that horror exerts its own kind of attraction, independent from beauty. It seems clear that Burke's ideas influenced the development of Gothic fiction. Horace Walpole celebrated Gothic architecture in part because it was grotesque in comparison with the more stately classical architecture of the eighteenth century, which was modeled on ancient Greek and Roman aesthetic ideas of beauty and dignity.

Romantic philosophy took a modified view of the sublime, largely inspired by the German Enlightenment philosopher Immanuel Kant (1724–1804). While Burke made the sublime an aspect of certain kinds of naturally occurring events, such as natural catastrophes, Kant saw the sublime as an aspect of the human mind. The mind, according to Kant, seeks to understand whatever it encounters in reality. Some encounters, however, are overwhelming; the event is simply too large or too powerful for the mind to comprehend. The mind falls short, but, in its failure, still finds something to admire in itself anyway: namely, the heroic effort of the mind to understand something far larger than itself. This mixed feeling of incomprehension and self-respect is what Kant considers the sublime. Later Romantic writers, including Samuel Taylor Coleridge, whose importance for horror fiction is considerable, would adopt something resembling Kant's idea, seeing the sublime in ways that mixed psychology with aesthetics.

Edgar Allan Poe provides a good example of the way this altered idea of the sublime affects horror fiction. He pays close attention to both the physical and psychological aspects of overwhelming experiences in order to depict them as intensely as possible, which gives his work its exceptional power. In his essay on horror fiction, *Supernatural Horror in Literature*, H. P. Lovecraft wrote: "Before Poe the bulk of weird writers had worked largely in the dark; without an understanding of the psychological basis of the horror appeal" (Lovecraft 2012, 55).

The sublime tends to fade in significance, while the psychological aspect of horror grows more important in horror criticism, as the twentieth century begins. The domain beyond, which was once considered sublime, is approached by more contemporary authors in a way having to do with the philosophy of existence, rather than aesthetic philosophy.

Michael Cisco

See also: Coleridge, Samuel Taylor; The Numinous; Poe, Edgar Allan; Romanticism and Dark Romanticism; Walpole, Horace.

Further Reading

Brown, Marshall. 1987. "A Philosophical View of the Gothic Novel." *Studies in Romanticism* 26: 275–301.

Burke, Edmund. [1756] 2013. *A Philosophical Enquiry into the Sublime and Beautiful.* Oxford: Oxford University Press.

Doran, Robert. 2015. *The Theory of the Sublime from Longinus to Kant.* Cambridge: Cambridge University Press.

Kilgour, Maggie. 1995. *The Rise of the Gothic Novel.* New York: Routledge.

Lovecraft, H. P. [1927] 2012. *The Annotated Supernatural Horror in Literature.* Edited by S. T. Joshi. New York: Hippocampus Press.

Mishra, Vijay. 2015. "The Gothic Sublime." In *A New Companion to the Gothic*, edited by David Punter, 288–306. Malden, MA: Wiley-Blackwell.

Voller, Jack G. 1994. *The Supernatural Sublime: The Metaphysics of Terror in Anglo-American Romanticism.* DeKalb: Northern Illinois University Press.

SUMMERS, MONTAGUE (1880–1948)

Augustus Montague Summers was an English author, vampirologist, demonologist, and clergyman of dubious religious orders. Enigmatic occultist and sometimes participant in the Black Mass in his earlier days, today Summers is primarily known for his scholarly works on Restoration drama and the Gothic and his occult works on vampires, witches, werewolves, and demons, figures in which he professed his firm belief. Summers was also responsible for the first English translation of the *Malleus Maleficarum* (1928), the infamous fifteenth-century witch hunter's manual.

The youngest of seven children, Summers was raised in Clifton, Bristol, then educated at Clifton College before going to Trinity College, Oxford, where he

---

A couple of brief excerpts from the first of Montague Summers's two books about vampires are enough to provide a good indicator of his characteristic style, tone, and approach to writing about supernatural and occult matters. In the now famous opening lines of the introduction to *The Vampire: His Kith and Kin*, Summers wrote, "In all the darkest pages of the malign supernatural there is no more terrible tradition than that of the Vampire, a pariah even among demons. Foul are his ravages; gruesome and seemingly barbaric are the ancient and approved methods by which folk must rid themselves of this hideous pest" (Summers 1929, ix). Then in the first sentence of the book's first chapter, titled "The Origins of the Vampire," he extended the theme: "Throughout the whole vast shadowy world of ghosts and demons there is no figure so terrible, no figure so dreaded and abhorred, yet dight with such fearful fascination, as the vampire, who is himself neither ghost nor demon, but yet who partakes the dark natures and possesses the mysterious and terrible qualities of both" (1).

Matt Cardin

Source: Summers, Montague. 1929. *The Vampire, His Kith and Kin.* New York: E. P. Dutton.

studied theology, intending to become a priest in the Church of England. After receiving a bachelor of arts degree in 1905, he attended the Lichfield Theological College to further his religious studies. In 1908, Summers was ordained a deacon in the Church of England, but following accusations of sexual impropriety he converted to Catholicism in 1909, supposedly obtaining holy orders in Italy, and thereafter passed himself off as a Catholic priest, self-styled as the Reverend Alphonsus Joseph-Mary Augustus Montague Summers. He wore clerical garments until the day he died in 1948.

Before turning to writing full-time, Summers worked as an English and Latin teacher at various schools in England and London for several years. Summers's prose, according to Gerard P. O'Sullivan, "was solemn, archaic, and often impenetrable" (O'Sullivan 2011, xxix). His other important occult works include *The History of Witchcraft and Demonology* (1926), *The Geography of Witchcraft* (1927), *The Vampire: His Kith and Kin* (1928), *The Vampire in Europe* (1929), *The Werewolf* (1933), *A Popular History of Witchcraft* (1937), *Witchcraft and Black Magic* (1946), and *The Physical Phenomena of Mysticism* (1947).

Perusing older as well as newer texts on the topical areas Summers pursued can scarcely be done without encountering his name and mention of his works, a fact owing as much to his curious demeanor, erudition, and rather quirky, ornate writing style as it does to the breadth of research he published in his lifetime. However, these same texts also reveal the curious absence of any real depth in Summers's work, and it is perhaps because of this that a stigma has been attached to Summers's writings for almost as long as they have been in print. Summers's rather orthodox belief in supernatural figures, his sometimes impenetrable writing style, and the documentation errors his works occasionally show have contributed to a partial and sometimes outright avoidance of his work by researchers.

Summers died suddenly in his home in Richmond, Surrey, on August 10, 1948, with only a handful of close friends in attendance at his simple graveside service three days later. After his death, Summers's contribution to the critical methodologies used for studying vampires has become undeniable. Without his frequently reprinted works, the image of the vampire that is widely recognized today might have had considerably less to do with comparative cultural studies and more to do with predominantly anglicized representations in film and literature. Indeed, it is because of Summers that the modern serious study of the vampire figure exists today.

John Edgar Browning

See also: Incubi and Succubi; Vampires; Witches and Witchcraft.

Further Reading

Jerome, Joseph. 1965. *Montague Summers: A Memoir*. London: Cecil and Amelia Woolf.

O'Sullivan, Gerard P. 2011. "Prologue: The Continuing Quest for Montague Summers." In *The Vampire, His Kith and Kin: A Critical Edition*, edited by John Edgar Browning, xxviii–lxxii. Berkeley, CA: Apocryphile Press.

Sewell, Brocard. 1991. *Tell Me Strange Things: A Memorial to Montague Summers*. Upton: Aylesford Press.

Summers, Montague. 1980. *The Galantry Show: An Autobiography*. London: Cecil Woolf.

Summers, Montague. 2011. *The Vampire, His Kith and Kin: A Critical Edition*. Edited by John Edgar Browning. Berkeley: Apocryphile Press.

Summers, Montague. 2014. *The Vampire in Europe: A Critical Edition*. Edited by John Edgar Browning. Berkeley: Apocryphile Press.

SURREALISM

Surrealism is a movement in poetry, painting, fiction, and film in which the artist attempts to tap directly into the subconscious, using such means as dreams or automatic writing to fuse subconscious and conscious thought to create a new type of reality. The movement was heavily influenced by Freudian theory and by the Gothic novel, which the founder of surrealism, the French poet Andre Breton, felt was a similar reaction against the art and social mores of an earlier era. These influences perhaps account for touches of horror that may surface in surrealist works.

Founded by Breton in 1924, surrealism grew to prominence between the two World Wars. It diverged from the earlier, nihilistic, Dadaist movement, in which artists rebelled against reason and logic in a disillusioned postwar Europe. The Surrealists sought to create something new and positive, if also shocking and discordant.

Because the term "surrealism" signifies a method of creation rather than a particular style or subject matter, there is little consistency in works so classified, but they do commonly feature strange and disquieting juxtapositions of objects and concepts, as often seen in surrealist paintings. Horrific imagery is often more apparent in film, as in *Andalusian Dog* (1929) by Luis Buñuel and Salvador Dalí, with its shocking scenes of a woman's eye being sliced by a razor and ants crawling out of a wound in a man's hand. Later Surrealist-influenced films include *L'Age d'Or* (1930) by Buñuel, *Beauty and the Beast* (1946) by Jean Cocteau, *Eraserhead* (1977) and *Blue Velvet* (1986) by David Lynch, and *El Topo* (1970) and *Sante Sangre* (1989) by Alejandro Jodorosky.

Surrealist fiction may also contain horrific elements. In *The Fashionable Tiger* (1947) by Jean Ferry, a vicious tiger is forced by hypnotism to dress and behave as a human in a circus performance. *The Rabbits* and *The Debutante* by Leonora Carrington (1939) respectively feature carnivorous rabbits and a hyena who eats a young woman and wears her torn-off face. *The Lost Traveller* (1943) by Ruthven Todd, based on a series of dreams, follows a man on a quest across a bizarre landscape with bleeding statues and faceless people.

Surrealism largely disappeared as an organized movement after World War II, but its effects were widespread. Some later writers, such as Rikki Ducornet, actually employed surrealist techniques, but the movement also had a more superficial influence on many writers such as William S. Burroughs, Nathanael West, William

Sansom, and J. G. Ballard, who often employed the type of disconcerting imagery or disjointedness seen in surrealist works.

The movement was one of many streams of influence on the development of weird fiction and in particular on writers such as Robert Aickman and Angela Carter. More recently, the influence can be seen in the work of the New Weird movement, including China Miéville, Thomas Ligotti, Michael Cisco, and Caitlín Kiernan.

Lee Weinstein

See also: Aickman, Robert; Ballard, J. G.; Carter, Angela; Dreams and Nightmares; Kiernan, Caitlín R.; Ligotti, Thomas; Miéville, China; New Weird.

Further Reading

Bradley, Fiona. 1997. *Surrealism*. Cambridge: Cambridge University Press.

Hopkins, David. 2004. *Dada and Surrealism: A Very Short Introduction*. Oxford: Oxford University Press.

VanderMeer, Ann, and Jeff VanderMeer. 2011. *The Weird: A Compendium of Strange and Dark Stories*. New York: Tor.

TEM, MELANIE (1949–2015)

The American author Melanie Tem was a renowned horror and dark fantasy writer known for her humane, insightful domestic horror, which was influenced by her career in social work. She received the Bram Stoker, International Horror Guild, British Fantasy, and World Fantasy awards for her writing, which included nearly a hundred short stories, twelve novels, and numerous plays, poems, and storytelling performances.

Tem's novels include *Prodigal* (1991), *Wilding* (1992), *Revenant* (1994), *The Yellow Wood* (2015), *Blood Moon* (1992), and *Black River* (1997). As a social worker and administrator, she worked with the elderly, the disabled, and adoptive children and parents, which provided her with unique insights into caring for damaged families. Her novels often locate the oppressive scenarios they explore in suburban houses, and she focuses on the domestic and on family interactions. The family's relationships are a prime location for her horror, which is an exposé of hypocrisy and repressive binary oppositions, taboos, and rituals that prioritize some behaviors while excluding, demonizing, and punishing others. In *Blood Moon* she explores the violent outbursts of a serially abused, neglected child, and in the short story (with writer husband Steve Rasnic Tem) "Mama" (1995), she identifies the domineering mother, every teenage girl's guilty secret, as a returned vampire eating flies in the kitchen, gnawing on her dominated husband. The disgusted teenage daughter nevertheless soon succumbs to her own vampire nature. In the lesbian Gothic *Wilding*, werewolves express hidden, socially unacknowledged passions. Tem deals sensitively with matriarchal power and problems of Othering, inclusivity, and exclusivity central to queer theory. In *The Yellow Wood* five father-dominated siblings struggle to cope with the traumatizing talents imposed on them, which Alexandra, who leaves, then returns, suspects is more than extreme parenting.

Tem's horror is based on her insights into families, social practices, and everyday relationships. She excavates the ways in which families and social groups Otherize those who are different, as seen in, for example, their responses of rejection, disgust, abjection, and destruction based on fears of difference, the body, the Other, the abject, the "not I." She also refuses to end her stories and novels on the kind of horror closure that restores a former state of order that is actually deeply flawed. In all this she undercuts neat reinforcement of the status quo, which some conventional horror embraces in its closure. Tem's work is caring, thoughtful, and concerned with human values, exposing the lack of all of these qualities in so many family and social settings. She refuses and exposes the demonizing of humanity's animal nature, other selves, and any easy maintenance of taboos, neat sets of behaviors, and beliefs. Melanie Tem died of metastatic breast cancer on February 9, 2015.

Gina Wisker

See also: Bram Stoker Award; International Horror Guild Award; Vampires; Werewolves; World Fantasy Award.

Further Reading

Simmons, William P. 2005. "A Conversation with Melanie Tem." *Cemetery Dance* 53: 70–75.
Wisker, Gina. 2009. "Devouring Desires: Lesbian Gothic Horror." In *Queering the Gothic*, edited by William Hughes and A. Smith, 123–141. Manchester, UK: Manchester University Press.

TERROR VERSUS HORROR

Both "terror" and "horror" have been used to name the affect that characterizes horror fiction. Critics trying to understand the genre better have had to reckon with the different ways in which people can be afraid.

Much of the critical discussion of horror and terror focuses on them as emotional reactions deliberately elicited by the writer. In an influential 1826 essay, Gothic novelist Ann Radcliffe wrote that terror was a kind of dread with no clear

---

Although a great many people have weighed in with varying opinions as to what constitutes the dividing line between terror and horror—from working horror authors themselves (such as Stephen King to Dennis Wheatley) to literary scholars and critics (such as Peter Penzoldt, Philip Van Doren Stern, and Devendra P. Varma)—no opinion has been more widely known or influential than that of Ann Radcliffe, who in her classic (and posthumously published) 1826 essay "On the Supernatural in Poetry" said this:

> Terror and Horror are so far opposite, that the first expands the soul and awakens the faculties to a high degree of life; the other contracts, freezes and nearly annihilates them. I apprehend, that neither Shakespeare nor Milton by their fictions, nor Mr. Burke by his reasoning, anywhere looked to positive horror as a source of the sublime, though they all agree that terror is a very high one; and where lies the great difference between horror and terror, but in uncertainty and obscurity, that accompany the first, respecting the dreaded evil? (Radcliffe 1826)

Matt Cardin

Source: Radcliffe, Ann. 1826. "On the Supernatural in Poetry." In *The New Monthly Magazine* 7, 145–152.

cause, while horror was a paralyzing or contracting emotion with a clear cause. Terror, according to Radcliffe, was a stimulating, expansive feeling, while horror deadened the mind. Stephen King, writing in his nonfiction survey of horror, *Danse Macabre*, likewise sees terror as a form of excitement associated with danger, while horror is an experience of helplessness or despair. However, it is not at all unlikely that any given writer might use these terms interchangeably, or reverse their senses.

On the other hand, terror and horror can also be understood in terms of the structure of a story. Terror is often the emotion a reader is meant to feel gathering strength as the story unfolds, while horror is the emotion that comes over the reader when the mystery is finally solved, and/or the evil exposed. In horror fiction, the reader is given a series of signs, which may be clues in a mystery, or moments of emotional revelation, or exploration of a place or relationship, and these signs all point toward the horror without naming it or making it too clear. Terror is the name one may give to the mounting impression created by these signs as they accumulate. Many of H. P. Lovecraft's stories have this structure, so that the final, horrifying revelation of the story comes as a surprise, but does not come out of nowhere. The astute reader, in gradually picking up the writer's signs, will have come to a vague suspicion that the hidden truth is nightmarish, will anticipate its being revealed, and will be both curious and reluctant to learn what it is. As long as the discovery is feared and postponed, the reader is enjoying the "terrifying" aspect of the story; however, as this unfolds, the "horror" of the story also comes increasingly into view. On re-reading, then, the reader would presumably experience primarily horror, the terror having given way to dramatic irony.

In everyday language, however, the word "terror" is often used to describe intense fear of some concrete or immediate danger, while "horror" is a feeling of denial, triggered by a more general state of affairs. For example, facing imminent death in an airplane crash would be cause for terror, while horror might better describe the sort of feeling one has contemplating one's own mortality. Seen in this way, horror is the word for a nightmarish situation or destiny that cannot be avoided, but is too painful to accept. Terror, then, would be some avoidable outcome, or a threat that can be faced and defeated. This means that certainty about outcomes is another way to tell these two emotions apart. If the outcome is certainly negative, then the feeling will be one of horror. If there is hope, then the feeling will be terror. Seen in this way, *Dracula* is primarily a novel of terror, because the vampire is finally defeated. *The Strange Case of Dr. Jekyll and Mr. Hyde*, however, is a horror story insofar as the reader identifies with the main character, because he ends up beyond help. Lovecraft cites Charles Lamb's essay "Witches and Other Night-Fears" at the opening of his own classic story, "The Dunwich Horror." In this extract, Lamb also points out that the terrors of fantasy, such as witches and demons, do not alarm us by threatening us with bodily harm, but in a more philosophical way, threatening our spirits, our sense of self.

Michael Cisco

See also: Dracula; "The Dunwich Horror"; King, Stephen; Lovecraft, H. P.; The Numinous; Radcliffe, Ann; Romanticism and Dark Romanticism; *The Strange Case of Dr. Jekyll and Mr. Hyde*; The Sublime; The Uncanny.

Further Reading

King, Stephen. [1981] 2010. *Danse Macabre*. New York: Gallery Books.

Lamb, Charles. *Witches and Other Night-Fears*. In *The Works of Charles and Mary Lamb, vol. 2: Elia and the Last Essays of Elia*, edited by E. V. Lucas, 65–69. New York: G. P. Putnam's Sons. https://ebooks.adelaide.edu.au/l/lamb/charles/elia/book1.13.html.

Radcliffe, Ann. [1826] 2004. "On the Supernatural in Poetry." In *Fantastic Literature: A Critical Reader*, edited by David Sandner, 41–50. Westport, CT, and London: Praeger.

TESSIER, THOMAS (1947–)

Thomas Tessier is an American author of horror fiction in a psychological vein, as opposed to the bloody, gory type of horror produced by many of the genre's other major figures. His books are concise and economical in their writing and plotting—he has never published a book with more than 400 pages—and his style of writing has drawn attention from critics for its lucidity and precision. He frequently leaves the reader suspended between supernatural and naturalistic understandings of the events in his novels, of which, to date, he has published ten. He has also published three volumes of poetry and numerous short stories. He is furthermore a playwright and has had several plays professionally staged, though they have never been published.

Tessier was born in Connecticut in 1947. For college he crossed the Atlantic to attend University College Dublin. He lived for several years in Dublin, and then in London (which later became the setting for several of his novels), before returning to the United States. He currently resides in his home state of Connecticut.

His first novel, *The Fates* (1978), explores the chilling impact that a strange force, possibly supernatural, has on a small town in America. It set the precedent for Tessier's later work by offering no final explanation for its frightening events, and by refusing to offer a happy ending. His second novel, *The Nightwalker*, published in 1979, featured the original American werewolf in London. Its protagonist is a quiet Vietnam veteran named Bobby Ives who is the victim of strange nightmares and violent impulses. It is unclear if Bobby's fears are due to his (probable) trauma from the war and mental illness, or if he really is turning into a werewolf.

More dark and disturbing fiction followed. Of Tessier's third novel, *Shockwaves* (1982), horror icon Ramsey Campbell called it "remarkably dark." Perhaps for this reason, Tessier's subsequent novel *Phantom*, published in the same year, features a child protagonist and actually ends on an optimistic note.

Nevertheless, it was back to familiar territory for Tessier's next novel, *Finishing Touches* (1986), which explores themes similar to *The Nightwalker*, focusing on a young American doctor's descent into a murderous madness. *Rapture* (1987) and

Secret Strangers (1990) were less supernatural and more conventional thrillers, and Tessier has been far less prolific in the years since they were published. His later novels are *Fogheart* (1997), *Father Panic's Opera Macabre* (2001), and *Wicked Things* (2007), though he has continued to publish short fiction since the turn of the millennium.

Tessier has received several award nominations and received an International Horror Guild Award for *Fogheart* in 1998. Though not the most prolific of horror writers, he continues to produce books, essays, and short stories, with his most recent production at the time of this writing being *Remorseless* (2013), a collection of his short fiction.

Carys Crossen

See also: Dreams and Nightmares; Psychological Horror; Werewolves.

Further Reading

Errickson, Will. 2014. "The Erotic Horrors of Thomas Tessier." Tor.com, June 20. http://www.tor.com/2014/06/20/summer-of-sleaze-the-erotic-horrors-of-thomas-tessier.

"Thomas (Edward) Tessier." 2002. *Contemporary Authors Online*. Detroit, MI: Gale.

"THERE'S A LONG, LONG TRAIL A-WINDING"

American writer, editor, and conservative political theorist Russell Kirk (1918–1994) had already produced one collection of ghost stories, *The Surly Sullen Bell* (1962), the Gothic novel *Old House of Fear* (1961), the picaresque black comedy *A Creature of the Twilight: His Memorials* (1966), and several seminal publications on social, political, and religious subjects before his story "There's a Long, Long Trail A-Winding" appeared in Kirby McCauley's anthology *Frights: New Stories of Suspense and Supernatural Terror* (1976). The story went on to win the World Fantasy Award for Best Short Fiction in 1977.

In the story, Frank Sarsfield is walking along a lonely stretch of highway when a blizzard forces him to seek shelter in an abandoned village beside the shell of a prison, where he finds a single dwelling unfelled by time. Sarsfield is a man of simple faith haunted by the belief that "there could be no grace for him" because of his failure to maintain contact with his parents and sister, his terms of imprisonment for raiding church poorboxes, and the degrading day-to-day existence of a vagabond. He has the stature of a Viking but shuns violence, and he loves children but mistrusts women too much to raise a family. Additionally, his untutored intelligence leans less towards making a life for himself or anyone else than toward poetry and the solipsistic daydreams in which his thoughts crowd out the outside world. Snowbound in a house where time and identity become dazzlingly fluid, he experiences an increasing sense of familiarity with his surroundings and its former denizens. He has always been prone to seeing things his fellows could not perceive, but he now notices that the odd movements seen out of the corner of his eye, certain distant sounds, and even the sense of having been touched when on the verge of a dream have taken on an added clarity before he is called upon to play a heroic role in events that coincide with the day of his birth, sixty years in the past.

Through this "signal act of contrition" Sarsfield remits the debt implied in the age-old Christian dilemma posed in the biblical Book of James whereby humanity is saved by faith, but justified by works. Kirk's heroes rarely play the passive role in uncovering and reacting to spectral phenomena that characterize the protagonists in most ghost stories, choosing rather to take an active, even aggressive stance toward the malignant forces arrayed against them. If Kirk's villains sometimes seem as transparent as an allegorical character out of Bunyan's *Pilgrim's Progress* (1678), his fallible heroes are more complex. Despite bearing the marks of the venal, violent world around them, they act decisively to protect the bodies and souls of the innocent, even when their fear is most acute. As John Webster stated in the seventeenth-century tragedy *The Duchess of Malfi*, "Man, like to cassia [that is, cinnamon], is proved best, being bruised" (Webster 1999, 52). As powerful as this tale is in isolation, it also fits into a larger body of work dramatizing concerns Kirk had voiced in his nonfiction. Working from a central Dantesque trilogy of which this story forms the Purgatorio, "Balgrummo's Hell" (1967) the Inferno, and "Saviourgate" (1976) the Paradiso, Kirk develops a Christian mythos drawing upon elements of medieval theology, the writings of the eighteenth-century Swedish mystic Emanuel Swedenborg, and others to produce a network of cross-references within his fiction, which reaches a focal and dramatic climax when Ralph Bain suddenly crashes into action in the supernatural thriller *Lord of the Hollow Dark* (1979) straight from his apparently fatal fall from a cliff-top at the end of 1952's "Sorworth Place." Frank Sarsfield's redemption, entire unto itself, requires no such apotheosis, though he does reappear briefly in Kirk's "Watchers at the Strait Gate" (1980).

Jim Rockhill

See also: Kirk, Russell.

Further Reading

Guroian, Vigen. 2004. "Introduction." In *Ancestral Shadows: An Anthology of Ghostly Tales* by Russell Kirk, vii–xvii. Grand Rapids, MI: William B. Eerdmans.

Herron, Don. 1985. "Russell Kirk: Ghost Master of Mecosta." In *Discovering Modern Horror Fiction I*, edited by Darrell Schweitzer, 21–47. Mercer Island, WA: Starmont House.

Kirk, Russell. 1984. "A Cautionary Note on the Ghostly Tale." In *Watchers at the Strait Gate*, ix–xiv. Sauk City, WI.

Pelan, John. 2002. "The Ghosts of Piety Hill." In *Off the Sand Road: Ghost Stories, Volume One* by Russell Kirk, ix–xvii. Ashcroft, British Columbia: Ash-Tree Press.

Webster, John. [1623] 1999. *The Duchess of Malfi*. Mineola, NY: Dover.

"THEY"

"They" is a short story by Rudyard Kipling, first published in *Scribner's Magazine* in 1904 and later collected in *Traffics and Discoveries* in 1904. It was influenced both by a personal bereavement of Kipling's and by his keen awareness of the thriving world of Spiritualism—centered on the practice of spirit mediums contacting and speaking for the spirits of the dead—in turn-of-the-century England and America.

The actual story of "They" is quite simple: the nameless narrator, driving in Sussex, makes a wrong turn, finds a beautiful old country house, and barely glimpses a number of children. The owner is a woman, Miss Florence, blind almost since birth; they speak of the children, and she reveals she loves but cannot see them. The narrator speaks of his children, one of whom (it is inferred) is dead, though he never sees faces in his dreams. Miss Florence's butler Madden, who helps him on his way, has also lost a child to the croup and will not accept a tip. The narrator returns again some months later, becoming emotionally closer with Miss Florence; when a distraught villager appears, the narrator assists by finding and fetching a doctor, then bringing in a nun to assist the dying child. A third visit, in autumn, permits him to see Miss Florence deal with a dishonest tenant; he and Miss Florence take tea, the children audible but not visible, and as he watches her and the farmer, his hand is kissed in a way known only to his dead daughter. He now knows who *They* are: the ghosts of dead children, visible only to those who have lost children, and Miss Florence tells him that he can never return.

Inspired by Kipling's loss of his daughter Josephine (1892–1899) to pneumonia, "They" is an elliptical work: the word "ghosts" is never used, and it is unclear until the conclusion if the story has a point or if it is simply a series of anecdotes involving life, death, and nature. Only at the conclusion is it revealed that "They" offers a glimpse into a world in which innocent love and its memories can keep alive the dead, and that those who care the most often cannot see what they care for. It is a poignant and moving story that Somerset Maugham described as "a fine and deeply moving effort of the imagination" (Maugham 1952, xxi). Kipling scholar William B. Dillingham characterizes "They" as "perhaps the most personally revealing of [Kipling's] stories" (Dillingham 2005, 140).

Richard Bleiler

See also: Kipling, Rudyard; "The Phantom 'Rickshaw"; "The Recrudescence of Imray"/"The Return of Imray"; Spiritualism.

Further Reading

Dillingham, William B. 2002. "Kipling: Spiritualism, Bereavement, Self-Revelation, and 'They.'" *English Literature in Transition, 1880–1920* 45, no. 4: 402–425.

Dillingham, William B. 2005. "The Immortal Woe of Life: Bereavement." In *Kipling: Hell and Heroism*, 101–157. New York: Palgrave Macmillan.

Maugham, Somerset. 1952. Introduction to *A Choice of Kipling's Prose*, vii–xxviii. New York: Macmillan.

"THRAWN JANET"

"Thrawn Janet" is a short story by Robert Louis Stevenson first published in the October 1881 issue of *The Cornhill Magazine*. It is narrated almost entirely in a thick Scottish dialect, which gives it the character of an old folk legend.

The story is set in 1712 in the moorland parish of Balweary, where the Reverend Murdoch Soulis has newly arrived from college. When he hires Janet M'Clour to be his housekeeper, the locals are aghast because Janet is rumored to be "si to the de'il" (that is, a witch). Soulis saves her from being dunked in the waters of the Dule to prove that she's a witch, and he has her swear before the townspeople that she renounces the devil. The next day, Janet appears with her head and neck twisted askew, as though she's been hanged or "thrawn." Soulis believes that she has suffered a palsy through the cruelty of the townspeople, but the townsfolk believe that something unholy has taken up residence in her body. One stormy evening, after Soulis has had a disturbing encounter with a strange Black Man in the churchyard, he enters Janet's room and sees her corpse hanging from a thread on a nail in the wall. When Soulis leaves the room, the corpse pursues him, and when he invokes the power of God, the corpse dissolves into ash. The next day, when the Black Man is seen leaving town, the locals reason that it was the devil himself who had possessed Janet's corpse the last few months. Thereafter, Soulis turns extremely dour and reclusive, and he frightens people with the intensity of his admonitions against the forces of evil.

In his introduction to *The Complete Stories of Robert Louis Stevenson*, Barry Menikoff praises "Thrawn Janet" as "a masterpiece of linguistic realism" and one of Stevenson's most complex considerations of the nature of evil. As he notes, neither the villagers' superstitiousness nor the minister's rationalism can explain the story's macabre events. "In effect," Menikoff writes, "the diabolic served Stevenson as a convenient frame for focusing attention on an aspect of life that appears to resist rational explanation" (Menikoff 2002, xliii). The story was one of Stevenson's personal favorites, and it moved him to reflect in his personal letters on whether it was wholesome for him to brood upon "the evil in the world and man."

Stefan R. Dziemianowicz

See also: Devils and Demons; Possession and Exorcism; Stevenson, Robert Louis; Witches and Witchcraft.

Further Reading

Arata, Stephen. 2010. "Stevenson and *Fin-de-Siècle* Gothic." In *The Edinburgh Companion to Robert Louis Stevenson*, edited by Penny Fielding, 53–69. Edinburgh: Edinburgh University Press.

Coleman, O. Parsons. 1946. "Stevenson's Use of Witchcraft in 'Thrawn Janet.'" *Studies in Philology* 43, no. 3 (July): 551–571.

Menikoff, Barry. 2002. "Introduction." *The Complete Stories of Robert Louis Stevenson*, edited by Barry Menikoff, xiii–liii. New York: Modern Library.

TRANSFORMATION AND METAMORPHOSIS

Transformation and metamorphosis are both words used to denote a change from one form or shape to another. The difference between the two terms is largely etymological: the Latin elements of "trans-" and "form" broadly correspond to the Greek elements of "meta-" and "morphosis" (meaning "between" and "form" respectively). Both words are used in English to refer to the process of change in a variety of contexts; however, in artistic works, metamorphosis generally connotes a more complete change of state or substance, often effected through supernatural or divine means. In fiction and art, the most common type of metamorphosis is the transformation of the human into another organism or inanimate object (and vice versa). Ideas of transformation have particular significance for the tradition of horror literature, as the enduring fascination with metamorphosis is reflected in numerous texts and narratives throughout the history of horror fiction.

Transformation and metamorphosis are among the earliest concerns of human art. Sculptures and cave paintings dating back to the last Ice Age (ca. 38,000–8000 BCE) depict creatures that are part human and part animal, suggesting species fluidity (either hybridity or metamorphosis). From the earliest examples, literature also evinces this fascination. The ancient Mesopotamian *Epic of Gilgamesh* (ca. 2100 BCE) contains, among other things, stories of scorpion-men, humans transformed into clay, and a shepherd turned into a wolf by an angry goddess. In the ancient Egyptian "Tale of Two Brothers" (ca. 1200–1194 BCE), a man is transformed into a bull and then into a tree after his death. In this latter case, metamorphosis intersects with resurrection and the afterlife, which is a recurrent motif in both Western and Eastern cultures. Ideas of metamorphosis frequently appear in classical Greek and Latin writing as well, with Homer's *Iliad* and *Odyssey* (ca. 760–710 BCE) containing numerous episodes of transformation. For Western fiction, Ovid's *Metamorphoses* (8 CE) is one of the most influential texts on transformation, with its unifying theme extending to episodes of human-animal, human-object, animal-human, and plant-human change, as well as to episodes of gender inversion and physical alteration. The mechanisms of transformation depicted in Ovid's work are also varied, with metamorphosis being effected by human, supernatural, and divine means, but also as a result of natural change. Ovid's work draws on earlier literature, but also on mythological and folkloric conceptions of transformation. Almost all known mythologies and folklores include some element of metamorphosis; magical practice, esotericism, and superstition also reflect a perennial concern with effecting transformation, including using rituals and spells to alter shape, status, or circumstance. Many stories are the result of an intermingling of Western and Eastern traditions. For example, *One Thousand and One Nights* (also known as the *Arabian Nights*) contains numerous stories in which voluntary and involuntary transformation is achieved through the will (or control) of a supernatural being. While some of these stories (such as "The Fisherman and the Jinni") appear in the oldest manuscripts of the text and probably draw on Persian and Indian folklore, others (such as "Aladdin's Lamp") were added by the eighteenth-century French translator, Antoine Galland. Galland was friends with Charles Perrault, one of the writers responsible for the popularity of the literary fairy tale, which has its roots in European folklore and fable. Physical transformation, supernatural alteration of circumstance, and species fluidity are key concerns in all these modes of storytelling.

As well as having folkloric and mythological roots, conceptions of metamorphosis have long been inflected by developments in religious and scientific thinking. In Western traditions, the centrality of an act of transformation to Christianity is significant. The doctrine of transubstantiation, while prescribed as a unique miracle in theological texts, is reflected in European narrative fiction from the twelfth century onward. Medieval romance texts (for example, Chrétien de Troyes's *Erec and Enide*) reveal a recurrent interest in the redemptive transformation of the individual (usually a man) and the potential for one substance to be translated into another through supernatural or divine will. At the same time as these developments in theology and literature, studies in biology (informed by Greek and Arabic scholarship) increased focus on natural processes of transformation such as digestion, reproduction, and growth. These intersecting influences continue to be a significant influence on fictional tales of metamorphosis.

Horror fiction retains this fascination with transformation and metamorphosis, and the influences of older traditions are visible. In the nineteenth century, a number of Gothic texts addressed the concept of metamorphosis through engagement with both supernatural and scientific ideas. Transformative creatures such as the vampire and the werewolf, whose previous incarnations had been mainly folkloric or theological, became staple figures of horror literature, and new understandings of biology, chemistry, and physics were interpreted through the lens of fiction. One of the best-known examples of such a text is Robert Louis Stevenson's *The Strange Case of Dr. Jekyll and Mr. Hyde*, in which a seemingly demonic act of horrific physical and psychological transformation is actually effected through secretive scientific experiments. Contemporary horror also often reflects current scientific concerns, incorporating new ideas of evolution, robotics, and genetic modification into older traditions of species fluidity, supernatural transformation, and ritual. For example, Harlan Ellison's "I Have No Mouth and I Must Scream" combines ideas of artificial intelligence with depictions of physical and mental transformation to depict the grotesque metamorphosis of human beings by a vengeful supercomputer. Elsewhere, arcane rites and supernatural evil are responsible for the distortion of the human form, and horrific transformation is a key theme in the works of writers such as H. P. Lovecraft, Clive Barker, and Thomas Ligotti. While Ellison's supercomputer represents the transformative potential of new technology, works such as Ligotti's "The Last Feast of Harlequin" draw on fears of ancient or repressed monstrosity and of the possibility of degeneration. Nevertheless, the basic premise of all these narratives—the possibility that a human might become something nonhuman—dates back to some of the earliest examples of artistic creation.

Hannah Priest

See also: Barker, Clive; Body Horror; The Grotesque; "I Have No Mouth and I Must Scream"; Kafka, Franz; "The Last Feast of Harlequin"; Ligotti, Thomas; Lovecraft, H. P.; *The Strange Case of Dr. Jekyll and Mr. Hyde*; Vampires; Werewolves.

Further Reading

Buzwell, Greg. "Gothic Fiction in the Victorian Fin de Siècle: Mutating Bodies and Disturbed Minds." The British Library. Accessed July 8, 2016. http://www.bl.uk/romantics -and-victorians/articles/gothic-fiction-in-the-victorian-fin-de-siecle.

Bynum, Caroline Walker. 2001. *Metamorphosis and Identity*. New York: Zone Books.

Cruz, Ronald Allan Lopez. 2012. "Mutations and Metamorphoses: Body Horror Is Biological Horror." *Journal of Popular Film & Television* 40, no. 4: 160–168.

Haddawy, Husain, trans. 1990. *The Arabian Nights*. New York and London: Norton.

Ovid. 1986. *Metamorphoses*. Translated by A. D. Melville. Oxford: Oxford University Press.

Paul-Choudhury, Sumit. 2013. "Ice-Age Art Hints at Birth of Modern Mind." *New Scientist*, February 13. Accessed March 12, 2016. https://www.newscientist.com/article/mg 21729042-300-ice-age-art-hints-at-birth-of-modern-mind/.

TRILBY

Trilby is an illustrated melodramatic novel by George du Maurier, a well-known cartoonist for *Punch* and other British periodicals. Published as a serial in 1894 and in volume form in 1895, it is largely set in Bohemian Paris.

Trilby O'Ferrall, the daughter of an Irish father and a French mother, models for a group of artistic British gentlemen who literally or nominally represent the remaining three nations of the United Kingdom. The most innocent of these, Little Billee, becomes enamored of the hybrid bilingual heroine, even in the knowledge that, to his respectable family at least, her occupations as a laundry maid and nude model render her little better than a prostitute. The mutual romance, though, is disrupted not by this consciousness but through the intervention of an Eastern European and polylingual Jew, Svengali, who hypnotizes Trilby under the pretense of curing her recurrent ocular neuralgia. While her pain is relieved, Svengali has gained control over her mind and is able to eclipse her everyday character with a "second" Trilby who is compliant with his commands and who remembers nothing of her other life. Under Svengali's tutelage Trilby, who is normally tone deaf, becomes a celebrated concert vocalist—her stage name of Madame Svengali intimating that the Jew's control may well extend to a possession of more than just her voice. Svengali humiliates Trilby's former admirers, Little Billee in particular, by having her ignore them while she is entranced, though when he dies during a concert his command over her is apparently negated. Reconciled with the British artists and Little Billee's family, Trilby is, however, a broken and confused personality, recalling her distant past as a laundress but not her recent stage career. Though she endures a long physical as well as mental decline, her end comes suddenly when a portrait of Svengali is delivered to her and its eyes command her to a final, fatal crescendo.

Trilby is a significant work for a number of reasons. Immediately, its interest in hypnotism draws upon the revived popularity of that technique in Parisian medical circles at the Victorian fin de siècle. The clinical work of J. M. Charcot, notably, was well publicized in Britain, though folk memories of stage mesmerism and rumors of sexual interference conducted under the guise of hypnotic séance remained as an implicit counterpart to any suggestion that hypnotism might ever be deployed as an analgesic or therapeutic tool. The double personality of Trilby, moreover, is suggestive of the doppelgänger, and du Maurier's novel ought to be regarded as an influence upon Stoker's *Dracula* (1897), given the facial resemblance that unites Svengali and Count Dracula, and their specific interest in gaining hypnotic ascendancy over (nominally) British women. Du Maurier's anti-Semitism reflects the rhetoric of his work's heyday, a period of pogroms and Jewish emigration from Eastern Europe to the crowded streets of London.

Trilby was dramatized in the United States by Paul Potter in 1895 and first staged in London in the same year. It has also been adapted for film, perhaps most memorably in the 1931 American film *Svengali*, starring John Barrymore as the eponymous villain.

William Hughes

See also: Doubles, Doppelgängers, and Split Selves; *Dracula*.

Further Reading

Berman, Avis. 1993. "George du Maurier's *Trilby* Whipped up a Worldwide Storm." *Smithsonian* 24, no. 9: 110.

Grossman, Jonathan H. 1996. "An Essay on Du Maurier's *Trilby*." *Studies in the Novel* 28.4 (Winter): 525–542. Rpt. in *Literature Resource Center*. 2016. Detroit, MI: Gale.

THE TURN OF THE SCREW

The Turn of the Screw is a novella by American writer Henry James, first published in 1898. It is now considered by many to be one of the finest examples of the ghost story ever written.

The main story is surrounded by a frame narrative in the style of the classic Gothic tale. Ghost stories are being told by the fireside at a house party; one guest tells a tale about a child being frightened by a ghost, then another guest offers a ghost story that, since it involves two children instead of one, amplifies the horror of the first guest's tale. In other words, he will give that horror an additional "turn of the screw."

The guest first speaks about a governess he once knew. She then takes over the narration in her own voice, although her name is never given. The governess is hired by a wealthy man to look after his young niece and nephew, to whom he is indifferent. Their parents have died, and he is unmarried and unwilling to take care of the children personally. The governess goes to live with the children at Bly,

[I find *The Turn of the Screw*] to be the most powerful, the most nerve-shattering ghost story I have ever read. . . . When I told the author exactly how I felt while reading it, and thanked him for giving me sensations that I thought no author could give me at my age, he said that he was made happy by my testimony. "For," said he, "I meant to scare the whole world with that story; and you had precisely the emotion that I hoped to arouse in everybody."

—William Lyon Phelps. 1916. *The Advance of the English Novel.*
New York: Dodd, Mead, and Company. 323–324.

The Turn of the Screw is such a deliberate, powerful, and horribly successful study of the magic of evil, of the subtle influence over human hearts and minds of the sin with which this world is accursed, as our language has not produced since Stevenson wrote his *Jekyll and Hyde* tale. . . . Mr. James's story is perhaps as allegorical as Stevenson's, but the allegory is not so clear. . . . These children are accursed, or all but damned, and are shown to have daily, almost hourly, communication with lost souls, the souls that formerly inhabited the bodies of a vicious governess and her paramour, who, in the flesh, began the degradation of their victims. . . . The strongest and most affecting argument against sin we have lately encountered in literature (without forcing any didactic purpose upon the reader) it is nevertheless free from the slightest hint of grossness.

—From "Magic of Evil and Love" (an anonymous review of
The Turn of the Screw). 1898. *The New York Times Saturday
Review of Books and Art,* October 15: 681–682.

Matt Cardin

her employer's country estate. They live there together with the housekeeper, Mrs. Grose. Very quickly the governess comes to the conclusion that Bly is haunted by the ghosts of Peter Quint, the former groundskeeper, and of the previous governess, Miss Jessel. Quint and Jessel were apparently having an affair. Quint died by violence under mysterious circumstances, while it appears that Miss Jessel might have taken her own life, possibly to escape the shame of pregnancy outside marriage.

The governess believes that Peter Quint, in particular, is exerting a corrupting influence over the children. The boy, Miles, has recently been expelled from school for reasons that aren't clear; all that emerges is that he was speaking to the other boys in an unacceptable way. As the story unfolds, the governess comes to suspect that the spirits of Peter Quint and Miss Jessel are trying to possess the children in order to renew their sexual relationship through them. The governess is determined to protect the children and reasons that, if she can compel them to admit that they are seeing Peter Quint and Miss Jessel, she can break the sinister influence of the ghosts. When the governess tries to compel the girl, Flora, to confess, she becomes distraught and seems to experience a hysterical episode that removes her from the story. Later, when the governess pressures Miles to a similar confession, he becomes so overwrought that he dies, possibly of heart failure. It may be that the ghost of Peter Quint has somehow claimed Miles as his victim, or it could be that the governess's emotional coercion of Miles, and what might be his fear of her rather than Quint, causes his death.

The narrative throws considerable doubt on the governess's interpretation of events. It is possible that Miles's behavior at school was only an expression of innocent high spirits. He might be imitating Peter Quint based solely on his memory of the living man, and there is no indication of any sexual activity between the children. So, *The Turn of the Screw* could be the story of a heroic governess fighting off a supernatural menace, which is the way she sees things, or it could be the story of a delusional governess inventing a terrible crisis when nothing is really wrong, simply to establish her own importance and to impress her employer. James plants a few indications in the story of the governess that suggest she unconsciously wishes to marry her employer and become the lady of the house. Clearly, the governess tends to dominate Mrs. Grose as if she were not essentially a servant of the household herself. The governess also only sees Miss Jessel after learning about her from Mrs. Grose, suggesting that she is embroidering her initial story.

James does not exclude the possibility of a supernatural influence at Bly. The governess sees a strange man at Bly very shortly after she first arrives at the estate. She describes this man's appearance in detail to Mrs. Grose, who recognizes him as Peter Quint, a man that the governess knew nothing about at the time. This is the one aspect of the story that cannot plausibly be accounted for, since Peter Quint is not an average-looking man, whose appearance might be hit upon by coincidence. The governess says "he's like nobody" and goes on to give this description of the man she saw:

> He has red hair, very red, close-curling, and a pale face, long in shape, with straight, good features and little, rather queer whiskers that are as red as his hair. His eyebrows are, somehow, darker; they look particularly arched and as if they might move a good deal. His eyes are sharp, strange—awfully; but I only know clearly that they're rather small and very fixed. His mouth's wide, and his lips are thin, and except for his little whiskers he's quite clean-shaven. He gives me a sort of sense of looking like an actor. (James 2009, 47)

The persistent ambiguity about the events at Bly is never resolved. While it is possible the governess might have run across Peter Quint or his description somewhere, that information is not included in the text. Also, the governess is originally from a small village and is not likely to have spent any time in the vicinity of Bly.

Franco-Bulgarian literary critic Tzvetan Todorov's classic book-length study of supernatural fiction, entitled *The Fantastic*, derives its definition of "fantastic" fiction almost entirely from a study of *The Turn of the Screw*. Todorov finds very few examples of what he would call the "pure" fantastic stories, and, because of its carefully constructed uncertainty about the existence of the supernatural, *The Turn of the Screw* is, for him, the most perfect expression of the "pure" fantastic tale.

The Turn of the Screw has been the subject of numerous adaptations in a variety of media. Benjamin Britten, the famous English composer, transformed the story into an opera. It was dramatized for the stage under the title *The Innocents*, debuting in 1950, and the play was adapted for a film of the same name in 1961. In 1972, director Michael Winner released *The Nightcomers*, a film meant to tell the story of Peter Quint and Miss Jessel before their deaths, starring Marlon Brando and Stephanie Beacham.

Michael Cisco

See also: Frame Story; James, Henry; Psychological Horror; Spiritualism; Unreliable Narrator.

Further Reading

Heller, Terry. 1989. *The Turn of the Screw: Bewildered Vision*. Boston: Twayne.

James, Henry. 2009. *The Turn of the Screw*. Edited by Peter G. Beidler. Case Studies in Contemporary Criticism. 3rd ed. Boston: Bedford/St. Martin's.

Smith, Allan L. 1993. "A Word Kept Back in *The Turn of the Screw*." In *Creepers: British Horror and Fantasy in the Twentieth Century*, edited by Clive Bloom, 47–63. London: Pluto Press.

Todorov, Tzvetan. *The Fantastic: A Structural Approach to a Literary Genre*. Ithaca, NY: Cornell University Press.

Wilson, Edmund. 1976. "The Ambiguity of Henry James." In *The Triple Thinkers: Twelve Essays on Literary Subjects*, 88–132. New York: Noonday.

U

THE UNCANNY

The uncanny is a concept used to describe something—an object, a place, an atmosphere—that is both strange and familiar at the same time. The overlapping of the known with the unknown generates an unsettling feeling for the reader (or viewer) that can range from discomfort to fear. The sense of what is "real" and "normal" is slightly unsettled by the presence of jarring elements in the narration, and it is uncertain, for both the reader/viewer and the characters, whether these elements have mundane, supernatural, or imaginative causes: a degree of ambiguity has to be maintained for the uncanny to exist. Borrowed from psychoanalysis, the concept has been widely used by literary criticism in the twentieth and twenty-first centuries to analyze any type of fiction that plays on this ambiguous feeling of unease, with Gothic fiction, horror literature, and weird fiction being examples. Instances of the uncanny include déjà-vu, time-loops, repetitions, doubles, twins, doppelgängers, ghosts, moving paintings, never-ending staircases, and living dolls. The sense of the uncanny can be compared to the "odd," the "weird," and the "incongruous."

One of the most well-known treatises on the uncanny is Sigmund Freud's 1919 essay *Das Unheimliche*, of which the English "uncanny" is a loose translation. The term *unheimliche* is a combination in German of the adjective *heimliche*—derived from *Heime,* or "home" in English—and the prefix *un. Heimliche* is used to refer to the house, the family, and everyday life, but also to what is intimate as well as concealed. As Freud observes, the concept of *Heimliche* is twofold, with the home a space of both comfort and secrecy. The negative prefix *un-* makes *unheimliche* an imperfect opposite of *Heimliche*: it describes a feeling of estrangement rooted within the familiar that is both threatening and alluring for the subject that experiences it.

Freud's essay was a response to previous theories of the uncanny, particularly that of the German psychiatrist Ernst Jentsch in his pioneering essay *On the Psychology of the Uncanny* (1906). Freud draws extensively from Jentsch's theory that the uncanny emerges from indecipherable circumstances and that fiction is the most efficient device to create such conditions. Most of Freud's response is dedicated to the intricate links between psychoanalysis and literature, expanding on the reading Jentsch offers of E. T. A. Hoffmann's short story "The Sand-man" (1817), which features childhood monsters, doppelgängers, and a living automata called Olympia. Freud agrees with Jentsch's opinion that Hoffmann's story is a landmark of uncanny fiction, but the conclusions he draws are slightly different: while Jentsch sees the living doll Olympia as the locus of the uncanny in the text, Freud believes that the character of the Sandman, a creature that steals children's eyes at night to feed them to its own offspring, is the central figure. Freud reads the haunting effects that the monster has on the main character as fictionalized versions of the psychoanalytical concepts of repression, repetition compulsion, and anxiety neurosis: repressed childhood fears and conflicts, when brought back to the surface by unexpected elements, trigger a feeling of anxiety that Freud identifies as the experience of the uncanny.

Freud's theory was highly influential both within and without the realm of psychoanalysis. It paved the way for Jacques Lacan's concept of the mirror stage in human psychological development, and it inspired psychoanalytical feminist philosophers such as Helen Cixous and Julia Kristeva to question the relationship between the "self" and the "other" in the cognitive space. It was also used widely in literary criticism, especially in attempts to define the genres of Gothic and horror fiction. Scholars such as Leslie Fiedler and David Punter consider it a key concept of the Gothic genre, tracing occurrences of the uncanny in foundational Gothic texts such as Ann Radcliffe's *Mysteries of Udolpho* (1794), Matthew Lewis's *The Monk* (1796), and Charles Brockden Brown's *Wieland* (1798). Later instances include Mary Shelley's *Frankenstein* (1818), Edgar Allan Poe's short stories such as "William Wilson," "The Tell-Tale Heart," and "The Black Cat," Henry James's *The Turn of the Screw* (1898), H. P. Lovecraft's "The Outsider" (1926), and Franz Kafka's *The Trial* (1925).

While written fiction was long the dedicated medium for the uncanny, cinema has also explored its potential. From the early days of the movie industry, directors such as F. W. Murnau (*Nosferatu the Vampyre*, *Faust*) and Fritz Lang (*Dr. Mabuse*, *M*, *Metropolis*), alongside other figures of expressionist cinema, sought to create feelings of unease through the distortion of reality on screen. Their use of oblique camera angles, stark black and white contrasts, heavy makeup, special effects, and crooked landscapes paved the way for other directors such as Emeric Pressburger (*The Red Shoes*), Orson Welles (*The Trial*, *Citizen Kane*, *The Lady of Shanghai*), Alfred Hitchcock (*The Birds*, *Vertigo*, *Psycho*), Stanley Kubrick (*The Shining*, *Lolita*) and David Lynch (*Mulholland Drive*, *Lost Highway*, *Inland Empires*).

Elsa Charléty

See also: Brown, Charles Brockden; Doubles, Doppelgängers, and Split Selves; Dreams and Nightmares; The Haunted House or Castle; Hoffmann, E. T. A. ; James, Henry; Kafka, Franz; *The Monk*; *The Mysteries of Udolpho*; "The Sand-man"; "Schalken the Painter"; Transformation and Metamorphosis.

Further Reading

Fiedler, Leslie A. [1960] 1997. *Love and Death in the American Novel*. Normal, IL: Dalkey Archive Press.

Freud, Sigmund. 2003. *The Uncanny*. New York: Penguin.

Kristeva, Julia. 1982. *Powers of Horror*. University Presses of California, Columbia, and Princeton.

Peel, Ellen. 1980. "Psychoanalysis and the Uncanny." *Comparative Literature Studies* 17, no. 4: 410–417. http://www.jstor.org/stable/40245653.

The Pervert's Guide to Cinema: Parts 1, 2, 3. 2006. Directed by Sophie Fiennes. Written and presented by Slavoj Žižek. London: P Guide Limited. DVD.

Punter, David. 1980. *The Literature of Terror: A History of Gothic Fictions from 1765 to the Present Day*. New York: Longman Publishing Group.

Tatar, Maria M. 1981. "The Houses of Fiction: Toward a Definition of the Uncanny." *Comparative Literature* 33, no. 2: 167.

UNRELIABLE NARRATOR

The term "unreliable narrator" refers to a narrative technique used in fiction when the story is told solely or partially through the single viewpoint of a first-person narrator who proves at some point to have failed to tell the entire truth, either intentionally or unintentionally. An unreliable narrator gives information to the reader that is biased, incomplete, fabricated, and/or insufficient. This type of narrator is especially common to, and significant in, Gothic romanticism, horror literature, and crime fiction.

Even though literary critic Wayne Booth coined the term "unreliable narrator" in his 1961 essay *The Rhetoric of Fiction,* the technique has existed as long as

---

"The Tell-Tale Heart"

Edgar Allan Poe's "The Tell-Tale Heart" (1843) epitomizes the narrative technique of the unreliable narrator and stands as probably the most famous and typical example of this technique in Poe's short fiction. In this case the narrator is an insane murderer, and Poe plunges the reader directly into this narrator's point of view and frame of mind right from the opening sentence and paragraph:

> True!—nervous—very, very dreadfully nervous I had been and am; but why *will* you say that I am mad? The disease had sharpened my senses—not destroyed— not dulled them. Above all was the sense of hearing acute. I heard all things in the heaven and in the earth. I heard many things in hell. How, then, am I mad? Hearken! and observe how healthily—how calmly I can tell you the whole story.

The narrator then proceeds to lay out a tale in which the very thoughts and actions that he vigorously presents as evidence of his own sanity and rationality indicate the exact opposite to the reader: that the narrator is hopelessly and incontrovertibly mad.

Matt Cardin

Source: Poe, Edgar Allan. 1902. *Complete Works of Edgar Allan Poe*. Vol. 3. New York: Fred De Fau & Company.

authors have written stories in which the narration, or part of it, is told from a subjective point of view. Early uses of a narrator's unreliability can be traced as far back as Homer's *Odyssey* (ca. eighth century BCE) and *The Arabian Nights* (ca. ninth century). With the rise of first-person narration in the eighteenth century and the publishing of novels such as Samuel Richardson's *Pamela* (1740) and Jean-Jacques Rousseau's *Julie, or the New Heloise* (French: *Julie, ou la nouvelle Héloïse*, 1761), the question of the narrator's reliability would become central in Western literature.

The fallibility of a narrator can be spotted through incongruities in his or her account such as repetitions, memory gaps, contradiction with other characters' versions, and apparent discrepancies between the narrator's statements and his or her actions. When made apparent, this unreliable quality of the narrator often leads to a complete overturn of the plot. It usually finds the narrator guilty of some dark deeds while he or she had painted himself or herself as innocent. It challenges heavily the reading experience, as a first-person narrator is the sole source of information for the reader.

Because such a narrator delivers skewed perspectives and heightens plot ambiguities, this technique offers a privileged way for authors to challenge the limit between reality and fantasy and intensify the mysterious atmosphere of a text. It allows exploring not just the moral failings of individuals, but also psychological instability. Indeed, in Gothic fiction, the first-person narrator is often proven to be unreliable due to being in a state of mental distress that makes him or her incapable of giving a trustworthy account of events.

For example, a narrator can be unreliable because he or she is a liar or delusional. In Emily Brontë's *Wuthering Heights* (1847), the character of Nelly Dean, the housekeeper, is presented to the reader as a mere chronicler of the drama that unfolds in the plot. However, she plays a greater role than what she says she does, as she is blinded by her emotional attachment to the family she works for. It takes a second narrator, an outsider, to show the cracks in her logic and have the reader question her impartiality.

An unreliable narrator can also be emotionally unstable, as in the case of Roderick Usher in Edgar Allan Poe's iconic Gothic tale "The Fall of the House of Usher" (1839). Described by the main narrator of the story as a feeble, depressed hypochondriac, Roderick Usher is a tortured man haunted by the memory of his dead sister Madeline. He is the only one to know the truth about her death, but his precarious emotional state forces the reader to compensate for his fallibility when he (Roderick) describes Madeline's death, and come up with his or her own interpretation of the mystery. It is also unclear, by the end of the novel, if the main narrator is completely trustworthy or, in fact, as mad as Usher himself. The reader, as is often the case with Poe's stories, has to draw his or her own conclusions.

Additional instances of mad narrators can be found in Poe ("The Black Cat," "William Wilson," "Berenice"), with the most representative being the "murderous maniac" of the "Tell-Tale Heart," a narrative *tour de force* that uses the whole potentiality of an unreliable narrator to delve into the depth of human madness. A short text written solely from the point of view of an unidentified "I," "The Tell-Tale Heart" sees the multiple attempts made by this anonymous narrator to convince the reader of his sanity as he sits in jail, accused of murdering his landlord. As the narration progresses and the narrator tells of the carefully calculated murder, as well as the dismembering and concealing of the body under the floorboards, he seems to have a harder time keeping his story in check. He eventually breaks into a hallucinatory rant and claims to have heard the beating heart of his dead victim through the floorboards. The first-person narrative makes it impossible for the reader to know where the truth lies: either the narrator is indeed mad, and his guilt-ridden conscience has made him fall into an acute paranoiac episode; or the narrator is, as he claims, not insane but the victim of some supernatural trick. Or he may be neither mad nor sane, but merely an avatar of Poe himself, who is playing with the conventions of narration and has invented the whole story from scratch.

"The Tell-Tale Heart" was the precursor for many other figures of "mad" unreliable narrators, including Humbert Humbert, the pervert maniac of Nabokov's *Lolita*; the haunted governess of Henry James's *The Turn of the Screw*; and the murderous German submarine commander of H. P. Lovecraft's "The Temple." Movie directors such as Alfred Hitchcock (*Psycho*, *Vertigo*), Orson Welles (*Citizen Kane*, *The Trial*), Stanley Kubrick (*The Shining*, *Lolita*) and David Lynch (*Mulholland Drive*, *Lost Highway*) have also relied on the point of view of unstable characters to challenge viewers' assumptions about the plot and create an atmosphere of mystery and fear through the medium of cinema.

Elsa Charléty

See also: The Brontë Sisters; Doubles, Doppelgängers and Split Selves; Faulkner, William; Gothic Hero/Villain; "The Horla"; *The Mysteries of Udolpho*; *The Other*; *The Shining*; *The Turn of the Screw*; "The Yellow Wall-Paper."

Further Reading

Booth, Wayne C. 1983. *The Rhetoric of Fiction*. Chicago: University of Chicago Press.

Nünning, Ansgar. 1997. "'But Why Will You Say That I Am Mad?' On the Theory, History, and Signals of Unreliable Narration in British Fiction." In *AAA: Arbeiten aus Anglistik und Amerikanistik* 22, no. 1: 83–105.

Punter, David. 1980. *The Literature of Terror: A History of Gothic Fictions from 1765 to the Present Day*. Longman Publishing Group.

V

VAMPIRES

As a figure in literary texts, vampires can be read as metaphors for whatever terrifies and disgusts, whatever is seen as Other. They are cultural indices of the concerns of different ages, contexts, and people. Part of what terrifies and disgusts is their liminal position, between life and death, active at night, invading hearth and home as well as the bodies and blood of loved ones, infecting them like a deadly plague. Vampires are embodiments of contagion and the abject (the aspects of bodily life that people tend to reject because they are felt to be distasteful or horrifying). While some characteristics of literary vampires are consistent across time and place—the blood-sucking, fear of the sun and the sacred, including crucifixes and holy water in Christian contexts (although each of these is questioned in contemporary texts)—they are used differently to represent culturally and historically inflected terrors. The vampire of war, for instance, is World War II propaganda, and in Indian culture the god Kali herself is vampiric. It is in their relation to issues of gender, sexuality, property, and racial purity that vampires are widely used in Western culture, their invasions and rejections of boundaries upsetting certainties, laws, and norms at a fundamental level. This particularly emerges in fears of loss of control over sexuality, women's bodies as property, and the purity of blood.

Early European literary vampires appear in German poetry of the *Sturm und Drang* period including Gottfried August Bürger's spectral ballad "Lenore" (1773), Johann Wolfgang Goethe's "Bride of Corinth" (1797), and Robert Southey's Oriental epic poem "Thalaba the Destroyer" (1801), in which the main character's dead bride turns into a vampire. Lord Byron mentions vampires in "The Giaour" (1813). In Samuel Taylor Coleridge's *Christabel* (1797), Geraldine, a lamia character (lamias were feminine demonic proto-vampires in ancient Greek mythology), bewitches and preys on young, innocent Christabel. The first vampire tale by a woman is believed to be Elizabeth Caroline Grey's Faustian penny dreadful *The Skeleton Count, or The Vampire Mistress* (1828). Malcolm Rymer's penny dreadful *Varney the Vampire* (1847) and John Polidori's Lord Ruthven in his short story "The Vampyre" (1819) build on the ambiguity represented by the vampire in an elegant/hideous, godlike/bestial form, but literary vampires have been more broadly popularized since Bram Stoker's *Dracula* (1897), aspects of which—primarily the eponymous vampire's name—were based on the bloodthirsty fifteenth-century Wallachian prince Vlad Tepes, who ruled Transylvania and who was popularly known as "Vlad the Impaler." *Dracula* touched a range of cultural, social, personal, and historical concerns. The character of Dracula himself represents an invasion of the modern

"For the Blood Is the Life"

If this 1905 vampire story by F. Marion Crawford may seem conventional to modern readers, they should bear in mind that it was written after *Dracula* but well before the advent of vampire movies or the existence of fantasy magazines such as *Weird Tales* in which the vampire could be rendered a cliché. Crawford's version is highly atmospheric and makes good use of its setting, a backwater village in Italy. The narrator dwells in a sixteenth-century tower, from which a grave-like mound is visible in a little valley nearby. A visitor notices it and remarks that there appears to be a corpse lying on it. But when he goes to investigate, there is only strangely clinging mist, leaving him to wonder if the corpse is an illusion.

The narrator then supplies the main story: A miser died, leaving a great sum of money that was stolen by two masons, thus dashing the prospects and marriage plans of the miser's much more decent son. Meanwhile a village girl longed for this young man, who never noticed her. By chance, she came upon the thieves burying their loot. They killed her and buried her with it. Driven by rage and restless need, she rose each night as a vampire, luring her beloved (the miser's son) to a slow death as she drained his life away. She was dispatched with holy water and a stake, but the ghostly outline of her corpse remains.

Crawford was born in Italy of American parents. He spent much of his life in that country, so he was familiar with the region described in the story, which at the time was one of the most backward and inaccessible parts of Europe. There was no reason vampires had to be found only in Transylvania.

Darrell Schweitzer

---

technological West by Otherness from Transylvania, part of little known, feared Eastern Europe, as Dracula buys up property in London, his coffins containing his broad vampire family delivered straight into the beating heart of Victorian London, when contemporary news reports indicate widespread anti-Semitism and fear of Jewish settlement. Dracula dramatizes the terror of invasion, both by hordes of others and through the blood of pure women. The vampire invades the home and the body of the beloved, bleeding her to undeath, subtly replacing the familiar loved one with a monster, no longer maternal, trustworthy, pure, and virginal.

Male vampires have generally been seen as dashing, frock-coated, alluring, and dangerously, sexually invasive. In popular fiction their predatory natures align them with dashing romantic leads, a version of relationships that, at its darkest, derives from and plays into sadomasochism. Stoker's Dracula, metamorphosing into bat or huge dog, is not an attractive figure, although his allure for the young Lucy and the vampire women at his castle is based on sexuality and engulfing power. There are exceptions to this rule, however. The loathsome title vampire in

Nosferatu (1922), the earliest (but unofficial) film adaptation of *Dracula*, is clearly more monster than man.

Female vampires have also played into some of these same tropes. The non-nurturing vampire mother, for instance, is also used to explore domestic horror. The three vampire women Dracula keeps in his castle would prefer to eat and bleed a child than nurture it, and Lucy Westenra, after being changed into a vampire by Dracula, is discovered about to devour a child in a graveyard. These are dangerously powerful, sexually voracious, and engulfing archaic mothers who refuse children independence and drain adults and children alike. Both configurations connote male fears of castration and disempowerment, the latter arising from fear of the mother, whose body is seen as disgusting in its fecundity and potentially overwhelming, engulfing. As Barbara Creed notes: "Vampirism combines a number of abject activities: the mixing of blood and milk; the threat of castration; the feminization of the male victim" (Creed 1993, 70).

Vampire mothers are both figures of horror and a vehicle through which more radical contemporary women horror writers undercut the stereotyping of conventional horror's gender roles. Women *disgust* in conventional vampire narratives, but are revisited in contemporary women's horror, such as by Angela Carter and Melanie Tem. In Tem's "Mama" (1998, with Steve Rasnic Tem), the revenant vampire mother eats flies in the kitchen, gnaws on her husband, and dominates her teenage daughter's life. Carter simultaneously punctures romance and the vampire role. In "The Lady of the House of Love" (1979), Dracula's last descendant is trapped by her vampire nature. Though she preys on travelers, she mostly devours small creatures. A victim of the fantasy of romance, she dies having fallen in love with a young wartime bicyclist, leaving the unaware young man a blood-filled rose.

Contemporary women writers have found in the figure of the vampire marvelous potential for radical reappropriation. Vampires and romantic relationships, both heterosexual and homoerotic, are aligned in Anne Rice's work (such as *Interview with the Vampire*, 1976), as they are in Poppy Z. Brite's *Lost Souls* (1992), in which, post–Vietnam War, transitory vampire teens adopt America's neglected children, offer community, and, performing as a rock band, devour at will. Brite authored several vampire novels and stories. Like Rice's, her work is infused with the disruptive power of the erotic, focusing on the performative vampire as rock star, flâneur, and gay/lesbian/queer, figures providing social critique and highlighting and questioning the fixity of roles and behaviors. Others splice representation of vampires with crime (Laurell K. Hamilton's *Anita Blake, Vampire Hunter* series, nineteen novels from 1993 to 2010; Sherry Gottlieb's *Love Bites,* 1994), time travel (Chelsea Quinn Yarbro's *Count Saint-Germain*, nineteen novels from 1978 to 2010), and romantic fictions building on the lesbian relations in J. Sheridan Le Fanu's *Carmilla* (1872) in the works of such writers as Jeanne Kalogridis (*The Diaries of the Family Dracul* series, 1995–1997), Jewelle Gomez (*The Gilda Stories,* 1992), and Victoria Brownworth's collection *Night Bites* (1996). In popular fiction and media, Charlaine Harris's *Sookie Stackhouse* novels (2008–2011, televised as *True Blood*, 2008–2014) built on the popularity of Joss Whedon's television series *Buffy the Vampire Slayer* (1997–2003), each problematizing representations of vampires as the Other, seeing them as likely to live alongside regular humans in small towns, high schools, and colleges. In this vein, Nina Auerbach celebrates their liberating potential: "Vampires were supposed to menace women, but to me at least, they promised protection against a destiny of girdles, spike heels and approval" (Auerbach 1995, 4). Latterly, Stephenie Meyer's *Twilight* series (since 2005) has taken an opportunity to reinforce conventional romantic traditions of the tall, dark, handsome demon lover interlacing teenage escape from boring marginality for Bella, stranded in school in Forks, Washington, with romantic involvement with the powerful, much older (128 years), assertive, masculine, protective vampire Edward Cullen. Meyer's Mormon religion–influenced series emphasizes conventional family values, a departure from the critique of vampire mothers.

In recent decades vampire literature has been taken in new and interesting directions that expand the field away from its former primary locus in European and American representations. Canadian/Jamaican/Trinidadian author Nalo Hopkinson uses soucouyants (shape-shifting witch-vampires of Caribbean folklore) to explore ageing and community values in "Greedy Choke Puppy" (2001). African American author Tananarive Due's series concerns underground African vampires known as the Life Brothers, who replay racism by treating mortals and women as worthless (*The Living Blood,* 2001). In its more radical form, the vampire is no longer abject, rejected with disgust to ensure identity (see Julia Kristeva, 1982, *The Powers of Horror),* but instead is a figure enabling recognition that the *Other* is constructed by and from a sense of self and personal fears. The vampire dramatizes endless potential for radical alternative behavior. Recent powerful examples are Moira Buffini's play/film (the latter directed by Neil Jordan) *Byzantium* (2013), which exposes historical sexual predation on women, and in contemporary times a mother and daughter reversing relationships of power with the liberation offered by vampire natures, adopted through the powers of a soucouyant. Ana Lily Amirpour's Persian-language film *A Girl Walks Home Alone at Night* (2014), which was also adapted as a graphic novel (also 2014), likewise builds on the radical female vampire figure, depicting a chadur (like a burkha)-clad, motorbike-riding female vampire in Iran.

Vampires are the epitome of metamorphosis. Transcending time, space, death, and the fixity of bodily shape, they are cultural indices of what is most questioned and feared, and they also offer radical potential to problematize whatever constrains, misrepresents, and denies.

Gina Wisker

See also: Byron, Lord; *Carmilla*; Carter, Angela; Coleridge, Samuel Taylor; *Dracula*; Due, Tananarive; *Interview with the Vampire*; Rice, Anne; Summers, Montague; Tem, Melanie; "The Vampyre"; *Varney the Vampire: or, The Feast of Blood*; Yarbro, Chelsea Quinn.

Further Reading

Auerbach, Nina. 1995. *Our Vampires, Ourselves*. Chicago, IL: University of Chicago Press.

Bunson, Matthew. 2000. *The Vampire Encyclopedia*. New York: Gramercy Books.

Carter, Margaret L. 1989. *The Vampire in Literature: A Critical Bibliography*. Ann Arbor, MI: UMI Research Press.

Creed, Barbara. 1993. *The Monstrous Feminine: Film, Feminism, Psychoanalysis*. London: Routledge.

Heldreth, Leonard G., and Mary Pharr, eds. 1999. *The Blood Is the Life: Vampires in Literature*. Bowling Green, OH: Bowling Green State University Popular Press.

Kristeva, Julia. 1982. *The Powers of Horror: An Essay on Abjection,* translated by Leon Roudiez. New York: Columbia University Press.

Punter, David. 1999. *A Companion to the Gothic*. Oxford: Blackwells.

Stoker, Bram. 1897. *Dracula*. Harmondsworth: Penguin.

Tem, Steve Rasnic, and Melanie Tem. 1995. "Mama." In *Sisters of the Night*, edited by Barbara Hambly and Martin H. Greenberg. New York: Warner Books.

"THE VAMPYRE"

"The Vampyre," an 8,000-word novelette that stands as the first vampire story in English literature, was written by Dr. John Polidori in 1816 near Lake Geneva, Switzerland, and was first published in *The New Monthly Magazine* for April 1, 1819. Polidori, Lord Byron's personal physician, had accompanied him to Lake Geneva and participated in the well-known ghost story contest during the wet summer of 1816, along with Byron and Mary and Percy Shelley.

Mary Shelley's contribution was *Frankenstein*. Byron wrote a fragment he intended to develop into a vampire story, but abandoned it after a few pages. Polidori began a novel, *Ernestus Berchtold*, but put it aside and later used Byron's fragment and knowledge of his intended outline as his inspiration to write "The Vampyre" for a lady friend. It is more notable today for its historical importance and its influence than for its literary quality. He had not intended it for publication, but the manuscript, by unclear means, came to the attention of the editor Henry Colburn, who published it without Polidori's knowledge or permission under Byron's name. It created a sensation, largely due to Byron's alleged authorship, despite protests by both Byron and Polidori. Colburn also published a chapbook version.

Polidori had taken the prevalent eighteenth-century European folk belief in vampires, corpses that leave their graves to feed on the blood of nearby living relatives, and adapted it to a Romantic literary sensibility. His character, Lord Ruthven, is no walking corpse, but a mysterious aristocratic gentleman, widely traveled, unemotional, immoral, yet fatally seductive to women. He was an obvious caricature of Byron himself. The name Ruthven came from a biting caricature of Byron in the popular novel *Glenarvon* by Byron's ex-lover, Lady Caroline Lamb.

Polidori's young protagonist, Aubrey, engages Ruthven as a mentor and tours Europe with him, but is soon appalled by his immoral behavior. Aubrey's love interest, Ianthe, is found dead from the bite of a vampire. Ruthven is later wounded by robbers, and as he dies, makes Aubrey swear an oath not to tell anyone of his death. Then Aubrey discovers Ruthven is Ianthe's murderer. Ruthven is brought back to life by moonlight, returns home, and courts Aubrey's sister, driving the oath-bound Aubrey to insanity and death. Aubrey's relationship with Ruthven has obvious parallels with Polidori's relationship with Byron.

"The Vampyre" was adapted for the French stage by Charles Nodier in 1819 and premiered as an opera in Leipzig in 1828. The story, with its image of a vampire as a seductive aristocrat, has been extremely influential, directly and indirectly, on all vampire fiction to follow, from *Varney the Vampire* (1845) through J. Sheridan Le Fanu's *Carmilla* (1871–1872) and Bram Stoker's *Dracula* (1897) down to the present day.

Lee Weinstein

See also: Byron, Lord; *Carmilla*; *Dracula*; Shelley, Mary; Vampires; *Varney the Vampire: or, The Feast of Blood.*

Further Reading

MacDonald, D. L. 1991. *Poor Polidori: A Critical Biography of the Author of "The Vampyre."* Toronto: University of Toronto Press.

Polidori, John W. 2005. *John William Polidori: "The Vampyre" and Other Writings.* Edited by Franklin Charles Bishop. Manchester: Carcanet Press.

Senf, Carol A. 1988. "Polidori's *The Vampyre*: Combining the Gothic with Realism." *North Dakota Quarterly* 56, no. 1 (Winter): 197–208.

VANDERMEER, JEFF (1968–)

Jeffrey Scott VanderMeer is a writer of fiction and nonfiction, an editor, and a publisher. He is best known for his cycle of stories and novels set in the fantastic city of Ambergris, for his *Southern Reach* trilogy of novels, and for his editorial work with his wife, Ann VanderMeer, with whom he produced a major attempt at establishing a canonical anthology of weird fiction.

VanderMeer was born in Pennsylvania, but spent some of his childhood in the Fiji Islands, where his parents worked; this stay and the subsequent trip back to the United States through Asia, Africa, and Europe had a formative impact on him, in particular on his early cycle of stories set in the fantastical city of Ambergris.

The Ambergris stories, collected in *City of Saints and Madmen* (2001), also bear the influence of Mervyn Peake's *Gormenghast* books (1946–1959) and M. John Harrison's *Viriconium* sequence (1971–1985). They bring decadence and experimental techniques to the urban fantastic mode. Two subsequent Ambergris novels have followed, *Shriek: An Afterword* (2006), which expands on the structural gameplaying of the earlier stories, and *Finch* (2009), which modernizes Ambergris and introduces noir elements.

VanderMeer's publishing and editorial work with his wife Ann has also had a significant influence on the horror field. In 1997 his publishing house, Ministry of Whimsy Press, published Stepan Chapman's award-wining *The Troika*, a novel that combines science fiction, surrealism, and body horror. Ministry of Whimsy Press has also published several anthologies of strange short fiction. With Ann, Vander-Meer has edited a number of encyclopedic anthologies, most significantly *The New Weird* (2008) and *The Weird: A Compendium of Strange and Dark Stories* (2012). *The New Weird* was an attempt to represent a mode of the fantastic that had been suggested in an earlier online discussion, a mode primarily featuring urban settings and written by authors using experimental techniques to expand the possibilities of what weird fiction, and the fantastic in general, can do. In their introduction to *The Weird*, the VanderMeers set out a thesis that the Weird is a nebulous, hybrid mode, a form of the fantastic that has mutated through contact with other types of surreal, decadent, and experimental fiction.

In 2014 VanderMeer published three novels, *Annihilation*, *Authority*, and *Acceptance*, which form the *Southern Reach Trilogy*. These works bring together cosmic horror and environmental concerns, and describe the gradual encroachment of an alien wilderness zone, Area X, on the world. VanderMeer is a long-time resident of Florida, and this location is an influence on the setting of these books. In 2016 VanderMeer published the novel *Borne*, a hallucinogenic take on apocalyptic science fiction.

VanderMeer's work in breaking down generic boundaries and opening up possibilities in the weird horror field has been of profound significance. He has won the Nebula Award, Rhysling Award, British Fantasy Award, BSFA Award, and three World Fantasy Awards, and has been a finalist for the Hugo Award.

Timothy J. Jarvis

See also: New Weird; World Fantasy Award.

Further Reading

VanderMeer, Jeff. 2008. "The New Weird: 'It's Alive?'" Introduction to *The New Weird*, edited by Ann and Jeff VanderMeer, ix–xviii. San Francisco, CA: Tachyon.

VanderMeer, Ann, and Jeff Vandermeer. 2011. Introduction to *The Weird: A Compendium of Strange and Dark Stories*, xv–xx. London: Corvus.

VARNEY THE VAMPIRE: OR, THE FEAST OF BLOOD

Varney thea Vampire: or, the Feast of Blood, by James Malcolm Rymer and Thomas Peckett Prest, is an influential English vampire narrative that appeared first as a series of penny dreadfuls in London between 1845 and 1847, when it was published as a book. One of the most popular of the Gothic horror narratives in Victorian England, Rymer and Prest's narrative drew on earlier vampire conventions and introduced new ones, influencing later writers and filmmakers.

Varney the Vampire is a long episodic tale of almost 900 pages that follows the adventures of Lord Francis Varney (the vampire) as he preys on a series of beautiful young daughters of aristocratic families in search of blood and wealth. In the course of 220 chapters, Varney stalks his victims through London, Bath, and the Continent, slowly becoming conscious of his own wretched fate and eventually committing suicide by throwing himself into Mt. Vesuvius.

Both the penny dreadful of 108 issues and the novel were highly successful, entertaining readers with tales of a wicked upper-class monster. In addition, Varney's self-awareness and despair at his condition made him sympathetic to Victorian readers, who could feel both horror of and sympathy for the vampire. Gothic horror, which combined pseudo-medieval settings with beautiful young women victimized by aristocratic men, or monsters, was a popular mid-nineteenth-century genre, and Rymer and Prest's work is an excellent example of the form in both popularity and narrative excess. They also made popular the essential structure of the vampire narrative: an unknown evil appears and threatens the young innocent women of a family and/or community; as the heroine sickens, or dies, a group of men must discover the nature of the evil, figure out how to destroy it, and finally chase it down. In the traditional narrative they succeed, but in the sympathetic variant on the vampire narrative they fail.

Like other penny dreadful writers, the authors of *Varney* were paid by the word, and as a result the narrative is full of long overwrought descriptions, convoluted plots, and formulaic language and imagery, the better to expand the word count. Despite these drawbacks, *Varney* remains important because the authors drew on earlier vampire narratives such as John Polidori's "The Vampyre" (1819) and European folklore for aspects of the vampire's character, while adding such new elements as superhuman strength, hypnotic power, the inability to eat or drink, and fangs that leave two marks in the victim's neck. These new elements were passed on to later writers whose work established them as standard conventions of the vampire narrative. Rymer and Prest should also be credited with creating the first sympathetic vampire, a character who would become an essential part of horror literature in more polished works such as J. Sheridan Le Fanu's *Carmilla* (1872), Anne Rice's *Vampire Chronicles* (1976–2014), and Stephenie Meyer's *Twilight* series (2005–2007).

Jim Holte

See also: *Carmilla*; *Dracula*; Penny Dreadful; Rice, Anne; Vampires; "The Vampyre."

Further Reading

Auerbach, Nina. 1995. *Our Vampires, Ourselves*. Chicago: University of Chicago Press.

Sensf, Carol. 2013. *The Vampire in Nineteenth Century Literature*. New York: Ace.

"The Vampire before Dracula." 2005. In *Bram Stoker's Dracula: A Documentary Volume*, edited by Elizabeth Miller, 29–97. *Dictionary of Literary Biography*, vol. 304. Detroit, MI: Gale.

VATHEK

Vathek is a Gothic novel by the English writer William Beckford, first published anonymously as *An Arabian Tale, from an Unpublished Manuscript* in 1786. Beckford claimed that it was originally composed in French, and that the published version was a translation by another hand, of which he disapproved. If that is true, he probably preferred to write in French partly as an affectation, partly because he obtained some assistance in its composition from Marianne Falque (ca. 1720–1785)—a defrocked nun forced to flee France by scandal, whose Oriental fantasy *Abbassai* (1753) is not dissimilar in style and manner, although far less excessive in its imagery—and partly because he feared that the book might not be publishable in English because it would be thought indecent.

Beckford had inherited property worth a million pounds, including the accident-prone neo-Gothic monstrosity of Fonthill Abbey. The life he led there was rumored to be debauched, but a shortage of ready money forced him to sell it before its famous tower collapsed for the last time. As nearly as any Englishman,

---

The following passages come from the closing scene of *Vathek*, in which the title character, a fabulously wealthy and decadent caliph who has sold himself to the powers of darkness, arrives at the underworld with his mistress Neuronihar. They descend through a portal and find an immense subterranean hall ruled by the demon Eblis. They soon discover that their fate is to be eternally tormented.

> In the midst of this immense hall, a vast multitude was incessantly passing, who severally kept their right hands on their hearts; without once regarding any thing around them. They had all, the livid paleness of death. Their eyes, deep sunk in their sockets, resembled those phosphoric meteors, that glimmer by night, in places of interment. Some stalked slowly on; absorbed in profound reverie: some shrieking with agony, ran furiously about like tigers, wounded with poisoned arrows; whilst others, grinding their teeth in rage, foamed along more frantic than the wildest maniac. They all avoided each other; and, though surrounded by a multitude that no one could number, each wandered at random unheedful of the rest, as if alone on a desert where no foot had trodden. (Beckford 1844, 543)
>
> . . . Almost at the same instant, the same voice announced to the Caliph, Nouronihar, the four princes, and the princess, the awful and irrevocable decree. Their hearts immediately took fire, and they, at once, lost the most precious gift of heaven—HOPE. These unhappy beings recoiled, with looks of the most furious distraction. Vathek beheld in the eyes of Nouronihar nothing but rage and vengeance; nor could she discern aught in his, but aversion and despair. (545)

Matt Cardin

Source: Beckford, William. [1786] 1844. *Vathek.* In *Cyclopaedia of English Literature.* Volume II, edited by Robert Chambers. Edinburgh: William and Robert Chambers.

Beckford lived in a fabulous palace, furnished with everything he might desire, fully equipped for the contemplation of absolutes. No one else was ever as well placed to fantasize *Vathek*.

Vathek is usually classified as a Gothic novel, and it does contain some of the same elements as the archetypal Gothic novels: a defiant and charismatic villain, a darkly obsessive interest in perverse sexuality, and a diabolical bargain that leads the eponymous protagonist to damnation. It is, however, a highly idiosyncratic production, differing from the run-of-the-mill Gothics not merely in the exoticism of its Oriental setting but the grotesquerie of its manner. Its most obvious literary debt is to Antoine Galland's *Thousand-and-One Nights*, but a more direct inspiration was probably the French Enlightenment writer and philosopher Voltaire, whom Beckford met in Paris in 1777, who had adapted Oriental tales to his satirical philosophical purposes. Within that tradition, *Vathek* is an intriguing precursor to the Marquis de Sade's elaborately extended *contes philosophiques* (philosophical fables), which proposed that morality is an arbitrary and hollow sham, and that there is nothing in Nature to deny the powerful the right to indulge themselves to the fullest in the perverse pleasure of perpetrating horrors. In the story, Caliph Vathek goes forth in search of a similar extreme.

Whereas the legendary philosopher-magician Faust bargained with the devil for enlightenment, pleasure, and profit, Vathek feels that he has little to gain in such mundane directions. He wants to go beyond mere matters of pleasure and profit toward some final and absolute evil. The fate that claims him at the end is not the kind of petty damnation that was later to claim such Gothic villains as Matthew Gregory Lewis's *The Monk* (1796), but the revelation that the archfiend Eblis has no such absolute to offer. Vathek's own hell is the realization that his boundless desires must remain forever unsatisfied, encapsulated in the limited hellfire that cages but never consumes the heart, leaving all the yearnings of the flesh intact while it mocks all ambition, emotion, and enlightenment. The only subsequent writer who came close to matching such imagery was Lord Byron in his own Faustian fantasy *Manfred* (1817).

Brian Stableford

See also: Devils and Demons; Gothic Hero/Villain; *The Monk*.

Further Reading

Birkhead, Edith. 1921. "The Oriental Tale of Terror: Beckford." In *The Tale of Terror: A Study of the Gothic Romance*, 94–99. New York: E. P. Dutton.

Garrett, John. 1992. "Ending in Infinity: William Beckford's Arabian Tale." *Eighteenth-Century Fiction* 5, no. 1 (October): 15–34.

Herrnstadt, Carol May. 1967. *The Gothic Villain in William Beckford's Vathek*. Chapel Hill: University of North Carolina Press.

Hubbard, Jennifer Lee. 2004. *The Function of the Grotesque in William Beckford's Vathek*. Seattle: University of Oregon Press.

W

WAGNER, KARL EDWARD (1945–1994)

Karl Edward Wagner was an American writer, editor, and publisher of fantasy and horror fiction whose career coincides with the ascent of horror and dark fantasy as popular categories in trade publishing in the 1970s and 1980s. Wagner's earliest published work—the novels *Darkness Weaves* (1970), *Bloodstone* (1975), and *Dark Crusade* (1976), and the collections *Death Angel's Shadow* (1973) and *Night Winds* (1978)—featured his immortal Byronic swordsman Kane, a character inspired partly by Robert E. Howard's Conan the Barbarian and Richard Maturin's *Melmoth the Wanderer*, whose adventures straddled the boundary between sword-and-sorcery and horror fiction. Wagner's interest in Howard would lead him to edit three collections of the restored texts of Howard's tales of Conan, all published in 1977: *The Hour of the Dragon, The People of the Black Circle,* and *Red Nails.*

Wagner's complete short tales of the supernatural were collected in three volumes: *In a Lonely Place* (1983), *Why Not You and I* (1987), and *Exorcisms and Ecstasies* (1997). The best of these stories are informed by his familiarity with classic supernatural fiction, including "In the Pines," a variation on the theme of Oliver Onions's "The Beckoning Fair One," and "The River of Night's Dreaming," which references the work of Robert W. Chambers. His best-known story, "Sticks," first published in 1974. was both a tribute to the work of *Weird Tales* artist Lee Brown Coye and a contribution to H. P. Lovecraft's Cthulhu Mythos. Its central concept and visual image of mysterious lattice-like stick formations that are discovered in the woods, and that seemingly hold horrific supernatural or occult significance, was borrowed for the first season of HBO's *True Detective* in 2014 and also, to all appearance, by the makers of *The Blair Witch Project* (1999). "The Fourth Seal" and "Into Whose Hands" are both macabre ruminations on the modern medical profession (for which Wagner, as a nonpracticing psychiatrist, had trained), while a number of his stories—"Neither Brute Nor Human," "The Last Wolf," "Silted In," "Lost Exits," and "The Slug," among others—are macabre tales about artists undone by their own flaws and vulnerabilities, a recurring theme in his later work.

With David Drake and Jim Groce, Wagner founded the publishing imprint Carcosa, which published four collections of pulp fiction by E. Hoffmann Price, Hugh B. Cave, and Manly Wade Wellman, including the World Fantasy Award–winning *Worse Things Waiting* (1973) and *Murgrunstrumm and Others* (1977). Wagner compiled three anthologies of classic sword-and-sorcery fiction in the Echoes of Valor series between 1987 and 1991, and an anthology of medical horror stories, *Intensive Scare* (1989). Between 1980 and his death in 1994, Wagner edited fifteen volumes of *The Year's Best Horror Stories*, an annual series that, in his hands, was instrumental for celebrating the small press's important contribution to modern horror fiction.

Stefan R. Dziemianowicz

See also: Chambers, Robert W.; Cthulhu Mythos; Dark Fantasy; Howard, Robert E.; Onions, Oliver; Wellman, Manly Wade.

Further Reading

Ashley, Mike. 1996. "Wagner, Karl Edward." *St. James Guide to Fantasy Writers*, edited by David Pringle, 583–584. Detroit, MI: St. James Press.

Drake, David. 1989. "A Brief Introduction to Karl Edward Wagner." *Weird Tales* 51, no. 1 (Spring/Fall): 110–112.

Howard, John. 2014. "In Lonely Places: The Essential Horror Fiction of Karl Edward Wagner." In *Touchstones: Essays on the Fantastic*, 187–202. Staffordshire, UK: Alchemy Press.

Mayer, John. 1997. "The Dark Muse of Karl Edward Wagner." *New York Review of Science Fiction* 112, no. 1 (December): 8–17.

Schweitzer, Darrell. 1985. "Karl Edward Wagner and the Haunted Hills (and Kudzu)." In *Discovering Modern Horror Fiction*, 86–91. Mercer Island, WA: Starmont House.

WAKEFIELD, H. R. (1888–1964)

Herbert Russell Wakefield was an English writer and editor, the best of whose work is noted for its intelligence, dark sensibilities, and clever variations on existing formulas for supernatural fiction. Wakefield matriculated at Marlborough College in Summerfield House from 1902 to 1906, then attended Oxford University, where he received a second-class degree in history, and from 1912 to 1914 he served as secretary to Lord Northcliffe. Wakefield's father was Bishop of Birmingham, and in 1920, following Wakefield's service in the First World War, where he achieved the rank of lieutenant, he briefly became his father's secretary. He later joined publisher Philip Allan (some say Collins) as editor, and in 1932, with Charles Birkin, Wakefield began the editorship of the *Creeps* series, some fourteen titles of which were published before the series concluded with *The Creeps Omnibus* (1935). This latter series contained twenty-nine stories, seven of which were by Wakefield.

Wakefield's first collection of ghost stories, *They Return at Evening* (1928), was jointly published by Philip Allan and an American publisher, Appleton, Century; in "Some Remarks on Ghost Stories," M. R. James praised the volume and described the contents as "a mixed bag, from which I should remove one or two that leave a very nasty taste. Among the residue are some admirable pieces, very inventive" (James 2009, 348). This was followed by additional collections of short stories and

"He Cometh and He Passeth By": Conflicting Magics and Rival Conjurors

Wakefield's "He Cometh and He Passeth By" was first published in 1928 in his supernatural fiction collection *They Return at Evening*. The story is a simple one and easily described: after his old friend Philip Franton is killed by magic sent by Oscar Clinton, successful barrister Edward Bellamy enlists the aid of rival magician Mr. Solan, studies magic himself, and ultimately causes Clinton to destroy himself via the same magic he used to destroy Franton.

The plot is clearly inspired by M. R. James's "Casting the Runes" (1911), in which a magical paper must be returned to its sender or the recipient will die miserably. Nevertheless, Wakefield's is in many ways superior. First, its world is not that of academia and scholarly societies but contemporary England, solidly drawn and clearly recognizable. In addition, while James kept his sorcerous villain (Karswell) largely offstage, letting others describe his powers and imagine his malevolence, Wakefield depicts Clinton at some length: modeled on Aleister Crowley, with perhaps a dash of Harry Crosby, the man is brilliantly amoral, openly indulging in every vice, and his demonstrations of his powers are eerie and convincing. Lastly, Wakefield's characters have backstories that add to the narrative: Bellamy and Franton have a history of friendship, as do Bellamy and Mr. Solan, and Solan and Clinton know of and respect each other; indeed, Clinton praises Solan's magical abilities, while Solan states that Clinton may have the best brain of any living person.

It is these touches that add depth to Wakefield's story, for "He Cometh and He Passeth By" is not simply a story about evading a curse but, rather, a tale of conflicting and maneuvering magics wielded by rival conjurors.

Richard Bleiler

a handful of crime novels. At the time of his death, Wakefield had published more than seventy-five short stories, many of them ultimately supernatural, though with a strong element of physical horror. His ghosts were rarely metaphysical.

Largely on the strength of "He Cometh and He Passeth By" (1928), a tale of rival magicians inspired by M. R. James's "Casting the Runes," Wakefield is sometimes considered one of the writers indebted to M. R. James and referenced somewhat dismissively as one of the "James Gang." This classification and categorization does him no service, for although he lacked James's enormous intelligence, he had a far greater palette than James, a far greater awareness of the world at large, and he was capable of telling more than one kind of ghost story. Wakefield recognized that hauntings did not necessarily need to involve medieval cathedrals and manuscripts or the English public schools; indeed, hauntings could occur in the twentieth century and did not need to involve the English upper classes. Wakefield thus occasionally made use of the traditional English country estate in such works as "The Red Lodge" (published in *They Return at Evening*), but his settings included golf courses ("The Seventeenth Hole at Duncaster" in *They Return at Evening*), and could involve even used cars and American gangsters ("Used Car," 1932).

Equally diverse were his characters: the misanthropic, seething, and murderous Pownall of "Professor Pownall's Oversight" (published as "The Unseen Player" in 1928) is beautifully characterized, and his murder of the amiable, better looking, and seemingly luckier Morisson, so that he might win a chess game, is convincingly detailed, as is his fate. At a time when most popular writers were incapable of recognizing the humanity of Asians, Wakefield's "And He Shall Sing . . ." (in *They Return at Evening*) matter-of-factly makes use of Japanese as characters, one of whom is a poet; and Agatha of "Damp Sheets" (1931) is not only a strong female character but one who precipitates the action. The relatively late "The Gorge of the Churels" (1951) in many ways epitomizes Wakefield's fiction: the protagonist is Indian, and when supernaturally threatened, he turns to his ancestral faith, which is superior to Christianity at dealing with local threats.

Wakefield could likewise see new elements in an established situation: the aforementioned "Professor Pownall's Oversight" does not follow the traditional pattern of supernatural fiction but extends Pownall's feud with Morisson to a new group of chess players. Finally, Wakefield had a pleasing and occasionally puckish sense of humor: those anticipating the titular story of his collection *Imagine a Man in a Box* (1931) to be horrific, and perhaps involving coffins and premature burials, will be pleasantly surprised.

In a letter to August Derleth, quoted in editor Peter Ruber's *Arkham's Masters of Horror*, Wakefield boasted: "I had over a million words published before you'd even written one word. I'd had articles in most ever leading English periodical on a variety of subjects from Gold to Economics, from water sports to Shakespearean criticism, from Pan-Uranianism to Fox farms" (Ruber 2000, 134). This material, as well as a number of shorter works of fiction, remains uncollected. It should also be noted that Wakefield's personal life and habits led to the estrangement of most of his family; in addition, he occasionally claimed the birth date of 1890, apparently fictionalized other aspects of his life, and thoroughly frustrated future researchers by destroying most of his papers and likenesses late in his life. Finally, the date of his death appears to be 1964 rather than the 1965 stated by some reference sources. His best fiction, however, remains timeless.

Richard Bleiler

See also: "Casting the Runes"; Derleth, August; James, M. R.

Further Reading

Indick, Ben P. 1992. "H. Russell Wakefield: The Man Who Believed in Ghosts." In *Discovering Classic Horror Fiction 1*, edited by Darrell Schweitzer, 73–93. San Bernardino, CA:

Borgo Press. Rpt. in *Twentieth-Century Literary Criticism*, Vol. 120, edited by Janet Witalec. Detroit, MI: Gale.

James, Henry. [1904] 2009. "M. R. James on Ghost Stories." In *Casting the Runes and Other Ghost Stories* by Henry James, edited by Michael Cox, 337–352. Oxford World's Classics. Oxford and New York: Oxford University Press.

Ruber, Peter. 2000. "H. Russell Wakefield." In *Arkham's Masters of Horror*, edited by Peter Ruber, 130–135. Sauk City, WI: Arkham House.

WALPOLE, HORACE (1717–1797)

The youngest son of Great Britain's first prime minister, Horace Walpole lived an extravagant life of opulence and privilege typical of many eighteenth-century aristocrats. He was also a voluminous writer whose letters have provided historians with much insight into the political, cultural, and social aspects of the eighteenth century, and his role in the development of the horror genre cannot be overlooked or overstated. It was not until he was in his late forties that he published *The Castle of Otranto* (1764), a strange work that established the genre of Gothic fiction. As the progenitor of the Gothic, Walpole laid the foundation for what would become the most popular type of literary fiction by the end of the century, directly influencing writers such as Ann Radcliffe and Matthew Lewis. Walpole's achievements have left a lasting impact on the horror genre, with writers such as Stephen King remarking on his importance to the field.

In the middle of the eighteenth century there was a resurgence of interest in the medieval period among historians, antiquarians, and other intellectuals. Walpole was among those who were fascinated with the Middle Ages, not seeing it as a dark period in history but rather as a more ideal era than previously believed. Using his vast wealth, Walpole constructed a Gothic castle at Strawberry Hill for his personal amusement. His castle, an artificial eighteenth-century construction designed to look ancient, not only influenced others to create similar structures in the eighteenth and nineteenth centuries, such as William Beckford's Fonthill Abbey and the Houses of Parliament, but it also served to inspire Walpole in his later literary endeavors. Claiming it came to him in a dream one night in Strawberry Hill, Walpole conceived of the idea to write a Gothic story, called so because of the word's association with the medieval period, which would take shape as *The Castle of Otranto*. Unsure of how the reading public would receive his text, Walpole published it anonymously under a fictitious identity who claimed it was a modern translation of a sixteenth-century Italian text. As his novel proved an immediate success, Walpole claimed ownership of his work and republished it in a new edition with an introduction that declared it was the first of a new genre of romance, one that blends the old and new: the Gothic. In 1766, Walpole wrote a Gothic play entitled *The Mysterious Mother*. However, because his play featured incest between a mother and son, he was again unsure how it would be received, and it was thus only distributed in small numbers to close friends during his lifetime.

Inheriting his family's earldom in 1791, Walpole died six years later in 1797 at the age of seventy-nine. He left behind a vast art collection, numerous writings, and a significant legacy in horror fiction.

Joel T. Terranova

See also: The Castle of Otranto; The Haunted House or Castle; Lewis, Matthew Gregory; Radcliffe, Ann.

Further Reading

Kallich, Martin. 1971. *Horace Walpole*. New York: Twayne.
Mowl, Timothy. 1998. *Horace Walpole: The Great Outsider*. London: Faber and Faber.
Sabor, Peter. 2013. *Horace Walpole: The Critical Heritage*. New York: Routledge.

WANDREI, DONALD (1908–1987)

To readers of horror, Donald Wandrei is first remembered as the co-founder of Arkham House publishers, and as co-editor of H. P. Lovecraft's *Selected Letters*. Less known is his genre fiction, produced in the 1930s with the encouragement of his friends, Lovecraft and Clark Ashton Smith, and made available in recent years in *Colossus* (1989), *Don't Dream: The Collected Fantasy and Horror of Donald Wandrei* (1997), and *Frost* (2000), which collect his science fiction, horror stories, and mysteries, respectively. While critics and readers mostly dismiss much of this work as being of poor quality, especially the bulk of the science fiction, the best of Wandrei's fiction is distinctive and exceptional.

Donald Albert Wandrei was born and raised in St. Paul, Minnesota, and he spent most of his life living there in his parents' house. He suffered a lifetime of vivid nightmares, which disposed him toward writing horror stories, stocked his psyche with unearthly imagery, and provided him an intuitive grasp of the Lovecraftian "stricken awe" that arises from glimpses of the nonhuman universe. Horror and science fiction legend Fritz Leiber, who, like Wandrei, was among the writers whose talent Lovecraft nurtured, famously said he thought Wandrei seemed Lovecraft's most obvious successor.

Though a few brief, moody pieces transcribe Wandrei's bizarre nightly visions—such as "The Crater" (1967), "Nightmare" (1965), and "The Lady in Gray" (1933—his best work finds Wandrei mining them for startling images, dreamlike strangeness, and incursions of the terrifying and the irrational. In "The Painted Mirror" (1937; dramatized on the horror television series *Night Gallery* in the 1970s), a young boy discovers such a thing in an attic, and chipping away the paint reveals a vague, terrible landscape with the figure of a girl in the distance. Each night as he scrapes, the girl draws closer; at the end of this Borgesian tale, the girl/entity switches souls with the boy and paints over the mirror. In "The Eye and the Finger" (1944), this pair of disembodied objects nightmarishly plagues the main character, hovering in his living room, staring, pointing. "Uneasy Lie the Drowned" (1937), a neglected classic of weird fiction, tells of revenge reaching out from an unlived other life.

While these true-felt horror stories are arguably his finest productions, Wandrei's best science fiction, like that of his friend Smith, is imbued with strong elements of horror as well. An exceptional set of otherwise widely different stories— "Giant-Plasm" (1939), "The Crystal Bullet" (1941), "Something from Above" (1930), and "The Monster from Nowhere" (1935)—finds characters terrified or destroyed by mere chance encounters with alien beings. The nightmarish intrusions here come not from the supernatural, but the abyss of space. One of Wandrei's last works is a fine novel of cosmic terror, *The Web of Easter Island* (1948), which has been out of print for more than fifty years, though an early draft (*Dead Titans, Awaken!*) has recently been made available.

Beyond prose, the young Wandrei was an acolyte of Smith and George Sterling, and produced Dark Romantic and fantastically themed poems of considerable quality. As can be said of much of Wandrei's work: these are difficult to find today, but are worth the search.

Steve Behrends

See also: Arkham House; Derleth, August; Leiber, Fritz; Lovecraft, H. P.; *Weird Tales.*

Further Reading

Behrends, Steve. 1988. "Something from Above: The Imaginative Fiction of Donald Wandrei." *Studies in Weird Fiction* 3 (Fall): 22–34.

Klein, T. E. D. 2009. "Donald Wandrei: A Haunted House." In *Conversations with the Weird Tales Circle*, edited by John Pelan and Jerard Walters, 541–543. Lake Wood, CO: Centipede Press. Originally published in *Studies in Weird Fiction* 6: 35–36 (Fall 1988).

Ruber, Peter. 2000. "Donald Wandrei." In *Arkham's Masters of Horror*, edited by Peter Ruber, 64–68. Sauk City, WI: Arkham House.

Schwartz, Julius. 2009. "Donald Wandrei." In *Conversations with the Weird Tales Circle*, edited by John Pelan and Jerard Walters, 534–540. Lake Wood, CO: Centipede Press.

Tierney, Richard L. 1989. "Introduction: Donald A. Wandrei." In *Colossus: The Collected Fiction of Donald A. Wandrei*, ix–xxix. Minneapolis: Fedogan & Bremer.

WEIRD TALES

Weird Tales was an American pulp fiction magazine published between 1923 and 1954 that, in its initial run of 279 issues, featured the work of most significant writers of horror and fantasy fiction in America in the first half of the twentieth century. Its impact on the shape and direction taken by modern weird fiction is incalculable.

Weird Tales debuted in March 1923 under the editorship of Edwin Baird, a fiction writer who also edited its sister magazine, *Real Detective Tales and Mystery*

Stories. Although *Weird Tales* was subtitled "The Unique Magazine," the thirteen issues that Baird edited through the mid-1924 issue were full of mostly run-of-the-mill neo-Gothic potboiler stories. Baird published little fiction of note, but under his editorship he introduced readers to the work of H. P. Lovecraft, Clark Ashton Smith, and Seabury Quinn, all of whom became distinguished contributors during the magazine's golden age.

Having failed to find a supportive readership—even after enlisting the services of celebrity magician Harry Houdini, who put his name on several ghost-written stories published in the magazine in early 1924—*Weird Tales* went on hiatus after the May/June/July 1924 issue. It resumed publication with the November 1924 issue with a new editor, former contributor and first reader Farnsworth Wright. Unlike Baird, Wright was enthusiastic about weird fiction, and the magazine flourished artistically, if not financially, under his stewardship. The 1930s were the magazine's greatest years as Wright published stories that attested to the diversity and variety of the weird tale as it had evolved in *Weird Tales*: Clark Ashton Smith's imaginary world fantasies, Robert E. Howard's sword-and-sorcery tales of Conan the Conqueror, Henry S. Whitehead's tales of occult marvels in the West Indies, August Derleth's traditional ghost stories, Mary Elizabeth Counselman's Southern Gothic tales, Seabury Quinn's psychic detective series featuring Jules de Grandin, Edmond Hamilton and C. L. Moore's scientific fantasies, and stories by H. P. Lovecraft that would later be acknowledged as the foundation for the shared fictional universe known today as the Cthulhu Mythos. Contributions to the Cthulhu Mythos also helped to launch the careers of Robert Bloch and Henry Kuttner, who would earn distinction for work independent of Lovecraft's influence. It was during these years that *Weird Tales* also enlisted the services of artists whose names would become synonymous with that of the magazine: Margaret Brundage, who was known for her cover images of scantily clad, sexually alluring women, and Virgil Finlay, whose black-and-white interior art had a distinctive photorealistic character.

Weird Tales was sold in late 1938 and its offices moved from Chicago to New York. Wright continued to edit the magazine through the March 1940 issue, after which he was replaced by Dorothy McIlwraith, who also edited the new publisher's general fiction magazine *Short Stories*. Nearly a year before Wright's departure the magazine had shifted from monthly to bi-monthly publication as a cost-saving measure. Although the character of *Weird Tales* changed during the McIlwraith years, the magazine continued to feature work from a lineup of stalwart contributors including Bloch, Derleth (under his own name and his Stephen Grendon pseudonym), and Quinn. Manly Wade Wellman became a regular contributor with his tales of supernatural investigator John Thunstone, as did Ray Bradbury with his modern American Gothic stories. Other contributors of note included Fritz Leiber, Joseph Payne Brennan, Harold Lawlor, and Alison V. Harding. Many stories first published in *Weird Tales* by these authors would be collected in books published by Arkham House, a publishing company started in 1939 by August Derleth and

Donald Wandrei with whom the magazine developed a close relationship in the 1940s and 1950s. Faced with the same financial pressures and competition from paperbacks and comic books that killed off other pulp magazines, *Weird Tales* shrank to digest size with the September 1953 issue and ceased publication after the September 1954 issue.

Weird Tales has been revived several times since its original run: for four issues edited by Sam Moskowitz between 1973 and 1974, and for four mass-market paperback anthologies edited by Lin Carter between 1981 and 1983. The two issues edited by Gordon M. D. Garb between 1984 and 1985 were notable for publishing mostly new stories rather than reprints, a trend that continued with subsequent revivals. Between 1988 and 2016, *Weird Tales* published seventy-two issues under a variety of editors, including four issues published between 1994 and 1996 when the magazine's name briefly changed to *Worlds of Fantasy & Horror*.

Stefan R. Dziemianowicz

See also: Arkham House; Bloch, Robert; Bradbury, Ray; Brennan, Joseph Payne; Derleth, August; Howard, Robert E.; Kuttner, Henry; Leiber, Fritz; Lovecraft, H. P.; Pulp Horror; Quinn, Seabury; Smith, Clark Ashton; Wellman, Manly Wade; Whitehead, Henry S.

Further Reading

Everett, Justin, and Jeffrey H. Shanks. 2015. *The Unique Legacy of Weird Tales: The Evolution of Modern Fantasy and Horror*. Lanham, MD: Rowman & Littlefield.

Weinberg, Robert. 1999. *The Weird Tales Story*. Berkeley Heights, NJ: Wildside Press.

WELLMAN, MANLY WADE (1903–1986)

Manly Wade Wellman was an American writer who is best remembered today for his supernatural fiction, especially for his stories of John the Balladeer, which appeared in *The Magazine of Fantasy and Science Fiction* in the 1950s and early 1960s and were collected in the Arkham House volume *Who Fears the Devil?* (1963).

Wellman was born to missionary parents in Portuguese East Africa (now Angola), where he lived with native children and spoke their language before he spoke English. His family returned to the United States, where he was educated in Washington, D.C., Salt Lake City, and Wichita, Kansas. In the 1920s he became friends with a noted folklorist and took many trips through the Ozark Mountains. Later, after a time in New York, Wellman settled with his own family in North Carolina. Culturally, Wellman was a Southerner and always identified himself as such.

He began writing for the pulps in his mid-twenties, with his first story appearing in *Thrilling Tales* in 1927. Soon he was contributing to *Astounding Science Fiction, Thrilling Wonder, Startling Stories*, and *Weird Tales*. He wrote one genuinely distinguished science fiction novel, *Twice in Time*, published in *Startling Stories* in

1940 and reprinted many times since, about a time-traveler who becomes the figure known to history as Leonardo Da Vinci. Wellman also contributed one novel in the Captain Future space-opera series, then moved on to comic books. He also wrote nonfiction and juvenile fiction about the South and its Civil War heroes.

His character John the Balladeer is a wandering singer who travels the backwoods of Appalachia, encountering folkloric spooks, many of which are the subjects of the songs that John sings. The lyrics quoted in the stories are more often than not Wellman's own and are excellent examples of what folklore scholars call "fakelore," that is, items or motifs that sound absolutely authentic but are not. In 2004 singer Joe Bethancourt released an album of the songs of John the Balladeer, with Wellman's lyrics occasionally expanded by Bethancourt and set to traditional melodies.

Wellman's other series characters, notably Judge Pursuivant and John Thunstone, whose adventures appeared in *Weird Tales* in the 1930s and 1940s, also regularly confront supernatural menaces. Pursuivant is retired, but, vastly learned in both legal and occult lore, he sallies forth from his home in West Virginia to do battle with evil. John Thunstone is a playboy Manhattanite who carries a sword cane, but he, too, is learned in the occult and adept at disposing of demonic menaces. Thunstone in particular is an idealization of Wellman himself, a huge, burly man with a moustache, a man of action who is also learned, sophisticated, and a proper gentleman. (Wellman was himself a large, muscular man with a moustache, educated, gracious, etc.)

The majority of the lore in the Wellman stories is by no means made up. Indeed, his greatest strength is the authenticity of the settings he depicts, drawn from those Ozark trips in his youth and from his own long residence in the North Carolina mountains. He was, like Stephen Vincent Benet, one of the genuinely American fantasy writers, drawing on uniquely American motifs and subject matter. Nevertheless, he does invent, sometimes very persuasively, most strikingly in the Thunstone series with the legend of the Shonokins, a dispossessed race that preceded the American Indians, perhaps descended from Neanderthals. The Shonokins are the ancient enemies of the rest of mankind, who work sinister magic but have strange limitations and seek to regain mastery of the Earth. As these stories appeared in *Weird Tales* at about the same time as Richard Shaver's "Shaver Mystery" stories (which pretended to be based on fact, also involving sinister ancient races), some readers who were duped by Shaver also began to wonder if the Shonokins might also be real.

After a hiatus in the 1960s, Wellman returned to the fantasy field to much acclaim in the 1970s. He wrote five novels about John the Balladeer (this remained Wellman's preferred term, despite the publisher's coinage of "Silver John"). There were also three John Thunstone novels. An expanded volume, *John the Balladeer*, containing additional stories written later in Wellman's career, appeared in 1988. Several of his stories have been adapted for television, most notably "The Valley Was Still" as "Still Valley" on *The Twilight Zone* in 1961. *Who Fears the Devil?* was filmed badly with the insulting title of *The Legend of Hillbilly John* in 1972. Wellman despised the film.

Darrell Schweitzer

See also: Arkham House; Dark Fantasy; *Weird Tales.*

Further Reading

Elliot, Jeffrey M. 1982. "Manly Wade Wellman: Better Things Waiting" (interview). In *Fantasy Voices: Interviews with American Fantasy Writers,* edited by Jeffrey M. Elliot, 5–18. San Bernardino, CA: Borgo Press.

Jones, Jeremy L. C. 2014. "Dark Hearts & Brilliant Patches of Honor: A Tribute to Manly Wade Wellman." *Clarkesworld* 89 (February). http://clarkesworldmagazine.com/wellman_interview.

Meyers, Walter E. 1985. "Manly Wade Wellman." In *Supernatural Fiction Writers,* edited by E. F. Bleiler, 947–954. New York: Scribner's.

Schweitzer, Darrell. 1994. "Manly Wade Wellman" (interview). In *Speaking of Horror: Interviews with Writers of the Supernatural,* 93–101. San Bernardino, CA: Borgo Press.

WELLS, H. G. (1866–1946)

Herbert George Wells was a prolific British author and social thinker. Through his imaginative blend of science and speculation, Wells laid the foundations for twentieth-century science fiction and horror literature. One of the most popular writers of his day, Wells published dozens of books and short stories, beginning with his early science fiction in the late nineteenth century. In later life he devoted himself more frequently to realist novels and political tracts, writing new work until his death in 1946.

Wells was born to a lower-middle-class family in Kent. Originally a draper's apprentice, the academically gifted Wells eventually succeeded in establishing a teaching career. After publishing short newspaper pieces, Wells produced a series of "scientific romances," beginning with *The Time Machine* in 1896. These imaginative fictions, heavily informed by contemporary scientific discoveries, launched his literary fame.

Most frequently in his fiction and commentary, Wells attacked the complacency of polite society, seeking to fire the imagination of his readers with novel imagery and perspectives. As a futurist, Wells called up visions of technologically advanced civilizations, often under the control of powerful political oligarchies (*When the Sleeper Wakes,* 1899), as well as utopian states built upon rational lines (*A Modern Utopia,* 1905; *The Shape of Things to Come,* 1933). Most often, these visions of the future emphasize the alienating and violent consequences of technological progress, confronting everyday life with strangely transformed human beings (as in 1897's *The Invisible Man* and the chemically produced giants of 1904's *The Food of the Gods*), or the ravages of technological warfare. Wells is often credited as the source for such concepts as the time machine, the tank ("The Land Ironclads," 1903), and the atomic bomb (*The World Set Free*, 1914).

From his training in biology, Wells also liberally applied concepts from natural history to his thought, most notably the pressures of evolution on humans and civilization (such as the splitting of humankind into two species in *The Time Machine*, or the Martian invaders of 1898's *The War of the Worlds*, evolved into ambulatory brains). Wells repeatedly emphasized the startling commonalities between human beings and the animal world, most strongly in 1896's *The Island of Doctor Moreau*.

Wells's influence since his death in London in 1946 has been significant and wide-reaching. His works are continually adapted and retold, owing to the continued relevance of the ethical and practical problems of technology and human identity that he proposed.

Miles Link

See also: *The Invisible Man*; *The Island of Doctor Moreau*; Mad Scientist; *The Night Land*.

Further Reading

Carey, John. 1992. *The Intellectuals and the Masses: Pride and Prejudice among the Literary Intelligentsia, 1880–1939*. London: Faber.

Hillegas, Mark. 1967. *The Future as Nightmare: H. G. Wells and the Anti-Utopians*. New York: Oxford University Press.

Wells, Herbert George. 1934. *Experiment in Autobiography*. London: Victor Gollancz.

West, Anthony. 1984. *H. G. Wells: Aspects of a Life*. New York: Random House.

WELTY, EUDORA (1909–2001)

In her ninety-two years, Eudora Alice Welty became a canonical American literary figure, who was also associated with the Southern Gothic genre. Welty was born in Jackson, Mississippi, on April 13, 1909 and died there on July 23, 2001. Southern settings constructed from both nostalgic dreams and twisted nightmares are a common backdrop for her fiction. She was an author who experimented with and had a complex relationship to genre fiction in its many forms. Some scholars, such as Mitch Frye, see traces of "Southern Fantastic" in Welty's style. Frye defines this categorization as a "mutant form that borrows provocatively from the speculative fiction genres of dystopia, fantasy, science fiction, and the weird tale" (Frye 2013, 75–76). Indeed, her special brand of domestic horror lapses into dark fantasy and the weird.

Welty is generally considered proximal to the horror genre: an important author who chose to "dabble in the supernatural and the psychotic" (Fonseca and Pulliam 1999, 24). Yet she had an understanding of and appreciation for horror fiction. As Suzanne Marrs has suggested, Welty's prose can be humorous and simultaneously "hauntingly enigmatic" (Marrs 2005, ix). Welty's narratives expose the deeply insightful within the everyday, through "the comic horror of the small town" (Marrs 2005, ix) or a "tortured interior monologue" (Marrs 2005, x). At times, as in "The Wanderers" (1949), her grotesque reflections juxtapose the horrors of life and love, always with a genteel, perceptive, and elusive lilt, even when decapitation is involved.

Welty produced a substantial corpus of literature during her lifetime, from her early short stories, such as "Death of a Traveling Salesman" and "Magic" (both published in 1936), to her later nonfiction, such as *One Writer's Beginning* (1984). Her major creative works include two novels, four collections, and four novellas.

Of Welty's vast literary output, critics such as David Pringle suggest that *The Wide Net and Other Stories* (1943) contains the best examples of her horror fiction. Darker elements run through "The Wide Net" that connect Welty's allusions to the rape and murder of a pregnant woman to a still more grim tradition of horror tales. "A Still Moment" conveys, in the narrated perception of one of its characters, "horror in its purity and clarity" (Welty 1998, 238), punctuated by an ephemeral surrealist vision that reinforces her dark aesthetic. She plays with notions of time, distorting them to evoke suspense, dread, or terror. *The Wide Net and Other Stories* initially divided critics. At the time, some reviewers concluded that the collection was filled with impropriety, while others argued that Welty had developed "her vision of *horror* to the point of nightmare" by examining "the clear day-to-day horror of actual life" and "the horror of dreams" (Trilling 1943, 386–387). Joyce Carol Oates sees strong horror themes in Welty's later works. She notes that Welty's short story "The Demonstrators" (1966), with its "unfocused horror" and depiction of racial tensions, "is horrible" and that "the grotesque has been assimilated deftly into the ordinary, the natural" (Oates 1969, 57).

Not only was Welty adept at portraying realistic horror, as in the evocation of the civil rights era in "The Demonstrators," but she effectively wrote fantastic fairy tale horror more reminiscent of the Brothers Grimm as well. Her first novella, *The Robber Bridegroom* (1942), is frequently analyzed for its use of dark fantasy. Studies by Eunice Glenn, Sally McMillan, Rosella Orzo, and Richard Gray explore Welty's morbid use of fairy tales and the manipulation or "conjuring" of what Glenn once called "scenes of horror" tinctured by Poe and Kafka (Glenn 1947, 81, 90). Sometimes dubbed a "Southern fried fairy tale," Welty's novella merges the Grimms' original fairy tales with American folklore. A unique blend of realistic and fantastic, *The Robber Bridegroom* depicts bloody violence, torture, and death in a Southern setting (the Natchez Trace) populated by legendary and savage outlaws. The violation of an unnamed native girl in the novella shocks the reader out of fairy tale mode, and through legend ties it to brutal realistic events. In her 1975 essay "Fairy Tales of the Natchez Trace," Welty describes how she embedded horror in her reimagining of "The Robber Bridegroom." But she contended that Grimm's horror exceeds even her own. Her use of these dark stories harkens back to their primary function as horror tales that shock and moralize through fable.

On her own admission, Welty led a sheltered life. Yet within her many macabre and fantastic fictional worlds, there is an undeniable magnitude and depth. Welty was radical and fearless in her exploration of genre, and this extended to her use of horror motifs. In 1969, Joyce Carol Oates extolled the beauty and brutality of what she deemed Welty's "unintended" horror fiction (54). However, Welty was well versed in horror literature, and her appreciation for and interest in classic horror is evident in reviews such as "Ghoulies, Ghosties, and Jumbees" (1944), where she examines "[g]ood, dependable horror conjurers" like M. R. James, Algernon Blackwood, August Derleth, John Collier, and H. P. Lovecraft, differentiating between "comfort horror" and weird tales (5).

Welty's strange fantasies and distorted realities have had a far-reaching impact. In a 2006 *New York Times* interview, Stephen King cites Welty as a new literary influence for his novel *Lisey's Story*. Michael McDowell's fiction has been shaped by the stylistic extravagance of Welty, through her use of Southern Gothic and horror. Her innovations, created by mixing genre conventions, garnered her much acclaim. Welty received a Pulitzer Prize in 1972, thirty-nine honorary degrees, eight O. Henry Awards, the Medal of Freedom, and numerous other prestigious accolades.

By the time Welty died in 2001 of cardiopulmonary failure, she had already cast a mythic shadow over the literary landscape. In recent years, scholarship on the Weird South, the Gothic South, and the Fantastic South has increased for a variety of complex reasons related to the institutionalization of Gothic studies in the American canon and changing notions of genre. As a result, there is renewed interest in the darker aspects of Welty's fiction.

Naomi Simone Borwein

See also: Dark Fantasy; Faulkner, William; The Grotesque; McDowell, Michael; Surrealism.

Further Reading

Fonseca, Anthony J., and June Michele Pulliam. 1999. *Hooked on Horror: A Guide to Reading Interests in Horror Fiction*. Westport, CT: Libraries Unlimited.

Frye, Mitch. 2013. "Astonishing Stories: Eudora Welty and the Weird Tale." *Eudora Welty Review* 5: 75–93.

Glenn, Eunice. 1947. "Fantasy in the Fiction of Eudora Welty." In *A Southern Vanguard*, edited by Allan Tate, 78–91. New York: Prentice-Hall.

Marrs, Suzanne. 2005. "Introduction." In *Eudora Welty: A Biography*, ix–xix. New York: Houghton Mifflin.

Oates, Joyce Carol. 1969. "The Art of Eudora Welty." *Shenandoah* 20 (Spring): 54–57.

Trilling, Diana. 1943. "Fiction in Review." *Nation* CLVII, October 2: 386–387.

Welty, Eudora. 1944. "Ghoulies, Ghosties, and Jumbees." *New York Times Book Review*, September 24: 5, 21.

Welty, Eudora. 1978. "Fairy Tales of the Natchez Trace." In *The Eye of the Story: Selected Essays and Reviews*, 306. New York: Vintage Books.

Welty, Eudora. 1998. *Eudora Welty: Stories, Essays & Memoir*. New York: Library of America.
Weston, Ruth D. 1994. *Gothic Traditions and Narrative Techniques in the Fiction of Eudora Welty*. Baton Rouge and London: Louisiana State University Press.

THE WEREWOLF OF PARIS

The Werewolf of Paris is a historical horror novel written by Guy Endore and published in 1933. The book is narrated by an unnamed American who travels to Paris to complete his PhD and discovers a testimony written in 1871 by Aymar Galliez in defense of a man called Sergeant Bertrand. Galliez's testimony tells the story of Bertrand Caillet, the werewolf of the title, and the various crimes this man has committed. It follows Bertrand into the National Guard during the Franco-Prussian War, ending with his capture and incarceration during the Paris Commune of 1870–1871.

The lycanthropic Bertrand was born to a servant in the employment of Galliez's aunt. The book's title leaves little mystery as to the nature of this young man, and so the early chapters are concerned with Galliez's attempts to come to terms with the "monster" who resides under his roof. Prior to the introduction of the main characters, the reader is told a family history from the Middle Ages. When Jehan Pitamont murdered two members of the rival noble Pitaval family, he was consigned to an *oubliette* (a small dungeon accessible only from a hatch in the ceiling), fed only on chunks of meat thrown into his prison, and gradually became little more than a wild animal. Centuries later, a descendant of Jehan Pitamont, a priest, raped a teenaged servant girl called Josephine, leaving her pregnant (Bertrand's mother). Lycanthropy in this novel is treated as a congenital condition—indeed, in a later chapter of the novel, a doctor misreads some of Bertrand's symptoms as those of "hereditary syphilis," before consigning him to a cell in an asylum that serves as a modern version of the *oubliette*.

The suggestion that lycanthropy is the product of the degenerate aristocracy fits with the setting of the Paris Commune. Particularly in the novel's early chapters, there is implicit criticism of the upper classes and the bourgeoisie. However, this is combined with a rather unsympathetic portrait of the communards and their cause, with Galliez coming to believe that the revolutionaries are themselves a race of werewolves. The book is characterized by brutality and violence, including sexual violence enacted toward women, and Bertrand ends up in a relationship with a masochistic young woman named Sophie whose relationship to the Commune is ambiguous. Nevertheless, the storytelling style, in which Galliez's matter-of-fact tone is mediated through the detached narration of the unnamed American, encourages the reader to view these acts with distaste and horror.

The Werewolf of Paris reached number 1 on the *New York Times* best-seller list when it was first published, and it remains a cult classic. It was adapted for the screen as *The Curse of the Werewolf* (1961), though the setting was altered and the political content removed.

Hannah Priest

See also: Monsters; Werewolves.

Further Reading

Martin, Carl Grey. 2014. "Guy Endore's Dialectical Werewolf." *Le Monde diplomatique*, September 15. http://mondediplo.com/outsidein/guy-endore-s-dialectical-werewolf.
Stableford, Brian. 1983. "The Werewolf of Paris." In *Survey of Modern Fantasy Literature*, vol. 5, edited by Frank N. Magill, 2102–2106. Englewood Cliffs, NJ: Salem Press.

WEREWOLVES

The werewolf has been a popular and ubiquitous presence in folklore, mythology, and literature for centuries, almost always taking the form of a human capable of shape-shifting into a wolf or wolf-like hybrid under certain conditions. Half-human and half-animal, the werewolf has long been a powerful and versatile symbol; a liminal figure (that is, one existing on the boundary or threshold between two distinct realms) representing the eruption of the wild into civilization, the beast within the human soul, the werewolf is unable to be fully reconciled with the human *or* the animal. It is, as such, an endlessly malleable symbol, appearing time and again in popular culture when chaos threatens to disturb an established order.

Some Notable Werewolf Fictions

Literary:

1896	*The Were-Wolf* by Clemence Housman
1933	*The Werewolf of Paris* by Guy Endore
1944	*Darker Than You Think* by Jack Williamson
1977	*The Howling* by Gary Brandner
1978	*The Wolfen* by Whitley Strieber
1979	*The Bloody Chamber* by Angela Carter (featuring "Wolf-Alice," "The Company of Wolves," and "The Werewolf")

Cinematic:

1935	*Werewolf of London*
1941	*The Wolf Man*
1961	*Curse of the Werewolf* (adapted from *The Werewolf of Paris*)
1981	*The Howling* (adapted from Guy Brandner's novel); *An American Werewolf in London*
1984	*The Company of Wolves* (based on Angela Carter's story)
1994	*Wolf*
2000	*Ginger Snaps*

Matt Cardin

The modern-day werewolf has its roots in ancient folklore, such as the Greek myth of Lycaon and the Mesopotamian *Epic of Gilgamesh* (ca. 2100 BCE), and also in ancient legends from the early Christian era (ca. first century CE), which portray the werewolf as a savage, bloodthirsty beast, afflicted with an insatiable hunger for human flesh. Roman works, such as Petronius's *Satyricon* (ca. late first century CE), later used the werewolf to comedic effect, depicting mysterious men who transform into wolves under the light of the moon. Some medieval romances, by contrast, viewed the werewolf in a benevolent light: several French *lais*, including "Bisclavret" by Marie de France and the anonymous "Melion" (ca. 1200) and "Guillame de Palerme" (ca. 1200), for instance, portrayed the werewolf as a dignified creature, a pathetic victim of circumstance.

In the sixteenth century, the bloodthirsty werewolf of antiquity was revived in legends circulated across the European countryside, which influenced later depictions of the werewolf in nineteenth-century Gothic novels such as Sutherland Menzies's *Hugue the Wer-Wolf* (1838), an early example of a psychological study of lycanthropy, and G. W. M. Reynolds's *Wagner the Wehr-Wolf* (1847), in which a lonely man makes a deal with the devil, becoming a werewolf in exchange for wealth and eternal youth. Though Wagner regrets his decision, he is condemned to prey upon the human species for eighteen months. Other nineteenth-century texts also drew on legends of the werewolf as a bloodthirsty, violent creature: the were-protagonist of Prosper Mérimée's novella "Lokis" (1869), for instance, murders his wife with a bite to the throat, while Arthur Conan Doyle's werewolf in "A Pastoral Horror" (1890) commits a string of bloody murders while in his wolf-like state. Female werewolves in nineteenth-century Gothic literature proved to be as savage as their male counterparts, often using their sexually enticing human forms as lures for potential male victims. In Clemence Housman's acclaimed Gothic novel *The Were-Wolf* (1896), the rapacious female werewolf can only be killed by one whose blood is as pure as Christ's.

The bloodthirsty werewolf of antiquity and of nineteenth-century Gothic literature continued to inform depictions of the werewolf in American and British literature of the first half of the twentieth century, despite the rise of the tragic, sympathetic werewolf in popular American horror films such as Stuart Walker's *Werewolf of London* (1935) and George Waggner's *The Wolf Man* (1941). In the first decades of the twentieth century, Algernon Blackwood published a number of werewolf and similar shape-shifter stories, such as "The Camp of the Dog" (1908), "The Wendigo" (1910), and "Running Wolf" (1921), while *Weird Tales* contributed to the figure's increasing popularity with works like H. Warner Munn's *The Werewolf of Ponkert* (1925) and "The Werewolf's Daughter" (1928) and Robert E. Howard's "Wolfshead" (1926).

The savage werewolf was memorably depicted in Guy Endore's critically acclaimed *The Werewolf of Paris* (1933), arguably the most important werewolf novel ever published and widely considered by many to have done for the werewolf what *Dracula* did for the vampire. Endore's werewolf Bertrand is a violent, sadistic beast, a product of the cursed Pitamont clan who were doomed to lycanthropy as punishment for a long-standing feud with a neighboring clan. Bertrand commits impulsive, violent acts against the backdrop of a chaotic Paris during the Franco-Prussian War, leading some critics to view the novel as an allegory. The murderous werewolf—albeit this time depicted in a more complicated manner—also appears in Jack Williamson's *Darker Than You Think* (1944), a noir-influenced dark fantasy in which humans and werewolves have been involved in an eternal war for control of the planet.

Though the murderous werewolf continued to make appearances in the latter half of the twentieth century in horror novels such as Gary Brandner's *The Howling* (1977), postmodern and contemporary werewolf texts have often taken a more complicated view of the figure, especially in light of the widespread and increasing popularity of environmental movements. Whitley Strieber's well-received novels *The Wolfen* (1978) and *The Wild* (1991), for instance, depict wolf-like creatures and werewolves as means through which humans can reconcile with nature. In *The Wolfen*, the eponymous lupine beings prey upon humans as a natural check to the human population, and in *The Wild*, the werewolf functions as a conduit for reintroducing humans to nature. Twentieth-century werewolf literature has also long recognized the werewolf's potent charge as a symbol of puberty and dawning sexuality. Angela Carter's *The Bloody Chamber* (1979) features a number of werewolf stories that invoke this theme to great effect, offering new takes on girlhood and puberty with "Wolf-Alice" and powerful, feminist inversions of the Little Red Riding Hood myth in "The Company of Wolves" and "The Werewolf."

The werewolf's perennial presence in mythology, folklore, literature, and cinema has contributed to its versatility in the horror genre as an enduring and ever-changing symbol of spiritual, sexual, and psychological transformation. Forced to stand at the boundary between human and animal, the werewolf's liminal status renders it forever ambiguous, forever mutable, and forever intriguing.

Brittany Roberts

See also: Carter, Angela; Monsters; Transformation and Metamorphosis; *Weird Tales*; *The Werewolf of Paris*.

Further Reading

Jones, Stephen, ed. 2009. *The Mammoth Book of Wolf Men*. Philadelphia: Running Press.

Lowder, James, ed. 2010. *Curse of the Full Moon: A Werewolf Anthology*. Berkeley, CA: Ulysses Press.

Otten, Charlotte F., ed. 2002. *The Literary Werewolf: An Anthology*. Syracuse, NY: Syracuse University Press.

Stypczynski, Brent. A. 2013. *The Modern Literary Werewolf: A Critical Study of the Mutable Motif*. Jefferson, NC: McFarland.

WHARTON, EDITH (1862–1937)

Edith Wharton, née Edith Newbold Jones, was born in New York, and her most famous works explore the city's haute society in intricate novels of manners like

The House of Mirth (1905) and *The Age of Innocence* (1920), which have critical, naturalist, and anthropological bents, despite her vexed relations with literary naturalism. But the supernatural was also a literary avocation for her; she published about a dozen supernatural short stories. These stories almost all first appeared in lucrative, prestigious magazines, and a few are in her short story collections. Shortly after her death, the nigh-complete collection *Ghosts* (1937) appeared.

Two major interpretations of Wharton's supernatural oeuvre compete. The first interpretation concerns the violence and stultifications of domestic life in the stories. In "Kerfol" (1916), a ghost dog pack avenges a French aristocrat's brutal treatment of them and their mistress. The second interpretation discerns the stories' anxiety over class division, servants' roles, and concepts of money, inheritance, and property. "The Looking Glass" (1935) overlays messages from the dead with Wharton's interest in con artists and business swindlers (from texts like "A Cup of Cold Water," 1899). Ghostly epistles also factor in "Pomegranate Seed" (1931); a wife intercepts a letter from her husband's dead first wife and, in an

"Afterward": A Classic Tale of Greed and Ghostly Retribution

The status of Wharton's "Afterward" (1910) as one of the great ghost stories in American literature is implied by its appearance in the 1996 collection *American Gothic Tales*, edited by Joyce Carol Oates. It is still taught at universities as paradigmatic of a ghost story standard: the return of an apparition who comes to claim a symbolic (in this case financial) debt.

One way to account for the unsettling effect of "Afterward" is to explore its intriguing time register. The story's plot is straightforward, but Wharton's conceptualization of the "afterward" remains intriguing. Mary and Edward (Ned) Boyne, newly rich Americans, emigrate to a rural mansion, Lyng, in Dorsetshire, England. After her husband is taken away by a visitor to Lyng, Mary, the central consciousness of the tale, comes to realize the visitant was the ghost of a dead man named Elwell whom Ned had secretly ruined in business.

The endurance and unconscious appeal of Wharton's story may be illuminated by referring to Sigmund Freud's theory of deferred action or afterwardness ("Nachträglichkeit" in German). This theory concerns itself with how the return to consciousness of a once forgotten act may collapse any temporality that has passed between the action and its reawakening. This is the temporal register of the ghost in "Afterward," and it is foreshadowed in the story's opening lines when Mary recalls the words of a friend, uttered several months before, regarding a ghostly inhabitant at Lyng. Only now, afterward, can she make some sense of what it means to be haunted, just as she realizes, once it is too late, that Elwell has taken her husband away forever.

Matt Foley

unnerving anticlimax, finds the writing too faint to discern. Sexual and economic anxieties intertwine in "The Eyes" (1910) as a haunted Henry James– or Dorian Gray–esque narrator is unveiled, to his audience's horror, as a sterile, exploitative parasite.

Wharton lacks many direct inheritors in horror, for during her lifetime pulps came to dominate in supernatural publishing rather than prestigious magazines. Yet her supernatural fiction's quality, subtlety, and frisson set her as a late apogee for the Anglo-American nineteenth- and early twentieth-century ghost story tradition. She is often associated with her older friends James and W. D. Howells, for the projects of all three involve both unsentimental novels of manners and supernatural short fiction. But the preface of *Ghosts* reserves Wharton's highest esteem for supernatural short stories for J. Sheridan Le Fanu, Fitz-James O'Brien, F. Marion Crawford, and the collection's dedicatee, Walter de la Mare. In one tribute, the U.K. television anthology series *Shades of Darkness* (1983) adapts a de la Mare tale and three of Wharton's (their only multiply adapted writer): "The Lady's Maid Bell" (1902), "Afterward" (1910), and "Bewitched" (1925).

Bob Hodges

See also: Crawford, F. Marion; de la Mare, Walter; Le Fanu, J. Sheridan; O'Brien, Fitz-James.

Further Reading

Jacobsen, Karen. 2008. "Economic Hauntings: Wealth & Class in Edith Wharton's Ghost Stories." *College Literature* 35.1: 100–127.

Killoran, Helen. 2001. *The Critical Reception of Edith Wharton*. Woodbridge: Boydell & Brewer.

McMullen, Bonnie. 2012. "Short Story Markets." *Edith Wharton in Context*, edited by Laura Rattray, 103–116. Cambridge: Cambridge University Press.

Shades of Darkness. 1983. Television. Pt. Washington: Koch, 2006. DVD.

WHEATLEY, DENNIS (1897–1977)

British author Dennis Wheatley fundamentally changed horror writing when he developed a form of occult- and satanic-influenced horror that has links to the work of H. P Lovecraft, Bram Stoker, Ambrose Bierce, and Arthur Machen. In Wheatley's work, the appearance of the Devil and his minions in the comfortable British shires and home counties (Berkshire, Essex, Surrey, and Hampshire) can be counteracted first by consulting complex reference tomes of magical lore, and then by the decisive acts of strong, chivalric, upper-middle-class men. Wheatley wrote more than 100 books and sold more than fifty million copies.

Born and raised in South London, Wheatley left his family's Mayfair wine business after being expelled from Dulwich College, joined the Merchant Navy, and was gassed in World War I. He worked in security in London during World War II, in Churchill's underground fortress, constructing false stories to mislead the Nazis. He wrote a mystery crime novel, adventure novels, and some science fiction, but is better known for his eight black magic novels—*The Devil Rides Out* (1934), *Strange Conflict* (1941), *The Haunting of Toby Jugg* (1948), *To the Devil a Daughter* (1953), *The Ka of Gifford Hillary* (1956), *The Satanist* (1960), *They Used Dark Forces* (1964), *Gateway to Hell* (1970)—plus his short stories and edited collections of horror tales. In the 1960s and 1970s each of his black magic books averaged yearly sales of 80,000 copies.

Wheatley's popularity waned, probably because of the values his novels promote: fear of the foreign, fear of disability (seen as degeneracy), and a patriarchal-based assertion of the need to preserve women's morality. Each of his novels is related to threats to British respectability, and each is ultimately controlled by the actions of dashing, upper- or upper-middle-class men (such as John in *To the Devil a Daughter* and the Duke of Richlieu and Rex in *The Devil Rides Out*). There are levels of voyeurism in Wheatley's work; for instance, in *To the Devil a Daughter* the morally righteous reader gains vicarious pleasure observing Christina, a semiclad young woman, rescued by a dashing young man from being sacrificed to the Devil, following a pact agreed by her father, at her birth. Speed, power, reason, and occult knowledge are used against the dark forces. David Punter notes that Wheatley can "smooth out the moments of terror and vision which comprise experience and render them into a unitary whole" (Punter 1980, 407).

While his conservatism, misogyny, and class distinction are rather controversial for today's readers, it can be argued that the investment in homeland security and leadership by powerful men underpinning such popular entertainments as the James Bond series reflect the same values that infused Wheatley's work. So do a host of horror and disaster movies, such as the *Die Hard* series, with each entry featuring Nazi-influenced fanatical villains. Wheatley's occult horror infuses the everyday and is resolved through strong values and action. Wheatley died of liver failure in November 1977.

Gina Wisker

See also: *The Devil Rides Out*; Devils and Demons.

Further Reading

Baker, Phil. 2011. *The Devil Is a Gentleman: The Life and Times of Dennis Wheatley*. Sawtry, UK: Dedalus.

Caines, Michael. 2013. "Feasting with Dennis Wheatley." *The TLS Blog at The Times Literary Supplement*. December 31. http://timescolumns.typepad.com/stothard/2013/12/feasting-with-dennis-wheatley.html.

Punter, David. 1980. *The Literature of Terror: A History of Gothic Fictions from 1765 to the Present Day*. London: Longman.

Wisker, G. 1993. "Horrors and Menaces to Everything Decent in Life: The Horror Fiction of Dennis Wheatley." In *Creepers: British Horror & Fantasy in the Twentieth Century*, edited by Clive Bloom, 99–110. London: Pluto.

"THE WHIMPER OF WHIPPED DOGS"

First published in 1973, Harlan Ellison's "The Whimper of Whipped Dogs" was inspired by the mainly inaccurate March 1964 report in the *New York Times* that claimed Katherine Susan "Kitty" Genovese was murdered outside of her Queens apartment in full view of thirty-seven of her neighbors, all of whom refused to render aid. Evidence since the initial publication of the story proves convincingly that no single individual witnessed the murder, which had initially been reported to the police as a domestic argument. Nevertheless, the incident became a kind of urban legend as it captured the idea of an apathetic populace made callous by the dehumanizing effects of life in the American city.

These themes of detachment and dehumanization inform "The Whimper of Whipped Dogs." Beth O'Neil, recently come to New York from rural Vermont, witnesses a brutal murder in her apartment building courtyard one evening. She notices that her neighbors are also watching and that some seem to take a perverse pleasure from the spectacle. She is further shaken by a fog that suddenly rises up from the courtyard and, if only for a moment, assumes almost human features. Soon afterwards Beth becomes romantically involved with a neighbor, Ray Gleeson, but as their relationship edges toward emotional and physical violence, Beth ends things. One night Beth awakens to the sound of someone moving about in her apartment. She encounters a burglar who, upon being discovered, attacks her. Their struggle takes them to the balcony, where, on the verge of losing consciousness, Beth notices her neighbors watching. Fearful that past events will replay themselves, Beth has a sudden revelation: In order for people to survive in the city, they must give part of their humanity to it. Ray's advances were actually an invitation to join a cult that worships the God of the City. She cries out to her neighbors that she understands and wishes to join them, and her assailant is suddenly whisked away, shredded into pieces yet somehow left alive, and dropped onto the courtyard below, which has become a type of sacrificial altar.

Ellison carefully builds toward his reveal, blending the grind of daily existence in the city with an encroaching dread. As with all of his work, the story is saturated with his characteristic judgmental anger. In this case, that fury is built upon a false foundation, but it gives Ellison the opportunity to chastise the world. The story received the 1974 Edgar Award by the Mystery Writers of America.

Javier A. Martinez

See also: Ellison, Harlan; "I Have No Mouth and I Must Scream."

Further Reading

Cook, Kevin. 2014. *Kitty Genovese: The Murder, the Bystanders, the Crime That Changed America*. New York: Norton.

Francavilla, Joseph, ed. 2012. *Critical Insights: Harlan Ellison*. Pasadena: Salem Press.

Weil, Ellen R., and Gary K. Wolfe. 2002. *Harlan Ellison: The Edge of Forever*. Columbus: Ohio State University Press.

"THE WHITE HANDS"

"The White Hands" is a short story from Mark Samuels's debut fiction collection, *The White Hands and Other Weird Tales* (2003). It was nominated for a British Fantasy Award for Short Fiction in 2004. It has subsequently been reprinted, notably in editor Stephen Jones's *The Mammoth Book of Best New Horror 15* (2004) and editors Ann and Jeff VanderMeer's *The Weird: A Compendium of Strange and Dark Stories* (2012). Probably the best-known of Samuels's tales, "The White Hands" is steeped in the author's knowledge of the supernatural fiction genre.

John Harrington, the narrator of the tale, tells of his association with Alfred Muswell, a disgraced and reclusive scholar, who has an obsession with a Victorian author of ghost stories, Lilith Blake. Harrington is drawn in by Muswell's enthusiasm, and he also develops a powerful interest in Blake, partly spurred by the delicacy and paleness of her hands in a surviving photograph. After Muswell dies, Harrington has Blake's corpse exhumed and, when he opens her coffin, finds her still living, though she swiftly crumbles to dust. Some time later, Harrington decides to attempt to transcribe and interpret *The White Hands and Other Tales*, Blake's last collection, dictated after death to Muswell. But the act drives Harrington mad.

"The White Hands" has an ambiguous ending—something common in Samuels's work, which often explores the transformative (as opposed to the destructive) aspects of an encounter with the Weird. Though it ends with Harrington confined to a psychiatric hospital, plagued by visions of disembodied white hands, there is in his madness much more of ecstasy than despair.

It is typical of Samuels's erudite work that his best-known tale should have a scholar of supernatural fiction at its heart. Muswell's thesis regarding the weird tale is expounded at the opening of the story. All great literature, he claims, is concerned with "the quest for hidden mysteries," and also "should unravel the secrets of life and death," and therefore bring about "some actual alteration in the structure of reality itself" (Samuels 2003, 2–3). In this statement can be seen Samuels's own authorial and philosophical approach.

Samuels has said his stories often evolve from a single image that he cannot shake off. In the case of "The White Hands," this image was that of Blake's disembodied hands. The image's source was literary rather than "real world"; it was inspired by Eddy C. Bertin's "Like Two White Spiders" (1973) and ultimately by the whole lineage of Gothic tales of preternaturally animated severed hands, including William Fryer Harvey's "The Beast with Five Fingers" and Guy de Maupassant's "The Hand." In addition to its intrinsic excellence, "The White Hands" is noteworthy because it has influenced the development of new writing in the weird field that is subtle and metatextual in its approach.

Timothy J. Jarvis

See also: "The Beast with Five Fingers"; Maupassant, Guy de.

Further Reading

Cardin, Matt. 2006. "Interview with Mark Samuels: A Sense of Charnel Glamour." *The Teeming Brain*, August. http://www.teemingbrain.com/interview-with-mark-samuels.

Samuels, Mark. 2003. *The White Hands and Other Weird Tales*. Leyburn, North Yorkshire: Tartarus Press.

"THE WHITE PEOPLE"

First published in 1904, Arthur Machen's story of a young girl's initiation into witch-craft was actually written in 1899, the same year as the publication of Sigmund Freud's *The Interpretation of Dreams*. It is nevertheless pre-Freudian and pre-Jungian (the latter term referring to the psychological system created by Freud's onetime colleague, Carl Jung), despite its extraordinarily suggestive imagery and barely sub-limated sexuality. The author was a mystic and a Catholic whose writings show no interest in psychoanalytical theory, even if he wrote about beautiful women achiev-ing sensuous ecstasy when covered by supernatural snakes.

As is a common technique for Machen, his characters talk out a philosophical idea, after which a narrative is presented to illustrate it. The philosophical idea under question in "The White People" is the nature of evil, which is framed in the

---

In a telling passage in the prologue to "The White People"—a passage quoted eighty-five years later by T. E. D. Klein in his deeply Machen-esque horror novel *The Ceremo-nies* (1984)—a man named Ambrose explains the real nature of sin and evil to a man named Cotgrave, in words that then resonate throughout the remainder of the story's primary narrative:

"We underrate evil. We attach such an enormous importance to the 'sin' of med-dling with our pockets (and our wives) that we have quite forgotten the awfulness of real sin."

"And what is sin?" said Cotgrave.

"I think I must reply to your question by another. What would your feelings be, seriously, if your cat or your dog began to talk to you, and to dispute with you in human accents? You would be overwhelmed with horror. I am sure of it. And if the roses in your garden sang a weird song, you would go mad. And suppose the stones in the road began to swell and grow before your eyes, and if the peb-ble that you noticed at night had shot out stony blossoms in the morning?

"Well, these examples may give you some notion of what sin really is." (Machen 1904, 58)

Matt Cardin

Source: Machen, Arthur. 1904. "The White People." *Horlick's Magazine*. Volume 1. London: James Elliott & Co.

opening debate between two characters as "the taking of heaven by storm . . . an attempt to penetrate into another and higher sphere in a forbidden manner" (Machen 1922, 117). Evil is a subversion of the natural order, as if roses began to sing. Sorcery and sanctity are "the only realities" (113). Great sinners are probably rarer than great saints.

To demonstrate his point, one debater hands the other the diary of a sixteen-year-old girl who was introduced to witchcraft at a young age by her nurse. Her narrative is near stream-of-consciousness and unparagraphed, which perfectly captures the naïveté of the character as she describes things she only half understands and repeats several sinister fairy tales that contain veiled warnings about her eventual plight. After visits with the sinister "white people," several ventures into strange, unworldly landscapes, and the occurrence of as yet harmless magical pranks such as overturning tables, she is found dead before an ancient pagan statue, poisoned "in time," as we learn in an epilogue (165).

H. P. Lovecraft, who regarded this as the second greatest weird story in English (the first being "The Willows" by Algernon Blackwood), found himself explaining the ending to correspondents. It is subtle: The girl has become pregnant with a monstrous thing, but feeling a mother's sympathy with her unborn child, she became aware of the abomination within her and so killed herself. When Lovecraft reworked this situation in "The Dunwich Horror," he was less subtle about it. "The White People" might be imagined as "The Dunwich Horror" from the point of view of a young, innocent Lavinia Whateley (the character in Lovecraft's tale who is impregnated by an other-dimensional entity). Here we see a major statement of Machen's "Little People" mythos, which also influenced Lovecraft and numerous others: the idea that the "fairies" of legend are survivals of some ancient race that has gone underground and turned to evil, never having lost its links to prehuman magic.

Apparently "The White People" was intended to be a part of a larger work, a fragment, cleverly made complete by its framing device. If this is true, then the circumstance may be deemed fortunate or even regarded as a stroke of genius, because the story's fascination stems precisely from Machen's refusal to go on too long or explain too much.

Darrell Schweitzer

See also: The Ceremonies; "The Dunwich Horror"; "The Great God Pan"; Machen, Arthur; "The Novel of the Black Seal"; "The Willows."

Further Reading

Joshi, S. T. 1990. "Arthur Machen: The Mystery of the Universe." In *The Weird Tale*. Austin: University of Texas Press.

Machen, Arthur. 1922. "The White People." In *The House of Souls*, 111–166. New York: Alfred A. Knopf.

WHITEHEAD, HENRY S. (1882–1932)

Henry St. Clair Whitehead, a frequent contributor to *Weird Tales* magazine and correspondent of H. P. Lovecraft, is best known for writing weird tales set in the West Indies. Born in Elizabethtown, New Jersey, Whitehead attended both Columbia College and Harvard University, but failing to earn a degree at either school, he entered Berkeley Divinity School, where he was ordained as a deacon in 1912, entering the priesthood a year later. It was Whitehead's profession that brought him to the West Indies, where he lived in St. Croix, serving as an archdeacon. Whitehead's tales, blurring the lines between fantasy, horror, and ethnography, focus on native magic of the West Indies.

Whitehead's stories explore colonial and native relations in the Caribbean through their investigation of island *jumbee*, a term related to *zombi* but here connoting any island spirit or ghost. His tales often involve an academic-minded protagonist who must act as a detective when confronted with irrational forces of native magic. Gerald Canevin, a New England writer living in the West Indies and an obvious stand-in for Whitehead, frequently narrates the West Indies stories. Canevin is an expert on the supernatural and uses his knowledge of island magic to solve mysteries that often shed light on the colonial history of the islands. In "The Shadows" (1927) it is Canevin's understanding that island magic is not mere superstition that allows him to uncover the story of Old Morris, a colonist whose attempt to harness the powers of an island fish-god for his own gain ends in his death, and in "Black Tancrède" (1929) Canevin discovers that the disturbance at a St. Thomas hotel is the work of the *jumbee* of a slave seeking revenge on the judge who sentenced him to death for his part in a slave revolt. While Whitehead's depictions of West Indies natives and native culture often rely on racist stereotypes, they also reveal a more complex understanding of racial relations in the colonial West Indies. Many of his tales reveal coercive practices of colonial representatives, and island magic is often portrayed as a means of resistance for the native population. In "Hill Drums" (1931), for example, when a colonial diplomat offends the native population, they use magic to possess him and force him to leave the islands.

Not all of Whitehead's tales, however, are set in the West Indies. Some take place in New England or Europe and adhere more to the mode of the antiquarian ghost tale. For example, "The Shut Room" (1930) is a haunted inn story set in England, and "The Trap" (1932) is a haunted mirror story set in a boarding school in Connecticut. However, these tales often refer to Canevin's time spent in the West Indies as the source of his understanding of supernatural events.

Whitehead spent the last years of his life in Dunedin, Florida, where he died, likely due to a gastric illness. His tales were collected posthumously by Arkham House in *Jumbee and Other Uncanny Tales* (1944) and *West India Lights* (1946).

Travis Rozier

See also: Arkham House; Lovecraft, H. P.; Lovecraftian Horror; *Weird Tales*; Zombies.

Further Reading

Searles, A. Langley. 1995. "Henry S. Whitehead: A Retrospection." *Fantasy Commentator* 8 (3–4): 186–200.

Whitehead, Henry S. 2012. *Voodoo Tales: The Ghost Stories of Henry S. Whitehead*. Hertfordshire: Wordsworth Editions.

"THE WILLOWS"

First published in Algernon Blackwood's 1907 collection *The Listener and Other Stories*, "The Willows" has a reputation as a seminal and definitive example of the classic weird tale. Praised by H. P. Lovecraft as a story "without a single strained passage or a single false note" (Lovecraft 2012, 88), its emphasis on carefully established mood and ambiguity contribute to a sustained atmosphere of dread. Its central mystery remains nebulous, adding to the potency of the overall effect.

The story has its origins in a 1901 account of one of Blackwood's expeditions written by him for *Macmillan's Magazine*, "Down the Danube in a Canadian Canoe."

At one point in "The Willows," the narrator observes strange shapes among the titular vegetation, "immense, bronze-coloured" shapes with "limbs and huge bodies melting in and out of each other . . . rising up in a living column into the heavens." His response conveys the essence of the numinous, that combined sense of fear and fascination before a preternatural reality that inspires a veritably religious sense of awe:

> Far from feeling fear, I was possessed with a sense of awe and wonder such as I have never known. I seemed to be gazing at the personified elemental forces of this haunted and primeval region. Our intrusion had stirred the powers of the place into activity. It was we who were the cause of the disturbance, and my brain filled to bursting with stories and legends of the spirits and deities of places that have been acknowledged and worshipped by men in all ages of the world's history. But, before I could arrive at any possible explanation, something impelled me to go farther out, and I crept forward on the sand and stood upright. I felt the ground still warm under my bare feet; the wind tore at my hair and face; and the sound of the river burst upon my ears with a sudden roar. These things, I knew, were real, and proved that my senses were acting normally. Yet the figures still rose from earth to heaven, silent, majestically, in a great spiral of grace and strength that overwhelmed me at length with a genuine deep emotion of worship. I felt that I must fall down and worship—absolutely worship. (Blackwood 1917, 153–154)

Matt Cardin

Source: Blackwood, Algernon. 1917. "The Willows." In *The Listener and Other Stories*. New York: Alfred A. Knopf.

"The Willows" begins similarly as a travelogue describing the canoe journey along the Danube undertaken by the narrator and his Swedish traveling companion. They become stormbound on an island in a desolate, sparsely populated region of marshland and ever-shifting sandbanks and islets; the surrounding wilderness seems to become imbued with a hostile intelligence. Their supplies unaccountably disappear, their equipment is sabotaged, and the narrator witnesses an indistinct, semimaterial presence somehow associated with the willows. They find odd "funnels" in the sand, and the banks of willows seem to encroach ever closer upon their camp. The mysterious assault intensifies until the Swede desperately attempts to drown himself to placate their persecutors, but is rescued by the narrator. Before the Swede passes out, he claims that the immediate threat has been lifted since "they've found another victim" (Blackwood 1973, 50). They later discover the drowned corpse of a peasant who had earlier attempted to warn them away from the island, and are horrified when they see the funnel-shaped wounds covering his face and chest.

The story's power is generated largely through Blackwood's refusal to specifically delineate the exact nature of the threat facing the two protagonists. The hostile forces in "The Willows" are tenebrous and obscure, in the tradition of Fitz-James O'Brien's "What Was It?" (1859), Guy de Maupassant's "The Horla" (1887), and Ambrose Bierce's "The Damned Thing" (1893). Even when the events are directly witnessed by the narrator, we are given little more information than that they are vague "shapes" or "presences." Although he continually tries to rationalize their experiences, he is ultimately unable to successfully do so. In contrast, the Swede, through his less hesitant recourse to supernatural or metaphysical speculation, is more immediately able to parse the nature of the encounter. At various points in the narrative, the Swede discusses hostile pagan forces suggestive of a malevolent *genius loci*, the numinous spirit of a particular place in ancient Roman religion, and themselves as interlopers within a sacred grove. Although Blackwood strongly hints at a supernatural explanation, the two opposing viewpoints create a sustained mood of queasy uncertainty. Blackwood's particular skill lies in his ability to sustain ambiguity without detriment to the narrative force of the tale. Its cumulative power is enhanced by the increasingly desperate speculation of the protagonists as they struggle to understand their experience.

Included by Dorothy Scarborough in her influential 1921 collection *Famous Modern Ghost Stories*, "The Willows" has been a staple of horror anthologies ever since. In the *Weird Tales* golden age of the 1920s and 1930s, the novella was repeatedly singled out for praise by H. P. Lovecraft and Clark Ashton Smith, who both identified it as among the best supernatural horror stories ever written. It retains its reputation to this day and is the third item in Ann and Jeff VanderMeer's seminal attempt at creating a canon of weird fiction, *The Weird: A Compendium of Dark and Strange Stories* (2012).

James Machin

See also: Blackwood, Algernon; "The Horla"; The Numinous.

Further Reading

Blackwood, Algernon. 1973. *Best Ghost Stories of Algernon Blackwood*, edited by E. F. Bleiler. New York: Dover.

Camara, Anthony. 2013. "Nature Unbound: Cosmic Horror in Algernon Blackwood's 'The Willows.'" *Horror Studies* 4, no. 1 (April): 43–62.

Joshi, S. T 1990. *The Weird Tale*. Holicong, PA: Wildside.

Lovecraft, H. P. [1927] 2012. *The Annotated Supernatural Horror in Literature*. Edited by S. T. Joshi. New York: Hippocampus Press.

VanderMeer, Ann, and Jeff VanderMeer, eds. 2012. *The Weird: A Compendium of Dark and Strange Stories*. London: Tor.

WILSON, F. PAUL (1946–)

F. Paul Wilson is an American horror and science fiction novelist who has also worked in a few other genres, including historical fiction and medical thrillers. Wilson was born in New Jersey in 1946 and has remained a lifelong resident. In his formative years, he sampled, among other eclectic works of art, the classic horror comic books from EC Comics in the 1950s, the stop-motion special effects extravaganza movies of Ray Harryhausen, and the stories and novels of H. P. Lovecraft, Richard Matheson, Ray Bradbury, and Robert Heinlein. He graduated from Georgetown University in 1968.

Wilson began selling short fiction as a first-year medical student. He sold a number of comic scripts to *Creepy* and *Eerie* during the 1970s, but generally concentrated on prose fiction. His short stories and novelettes have appeared in all the major markets and numerous best-of-the-year collections; his novels have made various national best-seller lists. His novels *The Keep* (1981) and *The Tomb* (1984) both were *New York Times* best-sellers. His novels and short fiction have appeared on the final ballots for the World Fantasy Award, the Nebula Award, and the Bram Stoker Award.

Wilson's first three novels, all science fiction, form what later came to be referred to as the LaNague Chronicles. Each reflects the author's libertarian leanings. They were followed by further forays into science fiction later in Wilson's career.

In 1981 Wilson published his first horror novel, *The Keep*, about Nazis accidentally awakening a supernatural evil in a remote castle in the Transylvanian Alps during World War II. After this novel, which was included as one of the one hundred best horror novels in the Stephen Jones–edited *Horror: 100 Best Books*, Wilson published five more books in what he called his "Adversary Cycle": *The Tomb* (1984), *The Touch* (1986), *Reborn* (NEL, 1990), *Reprisal* (1991), and *Nightworld* (1992). The Adversary Cycle introduced several concepts that came to form the core of much of Wilson's fictional universe: the ancient, evil entity called Rasalom, his eternal opponent Glaeken, the town of Monroe, Long Island, the wandering healing spirit known as the Dat-tay-vao (first seen in *The Touch*), and the modern pulp hero known as Repairman Jack.

The secretive Jack, who conceals his very existence from the world, made his first appearance in *The Tomb*. Not intending to establish a series character, Wilson left him near death at the end of that novel, only to have him reappear in *Nightworld*, playing a key role in frustrating Rasalom's bid to enslave humanity. Jack's fans proving persistent, Wilson responded with a new Repairman Jack novel titled *Legacies* in 1998. That book was followed by thirteen additional Repairman Jack novels, published from 1999 through 2011. Wilson also added six prequels to *The Tomb*, three set during Jack's formative years, and another three set during his first months in New York City. Set between the events in *The Tomb* and *Nightworld*, the books chronicle Jack's growing awareness of the battle between Rasalom and the entity he refers to as "the Otherness" or "the Ally," forming the core of what Wilson has come to call "The Secret History of the World."

The Keep was adapted as a horror movie by director Michael Mann in 1983. The movie version has attained something of a storied status due to its much-discussed history as a prototypical "troubled production," and the final result is mostly an incomprehensible mess, but aspects of its lush visual design, courtesy of director Mann and cinematographer Alex Thomson, as well as the hypnotic musical score by Tangerine Dream, have rendered it somewhat memorable.

James Machin

See also: Bradbury, Ray; Lovecraft, H. P.; Matheson, Richard.

Further Reading

Coker, Jennifer R. 2007. "F. Paul Wilson." *Guide to Literary Masters & Their Works* 1. *Literary Reference Center*, EBSCOhost (accessed August 6, 2016).

"F. Paul Wilson." 2015. *Contemporary Authors Online*. Detroit, MI: Gale.

Grossberg, Michael. 2011. "The Untrod Path: Interview with F. Paul Wilson." *Prometheus: Newsletter of the Libertarian Futurist Society* 29, no. 3 (Spring). http://lfs.org/news letter/029/03/FPWilson.shtml.

WITCHES AND WITCHCRAFT

The word "witch" derives from the Old English verb "wiccian," meaning to use sorcery or enchantment. "Witch" is often used as an umbrella term for all practitioners of magic, though this obscures historical and regional differences. Historically, the English terms "witch" and "witchcraft" have specifically referred to European traditions. Contemporary horror fictions that employ the words undeniably evoke the tradition of European witchcraft, though there is often some intermingling with other traditions (e.g., Louisiana Voodoo, Haitian Vodou). Additionally, as European witchcraft has a long and complex history, contemporary horror may approach the idea of the "witch" from varying perspectives.

The Hammer of the Witches

In 1487, Heinrich Kramer and Jacob Sprenger published a treatise on witchcraft entitled *Malleus Maleficarum* (*The Hammer of the Witches*). The book would come to be
one of the most infamous texts of the European witch-hunting period. Kramer was a
German Catholic clergyman who was expelled from Innsbruck after trying to conduct
witchcraft trials without authority. Sprenger was a Dominican Inquisitor who lectured at
the University of Cologne.

The *Malleus* is notorious for its detailed descriptions of witchcraft and for the fervor
with which it advocates the eradication of witches. The book describes the infernal pact
made by witches, making a direct connection between witches and Satan. It also describes (in graphic detail) the practices of witches, including the way in which witches
recruit one another through sexual temptation. The book accuses witches of cannibalism, infanticide, and castration, offering "real-life" examples of such cases. The book's
final section is a step-by-step guide to conducting a witch trial, including examples of
torture and execution techniques.

In 1490, the Catholic Church denounced the book. In 1538, the Spanish Inquisition
disowned its teachings as false. While the book claimed an endorsement from the
Faculty of Cologne, it seems many of the faculty condemned it for contradicting Catholic theology and promoting unethical and illegal procedures. Some historians claim that
Sprenger himself denounced the book and used his power and influence to make life
difficult for Kramer after its publication.

The book is now commonly cited as a key example of early modern beliefs about
women, witchcraft, and diabolical magic. However, the extent to which the book actually had any influence on historical trials is debatable.

Hannah Priest

European traditions of practicing and condemning witchcraft have their antecedents in antiquity. There is evidence that some practitioners of magic faced harsh
punishments in ancient Greece, Rome, Egypt, and Babylonia. There are also prohibitions against some forms of sorcery in the Old Testament. In these ancient texts,
there is a recurrent concern about malicious harm to men, livestock, and crops
caused by sorcery. The Christian tradition of condemning witchcraft began to be
codified with the Council of Elvira (ca. 305 CE), which decreed that the act of causing death through malicious intent could not be effected without "idolatry." This
decree associated witchcraft with devil or demon worship, and this association
continues throughout the European tradition.

Although most early legal prohibitions do not specifically gender witchcraft,
there is some evidence of a growing association of malicious sorcery with women
throughout the early Middle Ages. This may be a reflection of classical distinctions
between types of magic and their respective practitioners, but it may also draw on

classical mythology and literature, in which there are a number of malicious female sorcerers (for instance, Circe, a character in Homer's *Odyssey*, and Hecate, a Greek goddess). Many texts made the distinction between "necromancy" (learned or ceremonial magic) and "witchcraft" (possession by the devil). The former was the province of clerical and educated men, and the latter of uneducated peasants and women. This distinction was not a rigid one, but it had far-reaching consequences.

In order to draw a clear distinction between necromancy and witchcraft, clerical writers elaborated on the idea of diabolical witchcraft. Drawing on earlier legal codes, medieval writers increasingly began to associate witchcraft with a satanic pact to explain how "common" people might enact feats of magic to rival those of learned magicians. By the thirteenth century, this pact with the devil was imagined as a formal initiation rite or ceremony known as the Sabbat or "witches' sabbath," and clerics decried the rite in sermons. At the same time, the repertoire of crimes associated with witchcraft also expanded, incorporating transgressions previously included in accusations of heresy. As well as traditional complaints of malicious harm to livestock and crops, accusations of witchcraft now included references to sexual deviancy, cannibalism, and infanticide. The medieval connection of witchcraft to both idolatry and satanic pact also led to the idea that witches worshipped "familiars," or demonic spirits concealed in animal form.

In the fifteenth century, accusations of diabolical witchcraft began to become more systematic, and Europe entered a period of organized witch-hunting. Both Protestants and Catholics formed "Inquisitions," under which thousands of trials were conducted. In some regions, "werewolves" were tried alongside witches, as some Inquisitors (such as Henri Boguet) argued that witchcraft could include demonic shape-shifting—or at least the appearance of shape-shifting. Confessions were sometimes extracted under torture, though this varied dramatically by region, and death by burning, decapitation, or hanging was often the outcome. Corporal punishment, exile, and monetary fines were also passed as punishments. In most areas of Europe, the majority of the accused were women, though Iceland, Estonia, and Russia prosecuted more male than female witches. Throughout Europe, the majority of the accused belonged to lower socioeconomic classes. A number of witch trials were also conducted in European colonies, most famously in Salem, Massachusetts in 1692–1693. However, the fervor for witch trials abated toward the end of the seventeenth century, with a number of legal and religious edicts passed to curtail it. In England, for example, the Witchcraft Act of 1735 dismissed witchcraft as an impossibility and decreed that individuals purporting to practice the craft should be tried as confidence tricksters.

During the period of witch-hunting, numerous publications circulated that denounced and described the practices of witchcraft. In addition to religious and legal guidelines, broadsheets depicted (often in lurid detail) the various crimes of the witches. Additionally, fictional accounts of occult and demonic practice were popular in early modern Europe, and increased literacy meant that these fictions were more widely circulated. As well as behaviors, certain visual characteristics and accessories began to be associated with witches, such as the flying broomstick or distaff, black cats, and, later, the pointed hat.

By the end of the witch trials, the figure of the witch began to appear in other forms of literature. Witches appeared in children's chapbooks as early as 1710, foreshadowing their common role in folk and fairy tales. The Victorian era saw the beginnings of a more sympathetic understanding of the women tried during the witch-hunts; for instance, George Eliot's *The Mill on the Floss* (1860) has a heroine who revises an earlier narrative of persecution, identifying the witch-hunters as the guilty parties and the accused witch as an innocent victim. At the same time, an increasing interest in (reconstructed) pre-Christian beliefs, including Viking, Celtic, and Germanic folk traditions, paved the way for twentieth-century witchcraft "revivals" and modern paganism, such as the development of the contemporary pagan religion of Wicca in the 1920s–1940s. Associated with Neo-Druidism, countercultural movements, New Age philosophy, and reconstructionist pagan traditions, Wicca has also been heavily influenced by the second-wave feminism of the 1970s.

The history of European witchcraft is reflected in contemporary horror in a number of ways. Indeed, the complexity of the history allows for multiple and varied representations of witches. Arcane (often gendered) magical practices can be a source of horror, as in Fritz Leiber's *Conjure Wife* (1943); however, books such as Deborah Harkness's *A Discovery of Witches* (2011) blur genre boundaries by combining sinister occult practices with positive protagonists and fantasy creatures like the romantic vampire. The idea of the "coven" (either a family or social group of witches) often appears in contemporary fiction; for instance, Anne Rice's Lives of the Mayfair Witches series presents a matriarchal family of witches and the malevolent spirit with whom the witches are connected. Elsewhere, it is the practice of witch-hunting that is used to evoke terror and fear. Syd Moore's *Witch Hunt* (2012) depicts a present haunted by the specters of women killed during witch-hunts in Essex, and, though its specter is somewhat less sympathetic, "The Dreams in the Witch House" (1933) by H. P. Lovecraft draws on the history of the Salem witch trials. Demonic pacts, diabolical cannibalism, and infanticide also appear frequently in modern horror. As with much of the fiction that refers to witch-hunts and trials, there is a tradition of referencing historical and pseudohistorical cases of demonic witchcraft; for instance, Aldous Huxley's *The Devils of Loudun* (1952) is based on an alleged case of demonic possession (and its brutal punishment) in seventeenth-century France. The reclamation of the witch as a positive figure has also been subverted in recent fiction, with paganism and Wicca (rather than witchcraft) being a trope of folk horror fiction, such as Andrew Michael Hurley's *The Loney* (2014).

Hannah Priest

See also: Devils and Demons; Incubi and Succubi; Possession and Exorcism; Spiritualism.

Further Reading

Blumberg, Jess. 2007. "A Brief History of the Salem Witch Trials." *smithsonian.com*, October 23. Accessed March 26, 2016. http://www.smithsonianmag.com/history/a-brief-history-of-the-salem-witch-trials-175162489/?no-ist.

Clark, Stuart. 1997. *Thinking with Demons: The Idea of Witchcraft in Early Modern Europe*. Oxford: Oxford University Press.

Hutton, Ronald. 1996. "The Roots of Modern Paganism." In *Paganism Today*, edited by Graham Harvey and Charlotte Hardman, 4–15. London: Thorsons.

Kieckhefer, Richard. 1989. *Magic in the Middle Ages*. Cambridge: Cambridge University Press.

Purkiss, Diane. 1996. *The Witch in History*. London: Routledge.

THE WOMAN IN BLACK

Susan Hill's *The Woman in Black* (1983) revived the British ghost story, introducing social and historical concerns particularly affecting women and families. It enacts social and family cruelties and losses, using the ghostly figure of a woman in black who wreaks deadly revenge on a society whose shortsighted, gendered bigotry separated her from her own child, who drowned tragically when the pony and trap he was traveling in was overwhelmed by sea mist and fell into the marsh sea. The lives of those unlucky enough to come into range and consciousness of the revengeful dead are both haunted and blasted as the curse of Jennet Humfrye, the woman in black, leads to the death of local children.

The first-person narration of Arthur Kipps, solicitor, authenticates this traditional Christmas Eve ghost story (a formula reminiscent of M. R. James) as the book begins on that day with Kipps's step-children asking him to tell them a ghost story. Being too disturbed by the story he has to tell, he instead writes it down.

In his narrated story, Kipps is sent to the remote village of Crythin Gifford to settle the will of the reclusive, heirless Mrs. Drablow. Her home, Eel Marsh House, Lincolnshire, is isolated across a spit covered by sea at high tide. Readers are reminded of the law, inheritance, injustice, fog, and contagion in Charles Dickens's *Bleak House* (1853) and contradictory social values and growing up in Dickens's Gothic *Great Expectations* (1861), which also deals with damaging hauntings, and in which Miss Havisham's house resembles Mrs. Drablow's with its paralyzing past. *The Woman in Black* uses familiar ghost story strategies, including spectral visits, sounds in the night, empty rooms echoing with past activities, and an overwhelming atmosphere of dread.

Hill's novel has a feminist message concerning "fallen women," focusing on Jennet Humfrye, whose illegitimate son Nathaniel was adopted by her sister, Mrs. Drablow, and whose impoverishment, shame, and mental state disempowered her in life. Nathaniel was brought up at Eel Marsh House without connections to the real world or his increasingly desolate, maddened mother, product of a bigoted age that banished, silenced, and incarcerated unmarried mothers. Her fate, as well as her son's and subsequently that of the village children, are an indictment against the age.

Isolation is spatially represented by the landline, the narrow spit linking and dividing the house and its wealth from the village, as well as life from death. On his first visit to Eel Marsh House, isolated across the misty marshes, Kipps is traumatized by ghostly movements and sounds, particularly of pony and trap crashing, a terrified child crying, sounds of drowning, then silence. Nathaniel and his nurse Rose Judd, caught in the mist, drowned in the marshes and are condemned beyond death to repeat the fatal accident that drove Jennet to haunt graveyard, marsh, and village while the child's ghostly crying presence remains on the spit, and at night in the nursery.

Jennet lost everything, went mad, and died. But she returns and wanders as a ghost. Her revenge for her son's death is wreaked on those whose normal family structures condemned her to the margins. She haunts both graveyard and village, and the children begin to die, one by one. When attending Mrs. Drablow's funeral, Kipps hears of these losses. He also sees the woman in black.

The ghost actually gains a voice beginning when Kipps finds Jennet's letters begging to see her son. Finally Kipps, too, is caught up in her malevolent revenge cycle. When his wife and son visit and go for a spin in a pony trap he notices, all too late, the woman in black standing at one side. The trap crashes, killing his son and fatally wounding his wife.

The Woman in Black was adapted for the stage in 1987 by playwright Stephen Mallatratt. A British television adaptation was released in 1989 with a script adapted from Hill's novel by Nigel Kneale. A second film adaptation, directed by James Watkins and starring Daniel Radcliffe as Kipps, was released in 2012 and became a critical and financial success. A sequel, *The Woman in Black 2: Angel of Death*, was released in 2015.

Gina Wisker

See also: Frame Story; The Haunted House or Castle; Hill, Susan.

Further Reading

Cox, Donna. 2000. "'I Have No Story to Tell!': Maternal Rage in Susan Hill's *The Woman in Black*." *Intertexts* 4, no. 1: 74–89.

Jones, Alan. 2003. "Who Is Haunted by What in *The Woman in Black*? Alan Jones Considers the Multiple Relations of Susan Hill's Novel with Its Predecessors in the Gothic Tradition." *English Review* 13, no. 3: 10–12.

Kattelman, Beth A. 2014. "Still Scary after All These Years: Gothic Tropes and Theatricality in *The Woman in Black*." In *Frightful Witnessing: The Rhetoric and (Re)presentation of Fear*, edited by Beth A. Kattelman and Magdalena Hodalska, 37–54. Oxford, UK: Inter-Disciplinary Press.

WORLD FANTASY AWARD

The World Fantasy Awards are given annually by the World Fantasy Convention, an annual gathering of fantasy and horror professionals and enthusiasts. They are widely recognized as one of the most prestigious awards in the field of speculative fiction. Awards were given at the first convention in 1975 and at all subsequent ones (with some changes in the categories) for best novel, novella (this category was added in 1982), short story, story collection, anthology (added in 1988), artist, Special Award professional, Special Award non-professional, and Life Achievement. A Special Convention Award has sometimes been given. The award is juried by a panel of five judges (usually professional writers, editors, and critics) appointed by the Awards Administration, which is a subgroup of the World Fantasy Convention's board of directors. Popular nominations may add two items to the final ballot beyond the judges' choices.

Among prominent novels to have won the World Fantasy Award are *The Forgotten Beasts of Eld* by Patricia McKillip (1975), *Bid Time Return* by Richard Matheson (1976), *Our Lady of Darkness* by Fritz Leiber (1978), *The Shadow of the Torturer* by Gene Wolfe (1980), *Little, Big* by John Crowley (1982), *Towing Jehovah* by James Morrow (1995), *Jonathan Strange and Mr. Norrell* by Susanna Clarke (2005), and *Who Fears Death* by Nnedi Okorafor (2011). The Life Achievement Awards often reach beyond the usual genre suspects and have been given to Jorge Luis Borges, Italo Calvino, Madeleine L'Engle, and Angelica Gorodischer, in addition to such expected figures as Robert Bloch, Fritz Leiber, Ray Bradbury, Harlan Ellison, Ursula K. Le Guin, Stephen King, and more.

The short story category has also sometimes stretched beyond the expected. In 1989 it went to "Winter Solstice, Camelot Station," a narrative poem by John M. Ford, and in 1991 to "A Midsummer Night's Dream," a *Sandman* comic by Neil Gaiman and Charles Vess. The rumor has persisted that the rules were changed to prevent another comic book from winning. This is not true, though if a graphic novel were nominated today it would go in the Special Professional category.

The Special Awards are often given to scholars or editors for a body of effort, not a specific work. The Non-Professional special award often goes to publishers of small-press magazines or books, not amateur material by any means, but endeavors too small for anyone to be doing it for a living.

Given that the first World Fantasy Convention was held in Providence, Rhode Island, and its theme was H. P. Lovecraft and his Circle (with many of his old friends and protégés actually present), it was unsurprising that the award itself took the physical form of a bust of H. P. Lovecraft sculpted by Gahan Wilson. This remained the case for the next forty years, but in 2015, after some recipients expressed unease over Lovecraft's undeniable racism, the bust was retired amid considerable controversy. Lovecraft scholar S. T. Joshi (who has won twice) angrily returned his awards and announced a boycott of the convention. To date, no new design has been announced, but the award will continue.

Darrell Schweitzer

See also: Bram Stoker Award; International Horror Guild Award; Lovecraft, H. P.; Shirley Jackson Award.

Further Reading

Flood, Allison. 2015. "World Fantasy Award Drops HP Lovecraft as Prize Image." *The Guardian*, November 9. https://www.theguardian.com/books/2015/nov/09/world-fantasy-award-drops-hp-lovecraft-as-prize-image.

Leiber, Fritz, and Stuart David Schiff. 1980. *The World Fantasy Awards, Vol. 2*. New York: Doubleday.

Wilson, Gahan, ed. 1977. *The World Fantasy Awards*. New York: Doubleday.

World Fantasy Convention. 2016. http://www.worldfantasy.org.

WYNDHAM, JOHN (1903–1969)

Written during the time of the Cold War (1947–1991) between Russia, the United States, and the United Kingdom, the science fiction horror of British-born John Wyndham—whose full name was John Wyndham Parkes Lucas Beynon Harris—reinvigorated the theme of invasion and end of days, providing a link with and mutual influence between U.S. and British science fiction and fantasy. It also established the disaster focus popular in contemporary films including *Independence Day* (dir. Roland Emmerich, 1996), *2012* (dir. Roland Emmerich, 2009), and the 1953 and 2005 adaptations of H. G. Wells's *War of the Worlds* (1898), a major influence on Wyndham's own writing.

Wyndham's work depicts strong women as well as men and reflects an island nation's fear of the invasion of the Other, the terrors of invasion, and a sense of xenophobic powerlessness before the foreign Other with their strange ways. The invasion comes in *Day of the Triffids* (1951) in the shape of monstrous plants seemingly at home in people's gardens but actually turned into man-eating, ravenous, independently mobile creatures that prey on helpless people blinded by a meteor shower. In *The Midwich Cuckoos* (1957), an alien invasion takes place through insemination of human women and the birth of a race of beautiful, soulless blond children (similar to Adolf Hitler's Aryan youth) who are terrifying partly because of their extreme intelligence.

In *Billion Year Spree: The True History of Science Fiction* (1973), Brian Aldiss misleadingly labeled Wyndham's work "cosy catastrophe." The flowering of his science fiction horror (or "logical fantasy," or "reasoned fantasy" novels—a rejection of the Jules Verne–inspired, largely American label "science fiction") begins with *Day of the Triffids* and is followed by *The Kraken Wakes* (1953), named after Tennyson's poem "The Kraken" (1830), and serving as a possible influence on director James Cameron's science fiction action film *The Abyss* (1989). In Wyndham's novel the invasion is in the form of alien sea creatures, gas monsters landed from another planet by a meteor shower, which lie dormant inhabiting the sea depths. Living alongside them is impossible, as they harvest humans. The Japanese develop an ultrasonic destructive device that destroys the creatures, but climate change and depopulation have devastated the world. The U.K. edition is less bleak than the U.S. version, implying that humanity is rebuilding civilization.

Wyndham has been recognized as influencing such noted speculative fiction authors as John Christopher, J. G. Ballard, Brian Aldiss, and Christopher Priest. Don Siegel's *Invasion of the Body Snatchers* (filmed 1956, remade 1978 and 1993) reminds us of both *The Day of the Triffids*, an example of plant horror, and *The Midwich Cuckoos*, a changeling tale in which those like humans are in fact inhuman and could take over the world unless destroyed. Wyndham's final novel, *Web* (1963), published posthumously, is about spiders on a remote Pacific island that, like Daphne du Maurier's birds in "The Birds," suddenly turn en masse against human beings. Wyndham's invasion disaster horror tales continue to have a widespread influence on contemporary fiction and film.

Gina Wisker

See also: Wells, H. G.

Further Reading

Aldiss, Brian W. 1973. *Billion Year Spree: The True History of Science Fiction.* Garden City: Doubleday.

Ketterer David. 2004. "Questions and Answers: The Life and Fiction of John Wyndham." *New York Review of Science Fiction* 16 (March): 1, 6–10.

Manlove, Colin N. 1991. "Everything Slipping Away: John Wyndham's *The Day of the Triffids.*" *Journal of the Fantastic in the Arts* 4, no. 1: 29–53.

Moskowitz, Sam. 1966. "John Wyndham." In *Seekers of Tomorrow: Masters of Modern Science Fiction*, 118–132. Cleveland, OH: World Publishing.

Y

YARBRO, CHELSEA QUINN (1942–)

Chelsea Quinn Yarbro is a prolific American author who is probably best known for a series of historical vampire novels, although she writes in other genres as well. She has written (and published) more than sixty novels, numerous short stories, and several works of nonfiction. She was the first female president of the Horror Writers Association, and to date is one of only three female recipients of the World Horror Convention Grand Master's Award, the others being Anne Rice and Tanith Lee.

Yarbro's writing career has spanned over forty years, and in that time she written under a number of pseudonyms, including Quinn Fawcett (which represents the historical mysteries she has written, including a series centered on Sherlock Holmes's brother Mycroft); Camille Gabor (fantasy); T. F. C. Hopkins (works of historical nonfiction); and Trystam Kith (horror). Nonetheless, she is best known as Chelsea Quinn Yarbro and has published the majority of her work under that same. She has also collaborated with a number of different authors, notably Armin Shimerman (who is better known as an actor, having played Quark on *Star Trek: Deep Space Nine* and Principal Snyder on *Buffy the Vampire Slayer*). She also collaborated with fellow horror author Suzy McKee Charnas on the short story "Advocates," published in 1991.

Yarbro has contributed to many different genres of fiction, including science fiction, young adult, and Westerns, as well as a few poems. She has said she writes three to four books in a typical year, as advances for her work remain modest and she needs to earn a living. Arguably she is best known for her historical fantasy writing, and perhaps her best known creation is the aristocratic vampire the Comte de St. Germain. This character made his literary debut in 1978 in the novel *Hotel Transylvania*, only a few short years after Anne Rice revolutionized the literary vampire in *Interview with the Vampire* (1976). Although he has never quite attained the same level of fame as rock star vampire Lestat de Lioncourt from Rice's Vampire Chronicles, St. Germain is far more thoughtful and conscience-bound than the rebellious Lestat. He is also noticeably less violent than the majority of fictional vampires, despite facing some truly diabolical nemeses. Introduced amidst the corruption of pre-Revolutionary France in *Hotel Transylvania,* St. Germain is the prototypical "sympathetic vampire": he is sophisticated, philosophical, and compassionate, and spends much of his immortal life musing on the shortcomings and follies of mankind. Yarbro deliberately crafted her vampire to be at odds with traditional portrayals of the vampire such as in Stoker's *Dracula*, and yet still have him be recognizable as a member of the undead. Nor did she stint on the eroticism that has come to be associated with the modern vampire (with the exception of Stephenie Meyer's *Twilight* series). Although incapable of penetrative sexual intercourse (he has no blood flow), St. Germain finds satisfaction in pleasuring women, a bold stance to take at the time the first books in the series were written, but one that possibly demonstrates the influence of second-wave feminism and a new emphasis on female sexual pleasure.

St. Germain has been portrayed in settings that range from ancient Rome to post–World War II France, and Yarbro continues to plan novels featuring him. He has featured in several of her short stories as well. Yarbro has also produced two spin-off novels, *Out of the House of Life* (1990) and *In the Face of Death* (2004), featuring Madelaine de Montalia, St. Germain's protégé, whom he transforms into a vampire in *Hotel Transylvania*. A second spin-off series features another prominent lover of St. Germain's, Atta Olivia Clemens, who stars in a trilogy of her own: *A Flame in Byzantium* (1987), *Crusader's Torch* (1988), and *A Candle for D'Artagnan* (1989).

Of her other novels and short stories, Yarbro has not written much science fiction since the early 1980s, and much of her fictional output consists of horror and fantasy, including two books devoted to the vampire's close cousin, the werewolf: *Beastnights* (1989) and *The Lost Prince* (originally published as *The Godforsaken* in 1983). The former focuses on a bestial murderer and rapist stalking the streets of San Francisco, while the latter is a total contrast in that it focuses on the heir to the Spanish throne when the Inquisition was at its most powerful. These novels were inspired by a conversation with her then-editor in which she explained that lycanthropes did not interest her, as she perceived them as victims of fate who were incapable of dealing with their lycanthropy. She wondered why they would not simply end things if life became intolerable. When her editor queried what would happen if suicide was not an option, Yarbro was sufficiently intrigued to begin writing the story of the cursed Spanish prince. The novel is yet another example of how Yarbro typically endeavors to explore established horror themes and motifs from different perspectives and undermine the clichés that have arisen.

Of her nonfiction, Yarbro has authored a book on Middle Eastern history, entitled *Empires, Wars, and Battles: The Middle East* (2007), and on a naval battle between the Turks and European Crusaders, titled *Confrontation at Lepanto* (2006). Her works on Spiritualism, *Messages from Michael*, have also drawn considerable attention. What have become known as the Michael Teachings—a series of four books, the first published in 1979—record the three-decade-long conversations between a spiritual entity known as Michael and a group of friends based in San Francisco. The teachings endorse reincarnation and explore the experiences souls undergo during each lifetime.

She has received a number of award nominations for her writing and has been the recipient of three lifetime achievement awards: a Bram Stoker Lifetime Achievement Award, a World Fantasy Life Achievement Award, and an International Horror Guild Living Legend Award. Strangely, despite the popularity of St. Germain and other stories Yarbro has written, there have yet to be any TV or film adaptations of her work. She continues to be a prolific writer.

Carys Crossen

See also: Bram Stoker Award; International Horror Guild Award; Spiritualism; Vampires; Werewolves.

Further Reading

Bogstad, Janice M. 2003. "Yarbro, Chelsea Quinn 1942–" In *Supernatural Fiction Writers: Contemporary Fantasy and Horror*, 2nd ed. Vol. 2. Edited by Richard Bleiler, 993–1002. New York: Charles Scribner's Sons.

Fitzgerald, Gil. 1988. "History as Horror: Chelsea Quinn Yarbro." In *Discovering Modern Horror Fiction II*, edited by Darrell Schweitzer, 128–134. Mercer Island, WA: Starmont.

Howison, Del. 2015. "Inkslinger of the Highest Degree: Exclusive Interview with Chelsea Quinn Yarbro." *Blumhouse.com*, December 31. http://www.blumhouse.com/2015/12/31/inkslinger-of-the-highest-degree-exclusive-interview-with-chelsea-quinn-yarbro.

Phin, Vanessa Rose. 2015. "An Interview with Chelsea Quinn Yarbro." *Strange Horizons*, September 21. http://strangehorizons.com/2015/20150921/4yarbro-a.shtml.

Swift, Sondra F. 1999. "Toward the Vampire as Savior: Chelsea Quinn Yarbro's Saint-Germain Series Compared with Edward Bulwer-Lytton's *Zanoni*." In *The Blood Is the Life: Vampires in Literature*, edited by Leonard G. Heldreth and Mary Pharr, 155–164. Bowling Green, OH: Bowling Green State University Popular Press.

Interview with Chelsea Quinn Yarbro

October 2016

In this interview Yarbro shares some of the reasons behind several prominent aspects of her authorial career: her reasons for writing across a very broad spectrum of genres, her reasons for writing about vampires and werewolves, and her reasons for approaching established generic and mythic tropes in a way that subverts them. She also talks about her personal interest in Spiritualism and the occult, and she offers a list of recommended genre reading—not just horror but also science fiction, fantasy, and mystery. She closes with some thoughts on the purpose of horror fiction and the reasons why people seek it.

Matt Cardin: In a career spanning five decades, you have not only written a huge number of books, but you have written across a huge span of forms and genres. What is it that drives you toward such diversity in your authorial output? And is there any central impulse lying behind that diversity, a kind of core mission that threads its way through your work and unites it into an organic whole?

Chelsea Quinn Yarbro: Most simply put, I like to read in a wide variety of genres, and as a result, I like to write in a wide variety of genres. Doing the same mindset book after book tends to slow me down, but by genre-jumping and genre-straddling, my story sense stays fresh. As to a thematic element in my work, I'm sure there is one, but I don't worry about it, since paying attention to it would make me self-conscious and that is pure poison to fictionists.

MC: The character of Comte de St. Germain has now entered the canon of vampire literature. What led you to write about vampires in the first place? And why do you think they continue to exert such a mesmerizing power over the minds of not just the reading public but people in general? What's the fascination?

CQY: I wrote about vampires because there is something fascinating about them, and that's still true. As I have said before, after reading *Dracula* at fourteen, I read a lot more vampire fiction, and after a while, I wondered how far the Dracular model of vampires could be turned to the positive and still have a recognizable vampire. I'm still exploring that issue. I think some of the fascination comes from the high level of the ambiguity of the vampire—improperly dead, dependent on the living for its continued survival—which is at the heart of the whole vampire myth.

MC: How about werewolves, which have also played a part in your novels? What fascinates people about them? What fascinates *you* about them?

CQY: Werewolves are trickier beasties, and not nearly so engaging as vampires, although they, too, are ancient mythic archetypes in all known present and historical human societies. If vampires are The Other outside us, werecreatures are The Other within us. The most fun I've had with were-ness has been in *The Vildecaz Talents*, with Ninianee, who for the three nights of the full moon turns into a mammal, but she doesn't know which mammal until her first transformation for the month.

MC: In your horror writing you have tended to approach established themes, tropes, and motifs in a way that overturns and undermines them. You greet clichés and then explode them. Is this something you consciously set out to do? Is it perhaps linked to that core sense of authorial mission alluded to above?

CQY: Yes, you're right—I like to turn mythic figures upside down, back-to-front, inside-out, and so forth, and I do it deliberately, especially where there are inconsistencies in the archetype I'm dealing with. It lets me explore those figures in ways I couldn't do if I were dealing directly with the folkloric image, and what's the fun in that?

MC: The fact that you write supernatural horror while also writing about, and being personally involved in, Spiritualism, as expressed in your Messages from Michael series, puts you in relationship with a venerable line of authors in the horror and Gothic traditions—such as J. Sheridan Le Fanu, Edward Bulwer-Lytton, and Shirley Jackson—who have likewise held personal beliefs about the supernatural that worked its way into their written fictions. How do you personally understand the striking doubleness or duality of the supernatural, which in one context is the standard subject matter for stories about fear and horror, and in another is a source of much more benign and comforting notions and emotions about the nature of reality?

CQY: First, I don't believe in the supernatural—I believe everything that's happening, no matter how weird or creepy, is natural, or it wouldn't be able to occur. What is causing these things to happen is what interests me, and why I've been involved in occult studies for years, and so far, continue to do so. My work may reflect my interests in occult matters, but rarely do they reflect my opinions, since one of the most important aspect of writing, at least for me, is to take a story on its terms, and to reveal the experiences and opinions of the characters who inhabit it. The *Michael* material, which is taken from a real group and actual channeled information, is fictional only in that the identities of group members are not revealed, and most of those characters in the group in the *Michael* books are amalgamations of members, not portraits.

MC: Having made your mark on horror, what authors and works would you recommend in general to those who are looking to explore this wing of the literary universe? Or feel free to aim the question at the larger universe of speculative fiction as a whole, since you have worked for so long in all areas of it. Which books and authors strike you as especially important and profound both for speculative fiction and for literature as a whole?

CQY: I'm not very good at recommendations for newcomers to the various genres—I've read far too much over the years to be able to know what to point out as a first step. But I can make some generalities. If you haven't read *Dracula* and you like vampires, by all means do so. A lot of people like Lovecraft (I don't very much) for horror, and M. R. James (me, too). Of course, I recommend Robert Bloch for that most difficult of all forms, the funny horror story. If you like science fiction, Isaac Asimov, Alfred Bester, C. L. Moore, and Theodore Sturgeon were among my early favorites; Sturgeon and Moore remain so to this day. If you like mysteries, Agatha Christie, Edgar Allan Poe, Thorne Smith, James Ellroy, and Dick Francis are some writers whose work sticks with me. As fantasy goes, Roger Zelazny, Tanith Lee, and Ursula Le Guin held my interest more fully than some others. Sitting in his own multi-universe between fantasy and science fiction, R. A. Lafferty was a unique voice in my developmental period. I mention these because they were the ones I liked early in my career, when I was eager to see how the Big Names did it. On the other hand, some of my opinions are colored by having known a number of the ones listed, which probably flavors my understanding [of] their work. Almost all of them are senior citizens now, or no longer with us, and don't reflect the current array of Big Names, though I like Neil Gaiman very much, and Charles de Lint. I hope this might provide some useful ways to begin; they certainly did for me.

MC: Finally, do you have any thoughts on the purpose or meaning of horror fiction? What does it give us? Why do people actually seek the distressing emotional experiences of fright, dread, disgust, and dismay?

CQY: Most human beings don't mind being frightened if they're not in any real danger—think of roller-coasters and films—because it is thrilling to have that frisson that horror provides. A great many folk-stories and fairy tales are not only cautionary but scary because that cold finger down the spine is a lot of fun when it is imaginary, and we seek it out in stories for that reason. Such tales make it okay to be frightened and promise you a kind of vaccine against the very actual dangers and threats of real life. If you know how to handle a Lovecraftian sea monster, there's a chance that you can deal with dry rot under the deck or the political news from the Middle East.

"THE YELLOW WALL-PAPER"

"The Yellow Wall-Paper" is a horror story by Charlotte Perkins Gilman, written in June 1890 in Pasadena, California and published in the *New England Magazine*

(January 1892) under her married name, Stetson. She had suffered from postpartum depression while with her first husband in New England and was ordered by the prominent neurologist Dr. S. Weir Mitchell to take his rest cure, consisting of enforced bed rest for a month, followed by a prescription ordering her to limit her intellectual activities to two hours a day and never to write again. The result brought her to the edge of suicide, until she fought back, left the East Coast for California, and wrote the story over two days in 103-degree weather. She sent the published story to Mitchell, but contrary to rumor, he never responded or changed his therapy.

The semi-autobiographical story, in the form of a diary, recounts the experience of a clinically depressed woman given a rest cure similar to Mitchell's. The entire story is set in an upper room of a rented house where the woman is allowed nothing but rest, and she has nothing to do but stare at the ugly wallpaper. Eventually, she begins to see something moving behind the wallpaper's patterns. She soon realizes it is a woman who appears to be trapped behind the twisting pattern and is trying to get out. She decides to free the other woman by stripping off the wallpaper. By the end she has seemingly become the other woman.

More than two decades after the publication of "The Yellow Wall-Paper," Charlotte Perkins Gilman explained the "story behind the story" in a brief piece that she published in her magazine *The Forerunner*. "For many years," she said, "I suffered from a severe and continuous nervous breakdown tending to melancholia—and beyond." She described how a "noted specialist in nervous diseases, the best known in the country," gave her the "rest cure," sending her home and instructing her to curtail her intellectual life, "live as domestic a life as far as possible," and "never to touch pen, brush, or pencil again." The result of this treatment, she said, was well-nigh disastrous:

> I went home and obeyed those directions for some three months, and came so near the borderline of utter mental ruin that I could see over.
>
> Then, using the remnants of intelligence that remained, and helped by a wise friend, I cast the noted specialist's advice to the winds and went to work again—work, the normal life of every human being; work, in which is joy and growth and service, without which one is a pauper and a parasite—ultimately recovering some measure of power.
>
> Being naturally moved to rejoicing by this narrow escape, I wrote *The Yellow Wallpaper*, with its embellishments and additions, to carry out the ideal (I never had hallucinations or objections to my mural decorations) and sent a copy to the physician who so nearly drove me mad. He never acknowledged it.

Matt Cardin

Source: Gilman, Charlotte Perkins. 1913. "Why I Wrote the Yellow Wallpaper?" At *The Literature of Prescription: Charlotte Perkins Gilman and "The Yellow Wall-Paper."* U.S. National Library of Medicine, https://www.nlm.nih.gov/literatureofprescription/b2Reading.html. Originally published in *The Forerunner*, October 1913.

Several interpretations are possible. Initially "The Yellow Wall-Paper" was seen as a powerful, Poe-esque description of a woman's psychological descent into madness. This fits with the author's stated intention in writing it.

Gilman was a feminist activist, and a later view interprets it as a feminist allegory in which the hallucinated woman behind the wallpaper is the narrator's doppelgänger, and the imprisoning wallpaper pattern symbolizes the contemporary patriarchal social norms. The room where the protagonist is confined is described as a nursery, which has been interpreted as symbolizing the way women were treated as children.

It can also be interpreted as a tale of possession. The woman in the wallpaper is the spirit of a madwoman who had previously been imprisoned in the room and had died there. The room's barred windows, rings in the walls, nailed-down bed, and deep gouges in the plaster are more suggestive of a prison than a nursery. At the end, the madwoman's soul possesses the narrator's mind.

"The Yellow Wall-Paper" has been filmed more than once, by the BBC for *Masterpiece Theater* (1980) and as a student film by Alyssa Lundgren (2011). A feature film, *The Yellow Wallpaper* (2012), directed by Logan Thomas, is about Gilman's creation of the story.

Lee Weinstein

See also: Psychological Horror; Unreliable Narrator.

Further Reading

Dock, Julie Bates, ed. 1998. *Charlotte Perkins Gilman's "The Yellow Wallpaper" and the History of Its Publication and Reception: A Critical Edition and Documentary Casebook*. University Park: Pennsylvania State University Press.

Golden, Catherine, ed. 1992. *The Captive Imagination: A Casebook on 'The Yellow Wallpaper.'* New York: Feminist Press.

Scharnhorst, Gary. 1985. *Charlotte Perkins Gilman*. Boston: Twayne.

Wagner-Martin, Linda. 1989. "Gilman's 'The Yellow Wallpaper': A Centenary." In *Charlotte Perkins Gilman: The Woman and Her Work*, edited by Sheryl L. Meyering, 51–64. Ann Arbor: UMI Research Press.

"YOUNG GOODMAN BROWN"

The author of this story, Nathaniel Hawthorne, was one of the first writers to make use of the darker corners of America's Puritan past. He was uniquely suited to do so, born in Salem, Massachusetts, in 1804 and a descendant of John Hathorne, one of the judges involved in the Salem witch trials of 1692. Nathaniel later changed the spelling of the family name, adding the "w," to distance himself from his notorious ancestor.

Published in 1835, "Young Goodman Brown" is set about the time of the Salem witch panic; an offhand reference to "King William" dates the setting to 1688–1702.

The grim concluding passage of "Young Goodman Brown" describes the ruinous effect of the story's events on Goodman Brown—an effect that played out inexorably regardless of whether or not he had truly witnessed a satanic sabbat in the forest:

> Had Goodman Brown fallen asleep in the forest, and only dreamed a wild dream of a witch-meeting?
>
> Be it so, if you will. But, alas! it was a dream of evil omen for young Goodman Brown. A stern, a sad, a darkly meditative, a distrustful, if not a desperate man, did he become, from the night of that fearful dream. On the Sabbath-day, when the congregation were singing a holy psalm, he could not listen, because an anthem of sin rushed loudly upon his ear, and drowned all the blessed strain. When the minister spoke from the pulpit, with power and fervid eloquence, and with his hand on the open Bible, of the sacred truths of our religion, and of saint-like lives and triumphant deaths, and of future bliss or misery unutterable, then did Goodman Brown turn pale, dreading lest the roof should thunder down upon the gray blasphemer and his hearers. Often, awaking suddenly at midnight, he shrank from the bosom of Faith, and at morning or eventide, when the family knelt down at prayer, he scowled, and muttered to himself, and gazed sternly at his wife, and turned away. And when he had lived long, and was borne to his grave, a hoary corpse, followed by Faith, an aged woman, and children and grand-children, a goodly procession, besides neighbors, not a few, they carved no hopeful verse upon his tombstone; for his dying hour was gloom. (Hawthorne 1864, 104–105)

Matt Cardin

Source: Hawthorne, Nathaniel. 1864. "Young Goodman Brown." In *Mosses from an Old Manse.* Volume I. Boston: Ticknor and Fields.

The story is heavily allegorical, but anticipates much modern horror fiction. This and others of Hawthorne's works attracted the admiration of Edgar Allan Poe and had an enormous influence on H. P. Lovecraft.

The "goodman" (i.e., member of the Puritan community) of the title sets out from Salem into a dark forest at night. His wife, "aptly named" Faith, begs him not to go, but he has an urgent "errand." Once in the woods he meets a man who is clearly the Devil and who proceeds to disabuse him of the notion that the respectable members of Salem society are true Christians at all. Each of them is in league with Satan in one way or another. Brown overhears the conversation of two prominent clergymen as they ride by on horseback on their way to a witches' sabbat. Even as he comes to fear that all the world is corrupt, he clings to the hope that his wife, Faith, is pure; but a cloud passes over, he hears voices from it, and a ribbon like the ones Faith wears in her hair drifts down. When he reaches the sabbat itself, he is horrified to discover that just about everybody he knows, both sinners and the supposedly pious, including Faith, are present. He and Faith are to be initiated into the Devil's communion that night. A demonic preacher delivers a sermon to the effect that sin is the natural state of mankind, which is actually an orthodox Puritan view of things (thus generating a further irony: that the Devil's theology is quite sound). But right before the two are baptized into evil, Goodman Brown calls out to his wife to resist and look to heaven. The witches vanish. He is alone in the woods.

The implication is that it may have been a dream, and certainly, Goodman Brown gains no comfort from the notion. As he returns to Salem, he sees hypocrisy everywhere, and his ultimately long life ends in despair.

One of the great mysteries of this story is the question of what Goodman Brown was doing in the forest in the first place. Perhaps he was already planning to sell himself to the Devil, and he was only incidentally saved by his horror of seeing his wife succumb to similar corruption. Or perhaps the "gloom" that followed him for the rest of his days was a matter of guilt. As a Calvinist (as Puritans were), he would have believed in double predestination, the idea that some people are bound for heaven and others for hell, and nothing they can do will change the outcome. While it would not be possible to know who is going where, the events of this story are surely not a good sign. In this story, Hawthorne effectively captured the sense of spiritual dread that filled the Puritans' lives and formed the foundation for some of America's most sinister folklore.

Darrell Schweitzer

See also: Demons and Devils; Hawthorne, Nathaniel; *The Private Memoirs and Confessions of a Justified Sinner*; Witches and Witchcraft.

Further Reading

Magee, Bruce R. 2003. "Faith and Fantasy in 'Young Goodman Brown.'" *Nathaniel Hawthorne Review* 29, no. 1: 1–24.

Miller, Edwin Haviland. 1991. *Salem Is My Dwelling Place: Life of Nathaniel Hawthorne*, 111–120. Iowa City: University of Iowa Press.

Olson, Steven. 2009. "A History of the American Mind: 'Young Goodman Brown.'" *Journal of the Short Story in English* 52: 31–54.

"Overview: 'Young Goodman Brown.'" 1997. In *Literature and Its Times: Profiles of 300 Notable Literary Works and the Historical Events That Influenced Them, Vol. 1: Ancient Times to the American and French Revolutions (Prehistory–1790s)*, edited by Joyce Moss and George Wilson, 420–426. Detroit, MI: Gale.

"YOURS TRULY, JACK THE RIPPER"

"Yours Truly, Jack the Ripper" is a short story by Robert Bloch that was first published in the July 1943 issue of *Weird Tales* and collected in his first American short fiction collection, *The Opener of the Way* (1945). It has become Bloch's best-known short story, in part because it was instrumental in popularizing the theme of Jack the Ripper and his traits as a serial killer in horror fiction.

The story unfolds in (then) contemporary Chicago, where British Ripperologist Sir Guy Hollis enlists psychiatrist John Carmody (who narrates the story) in his search for Jack the Ripper, the infamous murderer of five women in London's Whitechapel district in 1888, who was never caught and whose identity has never been established. Sir Guy purports to have proof that Jack the Ripper's kills were blood sacrifices made to maintain his immortality, and that he is still alive. He believes that the Ripper's next cycle of murders is about to take place, and he enlists Carmody to introduce him to Chicago society where he thinks the Ripper may be hiding. The Ripper's identity, when revealed at the story's end, comes as a jarring surprise: he is none other than Carmody, the narrator, who has achieved immortality through his murders, which are actually blood sacrifices to dark gods.

"Your Truly, Jack the Ripper" is one of the earliest stories in which Bloch explored the psychology of a serial killer, an interest that would culminate in his renowned novel *Psycho* (1959). The story became part of an informal trilogy formed by Bloch's futuristic Ripper story "A Toy for Juliette" and Harlan Ellison's sequel "Prowler in the City on the Edge of Forever," both published in the anthology *Dangerous Visions* (1967). Bloch's novel *Night of the Ripper* (1984), an adjunct to "Yours Truly, Jack the Ripper," is a period tale about efforts to apprehend the Ripper at the time of his murders. Bloch also wrote the script for the 1967 *Star Trek* episode "Wolf in the Fold," featuring another take on an immortal Jack the Ripper. "Yours Truly, Jack the Ripper" has inspired several anthologies of horror stories on the theme of Jack the Ripper, notably Michel Parry's *Jack the Knife* (1975), Susan Casper and Jack Dann's *Jack the Ripper* (1988), and Ross Lockhart's *Tales of Jack the Ripper* (2013). The story has been adapted many times for extraliterary media, first for *The Kate Smith Radio Hour* in 1944 and, most memorably, as the April 11, 1961, episode of Boris Karloff's *Thriller*.

Stefan R. Dziemianowicz

See also: Bloch, Robert; Psychological Horror; Pulp Horror; *Weird Tales*.

Further Reading

Larson, Randall. 1986. *Robert Bloch: Starmont Reader's Guide 37.* Mercer Island, WA: Starmont House.

Zinna, Eduardo. "Yours Truly, Robert Bloch." *Casebook: Jack the Ripper.* Accessed July 5, 2016. http://www.casebook.org/dissertations/dst-bloch.html.

Z

ZOMBIES

The figure now known as the zombie has haunted the peripheries of folklore and narratives since the first stirrings of literature. Defying concrete definition, the figure has been in a state of flux, metamorphosing with each appearance, standing as a descriptive manifestation of cultural anxieties regarding selfhood and the transition from life to death. Its prominence in contemporary narratives is the result of a unique evolutionary development in which traditional stories were altered by popular fiction and film to form a new entry in the gallery of iconic monsters.

The concepts of death and the separation of the soul from the body, or the frightening prospect of a rampant body lacking the guiding reticence of a soul, have figured as themes within folklore and literature since *The Epic of Gilgamesh* (ca. 2100 BCE), in which the goddess Ishtar threatens to raise the dead so that they can feed upon the living. Revenants arise in folklore from such varied sources as the Chinese hopping corpse known as *Jiangshi* and the Scandinavian underworld figure called *draugr* to the Bible with its multiple examples of human resurrection in the name of God.

The first English appearance of the word "zombie" was in Robert Southey's three-volume *History of Brazil*, published between 1810 and 1819. The "zombie" to which Southey refers is the "nzambi" deity of Angolan folklore. It was not until 1929, however, that the notion of zombieism took hold of the American imagination with the publication of William Seabrook's anthropological account of Haiti, *The Magic Island*. Seabrook describes Haiti as an island of magic and Voodoo, detailing local accounts of bodies turned into zombies by Houngans, practitioners of Voodoo. These Haitian zombies are described as dead-eyed, laboring brutes, controlled with magic to fulfill the commands of the Voodoo master.

Seabrook's colorful account of Haiti and Voodoo went on to inspire further developments of the zombie figure, the most notable being the horror film *White Zombie* (1932), directed by Victor and Edward Halperin. Further examples of the Haitian zombie were depicted in similar films, such as in *King of the Zombies* (1941), *Revolt of the Zombies* (1936), and *I Walked with a Zombie* (1943).

Simultaneously, an alternative version of the zombie figure was emerging. Inspired by the proto-science fiction narrative of Mary Shelley's seminal Gothic novel *Frankenstein* (1818) and the somnambulist Cesare from Robert Wiene's film *The Cabinet of Dr. Caligari* (1920), H. P. Lovecraft's "Herbert West—Reanimator" (1922)

World War Z: Breaking the Zombie Mold

Max Brooks's 2006 novel *World War Z* was a pivotal novel in the renaissance of zombie fiction in the early twenty-first century, offering a distinct and influential approach to the living dead as a genre by exploring the fall of humanity and society as a result of governmental bureaucracy, ignorance, miscommunication, and global distrust that allowed the zombie virus to spread out of control. In writing the book as a follow-up to his best-selling *Zombie Survival Guide* (2003), Brooks deliberately chose to avoid the established zombie narrative that focuses on a group of survivors forced to protect themselves from the cannibalistic undead. Instead *World War Z* is structured as an oral history (modeled on Studs Terkel's 1984 nonfiction book *The Good War: An Oral History of World War II*) in which the battle for survival is presented as a global war against an enemy that is relentless and ever-growing.

Forgoing a traditional hero in favor of a multitude of narrators from around the world and across social strata, the novel is constructed as a series of eyewitness testimonies, recounting the firsthand experiences of each stage of a global zombie outbreak and war. While the war has ostensibly been won, this conglomeration of international voices, from military tacticians and CIA operatives to nurses, clerics, and those caring for the survivors, considers the war's global ramifications, reflecting on how it has reshaped international communities and identity. The novel offers an alternative to the Anglo-Eurocentrism of much of apocalyptic and horror literature, in which the apocalypse is usually equated with the fall of the Western world, by highlighting the impact of sociocultural, economic, and military decisions of global superpowers upon global citizens. It is on the scale of the apocalypse that the horror within the novel lies.

Stacey Abbott

saw a zombie-like figure emerge that connected scientific zombiefication with cannibalism. The zombie continued to appear as a figure straddling the boundary between Gothic horror and science fiction in films such as Ed Wood's *Plan 9 from Outer Space* (1959), where extraterrestrials resurrect the dead to wage war against humanity.

While film director George A. Romero is famously credited as the creator of the modern zombie, it was with the publication of Richard Matheson's novel *I Am Legend* in 1954 that the depiction of a zombie-like figure veered away from the familiar mind-controlled Haitian zombie toward a zombie imbued with new characteristics. Albeit not strictly a zombie novel, Matheson's vampiric figures served as the inspiration for the popular contemporary zombies that dominate film, literature, and video games today. Not only did Matheson's text invert the Gothic threat from something that haunts from within to an external threat attempting to invade the sanctuary of the Gothic edifice, but it further informed the zombie mythos by interpreting the figure within a dystopian framework, thereby linking the figure with the notion of apocalypse. Further, *I Am Legend* established the plague mythology as a replacement for Voodoo zombieism.

It was not until the 1964 film adaptation of Matheson's novel, retitled *The Last Man on Earth* and starring Vincent Price, that the early form of the zombie began to take shape. The trailer for the film makes multiple references to the creatures' zombie-like nature and opens with the title card, "This is the world of the living dead," a phrase that went on to inspire Romero's first installment of his zombie film series, *Night of the Living Dead*, a mere four years later.

In Romero's *Night of the Living Dead* (1968), radioactive contamination from a returning space probe is responsible for the dead rising from their graves. Following *Night of the Living Dead*, with its African American protagonist serving as social commentary on racial issues in America, and its basic plot and characterizations offering subtextual criticism of the Vietnam War (1955–1975), Romero continued to release zombie films that echoed the societal concerns of the time. *Dawn of the Dead* (1978) served as a critique of American capitalism and the cult of consumerism. *Day of the Dead* (1985) critiqued the Cold War, *Land of the Dead* (2005) questioned the unequal divide between the American rich and poor, *Diary of the Dead* (2007) commented on surveillance culture, and *Survival of the Dead* (2009) focused on patriarchal pride. Romero's use of the zombie as a figure of social criticism cemented the figure as a malleable representation of changing societal concerns.

Examples of living zombies can also be seen in Romero's *The Crazies* (1975, remade 2010), Danny Boyle's *28 Days Later* (2002), and the sequel, *28 Weeks Later* (2007), which depict the apocalyptic effects of untested bioweapons that turn the infected living into homicidal zombie figures. The upsurge of zombie narratives post-9/11 could be seen as a representation of violence against the dehumanized other, while comedic zombie films such as Edgar Wright's *Shaun of the Dead* (2004) exhibit social commentary on how the mindless regularity of daily routine has already disconnected humanity from reality; society is already in a zombiefied state.

The most recent development of the zombie figure has seen the zombie repositioned as the sympathetic hero, or antihero, as more narratives are frequently imbuing the zombie with sentience. Zombies like those in Isaac Marion's novel *Warm Bodies* (2010), adapted into a film of the same name in 2013, are given the capacity to redevelop the human qualities of self-awareness and conscience, and even fall in love. Dominic Mitchell's BBC drama series *In the Flesh* (2013–2014) depicts a society in which zombies can control their hunger through regulated doses of medicine, and in this condition attempt to reassimilate into the society they once ravaged, albeit as persecuted Others. This attempt to humanize the zombie reflects contemporary societal concerns with the isolation of "Others" within society and the restructuring of a more inclusive system of racial and gender rights.

Unlike the zombie's horror brethren, the vampire and the werewolf, who found their popularity in folklore and literature prior to their emergence in film, the zombie has always been a staple figure of the horror film genre and has only seen its popularity as a literary figure increased in the post-9/11 imagination. Alden Bell's *The Reapers Are the Angels* (2010), Mira Grant's *Feed* (2010), and the popular *World War Z* (2006) by Max Brooks serve as notable examples of classic zombie apocalypse novels; while John Ajvide Lindqvist's *Handling the Undead* (2005), Joe McKinney's Dead World series (2009–2014), and Brian Keene's The Rising series (2003–2015) contribute alternative approaches to the figure of the zombie. Keene's first novel, *The Rising* (2003), features bodies that have been possessed by evil spirits following a failed particle accelerator experiment; the theme of possession allows for sentient zombies with manipulative intelligence.

The zombie has also gained popularity as the literary subject of graphic novels, popularized by Robert Kirkman's comic book series *The Walking Dead* (2003–present), which has been adapted into a television series of the same name, and Chris Robertson and Michael Allred's comic book series *iZOMBIE* (2010–2012), featuring a sentient zombie named Gwen who works in a morgue, also adapted into a television series of the same name. The zombie has even invaded classic literature with the mash-up novel *Pride and Prejudice and Zombies* (2009), a parody by Seth Grahame-Smith that sees Elizabeth Bennet taking on the role of zombie hunter, as she and her four sisters fight off a horde of zombies.

The malleability of the zombie and the continued popularity of its use as a figure of social critique ensures that the zombie will continue to function in narratives that explore the sociopolitical concerns of contemporary humanity.

Kelly Gardner

See also: Ajvide Lindqvist, John; *Frankenstein*; *I Am Legend*; Keene, Brian.

Further Reading

Bishop, Kyle William. 2010. *American Zombie Gothic: The Rise and Fall (and Rise) of the Walking Dead in Popular Culture*. Jefferson, NC: McFarland.

Browning, John Edgar. 2010. "Survival Horrors, Survival Spaces: Tracing the Modern Zombie (cine)myth." *Horror Studies* 2, no. 1: 41–59.

Christie, Deborah, and Sarah Lauro Juliet, eds. 2011. *Better Off Dead: The Evolution of the Zombie as Post-Human*. New York: Fordham University Press.

Luckhurst, Roger. 2015. *Zombies: A Cultural History*. London: Reaktion Books.

Select Bibliography

Backer, Ron. 2015. *Classic Horror Films and the Literature That Inspired Them*. Jefferson, NC: McFarland.

Barron, Neil. 1990. *Horror Literature: A Reader's Guide*. New York: Garland.

Birkhead, Edith. 1921. *The Tale of Terror: A Study of the Gothic Romance*. London: Constable.

Bleiler, E. F. 1983. *The Guide to Supernatural Fiction*. Kent, OH: Kent State University Press.

Bleiler, E. F., ed. 1985. *Supernatural Fiction Writers*. 2 vols. New York: Scribner's.

Bleiler, Richard, ed. 2002. *Supernatural Fiction Writers: Contemporary Fantasy and Horror*. New York: Scribner's.

Bloom, Clive. 2010. *Gothic Histories: The Taste for Terror, 1764 to the Present*. London and New York: Continuum.

Briggs, Julia. 1977. *Night Visitors: The Rise and Fall of the English Ghost Story*. London: Faber & Faber.

Carroll, Noël. 1990. *The Philosophy of Horror; or Paradoxes of the Heart*. London and New York: Routledge.

Cavaliero, Glen. 1995. *The Supernatural in English Fiction*. Oxford: Oxford University Press.

Colavito, Jason, ed. 2008. *"A Hideous Bit of Morbidity": An Anthology of Horror Criticism from the Enlightenment to World War I*. Jefferson, NC, and London: McFarland.

Colavito, Jason. 2008. *Knowing Fear: Science, Knowledge, and the Development of the Horror Genre*. Jefferson, NC: McFarland.

Crow, Charles L., ed. 2014. *A Companion to American Gothic*. Malden, MA, and Oxford: Wiley-Blackwell.

Daniels, Les. 1975. *Living in Fear: A History of Horror in the Mass Media*. New York: Charles Scribner's Sons.

Docherty, Brian. 1990. *American Horror Fiction: From Brockden Brown to Stephen King*. New York: St. Martin's.

Fisher, Mark. 2017. *The Weird and the Eerie*. London: Repeater.

Fonseca, Anthony J., and June Michele Pulliam. 2003. *Hooked on Horror: A Guide to Reading Interests in Horror Fiction*. Englewood, CO: Libraries Unlimited.

Geary, Robert F. 1992. *The Supernatural in Gothic Fiction: Horror, Belief, and Literary Change*. Lewiston, Queenston, and Lampeter: Edward Mellon Press.

Gilbert, Jonathan Maximilian. 2008. "'The Horror, the Horror': The Origins of a Genre in Late Victorian and Edwardian Britain, 1880–1914." Ph.D. dissertation, Rutgers University. http://dx.doi.org/doi:10.7282/T3X065D6.

Halberstram, Judith. 1995. *Skin Shows: Gothic Horror and the Technology of Monsters.* Durham, NC: Duke University Press.

Heller, Terry. 1987. *The Delights of Terror: An Aesthetics of the Tales of Terror.* Urbana: University of Illinois Press.

Hogle, Jerrold E., ed. 2002. *The Cambridge Companion to Gothic Fiction.* Cambridge: Cambridge University Press.

Ingebretson, Edward J. 1996. *Maps of Heaven, Maps of Hell: Religious Terror as Memory from the Puritans to Stephen King.* New York and London: M. E. Sharpe.

Jackson, Rosemary. 1981. *Fantasy: The Literature of Subversion.* London: Methuen.

Jones, Stephen, and Kim Newman. 1998. *Horror: 100 Best Books.* New York: Carroll & Graf.

Jones, Stephen, and Kim Newman. 2005. *Horror: Another 100 Best Books.* New York: Carroll & Graf.

Joshi, S. T. 2001. *The Modern Weird Tale.* Jefferson, NC: McFarland.

Joshi, S. T. 2004. *The Evolution of the Weird Tale.* New York: Hippocampus Press.

Joshi, S. T., ed. 2007. *Icons of Horror and the Supernatural.* Westport: Greenwood Press.

Joshi, S. T. 2014. *Unutterable Horror: A History of Supernatural Fiction, Volume 1: From Gilgamesh to the End of the Nineteenth Century.* New York: Hippocampus Press.

Joshi, S. T. 2014. *Unutterable Horror: A History of Supernatural Fiction, Volume 2: The Twentieth and Twenty-first Centuries.* New York: Hippocampus Press.

Joshi, S. T., and Stefan Dziemianowicz, eds. 2005. *Supernatural Literature of the World: An Encyclopedia.* 3 vols. Westport: Greenwood Press.

Kendrick, Walter. 1991. *The Thrill of Fear: 250 Years of Scary Entertainment.* New York: Grove Weidenfeld.

Kerr, Howard, John W. Crowley, and Charles L. Crow, eds. 1983. *The Haunted Dusk: American Supernatural Fiction 1820–1920.* Athens: University of Georgia Press.

King, Stephen. [1981] 2010. *Danse Macabre.* New York: Gallery Books.

Lovecraft, H. P. [1927] 2012. *The Annotated Supernatural Horror in Literature.* Edited by S. T. Joshi. New York: Hippocampus Press.

Messent, Peter B., ed. 1981. *Literature of the Occult: A Collection of Critical Essays.* Englewood Cliffs, NJ: Prentice-Hall.

Mishra, Vijay. 1994. *The Gothic Sublime.* Albany: State University of New York Press.

Nelson, Victoria. 2001. *The Secret Life of Puppets.* Cambridge, MA: Harvard University Press.

Nelson, Vitoria. 2012. *Gothicka: Vampire Heroes, Human Gods, and the New Supernatural.* Cambridge and London: Harvard University Press.

Penzoldt, Peter. 1965. *The Supernatural in Fiction.* New York: Humanities Press.

Punter, David. 1980. *The Literature of Terror: A History of Gothic Fictions from 1765 to the Present Day.* London: Longman.

Punter, David, ed. 2015. *A New Companion to the Gothic.* Malden, MA: Wiley-Blackwell.

Robillard, Douglas, ed. 1996. *American Supernatural Fiction: From Edith Wharton to the* Weird Tales *Writers*. New York: Garland.

Sandner, David, ed. 2004. *Fantastic Literature: A Critical Reader*. Westport, CT, and London: Praeger.

Scarborough, Dorothy. 1917. *The Supernatural in Modern English Fiction*. New York and London: G. P. Putnam's Sons.

Schweitzer, Darrell, ed. 1985. *Discovering Modern Horror Fiction*. Mercer Island, WA: Starmont House.

Schweitzer, Darrell, ed. 1988. *Discovering Modern Horror Fiction II*. Mercer Island, WA: Starmont House.

Schweitzer, Darrell, ed. 1992. *Discovering Classic Horror Fiction*. Mercer Island, WA: Starmont House.

Skal, David J. 1993. *The Monster Show: A Cultural History of Horror*. New York: W. W. Norton.

Sullivan, Jack. 1978. *Elegant Nightmares: The English Ghost Story from Le Fanu to Blackwood*. Athens, OH: Ohio University Press.

Summers, Montague. 1938. *The Gothic Quest: A History of the Gothic Novel*. London: Fortune Press.

Thompson, G. R. 1974. *The Gothic Imagination: Essays in Dark Romanticism*. Washington: Washington State University Press.

Tibbetts, John C. 20121. *The Gothic Imagination: Conversations on Fantasy, Horror, and Science Fiction in the Media*. New York: Palgrave Macmillan.

Todorov, Tzvetan. 1973. *The Fantastic: A Structural Approach to a Literary Genre*. Translated by Richard Howard. Cleveland, OH: Press of Case Western Reserve University.

Tropp, Martin. 1990. *Images of Fear: How Horror Stories Helped Shape Modern Culture (1818–1918)*. Jefferson, NC: McFarland.

Twitchell, James B. 1985. *Dreadful Pleasures: An Anatomy of Modern Horror*. New York: Oxford University Press.

Tymn, Marshall B., ed. 1981. *Horror Literature: A Core Collection and Reference Guide*. New York: R. R. Bowker.

Varma, Devendra. 1957. *The Gothic Flame*. London: Arthur Barker.

Varnado, S. L. 1987. *Haunted Presence: The Numinous in Gothic Fiction*. Tuscaloosa: University of Alabama Press.

Voller, Jack G. 1994. *The Supernatural Sublime: The Metaphysics of Terror in Anglo-American Romanticism*. DeKalb: Northern Illinois University Press.

About the Editor and Contributors

The Editor

Matt Cardin is a writer, editor, college administrator, and college instructor specializing in the intersection of horror, religion, creativity, consciousness, and culture. In addition to teaching English and religion at Ranger College in Stephenville, Texas, he is the editor of ABC-CLIO's *Mummies around the World: An Encyclopedia of Mummies in History, Religion, and Popular Culture* (2014) and *Ghosts, Spirits, and Psychics: The Paranormal from Alchemy to Zombies* (2015). He also edited *Born to Fear: Interviews with Thomas Ligotti* (2014), for which he received a World Fantasy Award nomination. He is also the author of the horror collections *Divinations of the Deep*, *Dark Awakenings*, and *To Rouse Leviathan*. He blogs at The Teeming Brain.

The Contributors

Stacey Abbott is a Reader in Film and Television Studies at the University of Roehampton. A genre specialist, she writes extensively about cult television and has also written about vampires, science fiction, romantic comedies, and the horror genre. She is the author of, among others, *Undead Apocalypse: Vampires and Zombies in the 21st Century* (2016).

Aalya Ahmad holds a doctorate in Comparative Literary Studies, specializing in horror fiction. She teaches across several different disciplines on horror literature and film, and publishes work on various aspects of horror, including the pedagogy of horror, race, class, gender and horror, zombies, indigenization, and Canadian horror film. Her first love was Edgar Allan Poe.

Xavier Aldana Reyes is Senior Lecturer in English Literature and Film and a founding member of the Manchester Centre for Gothic Studies. He specialises in Gothic and Horror Studies, and his publications include *Spanish Gothic* (2017), *Horror: A Literary History* (editor, 2016), *Horror Film and Affect* (2016), *Digital Horror* (co-editor, 2015), and *Body Gothic* (2014).

Melanie R. Anderson is an Assistant Professor of English at Glenville State College. She is the author of *Spectrality in the Novels of Toni Morrison* (2013) and co-editor of *The Ghostly and the Ghosted in Literature and Film: Spectral Identities* (2013) and *Shirley Jackson, Influences and Confluences* (2016).

Eleanor Beal is Associate Lecturer in English Literature and Film at Manchester Metropolitan University. Her forthcoming publications include entries in the edited collections *Transmedia Creatures: Connecting Frankenstein's Afterlives* and *Divine Horror: The Cinematic Battle Between the Sacred and the Supernatural*. She is the author of the book *Postsecular Gothic* (forthcoming) for the Palgrave Gothic series.

Steve Behrends edited Clark Ashton Smith's fugitive fictions (*Strange Shadows*, 1989) and other Smith titles; contributed to the literary criticism of Smith, Donald Wandrei, and Darrell Schweitzer; and is an avid reader of the British New Wave. He trained in the field of particle physics and is currently employed as a technical analyst in the Boston area.

Richard Bleiler is collections librarian at the University of Connecticut. His most recent book, *The Strange Case of 'The Angels of Mons'* (McFarland 2015), describes the controversy following the September 30, 1914 publication of Arthur Machen's "The Bowmen" and collects for the first time many of the primary documents written to argue that angelic forces assisted the English troops.

Clive Bloom is an academic and author who has written widely on areas as diverse as popular culture, the Gothic, and political protest. He is the author of *Gothic Histories* and the editor in chief of Palgrave Gothic. His latest book, *Thatcher's Secret War: Coercion, Secrecy and Government, 1974–1990*, was listed for "Radical Book of the Year 2016."

Naomi Simone Borwein is a polymath disguised as a PhD candidate in English literature at the University of Newcastle, Australia. Her research interests include the Gothic, theory, and modern American literature, with a specialization in Southern literature. She engages with cultural and literary history, and quantitative methodologies.

Jason V Brock is an award-winning writer, editor, filmmaker, composer, and artist. He is the author of *Disorders of Magnitude: A Survey of Dark Fantasy* (2014), and he was art director/managing editor for *Dark Discoveries* magazine for more than four years. He also runs the biannual digest [NAMEL3SS], devoted to the macabre, weird, uncanny, and esoteric.

Simon Brown is Associate Professor of Film and Television at Kingston University and has written on various aspects of film and TV horror. He is currently completing a monograph entitled *Screening Stephen King: King Adaptations and the Horror Genre on Film and Television*, which is due for publication in 2018.

John Edgar Browning is a Marion L. Brittain Postdoctoral Fellow at the Georgia Institute of Technology. He is internationally recognized for his horror, *Dracula*, and vampire scholarship, with over fourteen published or forthcoming books and over sixty-five shorter works. He is also widely regarded as a chief expert on real vampirism in the United States and abroad.

Chloé Germaine Buckley is a Senior Lecturer at Manchester Metropolitan University, UK. She has a PhD in literature with a focus on contemporary Gothic fiction. She has published numerous articles and chapters on Gothic and horror literature and film, and is co-editor of *Telling It Slant: Critical Approaches to Helen Oyeyemi*.

Elsa Charléty is a PhD candidate in American literature at the Sorbonne University and in the Department of Comparative Literature at Brown University. Her areas of interest include the representation of gendered bodies and voices in nineteenth- and twentieth-century literature of the American South and the Caribbean, and the literary history of Gothic and horror narratives.

Michael Cisco is the author of various books, including *The Divinity Student*, *The Great Lover*, and *ANIMAL MONEY*. His scholarly work has appeared in *Iranian Studies*, *Lovecraft and Influence*, *Thinking Horror*, and elsewhere. He lives and teaches in New York City.

Carys Crossen was awarded her PhD in English and American Studies from the University of Manchester in 2012. Since then she has spent her time alternately studying to become a librarian, and researching and writing. Her favorite topics of study are vampires, gender, the Gothic, and, most particularly, werewolves.

Stephen Curtis has a PhD in English literature and specializes in the darker aspects of early modern literature, in particular the significance of blood in the period and the connections between tragedy and horror. He has written and presented on various aspects of early modern drama, contemporary Gothic literature, horror movies, and video games.

Dara Downey is a Lecturer in English Literature at the National University of Ireland, Maynooth. She is editor of *The Irish Journal of Gothic and Horror Studies*, and Vice-Chair of the Irish Association for American Studies. She is author of *American Women's Ghost Stories in the Gilded Age* (Palgrave 2014) and is currently working on a monograph on slaves and servants in American Gothic fiction.

Stefan R. Dziemianowicz has edited many horror fiction anthologies and written many articles and reviews for *The Washington Post Book World*, *Publishers Weekly*, *Lovecraft Studies*, and other journals. He is a senior editor at Barnes & Noble and has contributed to numerous reference works. He co-edited, with S. T. Joshi, *Supernatural Literature of the World: An Encyclopedia* (2005).

Benjamin F. Fisher, Emeritus Professor, English, University of Mississippi, has published much about horror and related topics, notably on topics abut Poe. He is a past president of the Poe Studies association and Chairman of the Speaker Series for the Edgar Allan Poe Society of Baltimore.

Matt Foley is a Lecturer in English at University of Stirling. He writes on the Gothic, transgression, and modernism. His most recent publication is an article on the acoustics of the Gothic romance for the journal *Horror Studies*. Current projects include writing a book on haunting modernisms and being the main academic contact for the Patrick McGrath archive at Stirling.

Kaja Franck's thesis at the University of Herfordshire looks at the werewolf in literature as an ecoGothic monster, concentrating on the relationship between wilderness, wolves, and werewolves, and how language is used to demarcate animal alterity. She co-organized the Company of Wolves conference in September 2015.

Kelly Gardner is an early career researcher and teaching fellow at the University of Stirling, Scotland. Her PhD thesis explored the emergence and development of the sentient zombie. Her research interests include Gothic literature, posthumanism, transhumanism, and speculative fiction. Her recent publications have focused on the historical zombie, apocalypse, and the use of sound in zombie-themed media.

Richard Gavin is an acclaimed Canadian author of horror fiction and esotericism. He has published seven books, including *Sylvan Dread: Tales of Pastoral Darkness* (Three Hands Press) and *The Benighted Path: Primeval Gnosis and the Monstrous Soul* (Theion Publishing). He welcomes readers at www.richardgavin.net.

Jon Greenaway is a PhD candidate at Manchester Metropolitan University researching theology, Gothic literature, and imaginative apologetics. He is also behind the popular online account @thelitcritguy, popularizing literary and critical theory.

Bob Hodges is a PhD candidate in literature and critical theory at University of Washington. His dissertation covers nineteenth- and early twentieth-century transatlantic detective fiction vis-à-vis political liberalism. He is co-editor of the forthcoming *The Weird and the Southern Imaginary*. He has contributed to *Critical Survey of Graphic Novels*, *ESQ*, *Poe Review*, and *Clues*.

Jerrold E. Hogle (PhD, Harvard) is University Distinguished Professor in English at the University of Arizona; past President of the International Gothic Association; author of, among other books, *The Undergrounds of The Phantom of the Opera* (2002); and editor of the *Cambridge Companions to Gothic Fiction* (2002) and *The Modern Gothic* (2014).

Jim Holte is a Professor of English and Film Studies at East Carolina University. He is editor of *The Fantastic Vampire* and author of *Dracula in the Dark: The Dracula Film Adaptations*. He has written extensively on film, horror, and fantasy.

Gary Hoppenstand is a professor in the Department of English at Michigan State University, and he currently serves as the Secretary for Academic Governance at MSU. He has published numerous books and articles in the field of popular culture studies, and has won Michigan State University's 2008 Distinguished Faculty Award.

William Hughes is Professor of Medical Humanities and Gothic Literature at Bath Spa University, England. He is the author, editor, or co-editor of seventeen books, including *That Devil's Trick: Hypnotism and the Victorian Popular Imagination* (2015), *The Historical Dictionary of Gothic Literature* (2013), and *EcoGothic* (with Andrew Smith, 2013).

Timothy J. Jarvis is a writer and a lecturer in creative writing. He has research interests, as a practitioner and critic, in the fields of the Gothic and weird fiction, innovative fiction, digital fiction, contemporary literature, and creative writing pedagogy. His novel, *The Wanderer*, was published in the summer of 2014.

Brian Johnson is an Associate Professor of English at Carleton University in Ottawa, Ontario. Recent publications include articles on posthumanism and ecology in Swamp Thing, H. P., Lovecraft, and Ridley Scott's *Alien* films. His current research focuses on superheroes and melodrama.

S. T. Joshi is the author of *The Weird Tale* (1990), *The Modern Weird Tale* (2001), *I Am Providence: The Life and Times of H. P. Lovecraft* (2010), and *Unutterable Horror: A History of Supernatural Fiction* (2012). He is the editor of *Supernatural Literature of the World: An Encyclopedia* (2005) and *American Supernatural Tales* (2007).

Ian Kinane is Lecturer in English Literature at the University of Roehampton, London. He researches and teaches in the areas of modern and contemporary literature, genre fiction, and global literatures.

Laura R. Kremmel holds a PhD from Lehigh University and is a visiting assistant professor at Lehigh. Her interests include Gothic literature, British Romanticism, medical humanities, history of medicine, and disability studies. She has published articles on Gothic studies, romanticism, and disability, and is co-editor of *The Handbook to Horror Literature*, forthcoming from Palgrave Macmillan.

Lisa Kröger is a writer and editor living on the Mississippi Gulf Coast. She has a PhD in Gothic literature, focusing on women writers. Most recently, she edited an essay collection on the writings of Shirley Jackson, published with Routledge. She is also a member of the Horror Writers Association.

Rob Latham is an independent scholar living in Los Angeles. He is the author of *Consuming Youth: Vampires, Cyborgs, and the Culture of Consumption* (Chicago 2002) and editor of *The Oxford Handbook of Science Fiction* (Oxford 2014) and *Science Fiction Criticism: Essential Writings* (Bloomsbury 2017).

Chun H. Lee is an instructor at Brazosport College in Lake Jackson Texas. His work has appeared in *Many Genres: One Craft, Dissections*, and many others. His favorite class to teach is creative writing because seeing imagination at work is always rewarding.

Miles Link is a Research Associate in the School of English in Fudan University, Shanghai. He received his doctorate from Trinity College Dublin. He has published on the popular literature, television, and film of the Cold War, as well as the works of H. G. Wells and John Wyndham.

Roger Luckhurst teaches at Birkbeck College, University of London, and is the author of *The Mummy's Curse* (2012) and *Zombies: A Cultural History* (2015).

James Machin undertook his doctoral thesis on late Victorian and Edwardian weird fiction at Birkbeck, University of London, where he also taught English literature. Since 2013, he has been the editor of *Faunus: The Journal of the Friends of Arthur Machen*.

Steven J. Mariconda's literary criticism on weird fiction, with an emphasis on close reading and prose style, has been published in a variety of periodicals and collections over the past thirty years. He is the author of *H. P. Lovecraft: Art, Artifact, and Reality* (Hippocampus Press, 2013).

Helen Marshall is a Lecturer of Creative Writing and Publishing at Anglia Ruskin University in Cambridge, England. She has won the Sydney J. Bounds Award, World Fantasy Award, and Shirley Jackson Award, and she edited the 2017 edition of *The Year's Best Weird Fiction*. Her debut novel *Everything That Is Born* will be published by Random House Canada in 2018.

Javier A. Martinez is an editor of the academic journal *Extrapolation*. His articles and reviews have appeared in *Dead Reckonings, Extrapolation, The Los Angeles Review of Books, Science Fiction Studies*, and elsewhere. He has served as department chair, college dean, and university provost, and is currently Associate Professor of English at the University of Texas Rio Grande Valley.

Sean Matharoo is a PhD student of comparative literature at the University of California, Riverside, where he studies francophone and anglophone speculative media, postcolonial theory, ecological philosophy, speculative realism, and noise. He has a forthcoming article in a special issue of *Horror Studies* devoted to sonic horror.

Neil McRobert is a researcher in contemporary horror and Gothic culture. He completed his doctorate at the University of Stirling. His particular interests are experimental horror fiction and film, and the role of technology and the Internet in contemporary horror. Recent publications have focused on found footage cinema and the growth of online horror folklore.

Sean Moreland is a writer, editor, and educator, much of whose research concerns Gothic and horror fiction in its literary, sequential art, and cinematic guises. He teaches in the English Department at the University of Ottawa.

Will Murray is a lifelong scholar of pulp fiction, a contributor to *Fangoria* magazine, and the author of several celebrated Cthulhu Mythos anthology stories. Enormously prolific, he has penned some seventy novels in series ranging from The Destroyer to The Wild Adventures of Doc Savage. His latest work is *King Kong vs. Tarzan*.

Sorcha Ní Fhlainn is Lecturer in Film Studies and American Literature, and a founding member of the Manchester Centre for Gothic Studies at Manchester Metropolitan University. She is the author/editor of numerous publications and Reviews Editor for *Gothic Studies*. Forthcoming publications include *Clive Barker: Dark Imaginer* (2017) and *Postmodern Vampires: Film, Fiction, and Popular Culture* (2018).

Keith M. C. O'sullivan is Senior Rare Books Librarian at the University of Aberdeen, UK. He earned an MA in English from the University of Sussex and has also studied at the Universities of Surrey, Wales, and Stirling. He is currently researching on Ramsey Campbell and the Gothic tradition at Manchester Metropolitan University.

Elizabeth Parker has a PhD in English literature from Trinity College Dublin. She has been published in *The Palgrave Companion to Literature and Horror* (2017) and elsewhere, and she co-edited *Between Space and Place: Landscapes of Liminality* (Rowman and Littlefield, 2016). She is currently the TV editor of the *Irish Journal of Gothic and Horror Studies*.

Bernard Perron is a Full Professor of Film and Game Studies at the University of Montreal, Canada. He is the editor of *Horror Video Games* (2009), the co-editor of

The Routledge Companion to Video Games Studies (2014) and *Video Games and the Mind* (2016), and the author of *Silent Hill: The Terror Engine* (2012). More information is at http://www.ludov.ca.

Hannah Priest is an academic writer and lecturer based in Manchester, UK. She has a PhD in late medieval literature, and her research interests include gender, violence, and monsters in popular culture. She has published on both medieval and contemporary popular fiction, including work on werewolves, cannibals, and fairies.

David Punter is a writer, poet, and critic, currently Professor of Poetry at the University of Bristol, UK. He has published critical monographs in many fields of literature, most notably the Gothic, but also including Romantic writing, contemporary fiction, and literary theory, as well as five small volumes of poetry.

Jean-Charles Ray is a PhD student in Film Studies at the Université de Montréal (Montreal, Canada) and in Comparative Literature at the Sorbonne Nouvelle (Paris, France). His main field of study is horror in literature and video games.

Brittany Roberts is a PhD candidate in Comparative Literature at the University of California, Riverside, where she studies Russian and Anglophone horror, science fiction, and weird fiction. She is particularly interested in eco-horror and is currently writing a dissertation that considers the ecological possibilities raised by dark speculative literature and cinema.

Jim Rockhill has contributed to books devoted to E. T. A. Hoffmann, M. R. James, J. Sheridan Le Fanu, Bob Leman, Jane Rice, and Clark Ashton Smith, as well as various encyclopedias and journals including *Supernatural Literature of the World*, *Ghosts in Popular Culture and Legend*, *Dead Reckonings*, and *Lost Souls*.

Travis Rozier earned his PhD in English at the University of Mississippi in 2015 and currently works as a lecturer in the English department at Texas A&M University. His areas of interest include literature of the U.S. South, Southern women writers, material culture, and weird fiction.

Darrell Schweitzer is a former editor of the legendary *Weird Tales* magazine, a critic, an essayist, and the author of books on Lord Dunsany and H. P. Lovecraft. He is also the author of three fantasy novels and about 300 short stories. A World Fantasy Award Winner, he lives in Philadelphia.

Brian J. Showers has written for publications such as *Rue Morgue*, *Supernatural Tales*, and *Wormwood*. He also edits *The Green Book*, a journal devoted to Irish writers of the fantastic, and runs the Swan River Press, Ireland's only publishing house dedicated to literature of the Gothic, strange, and supernatural. He lives in Dublin.

Michael Siefener has worked as a freelance writer since 1992, publishing several novels and short stories, mostly in the fantastical vein. He received his LLD in 1991 but never worked as a lawyer. He was born in Cologne and currently lives in a small village in the Eifel, one of the westernmost parts of Germany.

Brian Stableford has been publishing fiction and nonfiction for fifty years. His most recent nonfiction projects are *New Atlantis: A Narrative History of British Scientific Romance* (Wildside Press, 2016) and *The Plurality of Imaginary Worlds: The Evolution of French roman scientifique* (Black Coat Press, 2016).

E. Kate Stewart holds a PhD from the University of Mississippi and serves as Professor of English at the University of Arkansas at Monticello. She has published on Edgar Allan Poe and Transcendentalism, and has contributed to several volumes of the *Dictionary of Literary Biography*. Her primary research interests involve nineteenth-century American fiction.

Joel T. Terranova received his PhD in English from the University of Louisiana at Lafayette in 2015. Focusing on Gothic fiction of the eighteenth and nineteenth centuries, he has published a variety of scholarly works in this field. He also serves as the book review editor for *Studies in Gothic Fiction*.

Bev Vincent has a PhD in chemistry and is the author of forty peer-reviewed scientific articles. His work has been nominated for the Bram Stoker Award (twice), the Edgar Award, and the Thriller Award. He has been a contributing editor with *Cemetery Dance* magazine since 2001. His author site is bevvincent.com.

Hank Wagner is a respected critic and interviewer whose work has appeared in numerous genre publications such as *Dead Reckonings*, *Cemetery Dance*, *Mystery Scene*, and *Crimespree*. He is a co-author of *The Complete Stephen King Universe* and *Prince of Stories: A Guide to the Many Worlds of Neil Gaiman*. He also co-edited *Thrillers: 100 Must Reads* with David Morrell.

Mark Wegley currently teaches at Tacoma Community College and previously taught at the University of Arkansas at Monticello. He holds a bachelor's degree from the University of Washington and a master's from Boise State University, where he completed a graduate thesis on the short fiction of J. Sheridan Le Fanu.

Lee Weinstein is a retired librarian and a lifelong horror fan. His essays have appeared in *Studies in Weird Fiction*, *The New York Review of Science Fiction*, and elsewhere. He is a current contributor to *The Encyclopedia of Science Fiction* and has edited several short story collections.

Jillian Wingfield is a PhD candidate and visiting lecturer in the School of Humanities at the University of Hertfordshire. Her research project is focused on American twenty-first-century vampire fiction, investigating vampire-human as well as intra-vampiric dynamics for what they reveal about a dialogue between genre and post-9/11 culturally dominant fears.

Gina Wisker is Professor of Contemporary Literature & Higher Education at the University of Brighton, UK. She is the author of, among others, *Horror Fiction: An Introduction* (2005) and *Contemporary Women's Gothic Fiction*, and co-editor of the online horror journal *Dissections*. She is currently chair of the Contemporary Women's Writing Association, an HEA Principal Fellow, and a National Teaching Fellow.

Index

Page locators in **boldface** indicate main entries in the Encyclopedia.